Lecture Notes in Computer Science   10510

Commenced Publication in 1973
Founding and Former Series Editors:
Gerhard Goos, Juris Hartmanis, and Jan van Leeuwen

Editorial Board

Formal Methods

Subline of Lectures Notes in Computer Science

Subline Series Editors

Subline Advisory Board

More information about this series at http://www.springer.com/series/7408

Nadia Polikarpova · Steve Schneider (Eds.)

Integrated Formal Methods

13th International Conference, IFM 2017
Turin, Italy, September 20–22, 2017
Proceedings

 Springer

Editors
Nadia Polikarpova ⓘ
Massachusetts Institute of Technology
Cambridge, MA
USA

Steve Schneider ⓘ
University of Surrey
Guildford
UK

ISSN 0302-9743   ISSN 1611-3349   (electronic)
Lecture Notes in Computer Science
ISBN 978-3-319-66844-4   ISBN 978-3-319-66845-1   (eBook)
DOI 10.1007/978-3-319-66845-1

Library of Congress Control Number: 2017952382

LNCS Sublibrary: SL2 – Programming and Software Engineering

Printed on acid-free paper

This Springer imprint is published by Springer Nature
The registered company is Springer International Publishing AG
The registered company address is: Gewerbestrasse 11, 6330 Cham, Switzerland

Preface

Applying formal methods may involve the usage of different formalisms and different analysis techniques to validate a system, either because individual components are most amenable to one formalism or technique, because one is interested in different properties of the system, or simply to cope with the sheer complexity of the system. The iFM conference series seeks to further research into hybrid approaches to formal modeling and analysis; i.e., the combination of (formal and semi-formal) methods for system development, regarding both modeling and analysis. The conference covers all aspects from language design through verification and analysis techniques to tools and their integration into software engineering practice.

These proceedings document the outcome of the 13th International Conference on Integrated Formal Methods, iFM 2017, on recent developments toward this goal. The conference was held in Turin, Italy, on September 20–22, 2017, hosted by the University of Turin. Previous editions of iFM were held in York, UK (1999), Schloss Dagstuhl, Germany (2000), Turku, Finland (2002), Kent, UK (2004), Eindhoven, The Netherlands (2005), Oxford, UK (2007), Düsseldorf, Germany (2009), Nancy, France (2010), Pisa, Italy (2012), Turku, Finland (2013), Bertinoro, Italy (2014), and Reykjavik, Iceland (2016).

The conference received 61 submissions from authors in 24 countries. Papers were submitted in four categories: research papers, case study papers, regular tool papers, and tool demonstration papers. All papers were reviewed by at least three members of the Program Committee. After careful deliberation, the Program Committee selected 28 papers for presentation.

Among these papers, the Program Chairs, in consultation with the Program Committee, have selected winners for two awards. The contribution "Triggerless Happy: Intermediate Verification with a First-Order Prover" by YuTing Chen and Carlo A. Furia received the *Best Paper Award*. The contribution "Complexity Analysis for Java with AProVE" by Florian Frohn and Jürgen Giesl received the *Best Tool Paper Award*. Each award was accompanied by a EUR 500 prize, generously provided by Springer.

In addition to the 28 peer-reviewed papers, this volume contains contributions from each of the three invited keynote speakers:

- Jane Hillston (University of Edinburgh, UK): "Integrating Inference with Stochastic Process Algebra Models"
- André Platzer (Carnegie Mellon University, USA): "Logic & Proofs for Cyber-Physical Systems with KeYmaera X"
- Martin Vechev (ETH Zurich, Switzerland): "Machine Learning for Programming"

Invited presentations are always the highlights of a conference; these contributions are therefore gratefully acknowledged.

iFM was accompanied by a PhD Symposium, organized by the symposium chairs, Erika Ábrahám (RWTH Aachen University, Germany) and S. Lizeth Tapia Tarifa

(University of Oslo, Norway), as well as the following satellite events, managed by the workshop chairs, Wolfgang Ahrendt (Chalmers University of Technology, Sweden) and Michael Lienhardt (University of Turin, Italy):

- International Workshop on Formal Methods for Industrial Critical Systems and Automated Verification of Critical Systems (FMICS-AVoCS)
- Workshop on Architectures, Languages and Paradigms for IoT (ALP4IoT)
- Workshop on Actors and Active Objects (WAO)
- Workshop on Formal Verification of Autonomous Vehicles (FVAV)
- Second International Workshop on Pre- and Post-Deployment Verification Techniques (PrePost)
- Second International Workshop on Verification and Validation of Cyber-Physical Systems (V2CPS)

The conference would not have been possible without the enthusiasm and dedication of the iFM general chair, Ferruccio Damiani, and the support of the Computer Science Department at the University of Turin, Italy. The EasyChair conference management system was invaluable for conducting the peer review process and preparing the proceedings. Conferences like iFM rely on the willingness of experts to serve on the Program Committee; their professionalism and their helpfulness was exemplary. Finally, we would like to thank all the authors for their submissions, their willingness to continue improving their papers, and their presentations!

July 2017

Nadia Polikarpova
Steve Schneider

Organization

General Chair

Ferruccio Damiani   University of Turin, Italy

Program Chairs

Nadia Polikarpova   MIT, USA
Steve Schneider   University of Surrey, UK

Steering Committee

Erika Ábrahám   RWTH Aachen University, Germany
Elvira Albert   Complutense University of Madrid, Spain
John Derrick   University of Sheffield, UK
Marieke Huisman   University of Twente, Netherlands
Einar Broch Johnsen   University of Oslo, Norway
Dominique Mery   Université de Lorraine, LORIA, France
Luigia Petre   Åbo Akademi University, Finland
Steve Schneider   University of Surrey, UK
Emil Sekerinski   McMaster University, Canada
Marjan Sirjani   University of Reykjavik, Iceland
Helen Treharne   University of Surrey, UK
Heike Wehrheim   University of Paderborn, Germany

Program Committee

Erika Ábrahám   RWTH Aachen University, Germany
Elvira Albert   Complutense University of Madrid, Spain
Oana Andrei   University of Glasgow, UK
Borzoo Bonakdarpour   McMaster University, Canada
Barbora Buhnova   Masaryk University, Czech Republic
David Cok   GrammaTech, USA
John Derrick   Unversity of Sheffield, UK
Yliès Falcone   Univ. Grenoble Alpes, Inria, France
Leo Freitas   Newcastle University, UK
Carlo A. Furia   Chalmers University of Technology, Sweden
Jan Friso Groote   Eindhoven University of Technology, Netherlands
Reiner Hähnle   Technical University of Darmstadt, Germany
Ian J. Hayes   University of Queensland, Australia
Marieke Huisman   University of Twente, Netherlands
Rajeev Joshi   NASA Jet Propulsion Laboratory, USA

Laura Kovács	Vienna University of Technology, Austria
Juliana Küster Filipe Bowles	University of St. Andrews, UK
Axel Legay	IRISA/Inria Rennes, France
K. Rustan M. Leino	Microsoft Research, USA
Gerald Lüttgen	University of Bamberg, Germany
Dominique Mery	Université de Lorraine, LORIA, France
Stefan Mitsch	Carnegie Mellon University, USA
Rosemary Monahan	Maynooth University, Ireland
Luigia Petre	Åbo Akademi University, Finland
Adrian Riesco	Universidad Complutense de Madrid, Spain
Gerhard Schellhorn	Universität Augsburg, Germany
Gerardo Schneider	Chalmers University of Technology, University of Gothenburg, Sweden
Emil Sekerinski	McMaster University, Canada
Graeme Smith	University of Queensland, Australia
Martin Steffen	University of Oslo, Norway
Armando Tacchella	Università di Genova, Italy
Helen Treharne	University of Surrey, UK
Mark Utting	University of the Sunshine Coast, Australia
Frits Vaandrager	Radboud University Nijmegen, Netherlands
Heike Wehrheim	University of Paderborn, Germany
Kirsten Winter	University of Queensland, Australia

Additional Reviewers

Bodenmueller, Stefan	Flores-Montoya, Antonio	Pinisetty, Srinivas
Brett, Noel	Hallgren, Per	Schlaipfer, Matthias
Bubel, Richard	Isabel, Miguel	Siddique, Umair
Burton, Eden	Jakse, Raphaël	Suda, Martin
Camilleri, John J.	Kamburjan, Eduard	Talebi, Mahmoud
Caminati, Marco B.	Kragl, Bernhard	Töws, Manuel
Colvin, Robert	Modesti, Paolo	Traonouez, Louis-Marie
Do, Quoc Huy	Mueller, Andreas	Travkin, Oleg
Doménech, Jesús J.	Nazarpour, Hosein	de Vink, Erik
El-Hokayem, Antoine	Neele, Thomas	Yang, Fei
Enescu, Mike	Pagnin, Elena	Zanardini, Damiano
Fendrich, Sascha	Pfähler, Jörg	Zantema, Hans

Invited Talks

Integrating Inference into Stochastic Process Algebra Models

Jane Hillston

LFCS, School of Informatics, University of Edinburgh
jane.hillston@ed.ac.uk

Stochastic process algebras emerged in the early 1990s as a quantitative formal method. By incorporating information about probabilities and timing into a classical process algebra, it was possible to build models which allowed quantitative aspects of behaviour such as performance, reliability and availability to be evaluated in addition to qualitative aspects such as liveness and safety. Thus it became possible to answer questions such as the expected time until a failure in the system, or the proportion messages that are successfully delivered within 10 seconds. The language is equipped with a structured operational semantics giving rise to a labelled transition system that can be interpreted as a continuous time Markov chain. This class of stochastic processes is widely used in quantitative modelling and many efficient analysis techniques are available. Moreover the formality and structure of the process algebra has allowed new decompositions and approximations to be defined at the language level and automatically applied.

However one of the drawbacks of the stochastic process algebra approach is that the quantitative analysis of the model is dependent on the accuracy of the parameters used to capture the timings and probabilities that influence behaviour within the system. In some application domains this data can be obtained from monitoring or logging software, systems specifications etc. But in others, such as systems biology, not all aspects of behaviour are accessible to measurement and it can be very difficult to arrive at accurate parameters for the models.

Thus in recent years we have developed a stochastic process algebra, ProPPA, which allows parameters within the model to be left uncertain, specified by a distribution rather than a concrete value. Thus a ProPPA model describes not a single model, but a family of models, each associated with a probability that it is a good representation of the system. Moreover when evidence about the behaviour of the system is available, the language supports inference techniques from machine learning, which allow us to refine the uncertainty and generate a new family of models with different probabilities. The range of possible quantitative behaviours can be derived from the family of models together with an estimate of their likelihood.

Thus ProPPA, Probabilistic Programming Process Algebra, is a stochastic process algebra that combines elements of the data-driven modelling approach adopted in machine learning, with a more mechanistic modelling style from formal methods. Since different inference techniques are suited to different model characteristics, the ProPPA tool suite offers a modular approach with a number of different inference techniques which can be used to refine the estimate of the parameters of the model and therefore the possible quantitative behaviours that may be exhibited.

Logic & Proofs for Cyber-Physical Systems with KeYmaera X

André Platzer

Computer Science Department, Carnegie Mellon University, Pittsburgh, USA
aplatzer@cs.cmu.edu

1 Abstract of Invited Talk

Cyber-physical systems (CPS) combine cyber aspects such as communication and computer control with physical aspects such as movement in space, which arise frequently in many safety-critical application domains, including aviation, automotive, railway, and robotics [1, 2, 4–6, 8, 11, 16, 17, 24–28, 40, 42–44]. But how can we ensure that these systems are guaranteed to meet their design goals, e.g., that an aircraft will not crash into another one?

Borrowing from an invited paper at IJCAR [36] to which we refer for more detail, this talk will highlight some of the most fascinating aspects of cyber-physical systems and their dynamical systems models, such as hybrid systems that combine discrete transitions and continuous evolution along differential equations. Because of the impact that they can have on the real world, CPSs deserve proof as safety evidence.

Multi-dynamical systems understand complex systems as a combination of multiple elementary dynamical aspects [33], which makes them natural mathematical models for CPS, since they tame their complexity by compositionality. The family of differential dynamic logics [28–35, 37] achieves this compositionality by providing compositional logics, programming languages, and reasoning principles for CPS. Differential dynamic logics, as implemented in the theorem prover KeYmaera X [7], have been instrumental in verifying many applications, including the Airborne Collision Avoidance System ACAS X [9], the European Train Control System ETCS [39], automotive systems [13, 14, 20], aircraft roundabout maneuvers [38], mobile robot navigation [18, 19], and a surgical robot system for skull-base surgery [10].

In addition to serving as a basis for additional formal verification results in different CPS application domains, each of those case studies are chosen to demonstrate how characteristically new features can be verified in practice. Safety, controllability, reactivity, and liveness properties for the double integrator dynamics interacting with different discrete components are the basis for ETCS verification [39]. Combinations with distributed systems and communication systems are emphasized elsewhere

---

This talk is based on an overview of logic and proofs for cyber-physical systems from IJCAR [36] to which we refer for more details. The talk is augmented with more detail on the new theorem prover KeYmaera X, which is at http://keymaeraX.org/.This material is based upon work supported by the National Science Foundation under NSF CAREER Award CNS-1054246.

[13, 14, 20]. How safety properties of CPS with unsolvable dynamics can be verified rigorously is showcased for aircraft with fixed ground speed [38] and for mobile ground robot navigation with acceleration/braking [18, 19]. High precision results in the safe handling of data structures for an unbounded number of obstacles are showcased in medical robotics [10]. Systems whose decisions are based on table lookups from a machine-learned value table are studied in the context of elaborate characterizations of the safe region of the high-level vertical motion of aircraft [9]. The ACAS X results are also of interest for characterizations of last-resort safety, i.e., to restrict intervention to when the last chance for a corrective safety action has come.

The KeYmaera X prover implements a uniform substitution calculus for differential dynamic logic d$\mathscr{L}$ [35], which enables a prover with a very small soundness-critical core of just about 1 700 LOC of Scala [7]. To achieve high levels of confidence, this uniform substitution calculus has been cross-verified both in the Isabelle/HOL and in the Coq theorem provers [3]. Verification results about CPS models transfer to CPS implementations when generating provably correct runtime monitors with the ModelPlex approach [21], which is also implemented as a proof tactic in KeYmaera X. That approach makes it possible to rigorously develop correct CPS controllers for CPS models with a provable link to the safety monitors in the system implementation. The use of components for hybrid systems has been explored as well [15, 22, 23], which make it possible to benefit from safety proofs about components and inherit safety proofs for a compound system for free (under certain compatibility conditions). While differential dynamic logics are already inherently compositional for each of their composition operators, component notions add additional structuring principles for bigger pieces and provide simple safety notions for components. In order to bootstrap such a component approach without having to enlarge the small soundness-critical core of KeYmaera X, the safety of the composite is proved automatically by a KeYmaera X tactic from correctness proofs about its components [23].

More technical overviews are available in the literature [29, 33, 36, 41].

References

1. Alur, R.: Principles of Cyber-Physical Systems. MIT Press (2015)
2 Alur, R., Courcoubetis, C., Halbwachs, N., Henzinger, T.A., Ho, P.H., Nicollin, X., Olivero, A., Sifakis, J., Yovine, S.: The algorithmic analysis of hybrid systems. Theor. Comput. Sci. **138**(1), 3–34 (1995)
3. Bohrer, B., Rahli, V., Vukotic, I., Völp, M., Platzer, A.: Formally verified differential dynamic logic. In: Bertot, Y., Vafeiadis, V. (eds.) Certified Programs and Proofs - 6th ACM SIGPLAN Conference. CPP 2017, Paris, France, January 16–17, 2017, pp. 208–221. ACM (2017)
4. Clarke, E.M., Emerson, E.A., Sifakis, J.: Model checking: algorithmic verification and debugging. Commun. ACM **52**(11), 74–84 (2009)
5. Davoren, J.M., Nerode, A.: Logics for hybrid systems. IEEE **88**(7), 985–1010 (2000)
6. Doyen, L., Frehse, G., Pappas, G.J., Platzer, A.: Verification of hybrid systems. In: Clarke, E. M., Henzinger, T.A., Veith, H. (eds.) Handbook of Model Checking. Springer (2017)

7. Fulton, N., Mitsch, S., Quesel, J.D., Völp, M., Platzer, A.: KeYmaera X: An axiomatic tactical theorem prover for hybrid systems. In: Felty, A.P., Middeldorp, A. (eds.) CADE-25. LNAI, vol. 9195, pp. 527–538. Springer, Switzerland (2015)

8. Henzinger, T.A., Sifakis, J.: The discipline of embedded systems design. Computer 40(10), 32–40 (2007)

9. Jeannin, J., Ghorbal, K., Kouskoulas, Y., Schmidt, A., Gardner, R., Mitsch, S., Platzer, A.: A formally verified hybrid system for safe advisories in the next-generation airborne collision avoidance system. STTT (2016)

10. Kouskoulas, Y., Renshaw, D.W., Platzer, A., Kazanzides, P.: Certifying the safe design of a virtual fixture control algorithm for a surgical robot. In: Belta, C., Ivancic, F. (eds.) HSCC, pp. 263–272. ACM (2013)

11. Larsen, K.G.: Verification and performance analysis for embedded systems. In: Chin, W., Qin, S. (eds.) Third IEEE International Symposium on Theoretical Aspects of Software Engineering. TASE 2009, 29–31 July 2009, Tianjin, China, pp. 3–4. IEEE Computer Society (2009)

12. Proceedings of the 27th Annual ACM/IEEE Symposium on Logic in Computer Science, LICS 2012, Dubrovnik, Croatia, June 25–28, 2012. IEEE (2012)

13. Loos, S.M., Platzer, A., Nistor, L.: Adaptive cruise control: Hybrid, distributed, and now formally verified. In: Butler, M., Schulte, W. (eds.) FM 2011. LNCS, vol. 6664, pp. 42–56. Springer, Heidelberg (2011)

14. Loos, S.M., Witmer, D., Steenkiste, P., Platzer, A.: Efficiency analysis of formally verified adaptive cruise controllers. In: Hegyi, A., Schutter, B.D. (eds.) ITSC, pp. 1565–1570 (2013)

15. Lunel, S., Boyer, B., Talpin, J.P.: Compositional proofs in differential dynamic logic. In: ACSD (2017)

16. Lunze, J., Lamnabhi-Lagarrigue, F. (eds.): Handbook of Hybrid Systems Control: Theory, Tools, Applications. Cambridge University Press (2009)

17. Maler, O.: Control from computer science. Ann. Rev. Control 26(2), 175–187 (2002)

18. Mitsch, S., Ghorbal, K., Platzer, A.: On provably safe obstacle avoidance for autonomous robotic ground vehicles. In: Newman, P., Fox, D., Hsu, D. (eds.) Robotics: Science and Systems (2013)

19. Mitsch, S., Ghorbal, K., Vogelbacher, D., Platzer, A.: Formal verification of obstacle avoidance and navigation of ground robots (2016). CoRR abs/1605.00604

20. Mitsch, S., Loos, S.M., Platzer, A.: Towards formal verification of freeway traffic control. In: Lu, C. (ed.) ICCPS, pp. 171–180. IEEE (2012)

21. Mitsch, S., Platzer, A.: ModelPlex: Verified runtime validation of verified cyber-physical system models. Form. Methods Syst. Des. 49(1), 33–74 (2016). Special issue of selected papers from RV'14

22. Müller, A., Mitsch, S., Retschitzegger, W., Schwinger, W., Platzer, A.: A component-based approach to hybrid systems safety verification. In: Ábrahám, E., Huisman, M. (eds.) IFM 2016. LNCS, vol. 9681, pp. 441–456. Springer, Switzerland (2016)

23. Müller, A., Mitsch, S., Retschitzegger, W., Schwinger, W., Platzer, A.: Change and delay contracts for hybrid system component verification. In: Huisman, M., Rubin, J. (eds.) FASE 2017. LNCS, vol. 10202, pp. 134–151. Springer, Germany (2017)

24. Nerode, A.: Logic and control. In: Cooper, S.B., Löwe, B., Sorbi, A. (eds.) CiE 2007. LNCS, vol. 4497, pp. 585–597. Springer, Heidelberg (2007)

25. Nerode, A., Kohn, W.: Models for hybrid systems: Automata, topologies, controllability, observability. In: Grossman, R.L., Nerode, A., Ravn, A.P., Rischel, H. (eds.) Hybrid Systems. LNCS, vol. 736, pp. 317–356. Springer (1992)

26. NITRD CPS Senior Steering Group: CPS vision statement. NITRD (2012)

27. Pappas, G.J.: Wireless control networks: modeling, synthesis, robustness, security. In: Caccamo, M., Frazzoli, E., Grosu, R. (eds.) Proceedings of the 14th ACM International Conference on Hybrid Systems: Computation and Control, HSCC 2011, Chicago, IL, USA, April 12–14, 2011, pp. 1–2. ACM (2011)

28. Platzer, A.: Differential dynamic logic for hybrid systems. J. Autom. Reas. **41**(2), 143–189 (2008)

29. Platzer, A.: Logical Analysis of Hybrid Systems: Proving Theorems for Complex Dynamics. Springer, Heidelberg (2010)

30. Platzer, A.: Stochastic differential dynamic logic for stochastic hybrid programs. In: Bjørner, N., Sofronie-Stokkermans, V. (eds.) CADE 2011. LNCS, vol. 6803, pp. 431–445. Springer, Heidelberg (2011)

31. Platzer, A.: A complete axiomatization of quantified differential dynamic logic for distributed hybrid systems. Log. Meth. Comput. Sci. **8**(4), 1–44 (2012). Special issue for selected papers from CSL'10

32. Platzer, A.: The complete proof theory of hybrid systems. In: LICS 2012, pp. 541–550 (2012)

33. Platzer, A.: Logics of dynamical systems. In: LICS 2012, pp. 13–24 (2012)

34. Platzer, A.: Differential game logic. ACM Trans. Comput. Log. **17**(1), 1:1–1:51 (2015)

35. Platzer, A.: A complete uniform substitution calculus for differential dynamic logic. J. Autom. Reas. (2016)

36. Platzer, A.: Logic & proofs for cyber-physical systems. In: Olivetti, N., Tiwari, A. (eds.) IJCAR 2016. LNAI, vol. 9706, pp. 15–21. Springer, Switzerland (2016)

37. Platzer, A.: Differential hybrid games. ACM Trans. Comput. Log. **18**(3) (2017)

38. Platzer, A., Clarke, E.M.: Formal verification of curved flight collision avoidance maneuvers: A case study. In: Cavalcanti, A., Dams, D. (eds.) FM 2009. LNCS, vol. 5850, pp. 547–562. Springer, Heidelberg (2009)

39. Platzer, A., Quesel, J.D.: European Train Control System: A case study in formal verification. In: Breitman, K., Cavalcanti, A. (eds.) ICFEM 2009. LNCS, vol. 5885, pp. 246–265. Springer, Heidelberg (2009)

40. President's Council of Advisors on Science and Technology: Leadership under challenge: Information technology R&D in a competitive world. An Assessment of the Federal Networking and Information Technology R&D Program, August 2007

41. Quesel, J.D., Mitsch, S., Loos, S., Aréchiga, N., Platzer, A.: How to model and prove hybrid systems with KeYmaera: A tutorial on safety. STTT **18**(1), 67–91 (2016)

42. Tabuada, P.: Verification and Control of Hybrid Systems: A Symbolic Approach. Springer (2009)

43. Tiwari, A.: Logic in software, dynamical and biological systems. In: LICS, pp. 9–10. IEEE Computer Society (2011)

44. Wing, J.M.: Five deep questions in computing. Commun. ACM **51**(1), 58–60 (2008)

Machine Learning for Programming

Martin Vechev

Department of Computer Science, ETH Zurich, Switzerland
martin.vechev@inf.ethz.ch

In this talk I will discuss some of our latest research on creating probabilistic programming tools based on machine learning. These tools leverage the massive effort already spent by thousands of programmers and make useful predictions about new, unseen programs, helping solve difficult and important software tasks. I will illustrate several such probabilistic systems including statistical code synthesis and deobfuscation. Two of these de-obfuscation systems (jsnice.org and apk-deguard.com) are freely available, used daily and have more than 200,000 users from every country worldwide. I will also present new methods for creating probabilistic models that some of our systems are based on. These methods are more precise than neural networks and have applications to other domains, beyond code (e.g., to modeling natural language). Finally, I will conclude with what I believe are some of the more interesting, open problems in this area.

Contents

Cyber-Physical Systems

An Active Learning Approach to the Falsification of Black Box
Cyber-Physical Systems 3
  Simone Silvetti, Alberto Policriti, and Luca Bortolussi

Modelling and Verification of Timed Robotic Controllers 18
  Pedro Ribeiro, Alvaro Miyazawa, Wei Li, Ana Cavalcanti,
  and Jon Timmis

Spatial Reasoning About Motorway Traffic Safety with Isabelle/HOL 34
  Sven Linker

Formalising and Monitoring Traffic Rules for Autonomous Vehicles
in Isabelle/HOL 50
  Albert Rizaldi, Jonas Keinholz, Monika Huber, Jochen Feldle,
  Fabian Immler, Matthias Althoff, Eric Hilgendorf, and Tobias Nipkow

Software Verification Tools

Making Whiley Boogie! 69
  Mark Utting, David J. Pearce, and Lindsay Groves

Complexity Analysis for Java with AProVE 85
  Florian Frohn and Jürgen Giesl

The VerCors Tool Set: Verification of Parallel and Concurrent Software 102
  Stefan Blom, Saeed Darabi, Marieke Huisman, and Wytse Oortwijn

An Extension of the ABS Toolchain with a Mechanism for Type
Checking SPLs 111
  Ferruccio Damiani, Michael Lienhardt, Radu Muschevici,
  and Ina Schaefer

Safety-Critical Systems

Generalised Test Tables: A Practical Specification Language
for Reactive Systems 129
  Bernhard Beckert, Suhyun Cha, Mattias Ulbrich, Birgit Vogel-Heuser,
  and Alexander Weigl

Transient and Steady-State Statistical Analysis for Discrete
Event Simulators.   145
  Stephen Gilmore, Daniël Reijsbergen, and Andrea Vandin

Algebraic Compilation of Safety-Critical Java Bytecode.   161
  James Baxter and Ana Cavalcanti

Task-Node Mapping in an Arbitrary Computer Network Using SMT Solver. . .   177
  Andrii Kovalov, Elisabeth Lobe, Andreas Gerndt, and Daniel Lüdtke

Concurrency and Distributed Systems

Analysis of Synchronisations in Stateful Active Objects.   195
  Ludovic Henrio, Cosimo Laneve, and Vincenzo Mastandrea

BTS: A Tool for Formal Component-Based Development   211
  Dalay Israel de Almeida Pereira, Marcel Vinicius Medeiros Oliveira,
  Madiel S. Conserva Filho, and Sarah Raquel Da Rocha Silva

Testing and Verifying Chain Repair Methods for CORFU Using Stateless
Model Checking.   227
  Stavros Aronis, Scott Lystig Fritchie, and Konstantinos Sagonas

Synthesizing Coalitions for Multi-agent Games.   243
  Wei Ji, Farn Wang, and Peng Wu

Program Verification Techniques

Hoare-Style Reasoning from Multiple Contracts   263
  Olaf Owe, Toktam Ramezanifarkhani, and Elahe Fazeldehkordi

A New Invariant Rule for the Analysis of Loops with Non-standard
Control Flows.   279
  Dominic Steinhöfel and Nathan Wasser

Triggerless Happy: Intermediate Verification with a First-Order Prover   295
  YuTing Chen and Carlo A. Furia

SEMSLICE: Exploiting Relational Verification for Automatic
Program Slicing   312
  Bernhard Beckert, Thorsten Bormer, Stephan Gocht, Mihai Herda,
  Daniel Lentzsch, and Mattias Ulbrich

Formal Modeling

VBPMN: Automated Verification of BPMN Processes (Tool Paper)   323
  Ajay Krishna, Pascal Poizat, and Gwen Salaün

How Well Can I Secure My System? 332
 Barbara Kordy and Wojciech Wideł

MaxUSE: A Tool for Finding Achievable Constraints and Conflicts
for Inconsistent UML Class Diagrams 348
 Hao Wu

Formal Verification of CNL Health Recommendations. 357
 Fahrurrozi Rahman and Juliana Küster Filipe Bowles

Verified Software

Modular Verification of Order-Preserving Write-Back Caches. 375
 *Jörg Pfähler, Gidon Ernst, Stefan Bodenmüller, Gerhard Schellhorn,
 and Wolfgang Reif*

Formal Verification of ARP (Address Resolution Protocol)
Through SMT-Based Model Checking - A Case Study - 391
 *Danilo Bruschi, Andrea Di Pasquale, Silvio Ghilardi, Andrea Lanzi,
 and Elena Pagani*

Certified Password Quality: A Case Study Using Coq and Linux
Pluggable Authentication Modules 407
 *João F. Ferreira, Saul A. Johnson, Alexandra Mendes,
 and Phillip J. Brooke*

Verification of STAR-Vote and Evaluation of FDR and ProVerif 422
 Murat Moran and Dan S. Wallach

Author Index 437

Cyber-Physical Systems

An Active Learning Approach to the Falsification of Black Box Cyber-Physical Systems

Simone Silvetti[1,2(✉)], Alberto Policriti[2,3], and Luca Bortolussi[4,5,6]

[1] Esteco SpA, Trieste, Italy
silvetti@esteco.com
[2] DIMA, University of Udine, Udine, Italy
alberto.policriti@uniud.it
[3] Istituto di Genomica Applicata, Udine, Italy
[4] DMG, University of Trieste, Trieste, Italy
luca@dmi.units.it
[5] Modelling and Simulation Group, Saarland University, Saarbrücken, Germany
[6] CNR-ISTI, Pisa, Italy

Abstract. Search-based testing is widely used to find bugs in models of complex Cyber-Physical Systems. Latest research efforts have improved this approach by casting it as a falsification procedure of formally specified temporal properties, exploiting the robustness semantics of Signal Temporal Logic. The scaling of this approach to highly complex engineering systems requires efficient falsification procedures, which should be applicable also to black box models. Falsification is also exacerbated by the fact that inputs are often time-dependent functions. We tackle the falsification of formal properties of complex black box models of Cyber-Physical Systems, leveraging machine learning techniques from the area of Active Learning. Tailoring these techniques to the falsification problem with time-dependent, functional inputs, we show a considerable gain in computational effort, by reducing the number of model simulations needed. The effectiveness of the proposed approach is discussed on a challenging industrial-level benchmark from automotive.

Keywords: Model-based testing · Robustness · Gaussian Processes · Cyber-Physical Systems · Falsification

1 Introduction

Model Based Development (MBD) is a well known design framework of complex engineered systems, concerned with reducing cost and time of the prototyping process. Most prominently, this framework has been adopted in the industrial fields such as automotive and aerospace where the conformity of the end product is extremely important. The majority of systems in these areas are Cyber-Physical Systems (CPS) [5], where physical and software components interact

© Springer International Publishing AG 2017
N. Polikarpova and S. Schneider (Eds.): IFM 2017, LNCS 10510, pp. 3–17, 2017.
DOI: 10.1007/978-3-319-66845-1_1

producing complex behaviors. These systems can be described by appropriate mathematical models which are able to mime all the system behaviors. Moreover, it is necessary to have a suitable specification framework capable of analyzing the output of such models.

Hybrid Systems [13] are the mathematical framework usually adopted, while Temporal Logic [16], due to its ability to describe temporal events, is generally used as specification framework. The high level of expressivity of Hybrid Systems, which is the main reason for their success, is also the cause of their undecidability, even for simple logic formulas. Subclasses of Hybrid Systems which are decidable for specific temporal logic formulas exist and have been widely studied during the last 15 years, as well as model checking techniques capable of verifying them [3]. Unfortunately, the majority of CPS used nowadays in the industrial field are much more complex than decidable hybrid systems. They are mainly described by using block diagram tools (i.e. Simulink/Stateflow, Scade, LabVIEW, and so on) where several switch blocks, 2/3-D look-up tables and state transitions coexist. These CPS are generally not decidable and standard model checking techniques are not feasible, leading to the proposal of different techniques [4].

Testing procedures with the purpose of verifying the model on specific behaviors have been adopted for several years. These are feasible approaches whenever it is possible to write in advance collections of test cases which extensively cover all the possible events leading to system failure [21]. With the increase of complexity, such an *a priori* assumption is not viable in most of the real cases and for this reason different techniques, such as random testing and search-based testing, have been introduced [22]. The general idea consists in expressing the falsification procedure as an optimization process aiming at minimizing a target quantity which describes "how much" a given property is verified. For example, achieving a negative value of the robustness semantics of a given Signal Temporal Logic (STL) [9] formula means falsifying the system with respect to that formula.

In this paper we study the falsification problem of black box systems (i.e. block diagram models such as Simulink/Stateflow model or sets of ordinary differential equations generally used in automotive or aerospace industrial fields) which takes as input and produce as output continuous or Piecewise-Continuous (PWC) signals. The requirements are expressed by using STL.

Solving such falsification problems in a search-based framework poses two main challenges. Generally, the simulation of block diagram models is time consuming, hence it is necessary to falsify the model with as few simulations as possible. Moreover, the models accept continuous/PWC signals as inputs and an efficient finite dimensional parametrization is necessary to perform an optimization procedure. The contribution we propose in this paper is to tackle these challenges by a novel strategy leveraging Machine Learning techniques (Gaussian Processes and active learning) and by using a new adaptive version of the Control Points Parameterization approach.

The paper is organized as follows. In Sect. 2 we review the definition of Dynamical System, Signal Temporal Logic and Gaussian Processes. In Sect. 3 we discuss the Domain Estimation Problem which is solved by using Gaussian

Processes. Section 4 presents the Falsification Approach and the adaptive optimization strategy performed by using Gaussian Processes and adaptive function parameterization. In Sect. 5 we introduce the Probabilistic Approximation Semantics. In Sect. 6 we briefly introduce the test cases and discuss the results. Finally in Sect. 7 we provide the conclusions and discuss the future works.

2 Background

2.1 Dynamical System

We consider a system as a pair $\mathcal{M} = (\mathcal{S}, \mathtt{sim})$ where $\mathcal{S} = \mathcal{U} \times \mathcal{X}$, and $\mathcal{U}$ and $\mathcal{X}$ are finite (or infinite) sets representing respectively the input values of the system and the state (coinciding for us with the output). The system is equipped with a simulator, $\mathtt{sim}$, which will be considered as a black box (i.e. we can provide any input to the system and read the generated outputs). The input set is $\mathcal{U} = V_0 \times \cdots \times V_n \times W_1 \times \cdots \times W_m$ where V_i are finite sets and W_i are compact sets in $\mathbb{R}$, representing respectively the discrete input events and the continuous input signals. The dynamics of the system is described with two functions: the *state function* $\mathbf{x} : \mathcal{T} \to \mathcal{X}$ and the *input function* $\mathbf{u} : \mathcal{T} \to \mathcal{U}$ which map each time $t \in \mathcal{T}$ to a state $(\mathbf{x}(t) \in \mathcal{X})$ and input $(\mathbf{u}(t) \in \mathcal{U})$, and where $\mathcal{T} = [0, T] \subset \mathbb{R}$. We call $k-th$ *input signal* the u_k function belonging to the input function $\mathbf{u}$ and identify with $\{\mathcal{T} \to \mathcal{U}\}$ the set of function from $\mathcal{T}$ to $\mathcal{U}$.

The dynamics of the system is encoded in the *deterministic* simulator $\mathtt{sim}$, which takes as input an initial state $\mathbf{x}_0 \in \mathcal{X}$ and an input signal $\mathbf{u}(t)$, and returns as output a corresponding system trajectory $\mathbf{x} : \mathcal{T} \to \mathcal{X}$, with $\mathbf{x}(t_0) = \mathbf{x}_0$. We denote by $Path^{\mathcal{M}} \subseteq (\mathcal{T} \to \mathcal{S})$ the set of all possible simulations returned by $\mathtt{sim}$, described as pairs of state and input functions, for any possible different initial state and input signal. In any practical scenario, the simulator will operate in discrete time, returning a sequence of values at discrete time points $t_0, t_1, \ldots, t_k, \ldots$, which are then interpolated to produce a continuous output (e.g. by piecewise linear interpolation).

2.2 Signal Temporal Logic

Signal Temporal Logic (STL, [14]) is a discrete linear time temporal logic used to reason about the future evolution of a path in continuous time. Generally this formalism is used to qualitatively describe the behaviors of trajectories of differential equations or stochastic models. The temporal operators we consider are all time-bounded and this implies that time-bounded trajectories are sufficient to assess the truth of every formula. The atomic predicates of STL are inequalities on a set of real-valued variables, i.e. of the form $\mu(\boldsymbol{s}) := [g(\boldsymbol{s}) \geq 0]$, where $g : \mathcal{S} \to \mathbb{R}$ is a continuous function, $\boldsymbol{s} \in \mathcal{S}$ and consequently $\mu : \mathcal{S} \to \{\top, \bot\}$.

Definition 1. *A formula $\phi \in \mathcal{F}$ of STL is defined by the following syntax:*

$$\phi := \bot \mid \top \mid \mu \mid \neg\phi \mid \phi \vee \phi \mid \phi\mathbf{U}_{[T_1, T_2]}\phi, \tag{1}$$

where μ are atomic predicates as defined above, and $T_1 < T_2 < +\infty$.

Modal operators "eventually" and "globally" can be defined, as customary, as $\mathbf{F}_{[T_1,T_2]}\phi \equiv \top \mathbf{U}_{[T_1,T_2]}\phi$ and $\mathbf{G}_{[T_1,T_2]}\phi \equiv \neg\mathbf{F}_{[T_1,T_2]}\neg\phi$. STL formulae are interpreted over the dynamics $Path^{\mathcal{M}}$ of the model $\mathcal{M}$. We will consider the *quantitative* semantics [9] which, given a trajectory $\boldsymbol{x}(t)$, returns a real value capturing a notion of robustness of satisfaction whose sign captures the truth value of the formula (positive if and only if true), and whose absolute value gives a measure on how robust is the satisfaction.

Definition 2 (Quantitative Semantics). *The quantitative satisfaction function* $\rho : \mathcal{F} \times Path^{\mathcal{M}} \times [0, \infty) \to \mathbb{R}$ *is defined by:*

- $\rho(\top, \boldsymbol{s}, t) = +\infty$
- $\rho(\mu, \boldsymbol{s}, t) = g(\boldsymbol{s}(t))$ *where g is such that $\mu(\boldsymbol{s}) \equiv [g(\boldsymbol{s}) \geq 0]$*
- $\rho(\neg\phi, \boldsymbol{s}, t) = -\rho(\phi, \boldsymbol{s}, t)$
- $\rho(\phi_1 \vee \phi_2, \boldsymbol{s}, t) = \max(\rho(\phi_1, \boldsymbol{s}, t), \rho(\phi_2, \boldsymbol{s}, t))$
- $\rho(\phi_1 \mathbf{U}_{[T_1,T_2]}\phi_2, \boldsymbol{s}, t) = \sup\limits_{t' \in [t+T_1, t+T_2]} (\min(\rho(\phi_2, \boldsymbol{s}, t'), \inf\limits_{t'' \in [t,t')} \rho(\phi_1, \boldsymbol{s}, t'')))$

2.3   Gaussian Processes

Gaussian Processes (GPs) are probabilistic methods used for classification or regression purposes. More specifically, a GP is a collection of random variables $X(t) \in \mathbb{R}$ ($t \in T$, an interval of $\mathbb{R}$) of which any finite number define a multivariate normal distribution. A GP is uniquely defined by its mean and covariance functions (called also kernels) denoted respectively with $m : T \to \mathbb{R}$ and $k : \mathbb{R} \times \mathbb{R} \to \mathbb{R}$ such that for every finite set of points $(t_1, t_2, \ldots, t_n)$:

$$X \sim \mathcal{GP}(m, k) \iff (X(t_1), X(t_2), \ldots, X(t_n)) \sim \mathcal{N}(\mathbf{m}, K) \tag{2}$$

where $\mathbf{m} = (m(t_1), m(t_2), \ldots, m(t_n))$ is the vector mean and $K \in \mathbb{R}^{n \times n}$ is the covariance matrix, such that $K_{ij} = k(X(t_i), X(t_j))$. From a functional point of view, GP is a probability distribution on the set of functions $X : T \to R$. The choice of the covariance function is important from a modeling perspective because it determines the type of function that will be sampled with higher probability from a GP, see [18]. In this work we use the Neural Network kernel, which performed better than more classical choices, like Gaussian Radial Basis Function kernels, see [18] for further details.

GPs are successfully used to solve regression problems starting from a training set with noisy observations,

$$((t_1, x_1), (t_2, x_2), \ldots, (t_n, x_n)) \tag{3}$$

The goal is to find a function $x : T \to \mathbb{R}$ such that $\forall i \leq n, \quad x_i = x(t_i) + \epsilon$, and $\epsilon \sim \mathcal{N}(0, \sigma_n)$ (a Gaussian noise is a common choice for regression with real-valued outputs). In the GP paradigm a family of mean functions $m(x; h_1) : \mathbb{R} \times H_1 \to \mathbb{R}$ and of covariance functions $k(x_1, x_2; h_2) : \mathbb{R} \times \mathbb{R} \times H_2 \to \mathbb{R}$, where $h = (h_1, h_2)$ are called hyperparameters, are considered. The idea is to estimate the best hyperparameters which justify as much as possible, the observations provided in the training set. Mathematically it means to maximize the log marginal likelihood $\max_h log\, p(\boldsymbol{x}|\boldsymbol{t}; h)$. where $\boldsymbol{x} = (x_1, x_2, \ldots, x_n)$ and $\boldsymbol{t} = (t_1, t_2, \ldots, t_n)$ accordingly to (3). After having solved the previous optimization problem it is possible to predict the probability distribution of a new point as $x(t^*) \sim \mathcal{N}(m^*, k^*)$, where

$$m^* = (k(t, t_1), \ldots, k(t, t_N))K_N^{-1}x$$

$$k^* = k(t, t)(k(t, t_1), \ldots, k(t, t_N))K_N^{-1}(k(t, t_1), \ldots, k(t, t_N))^T$$

3 Domain Estimation with Gaussian Processes

Definition 3. *Consider a function $f : \mathcal{D} \to \mathbb{R}$ and an interval $I \subseteq \mathbb{R}$. We define the* domain estimation problem *as the task of identifying the set $\mathcal{B}$ of points $x \in \mathcal{D}$ such that $f(x) \in I$:*

$$\mathcal{B} = \{x \in \mathcal{D} | f(x) \in I\} \subseteq \mathcal{D}, \qquad (4)$$

In practice, if $\mathcal{B} \neq \emptyset$, we will limit us to identify a subset $B \subseteq \mathcal{B}$ of size n.

Gaussian Processes (GP) can be efficiently used to solve this task. Similarly to the Cross Entropy methods for optimization [19], the idea is to implement an iterative sample strategy in order to increase the probability to sample a point in $\mathcal{B}$, as the number of iterations increases. Consider the set $K(f) = \{(x_i, f(x_i))\}_{i \leq n}$ representing the partial knowledge we have collected after n iterations and the GP $f_K(x) \sim GP(m_K(x), \sigma_K(x))$ trained on $K(f)$. We can easily estimate $P(x \in \mathcal{B}) = P(f_K(x) \in I)$ by computing the probability of a Gaussian distribution with mean $m_K(x)$ and variance $\sigma_K^2(x)$. This corresponds to our uncertainty on the value of $f(x)$ belonging to I, as captured by the GP reconstruction of f. The previous probability can be effectively used to solve the domain estimation problem described in Definition 3. Our approach is described in Algorithm 1:

- During initialization (line 2), we set the iteration counter (i) and the minimum distance (d) from the interval I. The set (B) containing the elements of $(\mathcal{B})$ is set to empty, which ensures the algorithm is run at least once. The knowledge set $K(f)$ is initialized with some randomized points sampled from $\mathcal{D}$ (line 3).
- In the iterative loop, the algorithm first checks if the number of counterexamples (ce) or if the maximum number of iterations $(maxIter)$ has been reached. In this case, the method stops returning the estimated set (B) and the minimum distance from I that has been registered until that point. Otherwise new GPs are trained by using $K(f)$ (line 5) and a set composed by m points (D_{grid}) is generated by Latin Hypercube sampling [15], so to have a homogeneous distribution of points in space (line 6). For each of these points x, the probability $P(x \in \mathcal{B}) = P(f_K(x) \in I)$ is calculated and the set $\{(x, P(x \in \mathcal{B})), x \in D_{grid}\}$ is created. Afterwards, a candidate point x_{new} is

---

Algorithm 1

1: **procedure** $[B, d\ ] =$ DOMAINESTIMATION$(maxIter, ce, m, f, I)$
2:      $i \leftarrow 0,\ B \leftarrow \emptyset,\ d \leftarrow +\infty$
3:      INITIALIZE$(K(f))$
4:      **while** ($|B| \leq ce$ **and** $i \leq$ maxIter) **do**
5:          $f_{K(f)} \sim$ TRAINGAUSSIANPROCESS$(K(f))$
6:          $D_{grid} \leftarrow$ LHS(m)
7:          $x_{new} \leftarrow$ SAMPLE$\{(x, P(x \in \mathcal{B})), x \in D_{grid}\}$
8:          $f_{new} \leftarrow f(x_{new})$
9:          $d \leftarrow \min(d, $DISTANCE$(f_{new}, I))$
10:         $K(f) \leftarrow K(f) \cup \{(x_{new}, f_{new})\}$
11:         **if** $f_{new} \in I$ **then**
12:             $B = B \cup \{x_{new}\}$
13:         **end if**
14:         $i \leftarrow i + 1$
15:     **end while**
16: **end procedure**

---

sampled from D_{grid} proportionally to its associated probability (line 7) so to increase the sampling of points with higher estimated probability of belonging to $\mathcal{B}$. Consequently, $K(f)$ is upgraded and if $x \in \mathcal{B}$ then x is added to B (line 12). The procedure outputs also d, the minimum distance of the evaluated points from the interval I calculated during the procedure.

4   The Falsification Process

A big effort during the prototyping process consists in verifying the requirements usually expressed as safety property, such as:

$$\forall(\mathbf{u}, x_0) \in \{\mathcal{T} \to \mathcal{U}\} \times \mathcal{X}_0,\ \ \rho(\phi, (\mathbf{u}, \mathbf{x}), 0) > 0 \tag{5}$$

meaning that for each input function and initial state $x_0 \in \mathcal{X}_0 \subseteq \mathcal{X}$, the dynamics (Path$^{\mathcal{M}} = (\mathbf{u}, \mathbf{x})$) satisfies the STL formula ϕ. It is possible to interpret the safety condition (5) as a domain estimation problem associated with

$$\mathcal{B} = \{(\mathbf{u}, x_0) \in \{\mathcal{T} \to \mathcal{U}\} \times \mathcal{X}_0,\ \ \rho(\phi, (\mathbf{u}, \mathbf{x}), 0) < 0\} \tag{6}$$

with the purpose of verifying its emptiness, which entails that (5) is satisfied. We call $\mathcal{B}$ the *counterexample set* and its elements counterexamples.

Solving the previous domain estimation problem could be extremely difficult because of the infinite dimensionality of the input space, which is a space of functions. For this reason, it is mandatory to parameterize the input function by means of an appropriate finite dimensional representation. One of the most used parameterization—mainly for its simplicity—is the *fixed control point parameterization* (fixCP): after having fixed the times, $(t_1^k, \ldots, t_{n_k}^k)$ the control points

$\{(t_1^k, u_1^k), \ldots, (t_{n_k}^k, u_{n_k}^k)\}$ are chosen as parameter of the k-th input signals. Chosen an interpolation set of function with n_k degrees of freedom for each k-th input signals ($\mathcal{P}_{n_k}^k \subset \{\mathcal{T} \to \mathcal{U}_k\}$, e.g. piecewise linear, polynomials of degree n_k, and so on (see [20])), the fixCP parameterization will associate with each control point $c_k = \{(t_1^k, u_1^k), \ldots, (t_{n_k}^k, u_{n_k}^k)\}$ the unique function $P_{c_k} \in \mathcal{P}_{n_k}^k$ satisfying $\forall i \leq n, P_{c_k}(t_i^k) = u_i^k$. Let us denote by $\mathcal{P}_\mathbf{n} = (\mathcal{P}_{n_1}^1, \ldots, \mathcal{P}_{n_{|\mathcal{U}|}}^{|\mathcal{U}|})$, the set of interpolating functions.

It is clear that by increasing the number of control points, we will enlarge the set of approximant functions $\mathcal{P}_\mathbf{n}$: $\mathbf{n} \leq \mathbf{m}$ implies $\mathcal{P}_\mathbf{n} \subset \mathcal{P}_\mathbf{m}$, where $\mathbf{n} \leq \mathbf{m}$ is intended pointwise. As piecewise linear or polynomial functions are known to be dense in the space of continuous functions, by choosing an appropriately large $\mathbf{n}$, we can approximate any input function with arbitrary precision.

Considering an $\mathbf{n}$-fixCP, which is a fixCP where $\mathbf{n} = (n_1, \ldots, n_{|\mathcal{U}|})$ represents the number of control points used for each input variables, it is possible to introduce the domain estimation problem (6) associated with the following set:

$$\mathcal{B} = \{(\bar{c}, x_0) \in \mathcal{U}_1^{n_1} \times \cdots \times \mathcal{U}_{|\mathcal{U}|}^{n_{|\mathcal{U}|}} \times \mathcal{X}_0, \quad \rho(\phi, (P_\mathbf{n}(\bar{c}), x), 0) < 0\} \qquad (7)$$

which, differently from (6), is a finite dimensional set described by using $\sum_{j=1}^{|\mathcal{U}|} n_j + |\mathcal{X}_0|$ variables.

By the density argument it is clear that

(6) has at least one element $\iff \exists \mathbf{n} \in \omega^{|\mathcal{U}|}$, (7) has at least one element.

A possible strategy is to solve the domain estimation problem associated with (7) by choosing the minimum $\mathbf{n}$ such that $\mathcal{P}_\mathbf{n} \times \mathcal{X}_0$ contains a counterexample. Applying that strategy, even in simple cases, could be cumbersome as shown in the following example.

Toy Example. Consider a simple black box model which accepts a single piecewise-constant function $u : [0, 1] \to [0, 1]$ as input function and returning the same function $x = u$ as output. Considering the following requirement $\phi :=$ $\neg(\mathbf{G}_{[0,0.51]} 0 < x < 0.2 \wedge \mathbf{G}_{[0.55,1]} 0.8 < x < 1)$, it is evident that it could be falsified only in a control point parameterization having at least the point (t_i, u_i) such that $t_i \in [0.51, 0.55]$. Otherwise if this points does not exists it means the output signals will assume a constant values in $[0.51, 0.55]$ which implies that or $\mathbf{G}_{[0.55,1]} (0.8 < x < 1)$ or $\mathbf{G}_{[0,0.51]} (0 < x < 0.2)$ is false meaning that ϕ is not falsified. The minimum number of uniformed fixed control points necessary to achieve it is 9, which entails a considerable computational effort.

A natural way to overcome the limitation of the fixCP consists in considering the times of the control points as variables. An $\mathbf{n}$-*adaptive Control Points parameterization* ($\mathbf{n}$-adaCPP) consists in a function $\bar{P}_{n_k}^k : \mathcal{T}^{n_k} \times \mathcal{U}_k^{n_k} \to \mathcal{P}_{n_k}^k$, which has twice as much parameters than the fixed version: values at control points and times (which are constrained by $\forall i < n\ t_i \leq t_{i+1}$). The adaptive parameterization is preferable with respect to the fixed one because of its ability to describe functions with local high variability even with a low number of control points. In fact it is possible to concentrate any fraction of the available control points in a small time region, inducing a large variation in this region, while letting the parameterized function vary much less outside it.

4.1   Adaptive Optimization

The idea of the adaptive optimization approach consists in falsifying (5) starting from a simple input function and increasing its expressiveness by increasing the number of control points. Consider a model with input function $\mathbf{u}$ taking values in $\mathcal{U}_1 \times \cdots \times \mathcal{U}_m$ and with initial state x_0 taking values in a compact set $\mathcal{X}_0 \subset \mathbb{R}^k$. After having defined a parameterization for each of the m input signals, Algorithm 2 works as following:

- At the first iteration a parameterization $P_{\mathbf{n_0}} = \{P_1^0, \ldots, P_n^0\}$ with zero control points for each signals ($\mathbf{n_0} = (0, \ldots, 0)$) is considered (line 2). Zero control points means defining input signals which are constant functions. The final counterexample set (B) is set to empty, which ensures the optimization is run at least once (line 3).
- In the iterative loop, the algorithm first checks if the number of counterexamples (ce) or if the maximum global number of iterations (mgi) has been reached. In this case, the method stops returning the counter example set (B). Otherwise, the falsification problem is solved by using the domain estimation procedure DOMAINESTIMATION (Algorithm 1) which returns the counterexample set and the minimum value of the robustness found by using that parameterization (see Sect. 3 for details). The parameterization is then expanded by picking a coordinate of the input signal (lines 6–10) and adding a new control point (line 11), obtaining a new parameterization $P_{\mathbf{n_{i+1}}}$.

Algorithm 2

1: **procedure** $[B, d] = $ ADAPTIVEGPFALSIFICATION(mgi, mii, ce, m, ϕ)
2:     $\mathbf{n_0} \leftarrow (0, \ldots, 0)$
3:     $B \leftarrow \emptyset,\ k_0 \leftarrow 0,\ i \leftarrow 0,\ d_0 \leftarrow +\infty$
4:     **while** ($|B| \leq ce$ **and** $i \leq mgi$) **do**
5:         $[B^-, d_{i+1}] = $ DOMAINESTIMATION$(mii, \mathbf{n}_i, ce - |B|, m, \rho(\phi, \cdot, t), (-\infty, 0))$
6:         **if** $d_{i+1} > d_i$ **then**
7:             $k_{i+1} \leftarrow k_i$
8:         **else**
9:             $k_{i+1} \leftarrow (k_i + 1) \mod n$
10:         **end if**
11:         $\mathbf{n}_{i+1} \leftarrow \mathbf{n}_i + \mathbf{e}_k$
12:         $i \leftarrow i + 1$
13:         $B \leftarrow B \cup B^-$
14:     **end while**
15: **end procedure**

The general idea of this approach is to keep low the number of parameters by starting from constant signal and gradually increasing the number of control points of the input functions. In the adaptive control points parameterization, adding a control point means adding two new degrees of freedom (one for the time and one for the value of the control point). This means, on the one hand, having more expressiveness and so more chances to falsify the system, but on the other hand this complicates the optimization process and increases the dimension of the search space as well as, hence, the minimum number of simulations required to solve it. For this reason it is convenient to add control points only where it is truly necessary.

5   Probabilistic Approximation Semantics

Gaussian Processes can be used to estimate the probability that a given input falsifies a system as described in Sects. 3 and 4. This fact offers the possibility to define an approximate semantics which generalizes the concept of probability of falsification that we can infer considering the knowledge of the system we have collected. The basic idea is to decompose an STL formula as a Boolean combination of temporal modalities, propagating the probability of the temporal operators, estimated by GPs, through the Boolean structure. Formally, let $\mathcal{L}_0$ be the subset of STL containing only atomic propositions and temporal formulae of the form $\phi_1 \mathbf{U}_{[T_1,T_2]} \phi_2$, $\mathbf{F}_{[T_1,T_2]} \phi$ and $\mathbf{G}_{[T_1,T_2]} \phi$, that cannot be equivalently written as Boolean combinations of simpler formulae. For example $\mathbf{F}_T(\phi_1 \vee \phi_2)$ is not in $\mathcal{L}_0$ because $\mathbf{F}_T(\phi_1 \vee \phi_2) \equiv \mathbf{F}_T \phi_1 \vee \mathbf{F}_T \phi_2$. Furthermore, let $\mathcal{L}$ be the logic formed by the boolean connective closure of $\mathcal{L}_0$.[1]

For simplicity, let us denote by θ a parameter and describe the input function by u_θ and the initial state by $x_{0\theta}$. We write x_θ to indicate the path generated by the simulator, given as input u_θ and $x_{0\theta}$, accordingly to Sect. 2. We want to define an (approximate) semantics giving the probability that a path x_θ satisfies a given formula $\psi \in \mathcal{L}$ (without simulating it). The idea is to evaluate the quantitative semantics of the atomic formulae $\phi_j \in \mathcal{L}_0$ of ψ on a finite collection of parameters $(\Theta = \{\theta_i\}_{i \leq n})$, then building GPs in order to estimate the probability that the quantitative semantics of each formula ϕ_j is higher than zero on a target parameter. This is again a Domain Estimation Problem (Sect. 3), where the function is the robustness associated with the STL formula ϕ_j and the interval I is $(0, +\infty)$. We propagate this probability through the Boolean structure of ψ according to the following:

Definition 4 (Probabilistic Approximation Semantics of $\mathcal{L}$). *The probabilistic approximation function $\gamma : \mathcal{S} \times Path^{\mathcal{M}} \times [0, \infty) \to [0, 1]$ is defined by:*

- $\gamma(\phi, \theta, t) = P(f_{K(\phi)}(\theta) > 0)$
- $\gamma(\neg \psi, \theta, t) = 1 - \gamma(\psi, \theta, t)$

---

[1] $\phi \in \mathcal{L}$ iff $\psi := \phi \,|\, \neg \psi \,|\, \psi \vee \psi \,|\, \psi \wedge \psi$, with $\phi \in \mathcal{L}_0$.

- $\gamma(\psi_1 \wedge \psi_2, \theta, t) = \gamma(\psi_1, \theta, t) * \gamma(\psi_2, \theta, t)$
- $\gamma(\psi_1 \vee \psi_2, \theta, t) = \gamma(\psi_1, \theta, t) + \gamma(\psi_2, \theta, t) - \gamma(\psi_1 \wedge \psi_2, \theta, t)$

where $K(\phi) = \{\theta_i, \rho(\phi, \theta_i, t)\}_{i=1,..,n}$ is the partial knowledge of the satisfiability of $\phi \in \mathcal{L}_0$ that we have collected performing n simulations for parameters $(\theta_i)_{i=1,..,n}$. $f_{K(\phi)}$ is the GP trained on $K(\phi)$, and P refers to its probability. For simplicity we use $\gamma(\psi, \theta, t)$ to mean $\gamma(\psi, (u_\theta, x_\theta), t)$.

In the previous definition, the probability $P(f_{K(\phi)}(\theta) > 0)$ is easily computed, as $f_{K(\phi)}(\theta)$ is normally distributed.

Including the Probabilistic Approximation Semantics (PAS) in our falsification procedure (Algorithm 2) is straightforward. Given the formula we have to falsify, first we negate and decompose it in order to identify the $\mathcal{L}$ formula associated with it. Then we pass all the basic $\mathcal{L}_0$ formulas to the DOMAINESTIMATION procedure (Algorithm 1) and train a GP for each of them (instead of considering a single function (Algorithm 1, line 5). Subsequently we calculate its probabilistic approximation semantics to drive the sampling strategy (Algorithm 1, line 7). The rest of the algorithm remains the same.

Remark. Consider the STL formula $\phi = \mathbf{G}_{[0,30]}(v \leq 160 \wedge \omega \leq 4500)$. This formula is not in $\mathcal{L}_0$, as it can be rewritten as $\mathbf{G}_{[0,30]}(v \leq 160) \wedge \mathbf{G}_{[0,30]}(\omega \leq 4500)$. We could have defined the set $\mathcal{L}_0$ in different ways (e.g. by including also ϕ), our choice corresponding to the finer decomposition of temporal formulae. Even if this leads to an increased computational cost (more GPs have to be trained), it also provides more flexibility and allows us to exploit the boolean structure in more detail, as discussed in the following example.

Example. To clarify the advantages of the PAS, consider the functions $\rho(\phi_1, x, 0) = x^2 + 1$ and $\rho(\phi_2, x, 0) = -0.2 + 0.9(1 - h(x, 0.7, 0.035) - h(x, 0.85, 0.035))$ representing the robustness associated with the formulas ϕ_1 and ϕ_2 at time 0 and for input parameter x, respectively. Here $h(x, m, s)$ is a gaussian function with mean m and standard deviation s. We compare two approaches. In the first one, we calculate the probability of its negation i.e. $\gamma(\neg(\phi_1 \wedge \phi_2), x, 0) = 1 - \gamma((\phi_1 \wedge \phi_2), x, 0)$ by means of a single gaussian process. In the second one, we decompose the conjunction and calculate its PAS $\gamma(\neg(\phi_1 \wedge \phi_2), x, 0) = 1 - \gamma(\phi_1, x, 0) * \gamma(\phi_2, x, 0)$ by means of two separated Gaussian Processes. Functions used by the method to drive the sample are represented in Fig. 1(a). In the first case, the signal which is smooth in $[0, 0.65]$ and highly variable in $(0.65, 1]$ forces the method to sample many points near $x = 0$, as the function is close to zero near this point. This requires 55.35 ± 45.10 function evaluations. On the contrary the second approach shows a rapid discovery of the falsification area, i.e. 17.19 ± 7.71 evaluations, because the two components are treated independently, and the method quickly finds the minima regions of $\gamma(\phi_2, x, 0)$, after an initial phase of homogeneous exploration. In addition, the paraboloid $\gamma(\phi_1, x, 0)$ is smooth and requires few evaluations for a precise reconstruction.

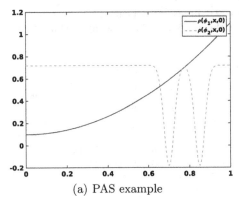

(a) PAS example

STL Formulae
$\phi_1^{AT}(\bar{v}, \bar{\omega}) = \mathbf{G}_{[0,30]}(v \le \bar{v} \wedge \omega \le \bar{\omega})$
$\phi_2^{AT}(\bar{v}, \bar{\omega}) = \mathbf{G}_{[0,30]}(\omega \le \bar{\omega}) \rightarrow \mathbf{G}_{[0,10]}(v \le \bar{v})$
$\phi_3^{AT}(\bar{v}, \bar{\omega}) = \mathbf{F}_{[0,10]}(v > \bar{v}) \rightarrow \mathbf{G}_{[0,30]}(\omega \le \bar{\omega})$

(b) Automatic Transmission Req.

Fig. 1. (a) Example on the use of the probabilistic semantics. The curve treating the formula as a single one is the minimum of the two curves. (b) Requirements for the Automatic Transmission example of Sect. 6.

6   Case Studies and Results

In this section we discuss a case study to illustrate our approach, taken from [20]. We will compare and discuss the performance of a prototype implementation in Matlab of our approach with S-TaLiRo toolbox [11]. We use S-TaLiRo to compute the robustness, and the implementation of Gaussian Process regression provided by Rasmussen and Williams [17].

Automatic Transmission (AT). We consider a Simulink model of a Car Automatic Gear Transmission Systems. There are two inputs: the throttle and the brake angle dynamics describing the driving style. Modes have two continuous state variables, describing vehicle (v) and engine (ω) speed. The Simulink model is initialized with a fixed initial state $(w_0, v_0) = (0, 0)$, it contains 69 blocks (2 integrators, 3 look-up tables, Stateflow Chart, ...). The requirements are described by means of STL formulae as reported in Fig. 1(b). The first requirement (ϕ_1^{AT}) is a so called *invariant* which says that in the next 30 s the engine and vehicle speed never reach $\bar{\omega}$ rpm and $\bar{v}$ km/h, respectively. The second requirement (ϕ_2^{AT}) says that if the engine speed is always less than $\bar{\omega}$ rpm, then the vehicle speed can not exceed $\bar{v}$ km/h in less than 10 s. Finally, the third requirement (ϕ_3^{AT}) basically says that if within 10 s the vehicle speed is above $\bar{v}$ km/h than from that point on the engine speed is always less than $\bar{\omega}$ rpm.

Results. We analyze the performance of our approach in terms of the minimum number of simulations and computational time needed to falsify the previous test cases. We have performed 50 optimization runs for each STL formula and compared its performance with the best statistics achieved among a Cross Entropy (CE), Montecarlo Sampling (SA) and Uniform Random Sampling (UR) approaches performed with the S-TaLiRo tool [4] and the GP-UCB algorithm

Table 1. Results. All the times are expressed in seconds. Legend - nval: number of simulations, times: time needed to falsify the property, Alg: the algorithm used as described in Sect. 6.

Req	Adaptive PAS		Adaptive GP-UCB		S-TaLiRo		
	nval	times	nval	times	nval	times	Alg
$\phi_1^{AT}(160, 4500)$	4.42 ± 0.53	2.16 ± 0.61	4.16 ± 2.40	0.55 ± 0.30	5.16 ± 4.32	0.57 ± 0.48	UR
$\phi_1^{AT}(160, 4765)$	6.90 ± 2.22	5.78 ± 3.88	8.7 ± 1.78	1.52 ± 0.40	39.64 ± 44.49	4.46 ± 4.99	SA
$\phi_2^{AT}(75, 4500)$	3.24 ± 1.98	1.57 ± 1.91	7.94 ± 3.90	1.55 ± 1.23	12.78 ± 11.27	1.46 ± 1.28	CE
$\phi_2^{AT}(85, 4500)$	10.14 ± 2.95	12.39 ± 6.96	23.9 ± 7.39	9.86 ± 4.54	59 ± 42	6.83 ± 4.93	SA
$\phi_2^{AT}(75, 4000)$	8.52 ± 2.90	9.13 ± 5.90	13.6 ± 3.48	4.12 ± 1.67	43.1 ± 39.23	4.89 ± 4.43	SA
$\phi_3^{AT}(80, 4500)$	5.02 ± 0.97	2.91 ± 1.20	5.44 ± 3.14	0.91 ± 0.67	10.04 ± 7.30	1.15 ± 0.84	CE
$\phi_3^{AT}(90, 4500)$	7.70 ± 2.36	7.07 ± 3.87	10.52 ± 1.76	2.43 ± 0.92	11 ± 9.10	1.25 ± 1.03	UR

applied to falsification as described in [2]. As the table shows, our approach (Adaptive PAS) has good results in terms of the minimum number of evaluations needed to falsify the systems with respect to the STL formulae, outperforming in almost all tests the methods of the S-TaLiRo suite and the Adaptive GP-UCB approach. This is the most representative index, as in real industrial cases the simulations can be considerably expensive (i.e. cases of real measurements on power bench, time and computation intensive simulations). In these cases the total computational time is directly correlated with the number of simulations and the time consumed by the optimizer to achieve its strategy becomes marginal. Furthermore, we are testing our method with a prototype implementation which has not been optimized, in particular for what concerns the use of Gaussian Processes. Despite this, the numerical results in terms of minimum number of simulations are outperforming S-TaLiRo and GP-UCB approach.

Conditional Safety Properties. When we define a conditional safety property i.e. $\mathbf{G}_T(\phi_{cond} \to \phi_{safe})$ we would like to explore cases in which the formula is falsified but the antecedent condition holds (see [2]). This is particular relevant when the formula cannot be falsified, as it reduces the search space, ignoring regions where the formula is trivially true due to a false antecedent. Focusing on the region where ϕ_{cond} holds requires a straightforward modification of the sampling routine of the Domain Estimation Algorithm (Algorithm 1, line 6–7). Instead of performing the sampling directly on the input provided by the Latin Hypercube Sampling Routine (Algorithm 1, line 6), we previously define a set of inputs verifying the antecedent condition (by the standard Domain Estimation Algorithm using the Gaussian Processes trained on the robustness of the antecedent condition) and then we sample from this set the candidate point (Algorithm 1, line 7).

To verify the effectiveness of this procedure, we calculate the percentage of sampled inputs satisfying the antecedent condition of the STL formula $\mathbf{G}_{[0,30]}(\omega \leq 3000 \to v \leq 100)$, which cannot be falsified. This percentage is 43% for the GP-UCB algorithm, but increases to 87% for the modified domain estimation algorithm.

7   Conclusions

In this paper we propose an adaptive strategy to find bugs in black box systems. We search in the space of possible input functions, suitably parameterized in order to make it finite dimensional. We use a separate parameterization for each different input signal, and we use an adaptive approach, increasing gradually the number of control points as the search algorithm progresses. This allows us to solve falsification problems of increasing complexity, looking first for simple functions and then for more and more complex ones. The falsification processes is then cast into the Domain Estimation Problem framework, which use the Gaussian Processes to constructs an approximate probabilistic semantics of STL formulae, giving high probability to regions where the formula is falsified. The advantage of using such an approach is that it leverages the Bayesian emulation providing a natural balance between exploration and exploitation, which are the key ingredients in a search-based falsification algorithm. In addition to a novel use of Gaussian Processes, we also rely on a new adaptive parameterization, treating the time of each control point as a variable, thus leading to an increase in expressiveness and flexibility, as discussed in Sect. 4. Moreover with a slight modification of our algorithm we efficiently manage the falsification of the condition safety properties, increasing the efficiency of the usual GP-UCB algorithm in focussing the search on the region of points satisfying the antecedent.

Future Work. The experimental results are quite promising, particularly as far as the number of simulations required to falsify a property is concerned, which is lower than other approaches. The computational time of the current implementation, however, is in some cases higher then S-TaLiRo. The main problem is in the cost of computing predictions of the function emulated with a Gaussian Process (GP). This cost, in fact, is proportional to the number of already evaluated inputs used to train the GP. To reduce this cost, we can leverage the large literature about sparse representation techniques for GP [18]. Furthermore, with the increase in the number of control points, we face a larger dimensional search space, reflecting in an increased number of simulations needed to obtain an accurate representation of the robustness for optimization, with a consequent increase of computational time. We can partially improve on this problem, typical of naive implementations of the Bayesian approach, by refining the choice of the covariance function and/or constraining some of its hyperparameters so as to increment the exploration propensity of the search. In the future, we also plan to improve the adaptive approach which is in charge of increasing the control points of an input signal, with the goal of dropping control points that are not useful. In the current paper, we use the GP-based sampling scheme to deal efficiently with falsification. However, our approach can be modified to deal with the coverage problem [10], i.e. the identification of a given number of counterexamples which are homogeneously distributed in the falsification domain. Our idea is to modify the sampling algorithm (Algorithm 1, line 7) by adding a memory of already visited areas, so to distribute samples homogeneously in space.

Related Work. Different approaches have been proposed to achieve the falsification of black box models, starting from test based approaches until recently, when search-based test approaches have become more popular. Stochastic local search [7], probabilistic Monte Carlo [1] and mixed coverage/guided strategy [10] approaches have been proposed and benchmark problems created [6,12]. Two software packages [4,8] implement the aforementioned techniques. Both these software tools assume a fix parameterization of the input function, differently from us. Similarly to our approach, in [7,10] the fixed parameterization is avoided. More specifically in [10] no parameterization has been used at all and the input signals are modified on the fly based on the robustness of the partial system trajectories. In [7] a uniform discretization of the input domains (both time and values) is dynamically applied to discretize the search space. The use of Gaussian Processes for falsification has been adopted in [2] but it is restricted to Conditional Safety Properties.

References

1. Abbas, H., Fainekos, G., Sankaranarayanan, S., Ivančić, F., Gupta, A.: Probabilistic temporal logic falsification of cyber-physical systems. ACM Trans. Embed. Comput. Syst. (TECS) **12**(2s), 95 (2013)
2. Akazaki, T.: Falsification of conditional safety properties for cyber-physical systems with Gaussian process regression. In: Falcone, Y., Sánchez, C. (eds.) RV 2016. LNCS, vol. 10012, pp. 439–446. Springer, Cham (2016). doi:10.1007/978-3-319-46982-9_27
3. Alur, R., Courcoubetis, C., Halbwachs, N., Henzinger, T.A., Ho, P.-H., Nicollin, X., Olivero, A., Sifakis, J., Yovine, S.: The algorithmic analysis of hybrid systems. Theo. Comput. Sci. **138**(1), 3–34 (1995)
4. Annpureddy, Y., Liu, C., Fainekos, G., Sankaranarayanan, S.: S-TaLiRo: a tool for temporal logic falsification for hybrid systems. In: Abdulla, P.A., Leino, K.R.M. (eds.) TACAS 2011. LNCS, vol. 6605, pp. 254–257. Springer, Heidelberg (2011). doi:10.1007/978-3-642-19835-9_21
5. Baheti, R., Gill, H.: Cyber-physical systems. Impact Control Technol. **12**, 161–166 (2011)
6. Bardh Hoxha, H.A., Fainekos, G.: Benchmarks for temporal logic requirements for automotive systems. In: Proceedings of ARCH, vol. 34, pp. 25–30 (2015)
7. Deshmukh, J., Jin, X., Kapinski, J., Maler, O.: Stochastic local search for falsification of hybrid systems. In: Finkbeiner, B., Pu, G., Zhang, L. (eds.) ATVA 2015. LNCS, vol. 9364, pp. 500–517. Springer, Cham (2015). doi:10.1007/978-3-319-24953-7_35
8. Donzé, A.: Breach, a toolbox for verification and parameter synthesis of hybrid systems. In: Touili, T., Cook, B., Jackson, P. (eds.) CAV 2010. LNCS, vol. 6174, pp. 167–170. Springer, Heidelberg (2010). doi:10.1007/978-3-642-14295-6_17
9. Donzé, A., Maler, O.: Robust satisfaction of temporal logic over real-valued signals. In: Chatterjee, K., Henzinger, T.A. (eds.) FORMATS 2010. LNCS, vol. 6246, pp. 92–106. Springer, Heidelberg (2010). doi:10.1007/978-3-642-15297-9_9
10. Dreossi, T., Dang, T., Donzé, A., Kapinski, J., Jin, X., Deshmukh, J.V.: Efficient guiding strategies for testing of temporal properties of hybrid systems. In: Havelund, K., Holzmann, G., Joshi, R. (eds.) NFM 2015. LNCS, vol. 9058, pp. 127–142. Springer, Cham (2015). doi:10.1007/978-3-319-17524-9_10

11. Fainekos, G.E., Sankaranarayanan, S., Ueda, K., Yazarel, H.: Verification of automotive control applications using S-TaLiRo. In: Proceeings of ACC, pp. 3567–3572. IEEE (2012)
12. Jin, X., Deshmukh, J.V., Kapinski, J., Ueda, K., Butts, K.: Powertrain control verification benchmark. In: Proceedings of HSCC, pp. 253–262. ACM (2014)
13. Maler, O., Manna, Z., Pnueli, A.: Prom timed to hybrid systems. In: Bakker, J.W., Huizing, C., Roever, W.P., Rozenberg, G. (eds.) REX 1991. LNCS, vol. 600, pp. 447–484. Springer, Heidelberg (1992). doi:10.1007/BFb0032003
14. Maler, O., Nickovic, D.: Monitoring temporal properties of continuous signals. In: Lakhnech, Y., Yovine, S. (eds.) FORMATS/FTRTFT -2004. LNCS, vol. 3253, pp. 152–166. Springer, Heidelberg (2004). doi:10.1007/978-3-540-30206-3_12
15. McKay, M.D., Beckman, R.J., Conover, W.J.: Comparison of three methods for selecting values of input variables in the analysis of output from a computer code. Technometrics **21**(2), 239–245 (1979)
16. Pnueli, A.: The temporal logic of programs. In: Proceedings of Foundations of Computer Science, pp. 46–57. IEEE (1977)
17. Rasmussen, C.E., Nickisch, H.: Gaussian processes for machine learning (GPML) toolbox. J. Mach. Learn. Res. **11**, 3011–3015 (2010)
18. Rasmussen, C.E., Williams, C.K.I.: Gaussian Processes for Machine Learning. MIT Press, New York (2006)
19. Rubinstein, R.Y., Kroese, D.P.: The Cross-Entropy Method: A Unified Approach to Combinatorial Optimization, Monte-Carlo Simulation and Machine Learning. Springer, New York (2013). doi:10.1007/978-1-4757-4321-0
20. Sankaranarayananm S., Fainekos, G.: Falsification of temporal properties of hybrid systems using the cross-entropy method. In: Proceedings of HSCC, pp. 125–134. ACM (2012)
21. Vinnakota, B.: Analog and Mixed-Signal Test. Prentice Hall, Upper Saddle River (1998)
22. Zhao, Q., Krogh, B.H., Hubbard, P.: Generating test inputs for embedded control systems. IEEE Control Syst. **23**(4), 49–57 (2003)

Modelling and Verification of Timed Robotic Controllers

Pedro Ribeiro[1]([✉]), Alvaro Miyazawa[1], Wei Li[2], Ana Cavalcanti[1],
and Jon Timmis[2]

[1] Department of Computer Science, University of York, York YO10 5GH, UK
pedro.ribeiro@york.ac.uk
[2] Department of Electronic Engineering, University of York, York YO10 5DD, UK

Abstract. Designing robotic systems can be very challenging, yet controllers are often specified using informal notations with development driven primarily by simulations and physical experiments, without relation to abstract models of requirements. The ability to perform formal analysis and replicate results across different robotic platforms is hindered by the lack of well-defined formal notations. In this paper we present a timed state-machine based formal notation for robotics that is informed by current practice. We motivate our work with an example from swarm robotics and define a compositional CSP-based discrete timed semantics suitable for refinement. Our results support verification and, importantly, enable rigorous connection with sound simulations and deployments.

Keywords: Semantics · Refinement · Process algebra · CSP · Robotics

1 Introduction

Robotic systems have applications in many real-life scenarios, ranging from household cleaning to critical search-and-rescue operations. Assessing their expected behaviour is challenging. In spite of that, typically controller software is developed in an ad-hoc manner, driven by simulations and physical experiments, but without a clear relation with models of requirements and design.

Standard state-machine notations, without underlying formal semantics, are often used [1,2] together with natural language annotations to specify more complex behaviours, involving aspects such as time and probabilities. State machines are often neither presented in an abstract way, nor do they contain precise and sufficient information to relate the designs to the simulations and deployments. In this scenario, the ability to faithfully replicate results, even just across different simulators, let alone using different robotic platforms, is significantly hampered.

In this paper we present a timed semantics for RoboChart [3], a state-machine based notation that can be characterised as a UML profile extended with time primitives and with a formal semantics. RoboChart provides constructs for capturing the architectural patterns of typical timed and reactive robotic systems.

© Springer International Publishing AG 2017
N. Polikarpova and S. Schneider (Eds.): IFM 2017, LNCS 10510, pp. 18–33, 2017.
DOI: 10.1007/978-3-319-66845-1_2

An abstract characterisation of a robot's operations and events is formalised via the notion of a robotic platform that decouples the software and hardware platform from controllers. A controller can encapsulate multiple state-machines, and is connected with a particular platform via the notion of a module. This enables an abstract and precise approach to the design of robotic systems, where high-level concepts can be mapped into low-level constructs of typical executable simulations, for example, as we have considered in [3].

Here we propose a compositional semantics for refinement using Timed CSP [4], enriched with deadline constructs from *Circus Time* [5], a discrete-time process algebra that combines constructs of Z [6], CSP [7], and Timed CSP, besides deadline operators. A semantics for the enriched Timed CSP is defined in the Unifying Theories of Programming [5,8].

For RoboChart models that make a modest use of data types, we translate the semantics to CSP using a special event *tock* to mark the time. This version of CSP, called *tock*-CSP [7], is supported by the model checker FDR [9]. We use it to validate the design of RoboChart and our semantics, and check timed properties of RoboChart models. With *tock*-CSP, we can give a discrete-time model for all constructs of Timed CSP and deadlines.

The encoding in *tock*-CSP is mechanised in RoboTool, a graphical editor for RoboChart models. Using RoboTool and the automatically generated semantics, we have tackled a number of examples, and present here four experiments: two chemical detectors [10], an alpha algorithm used in swarm robotics [11], and a transporter that works in a swarm to move an object to a goal position [1].

Our long-term objective is to use our semantics for verification by automated theorem proving using an Isabelle encoding of *Circus Time* [12], and prove that automatically generated simulations are sound, that is, refine the RoboChart models. Translation from Timed CSP with deadlines to *Circus Time* is not challenging, since *Circus Time* is a richer language.

In Sect. 2 we motivate our work by presenting an example of a typical timed robotic controller, as used in swarm robotics, and giving an insight into related work. In Sect. 3, we present RoboChart. We discuss in detail the RoboChart timed semantics in Sect. 4. In Sect. 5 we present verification results and discuss tool support. Finally, we summarize our contributions and provide pointers for future work in Sect. 6.

2   Modelling Robotic Controllers

We now present an example (Sect. 2.1) and related works (Sect. 2.2) to indicate the need for a specialised timed formal language.

2.1   Motivating Example

Our goal is not to propose an entirely novel notation, but to define a language that is akin to that currently adopted by roboticists in their informal approach.

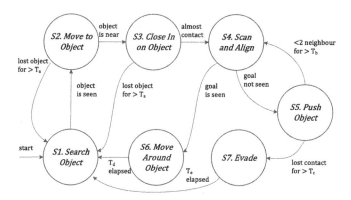

Fig. 1. Transport swarm state machine [1].

We present in this section an example, taken from the domain of swarm robotics, whose published model is representative of the current practice.

We consider an individual timed reactive controller used in robots of a swarm for cooperatively transporting tall objects towards a locally perceived goal [1]. The robotic platform has a camera that allows it to distinguish objects and the goal, and proximity sensors that can be used to estimate the distance to an object and to detect other nearby robots.

In Fig. 1 we reproduce the transport swarm controller in [1]. In state $S1$ the robot searches for an object and, once it sees one, it transitions to state $S2$. If the object is near, then it transitions to state $S3$. While in states $S2$ and $S3$, if the object is lost for a certain amount of time T_a, the robot initiates another search for the object by transitioning to state $S1$. When the robot is close enough to the object, by transitioning from state $S3$ to $S4$, it performs an alignment procedure and checks whether the goal can be seen. The underlying idea is that if the goal is occluded by the object, and the robot is close to the object, then it pushes the object towards the goal. While pushing, in state $S5$, the robot may lose contact with the object, in which case after a time threshold of T_c it evades the vicinity; or it may lose sight of nearby neighbours, in which case it tries to align itself again by transitioning to state $S4$. The transitions between states $S7$ and $S1$, and $S6$ and $S1$, are equally timed according to thresholds T_e and T_d.

We observe that the state machine in Fig. 1 is specified in natural language and a few aspects are unclear, such as the behaviour and time spent in each state, whether timed transitions take place immediately or need to wait until the behaviour has completed, and thresholds related to the distances to the object. Even when taking into account the implementation details [1], it is ultimately unclear whether the controller, as presented, could be independently and correctly implemented. In our experience, this is not an uncommon scenario in the development of robot applications. We refer, for instance, to [13,14] for examples of other applications modelled with similar state machines.

2.2   Related Work

According to a recent survey [15], there is increasing interest in domain-specific and model-driven approaches in robotics. We discuss below those closest to ours in tackling aspects such as architectural design, time, and verification.

$G^{en}{}_{o}M$ [16] provides a component-based approach for designing middleware-agnostic robotic controllers. Functional aspects are captured by recording the input and output parameters of functions together with their worst-case execution time. Implementations are provided by code fragments, for example, using C code. Verification of schedulability via model-checking is available using Fiacre [16], through the Timed Petri Net model-checker TINA, while deadlocks can be checked using BIP. $G^{en}{}_{o}M$ is primarily an executable language, whereas RoboChart is a modelling language catering for different levels of abstraction.

Proof techniques, including model-checking, have also been used to identify optimal configurations of adaptive architectures [17]. Related approaches such as CIRCA [18] tackle the problem of meeting real-time constraints given dynamic plan generation. Behavioural properties are not the main focus of these works.

ORCCAD [19] supports modelling, simulation, and programming, as well as verification of timed behavioural properties via translation into ESTEREL and Timed Argos. Unlike RoboChart, its support for graphical modelling is limited, while the modelling constructs employed are closest to those of our semantics.

UML has been used for model-based engineering of robotic systems [20]. The profile RobotML [21] supports design modelling and automatic generation of platform-independent code, but verification is not considered. On the other hand, several formal models of UML state machines exist; some of them use CSP [22,23]. However, none of these deal with time modelling.

UML has a simple notion of time. Its profile UML-MARTE [24] supports logical, discrete and continuous time through the notion of clocks. Specification of time budgets and deadlines, however, is focused on particular instances of behaviour via sequence and time diagrams. It is not possible to define timed constraints directly in terms of transitions and states as we require.

UML-RT [25], an extension to UML, includes the notion of capsules, which encapsulate state machines. Communication between capsules is governed by protocols. A timing protocol can raise timeouts, but it is not obvious how timed constraints, such as deadlines, can be specified directly on state machines. In [26] a semantics is given for a subset of UML-RT without considering time. An extension to UML-RT is considered in [27] with semantics given in CSP+T [28], an extension of CSP that records the timing of events.

Timed automata [29] use synchronous continuous-time clocks. Temporal logic properties can be checked using the model checker UPPAAL [30]. It is not directly comparable to RoboChart, which provides modelling abstractions catering for robotic applications and has a semantics for refinement. It is our aim to explore a semantics for RoboChart using UPPAAL for property verification.

3   RoboChart: A Formal Notation for Robotics

A system in RoboChart is characterised by a module that contains a robotic
platform, associated with one or more controllers. A controller is specified by one
or more state-machines. Our focus here is on the state machines, since that is
where we define the time properties. The untimed RoboChart semantics defined
in [31] already describes how CSP models of state machines can be composed
to define models for controllers, and how these can be composed to define a
complete module and provide a formal model of a robotic system.

A state-machine includes states and composite states with entry, during and
exit actions, junctions, and transitions, possibly guarded by expressions. The
language for actions is well defined to include assignments, operation calls, and
a primitive to raise events. In Fig. 2 we include part of the RoboChart metamodel
showing constructs related to time, whose syntax is summarized in Table 1. The
RoboChart Reference Manual [31] gives a complete description.

Table 1. Timed primitives of RoboChart.

Primitive	Metamodel element	Description
#C	ClockReset	Resets clock C.
since(C)	ClockExp	Time elapsed since the most recent reset of clock C.
sinceEntry(S)	StateClockExp	Time elapsed since state S was entered.
A <{d}	TimedStatement	Deadline on action A to terminate within d time units.
e <{d}	Transition	Deadline on event e to happen within d time units.
Wait(d)	Wait	Explicit time budget of d time units

We have a notion of Clock (see Fig. 2) that allows transitions to be guarded
by time expressions that define constraints relative to the occurrence of other
events via the since(C) (ClockExp in Fig. 2) and #C (ClockReset) primitives,
and relative to activation of a state via sinceEntry(S) (StateClockExp). We also
have primitives to impose a deadline d on action A (A <{d}) (TimedState-
ment), or transition trigger e (e <{d}) (Trigger), and to specify a budget d
(Wait(d)) (Wait) for an operation, where d is an Expression.

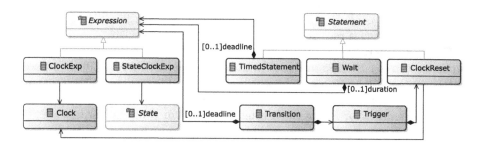

Fig. 2. Timed metamodel of RoboChart.

Similarly to timed automata, expressions involving clocks are restricted to comparing single timed primitives with constant expressions. We, however, allow conjunctive as well as disjunctive expressions involving more than one clock.

To illustrate the RoboChart notation we consider a robot that moves at constant speed in a square pattern while avoiding obstacles. The state machine is shown in Fig. 3, where the annotations T0 to T6 uniquely identifying the transitions are not actually part of RoboChart, but are included to guide the later discussion of the semantics in Sect. 4.

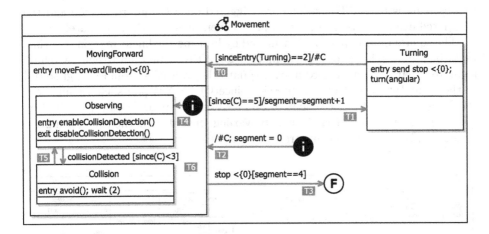

Fig. 3. Example of a square trajectory state machine controller.

When the robot is started, it transitions from the initial state, denoted by a black circle, to the state MovingForward, while resetting (#C) a clock C and assigning 0 to the local variable segment. The local declarations are elided in Fig. 3, but a RoboChart state machine is self-contained, in that it declares all the variables, events, and operations that it uses. The local variable segment records how many sides of the square have been covered so far; the robot stops when it completes the square (segment == 4). This is achieved by sending an event stop to the platform and transitioning to the final state: a white circle. The event stop is given a deadline 0, indicating that it is expected that the robotic platform is always ready to accept this event immediately.

In the composite state MovingForward, the motion is linear, unless an obstacle is detected. Linear motion is activated by calling the operation moveForward in the entry action with a constant value linear passed as a parameter. This operation is annotated with a deadline of 0, since moveForward can typically be implemented just as an assignment to a variable whose duration is regarded as negligible. Operations may be specified by other state machines or have their implementation provided by the robotic platform.

Before MovingForward is actually entered, its entry action executes, followed by that of its substate Observing, enabling the collision detection capability. Once a collision is detected, the event collisionDetected is raised by the robotic platform: the transition from Observing to the state Collision is then triggered, but only if there is enough time (since(C)<3) before the next turn, executing the exit action of Observing and subsequently the avoid operation that performs the actual collision avoidance. Here we do not specify this operation, but record its budget of 2 time units by sequentially composing it with the timed primitive wait(2). In RoboChart time elapses explicitly via budgets, unless a state has been entered and no transitions are enabled, or, every enabled transition is associated with an external event. Once the collision is resolved, a transition back to Observing is taken. Transitions are triggered once the guard is true and the associated event is raised, or, if there is no event associated, immediately.

The square motion pattern is achieved by limiting the linear motion to 5 time units before switching to angular motion for 2 time units, and then switching again to linear motion. Accordingly, we guard the transition from MovingForward to the state Turning with the expression since(C) == 5. Upon such a transition, the value of segment is incremented. Similarly, the angular motion is limited by guarding the transition from Turning to MovingForward using the timed primitive sinceEntry(Turning). Upon this transition, the clock is reset.

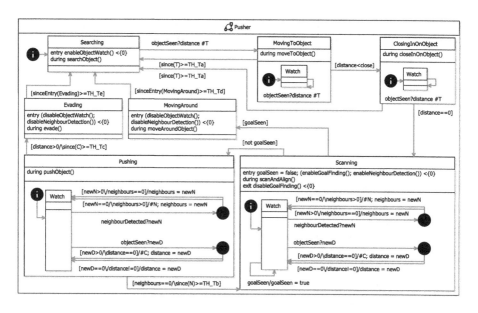

Fig. 4. RoboChart model of the transport swarm state machine.

In Fig. 4, we also show the RoboChart model for the transport swarm controller described in Sect. 1. We assume that the robotic platform can raise events: objectSeen, with a distance value passed as a parameter in response to seeing an object at an estimated distance; goalSeen in response to detecting the goal; and neighbourDetected, with a number of neighbours passed as a parameter. We also assume that the controller needs to enable the platform to receive those events, by calling appropriate operations, such as enableObjectWatch.

Operations likely to be implemented as assignments to variables have been annotated with zero deadlines. Overall we have the same structure as the original specification [1], with the same number of states, but with additional substates. This stems from interactions that are not clear in the original model, such as the need to keep counting neighbours while in states Pushing and Scanning, and the need to keep track of the object across multiple states.

The existing semantics of RoboChart deals with the structure (modules, controllers, and parallel state machines) of models. That semantics defines the visible behaviour of a module: the order and availability of the events of the platform. That semantics, however, ignores all time constructs of a model: clocks, and associated statements, waits, and deadlines. We address them in the next section.

4   Semantics

Here, we describe the semantics of RoboChart state machines (Sect. 4.1) [31]. We then focus on the semantics of each timed RoboChart construct, namely budgets and deadlines (Sect. 4.2) and clocks (Sect. 4.3).

Before defining the semantics, we first introduce the required CSP syntax. A communication on event e (also known as a channel), optionally parametrised by x, is defined as $e.x \rightarrow P$, with $e?x$ being syntactic sugar for allowing x to range over the type of e and introducing x in the scope of P, and with $e!v$ being used for a specific value v. Processes can be composed in parallel $(P \mid [s] \mid Q)$, where s is the set of events on which P and Q require agreement, and if s is empty this is an interleaving $(P \mid\mid\mid Q)$. An external choice $P \ \Box \ Q$ offers an initial choice between behaving as P or Q, while $P \bigtriangleup Q$ behaves as P but can be interrupted by Q at any time, with the timed version $P \bigtriangleup_d Q$ in addition also interrupting P exactly at d time units. $P \ \Theta_A \ Q$ initially behaves as P but can be interrupted by an event in A to behave as Q. Sequential composition of P and Q is $P \ ; \ Q$, with $SKIP$ being the unit. Hiding $(P \setminus h)$ makes the events in set h internal to P. Finally, the events in a process $P[f]$ can be renamed according to function f.

4.1   State Machines

A state machine is given a CSP semantics as the parallel composition of a process *States*, itself the parallel composition of processes that model a state, with a process *Initial*, that models the transition from the initial state. In Fig. 5 we illustrate the architecture of the CSP semantics of the example from Fig. 3. A state is modelled by a process *Entry*, modelling its entry action, sequentially composed with *During*, a model for its during action, that can be interrupted by a process *Transitions* that models the possible outgoing transitions.

A state machine defines a sequential and hierarchical control flow. To model this flow, there are *enter*, *entered*, *exit*, and *exited* events that model state activation and deactivation, with the associated entry and exit actions. Each event

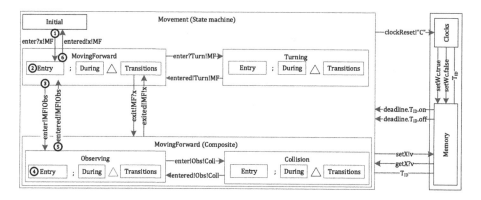

Fig. 5. Semantics Architecture based on Example of Fig. 3.

takes two parameters: the state that requested the activation or deactivation to start, and the target state of the request.

A state is modelled in a compositional way, capturing information only about itself, irrespective of whether it is inside a state machine or another state. In Fig. 5, the execution sequence is numbered. For example, the process modelling MovingForward offers events $enter?x!MF$ for any other state x, including the initial state to request it to enter, followed by the process that models its own entry action, a request on $enter!MF!Obs$ for the child Observing to enter, the entry action of Observing, and the acknowledgements $entered!MF!Obs$ and $entered!x!MF$. The process then offers an external choice of events that trigger its transitions.

Following a transition event, the $exit$ and $exited$ events to request and acknowledge deactivation are offered. For instance, in our example, following a transition triggered from state MovingForward, the process offers to synchronize on events $exit!MF.S$, where S ranges over all state identifiers except MF itself, as a way of requiring deactivation of either Observing or Collision.

Each state transition T is modelled by a process that synchronizes on T_{ID}, an event that uniquely identifies the transition in the state machine. If an event trigger e is associated with the transition, then at the outer level we rename the complete state machine process by mapping T_{ID} to e.

Variables declared in a state machine are modelled using a process *Memory* that exposes events get and set for each variable. In our example, *Memory* is parametrised by s, which holds the value of the variable segment, and offers the events $getSegment$ and $setSegment$ in an external choice followed by a recursion.

$$Memory(s) = \left(\begin{array}{l} getSegment!s \rightarrow Memory(s) \ \Box \ setSegment?y \rightarrow Memory(y) \\ \Box \ s == 4 \ \& \ T3 \rightarrow Memory(s) \end{array} \right)$$

Moreover, it also models transition guards by constraining synchronization on transition events (T_{ID}). In our example, the transition from MovingForward to the final state is guarded, so *Memory* captures this guard by only offering the event $T3$ that uniquely identifies the transition (Fig. 3) when *segment* is 4.

4.2   Budgets and Deadlines

As mentioned before, RoboChart budgets can be specified as part of actions. using the wait(d) construct. Its semantics is given by **Wait** t, a Timed CSP process that terminates exactly after t units of time elapse. Deadlines specified on actions are defined using the deadline operator $A \blacktriangleright t$ of *Circus Time*, where the process A modelling action A must terminate within t time units.

When a deadline is imposed on a transition trigger, however, it must be enforced only when the transition is enabled, that is, the transition's guard is true and the source state has been entered. In our model, we define a pair of events $deadline.T_{ID}.on$ and $deadline.T_{ID}.off$ for each transition T whose trigger has a deadline. Whenever T's guard is true, the *Memory* process offers the event $deadline.T_{ID}.on$, and when the guard is false, it offers $deadline.T_{ID}.off$. The *Memory* process of our example is defined as follows.

$$Memory(s) = \begin{pmatrix} ... \; \Box \; s == 4 \, \& \, deadline.T3.on \; \rightarrow \; Memory(s) \\ \Box \; \neg(s == 4) \, \& \, deadline.T3.off \; \rightarrow \; Memory(s) \end{pmatrix}$$

In addition to the *get* and *set* events for setting and getting the value of variable *segment*, and the guarded synchronization on $T3$, the event $deadline.T3.on$ is guarded by the expression corresponding to the guard on the transition identified by T3, and the negation of this expression guards the event $deadline.T3.off$.

For each process that models a state where an outgoing transition has a trigger with a deadline, we then compose in interleaving with the process modelling its during action, a $Dline_i$ process for each deadline d_i as defined below.

$$Dline_i = deadline.T_{ID}.on \; \rightarrow \; ((deadline.T_{ID}.off \; \rightarrow \; SKIP) \blacktriangleright d_i) \, ; \, Dline_i$$

$Dline_i$ initially synchronizes on $deadline.T_{ID}.on$, and thereafter must synchronize on $deadline.T_{ID}.off$ within d_i time units, followed by a recursion. The deadline is imposed on $deadline.T_{ID}.off$ rather than the transition identifier T_{ID}. The deadline can be satisfied either as a result of the transition's guard no longer being true, in which case the process synchronizes on $deadline.T_{ID}.off$, or as a result of the process being interrupted due to some transition out of the source state of T, modelled by a process *Transitions*, being triggered, possibly T itself. Effectively an enabled deadline on a transition becomes a deadline on the external choice between all enabled transitions out of the same state.

As an example, we show the process M for the state MovingForward.

$$M = enter?S!MF \rightarrow \begin{pmatrix} moveForward \, ; \, enter!MF!Obs \rightarrow \\ entered!MF!Obs \rightarrow entered!S!MF \rightarrow SKIP \, ; \\ ((SKIP \; ||| \; Dline_{MF}) \bigtriangleup Transitions_{MF}) \end{pmatrix} \, ; \, M$$

Initially it offers events $enter?S!MF$, so that any other state identified by S may request it to be entered. It then behaves as *moveForward*, the process that models the operation moveForward, and then requests the substate Observation to *enter* by synchronising on *enter*!MF!Obs, subsequently waiting for an acknowledgement via *entered*!MF!Obs and then acknowledging its own entry through *entered*!S!MF. M then behaves as an interleaving ($|||$) between the process modelling its during action, in this case $SKIP$ as there is none, and the process $Dline_{MF}$ that models the deadlines on triggers of every outgoing transition of state MovingForward, while offering for any event in $Transitions_{MF}$, the process that models every outgoing transition from this state, to interrupt the interleaving.

4.3   Clocks

As previously mentioned, RoboChart clocks allow conditions to be set relative to the time elapsed since a particular clock reset. To model a reset #C on clock C we introduce an event *clockReset.C*, where C is the name of the clock.

Although clocks could be explicitly modelled in the semantics, for example, by adding variables in the *Memory* process for each clock, this would make the model intractable for model-checking as the variables would have an unbounded domain. Since we assume clocks can only be compared with constant expressions, we adopt a model where a timed expression involving a comparison between a constant and constructs since(C) or sinceEntry(S) is encoded by a boolean variable together with an auxiliary CSP process synchronizing with the *Memory* process. For example, a transition with unique identifier T1 guarded by the expression x = 1 $\lor$ since(C)>= d is encoded in the *Memory* process as follows.

$$Memory(..., x, wc_{T1}) = \left(\begin{array}{l} ... \; \Box \; setWc_{T1}?wc \rightarrow Memory(..., x, wc) \\ \Box \; (x = 1 \lor wc_{T1}) \, \& \, T1 \rightarrow Memory(..., x, wc_{T1}) \end{array} \right)$$

A boolean variable wc_{T1} encodes the timed condition since(C)>=d, with channel $setWc_{T1}$ used to set it *true* or *false*. Synchronizing in parallel with the *Memory* process we introduce a *WaitingCondition* process WC_T1 defined below.

$WC\_T1 = Do(T1) \triangle WC\_T1\_reset$
$WC\_T1\_reset = clockReset.C \rightarrow setWc_{T1}!false \rightarrow WC\_T1\_body$
$WC\_T1\_body = (Do(T1) \triangle_d setWc_{T1}!true \rightarrow Do(T1)) \triangle WC\_T1\_reset$

This process ensures that while wc_{T1} is being updated the event $T1$ is not offered. Initially it is ready to synchronise on $T1$ indefinitely (as defined using the process $Do(e) = e \rightarrow Do(e)$), but can be interrupted by the event *clockReset*.C offered in the process WC_T1_reset. Whether $T1$ is actually enabled or not is controlled by *Memory* and not WC_T1. So, the availability of $T1$ in WC_T1 indicates only that wc_{T1} is not being updated. If there is a clock reset, WC_T1_reset sets the value of the *Memory* process variable wc_{T1} to *false* via the synchronization $setWc_{T1}!false$ and behaves as WC_T1_body. This ensures that, when the clock is reset, the transition cannot take place, even if the value of the condition is not yet updated. Initially this process continuously offers the event $T1$ until exactly d units elapse ($\triangle_d$), after which it sets wc_{T1}

to *true* via the synchronization $setWc_{T1}!true$ and then continuously offers the event $T1$. At any point the process may be interrupted by WC_T1_reset due to a *clockReset*.C.

The complete semantics of a timed state machine is given by the parallel composition of the process modelling the state machine, STM, the *Memory* process and a *Clocks* process whose definition is the parallel composition of all *WaitingCondition* processes as defined for each timed condition.

$$(((STM \mid [g \cup dc] \mid ((Memory \mid [w \cup t] \mid Clocks) \setminus w)) \setminus I)[f]) \, \Theta_{\{term\}} \, SKIP$$

Memory and *Clocks* synchronise on the events in the sets w, containing all *setWc* events, which are then subsequently hidden ($\setminus$). They also synchronise on the events of the set t of identifiers for transitions whose conditions are timed. This parallel process synchronises with STM on the events from g, containing the *get* and *set* events for reading and writing the value of state variables and the transition identifiers, and from dc, containing the *deadline* and *clockReset* events. This is illustrated by the lines on the top right corner of Fig. 5. The set of identifiers for internal transitions (I) are hidden ($\setminus$). Also, as explained, we use a function f to rename transition identifiers to external events of the platform. Finally if the state machine has a final state, the process STM can signal termination via the event *term*, which interrupts the process to behave as *SKIP*.

Our RoboTool presented next automatically calculates the timed semantics of a RoboChart model just described. Instead of Timed CSP, it uses *tock*-CSP for direct use of FDR. The time constructs are encoded as described in [4].

5   Tool Support and Model-Checking

To provide support for designing robotic systems using RoboChart, we have developed RoboTool[1], an Eclipse plugin that allows specifications to be input using both graphical and textual editors, implemented using the Sirius and Xtext[2] frameworks. RoboTool automatically generates the semantics of RoboChart models in CSP_M, the machine readable version of CSP used by FDR [9].

FDR includes facilities to translate untimed processes into *tock*-CSP. For example, the prefixing $a \rightarrow P$ is translated into an external choice offering *tock*, the event that marks the passage of time, in addition to a: $X = a \rightarrow P \, \square \, tock \rightarrow X$. Other operators are similarly accommodated, while more intricate concepts need to be manually specified using *tock*-CSP. For example, deadlines are encoded by timelocking once a deadline expires, that is, by refusing *tock*.

Using the timed semantics of RoboChart we can perform a number of core checks using FDR, namely, determinism and divergence freedom. In addition, for a given *tock*-CSP process STM_T modelling a state machine, and whose set

---

[1] https://www.cs.york.ac.uk/circus/RoboCalc.
[2] www.eclipse.org/sirius and www.eclipse.org/xtext.

of externally observable events is E, we can establish that there are no time-locks provided the following refinement is satisfied [7]. Since in our model unmet deadlines lead to timelocks this is a useful check to identify infeasible deadlines.

$$RUN(\{tock\}) \ ||| \ CHAOS(E) \sqsubseteq_F STM_T \upharpoonright (E \cup \{tock\})$$

With the above we require that STM_T, with every event other than those in E and $tock$ hidden (using the projection operator $\upharpoonright$), is a refinement ($\sqsubseteq_F$) in the failures model of the process $RUN(\{tock\})$, that is always offering $tock$, in interleaving ($|||$) with the process $CHAOS(E)$ that can perform any event in the set E nondeterministically. Zeno freedom, that is, the absence of a behaviour where an infinite sequence of events is performed in finite time, can be ascertained by checking that $STM_T \upharpoonright (E \cup \{tock\})$ is divergence free. Assertions to establish all these core properties are also automatically generated by RoboTool.

Using our semantics we have considered several case studies. We have verified core properties and also defined requirements directly in CSP and $tock$-CSP. A complete account of the experiments can be found in [32].

Table 2 summarises the results of checking for divergence freedom, a particularly expensive check in FDR, including state-space complexity (S/T) in terms of number of states (S) and transitions (T) visited, compilation time (C_T) and verification time (V_T). We also include the experimental results obtained with the untimed models, defined without using $tock$, for comparison. Results were obtained using FDR version 4.2.0 on a computer with 16GiB of RAM and an Intel i5-5287U CPU. Times correspond to an average of 5 runs. For the purpose of verification, in examples $E2$, $E3$ and $E4$ the types for reals and integers are instantiated in CSP_M as ranging from 0 to 1, whereas in $E1$ reals are instantiated within the range from -90 to 180 due to the specification using such values.

Table 2. Verification results of checking divergence freedom with FDR.

Examples	Untimed			Timed		
	S/T	C_T	V_T	S/T	C_T	V_T
E1. Chemical Detector	80/265	0.23 s	2.3 s	240/861	0.15 s	4.58 s
E2. Autonomous Chemical Detector	5/112	2.03 s	0.65 s	6/72	1.82 s	1.99 s
E3. Alpha Algorithm	52/184	0.26 s	1.28 s	12045/30918	0.66 s	1.30 s
E4. Transport Swarm	8/28	1.12 s	0.56 s	436/1085	2.49 s	0.17 s

Our results show that assertions in the failures-divergences model can typically be checked within a few seconds. Diligent application of compression functions significantly reduces the time required to compile and verify the assertions. We use *diamond*, which removes silent transitions from the LTS, and *wbisim*, that reduces the LTS by computing the maximal weak bisimulation.

To cope with additional variables in the *Memory* process, typically as the result of modelling timed conditions, we have optimized this process. Each variable is captured in separate, but parallel, "cell" processes, that synchronize with an auxiliary non-parametrised process, modelling the transitions' conditions, such that whenever a variable is changed it introduces in scope the current value of all variables. This yields a reduction in the number of possible states. The efficiency gain is particularly noticeable when a state machine has several variables, or timed conditions, which we have also optimized by generating equivalent timed expressions only once as a Waiting Condition CSP process.

As expected, the usage of *tock* increases the state-space complexity of examples compared to their untimed counterparts. The exception here is $E2$, likely due to *wbisim* that can yield better compression than *diamond* in some cases. We observe that *diamond* is not permitted by FDR within timed processes.

6   Conclusion

RoboChart can be viewed as a UML profile extended with timed primitives and a formal semantics. We have used constructs from *Circus Time* to capture budgets and deadlines in a timed semantics for refinement and model checking. Support for refinement is essential to our future plans to prove soundness of automatically generated simulation and deployment code.

To optimise model checking, clocks are modelled implicitly, with timed conditions modelled explicitly. Our use of clocks makes a translation into UPPAL feasible, and of interest for further analysis. For example, we have considered UPPAAL models of the transport swarm, including a model based on the architecture of our semantics and a simplified version. Both require additional states and transitions when compared to RoboChart to achieve a faithful model.

A semantic model generator has been implemented in RoboTool via translation into *tock*-CSP [7]. We have tackled several examples and verified whether the generated models satisfy expected system requirements, in addition to core properties like divergence freedom and zeno freedom. Results suggest an increase in complexity, but not necessarily in verification time, when compared to the verification of untimed models. The verifications are tractable given modest data ty pes and diligent use of FDR's compression functions. For realistic data types we do not expect scalability, instead we will consider theorem proving.

We have a precise account of the timed semantics of RoboChart embedded in RoboTool. We will capture this semantics via translation functions that generate *Circus Time* models suitable for use in Isabelle/UTP [12], which supports reasoning about the *Circus* family of languages via theorem proving. Furthermore, to account for the environment and probabilistic behaviour we will ultimately consider richer semantics models in the context of the UTP.

Acknowledgments. This work is funded by EPSRC grant EP/M025756/1. No new primary data was created during this study.

References

1. Chen, J., Gauci, M., Gross, R.: A strategy for transporting tall objects with a swarm of miniature mobile robots. In: 2013 IEEE International Conference on Robotics and Automation (ICRA), pp. 863–869, May 2013
2. Liu, W., Winfield, A.F.T.: Modeling and optimization of adaptive foraging in swarm robotic systems. Int. J. Robot. Res. **29**(14), 1743–1760 (2010)
3. Li, W., Miyazawa, A., Ribeiro, P., Cavalcanti, A.L.C., Woodcock, J.C.P., Timmis, J.: From formalised state machines to implementation of robotic controllers. In: Chong, N.-Y., Cho, Y.-J. (eds.) DARS 2016. Springer, London (2016)
4. Schneider, S.: Concurrent and Real-time Systems: the CSP Approach. Worldwide Series in Computer Science. Wiley, Chichester (2000)
5. Sherif, A., Cavalcanti, A.L.C., He, J., Sampaio, A.C.A.: A process algebraic framework for specification and validation of real-time systems. Formal Aspects Comput. **22**(2), 153–191 (2010)
6. Woodcock, J.C.P., Davies, J.: Using Z-Specification, Refinement, and Proof. Prentice-Hall, Englewood Cliffs (1996)
7. Roscoe, A.W.: Understanding Concurrent Systems. Texts in Computer Science. Springer, Heidelberg (2011)
8. Woodcock, J.: The miracle of reactive programming. In: Butterfield, A. (ed.) UTP 2008. LNCS, vol. 5713, pp. 202–217. Springer, Heidelberg (2010). doi:10.1007/978-3-642-14521-6_12
9. Gibson-Robinson, T., Armstrong, P., Boulgakov, A., Roscoe, A.W.: FDR3 — a modern refinement checker for CSP. In: Ábrahám, E., Havelund, K. (eds.) TACAS 2014. LNCS, vol. 8413, pp. 187–201. Springer, Heidelberg (2014). doi:10.1007/978-3-642-54862-8_13
10. Hilder, J.A., Owens, N.D.L., Neal, M.J., Hickey, P.J., Cairns, S.N., Kilgour, D.P.A., Timmis, J., Tyrrell, A.M.: Chemical detection using the receptor density algorithm. IEEE Trans. Syst. Man Cybern. C Appl. Rev. **42**(6), 1730–1741 (2012)
11. Dixon, C., Winfield, A.F.T., Fisher, M., Zeng, C.: Towards temporal verification of swarm robotic systems. Robot. Auton. Syst. **60**(11), 1429–1441 (2012)
12. Foster, S., Zeyda, F., Woodcock, J.: Isabelle/UTP: a mechanised theory engineering framework. In: Naumann, D. (ed.) UTP 2014. LNCS, vol. 8963, pp. 21–41. Springer, Cham (2015). doi:10.1007/978-3-319-14806-9_2
13. Nouyan, S., Gross, R., Bonani, M., Mondada, F., Dorigo, M.: Teamwork in self-organized robot colonies. IEEE Trans. Evol. Comput. **13**(4), 695–711 (2009)
14. Pini, G., Brutschy, A., Scheidler, A., Dorigo, M., Birattari, M.: Task partitioning in a robot swarm: object retrieval as a sequence of subtasks with direct object transfer. Artif. Life **20**(3), 291–317 (2014)
15. Nordmann, A., Hochgeschwender, N., Wigand, D., Wrede, S.: A survey on domain-specific modeling and languages in Robotics. J. Softw. Eng. Robot. **7**(1), 75–99 (2016)
16. Foughali, M., Berthomieu, B., Dal Zilio, S., Ingrand, F., Mallet, A.: Model checking real-time properties on the functional layer of autonomous robots. In: Ogata, K., Lawford, M., Liu, S. (eds.) ICFEM 2016. LNCS, vol. 10009, pp. 383–399. Springer, Cham (2016). doi:10.1007/978-3-319-47846-3_24
17. Fleurey, F., Solberg, A.: A domain specific modeling language supporting specification, simulation and execution of dynamic adaptive systems. In: Schürr, A., Selic, B. (eds.) MODELS 2009. LNCS, vol. 5795, pp. 606–621. Springer, Heidelberg (2009). doi:10.1007/978-3-642-04425-0_47

18. Musliner, D.J., Durfee, E.H., Shin, K.G.: CIRCA: a cooperative intelligent real-time control architecture. IEEE Trans. Syst. Man Cybern. **23**(6), 1561–1574 (1993)

19. Espiau, B., Kapellos, K., Jourdan, M.: Formal verification in robotics: why and how? In: Giralt, G., Hirzinger, G. (eds.) Robotics Research, pp. 225–236. Springer, London (1996)

20. Schlegel, C., Hassler, T., Lotz, A., Steck, A.: Robotic software systems: from code-driven to model-driven designs. In: International Conference on Advanced Robotics, ICAR 2009, 1–8 June 2009

21. Dhouib, S., Kchir, S., Stinckwich, S., Ziadi, T., Ziane, M.: RobotML, a domain-specific language to design, simulate and deploy robotic applications. In: Noda, I., Ando, N., Brugali, D., Kuffner, J.J. (eds.) SIMPAR 2012. LNCS (LNAI), vol. 7628, pp. 149–160. Springer, Heidelberg (2012). doi:10.1007/978-3-642-34327-8_16

22. Rasch, H., Wehrheim, H.: Checking consistency in UML diagrams: classes and state machines. In: Najm, E., Nestmann, U., Stevens, P. (eds.) FMOODS 2003. LNCS, vol. 2884, pp. 229–243. Springer, Heidelberg (2003). doi:10.1007/978-3-540-39958-2_16

23. Davies, J., Crichton, C.: Concurrency and refinement in the unified modeling language. Formal Aspects Comput. **15**(2–3), 118–145 (2003)

24. Selic, B., Grard, S.: Modeling and Analysis of Real-Time and Embedded Systems with UML and MARTE: Developing Cyber-Physical Systems. Morgan Kaufmann Publishers Inc., Burlington (2013)

25. Selic, B.: Using UML for modeling complex real-time systems. In: Mueller, F., Bestavros, A. (eds.) LCTES 1998. LNCS, vol. 1474, pp. 250–260. Springer, Heidelberg (1998). doi:10.1007/BFb0057795

26. Ramos, R., Sampaio, A., Mota, A.: A semantics for UML-RT active classes via mapping into *Circus*. In: Steffen, M., Zavattaro, G. (eds.) FMOODS 2005. LNCS, vol. 3535, pp. 99–114. Springer, Heidelberg (2005). doi:10.1007/11494881_7

27. Akhlaki, K.B., Tunon, M.I.C., Terriza, J.A.H., Morales, L.E.M.: A methodological approach to the formal specification of real-time systems by transformation of UML-RT design models. Sci. Comput. Program. **65**(1), 41–56 (2007)

28. Zic, J.J.: Time-constrained buffer specifications in CSP + T and timed CSP. ACM Trans. Program. Lang. Syst. **16**(6), 1661–1674 (1994)

29. Alur, R., Dill, D.L.: A theory of timed automata. Theoret. Comput. Sci. **126**(2), 183–235 (1994)

30. Bengtsson, J., Larsen, K., Larsson, F., Pettersson, P., Yi, W.: UPPAAL — a tool suite for automatic verification of real-time systems. In: Alur, R., Henzinger, T.A., Sontag, E.D. (eds.) HS 1995. LNCS, vol. 1066, pp. 232–243. Springer, Heidelberg (1996). doi:10.1007/BFb0020949

31. Miyazawa, A., et al.: RoboChart reference manual. Technical report, University of York (2017). http://bit.ly/2plUry4

32. RoboCalc Project: RoboChart Case Studies (2017). www.cs.york.ac.uk/circus/RoboCalc/case-studies/

Spatial Reasoning About Motorway Traffic Safety with Isabelle/HOL

Sven Linker[(✉)]

Department of Computer Science, University of Liverpool, Liverpool, UK
`s.linker@liverpool.ac.uk`

Abstract. Formal verification of autonomous vehicles on motorways is a challenging problem, due to the complex interactions between dynamical behaviours and controller choices of the vehicles. In previous work, we showed how an abstraction of motorway traffic, with an emphasis on spatial properties, can be beneficial. In this paper, we present a semantic embedding of a spatio-temporal multi-modal logic, specifically defined to reason about motorway traffic, into Isabelle/HOL. The semantic model is an abstraction of a motorway, emphasising local spatial properties, and parameterised by the types of sensors deployed in the vehicles. We use the logic to define controller constraints to ensure safety, i.e., the absence of collisions on the motorway. After proving safety with a restrictive definition of sensors, we relax these assumptions and show how to amend the controller constraints to still guarantee safety.

Keywords: Spatial logic · Isabelle · Interactive theorem proving · Motorway traffic · Verification · Safety

1 Introduction

Due to the current and ongoing interest in autonomous vehicles, proving that such vehicles will behave correctly is of growing importance. Since vehicles are complex, dynamical systems, proving properties about them often involves solving differential equations, where spatial elements, e.g., position and braking distance, are functions of time. However, safety is fundamentally a spatial property: the absence of collisions, i.e., no two vehicles occupy the same space.

To overcome the complexities of proving safety properties, we proposed to separate the dynamical behaviour from the concrete changes in space [1]. To that end, we defined *Multi-Lane Spatial Logic* (MLSL), which was used to express guards and invariants of controller automata defining a protocol for safe lane-change manoeuvres. Under the assumption that all vehicles adhere to this protocol, we proved that collisions were avoided. Subsequently, we presented an extension of MLSL to reason about changes in space over time, a system of

This work was supported by the EPSRC Research Programme EP/N007565/1 *Science of Sensor System Software (S4)*.

N. Polikarpova and S. Schneider (Eds.): IFM 2017, LNCS 10510, pp. 34–49, 2017.
DOI: 10.1007/978-3-319-66845-1_3

natural deduction, and formally proved a safety theorem [2,3]. This proof was carried out manually and dependent on strong assumptions about the vehicles' sensors.

In this paper, we define a semantic embedding of a further extension of MLSL into the theorem prover Isabelle/HOL [4]. That is, we present the first tool to mechanically assist reasoning with MLSL. Subsequently, we show how the safety theorem can be proved within this embedding. Finally, we alter this formal embedding by relaxing the assumptions on the sensors. We show that the previously proven safety theorem does *not* ensure safety in this case, and how the controller constraints can be strengthened to guarantee safety.[1]

Recently, many approaches to verify traffic safety have been published. A main distinction between them is the way they abstract properties of traffic. Loos et al. used the theorem prover KeYmaera [5] to verify safety of motorway scenarios [6]. The underlying logic of KeYmaera is *Differential Dynamic Logic* [7], where the dynamical behaviour of systems is explicitly encoded within hybrid programs. This contrasts with our approach, where the main focus is on spatial aspects of traffic. However, they abstract away from the way real vehicles change lanes, i.e., vehicles may change to any lane, not only adjacent ones, in one step. We restrict the possibilities of lane changes to exactly the adjacent lanes.

Rizaldi and Althoff presented a formal implementation of traffic rules [8]. Similar to our work, they choose Isabelle/HOL to analyse several laws from the Vienna Convention on Road Traffic. However, they focus on whether the behaviour of vehicles is compliant with these laws. Our formalisation does not take legal issues into account, and concentrates only on the absence of collisions.

The distinction between dynamical behaviour and a higher-level is not unique to our work. Kamali et al. [9] used a combination of the *Belief-Desire-Intention* approach to model agents, and Timed Automata [10]. They distinguish between the planning component of a vehicle and its underlying dynamics. The planning component creates the new intentions of a vehicle according to its current belief about the situation on the road, and its general desires. The underlying dynamics then implement the plan constructed by the planning component. Both components can be verified on their own, the planning component with the model checker AJPF [11], and the dynamics with Uppaal [12]. Our spatial abstraction could serve as a middle tier between their planning component and the dynamics, by abstracting concrete values (e.g., distances) to spatial properties.

In a similar fashion, Campbell et al. used π-calculus processes to define and reason about the communication structure of vehicle networks [13]. The lower level dynamics are implemented as Hybrid Automata [14], and the connection between both levels is given by connecting the messages in the higher level with input and output messages of the automata. Our results imply that the amount of necessary communication between vehicles depends on sensor capabilities of each vehicle. Hence our results could inform the instantiations of their models.

---

[1] The code of the formalisation can be found at www.github.com/svenlinker/HMLSL. It is compatible with Isabelle2016-1.

The structure of our paper is as follows. Section 2 presents the semantic embedding of MLSL into Isabelle/HOL. In Sects. 3 and 4 we discuss the proofs for safety with different sensor capabilities. Section 5 concludes the paper.

2   Embedding MLSL into Isabelle/HOL

In this section, we present our abstraction of motorway traffic, as well as *Hybrid Multi-Lane Spatial Logic* (HMLSL), an extension of *Multi-Lane Spatial Logic* (MLSL), by introducing concepts from *Hybrid Logic* [15] and universal modalities. In the majority of the paper, we will only present the formalisation within Isabelle, but explain the relation to previous work [1–3].

Notations. Isabelle/HOL is based on type theory, hence every term t has a specific type τ, denoted by $t :: \tau$. The type of a function from τ to τ' is written as $\tau \Rightarrow \tau'$. Within Isabelle, we have to distinguish between the meta-logic and the object logic. In the case of Isabelle/HOL, both are instantiations of Higher-Order logic. Implication and equivalence of the meta-logic is denoted by $\Longrightarrow$ and $\equiv$, respectively. They are generally used to define terms. The object level implication is $\longrightarrow$, which is used within lemmas and theorems. In this paper, conjunction, disjunction and existential quantification will generally be used within the object logic, denoted by the operators $\wedge$, $\vee$, and $\exists$. Finally, function application will typically be denoted without parentheses, i.e., instead of $f(t)$, we will write $f\ t$.

2.1   Semantic Model

The semantics of HMLSL reflects situations as depicted in Fig. 1. That is, we consider vehicles driving on a motorway with possibly several lanes. All vehicles are assumed to drive in one direction (to the right in the figure). The *safety envelope* comprises the physical size of c as well as the distance needed for an emergency braking. Within the model, we distinguish between two spatial properties of vehicles. The *reservation* of a vehicle c is the part of the motorway that c currently drives on, defined by the lanes c uses and its safety envelope. Reservations may occupy space on up to two adjacent lanes, which indicates that the vehicle is currently performing a lane-change manoeuvre, see, e.g., vehicle a in Fig. 1. A *claim*, depicted by the dotted lines in the figure, is a formalisation of setting the turn signal, i.e., it is an indicator that c wants to change its lane. Vehicles may only hold claims while not engaged in a lane change, i.e., as long as the reservation only contains space on a single lane. A claim of a vehicle is always adjacent to its reservation and of the same length.

The semantic model we use is twofold. We use *traffic snapshots* to formalise the current situation on the whole motorway. The motorway is of infinite length, modelled by the real numbers, and consists of an arbitrary, but fixed number of discrete lanes. Furthermore, we assume an infinite number of vehicles, each of which has a position and dynamic behaviour, e.g., its velocity and current acceleration. On top of the snapshots, *views* denote a finite part of the motorway

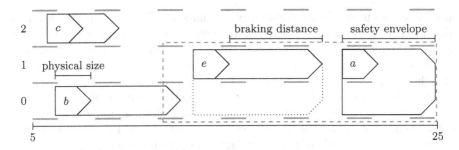

Fig. 1. Situation on a motorway at a single point in time

perceived by a vehicle. To that end, they consist of a closed real-valued interval, and a finite discrete interval of lanes. Each view is associated with a distinct vehicle, its *owner*. In Fig. 1, the traffic snapshot contains three lanes. A possible view v of the vehicle e is depicted as a dashed rectangle, and contains the two lower lanes. While both vehicle a and e are fully contained in v, only the safety envelope of vehicle b is within this view. If we assume an idealised world, where each vehicle can perceive the full safety envelope of other vehicles, i.e., both their physical size and braking distance, then e can sense the presence of b. We call this type of information *perfect*. Of course, this assumption is rather strong. If we assume that vehicles know about their own safety envelope, but only about the physical size and position of other vehicles, e cannot perceive b. We will refer to this situation as *regular information* [1].

2.2 Preliminary Definitions

Formally, we introduce two new types, one for real-valued intervals and another for discrete intervals. For real valued intervals, we use the type *real_int*, which is a tuple of two real values (x, y), with the condition $x \le y$. The discrete intervals use a definition within the *Main* library of Isabelle to define a consecutive sequence of numbers between m and n. If $m > n$, this will result in the empty set.

$$\textbf{typedef } real\_int = \{r :: (real * real).fst\ r \le snd\ r\}$$
$$\textbf{typedef } nat\_int = \{i.(\exists(m :: nat)n.\{m..n\} = i)\}$$

For both of these types, we define several auxiliary functions and predicates. The function *right* (*left*) returns the right (left, resp.) end point of a real-valued interval. We define a partial order on *real_int* to denote subintervals, i.e., $r \le s$ if, and only if, *left* $r \ge$ *left* s and *right* $r \le$ *right* s. Within Isabelle, we define this relation and show that *real_int* instantiates the abstract class *order*, i.e., we show reflexivity, transitivity and anti-symmetry. For *nat_int*, we prove more structure. We define the infimum $i \sqcap j$ of two intervals i and j by lifting set intersection to *nat_int*. Similarly, we can lift the subset relation on sets to *nat_int*, to constitute a partial order $\sqsubseteq$ with a least element, the empty set. Since discrete intervals are not closed under arbitrary unions, we introduce a new predicate *consec i j*, to denote that two intervals are non-empty and $\max(i) + 1 = \min(j)$. We can then define $i \sqcup j$ as the union of i and j. Furthermore, we need *measures* for both types of intervals. For discrete intervals, the measure is its cardinality lifted from sets, while the measure for real valued intervals is the difference between the left and right end points, i.e., $\|r\| \equiv right\ r - left\ r$.

Furthermore, we introduce the notion of *chopping* an interval into two sub-intervals. The predicate $R\_Chop(r, s, t)$ is similar to the chopping operation of Interval Temporal Logic [16]. For discrete intervals, we implemented a ternary predicate $N\_Chop(i, j, k)$, which was taken from previous work [2,3].

$$R\_Chop(r, s, t) \equiv left\ r = left\ s \land right\ s = left\ t \land right\ r = right\ t$$
$$N\_Chop(i, j, k) \equiv i = j \sqcup k \land (j = \emptyset \lor k = \emptyset \lor consec\ j\ k)$$

Finally, we get a countably infinite type *cars* by a bijection on natural numbers.

2.3   Views

Using these definitions, we construct a type *view* as a record of three elements: a real-valued interval modelling the *extension* along the lanes, a discrete interval denoting the perceived *set of lanes*, and an identifier for the *owner* of the view.

record $view = ext :: real\_int \quad lan :: nat\_int \quad own :: cars$

We lift the chopping on intervals to views. For example, *horizontal chopping*, i.e., dividing the extension of the view while keeping the set of visible lanes and the owner, is defined as follows.

$$v = u \| w \equiv R\_Chop(ext\ v, ext\ u, ext\ w) \land lan\ v = lan\ u \land lan\ v = lan\ w$$
$$\land\ own\ v = own\ u \land own\ v = own\ w$$

The functions *lan*, *ext* and *own* are automatically generated by Isabelle, to refer to the respective parts of the views. The predicate $v = u\text{--}w$ denotes *vertical chopping*. Furthermore, we introduce a relation $v = c > u$ to change the owner of the view v to c, while keeping the spatial borders.

$$(v = c > u) \equiv ext\ v = ext\ u \land lan\ v = lan\ u \land own\ u = c$$

We can prove several lemmas about views and their relationships. For example, if we can chop a view v vertically into u and w and can switch v to a view v' with the owner c, we can chop v' into counterparts to u and w.

lemma $v = u\text{--}w \land v = c > v' \longrightarrow (\exists u'\ w'. u = c > u' \land w = c > w' \land v' = u'\text{--}w')$

2.4   Traffic Snapshots

The formalisations of the underlying traffic situations, called *traffic snapshots*, have to capture the intuitions given in Sect. 2.1, i.e., reservations, claims, positions, physical sizes, braking distances and the dynamical behaviour of vehicles.

For all of these, we use functions whose domain is the type *cars*. Since the definitions for traffic snapshots are long, but straightforward, we mostly refrain from providing the Isabelle code, but describe the formal concepts. Reservations and claims are given by the functions $res, clm \colon cars \Rightarrow nat\_int$, positions, physical sizes and braking distances are given by $pos, ps, bd \colon cars \Rightarrow real$. The dynamic behaviours over time, i.e., the increases in the cars' positions, are given by a real-valued function for each vehicle: $dyn \colon cars \Rightarrow (real \Rightarrow real)$. Traffic snapshots are tuples $ts = (pos, res, clm, dyn, ps, bd)$, with the following conditions:

1. $res\ c \cap clm\ c = \emptyset$,
2. $|res\ c| \geq 1$,
3. $|res\ c| \leq 2$,
4. $|clm\ c| \leq 1$,
5. $|res\ c| + |clm\ c| \leq 2$,
6. $clm\ c \neq \emptyset \longrightarrow$
    $\exists n \colon res\ c \cup clm\ c = \{n, n+1\}$,
7. $ps\ c > 0$,
8. $bd\ c > 0$.

Conditions 1–6 are the *sanity conditions* from previous work [2,3], that vehicles have to respect to be spatially well-defined. For example, we require reservations and claims to be adjacent, that vehicles have at most one claim, and so forth. Condition 7 denotes that vehicles have to be physically present (even though they may be arbitrarily small), while 8 ensures that a vehicle needs some leading safe space. Subsequently, we will refer to the reservation function of a traffic snapshot ts by $res\,ts$, and also respectively notate the other functions.

Example 1. The traffic situation ts in Fig. 1 can be formalised as follows.

$pos\ ts\ a = 22$	$pos\ ts\ b = 7$	$pos\ ts\ c = 6$	$pos\ ts\ e = 17$
$res\ ts\ a = \{0,1\}$	$res\ ts\ b = \{0\}$	$res\ ts\ c = \{2\}$	$res\ ts\ e = \{1\}$
$clm\ ts\ a = \emptyset$	$clm\ ts\ b = \emptyset$	$clm\ ts\ c = \emptyset$	$clm\ ts\ e = \{0\}$
$bd\ ts\ a = 3$	$bd\ ts\ b = 6$	$bd\ ts\ c = 2$	$bd\ ts\ e = 6$

As an example, we further set $ps\ ts\ d = 1$ and $dyn\ ts\ d\ x = \frac{1}{2} \cdot a_d \cdot x^2$ for all vehicles d. That is, we assume that each vehicle has its own acceleration a_d. The view v indicated by the dashed rectangle is given by $ext\ v = (13, 25)$, $lan\ v = \{0,1\}$ and $own\ v = e$. Observe that the concrete values of the functions are less important than the relations between them. In particular, we do not instantiate dyn in any proofs in this paper, and use it as an abstraction of the cars' dynamics.

Between two traffic snapshots ts and ts', different *global* and *local* transitions are possible. The only type of global transition is the passing of time, i.e., ts' is the result of purely dynamical behaviour of vehicles, starting at ts. The passing of x time units is denoted by $ts-x \rightarrow ts'$, during which only the vehicles' position is updated according to their dynamic behaviour, with the precondition that $dyn\ ts\ c\ y \geq 0$ for all c and $0 \leq y \leq x$. This ensures that cars only drive forward. Furthermore, single vehicles can perform *local* transitions. A vehicle c can

1. *create a new claim*, residing on a lane adjacent to its current reservation, which may only consist of a single lane, denoted by $ts-c(c, n) \rightarrow ts'$,

2. *create a new reservation*, i.e., it has to currently possess a claim and mutates this claim to a reservation, denoted by $ts-r(c) \rightarrow ts'$,
3. *withdraw its claim*, i.e., remove a currently existing claim from the road, denoted by $ts-wdc(c) \rightarrow ts'$,
4. *withdraw a reservation*, i.e., if its current reservation comprises two lanes, c shrinks its reservation to a single lane, denoted by $ts-wdr(c, n) \rightarrow ts'$, or
5. *adjust its dynamics*, i.e., change the function responsible for its dynamic behaviour to a given function $f\colon real \rightarrow real$, denoted by $ts-dyn(c, f) \rightarrow ts'$.

All of these relations can be straightforwardly defined using the notion of traffic snapshots. For example, we define creation of a claim as follows.[2]

$$ts-c(c, n) \rightarrow ts' \equiv (pos\ ts') = (pos\ ts) \wedge (res\ ts') = (res\ ts)$$
$$\wedge\,(dyn\ ts') = (dyn\ ts) \wedge (ps\ ts') = (ps\ ts) \wedge (bd\ ts') = (bd\ ts)$$
$$\wedge\,|clm\ ts\ c| = 0 \wedge |res\ ts\ c| = 1$$
$$\wedge\,((n+1 \in res\ ts\ c) \vee (n-1 \in res\ ts\ c))$$
$$\wedge\,(clm\ ts') = (clm\ ts)(c := Abs\_nat\_int\{n\})$$

The definition ensures that except for the claim of c, all parts of ts are equal to their counterparts in ts'. Furthermore, it requires that within ts, the vehicle c may only possess a single reservation, and no claim at all. The claim on lane n may only be created, if the reservation consists of a lane adjacent to n. Finally, the claims in ts' are the claims in ts, except for the newly created claim of c.

With these relations, we create two additional types of transition. *Evolutions* consists of arbitrary sequences of time passing and dynamic adjustments. We denote the evolution from ts to ts' by $ts \rightsquigarrow ts'$. Within Isabelle, we use an inductive definition to enable reasoning about evolutions. An *abstract transition* is an arbitrary transition sequence between ts and ts'. We denote such sequences by $ts \Rightarrow ts'$. Similarly to evolutions, we can define abstract transitions inductively.

Example 2. Consider again the traffic snapshot ts depicted in Fig. 1. The vehicle b can create a claim on lane 1, since its reservation contains only the lane 0. That is, there is a ts', such that $ts-c(b, 1) \rightarrow ts'$. However, there is no possibility for b to create a claim on lane 2.

Since views are intended to be relative to their owner, we have to consider the position of a view if the owner moves. Let v be a view with owner e. If time passes between snapshots ts and ts', we have to compute the difference between the position of e in ts and ts' and add it to the borders of the extension of v. Within Isabelle, we define a suitable function *move ts ts' v*.

---

[2] The function Abs_nat_int takes a set of natural numbers as its input, and returns an element of type nat_int. It is automatically created by Isabelle as a result of the type definition in Sect. 2.2. Subsequently, we will silently omit these functions.

2.5   Sensors

The preceding definitions are independent of the types of sensor the vehicles possess. The sensors, however, define the information each vehicle may use to decide, whether manoeuvres on the road can be safely performed, e.g., a lane change manoeuvre. We parameterise our model with a function representing the distances obtained from the sensors, i.e., a function returning the perceived length of a vehicle c by a vehicle e at the current traffic snapshot ts.

$$sensors :: cars \Rightarrow traffic \Rightarrow cars \Rightarrow real$$

We require $sensors$ to return a non-zero length for each vehicle. That is, for all vehicles e, c and all traffic snapshots ts, we have $sensors\ e\ ts\ c > 0$. Using the sensor definition as a parameter implies that all vehicles use the same definition of the sensor function. In general, however, this function can be as complicated as necessary. We then define the space used by a vehicle c as observed by e.

$$space\ ts\ v\ c \equiv (pos\ ts\ c,\ pos\ ts\ c + sensors\ (own\ v)\ ts\ c)$$

2.6   Restriction to Views

Our intention when using views together with traffic snapshots is to limit the space a vehicle can perceive at any time, since it can only take a limited amount of information into account. We need to restrict the perceived length of a vehicle to the view, as well as the lanes used for claims and reservations.

We denote the perceived length of a vehicle c by the owner of a given view v by $len\ v\ ts\ c$. Consider Fig. 1, and the indicated view v owned by the vehicle e. For the vehicles e and a, we intend that $space$ and len coincide on v. However, for c, we have to ensure that len is empty, since it drives outside of v. The size of len for b depends on the type of information we assume: with perfect information, we want that len is not empty and describes the small part of the safety envelope of b within in v, while with regular information, we intend that len returns an empty interval. We therefore define the perceived length as follows.

$$
\begin{aligned}
len\ v\ ts\ c \equiv\ &\textbf{if}\ (left\ (space\ ts\ v\ c)) > right\ (ext\ v)) \\
&\textbf{then}\ (right\ (ext\ v), right\ (ext\ v)) \\
&\textbf{else if}\ (right\ (space\ ts\ v\ c) < left\ (ext\ v)) \\
&\quad\textbf{then}\ (left\ (ext\ v), left\ (ext\ v)) \\
&\quad\textbf{else}\ (\max\ (left\ (ext\ v))\ (left\ (space\ ts\ v\ c)), \\
&\qquad\quad \min\ (right\ (ext\ v))\ (right\ (space\ ts\ v\ c)))
\end{aligned}
$$

The first two cases ensure that vehicles not visible in the view v (either to the left or to the right) will be represented by an empty interval. The last case is defined such that len is always a sub-interval of the extension of the view.

We have proved several properties about *len* needed in the safety proofs. For example, if the perceived length of a vehicle fills the extension of a given view, then it does the same for the horizontal sub-views.

$$\textbf{lemma } len\ v\ ts\ c = ext\ v \wedge v = u \,\|\, w \longrightarrow len\ u\ ts\ c = ext\ u$$

$$\textbf{lemma } len\ v\ ts\ c = ext\ v \wedge v = u \,\|\, w \longrightarrow len\ w\ ts\ c = ext\ w$$

The restriction of the claims and reservations to a view is the intersection with the lanes visible in the view. Within Isabelle, we use the following definition.

$$restrict\ v\ f\ c \equiv (f\ c) \sqcap lan\ v$$

To use this function we partially evaluate one of the functions *res* or *clm*. For example, the restriction of reservations contains at most two lanes at any time.

$$\textbf{lemma } |restrict\ v\ (res\ ts)\ c| \leq 2$$

However, most properties of *restrict* hold for any possible function from *cars* to *lanes*. E.g., if a view v can be vertically chopped into sub-views u and w, the restriction of a function f to v is the union of the restriction of f on u and w.

$$\textbf{lemma } v = u\text{--}w \longrightarrow restrict\ v\ f\ c = restrict\ u\ f\ c \sqcup restrict\ w\ f\ c$$

2.7 Hybrid Multi-Lane Spatial Logic

The logic HMLSL is a modal extension of first-order logic. In addition to first-order operators, HMLSL contains two spatial predicates $re(c)$ and $cl(c)$, which are true, if, and only if, the current view consists of a single lane that is completely filled with the reservation of the vehicle denoted by c (or its claim, respectively). To reason about views with more lanes, and different topological relations between vehicles, we can *chop* views either horizontally with the binary modality $\frown$, or vertically using $\smile$. Intuitively, $\phi \frown \psi$ splits the extension of a view into two disjoint sub-views, where ϕ holds on the left interval and ψ on the right, while the set of lanes and the owner is kept. For each type of spatial transition $*(c)$, we use a family of modalities $\Box*(c)$. I.e., the modalities are parameterised and this parameter will be evaluated like other variables in the formulas. Furthermore, we use a single modality to refer to evolutions between snapshots, i.e., the passing of time and changes in the dynamical behaviour of the vehicles. The universal modality $\mathbf{G}$ is defined with respect to abstract transitions, i.e., it can be used to define invariance properties. Finally, we employ a modality @c in the fashion of Hybrid Logic (HL) [15]. In HL, @c is used to switch to the world c, regardless of the accessibility relation of the logic. Within MLSL, we use @c to exchange the owner of the current view, which allows to reason about different perspectives on parts of the motorway. The information we have at our disposal may change for different perspectives, depending of the type of sensors in the vehicles. For a given view v, while we evaluate the formula @$c\ \varphi$, we switch to a view v' with the same extension and lanes as v, but whose owner is c.

Definition 1 (Syntax of HMLSL). *The syntax of formulas of the* hybrid multi-lane spatial logic *is given as follows, where c, d are variables of type cars:*

$$\phi ::= \bot \mid c = d \mid re(c) \mid cl(c) \mid \phi_1 \rightarrow \phi_2 \mid \forall c \bullet \phi_1 \mid \phi_1 \frown \phi_2 \mid \phi_1 \smile \phi_2 \mid M\phi$$

where $M \in \{\Box r(c), \Box c(c), \Box wd\ c(c), \Box wd\ r(c), \Box \tau, \mathbf{G}, @c\}$, and c, d are variables.

To define HMLSL within Isabelle, we follow an approach of Benzmüller and Paulson to embed quantified multi-modal logics into HOL [17]. Essentially, we encode formulas as functions from the set of worlds to truth values. Since our semantic model consists of both views and traffic snapshots, we define the formulas of HMLSL to be functions taking both of these entities as parameters, i.e., we translate them directly into HOL. This allows for a natural definition and notation of the operators, while still enabling us to use the automatic proof methods of Isabelle. For brevity, we define a type synonym $\sigma = traffic \Rightarrow view \Rightarrow bool$.

Most operators combine several terms of type σ, and return a new term of type σ. For example, negation is of type $\sigma \Rightarrow \sigma$. Conjunction and the chopping modalities have the type $\sigma \Rightarrow \sigma \Rightarrow \sigma$, since they are just binary connectives. The box modalities, however, also take a vehicle as a parameter, i.e., their type is $cars \Rightarrow \sigma \Rightarrow \sigma$. Due to space limitations, we only provide some examples.

$$\neg\varphi \equiv \lambda\ ts\ v.\neg\varphi(ts)(v)$$
$$\varphi \frown \psi \equiv \lambda\ ts\ v.\exists u\ w.(v = u \,\|\, w) \wedge \varphi(ts)(u) \wedge \psi(ts)(w)$$
$$\Box c(c)\ \varphi \equiv \lambda\ ts\ v.\forall ts'\ n.(ts - c(c, n) \rightarrow ts') \longrightarrow \varphi(ts')(v)$$
$$\mathbf{G}\ \varphi \equiv \lambda\ ts\ v.\forall ts'.(ts \Rightarrow ts') \longrightarrow \varphi(ts')(move\ ts\ ts'\ v)$$
$$@c\varphi \equiv \lambda\ ts\ v.\forall u.(v = c > u) \longrightarrow \varphi(ts)(u)$$

To avoid confusion with the object logic of Isabelle/HOL, we use bold symbols for the operators of HMLSL. While the Boolean operators are just translations to operators of HOL, the operators specific to HMLSL refer to the elements of the models given in the previous section. E.g., the semantics of the chop modalities refer to the chopping operations of Sect. 2.3. The behavioural modalities use the transition relations of Sect. 2.4, e.g., the modality $\mathbf{G}$ is defined with respect to all abstract transitions leaving the current traffic snapshot. The semantics of atomic formulas refers to the measures of intervals and restrictions to views.

$$re(c) \equiv \lambda\ ts\ v.\ len\ v\ ts\ c = ext\ v \wedge restrict\ v\ (res\ ts)\ c = lan\ v$$
$$\wedge \|ext\ v\| > 0 \wedge |lan\ v| = 1$$

These abbreviations correspond directly to the original definitions of MLSL [1,2]. Furthermore, we can define the *somewhere* modality as an abbreviation.

$$\langle\varphi\rangle \equiv \top \frown (\top \smile \varphi \smile \top) \frown \top$$

Finally, we also introduce notions for validity and satisfaction, which allow us to state lemmas comfortably, but can also be used within proofs of these lemmas.

$$\models \varphi \equiv \forall ts.\forall v.\varphi(ts)(v) \qquad\qquad ts, v \models \varphi \equiv \varphi(ts)(v)$$

We prove several lemmas to show that the definitions work as intended. For example, somewhere distributes over disjunction, which can be proven by a single application of the *blast* proof method. Furthermore for each vehicle, there can be at most two reservations visible anywhere on the motorway. Finally, we show how the transitions to create reservations are connected to the claims and reservations on the road. The proof of these lemmas need manual intervention, but mainly to guide the automatic methods.

> **lemma** $\models \langle \varphi \vee \psi \rangle \leftrightarrow \langle \varphi \rangle \vee \langle \psi \rangle$
>
> **lemma** $\models \neg \langle re(c) \rangle \smile \langle re(c) \rangle \smile \langle re(c) \rangle$
>
> **lemma** $reservation : \models (\Box r(c)\ re(c)) \leftrightarrow (re(c) \vee cl(c))$

3   Safety with Perfect Information

In this section, we instantiate the sensor function of the semantic model such that each vehicle possesses ideal and unrestricted sensors and can thus obtain *perfect information* of the space visible in its view. Formally, the sensor function consists of the sum of the physical size of a vehicle and its safety distance.

$$sensors\ e\ ts\ c \equiv ps\ ts\ c + bd\ ts\ c$$

Observe that the sensors do not distinguish between the owner of the view and any other vehicle. That is, they always return the full safety envelope of a vehicle.

Safety in our model is modelled by the absence of overlapping reservations. That is, our safety predicate can be defined as follows.

$$safe\ e \equiv \forall c.\neg(c = e) \rightarrow \neg \langle re(c) \wedge re(e) \rangle$$

To restrict the allowed behaviour of vehicles on the road, we require them to adhere to certain protocol specifications. Vehicles have to respect reservations as long as they only drive on the road without changing lanes, i.e., during evolutions. This is ensured by the *distance controller DC*.

$$DC \equiv \mathbf{G}\ (\forall c\ d.\neg(c = d) \rightarrow \neg \langle re(c) \wedge re(d) \rangle \rightarrow \Box \tau\ \neg \langle re(c) \wedge re(d) \rangle)$$

Intuitively, *DC* ensures that two different vehicles c and d, whose reservations do not overlap initially, will keep their distances so that no overlap occurs, as long as only time passes and dynamics are adjusted.

The only transition after which new reservations appear on the road is the creation of reservations. Observe that a unsafe situation can only occur, if there was already a claim overlapping with a reservation before the transition happened. Hence we have to forbid the creation of reservations in this case. To that end, we define the *potential collision check*.

$$pcc\ c\ d \equiv \neg(c = d) \wedge \langle cl(d) \wedge (re(c) \vee cl(c)) \rangle$$

Finally, the *lane change controller* restricts the vehicles such that if a vehicle holding a claim created a reservation, while a potential collision exists, we would get a contradiction. Hence, such a transition cannot occur.

$$LC \equiv \mathbf{G}\,(\forall d.(\exists c.pcc\ c\ d) \rightarrow \Box r(d)\ \bot)$$

Observe that this formula is slightly more restrictive than necessary. The potential collision check is already satisfied, if two claims overlap, which does not immediately lead to overlapping reservations, if only one of the vehicles changes the claim to a reservation. That is, in a model with interleaving semantics, as we defined in Sect. 2.4, we could reduce this check to only be satisfied, if the claim overlaps with a reservation. However, the given formula even ensures safety, if we allowed for synchronous creation of reservations [18].

Our safety theorem is as follows. If the initial situation is safe, and all vehicles adhere to DC and LC, safety is an invariant along all possible transitions.

theorem *safety* : $\models (\forall e.safe\ e) \wedge DC \wedge LC \rightarrow \mathbf{G}\,(\forall e.safe\ e)$

Proof. We only present a proof sketch, since the proof itself consists of roughly 200 lines of Isar proof script. We fix an arbitrary traffic snapshot ts and view v, and proceed by induction on transition sequences $ts \Rightarrow ts'$. The base case follows by the assumption $\forall e.safe\ e$. The induction step consists of a case distinction for the different transition types, where we assume that $ts \Rightarrow ts'$ holds for some ts' and $ts', v \models \forall e.safe\ e$. In all cases, we prove the theorem by contradiction.

For evolutions, fix a ts'' with $ts' \rightsquigarrow ts''$ and $ts'', move\ ts\ ts''\ v \models \neg \forall e.safe\ e$. That is, there are c and e, such that $ts'', move\ ts'\ ts''\ v \models \langle re(c) \wedge re(e) \rangle$. By the induction hypothesis and DC, we get $ts', move\ ts\ ts'\ v \models \Box_T \neg \langle re(c) \wedge re(e) \rangle$, and thus $ts'', move\ ts\ ts''\ v \models \neg \langle re(c) \wedge re(e) \rangle$. This yields the contradiction.

For creations of reservations, fix d and ts'', such that both $ts - r(d) \rightarrow ts''$ and $ts'', move\ ts\ ts''\ v \models \neg \forall e.safe\ e$. That is, there are c and e, such that $ts'', move\ ts\ ts''\ v \models \langle re(c) \wedge re(e) \rangle$. Subsequently, we have to distinguish the cases whether $d = c$ or $d = e$, or neither. In the latter case, we have that the overlap exists on ts' as well and get a contradiction. The other two cases are similar, and we only discuss the case $d = e$. In this case, we get that on ts', a claim or a reservation of e was overlapping with the reservation of c, i.e., $ts', move\ ts\ ts'\ v \models (\langle re(c) \wedge re(e) \rangle \vee \langle re(c) \wedge cl(e) \rangle)$. The first case contradicts the induction hypothesis. The latter case implies $ts', move\ ts\ ts'\ v \models \langle re(c) \wedge (re(e) \vee cl(e)) \rangle$ This is exactly the potential collision check $pcc\ e\ c$. With LC, we get the contradiction. The other cases are all proved in similar ways, by concluding that the overlap existed on ts', contradicting the induction hypothesis.   □

The safety theorem states that our controllers ensure safety, from the perspective of a single vehicle, since we never employ the hybrid modality @c. However, with our assumption of perfect knowledge, we can prove the following theorem, which shows that switching to a different owner does not impact safety.

lemma $\models (\forall e.safe\ e) \rightarrow @c\,(\forall e.safe\ e)$

Hence, no vehicle perceives a collision, which implies that safety is an invariant along all transitions for all vehicles.

4   Safety with Regular Information

In this section, we discuss how the proof given previously is affected, if we assume regular sensors. That is, while a vehicle can compute its own braking distance, it is not able to refer to the braking distance of other vehicles. However, we assume that the sensors can identify the physical size of other vehicles.

$$sensors\ e\ ts\ c\ \equiv \textbf{if}\ (e = c)\ \textbf{then}\ ps\ ts\ c + bd\ ts\ c\ \textbf{else}\ ps\ ts\ c$$

Hence, each vehicle e has complete information about its own safety envelope (the sum of its physical size and braking distance), but does not know anything about the braking distance of other vehicles. Note that the sensor function is a global parameter of HMLSL, i.e., all vehicles use the same function. With this sensor definition, we can still proceed to prove the safety theorem given in Sect. 3. However, since we neither refer to views with different owners in the safety property, nor in the theorem itself, we cannot prove the invariance of safety if we switch owners. Instead, we can prove the following lemma.

$$\textbf{lemma}\ \exists ts\ v.\ ts,v \models \forall e.safe\ e \wedge (\exists c.@c\ \neg(\forall e.safe\ e))$$

The proof consists of a straightforward, but tedious, construction of a suited traffic snapshot ts and view v. The essential parts of ts and v are shown in Fig. 2. Vehicle e is currently engaged in a lane change, while the vehicle c drives behind e on one lane. The view v indicated by the dashed rectangle is owned by e, hence e can only perceive the physical size of c, and not its full safety envelope, denoted by the dashed lines in front of c. For e, the situation seems perfectly safe, since the part of c visible to e is disjoint from e's reservation. In particular, we get $ts,v \models \forall e.safe\ e$. However, if we switch the view to be owned by c, we get overlapping reservations, i.e., we also have $ts,v \models \exists c.@c\neg(\forall e.safe\ e)$.

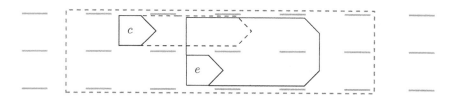

Fig. 2. Unsafe situation with regular information

We can amend our controller specification, however, to also take the perspective of other vehicles into account.

$$DC' \equiv \textbf{G}\ (\forall c\ d.\neg(c = d) \rightarrow @d\neg\langle re\,(c) \wedge re(d)\rangle \rightarrow \Box_\tau\ @d\neg\langle re(c) \wedge re(d)\rangle)$$
$$LC' \equiv \textbf{G}\ (\forall d.(\exists c.@c\,(pcc\ c\ d) \vee @d\,(pcc\ c\ d)) \rightarrow \Box r(d)\ \bot)$$

Note that within the distance controller, we still only refer to the perspective of a single vehicle, i.e., this specification can be implemented without coordinating

with other vehicles. In the lane change controller, however, we specifically refer
to views with different owners to restrict the possible transitions of one vehicle.
For implementations, this implies that information has to be passed between
vehicles. This is in line with our previous automata based specification of the
lane change controller for regular sensors [1].

With these definitions, we can prove a slightly refined safety theorem. We not
only require that *safe e* is satisfied for all vehicles *e*, but that *safe e* is satisfied,
after we switch to the view owned by e. This addition is sufficient, since for each
e, the views it owns contain the maximum amount of information about *e*.

theorem *safety* $: \models (\forall e.@e\,(safe\ e)) \wedge DC' \wedge LC' \rightarrow \mathbf{G}\,(\forall e.@e\,(safe\ e))$

The proof of this theorem is then similar to the safety proof in Sect. 3, insofar that
we start by induction on the length of transition sequences, and then proceed
by contradiction. We need to distinguish several more cases, but these cases
themselves are proven analogously to the original proof.

5 Conclusion

We presented a semantical embedding of the spatio-temporal logic HMLSL,
specifically designed to reason about motorway traffic, into Isabelle/HOL,
and thus implemented the first computer-based assistance for reasoning with
HMLSL. Isabelle/HOL as a framework enabled us to use its highly sophisticated automatic proof methods. Within this embedding, we proved the absence
of collisions, if the controllers of all vehicles adhere to a certain set of constraints.
The constraints needed for proving safety differ, if we reduce the capability of
the sensors deployed in the vehicles. Parameterising our embedding with the
types of sensors allowed us to prove general theorems and rules of MLSL, which
could subsequently be used by all instantiations of HMLSL.

Of course, our level of abstraction is high, since we focus on the spatial aspects
of the motorway. However, our safety theorems show which capabilities vehicles
have to possess, to ensure safety on a motorway. E.g., for perfect information, the
controllers only have to adhere to the constraints implied by the reservations. For
regular information, the vehicles need more capabilities, in particular, the ability
to pass information between them. Olderog et al. examined ways to link a formal
model very similar to ours (i.e., based on similar notions of traffic snapshots and
views) with concrete controller implementations [19]. They specify high-level
controllers, where MLSL formulas may be used as guards and invariants. To
link our presentation to their work, the semantics of these controllers, as well as
the *linking predicates* that specify the connection between the dynamics and the
high-level controllers would have to be formalised within Isabelle/HOL. Then,
proving safety amounts to proving that the controllers satisfy our requirements.
Since Olderog et al. assumed perfect information for the controllers, their general
approach has to be refined to take less idealistic information into account.

Our current proofs show safety of motorway traffic, which can be achieved,
if the vehicles do not drive at all. Hence, proving liveness properties would be

an interesting extension of our current approach. Both sensor definitions we presented are very idealistic. For example, we did not take imprecision or probabilistic failures into account. However, such properties could be encoded into more complex sensor functions, e.g., by using probability measures in Isabelle/HOL as defined by Hölzl [20]. Since our definition of HMLSL is parametric in the sensor definition, the main properties of the logic can be reused, and only the new implications of the sensor definition have to be proven.

Furthermore, the embedding is designed for motorway traffic, i.e., vehicles driving into one direction on a multi-lane highway. A natural extension would be to take oncoming traffic into account and could be done along lines of previous work [21]. In this case, the model would probably just need slight adjustments, e.g., to distinguish vehicles driving in different directions. Extensions to model urban traffic could be defined following, e.g., Hilscher and Schwammberger [22] or Xu and Li [23]. However, the models in both of these approaches differ strongly from the model for motorway traffic.

References

1. Hilscher, M., Linker, S., Olderog, E.-R., Ravn, A.P.: An abstract model for proving safety of multi-lane traffic manoeuvres. In: Qin, S., Qiu, Z. (eds.) ICFEM 2011. LNCS, vol. 6991, pp. 404–419. Springer, Heidelberg (2011). doi:10.1007/978-3-642-24559-6_28

2. Linker, S., Hilscher, M.: proof theory of a multi-lane spatial logic. LMCS **11** (2015)

3. Linker, S.: Proofs for traffic safety: combining diagrams and logic. Ph.D. thesis, University of Oldenburg (2015). http://oops.uni-oldenburg.de/2337/

4. Nipkow, T., Paulson, L.C., Wenzel, M.: Isabelle/HOL–A Proof Assistant for Higher-Order Logic. LNCS, vol. 2283. Springer, Heidelberg (2002)

5. Platzer, A., Quesel, J.-D.: KeYmaera: a hybrid theorem prover for hybrid systems (system description). In: Armando, A., Baumgartner, P., Dowek, G. (eds.) IJCAR 2008. LNCS (LNAI), vol. 5195, pp. 171–178. Springer, Heidelberg (2008). doi:10.1007/978-3-540-71070-7_15

6. Loos, S.M., Platzer, A., Nistor, L.: Adaptive cruise control: hybrid, distributed, and now formally verified. In: Butler, M., Schulte, W. (eds.) FM 2011. LNCS, vol. 6664, pp. 42–56. Springer, Heidelberg (2011). doi:10.1007/978-3-642-21437-0_6

7. Platzer, A.: The complete proof theory of hybrid systems. In: LICS, pp. 541–550. IEEE (2012)

8. Rizaldi, A., Althoff, M.: Formalising traffic rules for accountability of autonomous vehicles. In: ITSC, pp. 1658–1665. IEEE (2015)

9. Kamali, M., Dennis, L.A., McAree, O., Fisher, M., Veres, S.M.: Formal verification of autonomous vehicle platooning. arXiv preprint arXiv:1602.01718 (2016)

10. Alur, R., Dill, D.L.: A theory of timed automata. TCS **126**, 183–235 (1994)

11. Dennis, L.A., Fisher, M., Webster, M.P., Bordini, R.H.: Model checking agent programming languages. ASE **19**, 5–63 (2012)

12. Larsen, K.G., Pettersson, P., Yi, W.: UPPAAL in a nutshell. STTT **1**, 134–152 (1997)

13. Campbell, J., Tuncali, C.E., Liu, P., Pavlic, T.P., Ozguner, U., Fainekos, G.: Modeling concurrency and reconfiguration in vehicular systems: a π-calculus approach. In: CASE, pp. 523–530 IEEE (2016)

14. Alur, R.: Principles of Cyber-Physical Systems. MIT Press, Cambridge (2015)
15. Braüner, T.: Hybrid Logic and Its Proof-Theory. Springer, Netherlands (2010)
16. Moszkowski, B.C.: A temporal logic for multilevel reasoning about hardware. Computer **18**, 10–19 (1985)
17. Benzmüller, C., Paulson, L.: Quantified multimodal logics in simple type theory. Log. Univers. **7**, 7–20 (2013)
18. Bochmann, G.V., Hilscher, M., Linker, S., Olderog, E.R.: Synthesizing and verifying controllers for multi-lane traffic maneuvers. FAC **29**, 583–600 (2017)
19. Olderog, E.-R., Ravn, A.P., Wisniewski, R.: Linking discrete and continuous models, applied to traffic manoeuvrers. In: Hinchey, M.G., Bowen, J.P., Olderog, E.-R. (eds.) Provably Correct Systems. NMSSE, pp. 95–120. Springer, Cham (2017). doi:10.1007/978-3-319-48628-4_5
20. Hölzl, J.: Markov processes in Isabelle/HOL. In: CPP 2017, pp. 100–111. ACM (2017)
21. Hilscher, M., Linker, S., Olderog, E.-R.: Proving safety of traffic manoeuvres on country roads. In: Liu, Z., Woodcock, J., Zhu, H. (eds.) Theories of Programming and Formal Methods. LNCS, vol. 8051, pp. 196–212. Springer, Heidelberg (2013). doi:10.1007/978-3-642-39698-4_12
22. Hilscher, M., Schwammberger, M.: An abstract model for proving safety of autonomous urban traffic. In: Sampaio, A., Wang, F. (eds.) ICTAC 2016. LNCS, vol. 9965, pp. 274–292. Springer, Cham (2016). doi:10.1007/978-3-319-46750-4_16
23. Xu, B., Li, Q.: A spatial logic for modeling and verification of collision-free control of vehicles. In: ICECCS, pp. 33–42. IEEE (2016)

Formalising and Monitoring Traffic Rules for Autonomous Vehicles in Isabelle/HOL

Albert Rizaldi[1]([✉]), Jonas Keinholz[1], Monika Huber[1], Jochen Feldle[2],
Fabian Immler[1], Matthias Althoff[1], Eric Hilgendorf[2], and Tobias Nipkow[1]

[1] Institut für Informatik, Technische Universität München, Munich, Germany
`rizaldi@in.tum.de`
[2] Forschungsstelle RobotRecht, Julius-Maximilians-Universität Würzburg,
Würzburg, Germany

Abstract. Recent accidents involving autonomous vehicles prompt us to consider how we can engineer an autonomous vehicle which always obeys traffic rules. This is particularly challenging because traffic rules are rarely specified at the level of detail an engineer would expect. Hence, it is nearly impossible to formally monitor behaviours of autonomous vehicles—which are expressed in terms of position, velocity, and acceleration—with respect to the traffic rules—which are expressed by vague concepts such as "maintaining safe distance". We show how we can use the Isabelle theorem prover to do this by first codifying the traffic rules abstractly and then subsequently concretising each atomic proposition in a verified manner. Thanks to Isabelle's code generation, we can generate code which we can use to monitor the compliance of traffic rules formally.

1 Introduction

Formalising law in a logical language is hard. Since the formalisation of the British Nationality Act in PROLOG [19], there has yet to be another major breakthrough in the formalisation of law. Even formalising traffic rules for highway scenarios, which seems straightforward on the surface, possesses many challenges. The challenges are not so much representing natural language specifications as logical entities—which we term "codification"—as concretely interpreting predicates such as *overtaking*, *maintaining safe distance*, or *maintaining enough side clearance*—which we term "concretisation". For example, how large is a distance in order to be categorised as safe?

We are mainly motivated to formalise traffic rules for two purposes: (1) holding autonomous vehicles legally accountable; and (2) clarifying requirements for engineering autonomous vehicles. It is necessary that traffic rules are codified in a logical language so that engineers have a clear and well-defined specification

A. Rizaldi—This work is partially supported by the DFG Graduiertenkolleg 1480 (PUMA), DFG NI 491/16-1, European Commission project UnCoVerCPS 643921.

N. Polikarpova and S. Schneider (Eds.): IFM 2017, LNCS 10510, pp. 50–66, 2017.
DOI: 10.1007/978-3-319-66845-1_4

against which the autonomous vehicles will be verified. However, codifying traffic rules can be done abstractly by leaving predicates such as *overtaking, safe-distance*, and *side clearance* undefined which still makes traffic rules unclear. Therefore, these predicates need to be concretised through legal and engineering analyses.

Formalising traffic rules entails choosing the logical language to codify the rules. It must be expressive enough to codify natural language yet simple enough to have automation for checking whether the behaviours of autonomous vehicles satisfy (obey) the formulas (traffic rules). In line with our previous works for formalising traffic rules [17], we advocate the use of higher-order logic (HOL) as follows: we codify the rules in linear temporal logic (LTL)—which can be defined in HOL—by assuming each predicate found in the legal text to be an atomic proposition. We then define these predicates concretely in higher-order logic (HOL). In this setting, HOL provides expressiveness while LTL allows automation.

In this paper, we focus on the German traffic rules *Straßenverkehrsordnung* (StVO) especially on the paragraph about overtaking. We choose this specific paragraph, because we think that it represents the general challenge of codification and concretisation of formalising traffic rules. The formalisation is performed with the help of the Isabelle theorem prover in order to achieve a higher level of trustworthiness. Our contributions are as follows:[1]

- We codify a part of the German overtaking traffic rules in LTL and show that these formalise the traffic rules faithfully (Sect. 3).
- We provide a verified checker for detecting the occurrence of an overtaking from a trace of a vehicle (Sect. 4). This requires a formal model of road network—we use lanelets [3]—and functions for detecting lane occupied by a vehicle.
- We provide a verified checker for determining a safe distance by considering the reaction time of the vehicle (Sect. 5); this is an improvement of our previous work [18].
- We provide a trustworthy Standard ML code for overtaking and safe distance checkers and that for monitoring the satisfaction of a trace against LTL formulas (Sect. 6).

2   Preliminaries

Notations used in this paper closely resemble Isabelle/HOL's syntax. Function application is always written in an uncurried form: instead of writing $f\ x\ y$ as in the λ-calculus, we always write $f(x, y)$. We write $t :: \tau$ to indicate that term t has type τ. Types used in this paper could either be a base type such as $\mathbb{R}$ for real numbers, or constructed via type constructors such as α *list* and *set* α for list of type α and set of type α, respectively. For an $xs :: \alpha$ *list*, we can (1) obtain its n-th element by writing $xs\,!\,n$; (2) obtain its length by writing $|xs|$;

---

[1] Our Isabelle formalisation is in https://github.com/rizaldialbert/overtaking.

(3) drop its first n elements by writing *drop*(n, xs); (4) obtain the first and the last element by writing *hd*(xs) and *last*(xs), respectively. We use $\{t \mid x. P\}$ as the set builder notation where t is a term, P is a predicate, and x is a free variable in t, which occurs in P. Another frequently used type in this work is a pair; we can obtain the first element of a pair $p :: \alpha \times \beta$ by the *fst* operator, *fst*$(p) :: \alpha$, and the second element by the *snd* operator, *snd*$(p) :: \beta$. For option data type, we use *None* and *Some* instead of Haskell's *Nothing* and *Maybe*; but we use Haskell's **do**-notation for monadic computation. In higher-order logic, a deduction with a single premise is written as $P \implies Q$, and if there are n premises, we write $P_1 \implies P_2 \implies \ldots \implies P_n \implies Q$. In linear temporal logic, we shall use $\mathsf{G}(\phi)$ to denote properties that atomic proposition ϕ should be true at all times.

3   Codification of Traffic Rules

The *Straßenverkehrsordnung* (StVO)—or German traffic rules—is the main traffic code for regulating the behaviours of motorised vehicles in Germany. It covers both the scenarios for urban and highway driving: here we focus on the paragraph about overtaking (§ 5 StVO) on highway scenarios. The English version of § 5(4) StVO is:

> When changing the lane to the left lane during overtaking, no following road user shall be endangered. [...] During overtaking, the driver has to change from the fast lane to the right lane as soon as possible. The road user being overtaken shall not be obstructed.

3.1   Legal Analysis

Overtaking in right-hand-traffic countries could be divided roughly into three parts: changing to the left lane, passing the vehicle in front, and returning back to the original lane (see Fig. 1). Whenever a vehicle changes to the left lane to overtake another road user, the driver has to ensure that those on the fast lane will not be endangered. If a vehicle that becomes a following vehicle might be endangered in any way, overtaking is prohibited [5, § 5 StVO, recital 33]. However, this does not mean that any interference with the following traffic needs to be avoided. If, by the overtaking manoeuvre, the following road user is led to reduce its speed safely and will not collide with the overtaking vehicle [4, p. 481], [15, p. 248], the vehicle is allowed to change to the left lane. This overtaking decision must consider the speed difference of the overtaking and the following car.

After overtaking a slower vehicle in front, the overtaking vehicle needs to return to the right lane. This is a special manifestation of the "drive on the right"-rule in § 2(2) StVO [7, § 5 StVO Rn. 32]. When returning to the right lane, other road users must not be forced to brake. The overtaking vehicle also needs to keep a safe distance to the following traffic. However, there is no fixed value for this distance and the decisive factor is that, in the case of an unexpected

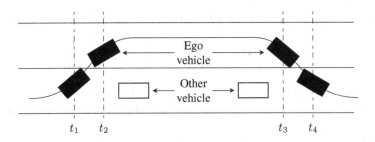

Fig. 1. Illustration of overtaking. The curve represents the overtaking trajectory. We show the positions of the ego vehicle (filled rectangle) at four different time points t_1, t_2, t_3, and t_4. The positions of the other vehicle (empty rectangle) are shown only for t_1 and t_4.

emergency brake, the following vehicle must be able to stop behind the vehicle in front. This depends on the road surface and the speed of both cars [9, § 4 StVO recital 5]. With human drivers, the response time needs to be taken into account.

The last sentence regarding obstruction serves as a protection of the slower vehicle being overtaken. This "no obstruction" rule has the same meaning of keeping a safe distance to the vehicle being overtaken as in the previous paragraphs.

3.2 LTL Formulas of Traffic Rules

In order to codify traffic rules in LTL, we need to identify relevant atomic propositions first. By using the previous legal analysis, we list required atomic propositions with their intended interpretation in Table 1; references to time points t_1, t_2, t_3, and t_4 should be seen in conjunction with illustration in Fig. 1. The LTL formulas of the traffic rules are:

Table 1. Atomic propositions and its intended interpretation

Atomic proposition	Interpretation
overtaking	Performing an overtaking manoeuvre—$[t_1; t_4)$
begin-overtaking	Overtaking and starting to move to the next lane—$[t_1; t_2)$
merging	Starting to merge to the original lane—t_3
finish-overtaking	Overtaking and returning back to the original lane—$[t_3; t_4)$
sd-rear	Maintaining a safe distance to the rear vehicle on all lanes
safe-to-return	Leave large enough distance for merging to the original lane

1. *When changing the lane to the left lane during overtaking, no following road user shall be endangered.*

$$\Phi_1 := \boxed{\text{G (begin-overtaking} \longrightarrow \text{sd-rear)}}$$

As mentioned in the previous legal analysis, the word 'endangered' can be concretely interpreted as maintaining a safe distance to the vehicles in the fast lane.

2. *During overtaking, the driver has to change from the fast lane to the right lane as soon as possible.*

$$\Phi_2 := \boxed{\text{G (merging} \longleftrightarrow \text{safe-to-return)}}$$

The phrase 'as soon as possible' in this rule is interpreted as the time at which the ego vehicle has left a large enough distance. From this formula, one can infer that atomic proposition safe-to-return and merging must evaluate to true at the same time; this agrees with the natural language interpretation of the phrase 'as soon as possible' too.

3. *The road user being overtaken shall not be obstructed.*

$$\Phi_3 := \boxed{\text{G (finish-overtaking} \longrightarrow \text{sd-rear)}}$$

Here the word 'obstructed' is interpreted as maintaining safe distance to the vehicle being overtaken; hence the atomic proposition sd-rear in the conclusion of the implication.

3.3   Monitoring Traffic Rules

One intended application of our work is to determine whether the behaviours of an autonomous vehicle recorded in a black box comply with (overtaking) traffic rules or not. This black box is assumed to record not only data from the ego vehicle but also those from other road users observed by the ego vehicle or obtained from vehicle-to-vehicle (V2V) communication. In order to analyse this black box formally, we model the recorded data as discrete time *runs* (or *paths*). Each run is the evolution of a vehicle's state consisting of continuous data such as position, velocity, and acceleration—all comprise values in x- and y-dimensions. We assume that the black box also contain information about the occupancies of a vehicle; they are represented by rectangles with time-varying width and length.

For formal analysis purposes, we need to convert these runs into *traces*; a corresponding trace of a run is defined here as the evolution of the Boolean values (truth values) over the predefined set of atomic propositions (a word over the set of atomic propositions). This is the next challenge for formalising traffic rules: concretely defining each atomic proposition in Table 1 in terms of the continuous and discrete variables in the runs. Section 4 concretises the first four atomic propositions in Table 1 and Sect. 5 concretises the last two atomic propositions.

4   Concretising the Overtaking Predicate

In this paper, we improve our previous definition of overtaking in [17] by defining four instead of two time points; these points are labelled from t_1 to t_4 in Fig. 1. This is required for concretising begin-overtaking, merging, and finish-overtaking. Overtaking starts at time point t_1, which is the earliest time to touch the lane divider; in $[t_0; t_1)$ the vehicle always stays in the same lane. It then continues until t_2, at which it enters the next lane completely, and stays in this lane until t_3, at which it touches the lane divider again. Overtaking is finished at t_4 when it re-enters the original lane completely. In order to detect and formalise such geometrical interpretations, we need a formal model of lanes and a verified function for lane detection. At t_1 in Fig. 1, for example, the lane detection should tell us that it is in the rightmost lane and starts to touch the lane boundary, and at t_2, it is only in the leftmost lane.

4.1   Lanelets

We use lanelet [3] as a formal model of a lane in this work. A lanelet consists of two nonempty monotone polygonal chains, each for representing the left and right boundary.

Definition 1 (Polygonal chains). *An $xs :: (\mathbb{R}^2 \times \mathbb{R}^2)$ list is a polygonal chain if and only if*

$$\forall i.\ i+1 < |xs| \ \longrightarrow \ \mathit{snd}\ (xs\,!\,i) = \mathit{fst}\ (xs\,!\,(i+1)).$$

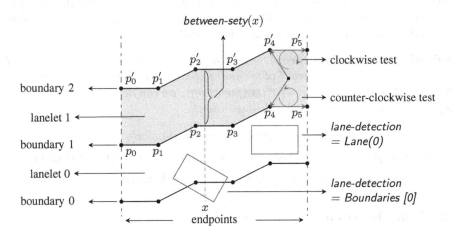

Fig. 2. An example of two lanelets with the direction to the *right*. The upper and lower polygonal chains for lanelet 1 is *points-le* $= [(p_0', p_1'), (p_1', p_2'), \ldots, (p_4', p_5')]$ and *points-ri* $= [(p_0, p_1), (p_1, p_2), \ldots, (p_4, p_5)]$, respectively. One restriction used in this formalisation is that the endpoints have the same value in x-dimension i. e. *fst*$(p_0) =$ *fst*(p_0') and *fst*$(p_5) =$ *fst*(p_5'). The grey area is the drivable area for lanelet 1. Both the rightmost lanelet and the rightmost boundary are identified with 0, and they increase as we move to the leftmost lanelet and boundary.

Definition 2 (Monotone polygonal chains w.r.t x-dimension). *A monotone polygonal chain w.r.t x-dimension is a polygonal chain whose x-element always increases:*

$$\forall\, i < |xs|. \quad \mathsf{fst}\,(\mathsf{fst}\,(xs\,!\,i)) \;<\; \mathsf{fst}(\mathsf{snd}\,(xs\,!\,i)).$$

The property of being monotone for a polygonal chain ensures that for each x, we have a unique y such that (x, y) is in the polygonal chain. Therefore, given a polygonal chain *points*, we can always create a function *f-of-x* from the set of all real numbers in x-dimension to the set of real numbers in y-dimension.

Definition 3 (Lanelets). *A lanelet consists of two nonempty monotone polygonal chains w.r.t. x-dimension, points-le and points-ri, which do not intersect and have the same endpoints in x-dimension.*

As defined in [3], there is no requirement of the relative placement between the two polygonal chains; *points-le* could be positioned above *points-ri* (from a bird's-eye view) or vice-versa. If it is the former then the lanelet has the direction to the right and to the left if it is the latter. Two polygonal chains *points*$_1$ and *points*$_2$ are called non-intersecting if there does not exist any two intersecting chains $c_1 \in \mathsf{set}\,\mathsf{points}_1$, $c_2 \in \mathsf{set}\,\mathsf{points}_2$.

Note that, with this definition, we could not model a lane which has a 90° turn. This is because our definition of monotone polygonal chain is fixed w.r.t. x-dimension. Lanelets in [3] do not have this restriction, but we can circumvent this problem by using a more general definition of monotone polygonal chains w.r.t to line l and split a polygonal chain into a minimal number of monotone polygonal chains [16]; each with its own coordinate system. We impose this restriction because it eases the following definition of drivable areas and makes the checking of intersecting polygonal chains easier.

Definition 4 (Drivable area). *By using the function representation of the left and right boundary f-of-x$_l$ and f-of-x$_r$, and defining first-point := fst(hd(points-le)), last-point := fst(last(points-le)), we can define the drivable area as follows (see Fig. 2 for graphical illustration).*

$$\mathsf{setx} \;:=\; \big\{x \mid x.\ \mathit{first\text{-}point} \le x \le \mathit{last\text{-}point}\big\},$$
$$\mathsf{between\text{-}sety}(x) \;:=\; \big(\min(\mathit{f\text{-}of\text{-}x}_l(x), \mathit{f\text{-}of\text{-}x}_r(x));\ \max(\mathit{f\text{-}of\text{-}x}_l(x), \mathit{f\text{-}of\text{-}x}_r(x))\big),$$
$$\mathsf{drivable\text{-}area} \;:=\; \big\{(x, y) \mid x\,y.\ x \in \mathsf{setx} \wedge y \in \mathsf{between\text{-}sety}(x)\big\}.$$

4.2   Lane Detection

In order to detect the lanelet a rectangle is currently occupying, we need first to test whether there is a lanelet in which a rectangle is located completely inside. To achieve this, we need to test whether the four vertices of a rectangle are located in the lanelet, and none of the four edges intersects with any lane boundary of the lanelet. Hence, we need two primitives here: *segment intersection* and *point-in-lanelet test*.

Segments Intersection. First, we differentiate between lines and segments. A line in $\mathbb{R}^2$ is characterised by the line equation $ax + by = c$; a segment is a contiguous subset of a line.

Definition 5 (Closed Segment). *A segment is a pair of points* $(p, q) :: \mathbb{R}^2 \times \mathbb{R}^2$ *and the set of all points on this segment is*

$$closed\text{-}segment\,(p, q) \;=\; \{(1 - u) \cdot p + u \cdot q \,|\, u :: \mathbb{R}. \quad 0 \le u \le 1\}.$$

With this definition, we can give the correctness and completeness condition for the function *segment-intersect* we wish to define as follows:

$$segment\text{-}intersect(s_1, s_2) \iff \exists p.\; p \in closed\text{-}segment(s_1) \wedge p \in closed\text{-}segment(s_2)$$

By using the definition of closed segment above, the formula on the right hand side of the bi-implication above can be reformulated as:

$$\exists u_1\, u_2.\; 0 \le u_1 \le 1 \wedge, 0 \le u_2 \le 1 \;\wedge\; (1 - u_1) \cdot s_1 + u_1 \cdot s_2 = (1 - u_2) \cdot s_1 + u_2 \cdot s_2,$$

which is a linear arithmetic formula. Therefore, we can use decision procedures for linear arithmetic problem to define *segment-intersect*. In this work, we implement a specialised instance of Fourier–Motzkin variable elimination algorithm for this problem; readers are encouraged to consult [12] and our implementation in Isabelle for the detailed implementation. We have proved with Isabelle theorem prover that this function indeed satisfies the correctness and completeness condition above.

Point-in-Lanelet Test. Let us consider a lanelet which has the direction to the right and is parameterised by *points-le* and *points-ri* as its left and right boundary, respectively, as defined in Definition 3. To check whether a point is in a lanelet, we need to perform clockwise and counter-clockwise tests. The clockwise test (*cw*) for a triple (p_1, p_2, p_3) checks whether the sequence of points in the triple has a clockwise orientation; the counter-clockwise (*counter-cw*) test does the opposite (see Fig. 2). The point-in-lanelet test is defined by the following function.

$$point\text{-}in\text{-}lanelet(p) \;:=\; \textbf{let } c_1 = find\text{-}segment(points\text{-}le, p);$$
$$c_2 = find\text{-}segment(points\text{-}ri, p)$$
$$\textbf{in } cw(p, fst(c_1), snd(c_1)) \;\wedge\; counter\text{-}cw(p, fst(c_2), snd(c_2))$$

The *point-in-lanelet(p)* first finds the two segments c_1 and c_2 in the left and right polygonal chains, respectively, such that *in-x-interval*(c_1, x) and *in-x-interval*(c_2, x) hold (for instance $c_1 = (p_4', p_5')$ and $c_2 = (p_4, p_5)$ in Fig. 2). With these two segments, we only need to perform a counter-clockwise test for the triple $(p, fst(c_2), snd(c_2))$ and a clockwise test for the triple $(p, fst(c_1), snd(c_1))$ (see Fig. 2). This will guarantee that the point (x, y) is between the segments c_1 and c_2, which in turn ensures that the point is in the drivable area.

Theorem 1. *For a right-direction lanelet defined in Definition 3 with* **points-le** *and* **points-ri** *as its left and right boundary, respectively, we have*

$$\text{point-in-lanelet}(p) \implies p \in \text{drivable-area}.$$

Previously, we have explained how to test whether a rectangle is located inside a lanelet completely. However, this is not the only possible result of lane detection; we define a new data type to represent all possible results of our lane detection:

datatype *detection-opt* $=$ *Outside* | *Lane* $(n :: \mathbb{N})$ | *Boundaries* $(ns :: \mathbb{N}\ list)$

Each argument in the constructor *Lane* and *Boundaries* represents the lanelet identifier at which it is currently located or a list of boundaries with which a rectangle is intersecting, respectively. Figure 2 provides two examples of lane detection. The first rectangle intersects with boundary 0 only and hence our lane detection primitive returns *Boundaries*$([0])$. The second rectangle meanwhile is located inside lanelet 0 and hence our lane detection primitive returns *Lane*(0).

The function *lane-detection* takes a rectangle and lane boundaries as arguments and returns an element of type *detection-opt*. It checks first whether there is any lanelet in which a rectangle is completely located and, if there is no such lanelet, it tests for the intersections between the lane boundaries and rectangles. This can be easily done by checking intersections between relevant segments in the lane boundaries and edges in the rectangle. If there is no such lane boundary, we conclude that the rectangle is outside of any lanelet.

4.3   Overtaking Detection

We can use the previously described lane detection function for detecting overtaking as follows. Assuming that the vehicle is located in lane n initially, we use the following function to detect t_1 and t_2:

$$\textit{increase-lane } \textit{rects} := \mathbf{do}\,\{(t_1, r_1) \leftarrow \textit{start-inc-lane}(\textit{rects}, n, 0);$$
$$(t_2, r_2) \leftarrow \textit{finish-inc-lane}(r_1, (n+1), (t_1+1));$$
$$\textit{Some } ((t_1, t_2), r_2)\}$$

The function *start-inc-lane* detects t_1 by continuously checking whether the occupied lane is still n and stops immediately whenever the lane detection returns the boundary $n + 1$. Function *finish-inc-lane* detects t_2 by checking whether the lane is still on the boundary $n + 1$ and stops immediately on the first occurrence of the lane $n + 1$. Notice that $[t_0; t_2)$ and $[t_2; t_4)$ are identical and we can therefore detect t_3 and t_4 similarly as we do for t_1 and t_2, respectively, with function *decrease-lane*. The correctness of the function *increase-lane*[2] is shown next.

---

[2] We also have similar theorems for decrease-lane but they are omitted for brevity.

Theorem 2. *Assuming that the initial lane is n, we have the following deduction:*

$$\textit{increase-lane rects} = \textit{Some}(t_1, t_2, \textit{rest}) \implies \textit{rects}' = \textit{drop}(t_1 + 1, \textit{rects}) \implies$$
$$\wedge \ t_1 < |\textit{rects}| \ \wedge \ t_1 < t_2 \ \wedge \ t_2 < t_1 + |\textit{rects}'|$$
$$\wedge \ \textit{lane-detection}\,(\textit{rects}\,!\,t_1) = \textit{Boundaries}\,[n + 1]$$
$$\wedge \ \forall m. \ m < t_1 \longrightarrow \textit{lane-detection}\,(\textit{rects}\,!\,m) = \textit{Lane}\,(n)$$
$$\wedge \ \textit{lane-detection}\,(\textit{rects}\,!\,t_2) = \textit{Lane}\,(n + 1)$$
$$\wedge \ \forall m > t_1. \ m < t_2 \longrightarrow \textit{lane-detection}\,(\textit{rects}\,!\,m) = \textit{Boundaries}\,[n + 1]$$

The overtaking detection can be defined by using *increase-lane* and *decrease-lane* as follows. The primitive looks for t_1 and t_2 with *increase-lane* first and—if we have found this—continues to search for t_3 and t_4 with *decrease-lane*. If it cannot find t_1 and t_2 initially, we can conclude that there is no occurrence of overtaking at all. It could also be that we found t_1 and t_2 without the corresponding pair t_3 and t_4. In this case, we discard t_1 and t_2 and start to look for a new occurrence of overtaking from one lane to the left of the original lane.

5 Concretising the Safe Distance Predicate

The safe distance problem has been previously explored in our previous work [18] and, in this work, we improve it by considering nonzero reaction time. In this problem, we are interested in the scenario where there are two vehicles involved: *ego* and *other* vehicle which are located at $s_{0,e}$ and $s_{0,o}$, respectively. These positions are the frontmost part of the ego vehicle and the rearmost part of the other vehicle, respectively. We assume that the other vehicle is located in front of the ego vehicle initially, $s_{0,e} < s_{0,o}$, and the other vehicle performs an emergency brake with maximum deceleration $a_o < 0$. After $0 < \delta$ seconds of reaction time, the ego vehicle also performs an emergency brake with maximum deceleration $a_e < 0$. We can define the braking movement of the other vehicle mathematically as follows:

$$s_o(t) := \begin{cases} p_o(t) & \text{if } 0 \leq t \leq t_{\text{stop,o}} \\ p_o(t_{\text{stop,o}}) & \text{if } t_{\text{stop,o}} \leq t \end{cases} \tag{1}$$

where $p_o(t) := s_{0,o} + v_o t + \frac{1}{2} a_o t^2$ and $t_{\text{stop,o}} := -\frac{v_o}{a_o}$. To cater for the reaction time delay, the braking movement of the ego vehicle defined here is slightly different than what we have defined in our previous work [18]:

$$u_e(t) := \begin{cases} q_e(t) & \text{if } 0 \leq t \leq \delta \\ p_e^*(t - \delta) & \text{if } \delta \leq t \leq t_{\text{stop,e}} + \delta \\ p_e^*(t_{\text{stop,e}}) & \text{if } t_{\text{stop,e}} - \delta \leq t \end{cases} \tag{2}$$

with $q_e(t) := s_{0,e} + v_e t$, $p_e^*(t) := q_e(\delta) + v_e t + \frac{1}{2} a_e t^2$, and $t_{\text{stop,e}} := -\frac{v_e}{a_e}$. As the definition of q_e shows, we can now model that the ego vehicle maintains its current speed for δ seconds before performing an emergency brake. The stopping distances for both vehicles $u_{stop,e}$ and $s_{stop,o}$ are the positions where the derivative of $u_e(t)$ and $s_o(t)$, respectively, are equal to zero; we prove that these are

$$u_{stop,e} := q_e(\delta) - \frac{v_e^2}{2 \cdot a_e} \quad \text{and} \quad s_{stop,o} := s_{0,o} - \frac{v_o^2}{2 \cdot a_o}. \tag{3}$$

The problem now is to determine a sufficient distance $s_{0,o} - s_{0,e}$ such that for $T = [0; \infty)$ the predicate *no-collision-react*$(T) := \neg (\exists t \in T.\ u_e(t) = s_o(t))$ is true.

Following the methodology in our previous work [18], we analyse all possible cases to obtain the lower bound of the distance that is still safe. There are five possible cases as shown in Fig. 3. These five cases are obtained from case distinction based on stopping distances $u_{stop,e}$. In case ①, the ego vehicle stops before the initial position of the other vehicle and in case ② it stops after the stopping position of the other vehicle; in case ③, ④, and ⑤, it stops in between. Case ③ is characterised by the condition where the ego position at time δ is already in front of the other vehicle while the fourth and the fifth is not. In case ④, the ego vehicle stops after $s_o(\delta)$ i.e. the position of the other vehicle at time $t = \delta$, while in case ⑤, the ego vehicle stops before.

As Fig. 3 shows, we can deduce that there will be no collision for case ① because the ego vehicle stops before the starting position of the other vehicle.

Theorem 3 (Case ①). $u_{stop,e} < s_{0,o} \implies$ *no-collision-react* $[0; \infty)$

From this theorem, we can replace the definition of $u_{stop,e}$ with the expression in Eq. 3 so that we obtain *safe-distance*$_0 := v_e \cdot \delta - v_e^2/(2 \cdot a_e)$ as our zeroth safe distance expression. In cases ② and ③, the stopping positions of the ego vehicle are after those of the other vehicles'. Hence, we can deduce collisions by using the Intermediate Value Theorem (IVT). In case ④, we cannot deduce a

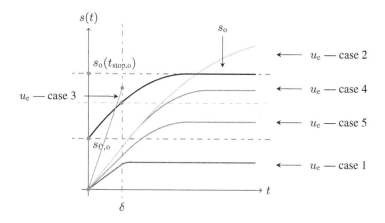

Fig. 3. Cases obtained according to relative positions of ego's stopping distance to that of the other vehicle.

collision or a collision freedom just by looking at the stopping distances of the ego vehicle relative to the other vehicle; the following theorem helps to deduce these.

Theorem 4 (Case ④). *By defining*

$$v_o^* := \begin{cases} v_o + a_o\delta & \text{if } \delta \leq t_{\text{stop},o} \\ 0 & \text{otherwise} \end{cases} \tag{4}$$

and $t_{\text{stop},o}^* := -\frac{v_o^*}{a_o}$, $s_{0,o}^* := s_o(\delta)$, *and* $s_{0,e}^* := q_e(\delta)$, *we have*

$$s_{0,o} \leq u_{\text{stop},e} \implies u_{\text{stop},e} < s_{\text{stop},o} \implies \textit{no-collision-react}\,[0;\infty) \iff$$

$$\neg\left(a_o > a_e \wedge v_o^* < v_e \wedge s_{0,o}^* - s_{0,e}^* \leq \frac{(v_o^* - v_e)^2}{2 \cdot (a_o - a_e)} \wedge t_{\text{stop},e} < t_{\text{stop},o}^* \right).$$

Note that the definition of v_o^* depends on the condition whether the reaction time is smaller than the stopping time of the other vehicle $t_{\text{stop},o}$. When $\delta \leq t_{\text{stop},o}$, we can rearrange the deduction by first weakening the bi-implication into implication and replacing the definition of $u_{\text{stop},e}$ and $s_{\text{stop},o}$ with their respective definitions in Eq. 3, and then use de Morgan's rule into:

$$s_{0,o} \leq u_{\text{stop},e} \implies \left(a_o > a_e \wedge v_o^* < v_e \wedge t_{\text{stop},e} < t_{\text{stop},o}^* \right)$$

$$s_{0,o} - s_{0,e} > \underbrace{v_e\delta - \frac{v_e^2}{2a_e} + \frac{v_o^2}{2a_o}}_{\textit{safe-distance}_1} \implies s_{0,o} - s_{0,e} > \underbrace{\frac{(v_o + a_o\delta - v_e)^2}{2 \cdot (a_o - a_e)} - v_o\delta - \frac{1}{2}a_o\delta^2 + v_e\delta}_{\textit{safe-distance}_2}$$

$$\implies \textit{no-collision-react}\,[0;\infty).$$

If the first assumption in the deduction above is false, then we are in case ① and Theorem 3 guarantees the situation to be collision free. Hence, to derive a checker, we can safely ignore the first assumption above and put the second assumption as a condition in an **if** statement. Now, we are left with two expressions for safe distance, which can be chosen with the following lemma.

Lemma 1. $a_o > a_e \implies \textit{safe-distance}_1 \leq \textit{safe-distance}_2$.

From this lemma, we check whether the distance is larger than *safe-distance*$_2$ when $a_o > a_e \wedge v_o^* < v_e \wedge t_{\text{stop},e} < t_{\text{stop},o}^*$ is true. Otherwise, we check the distance against *safe-distance*$_1$ because Theorem 4 suggests that this will lead to collision freedom.

In case ⑤, we can deduce a collision freedom. To see this, we can reformulate the problem into a safe distance problem without reaction time delay as we did in our previous work [18] with δ is set to zero. Graphically speaking, we ignore any behaviour that has happened to the left of δ in Fig. 3 and, in this reformulation, case ⑤ becomes case ① in zero reaction time delay setting. As the deduction in [18] suggests, there will be no collision.

Theorem 5 (Case ⑤).

$$s_o \leq u_{\text{stop,e}} \implies u_{\text{stop,e}} < s_{\text{stop,o}} \implies u_{\text{stop,o}} < s_o(\delta) \implies \textit{no-collision-react}\,[0;\infty)$$

By using Eq. 3, the premise $u_{\text{stop,o}} < s_o(\delta)$ in the deduction above can be reformulated so that we can obtained the third safe distance expression for $\delta \leq t_{\text{stop,o}}$ as *safe-distance*$_3$ $:= v_e\delta - v_e^2/2a_e - v_o\delta - a_o\delta^2/2$. To summarise, we can combine all the logical analyses above into the following checker which we have proved in Isabelle theorem prover to be sound and complete.

checker :=

> **let** *dist* $= s_{0,o} - s_{0,e}$ **in**
>
> **if** $\underline{\textit{dist} > \textit{safe-distance}_0} \vee (\delta \leq t_{\text{stop,o}} \wedge \underline{\textit{dist} > \textit{safe-distance}_3})$ **then** *True*
>
> **elseif** $\delta \leq t_{\text{stop,o}} \wedge a_0 > a_e \wedge v_o^* < v_e \wedge t_{\text{stop,e}} < t_{\text{stop,o}}^*$ **then**
>
> $\underline{\textit{dist} > \textit{safe-distance}_2}$ **else** $\underline{\textit{dist} > \textit{safe-distance}_1}$

We can now define the atomic proposition sd-rear and safe-to-return simply as an application of the safe distance checker. However, the analysis above have the opposite assumption about the relative position of the ego and the other vehicle. Therefore, we have to properly swap the values of position, velocity, and maximum deceleration between the ego and the other vehicle. The key difference between the definition of atomic proposition sd-rear and safe-to-return is that the former uses the checker w.r.t. the vehicle in the left lanelet, while the latter is w.r.t. the vehicle in the right lanelet.

Since both sd-rear and safe-to-return are defined by using the notion of safe distance, readers might think that the rule of returning to the right lane as soon as possible (Φ_2) might not be valid because the safe distance condition might hold immediately after the change to the left lane. This would not happen due to the assumption $s_{0,e} < s_{0,o}$ in the safe distance problem explained in the beginning of this section; our checker checks this condition implicitly[3]. Hence, during the monitoring of Φ_2, the values between the ego and the other vehicle are swapped and the previous condition becomes $s_{0,o} < s_{0,e}$. After the ego vehicle change to the left lane and is still behind the other vehicle, this condition will be false and hence our formalisation of Φ_2 excludes this scenario.

6   Monitoring Overtaking Traffic Rules

With the concrete definition of the atomic propositions in Table 1, we can define a converter from a run to a trace for each atomic proposition. These traces are then combined into a word over the set of all atomic propositions for monitoring the satisfaction of the codified traffic rules in LTL. For this purpose, we need to define the semantics we use in this work. Since runs from an autonomous vehicles' planners are usually finite, we use the semantics in [6][4] which interprets LTL formulas over finite traces.

---

[3] This can be checked in our Isabelle formalisation.

[4] The semantics for LTL is pretty standard and, hence, we omit them for brevity.

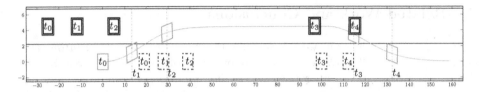

Fig. 4. Example of overtaking scenario. The curve is the trajectory of the ego vehicle we want to monitor. All vehicles drive to the right direction. Ego vehicle (solid rectangle) is positioned at $(0,0)$ and the first vehicle (double rectangle) at $(-25, 4.5)$ initially. Both vehicles have initial velocity of $16.7\,\mathrm{ms}^{-1}$. The second vehicle (dashed rectangle) is located at $(19, 0)$ with initial velocity of $11.1\,\mathrm{ms}^{-1}$. All vehicles except the ego vehicle drive with constant velocity. For each vehicle we show the position at time $t_1 = 0.8\,\mathrm{s}$, $t_2 = 1.8\,\mathrm{s}$, $t_3 = 7.3\,\mathrm{s}$, and $t_4 = 8.4\,\mathrm{s}$.

As a numerical example, we consider a situation with two lanelets (Fig. 4) in which the first vehicle (double rectangle) is positioned behind the ego vehicle in the leftmost lane. The ego vehicle (solid rectangle) intends to overtake the second vehicle (dashed rectangle); both are at the rightmost lane initially. Each vehicle has the same width $(2\,\mathrm{m})$, length $(4.8\,\mathrm{m})$, reaction time $(1\,\mathrm{s})$, and maximum deceleration $(-8\,\mathrm{ms}^{-2})$. The run for this numerical example is produced by the controller for autonomous vehicles found in [20].

In order to monitor this run on the code level, we need to generate the code for the environment (lanelets). From Definition 3, we need to ensure that the two boundaries of each lanelet are not intersecting. To achieve this, we have implemented a polygonal chain intersection test according to the algorithm in [16] and proved its correctness. The algorithm is based on a sweep-line algorithm which, as the sweeping progresses, it checks whether each pair of chain in each boundary are relevant or not and, if the pair is relevant, it performs an intersection check as explained in Sect. 4.

All code required for monitoring the codified traffic rules, including the semantics of the LTL, are generated automatically by using Isabelle's code generator [8]. Therefore, we only have to trust the Isabelle's code generator for the correctness of our Standard ML's code. However, most of the formalised functions used for monitoring traffic rules require real numbers data type, and code generation with real numbers is usually done with the help of Interval Arithmetic [10] or Affine Arithmetic [11]. Since this is a numerical example only, mapping real numbers to machine's floating-point numbers is sufficient.

The results of the simulation show that all overtaking traffic rules except the merging rule (Φ_2) are satisfied. Particularly, rule Φ_2 is not satisfied due to the 'if' ($\longleftarrow$) fragment. If we weaken rule Φ_2 into $\Phi_2' := \mathsf{G}\,(\mathtt{merging} \longrightarrow \mathtt{safe\text{-}to\text{-}return})$, the run from the controller still satisfies rule Φ_2'.

7   Related Work and Conclusions

The monitoring part of our work belongs to the research area called *runtime verification*; Küster [13] provides a complete overview of this research area. Specifically, our work can be categorised as *runtime monitoring*. Our work does not construct a monitor automaton [2] as in most monitoring techniques but simply executes the semantics of LTL over finite-length traces. This is sufficient because we wish to verify traces produced by autonomous vehicles' planners whose duration are usually not very long. The other intended application of our work is to perform automated offline checking of a recorded trace for compliance with traffic rules.

In terms of the logic used for specifying properties, there is signal temporal logic (STL) [14] which is expressive enough to specify real-time properties. This is particularly useful for relaxing the requirement to satisfy a rule within a certain duration of time such as in the 'if' part of Φ_2. Another expressive logic for runtime monitoring is metric first-order temporal logic (MFOTL) [1] which is capable of handling relations that change over time such as safe distance. However, we stick to logic without first-order fragment because we do not need to reason about first-order structure for formalising the presented subset of traffic rules.

In comparison to [18], we have improved the analysis by taking the reaction time into consideration. This is required because autonomous vehicles will interact with human drivers and they clearly do not have zero reaction time. To achieve this, we have to perform five instead of three case analyses in terms of the relative stopping distance between the ego and the other vehicles. Additionally, during our formalisation effort, we found out that we need two additional case analyses regarding the relative duration of the stopping time and reaction time. As a result, we obtain a general checker (safe distance expression) which has been proved to be sound and complete in Isabelle/HOL.

In comparison to [17], we now have identified four instead of two time points when detecting overtaking occurrences. To achieve this, we need to implement two additional checkers for detecting the additional time points and formally verify them in Isabelle/HOL. As a result, we are now able to specify traffic rules which requires these two time points: safe distance during the beginning of the overtaking manoeuvre and merging.

To conclude, we have formalised a subset of overtaking traffic rules in Isabelle/HOL. By formalising traffic rules, we do not mean only the codification of traffic rules in a logical language where abstract concepts such as overtaking and safe distance are left unspecified: we went deeper by concretising these abstract concepts through legal and mathematical analysis. Through these two analyses, we obtain unambiguous, precisely defined specifications from overtaking traffic rules for autonomous vehicles. Furthermore, from these formalised traffic rules, we show how to monitor the satisfaction of a run obtained from a planner for autonomous vehicles.

References

1. Basin, D.A., Klaedtke, F., Müller, S., Zalinescu, E.: Monitoring metric first-order temporal properties. J. ACM **62**(2), 15:1–15:45 (2015)
2. Bauer, A., Leucker, M., Schallhart, C.: Runtime verification for LTL and TLTL. ACM Trans. Softw. Eng. Methodol. **20**(4), 14:1–14:64 (2011)
3. Bender, P., Ziegler, J., Stiller, C.: Lanelets: efficient map representation for autonomous driving. In: Proceedings of the IEEE Intelligent Vehicles Symposium, Michigan, MI, USA, pp. 420–425 (2014)
4. Bundesgerichtshof: Sorgfaltspflichten beim überholen auf der autobahn, pp. 481–482. Neue Juristische Wochenschrift: NJW (1954)
5. Burmann, M., Heß, R., Hühnermann, K., Jahnke, J., Janker, H.: Straßenverkehrsrecht: Kommentar, 24th edn. C.H. Beck (2016)
6. Giannakopoulo, D., Havelund, K.: Automata-based verification of temporal properties on running programs. In: Proceedings of the 16th Annual International Conference on Automated Software Engineering (ASE), San Diego, CA, USA, pp. 412–416 (2001)
7. Gutt, S.: Gesamtes Verkehrsrecht, 1st edn. Nomos (2014)
8. Haftmann, F., Nipkow, T.: Code generation via higher-order rewrite systems. In: Blume, M., Kobayashi, N., Vidal, G. (eds.) FLOPS 2010. LNCS, vol. 6009, pp. 103–117. Springer, Heidelberg (2010). doi:10.1007/978-3-642-12251-4_9
9. Hentschel, P., König, P., Dauer, P.: Straßenverkehrsrecht: Kommentar, 43rd edn. C.H. Beck (2015)
10. Hölzl, J.: Proving inequalities over reals with computation in Isabelle/HOL. In: Proceedings of the ACM SIGSAM International Workshop on Programming Languages for Mechanized Mathematics Systems (PLMMS 2009), Munich, pp. 38–45 (2009)
11. Immler, F.: A verified algorithm for geometric zonotope/hyperplane intersection. In: Proceedings of the International Conference on Certified Programs and Proofs (CPP), Mumbai, India, pp. 129–136 (2015)
12. Kroening, D., Strichman, O.: Decision Procedures - An Algorithmic Point of View. Texts in Theoretical Computer Science. EATCS Series, 2nd edn. Springer, Heidelberg (2016)
13. Küster, J.C.: Runtime verification on data-carrying traces. Ph.D. thesis, The Australian National University, October 2016
14. Maler, O., Nickovic, D.: Monitoring temporal properties of continuous signals. In: Lakhnech, Y., Yovine, S. (eds.) FORMATS/FTRTFT -2004. LNCS, vol. 3253, pp. 152–166. Springer, Heidelberg (2004). doi:10.1007/978-3-540-30206-3_12
15. Oberlandesgericht Karlsruhe: Gefährdung des Nachfolgendes beim Überholen. Neue Zeitschrift für Verkehrsrecht (NZV), pp. 248–249 (1992)
16. Park, S.C., Shin, H.: Polygonal chain intersection. Comput. Graph. **26**(2), 341–350 (2002)
17. Rizaldi, A., Althoff, M.: Formalising traffic rules for accountability of autonomous vehicles. In: Proceedings of the 18th IEEE International Conference on Intelligent Transportation Systems, Las Palmas de Gran Canaria Canary Islands, Spain, pp. 1658–1665 (2015)
18. Rizaldi, A., Immler, F., Althoff, M.: A formally verified checker of the safe distance traffic rules for autonomous vehicles. In: Rayadurgam, S., Tkachuk, O. (eds.) NFM 2016. LNCS, vol. 9690, pp. 175–190. Springer, Cham (2016). doi:10.1007/978-3-319-40648-0_14

19. Sergot, M.J., Sadri, F., Kowalski, R.A., Kriwaczek, F., Hammond, P., Cory, H.T.: The British Nationality Act as a logic program. Commun. ACM **29**(5), 370–386 (1986)
20. Werling, M., Ziegler, J., Kammel, S., Thrun, S.: Optimal trajectory generation for dynamic street scenarios in a frenet frame. In: Proceedings of the IEEE International Conference on Robotics and Automation, Anchorage, AK, USA, pp. 987–993 (2010)

Software Verification Tools

Making Whiley Boogie!

Mark Utting[1]([✉]), David J. Pearce[2], and Lindsay Groves[2]

[1] University of the Sunshine Coast, Sippy Downs, Australia
utting@usc.edu.au
[2] Victoria University of Wellington, Wellington, New Zealand
{david.pearce, lindsay}@ecs.vuw.ac.nz

Abstract. The quest to develop increasingly sophisticated verification systems continues unabated. Tools such as Dafny, Spec#, ESC/Java, SPARK Ada, and Whiley attempt to seamlessly integrate specification and verification into a programming language, in a similar way to type checking. A common integration approach is to generate verification conditions that are handed off to an automated theorem prover. This provides a nice separation of concerns, and allows different theorem provers to be used interchangeably. However, generating verification conditions is still a difficult undertaking and the use of more "high-level" intermediate verification languages has become common-place. In particular, Boogie provides a widely used and understood intermediate verification language. A common difficulty is the potential for an impedance mismatch between the source language and the intermediate verification language. In this paper, we explore the use of Boogie as an intermediate verification language for verifying programs in Whiley. This is noteworthy because the Whiley language has (amongst other things) a rich type system with considerable potential for an impedance mismatch. We report that, whilst a naive translation to Boogie is unsatisfactory, a more abstract encoding is surprisingly effective.

Keywords: Whiley · Boogie · Verifying compiler · Intermediate verification language · Semantic translation · Impedance mismatch

1 Introduction

The idea of verifying that a program meets a given specification for all possible inputs has been studied for a long time. According to Hoare's vision, a verifying compiler *"uses automated mathematical and logical reasoning to check the correctness of the programs that it compiles"* [15]. A variety of tools have blossomed in this space, including ESC/Java [14], Spec# [4], Dafny [18], Why3 [13], VeriFast [16], SPARK Ada [20], and Whiley [26,30]. Automated Theorem Provers are integral to such tools and are responsible for discharging proof obligations [4,7,14,16]. Various Satisfiability Modulo Theory (SMT) solvers are typically used for this, such as Simplify [9] or Z3 [21]. These provide hand-crafted implementations of important decision procedures, e.g. for linear arithmetic [12],

© Springer International Publishing AG 2017
N. Polikarpova and S. Schneider (Eds.): IFM 2017, LNCS 10510, pp. 69–84, 2017.
DOI: 10.1007/978-3-319-66845-1_5

congruence [24] and quantifier instantiation [22]. Different solvers are appropriate for different tasks, so the ability to utilise multiple solvers can improve the chances of successful verification.

Verifying compilers often target an *intermediate verification language*, such as Boogie [3] or WhyML [6,13], as these provide access to a range of different solvers. SMT-LIB [29] provides another standard readily accepted by modern automated theorem provers, although it is often considered rather low-level [6]. One issue faced by intermediate verification languages is the potential for an *impedance mismatch* [26]. This arises when constructs in the source language cannot be easily translated into those of the intermediate verification language. In this paper, we explore Boogie as an intermediate verification language for the Whiley verifying compiler. A particular concern is the potential for an impedance mismatch arising from Whiley's expressive type system which, amongst other things, supports *union, intersection* and *negation types* [25]. The obvious translation between Whiley and Boogie is rather unsatisfactory, but with care, a suitable encoding can be found that works surprisingly well.

The contributions of this paper include:

- a novel translation from Whiley programs to Boogie. Whilst in many cases this is straightforward, there are a number of challenges to overcome arising from the impedance mismatch between Whiley and Boogie.
- the results of an empirical comparison between Boogie/Z3 and the native Whiley verifier. The results indicate that using Boogie to verify Whiley programs (via our translation) is competitive with the native Whiley verifier.

2   Background

We begin with a brief overview of Whiley and a more comprehensive discussion of Boogie.

2.1   Whiley

The Whiley programming language has been developed to enable compile-time verification of programs and, furthermore, to make this accessible to everyday programmers [26,30]. The Whiley Compiler (WyC) attempts to ensure that all functions in a program meet their specifications. When this succeeds, we know that: (1) all function postconditions are met (assuming their preconditions held on entry); (2) all invocations meet their respective function's precondition; (3) runtime errors such as divide-by-zero, out-of-bounds accesses and null-pointer dereferences cannot occur. Notwithstanding, such programs may still loop indefinitely and/or exhaust available resources (e.g. RAM).

Figure 1 provides an interesting example which illustrates many of the salient features of Whiley:

- **Preconditions** are given by **requires** clauses and **postconditions** by **ensures** clauses. Multiple clauses are simply conjoined together. We found

```
1  type nat is (int n) where n >= 0
2
3  function indexOf(int[] items, int item) -> (int|null r)
4  // If valid index returned, element at r matches item
5  ensures r is int ==> items[r] == item
6  // If invalid index return, no element matches item
7  ensures r is null ==> all{i in 0..|items| | items[i] != item}:
8      //
9      nat i = 0
10     while i < |items|
11         where all { k in 0 .. i | items[k] != item }:
12         //
13         if items[i] == item:
14             return i
15         i = i + 1
16     //
17     return null
```

Fig. 1. Implementation of indexOf() in Whiley, returning the least index in items which matches item, or **null** if no match exists.

that allowing multiple **requires** and/or **ensures** clauses can help readability, and note that JML [8], Spec# [4] and Dafny [18] also permit this.

- **Loop Invariants** are given by **where** clauses. Figure 1 illustrates an inductive loop invariant covering indices from zero to i (exclusive).
- **Type Invariants** can be included with **type** declarations, as illustrated by type nat. This is the declared type of variable i, meaning no loop invariant of the form i >= 0 is necessary. We consider good use of type invariants as critical to improving the readability of function specifications.
- **Flow Typing & Unions**. An unusual feature of Whiley is the use of a *flow typing system* [25] coupled with *union types*. This is illustrated by the return type "**int|null**" and the use of a type test in the postcondition. Specifically, in the predicate "x **is** T ==> e" it follows that x has type T within the expression e.

2.2 Boogie

Boogie [3] is an intermediate verification language developed by Microsoft Research as part of the Spec# project [4]. Boogie is intended as a back-end for other programming language and verification systems [19] and has found use in various tools, such as Dafny [18], VCC [7], and others (e.g. [5]). Boogie is both a specification language (which shares some similarity with Dijkstra's language of guarded commands [11]) and a tool for checking that Boogie "programs" are correct.

The original Boogie language was *"somewhat like a high-level assembly language in that the control-flow is unstructured but the notions of statically-scoped locals and procedural abstraction are retained"* [3]. However, later versions support structured **if** and **while** statements to improve readability. Nevertheless, a non-deterministic **goto** statement is retained for encoding arbitrary control-flow, which permits multiple target labels with non-deterministic choice. Boogie provides various primitive types including **bool**, **int** and map types, which can be used to model arrays and records. Concepts such as a "program heap" can also be modelled using a map from references to values.

Boogie supports **function** and **procedure** declarations which have an important distinction. In general, **function**s are pure and intended to model fundamental operators in the source language. In contrast, **procedure**s are potentially impure and are intended to model methods in the source language. A **procedure** can be given a specification composed of **requires** and **ensures** clauses, and also a **modifies** clause indicating non-local state that can be modified. Most importantly, a **procedure** can be given an **implementation**, and the tool will attempt to ensure this implementation meets the given specification. The **requires** and **ensures** for **procedure**s demarcate proof obligations, for which Boogie emits verification conditions in first-order logic, to be discharged by Z3. In addition, the implementation of a **procedure** may include **assert** and **assume** statements. The former lead to proof obligations, whilst the latter give properties which the underlying theorem prover can exploit.

Figure 2 provides an example encoding of the indexOf() function in Boogie. At first glance, it is perhaps surprising how close to an actual programming language Boogie has become. Various features of the language are demonstrated

```
1  function len(arr:[int]int) returns (r: int); // array length operator
2
3  axiom (forall A:[int]int :: len(A) >= 0); // no negative length arrays
4
5  procedure indexOf(xs: [int]int, x: int) returns (r: int)
6  ensures r >= 0 && r <= len(xs);
7  ensures (r < len(xs)) ==> (xs[r] == x);
8  ensures (forall k:int :: (0<=k && k<r) ==> xs[k] != x); {
9    var i : int;
10   i := 0;
11   while (i < len(xs))
12   invariant i >= 0 && i <= len(xs);
13   invariant (forall k:int :: (0<=k && k<i) ==> xs[k] != x); {
14     if(xs[i] == x) { break; }
15     i := i + 1;
16   }
17   r := i;
18 }
```

Fig. 2. Simple Boogie program encoding an implementation of the indexOf() function, making extensive use of the structured syntax provided in later versions of Boogie

```
1   procedure indexOf(xs: [int]int, x: int) returns (r: int) ... {
2     var i : int;
3     i := 0;
4     assert i >= 0 && i <= len(xs); // assert invariant on entry
5     assert (forall k:int :: (0<=k && k<i)==> xs[k] != x);
6   head:
7     havoc i;
8     assume i >= 0 && i <= len(xs); // assume invariant
9     assume (forall k:int :: (0<=k && k<i)==> xs[k] != x);
10    goto body,exit;
11  body:
12    assume i < len(xs); // assume loop condition
13    if(xs[i] == x) { goto exit; }
14    i := i + 1;
15    assert i >= 0 && i <= len(xs); // assert invariant
16    assert (forall k:int :: (0<=k && k<i)==> xs[k] != x);
17    goto head;
18  exit:
19    assume i >= len(xs); // assume negated condition
20    r := i;
21  }
```

Fig. 3. Unstructured encoding of the example from Fig. 2—the pre/postconditions are omitted as they are unchanged from above, and likewise for len().

with this example. Firstly, an array length operator is encoded using an uninterpreted function len(), and accompanying **axiom**. Secondly, the input array is modelled using the map **[int]int**, the meaning of which is somewhat subtle, in that it is not describing an array as in a programming language. Rather, it is a total mapping from *arbitrary integers* to *arbitrary integers*. For example, xs[-1] identifies a valid element of the map despite -1 not normally being a valid array index. We can refine this to something closer to an array through additional constraints, as shown in the next section.

Whilst the structured form of Boogie is preferred, where possible, it is also useful to consider the unstructured form, which we use for a few Whiley constructs such as **switch** (Sect. 3.2). Figure 3 provides an unstructured encoding of the indexOf() function from Fig. 2. In this version, the **while** loop is decomposed using a non-deterministic **goto** statement. Likewise, the loop condition and invariant are explicitly assumed (lines 8, 9, 12) and asserted (lines 15, 16), rather than being done implicitly by the tool (as in Fig. 2). The **havoc** statement *"assigns an arbitrary value to each indicated variable"* [3], so is used here to indicate that variable i contains an arbitrary integer value at this point.

3   Modeling Whiley in Boogie

Our goal is to model as much of the Whiley language as possible in Boogie, so that we can utilise Boogie for the verification of Whiley programs, hopefully leading to better overall results compared with Whiley's native (and relatively adhoc) verifier. The key challenge here is the impedance mismatch between Whiley and Boogie. Despite their obvious similarities, there remain some significant differences:

- **Types.** Whiley has a relatively rich (structural) type system which includes: *union, intersection* and *negation* types.
- **Flow Typing.** Whiley's support for flow typing is also problematic, as a given variable may have different types at different program points [25].
- **Definedness.** Unlike many other tools (e.g. Dafny), Whiley implicitly assumes that specification elements (e.g. pre-/postconditions and invariants) are *well defined*.

To understand the **definedness** issue, consider a precondition that contains an array reference, like "**requires** a[i] == 0". In a language like Dafny, one would additionally need to specify "i >= 0 && i < |a|" to avoid the verifier reporting an out-of-bounds error. Such preconditions are implicit in Whiley, so must be extracted and made explicit in a translation to Boogie.

We now present the main contribution of this paper, namely a mechanism for translating Whiley programs into Boogie. These are implemented in our translator program, called Wy2B.[1] Whilst, in some cases, this process is straightforward, there are a number of subtle issues to be addressed, such as the representation of Whiley types in Boogie.

3.1   Types

Finding an appropriate representation of Whiley types is a challenge. We begin by considering the straightforward (i.e. naive) translation of Whiley types into Boogie, and highlight why this fails. Then, we present a new and more sophisticated approach, which we refer to as the *set-based translation*.

Naive Translation of Types. The simple and obvious translation of Whiley types into Boogie is a direct translation to the built-in types of Boogie. Here, an **int** in Whiley is translated into a Boogie **int**, whilst a Whiley array (e.g. **int**[]) translates to a Boogie map (e.g. [**int**]**int**, with appropriate constraints). Similarly, records in Whiley can be translated using Boogie's map type. However, this approach immediately encounters some serious impedance mismatch problems. For example, the type "**int**|**null**" cannot be represented in Boogie because there is no corresponding Boogie type. In addition, a Whiley type test such as "x **is int**" cannot be translated. To resolve these issues requires an altogether different approach.

---

[1] Source code and test programs are viewable at https://github.com/utting/WhileyCompiler/tree/wyboogie and are based on Whiley release 0.4.0.

Set-Based Translation of Types. Our second approach to modeling Whiley types and data values uses a *set-based* approach. That is, we model *all* Whiley values as members of a single set, called WVal (short for *Whiley Value*), and model the various Whiley types as being subsets of this universal set. We also define several helper types for Whiley record labels and higher-order function/method names:

```
1  type WVal;          // The set of ALL Whiley values.
2
3  type WField;        // field names for records and objects.
4  type WFuncName;     // names of functions
5  type WMethodName;   // names of methods
```

For each distinct Whiley type T, we define a subset predicate isT() that is true for values in T, an extraction function toT() that maps a WVal value to a Boogie type, and an injection function fromT() which does the reverse mapping. We axiomatize these two functions to define a partial bijection between T and the subset of WVal that satisfies isT().

For example, the functions for the Whiley **int** type of unbounded integers (recall "int" is also the Boogie name for integers) are as follows. We also add Boogie axioms to ensure that the WVal subsets that correspond to each basic Whiley type (int, bool, array, etc.) are mutually disjoint.

```
1  function isInt(WVal) returns (bool);
2  function toInt(WVal) returns (int);
3  function fromInt(int) returns (WVal);
4
5  axiom (forall i:int :: isInt(fromInt(i)));
6  axiom (forall i:int :: toInt(fromInt(i)) == i);
7  axiom (forall v:WVal :: isInt(v) ==> fromInt(toInt(v)) == v);
```

The set-based approach has several advantages. Firstly, it is easy to define a Whiley user-defined subtype SubT by defining a predicate isSubT(v) = (isT(v) $\wedge$ ...). Secondly, the Whiley union, intersection and negation types simply map to disjunction, conjunction and negation of these type predicates. Thirdly, Boogie sees all Whiley values as WVal objects, so can prove equality of two of those objects only if they are constructed using the same fromT injection function from values that are equal. This is a weak notion of equality, which can be strengthened by adding type-specific axioms where needed, as we shall now demonstrate for arrays.

Whiley arrays are fixed length, whereas Boogie maps are total. To represent Whiley arrays, we model them using a Boogie map [int]WVal from integers to WVal objects, plus the explicit length of the array, but we encode these two values as a single WVal value, using Boogie equality axioms, as follows. We provide an extraction function for each of these components (toArray() and arraylen(), respectively), and an injection function that takes both components and constructs the corresponding fixed length array in WVal.

```
1  function toArray(WVal) returns ([int]WVal);
2  function arraylen(WVal) returns (int);
3  function fromArray([int]WVal,int) returns (WVal);
4
5  axiom (forall s:[int]WVal, len:int :: 0 <= len
6         ==> isArray(fromArray(s,len)));
7  axiom (forall s:[int]WVal, len:int :: 0 <= len
8         ==> arraylen(fromArray(s,len)) == len);
9  axiom (forall v:WVal :: isArray(v)
10        ==> fromArray(toArray(v), arraylen(v)) == v);
11 axiom (forall v:WVal :: isArray(v)
12        ==> 0 <= arraylen(v));
```

We also provide a convenience function for updating one element of an array, by using Boogie's a[i := v] map update function, which returns a with index i updated to be v with the necessary conversion functions.

```
1  function arrayupdate(a:WVal, i:WVal, v:WVal) returns (WVal) {
2      fromArray(toArray(a)[toInt(i) := v], arraylen(a)) }
```

Whiley records are also modeled using Boogie maps, with all unknown fields mapping to a special undef_field value. To create records dynamically, we start from the empty record (no fields) called empty_record, and update the required fields with their values. Whiley objects are similar to records, but have an extensible set of field names, so that "subtypes" can have more fields than "supertypes" (note that Whiley uses structural subtyping, so it is not necessary to declare subtype relationships explicitly).

```
1  // Record literals use empty_record[f1 := v1][f2 := v2] etc.
2  const unique empty_record : [WField]WVal;
3  const unique undef_field:WVal;
4  axiom (forall f:WField :: empty_record[f] == undef_field);
```

Overall, this "types-as-subsets" approach has avoided the impedance mismatch of the naive translation and made it easy to map the rich value and type system of Whiley into Boogie. One minor practical issue, however, was that our first version of the translator tended to produce deeply nested unreadable sequences of redundant extraction and injection functions; this was because all subexpressions were converted to WVal results. For example, x := 2 * x + 1 was translated to:

```
1      x := fromInt(toInt(fromInt(toInt(fromInt(2)) * toInt(x)))
2                  + toInt(fromInt(1)))
```

We solved this problem by tracking the Boogie type of each subexpression and inserting these coercion functions lazily, only where needed, giving a more concise and readable translation:

```
1    x := fromInt(2 * toInt(x) + 3)
```

3.2 Control Flow

Translating most Whiley declarations and statements into Boogie is straightforward (see the similarities between Figs. 1 and 2). Here, we describe the interesting cases that illustrate impedance mismatches between Whiley and Boogie.

The first issue is that Whiley function bodies are defined by code (with restrictions to ensure no external side-effects are possible), whereas Boogie functions are either uninterpreted or have a single expression as their body. To overcome this, we translate each Whiley function $f(i) \rightarrow (o)$: body (where i and o are vectors of variables, possibly empty) into *four* Boogie definitions:[2]

1. A pure function "f__pre(i) returns (bool)" with an expression body that is the Whiley precondition of f, including any type invariants on the input parameters i. This is useful for generating proof obligations for calls to f;
2. A pure function "f(i) returns (o)", which is called whenever a Whiley expression calls f, with an axiom "$\forall i, o : \text{WVal} :: f(i) == o \land f\_\_\text{pre}(i) \implies$ post" (where post is the Whiley postcondition of f).
3. A procedure specification "f__impl(i) returns (o)" with precondition f__pre(i) and a postcondition of post;
4. A procedure implementation of "f__impl(i) returns (o)", which contains the translated body code of the Whiley function f.

This approach causes Boogie to generate proof obligations to ensure that body satisfies the procedure specification. A call to f(i) within a Whiley expression is translated to a Boogie function call to f(i), which has the desired precondition and postcondition properties, but none of the extra properties of code. This is acceptable, since Boogie supports only *modular* verification, which means that calls to a function or procedure must be verified using its specification, not its implementation.

We translate Whiley *methods* (procedures) in the same way, but omit step 2 (the pure function), because Whiley methods typically have side effects. However, a complication is that expressions in executable Whiley code can call methods as well as functions, whereas Boogie only allows methods (procedures) to be called via a "call" statement, and not from within expressions. We currently translate simple method calls (those that appear at the outermost level of the right-hand-side of an assignment) into call statements, and throw a translation error for method calls within expressions. Extending the translator to handle these will require doing a pre-pass of all expressions to pull those methods calls out into separate call statements, and even this will not handle some scenarios of side-effect method calls within short-circuit boolean operators.

---

[2] Note that Boogie always separates procedure specifications and implementations, which are our definitions (3) and (4).

Another aspect of the impedance mismatch is that, unlike Whiley, Boogie has no do-while statement. We initially translated "**do:** code **while c**" as "code; **while**(c) {code}" in Boogie. But this did not handle **break** and **continue** statements within code. Next we tried translating do-while into a single while loop with a boolean flag to force a first iteration. However, this gave the wrong semantics for loop invariants—in a Whiley do-while loop the invariant need not be true before the first iteration of code (this makes some proofs easier). We now translate do-while statements into code; **while**(c){code}, but generate explicit labels for blocks in order to implement **break/continue** statements using gotos.

The Whiley switch statement posed similar challenges, since Boogie has no switch statement. Rather than translating this to a sequence of if-else statements, we translate it to a non-deterministic goto to all the available cases. Thus, we can use labels and goto statements to implement the Whiley semantics of break/continue statements (in Whiley, break exits the whole switch statement, while continue falls through to the following case).[3]

Other minor impedance mismatches that we encountered were:

- Function overloading is supported in Whiley, but not in Boogie. So we mangle the names of any overloaded functions.
- Function/procedure inputs are treated as mutable local variables in Whiley, but not in Boogie. To overcome this, for any input that is mutated, the translator generates a local variable that contains a copy of the input value.
- Boogie does not provide lambda expressions for functions (only for maps), so the translator has to convert Whiley lambda expressions to named functions (not yet implemented). This is adequate for simple lambda expressions, but not for lambda expressions that capture local variables.
- Boogie requires all local variables to be declared at the start of a procedure body, which makes it harder to generate temporary variables during translation of expressions.
- Typing versus proof. The Whiley compiler uses typing algorithms to distinguish bytes from integers (which are unbounded), and gives the bitwise operators different semantics on those two types. This proved hard to do in Boogie when we treated bytes as a subrange of integers and overloaded the bitwise operators, so we had to generate separate operators for byte and integer values, and axiomatise them differently.

4   Generating Verification Conditions

After translating a Whiley program into Boogie, we use the Boogie tool to generate and check proof obligations to ensure the usual correctness condition for each procedure: pre $\implies$ wp(body, post) [3]. In addition to the inherent proof

---

[3] Our translator does not yet implement the translation of continue statements within switch statements, because it is rarely needed, but there are no technical obstacles to doing this.

obligations, we generate several kinds of Whiley-specific proof obligations by inserting **assert** statements in the generated Boogie code. Boogie then attempts to prove each of these assert statements.

The additional proof obligations we generate include any explicit assert statements included in the Whiley program, plus assertions to check three Whiley runtime correctness conditions that Boogie does not check automatically:

1. function calls satisfy their preconditions (Boogie functions are total, but Whiley functions have **requires** conditions, so we generate an assertion before any expression that calls a function, to check that its precondition is satisfied);
2. array indexes are in bounds; and
3. the divisor is non-zero in division and modulo expressions.

Since these assertions may be generated from subexpressions that are deeply nested inside complex predicates, we need to carefully define the assumptions that are available for each proof obligation. This is achieved via a recursive descent into each predicate and expression, collecting the context assumptions using the following window-inference rules [27]. A premise of the form $assert(A \implies P)$ means that this assertion is inserted into the generated Boogie program as a proof obligation.

$$\frac{A \vdash check(P) \qquad A, P \vdash check(Q)}{A \vdash check(P \wedge Q)} \qquad \frac{A \vdash check(P) \qquad A, \neg P \vdash check(Q)}{A \vdash check(P \vee Q)} \qquad \frac{A, x : int; a \leq x; x \leq b \vdash check(P)}{A \vdash check(\forall x : a \ldots b :: P)}$$

$$\frac{assert(A \implies d \neq 0) \qquad A \vdash check(e) \qquad A \vdash check(d)}{A \vdash check(e/d)} \qquad \frac{assert(A \implies f\_pre(a)) \qquad A \vdash check(a)}{A \vdash check(f(a))} \qquad \frac{assert(A \implies 0 \leq i \\ \wedge\, i < arraylen(a)) \qquad A \vdash check(a) \qquad A \vdash check(i)}{A \vdash check(a[i])}$$

The conjunction and disjunction rules are not symmetric—they assume the left-hand predicate while checking the right-hand predicate, but not vice versa. This is done to reflect the execution semantics of Whiley expressions, which is to execute subexpressions left-to-right.

5 Experimental Results

In this section, we discuss the effectiveness of the Wy2B translator as an alternative verification path, in terms of what Whiley language features can be translated, the limitations and challenges of the approach, and what percentage of valid Whiley programs can be verified using the Wy2B+Boogie+Z3 toolchain (using Boogie v2.3.0.61016 and Z3 v4.4.0, with no custom triggers on axioms).

Figure 4 shows statistics comparing how the native Whiley verifier (the y-axis) and the new Wy2B+Boogie+Z3 verifier (the x-axis) handle the nearly 500 valid test case programs in the Whiley distribution, which are intended to methodically test all Whiley language features. Each of these short test programs (ranging from 3 to 100 lines of Whiley code, with an average length of 18 lines) typically contains multiple function and method definitions, and each definition can generate several proof obligations. We classify the results according to whether the verifier: (i) fully verifies *all* the proof obligations for that program (**Fully**); (ii) fails to verify one or more of the proof obligations (**Partial**); (iii) generates proof obligations that cause Boogie errors (**Errors**)—this may be due to accidental use of reserved words, or Whiley constructs that are too complex for Boogie; (iv) the test program uses Whiley features that are not yet able to be translated to Boogie by our Wy2B translator (**NotImpl**).

All of these test programs are intended to be verifiable, but some have not yet been verified by either prover because they use language features that are not yet fully supported in the verifiers. For example, neither prover fully models the semantics of bitwise operators, lambda expressions, or heap allocation and the address-of operator yet. Instead, these features are modelled as uninterpreted functions, which means that general properties of those operators are sometimes provable, but assertions that depend upon the specific semantics of those operators are not yet provable.

Wy2B+Boogie+Z3

Whiley Verifier	NotImpl	Errors	Partial	Fully	Total	Total%
Partial	5	7	22	54	88	17.8%
Fully	38	13	9	345	405	82.2%
Total	43	20	31	399	493	
Total%	8.7%	4.1%	6.3%	80.9%		100.0%

Fig. 4. Comparison of Whiley Verifier results (y-axis) with Boogie+Z3 results (x-axis).

Overall, the Whiley verifier can fully verify 82.2% of the programs, while the Wy2B+Boogie tools can fully verify only 80.9%. Part of the reason for this difference is that there are several language constructs such as lambda expressions, multiple return values and calling methods (with side-effects) from within non-specification expressions, that are not yet implemented in the Wy2B translator (8.7% of programs). So there are opportunities for improvement in the Wy2B+Boogie path.

Considering a detailed breakdown of results, the largest result category is that there are 345 programs (70%) that can be fully verified with both verifiers. There are also 54 programs (11%) that can be fully verified with Wy2B+Boogie but only partially with the Whiley verifier, and 9 programs (1.8%) that can be fully verified with the Whiley verifier, but Boogie fails to fully verify. These nine cases are as follows:

Complex_Valid_5.whiley: Boogie fails to instantiate axioms to prove a subtype condition.

ConstrainedList_Valid_14.whiley: Boogie fails to prove a typing condition containing $(\exists i : int \,|\, 0 \leq i < |xs| \bullet xs[i] > 0)$, after the assignment "`xs[0]=1`".

DoWhile_Valid_6.whiley: Boogie cannot reestablish an invariant in a do-while loop.

DoWhile_Valid_8.whiley: similar problem, but with a **break** inside the loop.

FunctionRef_Valid_9.whiley: cannot establish a result type for an indirect function call of a function inside a record, inside the heap.

MessageSend_Valid_2.whiley: cannot establish result type of a heap reference.

MessageSend_Valid_5.whiley: ibid.

RecursiveType_Valid_19.whiley: complex recursive subtypes. 10 s timeout.

RecursiveType_Valid_20.whiley: ibid.

The Wy2B+Boogie toolchain takes 502 s to translate and verify the 493 test programs (9040 lines of Whiley code) on a MacBook Pro (Intel Core i5-4258U 2.4 GHz). This is approximately one second per program, which is acceptable performance for real-world usage. We run Boogie with a timeout of 10 s, but only three programs failed to verify due to timeouts.

6 Related Work

ESC/Modula-3 was one of the earliest tools to use an intermediate verification language [10]. This was based on Dijkstra's language of guarded-commands [11] and, in many ways, is Boogie's predecessor. Such a language typically includes assignment, **assume** and **assert** statements and non-deterministic choice. It is notable that the guarded-command language used in ESC/Modula-3 lacked type information and used a similar encoding of types as ours, although Modula-3 has a simpler type system than Whiley. For example, a predicate isT was defined for each type to determine whether a given variable was in the type T. A similar approach was also taken in Leino's Ecstatic tool, where the subtyping relation was encoded using a subtype() predicate [17].

The ESC/Java tool followed ESC/Modula-3 in using guarded commands, but employed a multi-stage process allowing "high-level" guarded command programs to be desugared into a lower-level form [14]. Spec# followed this lineage of tools and the language of guarded commands used previously was reused in Boogie [4]. Boogie was described as an *"effective intermediate language for verification condition generation of object-oriented programs because it lacks the complexities of a full-featured object-oriented programming language"* [3]. In essence, Boogie was a version of the guarded command language from ESC/Java which also supported a textual syntax, type checking, and a static analysis for inferring loop invariants. Other important innovations include the ability to specify *triggers* to help guide quantifier instantiation, and the use of a trace semantics to formalise the meaning of Boogie.

In addition to Boogie, the other main intermediate verification language in use is WhyML [6,13]. This is part of the Why3 verification platform which specifically exploits external theorem provers. WhyML is a first-order language with polymorphic types, pattern matching, inductive predicates, records and type invariants. It has also been used in the verification of C, Java and Ada programs (amongst others). Like Boogie, WhyML provides structured statements (e.g. **while** and **if** statements). In addition, a standard library is included which provides support for different theories (e.g. integer and real arithmetic, sets and maps).

Research on intermediate verification languages has often encountered impedance mismatch. Ameri and Furia present a translation from Boogie to WhyML which, although largely successful, did expose some important mismatches between them [1]. The structured nature of WhyML presented some problems in handling Boogie's unstructured branching, and aspects of Boogie's polymorphic maps and bitvectors were problematic. They showed that Why3 could verify 83% of the translated programs with the same outcome as Boogie.

Segal and Chalin [28] attempted a systematic comparison of two intermediate verification languages: Boogie and Pilar. They stated that it is *"not trivial to define a common intermediate language that can still support the syntax and semantics of many source languages"*. Their research method was to develop translations from Ruby into both Boogie and Pilar, and then compare. Various aspects of Ruby proved challenging for Boogie, including its dynamically-typed nature and arrays. Their solution bears similarity to ours, as they defined an abstract Boogie type as the root of all Ruby values.

Müller *et al.* [23] argue that existing systems (e.g. Boogie, Why3) do not support separation logics and related permission-based logics. They identify that such systems have a "higher-order nature" than typical software verification problems, and make extensive use of recursive predicates (which Boogie/Z3 does not support well). They developed an alternative intermediate verification language designed specifically for this. Finally, Arlt *et al.* [2] presented a translation from SOOT's intermediate bytecode language (Jimple) to Boogie, with an aim of identifying unreachable code. They found many aspects of the translation straightforward. For example, Java's `instanceof` operator was modelled using an uninterpreted function. However, some aspects of impedance mismatch were present and they had difficulty with monitor bytecodes, exceptions, certain chains of **if-else** statements and **finally** blocks.

7   Conclusion

Using Boogie as an intermediate verification language eases the development of a verifying compiler, particularly as it handles verification condition generation, and offers high-level structures such as while loops and procedures with specifications. However, as with any intermediate language, there is potential for an impedance mismatch when Boogie structures do not exactly match the source language (e.g. the Whiley **do-while** loop). Fortunately, this impedance mismatch can be circumvented by translating to lower-level Boogie statements, such as labels and gotos. Boogie provides a good level of flexibility to define the "background theory" of a source language, such as its type system, its object structure, and support for heaps. This background theory is at a similar level of abstraction in Boogie as it would be in SMT-LIB so, whilst Boogie offers no major advantages in this area, it also has no disadvantages.

Our work shows that the encoding one chooses when translating source language types and values into Boogie has a major impact on the effectiveness of the resulting system. It would be beneficial to have a repository of knowledge about different ways of encoding various language constructs. Some alternatives (particularly for various heap encoding techniques and procedure framing axioms) are discussed in the published Boogie papers, but there is no central repository of techniques or publications comparing encoding techniques. A major benefit of Boogie is, of course, its easy access to Z3. We have shown that Wy2B+Boogie+Z3 is competitive with the native Whiley verifier in terms of the percentage of programs that it can verify automatically. Finally, interesting future work would be to explore translating Boogie's *counter-example models* back into Whiley-like notation to improve error reporting. Other priorities are to add support for a few remaining Whiley language features to our Wy2B translator, and to continue to improve the Whiley verifier.

References

1. Ameri, M., Furia, C.A.: Why just Boogie? In: Ábrahám, E., Huisman, M. (eds.) IFM 2016. LNCS, vol. 9681, pp. 79–95. Springer, Cham (2016). doi:10.1007/978-3-319-33693-0_6
2. Arlt, S., Rümmer, P., Schäf, M.: Joogie: from Java through Jimple to Boogie. In: Proceedings of SOAP (2013)
3. Barnett, M., Chang, B.-Y.E., DeLine, R., Jacobs, B., Leino, K.R.M.: Boogie: a modular reusable verifier for object-oriented programs. In: Boer, F.S., Bonsangue, M.M., Graf, S., Roever, W.-P. (eds.) FMCO 2005. LNCS, vol. 4111, pp. 364–387. Springer, Heidelberg (2006). doi:10.1007/11804192_17
4. Barnett, M., Fähndrich, M., Leino, K.R.M., Müller, P., Schulte, W., Venter, H.: Specification and verification: the Spec# experience. CACM 54(6), 81–91 (2011)
5. Betts, A., Chong, N., Donaldson, A.F., Qadeer, S., Thomson, P.: GPUVerify: a verifier for GPU kernels. In: Proceedings of the OOPSLA, pp. 113–132. ACM Press (2012)
6. Bobot, F., Filliâtre, J.C., Marché, C., Paskevich, A.: Why3: Shepherd your herd of provers. In: Workshop on Intermediate Verification Languages (2011)
7. Cohen, E., Dahlweid, M., Hillebrand, M., Leinenbach, D., Moskal, M., Santen, T., Schulte, W., Tobies, S.: VCC: a practical system for verifying concurrent C. In: Berghofer, S., Nipkow, T., Urban, C., Wenzel, M. (eds.) TPHOLs 2009. LNCS, vol. 5674, pp. 23–42. Springer, Heidelberg (2009). doi:10.1007/978-3-642-03359-9_2
8. Cok, D.R., Kiniry, J.R.: ESC/Java2: uniting ESC/Java and JML. In: Barthe, G., Burdy, L., Huisman, M., Lanet, J.-L., Muntean, T. (eds.) CASSIS 2004. LNCS, vol. 3362, pp. 108–128. Springer, Heidelberg (2005). doi:10.1007/978-3-540-30569-9_6
9. Detlefs, D., Nelson, G., Saxe, J.B.: Simplify: a theorem prover for program checking. JACM 52(3), 365–473 (2005)
10. Detlefs, D.L., Leino, K.R.M., Nelson, G., Saxe, J.B.: Extended static checking. SRC Research Report 159, Compaq Systems Research Center (1998)
11. Dijkstra, E.W.: Guarded commands, nondeterminancy and formal derivation of programs. CACM 18, 453–457 (1975)

12. Dutertre, B., Moura, L.: A fast linear-arithmetic solver for DPLL(T). In: Ball, T., Jones, R.B. (eds.) CAV 2006. LNCS, vol. 4144, pp. 81–94. Springer, Heidelberg (2006). doi:10.1007/11817963_11

13. Filliâtre, J., Paskevich, A.: Why3 – where programs meet provers. In: Proceedings of ESOP, pp. 125–128 (2013)

14. Flanagan, C., Leino, K.R.M., Lillibridge, M., Nelson, G., Saxe, J.B., Stata, R.: Extended static checking for Java. In: Proceedings of PLDI, pp. 234–245 (2002)

15. Hoare, C.: The verifying compiler: a grand challenge for computing research. JACM 50(1), 63–69 (2003)

16. Jacobs, B., Smans, J., Philippaerts, P., Vogels, F., Penninckx, W., Piessens, F.: VeriFast: a powerful, sound, predictable, fast verifier for C and Java. In: Bobaru, M., Havelund, K., Holzmann, G.J., Joshi, R. (eds.) NFM 2011. LNCS, vol. 6617, pp. 41–55. Springer, Heidelberg (2011). doi:10.1007/978-3-642-20398-5_4

17. Leino, K.R.M.: Ecstatic: an object-oriented programming language with an axiomatic semantics. In: Workshop on Foundations of Object-Oriented Languages (FOOL 4) (1997)

18. Leino, K.R.M.: Dafny: an automatic program verifier for functional correctness. In: Clarke, E.M., Voronkov, A. (eds.) LPAR 2010. LNCS (LNAI), vol. 6355, pp. 348–370. Springer, Heidelberg (2010). doi:10.1007/978-3-642-17511-4_20

19. Leino, K.R.M.: Program proving using intermediate verification languages (IVLs) like Boogie and Why3. In: Proceedings of HILT, pp. 25–26 (2012)

20. McCormick, J.W., Chapin, P.C.: Building High Integrity Applications with SPARK. Cambridge University Press, Cambridge (2015)

21. Moura, L., Bjørner, N.: Z3: an efficient SMT solver. In: Ramakrishnan, C.R., Rehof, J. (eds.) TACAS 2008. LNCS, vol. 4963, pp. 337–340. Springer, Heidelberg (2008). doi:10.1007/978-3-540-78800-3_24

22. Moura, L., Bjørner, N.: Efficient E-matching for SMT solvers. In: Pfenning, F. (ed.) CADE 2007. LNCS (LNAI), vol. 4603, pp. 183–198. Springer, Heidelberg (2007). doi:10.1007/978-3-540-73595-3_13

23. Müller, P., Schwerhoff, M., Summers, A.J.: Viper: a verification infrastructure for permission-based reasoning. In: Jobstmann, B., Leino, K.R.M. (eds.) VMCAI 2016. LNCS, vol. 9583, pp. 41–62. Springer, Heidelberg (2016). doi:10.1007/978-3-662-49122-5_2

24. Nelson, G., Oppen, D.C.: Fast decision procedures based on congruence closure. JACM 27, 356–364 (1980)

25. Pearce, D.J.: Sound and complete flow typing with unions, intersections and negations. In: Giacobazzi, R., Berdine, J., Mastroeni, I. (eds.) VMCAI 2013. LNCS, vol. 7737, pp. 335–354. Springer, Heidelberg (2013). doi:10.1007/978-3-642-35873-9_21

26. Pearce, D.J., Groves, L.: Designing a verifying compiler: lessons learned from developing Whiley. Sci. Comput. Program. 113, 191–220 (2015)

27. Robison, P.J., Staples, J.: Formalizing a hierarchical structure of practical mathematical reasoning. J. Logic Comput. 3(1), 47–61 (1993). http://dx.doi.org/10.1093/logcom/3.1.47

28. Segal, L., Chalin, P.: A comparison of intermediate verification languages: Boogie and Sireum/Pilar. In: Joshi, R., Müller, P., Podelski, A. (eds.) VSTTE 2012. LNCS, vol. 7152, pp. 130–145. Springer, Heidelberg (2012). doi:10.1007/978-3-642-27705-4_11

29. The SMT-LIB standard: Version 2.0

30. The Whiley programming language. http://whiley.org

Complexity Analysis for **Java** with AProVE

Florian Frohn and Jürgen Giesl[✉]

LuFG Informatik 2, RWTH Aachen University, Aachen, Germany
florian.frohn@cs.rwth-aachen.de, giesl@informatik.rwth-aachen.de

Abstract. While AProVE is one of the most powerful tools for termination analysis of Java since many years, we now extend our approach in order to analyze the complexity of Java programs as well. Based on a symbolic execution of the program, we develop a novel transformation of (possibly heap-manipulating) Java programs to integer transition systems (ITSs). This allows us to use existing complexity analyzers for ITSs to infer runtime bounds for Java programs. We demonstrate the power of our implementation on an established standard benchmark set.

1 Introduction

Our verifier AProVE [14] is one of the leading tools for termination analysis of languages like Java, C, Haskell, Prolog, and term rewrite systems, as witnessed by its success at the annual *Termination Competition* and the termination category of the *SV-COMP* competition.[1] However, in many cases one is not only interested in termination, but in estimating the runtime of a program. Thus, *automated complexity analysis* has become an increasingly important subject and there exist several tools which analyze the complexity of programs in different languages and formalisms, e.g., [1,3,4,8,10–12,15,17,18,21,23].[2]

In this paper, we adapt our previous approach for termination analysis of Java [5,6,22] in order to infer complexity bounds. In particular, the contributions of the current paper and their implementation in AProVE are crucial in our joint project *CAGE* [9,24] with Draper Inc. and the University of Innsbruck. In this project, AProVE is used interactively to analyze the complexity of large Java programs in order to detect vulnerabilities. To the best of our knowledge, COSTA [1] is currently the only other tool which analyzes the complexity of (possibly heap manipulating) Java programs fully automatically. However, COSTA's notion of "size" for data structures significantly differs from ours and hence our technique can prove bounds for many programs where COSTA is bound to fail. See Sect. 6 for a more detailed comparison with related work.

In Sect. 2, we explain the notion of *complexity* that we analyze for Java and recall *symbolic execution graphs* (SE graphs) [5,6,22], which represent all possible executions of the analyzed Java program. Up to now, AProVE automatically

---

Support by DFG grant GI 274/6-1 and the Air Force Research Laboratory (AFRL).

[1] See http://www.termination-portal.org/wiki/Termination_Competition and http://sv-comp.sosy-lab.org.

[2] The work on worst-case execution time (WCET) for real-time systems [25] is largely orthogonal to the inference of symbolic loop bounds.

© Springer International Publishing AG 2017
N. Polikarpova and S. Schneider (Eds.): IFM 2017, LNCS 10510, pp. 85–101, 2017.
DOI: 10.1007/978-3-319-66845-1_6

transformed these SE graphs into *term rewrite systems* with built-in integers to analyze termination. However, this transformation is not complexity preserving for programs with non-tree shaped objects and moreover, existing techniques for termination analysis of term rewriting with built-in integers have not yet been adapted to complexity analysis. Therefore, in Sect. 3 we present a novel[3] transformation of SE graphs to *integer transition systems* (ITSs), a simple representation of integer programs suitable for complexity analysis. These ITSs are then analyzed by standard complexity analysis tools for integer programs like CoFloCo [12] and KoAT [8]. In our implementation in AProVE, we coupled our approach with these two tools to obtain an automatic technique which infers upper complexity bounds for Java programs. So in our approach, we model a Java program in several different ways (as Java (Bytecode), SE graphs, and ITSs), where the reason for the new modeling of Java programs by ITSs is their suitability for complexity analysis. Section 4 explains how to avoid the analysis of called auxiliary methods by providing *summaries*. This allows us to use AProVE in an interactive way and it is crucial to scale our approach to large programs within the *CAGE* project. In Sect. 5, we show how our transformation to ITSs also handles Java programs which manipulate the heap. Finally, in Sect. 6 we evaluate the power of our implementation in AProVE by experiments with an established standard benchmark set and compare AProVE's performance with COSTA.

2   Complexity of **Java** and Symbolic Execution Graphs

Example 1 (Variant of SortCount *from the* Termination Problem Data Base (TPDB)[4]). *To illustrate our approach, consider the following program. The method* sort *sorts a list* l *of natural numbers. To this end, it enumerates* $0, \ldots, \max(l)$ *and adds each number to the result list* r *if it is contained in* l. *Its runtime complexity is in* $\mathcal{O}(\text{length}(l) \cdot \max(l))$. *In this paper, we show how AProVE infers similar complexity bounds automatically.*

```
1   class List{
2     private int val; private List next;
3     static boolean mem(int n,
4                        List l){...}
5
6     static int max(List l) {
7       int m = 0;
8       while (l != null) {
9         if (l.val > m) {
10          m = l.val;
11        }
12        l = l.next;
13      }
14      return m;
15    }
```

```
16    static List sort(List l) {
17      int n = 0;
18      List r = null;
19      while (max(l) >= n) {
20        if (mem(n, l)) {
21          List rNew = new List();
22          rNew.next = r;
23          rNew.val = n;
24          r = rNew;
25        }
26        n++;
27      }
28      return r;
29    } ... }
```

---

[3] We presented a preliminary extended abstract with our "size" definition at the *15th Int. Workshop on Termination*, an informal workshop without formal reviewing or published proceedings, cf. http://cl-informatik.uibk.ac.at/events/wst-2016.

[4] The TPDB is the collection of examples used for the annual *Termination Competition*, available from http://termination-portal.org/wiki/TPDB.

We restrict ourselves to Java programs without arrays, exceptions, static fields, floating point numbers, class initializers, recursion, reflection, and multi-threading to ease the presentation. However, our implementation supports full Java except for floating point numbers, reflection, multi-threading, and recursion (which is currently only supported for termination analysis). Moreover, we abstract from the different types of integers in Java and consider unbounded integers instead, i.e., we do not handle problems related to overflows.

Symbolic execution is a well-known technique in program verification and transformation [19]. We recapitulate the notion of SE graphs used in AProVE and refer to [5,6,22] for details on their automated construction. First, the Java program is compiled to Java Bytecode (JBC) by any standard compiler.

Example 2 (Java Bytecode for the Method max from Example 1).

```
1 iconst_0      //load 0 to opstack       10 getfield val //load l.val to opstack
2 istore_1      //store 0 to var 1 (m)    11 istore_1      //store l.val into m
3 aload_0       //load l to opstack       12 aload_0       //load l to opstack
4 ifnull 16     //jump if l is null       13 getfield next //load l.next to opstack
5 aload_0       //load l to opstack       14 astore_0      //store l.next into l
6 getfield val//load l.val to opstack     15 goto 3
7 iload_1       //load m to opstack       16 iload_1       //load m to opstack
8 if_icmple 12//jump if l.val <= m        17 ireturn       //return m
9 aload_0       //load l to opstack
```

The SE graph is a finite graph that represents all executions of a JBC program. Its nodes are *abstract states* which differ from concrete program states by also allowing "symbolic" (unknown) values for integers and references (i.e., addresses in the heap). In the following, $\bar{\ell}, \bar{f}$ etc. denote sequences, $|\bar{\ell}|$ is the length of $\bar{\ell}$, and $\bar{\ell}|_j$ is the jth element of $\bar{\ell}$, where $\bar{\ell}$'s first element has index 0.

Definition 3 (Abstract State). *Let* REF *be the set of all* symbolic references, *let* INT *be the set of all* symbolic integers,[5] *and let* SYM = REF ⊎ INT *be the set of all* symbolic variables. *We write* $o, \tilde{o}, \ldots$ *for elements of* REF, $i, \tilde{i}, \ldots$ *for elements of* INT, *and* $x, \tilde{x}, \ldots$ *for arbitrary symbolic variables from* SYM. *An abstract state has the form* $s = (pp, \bar{\ell}, \overline{op}, h, p) \in$ STATE, *where* $pp \in \mathbb{N}$ *is the program position, i.e., the index of the next instruction to evaluate. The sequences* $\bar{\ell}, \overline{op} \in$ SYM* *represent the symbolic variables stored in the local (program) variables resp. the entries of the operand stack. Here,* $\bar{\ell}|_j$ *is the value of the* j^{th} *local variable, for all* $0 \leq j < |\bar{\ell}|$.[6] *Similarly,* $\overline{op}|_0$ *is the top entry of the operand stack. The partial function* $h :$ REF $\rightarrowtail$ OBJECT *maps symbolic references to abstract objects (i.e.,* $h(o)$ *expresses information about the object at address* o *in the heap). An abstract object is either* null *or a pair* (cl, vl) *of a class name* cl *and a function* $vl : Fields(cl) \rightarrow$ SYM *that maps all fields of* cl *to symbolic variables. The last component of* s *is a set of* predicates p. *Predicates specify heap shapes and are of the form* $o!$ *("o may point to a non-tree shaped object"),* $o =^? \tilde{o}$ *("o and $\tilde{o}$ may alias"), or* $o \searrow \tilde{o}$ *("o and $\tilde{o}$ may share"). We write* $o \xrightarrow{f}_h x$ *if* $h(o) = (cl, vl)$,

---

[5] As we do not regard floats, JBC represents all primitive Java types as integers.

[6] For the sake of simplicity, we assume that all states are well typed throughout this paper, i.e., local variables of type int always store symbolic integers, etc.

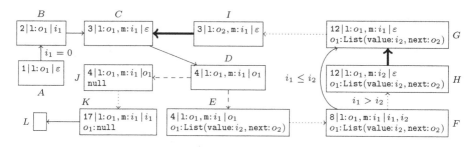

Fig. 1. SE graph for `max`

$f \in \mathit{Fields}(cl)$, and $vl(f) = x$, where we omit f if it is irrelevant. For a state $s = (pp, \overline{\ell}, \overline{op}, h, p)$, we define $\mathrm{REF}(s) = \{o \in \mathrm{REF} \mid 0 \le j < |\overline{\ell}|, \overline{\ell}|_j \rightarrow_h^* o\} \cup \{o \in \mathrm{REF} \mid 0 \le j < |\overline{op}|, \overline{op}|_j \rightarrow_h^* o\}$, where $\rightarrow_h^*$ is the reflexive–transitive closure of $\rightarrow_h$. $\mathrm{INT}(s)$ and $\mathrm{SYM}(s)$ are defined analogously.

Intuitively, an abstract state $(pp, \overline{\ell}, \overline{op}, h, p)$ can be seen as a collection of invariants. For example, if $\overline{\ell}|_0, \overline{\ell}|_1 \notin \mathrm{Dom}(h)$ (i.e., we have no concrete information about the objects at $\overline{\ell}|_0$ and $\overline{\ell}|_1$), then the *absence* of the predicate $\overline{\ell}|_0 \curlyvee \overline{\ell}|_1$ in p means that the first two local variables do not share at program position pp, i.e., there is no path from $\overline{\ell}|_0$ to $\overline{\ell}|_1$ or vice versa, and $\overline{\ell}|_0$ and $\overline{\ell}|_1$ do not have a common successor. Let $\mathcal{T}(\mathcal{V})$ resp. $\mathcal{F}(\mathcal{V})$ be the set of all arithmetic terms resp. quantifier-free formulas over the set of variables $\mathcal{V}$ (where we only consider integer arithmetic). The edges $s \xrightarrow{\varphi} \tilde{s}$ of an SE graph are directed and labeled with formulas $\varphi \in \mathcal{F}(\mathrm{INT})$ which restrict the control flow.

Figure 1 shows an SE graph for `max`. The first line "$pp \mid \overline{\ell} \mid \overline{op}$" of a state in Fig. 1 describes its first three components, where "$\mathbf{1} : o_1, \mathbf{m} : i_1$" means that $\overline{\ell}$ is (o_1, i_1), $\mathbf{1}$ is the 0th local variable, and $\mathbf{m}$ is the first local variable. In the next lines of a state, we show information about the heap, i.e., key-value pairs "$o : \ldots$" for each $o \in \mathrm{Dom}(h)$, and the predicates in p.

In State A, o_1 points to a (tree-shaped and hence acyclic) `List` or `null`, as $\mathbf{1}$ is of type `List` and $o_1 \notin \mathrm{Dom}(h)$. To express that o_1 may also point to non-tree shaped `List`s, one would need the predicate $o_1!$. Evaluating "`iconst_0`" at the program position 1 pushes the constant 0 to the operand stack, resulting in State B. This is indicated by a (solid) *evaluation edge* from A to B, labeled with the condition $i_1 = 0$ which is required to perform this evaluation step. Afterwards, i_1 is stored in the local variable $\mathbf{m}$ which yields State C. Evaluating "`aload_0`" in Line 3 pushes o_1 to the operand stack in State D. The next instruction "`ifnull 16`" jumps to Instruction 16 if the top operand stack entry is `null`. The dashed *refinement edges* connecting D with J (where o_1 is `null`) and E (where o_1 points to a `List`) correspond to a case analysis. Evaluating J results in K after two more evaluation steps (we abbreviate several evaluation edges by dotted edges). Finally, evaluating "`ireturn`" in Line 17 results in the end state L. In State E, the next four evaluation steps push `1.value` (i_2) and $\mathbf{m}$ (i_1) to the operand stack in order to compare them afterwards. In F, another case analysis is required. If $1.\mathtt{value} \leq \mathtt{m}$, the next instruction is 12 (State G). Otherwise, the instructions 9 – 11 update $\mathtt{m}$ to $1.\mathtt{value}$ (i.e., $\mathtt{m}$ stores i_2 in State H) before reaching Instruction 12. Note that when evaluating F, the case analysis is not modeled by refining F, as conditions like $i_2 \leq i_1$ cannot be expressed in STATEs. Instead, the edges connecting F with G and H are labeled with the corresponding conditions. The only difference between G and H is that we have $\mathtt{m} = 1.\mathtt{value}$ in H, whereas $\mathtt{m}$ and $1.\mathtt{value}$ can be arbitrary in G. Hence, G is *more general* than H (denoted $H \sqsubseteq G$) and thus there is a (thick) *generalization edge* from H to G.

See [2] for a formal definition of when a state $\tilde{s} = (pp, \overline{\ell}, \overline{op}, \tilde{h}, \tilde{p})$ is "more general" than $s = (pp, \overline{\ell}, \overline{op}, h, p)$. Essentially, s and $\tilde{s}$ have to be at the same position pp and in both s and $\tilde{s}$, the same symbolic variables must be used for the local variables and the operand stack. We also require that all information on the heap of $\tilde{s}$ holds for s as well (i.e., we must have $\mathrm{REF}(\tilde{s}) \subseteq \mathrm{REF}(s)$, and $h(o) = \tilde{h}(o)$ for all $o \in \mathsf{Dom}(\tilde{h})$). In addition, concrete sharing (e.g., $o_1 \rightarrow_h o_3$ and $o_2 \rightarrow_h o_3$) and abstract sharing (as expressed by predicates like $(o_1 \searrow\!\!\!\!\nearrow o_2) \in p$) in s must be permitted in $\tilde{s}$ (e.g., by the predicate $(o_1 \searrow\!\!\!\!\nearrow o_2) \in \tilde{p}$) and, similarly, concrete and abstract non-tree shapes in s must be permitted in $\tilde{s}$, too. To weaken the requirement that s and $\tilde{s}$ must use the same symbolic variables, we also allow to rename the symbolic variables of the abstract state $\tilde{s}$. So we also have $s \sqsubseteq \tilde{s}$ if there is a renaming function $\mu : \mathrm{SYM} \rightarrow \mathrm{SYM}$ such that $s \sqsubseteq \mu(\tilde{s})$ (where we lift μ to abstract states in the obvious way). Then we say that μ *witnesses* $s \sqsubseteq \tilde{s}$. However, we only allow renaming functions μ where $\mu(o_1) = \mu(o_2)$ implies $(o_1 =^? o_2) \in \tilde{p}$ for all $o_1, o_2 \in \mathrm{REF}(\tilde{s})$ with $o_1 \neq o_2$. So symbolic references $o_1, o_2 \in \mathrm{REF}(\tilde{s})$ may only be unified by μ if aliasing is explicitly allowed by a corresponding predicate $o_1 =^? o_2$ in $\tilde{s}$. In contrast, $\mu(i_1) = \mu(i_2)$ is possible for any $i_1, i_2 \in \mathrm{INT}(\tilde{s})$ (since different symbolic integers could represent the same number). If no renaming is required, then the witness of $s \sqsubseteq \tilde{s}$ is the identity.

Example 4 (Generalizing States). In Fig. 1, the witness for $H \sqsubseteq G$ is $\mu = \{i_1 \mapsto i_2\}$ (i.e., $\mu(i_1) = i_2$ and $\mu(x) = x$ for $x \in \{o_1, o_2, i_2\}$).

$\ldots\mid\ldots\mid o_1$	M	N	$\ldots\mid\ldots\mid o_1$
$o_1\!:\!\mathtt{List(value}\!:i_1,\mathtt{next}\!:o_2\mathtt{)}$			$o_1\!:\!\mathtt{List(value}\!:i_1,\mathtt{next}\!:o_1\mathtt{)}$
$o_1!,\ \ o_1 =^? o_2$			

To see the effect of predicates, consider the states M and N on the side, where $N \sqsubseteq M$. Here, the predicate $o_1!$ is needed in M, as o_1 is cyclic and hence non-tree shaped in N since o_1's field $\mathtt{next}$ points to o_1 itself. Thus, $N \sqsubseteq M$ is witnessed by $\mu = \{o_2 \mapsto o_1\}$. This witness function is valid, as we have $o_1 =^? o_2$ in M.

In Fig. 1, I results from G by setting 1 to $1.\mathtt{next}$ (Instructions 12 – 14) and going back to Step 3 ("goto 3" in Line 15). We draw a generalization edge from I to C, as I is a variable-renamed version of C, i.e., $I \sqsubseteq C$ with witness $\{o_1 \mapsto o_2\}$.

To see the connection between JBC and SE graphs, we now define which concrete JBC states are represented by an abstract state.

Definition 5 (Concrete State). *A* concrete state (c, τ) *is a pair of an abstract state* $c = (pp, \overline{\ell}, \overline{op}, h, \varnothing) \in \text{STATE}$ *with* $\text{REF}(c) \subseteq \text{Dom}(h)$ *and a valuation* $\tau : \text{INT}(c) \to \mathbb{Z}$. *We say that* (c, τ) *is* represented *by a state* $s \in \text{STATE}$ *if* $c \sqsubseteq s$.

So the heap of a concrete state has to be completely specified ($\text{REF}(c) \subseteq \text{Dom}(h)$) and hence predicates are not needed for c. The additional component τ determines the values of symbolic integers. For example, $(J, \{i_1 \mapsto n\})$ is a concrete state for all $n \in \mathbb{Z}$. Since $\sqsubseteq$ is transitive, $s \sqsubseteq \tilde{s}$ always guarantees that all concrete states represented by a state s are also represented by the state $\tilde{s}$.

As shown in [5, 6, 22], for any JBC program $\mathcal{P}$ one can automatically construct an SE graph $\mathcal{G}$ such that every JBC execution sequence can be *embedded* into $\mathcal{G}$. This means that if $(c, \tau) \xrightarrow{jbc}_{\mathcal{P}} (\tilde{c}, \tilde{\tau})$ is a JBC execution step for two concrete states and $c \sqsubseteq s$ holds for some state s in $\mathcal{G}$, then $\mathcal{G}$ has a non-empty path from s to a state $\tilde{s}$ with $\tilde{c} \sqsubseteq \tilde{s}$. Hence, the paths in $\mathcal{G}$ are at least as long as the corresponding JBC sequences and therefore, SE graphs are a suitable representation for inferring upper bounds on the runtime complexity of JBC programs.

The complexity of a JBC program is a function from its inputs to its runtime. Our goal is to infer a representation of this function which is intuitive and as precise as possible. To this end, we over-approximate the complexity by a function on integers in closed form. As the inputs of a Java program can be arbitrary objects, we need a suitable mapping from objects to integers to achieve such a representation. Hence, we now define how we measure the size of objects.

Definition 6 (Size $\| \cdot \|$). *For a concrete state* (c, τ) *with heap* h *and* $o \in \text{REF}(c)$, *let* $intSum(o) = 1 + \sum_{f \in Fields(cl), vl(f) = i \in \text{INT}} |\tau(i)|$ *if* $h(o) = (cl, vl)$ *and* $intSum(o) = 0$ *if* $h(o) = \texttt{null}$. *We define* $\|o\|_{(c, \tau)} = \sum_{o \to_h^* \tilde{o}} intSum(\tilde{o})$.

So the size $\|o\|_{(c, \tau)}$ of the object at the address o in (c, τ) is the number of all reachable objects $\tilde{o}$ plus the absolute values of all integers in their fields. If the same symbolic integer i is in several fields of $\tilde{o}$, then $|\tau(i)|$ is added several times.

In our opinion, this is the notion of "size" that is most suitable for measuring the runtime complexity of programs. The addend "1" in the definition of $intSum$ covers features like the length of lists (i.e., an acyclic list is always greater than any of its proper sub-lists) or the number of nodes of trees. But in contrast to measures like "path length", we also take the elements of data structures into account (i.e., $\| \cdot \|$ is similar to "term size", see e.g., [13]). Since the second addend of $intSum$ measures integer elements of data structures, we can analyze the complexity of algorithms like $\texttt{sort}$ from Example 1 whose runtime (also) depends on the numbers that are stored in a list. Moreover in contrast to "path length", our notion of size is also suitable for cyclic objects. For example, consider a concrete state (N, τ) for State N of Example 4. Here, we have $\|o_1\|_{(N,\tau)} = intSum(o_1) = 1 + |\tau(i_1)|$, i.e., the size of such a cyclic list is finite.[7]

Now we can define the notion of complexity that we analyze. The *derivation height* $\mathsf{dh}_\mathcal{P}(c, \tau)$ of a concrete state is the length of the longest JBC execution sequence in the program $\mathcal{P}$ that starts in (c, τ). This corresponds to the usual definition of "derivation height" for other programming languages, cf. [16]. A *complexity bound* for an abstract state s is an arithmetic term $b_\mathcal{P}(s)$ over the variables $\mathcal{V}(s) = \{x_o \mid o \in \mathrm{REF}(s)\} \cup \mathrm{INT}(s)$. Here, the variable x_o represents the *size* of the object at the symbolic reference o. Then for any valuation σ of $\mathcal{V}(s)$, $\sigma(b_\mathcal{P}(s))$ should be greater or equal to the length of the longest JBC execution sequence starting with a concrete state (c, τ) that is represented by s, where the values of all $i \in \mathrm{INT}(c)$ and the sizes of all $o \in \mathrm{REF}(c)$ correspond to the valuation σ. In the following, $\omega > n$ holds for all $n \in \mathbb{N}$ and for any $M \subseteq \mathbb{N} \cup \{\omega\}$, $\sup M$ is the least upper bound of M, where $\sup \varnothing = 0$.

Definition 7 (Derivation Height, Complexity Bound). *Let $\mathcal{P}$ be a JBC program. For every concrete state (c_0, σ_0) of $\mathcal{P}$, we define its* derivation height *as*

$$\mathsf{dh}_\mathcal{P}(c_0, \sigma_0) = \sup\{n \mid \exists (c_1, \sigma_1), \dots, (c_n, \sigma_n) : (c_0, \sigma_0) \xrightarrow{jbc}_\mathcal{P} \dots \xrightarrow{jbc}_\mathcal{P} (c_n, \sigma_n)\}.$$

Let $s \in \mathrm{STATE}$. A term $b_\mathcal{P}(s) \in \mathcal{T}(\mathcal{V}(s)) \cup \{\omega\}$ is a complexity bound *for s in $\mathcal{P}$ if for all valuations $\sigma : \mathcal{V}(s) \to \mathbb{Z}$ we have $\sigma(b_\mathcal{P}(s)) \geq \mathsf{dh}_\mathcal{P}(c, \tau)$ for any concrete state (c, τ) where some function μ witnesses $c \sqsubseteq s$, $\sigma(x_o) = \|\mu(o)\|_{(c,\tau)}$ for all $o \in \mathrm{REF}(s)$, and $\sigma(i) = \tau(\mu(i))$ for all $i \in \mathrm{INT}(s)$.*

So if s is an abstract state that represents all possible concrete states at the start of a Java method in a program $\mathcal{P}$, then a complexity bound $b_\mathcal{P}(s)$ describes an upper bound for the runtime complexity of the Java method.

Example 8 (Runtime Complexity of max*).* *For any state $c \sqsubseteq A$ where o_1 is a list of length n, we get $\mathsf{dh}_\mathcal{P}(c, \tau) \leq 13 \cdot n + 6 \leq 13 \cdot \|o_1\|_{(c,\tau)} + 6$ for all valuations τ. Hence, $b_\mathcal{P}(A) = 13 \cdot x_{o_1} + 6$ is a complexity bound for A, which means that $13 \cdot \|1\| + 6$ is an upper bound for the runtime complexity of* max(1) *from Example 2.*

3   From SE Graphs to ITSs

Now we introduce a new complexity-preserving transformation from SE graphs to *integer transition systems*. This allows us to use existing tools for complexity analysis of integer programs to infer bounds on the runtime of JBC programs.

---

[7] With this notion of *size*, the transformation from objects to *terms* that we used for termination analysis in [22] is unsound for complexity analysis, as it duplicates objects that can be reached by different fields: Consider a binary "tree" of n nodes where the left and right child of each inner node are the same. The size $\| \cdot \|$ of this object is linear in n, but the resulting transformed term would be exponential in n. This problem is avoided by our new transformation to *integers* instead of terms in Sect. 3.

Definition 9 (Integer Transition System). *Let $\mathcal{V}$ be a set of variables and let $\mathcal{V}' = \{x' \mid x \in \mathcal{V}\}$ be the corresponding* post-variables. *An ITS $\mathcal{I}$ is a directed graph $(\mathcal{L}, \mathcal{R})$ where $\mathcal{L}$ is the set of nodes (or* locations*) and $\mathcal{R}$ is the set of edges (or* transitions*). A transition $(s, \varphi, w, \tilde{s}) \in \mathcal{R}$ consists of a source location $s \in \mathcal{L}$, a condition $\varphi \in \mathcal{F}(\mathcal{V} \cup \mathcal{V}')$, a weight $w \in \mathcal{T}(\mathcal{V})$, and a target location $\tilde{s} \in \mathcal{L}$. Any valuation $\sigma : \mathcal{V} \to \mathbb{Z}$ induces a post-valuation $\sigma' : \mathcal{V}' \to \mathbb{Z}$ with $\sigma'(x') = \sigma(x)$ for all $x \in \mathcal{V}$. The transition relation $\to_\mathcal{I}$ of an ITS $\mathcal{I}$ operates on configurations (s, σ), where $s \in \mathcal{L}$ and σ is a valuation. For any $s, \tilde{s} \in \mathcal{L}$ and any valuations $\sigma, \tilde{\sigma} : \mathcal{V} \to \mathbb{Z}$, we have $(s, \sigma) \xrightarrow{m}_\mathcal{I} (\tilde{s}, \tilde{\sigma})$ if there exists a transition $(s, \varphi, w, \tilde{s}) \in \mathcal{R}$ such that $\sigma(w) = m$ and $\sigma \cup (\tilde{\sigma})'$ satisfies φ (i.e., φ is satisfied if all $x \in \mathcal{V}$ are instantiated by σ and all $x' \in \mathcal{V}'$ are instantiated according to $\tilde{\sigma}$).*

For any location s, a term $b_\mathcal{I}(s) \in \mathcal{T}(\mathcal{V}) \cup \{\omega\}$ is a complexity bound *for s in $\mathcal{I}$ if for all valuations $\sigma : \mathcal{V} \to \mathbb{Z}$ we have $\sigma(b_\mathcal{I}(s)) \geq \sum_{1 \leq j \leq n} m_j$ whenever $(s, \sigma) \xrightarrow{m_1}_\mathcal{I} \dots \xrightarrow{m_n}_\mathcal{I} (\tilde{s}, \tilde{\sigma})$ holds for some $(\tilde{s}, \tilde{\sigma})$.*

Example 10 (ITS). Consider the ITS $\mathcal{I}$ on the right where each edge $(s, \varphi, w, \tilde{s})$ is labeled with "$w : \varphi$". It corresponds to a loop where a counter x is decremented (transition from P to O) as long as it is positive (transition from O to P). Due to the weight x of the transition from P to O, $b_\mathcal{I}(O) = \frac{(x+1) \cdot x}{2}$ is a complexity bound for O.

So given an initial state s, a complexity bound $b_\mathcal{I}(s)$ is an upper bound for the runtime complexity of $\mathcal{I}$. For instance, the complexity bound $b_\mathcal{I}(O)$ in Example 10 means that the runtime complexity of the ITS $\mathcal{I}$ is quadratic in x. We will now show how to automatically translate the SE graph of a Java program $\mathcal{P}$ into a corresponding ITS $\mathcal{I}$ such that any complexity bound $b_\mathcal{I}(s)$ for $\mathcal{I}$ is also a complexity bound $b_\mathcal{P}(s)$ for $\mathcal{P}$. We first consider programs that do not modify the heap and handle heap-manipulating programs in Sect. 5.

Let $\mathcal{G}$ be an SE graph with the states STATE and the edges EDGE. To transform SE graphs to ITSs, we fix $\mathcal{V} = \bigcup_{s \in \text{STATE}} \mathcal{V}(s)$ and $\mathcal{L} = \text{STATE}$. Essentially, we define $(s, \nu_{s,\tilde{s}}(\varphi) \wedge \psi_s \wedge \rho, w, \tilde{s}) \in \mathcal{R}$ iff $s \xrightarrow{\varphi} \tilde{s} \in \text{EDGE}$ where $w = 0$ if $s \xrightarrow{\varphi} \tilde{s}$ is a refinement or generalization edge and $w = 1$ if $s \xrightarrow{\varphi} \tilde{s}$ is an evaluation edge.

The substitution $\nu_{s,\tilde{s}}$ is defined as $\nu_{s,\tilde{s}}(x) = x'$ for $x \in \mathcal{V}(\tilde{s}) \setminus \mathcal{V}(s)$ and $\nu_{s,\tilde{s}}(x) = x$ for $x \in \mathcal{V}(s)$. Then $\nu_{s,\tilde{s}}(\varphi)$ is a condition on the values of the symbolic integers that must be satisfied in order to use the transition from s to $\tilde{s}$. For example, if the evaluated instruction is `iadd` (i.e., adding the two top elements of the operand stack), the operand stack of s starts with "i_1, i_2", and the operand stack of $\tilde{s}$ has the fresh symbolic integer "i_3" on top, then the edge $s \to \tilde{s}$ in the SE graph is labeled with $i_3 = i_1 + i_2$ and the corresponding transition in the ITS has the condition $i_3' = i_1 + i_2$. Thus, in the location $\tilde{s}$, the value of i_3 must be the sum of the values that i_1 and i_2 had in s.

While the semantics of arithmetic operations is captured by φ, the formula ψ_s expresses conditions on the variables x_o that represent the *sizes* $\|o\|$ of the objects in s. We define ψ_s to be the following formula, where h is the heap of s:

$$\bigwedge_{\substack{o\in\text{REF}(s)\cap\text{Dom}(h) \\ h(o)=\texttt{null}}} x_o = 0 \quad \wedge \quad \bigwedge_{\substack{o\in\text{REF}(s)\cap\text{Dom}(h) \\ h(o)\neq\texttt{null}}} x_o \geq 1 \quad \wedge \quad \bigwedge_{o\in\text{REF}(s)\setminus\text{Dom}(h)} x_o \geq 0$$

While this encoding might seem rather coarse, we achieve precision by defining a suitable formula ρ which encodes the relation between the values of the variables $x \in \mathcal{V}(s)$ and the post-variables x' (i.e., the values of the variables in $\tilde{s}$). The definition of ρ is straightforward for evaluation edges that do not modify the heap, because here the values of the symbolic variables do not change.

Definition 11 (Encoding Evaluation Edges). *Let $e = s \xrightarrow{\varphi} \tilde{s} \in$ EDGE be an evaluation edge with $s = (pp, \overline{\ell}, \overline{op}, h, p)$ such that the instruction at program position pp is neither* `putfield` *nor* `new`. *Then the edge e is translated into the ITS transition $tr(e) = (s, \nu_{s,\tilde{s}}(\varphi) \wedge \psi_s \wedge \bigwedge_{x\in\mathcal{V}(s)\cap\mathcal{V}(\tilde{s})} x' = x, 1, \tilde{s})$.*

Example 12 (Encoding Evaluation Edges). For Fig. 1, we have $tr(C \rightarrow D) = (C, x_{o_1} \geq 0 \wedge x'_{o_1} = x_{o_1} \wedge i'_1 = i_1, 1, D)$ and $tr(F \xrightarrow{i_2 \leq i_1} G) = (F, i_2 \leq i_1 \wedge x_{o_1} \geq 1 \wedge x_{o_2} \geq 0 \wedge \rho, 1, G)$ where ρ is $x'_{o_1} = x_{o_1} \wedge x'_{o_2} = x_{o_2} \wedge i'_1 = i_1 \wedge i'_2 = i_2$.

When transforming refinement edges to ITS transitions, we encode our knowledge about the object at the reference o that is "refined". We exploit that, by construction of $\|\cdot\|$, the size of any $\tilde{o}$ with $o \rightarrow^* \tilde{o}$ is bounded by the size of o.

Definition 13 (Encoding Refinement Edges). *Let $e = s \rightarrow \tilde{s} \in$ EDGE be a refinement edge with $s = (pp, \overline{\ell}, \overline{op}, h, p)$, $\tilde{s} = (pp, \overline{\ell}, \overline{op}, \tilde{h}, \tilde{p})$, and let $o \in$ REF(s) be the symbolic reference of the object that was refined. Then $tr(e) = (s, \nu_{s,\tilde{s}}(\psi_{\tilde{s}}) \wedge \rho, 0, \tilde{s})$ where ρ is $\bigwedge_{x\in\mathcal{V}(s)} x' = x$ if $\tilde{h}(o) = \texttt{null}$. Otherwise, ρ is*

$$\bigwedge_{x\in\mathcal{V}(s)} x' = x \quad \wedge \quad \bigwedge_{\tilde{o}\in\text{REF}(\tilde{s}),\, o\rightarrow_{\tilde{h}}\tilde{o}} x_o \underset{(-)}{\geq} x'_{\tilde{o}} \quad \wedge \quad \bigwedge_{i\in\text{INT}(\tilde{s}),\, o\rightarrow_{\tilde{h}}i} x_o > i' > -x_o.$$

Here, "$\underset{(-)}{\geq}$" is "$\geq$" if $o! \in p$ and "$>$" if $o! \notin p$.

Note that we can encode the knowledge from the more specialized state $\tilde{s}$ (i.e., we use $\psi_{\tilde{s}}$ instead of ψ_s), as the transition just has to be applicable in the case represented by $\tilde{s}$. The sizes of o's successor references $\tilde{o}$ are strictly smaller than $\|o\|$ if o is guaranteed to be acyclic (i.e., if $o! \notin p$), since in this case, $\tilde{o}$ reaches less objects than o. Otherwise, there might be a path from $\tilde{o}$ to o and hence we might have $\|\tilde{o}\| = \|o\|$. For symbolic integers $i \in$ INT reachable from o, we know that $\|o\| > |i|$ holds due to the definition of $\|\cdot\|$. In Definition 13 we express this without using absolute values explicitly, since they are not supported by current complexity tools for ITSs.

Example 14 (Encoding Refinement Edges). For Fig. 1, we have $tr(D \rightarrow J) = (D, x_{o_1} = 0 \wedge x'_{o_1} = x_{o_1} \wedge i'_1 = i_1, 0, J)$. Transforming $D \rightarrow E$ yields $(D, x_{o_1} \geq 1 \wedge x'_{o_2} \geq 0 \wedge \rho, 0, E)$ where ρ is $x'_{o_1} = x_{o_1} \wedge i'_1 = i_1 \wedge x_{o_1} > x'_{o_2} \wedge x_{o_1} > i'_2 > -x_{o_1}$.

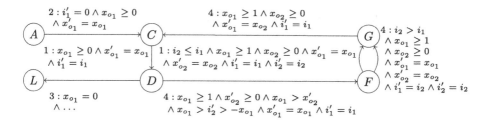

Fig. 2. ITS for the SE graph of Fig. 1

For generalization edges $s \rightarrow \tilde{s}$ where μ witnesses $s \sqsubseteq \tilde{s}$, the renaming μ describes how the names of the symbolic variables in s and $\tilde{s}$ are related.

Definition 15 (Encoding Generalization Edges). *Let* $e = s \rightarrow \tilde{s} \in \mathrm{EDGE}$ *be a generalization edge and let* μ *witness* $s \sqsubseteq \tilde{s}$. *We extend* μ *to* $\{x_o \mid o \in \mathrm{REF}(\tilde{s})\}$ *by defining* $\mu(x_o) = x_{\mu(o)}$. *Then* $tr(e) = (s, \psi_s \wedge \bigwedge_{x \in \mathcal{V}(\tilde{s})} x' = \mu(x), 0, \tilde{s})$.

Example 16 (Encoding Generalization Edges). The witness of $H \sqsubseteq G$ *is* $\{i_1 \mapsto i_2\}$. *Hence, we get* $tr(H \rightarrow G) = (H, x_{o_1} \geq 1 \wedge x_{o_2} \geq 0 \wedge x'_{o_1} = x_{o_1} \wedge x'_{o_2} = x_{o_2} \wedge i'_1 = i_2 \wedge i'_2 = i_2, 0, G)$. *Similarly, the witness of* $I \sqsubseteq C$ *is* $\{o_1 \mapsto o_2\}$. *Hence, we get* $tr(I \rightarrow C) = (I, x_{o_2} \geq 0 \wedge x'_{o_1} = x_{o_2} \wedge i'_1 = i_1, 0, C)$.

Example 17 (ITS for `max`*). Figure 2 shows the ITS* $\mathcal{I}$ *obtained from the SE graph in Fig. 1 after simplifying it via chaining, i.e., subsequent transitions* $(s_1, \varphi_1, w_1, s_2), (s_2, \varphi_2, w_2, s_3)$ *are combined to a single transition that corresponds to first applying* $(s_1, \varphi_1, w_1, s_2)$ *and then* $(s_2, \varphi_2, w_2, s_3)$. *In our implementation, we only chain such transitions if* s_2 *has exactly one incoming and one outgoing transition. Further chaining changes the original control flow of the program which was disadvantageous in our experiments. Again, each transition* $(s, \varphi, w, \tilde{s})$ *is labeled with "*$w : \varphi$*" in Fig. 2. State-of-the-art complexity analysis tools like* CoFloCo *[12] and* KoAT *[8] can easily infer a complexity bound* $b_{\mathcal{I}}(A)$ *which is linear in* x_{o_1}. *In Theorem 24 we will show that complexity bounds* $b_{\mathcal{I}}(A)$ *for the obtained ITS* $\mathcal{I}$ *are also upper bounds* $b_{\mathcal{P}}(A)$ *on the complexity of the original* Java *program* $\mathcal{P}$.

Slight modifications of our transformation tr from the SE graph to ITSs allow us to analyze different notions of complexity. For *space complexity*, we can simply change the weight of all evaluation edges to 0 except those that correspond to **new** instructions (i.e., in this way we infer an upper bound on the auxiliary heap space required by the method when ignoring any deallocation of memory by the garbage collector). Our technique can also easily analyze the *size* of a function's result. To this end, all transitions get weight 0 except evaluation edges that correspond to `ireturn` or `areturn` (returning an integer or a reference). Their weight is simply the top entry of the operand stack. Applying this transformation to Fig. 1 yields an ITS $\mathcal{I}'$ like Fig. 2, but the edge from D to L has weight i_1 and all other edges have weight 0. Then complexity tools can infer an upper bound like $b_{\mathcal{I}'}(A) = |x_{o_1}|$. This proves that the result of `max` is bounded by $\|1\|$.

4   Summarizing Method Calls

In [5], we extended abstract states to represent the call stack. In this way, our implementation can analyze programs with method invocations like Example 1 fully automatically. As an alternative, we now introduce the possibility to use *summaries*, which is crucial for a modular incremental (possibly interactive) analysis of large programs. Summaries approximate the effect of method calls. Thus, AProVE can now use information about called methods without having to analyze them. Currently, such summaries have to be provided by the user as JSON files, but they can contain information obtained by previous runs of AProVE.

Example 18 (Summarizing max*). A possible summary for* max *looks as follows.*

```
1   "class": "List",                    10      "upperSize": [{
2   "methods": [{                       11        "pos": "ret",
3   "name": "max",                      12        "bound": "arg0"
4   "descriptor": "(LList;)I",          13      }],
5   "static": true,                     14      "lowerSize": [{
6   "complexity": {                     15        "pos": "ret",
7     "upperTime": "13 * arg0 + 6",     16        "bound": "0"
8     "upperSpace": "0"                 17      }]
9   },                                  18   }]
```

So for a given class, each summarized method is identified by its name and descriptor.[8] *Upper bounds for the method's time and auxiliary heap space complexity can be provided as polynomials over* arg0, . . . , argn *for static methods resp.* this, arg0, . . . , argn *for non-static methods, where* argi *refers to the size of the method's i^{th} argument if it is an object resp. the value of the ith argument if it is an integer. Similarly, one can provide bounds (*upperSize *and* lowerSize*) on the size of the method's result (*ret*).*

Our summaries are not yet expressive enough to describe heap shapes (we will improve them in future work). So for simplicity we assume that one only summarizes methods which do not manipulate the heap. Moreover, the summary for max is only correct if its argument is acyclic (otherwise, max fails to terminate). For soundness, one has to ensure that the pre-conditions of the summary are invariants of the respective class (e.g., that List only implements acyclic lists).

Figure 3 shows the SE graph for sort. Here, we assume a summary for mem where upperTime is "10 * arg1 + 4", i.e., computing mem(n,l) takes at most $10 \cdot \|1\| + 4$ steps. For readability of Fig. 3, instead of program positions we described the respective JBC instructions and omitted the case n > max(l) (indicated by the edge $S \xrightarrow{i_1 > i_2} \ldots$) and the case where mem returns false. The *summarization edge* $Q \to R$ is labeled with the *size condition* $x_{o_1} \geq i_2 \geq 0$ restricting the size of max's result i_2 and the *weight* $13 \cdot x_{o_1} + 6$ which correspond to the summary from Example 18. Such summarization edges are only permitted for methods whose summary contains a finite upper runtime bound $(< \omega)$. The

---

[8] The descriptor specifies the argument types and return type of a method ("LList;" stands for the argument type List and "I" stands for the result type int), see docs.oracle.com/javase/specs/jvms/se7/html/jvms-4.html#jvms-4.3.3.

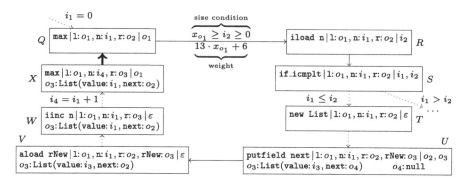

Fig. 3. SE graph for `sort`

(omitted) summarization edge for `mem` is labeled with the weight $10 \cdot x_{o_1} + 4$. The SE graph clearly reflects the quadratic complexity of `sort`: in each iteration, i_4 is set to $i_1 + 1$ (on the path from W to X) and afterwards i_4 is renamed back to i_1 (on the generalization edge $X \to Q$), i.e., i_1 is incremented. The program terminates as soon as the value of i_1 exceeds i_2, where i_2 is bounded by $\|o_1\|$. As $\|o_1\|$ never changes and i_1 is initialized to 0, the loop cannot be executed more than $\|o_1\|$ times. Since the complexity of each iteration is linear in $\|o_1\|$ due to the weights of `max` and `member`, the complexity of `sort` is quadratic. To show how we infer this quadratic bound for `sort` automatically, it remains to explain how we transform summarization edges and evaluation edges with `new` and `putfield` to ITS transitions. Encoding summarization edges is straightforward.

Definition 19 (Encoding Summarization Edges). *Let $e = s \to \tilde{s} \in \mathrm{EDGE}$ be a summarization edge with size condition φ and weight w. It is transformed into the ITS transition $tr(e) = (s, \nu_{s,\tilde{s}}(\varphi) \wedge \psi_s \wedge \bigwedge_{x \in \mathcal{V}(s) \cap \mathcal{V}(\tilde{s})} x' = x, w, \tilde{s})$.*

Example 20 (Encoding Summarization Edges). We have $tr(Q \to R) = (Q, x_{o_1} \geq i_2' \geq 0 \wedge x_{o_1} \geq 0 \wedge x_{o_2} \geq 0 \wedge x_{o_1}' = x_{o_1} \wedge x_{o_2}' = x_{o_2} \wedge i_1' = i_1, 13 \cdot x_{o_1} + 6, R)$.

5   Encoding Heap Modifications

Now we show how to encode the only instructions that modify the heap as ITS transitions. To encode the instruction `new`, we simply add the constraint $x_o' = 1$ for the newly created object o.

Example 21 (Encoding new). For the (omitted) successor T' of T in Fig. 3 we have $tr(T \to T') = (T, x_{o_1} \geq 0 \wedge x_{o_2} \geq 0 \wedge x_{o_1}' = x_{o_1} \wedge x_{o_2}' = x_{o_2} \wedge x_{o_3}' = 1 \wedge i_1' = i_1, 1, T')$.

The only instruction that changes the size of objects is `putfield`. Note that `putfield` also changes the size of all predecessors $\tilde{o}$ of the object affected by the write access. However, our size measure $\|\cdot\|$ was defined in such a way that we can easily provide lower and upper bounds for the affected variables $x_{\tilde{o}}$.

Definition 22 (Encoding putfield for Object Fields). *Let* $e = s \to \tilde{s} \in$ EDGE *be an evaluation edge with* $s = (pp, \bar{\ell}, \overline{op}, h, p)$, *let* $\tilde{o}_f$ *and* o *be the two top entries of* $\overline{op}$, *and let* putfield f *be the instruction at program position* pp *(i.e.,* $\tilde{o}_f \in$ REF *is written to the field* f *of* $h(o)$*). Moreover, let* $o \xrightarrow{f}_h o_f$ *(i.e.,* o_f *is the former value of* $h(o)$*'s field* f*) and* PotPred $= \{\tilde{o} \in$ REF$(\tilde{s}) \mid \tilde{o} \rightsquigarrow o\}$ *where* $\tilde{o} \rightsquigarrow o$ *iff* $\tilde{o} \to^*_h o$ *or* $\tilde{o} \to^*_h \hat{o}$ *and* $(\hat{o} \setminus\!\!\!\diagup o) \in p$ *for some* $\hat{o} \in$ REF.[9] *Then* $tr(e) = (s, \psi_s \wedge \bigwedge_{x \in \mathcal{V}(\tilde{s}) \setminus \{x_{\tilde{o}} \mid \tilde{o} \in \text{PotPred}\}} x' = x \wedge \bigwedge_{\tilde{o} \in \text{PotPred}} x_{\tilde{o}} + x_{\tilde{o}_f} \geq x'_{\tilde{o}} \geq x_{\tilde{o}} - x_{o_f}, 1, \tilde{s})$.

So the size of all potential predecessors $\tilde{o}$ of o (captured by $\rightsquigarrow$) may change, but by definition of $\|\cdot\|$, the new size of $\tilde{o}$ is between $\|\tilde{o}\| - \|o_f\|$ and $\|\tilde{o}\| + \|\tilde{o}_f\|$.

If an integer $\tilde{i}_f$ is written to a field by putfield, then we need to take the signs of $\tilde{i}_f$ and of the previous value i_f of the field into account, since integers contribute to $\|\cdot\|$ with their absolute value. To avoid case analyses, we infer integer invariants using standard techniques which often allow us to determine the signs of integers statically. Moreover, for simplicity we just encode the upper bound and use $x_{\tilde{o}} + \tilde{i}_f \geq x'_{\tilde{o}} \geq 0$ if $\tilde{i}_f$ is non-negative resp. $x_{\tilde{o}} - \tilde{i}_f \geq x'_{\tilde{o}} \geq 0$ if $\tilde{i}_f$ is negative, since 0 is a trivial lower bound for $\|\tilde{o}\|$. Hence, our encoding yields just one rule if the sign of $\tilde{i}_f$ can be determined statically and two rules, otherwise.

Example 23 (Encoding putfield*).* We have $tr(U \to V) = (U, x_{o_1} \geq 0 \wedge x_{o_2} \geq 0 \wedge x_{o_3} \geq 1 \wedge x_{o_4} = 0 \wedge \rho, 1, V)$ *where* ρ *is* $x'_{o_1} = x_{o_1} \wedge x'_{o_2} = x_{o_2} \wedge i'_1 = i_1 \wedge i'_3 = i_3 \wedge x_{o_3} + x_{o_2} \geq x'_{o_3} \geq x_{o_3} - x_{o_4}$.

The following theorem states that our transformation is sound for complexity analysis. For the proof, we refer to [2].

Theorem 24 (Soundness Theorem). *Let* $\mathcal{P}$ *be a* JBC *program and* $\mathcal{I}$ *be the ITS which results from the SE graph for* $\mathcal{P}$*. Then for all* $s \in$ STATE*, any complexity bound* $b_{\mathcal{I}}(s)$ *for* s *in* $\mathcal{I}$ *is also a complexity bound for* s *in* $\mathcal{P}$*.*

For the initial state of the ITS resulting from the SE graph in Fig. 3, CoFloCo and KoAT infer complexity bounds in $\mathcal{O}(x_{o_1}^2)$. By Theorem 24, this proves that the runtime of sort(1) is quadratic in $\|\mathbf{l}\|$.

6   Experiments and Conclusion

Building upon AProVE's symbolic execution, we presented a new complexity-preserving transformation from heap-manipulating Java programs with user-defined data structures to integer transition systems. Furthermore, we explained how we achieve modularity using summaries. In contrast to AProVE's termination analysis which transforms Java to term rewrite systems with built-in integers, our new transformation allows us to apply powerful off-the-shelf solvers for

---

[9] While s may have the predicate $\hat{o} \setminus\!\!\!\diagup o$, it cannot contain $\hat{o} =^? o$, as our symbolic execution rules require that if a field of o is written by putfield, then predicates of the form $\hat{o} =^? o$ first have to be removed by refinement steps, cf. [5]. Similarly, $o \in$ Dom(h) is enforced by refinements before symbolically evaluating putfield.

integer programs like CoFloCo [12] and KoAT [8]. In our implementation, we run CoFloCo and KoAT in parallel to obtain complexity bounds that are as small as possible.

Clearly, our translation is also sound for termination analysis. In fact, AProVE was not able to prove termination of Example 1 so far. Coupling our translation with dedicated termination analysis tools for ITSs like T2 [7] is subject of future work.

Related approaches are presented in [1,3,4,10,15,17,18]. [3] analyzes the complexity of a Java-like language, but in contrast to our technique, it requires user-provided loop invariants. [17] analyzes ML, i.e., the considered input language differs significantly from ours. [15] regards C programs, but requires user-provided "quantitative functions over data structures" (which are similar to our optional summaries, cf. Sect. 4) and hence cannot analyze programs with data structures fully automatically. The approach in [10] also relies on user annotations to handle resource bounds that depend on the contents of the heap. The tool [4] analyzes Jinja [20], which is similar (but not equal) to a restricted subset of Java. Therefore, transforming Java to Jinja is non-trivial and no suitable tool to accomplish such a transformation is available.[10] Similarly, [18] analyzes the complexity of a language related to Java (RAJA), but a (possibly automated) transformation from full Java to RAJA is not straightforward.

Hence, we compare our implementation with COSTA [1], the only other tool for fully automated complexity analysis of Java we are aware of. Like our technique, COSTA transforms Java to an integer-based formalism (called *cost relations*). However, COSTA uses *path length* to measure the size of objects, i.e., lists are measured by length, trees by height, etc. Thus, COSTA fails for programs like Example 1 where one has to reason both about data structures and their elements, as `sort`'s runtime is not bounded by the length of the input list. So both COSTA and AProVE estimate how the number of executed instructions depends on the size of the program input. But as the tools use different size measures, the semantics of their results are incomparable. Thus, our experimental evaluation is just meant to give a rough impression of the capabilities of the tools.

To assess the power of our approach, we ran AProVE on all 300 non-recursive examples from the category "Java Bytecode" of the *Termination Problem Data Base* (TPDB), a well-established benchmark for automated termination analysis used at the annual *Termination Competition*, cf. Footnote 4. (So we did not include the 286 examples from the category "Java Bytecode Recursive".) We omitted 80 examples from two sub-collections of the TPDB which mainly consist of non-terminating examples as well as 8 further examples where AProVE proves non-termination and consequently fails to infer an upper bound. The remaining 212 examples contain 131

Table 1. Results on the TPDB

$\mathcal{O}(1)$	$\mathcal{O}(n)$	$\mathcal{O}(n^2)$	$\mathcal{O}(n^3)$	$\mathcal{O}(n^{>3})$	?
31	102	15	1	5	58

---

[10] Java2Jinja (http://pp.ipd.kit.edu/projects/quis-custodiet/Java2Jinja) generates JinjaThreads-code, which is a superset of Jinja and cannot be handled by [4].

heap-manipulating and 81 numeric programs. AProVE finds runtime bounds for 78 heap-manipulating and 76 numeric examples, i.e., for 154 (73%) of all 212 examples, cf. Table 1. Here, n is the sum of the sizes of all object arguments and of the absolute values of all integer arguments. On average, AProVE needs 7.2 s to prove an upper bound and the median of the runtime is 4.6 s.

Unfortunately, we cannot compare AProVE with COSTA on the TPDB directly. The reason is that the TPDB examples simulate numeric inputs by the lengths of the strings in the argument of the entry point `main(String[] args)` of the program. As COSTA abstracts arrays to their length, it loses all information about the elements of `args` and hence fails for almost all TPDB examples.

So we adapted the 212 examples[11] of the TPDB such that they do not rely on `main`'s argument to simulate numeric inputs anymore. Instead, now a new

Table 2. Comparison with COSTA

	$\mathcal{O}(1)$	$\mathcal{O}(\log n)$	$\mathcal{O}(n)$	$\mathcal{O}(n \cdot \log n)$	$\mathcal{O}(n^2)$	$\mathcal{O}(n^3)$	$\mathcal{O}(n^{>3})$	?
AProVE	28	0	102	0	13	2	4	62
COSTA	10	4	45	3	5	0	1	143

entry point method with a suitable number of integer arguments is analyzed directly. However, this adaption is not always equivalent, as `main`'s argument array can be arbitrarily long (and hence can be used to simulate arbitrarily many numeric inputs), whereas the arity of the new entry point method is fixed. Thus, AProVE's results on these modified examples differ from the results on the TPDB in some cases. Table 2 compares both tools on these examples. AProVE succeeds in 149 cases, whereas COSTA proves an upper bound in 68 cases and infers a smaller bound than AProVE in 4 cases. Besides our novel size abstraction, further reasons why AProVE often yields better results are its precise symbolic execution and the use of more powerful back end tools (CoFloCo and KoAT) instead of COSTA's back end PUBS. On the other hand, COSTA can infer logarithmic bounds, which are not supported by AProVE. If instead of CoFloCo and KoAT we use COSTA's back end PUBS to analyze the ITSs generated by AProVE, then this modified version of AProVE still succeeds in 101 cases.

For more details on our experiments (including a selection of typical heap-manipulating programs where AProVE succeeds, but COSTA fails), the examples used to compare with COSTA, a web interface to access our implementation, and to download a virtual machine image of AProVE, we refer to [2].

References

1. Albert, E., Arenas, P., Genaim, S., Puebla, G., Zanardini, D.: Cost analysis of object-oriented bytecode programs. Theor. Comp. Sci. **413**(1), 142–159 (2012)
2. AProVE. https://aprove-developers.github.io/jbc-complexity/
3. Atkey, R.: Amortised resource analysis with separation logic. Logical Methods Comput. Sci. **7**(2) (2011)

---

[11] We could not adapt `Julia_10_Iterative/RSA` as its sources are missing.

4. Avanzini, M., Moser, G., Schaper, M.: TcT: Tyrolean complexity tool. In: Chechik, M., Raskin, J.-F. (eds.) TACAS 2016. LNCS, vol. 9636, pp. 407–423. Springer, Heidelberg (2016). doi:10.1007/978-3-662-49674-9_24

5. Brockschmidt, M., Otto, C., Essen, C., Giesl, J.: Termination graphs for Java Bytecode. In: Siegler, S., Wasser, N. (eds.) Verification, Induction, Termination Analysis. LNCS, vol. 6463, pp. 17–37. Springer, Heidelberg (2010). doi:10.1007/978-3-642-17172-7_2

6. Brockschmidt, M., Musiol, R., Otto, C., Giesl, J.: Automated termination proofs for Java programs with cyclic data. In: Madhusudan, P., Seshia, S.A. (eds.) CAV 2012. LNCS, vol. 7358, pp. 105–122. Springer, Heidelberg (2012). doi:10.1007/978-3-642-31424-7_13

7. Brockschmidt, M., Cook, B., Ishtiaq, S., Khlaaf, H., Piterman, N.: T2: temporal property verification. In: Chechik, M., Raskin, J.-F. (eds.) TACAS 2016. LNCS, vol. 9636, pp. 387–393. Springer, Heidelberg (2016). doi:10.1007/978-3-662-49674-9_22

8. Brockschmidt, M., Emmes, F., Falke, S., Fuhs, C., Giesl, J.: Analyzing runtime and size complexity of integer programs. ACM TOPLAS 38(4), 13:1–13:50 (2016)

9. Complexity Analysis-Based Guaranteed Execution. http://www.draper.com/news/draper-s-cage-could-spot-code-vulnerable-denial-service-attacks

10. Carbonneaux, Q., Hoffmann, J., Shao, Z.: Compositional certified resource bounds. In: Proceedings of the PLDI 2015, pp. 467–478 (2015)

11. Debray, S., Lin, N.-W.: Cost analysis of logic programs. ACM TOPLAS 15(5), 826–875 (1993)

12. Flores-Montoya, A., Hähnle, R.: Resource analysis of complex programs with cost equations. In: Garrigue, J. (ed.) APLAS 2014. LNCS, vol. 8858, pp. 275–295. Springer, Cham (2014). doi:10.1007/978-3-319-12736-1_15

13. Genaim, S., Codish, M., Gallagher, J., Lagoon, V.: Combining norms to prove termination. In: Cortesi, A. (ed.) VMCAI 2002. LNCS, vol. 2294, pp. 126–138. Springer, Heidelberg (2002). doi:10.1007/3-540-47813-2_9

14. Giesl, J., Aschermann, C., Brockschmidt, M., Emmes, F., Frohn, F., Fuhs, C., Hensel, J., Otto, C., Plücker, M., Schneider-Kamp, P., Ströder, T., Swiderski, S., Thiemann, R.: Analyzing program termination and complexity automatically with AProVE. J. Autom. Reasoning 58(1), 3–31 (2017)

15. Gulwani, S., Mehra, K.K., Chilimbi, T.M.: SPEED: precise and efficient static estimation of program computational complexity. In: Proceedings of the POPL 2009, pp. 127–139 (2009)

16. Hofbauer, D., Lautemann, C.: Termination proofs and the length of derivations. In: Dershowitz, N. (ed.) RTA 1989. LNCS, vol. 355, pp. 167–177. Springer, Heidelberg (1989). doi:10.1007/3-540-51081-8_107

17. Hoffmann, J., Das, A., Weng, S.-C.: Towards automatic resource bound analysis for OCaml. In: Proceedings of the POPL 2017, pp. 359–373 (2017)

18. Hofmann, M., Rodriguez, D.: Automatic type inference for amortised heap-space analysis. In: Felleisen, M., Gardner, P. (eds.) ESOP 2013. LNCS, vol. 7792, pp. 593–613. Springer, Heidelberg (2013). doi:10.1007/978-3-642-37036-6_32

19. Ji, R., Hähnle, R., Bubel, R.: Program transformation based on symbolic execution and deduction. In: Hierons, R.M., Merayo, M.G., Bravetti, M. (eds.) SEFM 2013. LNCS, vol. 8137, pp. 289–304. Springer, Heidelberg (2013). doi:10.1007/978-3-642-40561-7_20

20. Klein, G., Nipkow, T.: A machine-checked model for a Java-like language, virtual machine and compiler. ACM TOPLAS 28(4), 619–695 (2006)

21. Noschinski, L., Emmes, F., Giesl, J.: Analyzing innermost runtime complexity of term rewriting by dependency pairs. J. Autom. Reasoning 51(1), 27–56 (2013)

22. Otto, C., Brockschmidt, M., von Essen, C., Giesl, J.: Automated termination analysis of Java Bytecode by term rewriting. In: Proceedings of the RTA 2010, LIPIcs 6, pp. 259–276 (2010)
23. Sinn, M., Zuleger, F., Veith, H.: Complexity and resource bound analysis of imperative programs using difference constraints. J. Autom. Reasoning 59(1), 3–45 (2017)
24. Space/Time Analysis for Cybersecurity (STAC). http://www.darpa.mil/program/space-time-analysis-for-cybersecurity
25. Wilhelm, R., Engblom, J., Ermedahl, A., Holsti, N., Thesing, S., Whalley, D.B., Bernat, G., Ferdinand, C., Heckmann, R., Mitra, T., Mueller, F., Puaut, I., Puschner, P.P., Staschulat, J., Stenström, P.: The worst-case execution-time problem - overview of methods and survey of tools. ACM TECS 7(3), 36:1–36:53 (2008)

The VerCors Tool Set: Verification of Parallel and Concurrent Software

Stefan Blom, Saeed Darabi, Marieke Huisman, and Wytse Oortwijn[✉]

University of Twente, Enschede, The Netherlands
{s.c.c.blom,s.darabi,m.huisman,w.h.m.oortwijn}@utwente.nl

Abstract. This paper reports on the VerCors tool set for verifying parallel and concurrent software. Its main characteristics are *(i)* that it can verify programs under different concurrency models, written in high-level programming languages, such as for example in Java, OpenCL and OpenMP; and *(ii)* that it can reason not only about race freedom and memory safety, but also about functional correctness. VerCors builds on top of existing verification technology, notably the Viper framework, by transforming the verification problem of programs written in a high-level programming language into a verification problem in the intermediate language of Viper. This paper presents three examples that illustrate how VerCors support verifying functional correctness of three different concurrency features: heterogeneous concurrency, kernels using barriers and atomic operations, and compiler directives for parallelisation.

1 Introduction

In a parallel or concurrent program, multiple program threads proceed in parallel while they access and write to a globally shared memory. Such programs are notoriously error-prone, because the set of possible program behaviours is exponential in the programs' size, containing all possible interleavings of the atomic steps of the individual threads. As a consequence, for developers it is easy to overlook a problem that occurs in only a few of these behaviours. Moreover, systematically testing all possible program behaviours is unfeasible for most concurrent programs. Nonetheless, parallel and concurrent programming is nowadays ubiquitous due to increased performance demands as well as the vast increase in availability of multi-core hardware. Tools and techniques are therefore needed that support the developers of such software to increase its reliability.

This paper discusses recent developments of the VerCors tool set, which aims to support developers in writing reliable concurrent software. VerCors allows *practical mechanised verification under different concurrency models*; notably *heterogeneous* concurrency (e.g. Java programs) and *homogeneous* concurrency (e.g. GPU kernels). Multiple widely-used languages with parallelism and concurrency features are targeted, such as Java, OpenCL, and OpenMP for C. It allows reasoning about data race freedom, memory safety, and functional properties of (possibly non-terminating) concurrent programs. Moreover, it can handle advanced language features such as compiler directives and atomic operations.

© Springer International Publishing AG 2017
N. Polikarpova and S. Schneider (Eds.): IFM 2017, LNCS 10510, pp. 102–110, 2017.
DOI: 10.1007/978-3-319-66845-1_7

An earlier paper on the VerCors tool set has appeared in Formal Methods 2014 [5], where we showed how VerCors is used to prove data race freedom and basic functional correctness of concurrent Java [2] and OpenCL [6] programs. This paper extends on [5] and illustrates more advanced verification features of VerCors. First, we demonstrate our model-based approach to functional verification of concurrent Java programs, where an abstract model captures all concurrent behaviours of a program w.r.t. a set of shared variables [7,16]. We then use program logic-based verification to show the correspondence between the program and its abstraction, while algorithmic verification is used to reason about the abstract model. We also illustrate how VerCors is used to verify OpenCL kernels (OpenCL programs that run on GPUs) that use barriers and atomics for synchronisation [1]. Finally, programs with homogeneous threading are often constructed by developing a sequential program and adding suitable compiler directives, as is done in OpenMP. VerCors provides support to prove correctness of such compiler directives, i.e. ensuring that they will not change the functional behaviour of a program [4,10]. We also illustrate this by an example.

The VerCors tool set supports static verification in a design-by-contract fashion: programmers annotate their code and VerCors transforms verification of this annotated program into a verification problem in the intermediate verification language Silver [14]. The Viper verification technology (that works on Silver programs) is then used to verify the Silver specification with respect to its implementation. If this succeeds, we can conclude that the original program satisfies its annotations. Thus, the focus of VerCors is not so much on developing new verification technology, but rather on making existing verification technology usable for realistic programming languages and advanced language features. The specification language builds on *permission-based separation logic (PBSL)* [2,8], an extension of Hoare logic that explicitly considers where an object is stored in memory, which enables thread-modular verification of concurrent programs.

Section 2 provides a quick description of the tool architecture, focusing on its extendability. Section 3 discusses several examples to illustrate advanced features supported by VerCors. Section 4 concludes with a discussion of related and future work, and gives information about how to try VerCors yourself.

2   The VerCors Architecture

Our main goal is to make existing program verification technology usable for high-level programming languages and advanced language features. This is reflected in the design of VerCors, which is implemented as a collection of compiler transformations and uses the existing Viper technology as back-end [14], see Fig. 1. Viper supports the intermediate verification language Silver, which allows reasoning about programs with persistent mutable state, annotated with separation logic-style specifications. The compiler transformations are used to transform different high-level language/concurrency features into Silver code. The Viper technology provides two styles of reasoning: verification condition generation (via Boogie), and symbolic execution. The symbolic execution engine

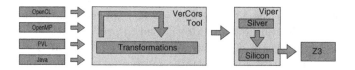

Fig. 1. The architecture of the VerCors tool set.

is the most powerful and provides support for e.g. quantified permissions, which we heavily rely upon. In earlier versions of VerCors, Chalice [13] was used as the main back-end, but its functionality is subsumed by Viper.

VerCors takes as input a program in a high-level programming language, annotated with JML-style specifications, and transforms this into verification problems encoded in Silver. The current input languages are Java, PVL, OpenCL, and OpenMP for C; it supports reasoning about the main concurrency-related features of these languages. The support for OpenCL covers only the verification of kernels, including barrier synchronisation and atomic operations, but not host code (which would mostly require engineering). PVL is a Java-like procedural toy language used for quick prototyping of new verification features. Notably, it has support for kernels and hostcode. VerCors also supports a substantial subset of OpenMP, essentially characterising deterministic parallel programming. The annotation language of VerCors is the same across all supported languages.

VerCors can easily be extended with new parallel or concurrent pointer languages, by providing a parser that transforms input programs and their specifications into the *intermediate language* of VerCors. All further program transformations are defined over the intermediate language of VerCors, thereby automatically providing verification support for the features of the extended language.

3   Verification Highlights

This section discusses three verification examples to illustrate the most interesting features supported by VerCors. For clarity of presentation the example annotations are somewhat simplified; the full, verifiable programs are available at http://www.utwente.nl/vercors. Also a detailed list of case studies and verified example programs is available, together with statistics about performance and required amounts of specification code relative to program code.

Model-Based Verification. In the context of heterogeneous threading, verification of functional properties is a major challenge and requires suitable abstractions. Our model-based verification technique captures the behaviour of a shared memory concurrent program by means of a *process algebra term with data* [7,16]. All accesses to the relevant shared memory locations are abstracted by *actions*. The process algebra term specifies the legal sequences of actions that are allowed to occur, and the program logic is used to verify that the process algebra term is indeed a correct program abstraction. Functional properties about the program can then be verified by reasoning algorithmically on the process algebra term.

We illustrate this on the parallel GCD challenge from the VerifyThis 2015 program verification competition [11]. The standard sequential Euclidean algorithm is described as a function **gcd** which, given two positive integers a and b, $\mathsf{gcd}(a, a) = a$, $\mathsf{gcd}(a, b) = \mathsf{gcd}(a - b, a)$ if $a > b$, and $\mathsf{gcd}(a, b) = \mathsf{gcd}(a, b - a)$ if $b > a$. The parallel version we consider uses two concurrent threads: one thread to repeatedly decrease a when $a > b$, and one thread to repeatedly decrease the value of b when $b > a$. This process continues until a and b converge to $\mathsf{gcd}(a, b)$.

```
1  int x, y;
2
3  guard y > 0 ∧ x > y; effect x = old(x) − old(y); action decrX();
4  guard x > 0 ∧ y > x; effect y = old(y) − old(x); action decrY();
5  guard x = y; action done();
6
7  requires x > 0 ∧ y > 0;
8  ensures x = y ∧ y = gcd(old(x), old(y));
9  process pargcd() := tx() ∥ ty();
10
11 process tx() := decrX() · tx() + done();
12 process ty() := decrY() · ty() + done();
```

Fig. 2. The process algebraic description of the gcd algorithm.

To prove that the parallel algorithm computes $\mathsf{gcd}(a, b)$ we first model **gcd** as a process algebra term, named **pargcd**, by using two actions, named **decrX** and **decrY**. The **decrX** action corresponds to the assignment $x := x - y$ in the program code, and **decrY** corresponds to $y := y - x$. Action behaviour is defined in terms of *guard* and *effect* clauses, which logically describe the (guarded, conditional) effects of an action on the shared memory. A third action **done** indicates termination of the process term. Figure 2 shows the abstract model.

We use existing process-algebraic reasoning techniques to analyse the process **pargcd**: by giving any two positive integers as input, their **gcd** has been found when the action **done** has been performed. This is currently done by translating the analysis into an SMT problem, by encoding it into Silver. Finally, we prove the connection between **pargcd** and the concrete program code, presented in Fig. 3. In future work we plan to analyse the processes via the mCRL2 toolset.

The `calcgcd` function creates a new *model* named m via the invocation on line 4. The model m is *split* along the parallel composition tx() ∥ ty() on line 5 to match the forking of the two program threads T_0 and T_1 (where the body of thread T_1 is omitted for brevity). The thread T_0 requires that part of the model that executes the process term tx(); the thread T_1 requires the term ty(). The connection between program execution and process execution is made via action

```
1   requires x > 0 ∧ y > 0;
2   ensures \result = gcd(a, b);
3   int calcgcd(int a, int b) {
4      model m := pargcd() with [x := a, y := b];
5      split m into (½, tx()) and (½, ty());
6      invariant inv(m.x ↪₁ₚ v * m.y ↪₁ₚ w * v > 0 * w > 0) {
7         requires Proc(m, ½, tx()); ensures Proc(m, ½, ε);
8         par T₀() {
9            bool run := true;
10           loop-invariant run ? Proc(m, ½, tx()) : Proc(m, ½, ε);
11           while (run) {
12              atomic (inv) {
13                 if (m.x > m.y) action decrX() { m.x := m.x − m.y; };
14                 if (m.x = m.y) action done() { run := false; };
15           } } }
16           requires Proc(m, ½, ty()); ensures Proc(m, ½, ε);
17           and par T₁ { ⋯ }
18        }
19        merge (m, ½, ε) and (m, ½, ε); finish m;
20        return m.x;
21   }
```

Fig. 3. The annotated implementation of the parallel GCD algorithm.

annotations in the code. To this end, the actions decrX, decrY, and done are linked to concrete statements in the language via **action** blocks. Correctness of the connection is shown by applying the rules of our extended separation logic.

GPU Kernels and Atomics. VerCors supports verifying race freedom and functional correctness of GPU kernels that use atomic operations and barriers [1,6]. In a GPU kernel, threads are organised in workgroups, which consist of multiple threads. Threads within a workgroup can synchronise by means of a barrier; threads in different workgroups can only synchronise using atomic operations.

The VerCors tool set supports a kernel-specific version of PBSL; kernels are specified with the permissions available for them, in addition to their functional behaviour contract. The available permissions are distributed over the different workgroups, which in turn are specified with a permission distribution for its threads. We verify that these permission distributions are correct, meaning that kernels and workgroups do not distribute more permissions than are available. When threads within a workgroup synchronise on a barrier, they may redistribute permissions and exchange knowledge about their thread-local state.

We illustrate this approach on a kernel that calculates the sum of the elements of an array. The PVL encoding of this kernel is shown in Fig. 4 (the clause **context** P abbreviates **requires** P; **ensures** P). This example shows how race

```
1  invariant A ≠ null ∧ m > 0 ∧ n > 0;
2  context Perm(result, write) * (\forall int i;  0 ≤ i < m * n;  Perm(A[i], read);
3  requires result = 0;
4  int calculate-sum(int m, int n, int[m*n] A) {
5    invariant outer(Perm(result, write)) {
6      par kernel(int gid ∈ [0, . . . , m))
7      context (\forall int i;  0 ≤ i < n;  Perm(A[gid*n+i], read); {
8      int[1] temp := new int[1] { 0 };
9      invariant inner(\array(temp, 1) * Perm(temp[0], write)) {
10       par workgroup(int tid ∈ [0, . . . , n))
11       requires Perm(A[gid*n+tid], read);
12       ensures tid = 0 ⇒ (\forall int i;  0 ≤ i < n;  Perm(A[gid*n+i], read)); {
13       atomic(inner) { temp[0] := temp[0] + ar[gid*n +tid]; }
14       barrier (workgroup) {
15         requires Perm(A[gid*n+tid], read);
16         ensures tid = 0 ⇒ (\forall int i; 0 ≤ i < n; Perm(A[gid*n+i], read)); }
17       if (tid = 0) {
18       int tmp; atomic(inner) { tmp := temp[0]; }
19       atomic(outer) { result := result + tmp; }
20  } · · · }
```

Fig. 4. Summing up the elements of the input array A.

freedom of kernels with barriers and atomics is verified, the interested reader can see the functional specification in [1]. The program uses two nested parallel blocks: the outer **par**-block resembles kernel execution, and the inner **par**-block resembles workgroup execution. First, each workgroup atomically adds the values in its part of the input array A to a *local* memory buffer *temp*. After writing to *temp*, each thread enters a barrier. After leaving the barrier, the first thread of each workgroup adds the local sum (stored in *temp*) to the *global* result. Each parallel block has a contract, denoting the requirements and the contributions of the workgroups and threads, respectively. In particular, each workgroup requires permission to read its share of A and each thread in a workgroup requires read permission to one entry of A. In the barrier, the read permission of each thread is transferred to the first thread in the workgroup.

To make the algorithm correct, addition to the shared intermediate result must be performed atomically (on line 20). In PVL this is expressed by putting the addition in an atomic block. Reasoning about atomic operations is an adaptation of the classical verification technique for atomic operations [15, 19]. The specification language supports kernel and group invariants, which capture the behaviour of the atomic operations accessing the shared locations.

Deterministic Parallelism. Parallel programs are commonly written by using compiler directives, like done in OpenMP [17]. Compiler directives indicate code that may be executed in parallel, so that the compiler can generate parallelised

```
1  given seq⟨seq⟨int⟩⟩ data;
2  invariant m > 0 ∧ n > 0 ∧ p > 0 ∧ \matrix(M, m, n) ∧ \array(H, p);
3  context (\forall int i ∈ [0..m), j ∈ [0..n); Perm(M[i][j], read));
4  context (\forall int i ∈ [0..m), j ∈ [0..n); M[i][j] = data[i][j] ∧ 0 ≤ M[i][j] < p);
5  context (\forall int i ∈ [0..p); Perm(H[i], write));
6  ensures (\forall int k ∈ [0..p); H[k] = (\count int i ∈ [0..m), j ∈ [0..n); data[i][j] = k));
7  void histogram(int m, int n, int[m][n] M, int p, int[p] H) {
8    for (int k := 0; k < p; k++)  context Perm(H[k], write); ensures H[k] = 0;
9    { H[k] := 0; }
10   for (int i := 0; i < m; i++)
11     requires (\forall int k ∈ [0..p); Reducible(H[k], +));
12     context Perm(M[i][j], read) * 0 ≤ M[i][j] < p * M[i][j] = data[i][j];
13     ensures (\forall int k ∈ [0..p); Contribution(H[k], data[i][j] = k ? 1 : 0)); {
14       for (int j := 0; j < n; j++) { H[M[i][j]] += 1; } } }
```

Fig. 5. The implementation of the histogram example, written in C.

code. VerCors provides support to prove that these compiler directives do not change the meaning of the program, meaning that functional correctness of the original program implies functional correctness of the parallelised program.

We illustrate this by means of a `histogram` example, see Fig. 5, which outputs an array H such that $H[k]$ contains the number of occurrences of the integer k in the input matrix M. We use VerCors to show that the **for**-loops can be parallelised without changing the functional program behaviour. We do this by specifying an *iteration contract* [4], which denotes the pre- and postcondition for each iteration of the loop. The iteration contract of the first loop expresses that each iteration k requires writing permission for $H[k]$ and sets $H[k]$ to zero. From the iteration contract we can derive that each loop iteration is independent, and thus that the loop can be parallelised without changing its functional behaviour. In a similar way, also for the second loop the iteration contract is used to capture independence of the iterations. The specification language provides extra annotations to deal with several typical scenarios; in this case, the Reducible and Contributes predicates are used to denote the reduction pattern.

4 Conclusion and Related Work

This paper gives a concise overview of the most interesting features of the VerCors toolset for verifying concurrent software. For more verification examples, statistical information, an indication of supported features, and for trying out the verification technology yourself, we refer to http://utwente.nl/vercors.

The VerCors tool set is currently used for teaching, as part of an advanced Master-level course on program verification. In addition, we also have several students working individually on interesting verification case studies, for example verifying the correctness of a parallel prefix sum implementation. Having non-developers of VerCors use the tool has been very useful to improve the maturity of the tool, to understand how people use the tool, and to see which features could be improved further. We are working on the development of a regression test suite, containing examples that *should* and that *should not* verify, which is automatically evaluated whenever the tool is updated. One particular challenge that we encountered is that we depend on the Viper framework, which is also still under development. Therefore, sometimes bug fixes for VerCors depend on Viper updates, and good communication with the group behind Viper is essential.

There exist several other tools for the verification of concurrent software, such as VeriFast [12] (for concurrent C and Java programs), VCC [9] (for C programs), Chalice [13] (for a concurrent toy language, not maintained anymore), Cave [18] (proving memory safety and linearizability), and GPUVerify [3] (automatic data race detection of GPU Kernels). The main distinguishing feature of the VerCors tool set is that it generalises the verification of concurrent software to a language-independent setting, where new front-ends can be added easily.

There are many directions we plan to explore to further increase usability of VerCors. We are currently investigating how our model-based verification technique can be used to reason about distributed software, focusing in particular on message passing. To improve scalability of the verification process we plan to experiment with different techniques for annotation generation and to generate meaningful error messages. Ultimately, our goal is to support complete programming languages, not just subsets. Since this is a large engineering effort, we hope to reuse existing verification technology as much as possible.

Acknowledgements. The work in this paper is partially supported by the ERC grant 258405 for the VerCors project, by the EU FP7 STREP 287767 project CARP, and by the NWO TOP 612.001.403 project VerDi.

References

1. Amighi, A., Darabi, S., Blom, S., Huisman, M.: Specification and verification of atomic operations in GPGPU programs. In: Calinescu, R., Rumpe, B. (eds.) SEFM 2015. LNCS, vol. 9276, pp. 69–83. Springer, Cham (2015). doi:10.1007/978-3-319-22969-0_5
2. Amighi, A., Haack, C., Huisman, M., Hurlin, C.: Permission-based separation logic for multithreaded Java programs. LMCS **11**(1) (2015)
3. Betts, A., Chong, N., Donaldson, A., Qadeer, S., Thomson, P.: GPUVerify: a verifier for GPU kernels. In: OOPSLA, pp. 113–132. ACM (2012)
4. Blom, S., Darabi, S., Huisman, M.: Verification of loop parallelisations. In: Egyed, A., Schaefer, I. (eds.) FASE 2015. LNCS, vol. 9033, pp. 202–217. Springer, Heidelberg (2015). doi:10.1007/978-3-662-46675-9_14
5. Blom, S., Huisman, M.: The VerCors Tool for verification of concurrent programs. In: Jones, C., Pihlajasaari, P., Sun, J. (eds.) FM 2014. LNCS, vol. 8442, pp. 127–131. Springer, Cham (2014). doi:10.1007/978-3-319-06410-9_9
6. Blom, S., Huisman, M., Mihelčić, M.: Specification and Verification of GPGPU programs. Sci. Comput. Program. **95**, 376–388 (2014)
7. Blom, S., Huisman, M., Zaharieva-Stojanovski, M.: History-based verification of functional behaviour of concurrent programs. In: Calinescu, R., Rumpe, B. (eds.) SEFM 2015. LNCS, vol. 9276, pp. 84–98. Springer, Cham (2015). doi:10.1007/978-3-319-22969-0_6

8. Bornat, R., Calcagno, C., O'Hearn, P.W., Parkinson, M.J.: Permission accounting in separation logic. In: POPL, pp. 259–270 (2005)

9. Cohen, E., Dahlweid, M., Hillebrand, M., Leinenbach, D., Moskal, M., Santen, T., Schulte, W., Tobies, S.: VCC: a practical system for verifying concurrent C. In: Berghofer, S., Nipkow, T., Urban, C., Wenzel, M. (eds.) TPHOLs 2009. LNCS, vol. 5674, pp. 23–42. Springer, Heidelberg (2009). doi:10.1007/978-3-642-03359-9_2

10. Darabi, S., Blom, S.C.C., Huisman, M.: A verification technique for deterministic parallel programs. In: Barrett, C., Davies, M., Kahsai, T. (eds.) NFM 2017. LNCS, vol. 10227, pp. 247–264. Springer, Cham (2017). doi:10.1007/978-3-319-57288-8_17

11. Huisman, M., Klebanov, V., Monahan, R., Tautschnig, M.: VerifyThis 2015: a program verification competition. Int. J. Softw. Tools Technol. Transfer (2016)

12. Jacobs, B., Smans, J., Philippaerts, P., Vogels, F., Penninckx, W., Piessens, F.: VeriFast: a powerful, sound, predictable, fast verifier for C and Java. In: Bobaru, M., Havelund, K., Holzmann, G.J., Joshi, R. (eds.) NFM 2011. LNCS, vol. 6617, pp. 41–55. Springer, Heidelberg (2011). doi:10.1007/978-3-642-20398-5_4

13. Leino, K.R.M., Müller, P., Smans, J.: Verification of concurrent programs with chalice. In: Aldini, A., Barthe, G., Gorrieri, R. (eds.) FOSAD 2007-2009. LNCS, vol. 5705, pp. 195–222. Springer, Heidelberg (2009). doi:10.1007/978-3-642-03829-7_7

14. Müller, P., Schwerhoff, M., Summers, A.J.: Viper: a verification infrastructure for permission-based reasoning. In: Jobstmann, B., Leino, K.R.M. (eds.) VMCAI 2016. LNCS, vol. 9583, pp. 41–62. Springer, Heidelberg (2016). doi:10.1007/978-3-662-49122-5_2

15. O'Hearn, P.W.: Resources, concurrency and local reasoning. Theoret. Comput. Sci. **375**(1–3), 271–307 (2007)

16. Oortwijn, W., Blom, S., Gurov, D., Huisman, M., Zaharieva-Stojanovski, M.: An abstraction technique for describing concurrent program behaviour. In: VSTTE (2017, to appear)

17. OpenMP Architecture Review Board, OpenMP API Specification for Parallel Programming. http://openmp.org/wp/. Accessed 18 Oct 2016

18. Vafeiadis, V.: Automatically proving linearizability. In: Touili, T., Cook, B., Jackson, P. (eds.) CAV 2010. LNCS, vol. 6174, pp. 450–464. Springer, Heidelberg (2010). doi:10.1007/978-3-642-14295-6_40

19. Vafeiadis, V.: Concurrent separation logic and operational semantics. In: MFPS. ENTCS, vol. 276, pp. 335–351 (2011)

An Extension of the ABS Toolchain
with a Mechanism for Type Checking SPLs

Ferruccio Damiani[1(✉)], Michael Lienhardt[1], Radu Muschevici[2],
and Ina Schaefer[3]

[1] University of Torino, Torino, Italy
{ferruccio.damiani,michael.lienhardt}@unito.it
[2] Technische Universität Darmstadt, Darmstadt, Germany
radu@cs.tu-darmstadt.de
[3] Technische Universität Braunschweig, Braunschweig, Germany
i.schaefer@tu-braunschweig.de

Abstract. A Software Product Line (SPL) is a set of similar programs, called variants, with a common code base and well documented variability. Because the number of variants in an SPL can be large, checking them efficiently (e.g., to ensure that they are all well-typed) is a challenging problem. Delta-Oriented Programming (DOP) is a flexible approach to implement SPLs. The Abstract Behavioral Specification (ABS) modeling language and toolchain supports delta-oriented SPLs. In this paper we present an extension of the ABS toolchain with a mechanism for checking that all the variants of an SPL can be generated and are well-typed ABS programs. Currently we have implemented only part of this mechanism: our implementation (integrated in version 1.4.2 of the ABS toolchain and released in April 2017) checks whether all variants can be generated, however it does not check, in particular, whether the bodies of the methods are well-typed. Empirical evaluation shows that the current implementation allows for efficient partial type checking of existing ABS SPLs.

1 Introduction

Recent fundamental changes of deployment platforms (cloud, multi-core) together with the emergence of cyber-physical systems and the internet of things imply that modern software must support variability [22] and emphasize the need for modeling languages capturing system diversity.

The *Abstract Behavioral Specification* (ABS) [7] modeling language and toolchain has been designed to fill the gap between structural high-level modeling

This work has been partially supported by: EU Horizon 2020 project HyVar (www.hyvar-project.eu), GA No. 644298; ICT COST Action IC1402 ARVI (www.cost-arvi.eu); Ateneo/CSP D16D15000360005 project RunVar (runvar-project.di.unito.it); LOEWE initiative to increase research excellence in the state of Hesse, Germany as part of the LOEWE Schwerpunkt CompuGene.

© Springer International Publishing AG 2017
N. Polikarpova and S. Schneider (Eds.): IFM 2017, LNCS 10510, pp. 111–126, 2017.
DOI: 10.1007/978-3-319-66845-1_8

languages (e.g., UML) and implementation-close formalisms (including programming languages such as C/C++, C#, or Java). It facilitates the precise modelling of the behaviour of highly configurable distributed systems, and has been successfully used in industry [1,17,19].

Figure 1 illustrates the different languages comprised in ABS. The basis, *Core ABS*, is a strongly typed, abstract, object-oriented, concurrent, fully executable modeling language. The other three languages support the implementation of delta-oriented *Software Product Lines* (SPLs) of Core ABS programs.

Language	Role
Core ABS	Specifies base behavioural models
Micro Textual Variability Language Feature (μTVL)	Feature models
Delta Modelling Language (DML)	Modifications to base behavioural models
Product Line Configuration Language (CL)	Links features and delta modules, configures deltas with attributes

Fig. 1. Language definitions in ABS

An SPL is a set of similar programs, called *variants*, with a common code base and well documented variability [8]. *Delta-Oriented Programming* (DOP [2, Sect. 6.6.1] and [5,21]) is a flexible and modular approach to implement SPLs. A delta-oriented SPL comprises a *feature model*, an *artifact base*, and *configuration knowledge*. The feature model provides an abstract description of variants in terms of *features*: each feature represents an abstract description of functionality and each variant is identified by a set of features, called a *product*. The artifact base provides language dependent artifacts that are used to build the variants: it consists of a *base program* (written in the same language in which variants are written) and of a set of *delta modules* (*deltas* for short), which are containers of modifications to a program—for Core ABS programs, a delta can add, remove or modify classes, interfaces, fields and methods. Configuration knowledge connects the feature model with the artifact base by associating with each delta an *activation condition* over the features and specifying an *application ordering* between deltas. Once a user selects a product, the corresponding variant is derived by applying the deltas with a satisfied activation condition to the base program according to the application ordering. To avoid over-specification the application ordering can be partial—this opens the issue of ensuring *unambiguity* of the product line, i.e., for each product, any total ordering of the activated deltas that respects the partial ordering must generate the same variant.

With respect to the languages in Fig. 1: Core ABS is for writing base programs; μTVL is for feature models; DML is for deltas; and CL is for configuration knowledge.

As the number of variants in an SPL can be large, checking them efficiently (e.g., to ensure that they are all well-typed) is a challenging problem. Until the release of version 1.4.2 in April 2017, the ABS toolchain[1] did not officially

---

[1] ABS language & tools: http://abs-models.org/.

provide any dedicated support for checking that an SPL is unambiguous (cf. the discussion above) and for *type checking an SPL* (i.e., to ensure that all its variants are generable[2] and well-typed).[3] In order to type check an SPL developers had to generate all its variants and type check each of them in isolation using the Core ABS type checker. Evaluation of ABS against industrial requirements [13,16] repeatedly identified lack of tool support for SPL unambiguity checking and SPL type checking as a major usability issue.

In this paper we present an extension of the ABS toolchain with an *SPL unambiguity and type checking mechanism* (*SPL checking mechanism*, for short). This mechanism is an adaptation to ABS of an approach formalized for IMPERATIVE FEATHERWEIGHT DELTA JAVA (IFΔJ) [5,12], a minimal core calculus for delta-oriented SPLs where variants are written in IFJ [5], an imperative version of FJ [18]. Currently we have implemented only part of the checking mechanism: our implementation checks whether the SPL is unambiguous and whether all variants can be generated, however it does not check, in particular, whether the bodies of the methods are well-typed.

Empirical evaluation shows that the extended toolchain allows for efficient partial checking of existing ABS product lines, providing a significant performance increase with respect to generating and fully type checking each variant in isolation using the Core ABS type checker. This result raises our confidence that the (currently under development) implementation of the full SPL checking mechanism will remain similarly performant.

The paper is organized as follows. In Sect. 2 we provide an overview of ABS and recall its minimal fragment FDABS [9]. In Sect. 3 we illustrate the SPL checking mechanism by means of FDABS. In Sect. 4 we present the implementation of part of the SPL checking mechanism for the complete ABS language and its integration in the ABS toolchain. In Sect. 5 we show how the extended ABS toolchain is applied to check two SPLs developed in two different industrial modeling scenarios. In Sect. 6 we discuss related work and conclude in Sect. 7.

2 FDABS: A Minimal Language for Core ABS and Deltas

In this section we provide an overview of ABS product lines and of the FEATHERWEIGHT DELTA ABS (FDABS) [9] language, the minimal fragment of ABS used in Sect. 3 to illustrate the SPL checking mechanism.

---

[2] The generation of a variant fails whenever the application of an activated delta fails. The application of a DML delta to a Core ABS program fails, e.g., if the delta tries to add a class that is already present in the program, or tries to remove or modify a class that is not present in the program.

[3] The development of the SPL checking mechanism described in this paper started in 2015 and a prototypical version has been made available since June 2015.

We illustrate ABS product lines by means of a version of the *Expression Product Line* (EPL) benchmark [20] (see also [5]) defined by the following grammar which describes a language of numerical expressions:

Exp ::= Lit | Add   Lit ::= <non−negative−integers>   Add ::= Exp "+" Exp

Each variant of the EPL contains an interface `Exp` that represents an expression equipped with a subset of the following operations: `eval`, which returns the value of the expression as an integer; and `toString`, which returns the expression as a `String`.

Figure 2 shows the feature model of the EPL depicted as a feature diagram. The EPL has four products, described by four features: the mandatory features `Flit` and `Feval` correspond to the presence of literal expression (i.e., numbers) and the `eval` method, respectively; the optional features `Fadd` and `Fprint` provide the `Add` class (for sum expression) and the `toString` method, respectively.

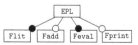

Fig. 2. EPL feature model

// Feature model (written in μTVL)	// Configuration knowledge (written in CL)
productline EPL;	delta Dadd when Fadd;
features Flit , Fadd, Feval, Fprint;	delta Dlit_NOprint when !Fprint;
root EPL { group allof {	delta Dadd_NOprint after Dadd
Flit , opt Fadd, Feval, opt Fprint }}	when Fadd && !Fprint;

```
 1  // Base program (written in the FABS      17  // Deltas (written in the FDML subset of DML)
 2  // subset of Core ABS)                     18  delta Dadd;
 3  interface Exp {                            19  adds class Add implements Exp {
 4    Int eval();                              20    Exp a;      Exp b;
 5    String toString();                       21    Exp set(Exp a, Exp b) { this.a=a; this.b=b; return this;}
 6  }                                          22    Int eval() { return this.a.eval() + this.b.eval(); }
 7  class Lit implements Exp {                 23    String toString() {
 8    Int val;                                 24      return this.a.toString() + "+" + this.b.toString(); }
 9    Exp set(Int x) {                         25  }
10      this.val=x; return this;               26
11    }                                        27  delta Dlit_NOprint;
12    Int eval() { return this.val; }          28  modifies interface Exp { removes toString; }
13    String toString() {                      29  modifies class Lit { removes toString; }
14      return this.val.toString();            30
15    }                                        31  delta Dadd_NOprint;
16  }                                          32  modifies class Add { removes toString; }
```

Fig. 3. ABS code for the EPL: feature model (top left, cf. the graphical representation in Fig. 2); configuration knowledge (top right); and artifact base (bottom)

Figure 3 illustrates the ABS code implementing the EPL. Configuration knowledge (Fig. 3, top right) lists the names of the deltas and specifies when and how each delta must be applied to generate a given variant: the **when** clause declares the activation condition of a delta, while the **after** clauses specify the application ordering between deltas (cf. the description of DOP in Sect. 1). The artifact base comprises the base program and three deltas. The base program (Fig. 3, bottom left) declares the interface `Exp` and the class `Lit` (for literals)— note that both `Exp` and `Lit` declare the `toString` method. The delta `Dadd` (activated when feature `Fadd` is selected) adds the `Add` class for sum expression, with the methods `eval` and `toString`. The delta `Dlit_NOprint` (activated when feature `Fprint` is not selected) removes the `toString` method from the `Exp` interface and `Lit` class, while the delta `Dadd_NOprint` removes it from the `Add` class.

The abstract syntax of FDABS is given in Fig. 4. An FDABS product line L, see Fig. 4 (top left), consists of: a feature model $\mathcal{M}$, configuration knowledge $\mathcal{K}$, a base program P, and a (possibly empty) set $\overline{\Delta}$ of deltas—following Igarashi et al. [18], $\overline{X}$ denotes a finite (possibly empty) sequence of syntactic elements of kind X, and the empty sequence is denoted by $\emptyset$. In FDABS there is no syntax for feature models and configuration knowledge.

$L ::= \mathcal{M}\ \mathcal{K}\ P\ \overline{\Delta}$	$\Delta\ \ ::= \texttt{delta d;}\ \overline{IO}\ \overline{CO}$
	$IO\ ::= \texttt{adds}\ ID\ \mid\ \texttt{removes I;}\ \mid\ \texttt{modifies I [extends }\overline{\texttt{I}}\texttt{] \{ }\overline{HO}\texttt{ \}}$
	$HO\ ::= \texttt{adds}\ HD;\ \mid\ \texttt{removes m;}$
	$CO\ ::= \texttt{adds}\ CD\ \mid\ \texttt{removes C;}\ \mid\ \texttt{modifies C [implements }\overline{\texttt{I}}\texttt{] \{ }\overline{AO}\texttt{ \}}$
	$AO\ ::= \texttt{adds}\ FD\ \mid\ \texttt{removes f;}\ \mid\ \texttt{adds}\ MD\ \mid\ \texttt{removes m;}\ \mid\ \texttt{modifies}\ MD$
$P ::= \overline{ID}\ \overline{CD}$	$ID\ ::= \texttt{interface I [extends }\overline{\texttt{I}}\texttt{] \{ }\overline{HD;}\texttt{ \}}$ $AD ::= FD\ \mid\ MD$
	$CD ::= \texttt{class C [implements }\overline{\texttt{I}}\texttt{] \{ }\overline{AD}\texttt{ \}}$ $FD\ ::= \texttt{I f;}$
	$HD ::= \texttt{I m(}\overline{\texttt{I x}}\texttt{)}$ $MD ::= HD\ \texttt{\{ }\overline{s}\ \texttt{return e; \}}$

Fig. 4. Syntax of FDABS (top left), FDML (top right) and FABS (bottom)

The language for base programs, FEATHERWEIGHT CORE ABS (FABS), is given in Fig. 4 (bottom). The non-terminal P represents programs, ID interface declarations, CD class declarations, HD method headers, AD attribute declarations, FD field declarations, MD method declarations, e expressions, and s statements. To save space, we do not specify expression and statement syntax.

The language for deltas, FEATHERWEIGHT DML (FDML), is given in Fig. 4 (top right). A delta Δ comprises a name d and a set of operations IO on interfaces and operations CO on classes. These operations can add or remove interfaces and classes, or modify their content by adding or removing attributes. Moreover, these operations can also change the set of interfaces implemented by a class or extended by an interface by means of an optional `implements` or `extends` clause in the `modifies` operation, respectively. Finally, it is also possible to *modify* the body of a method with the `modifies` operation, where the new method may call the original implementation of the method using the keyword `original`.

3   The Checking Mechanism for FDABS Product Lines

SPL analysis approaches can be classified into three main categories [25]: *product-based* analyses work only on generated variants (or models of variants); *family-based* analyses work on the artifact base, without generating any variant or model of variant, by exploiting feature model and configuration knowledge to derive results about all variants; *feature-based* analyses work on the reusable artifacts in the artifact base (base program and deltas in DOP) in isolation, without using feature model and configuration knowledge, to derive results on all variants.

In this section we outline how the SPL unambiguity and type checking mechanism formalized for IFΔJ by Bettini et al. [5,12], can be reformulated for FABS. The type checking mechanism comprises three steps: (i) a feature-based analysis step that extracts suitable constraints from the base program and the deltas; (ii) a family-based step that builds a data structure, called the *product family generation trie* (PFGT) of the SPL, that is exploited (in the next step) to optimize generation and check of the constraints; and (iii) a product-based step that uses the constraints extracted in the first step to generate and check, for each product of the SPL, constraints that are satisfiable if and only if the associated variant is well-typed.

3.1 Unambiguity Checking

In the formalization of DOP by Bettini et al. [5,12] the application ordering is specified by providing a totally ordered partition of the set of the deltas, which is interpreted as defining the partial ordering such that: *two deltas in the same set are not comparable, and two deltas in different sets are ordered according to the partition ordering*. Bettini et al. [5] pointed out that, if the application ordering is specified (as described above) by a totally ordered partition of the deltas, then unambiguity of the SPL is implied by a stronger condition, called *strong unambiguity*, which states that: (i) if a delta in a set of the partition adds or removes a class/interface then no other delta in the same set adds, removes or modifies the same class/interface; and (ii) the modifications of the same class/interface in different deltas in a same set are disjoint (i.e., there is at most one delta operation for each field, method, implements clause, method header, and extends clause). They also pointed out that strong unambiguity can be efficiently checked by only analyzing the *delta signature table* (DST) of a product line, which is a table that has an entry for each delta declared in the artifact base: it associates with each delta name a data structure, called *delta signature*, containing the information provided by the delta deprived of the bodies of its methods.

The ABS toolchain uses the after clauses (cf. Sect. 2) to compute a totally ordered partition of the set of deltas, that we call the *canonical partition*, which in turn defines the application ordering as described above—we call it the *canonical application ordering*. Therefore, we can directly exploit the result on strong unambiguity [5]. The canonical partition is computed by: building the after graph (i.e., a direct graph where the nodes are the names D of the deltas, and there is an edge from D_1 to D_2 iff there is a clause D_2 after D_1); checking whether the after graph is acyclic; computing for each delta the length l of the longest path from a source node in the after graph; and putting in the same set all the deltas that have the same l.

3.2 Type Checking Step (i): Extracting Constraints

The constraints extracted from a FABS program, called *program constraints*, encode its typing requirements. Figure 5 lists the constraints extracted from method bodies (i.e., from expressions and statements). These constraints are associated with the corresponding method

class(C)	*class* C *must be defined*
interface(I)	*interface* I *must be defined*
subtype(C, I)	C *must implement (directly or not)* I
subtype(I, I′)	I *must extend (directly or not)* I′
field(C, f, I)	C *must have field* f *of type* I
meth(C, m, $\bar{\text{I}}$ → I′)	C *must have method* m *of type* $\bar{\text{I}}$ → I′
meth(I, m, $\bar{\text{I}}$ → I′)	I *must have method* m *of type* $\bar{\text{I}}$ → I′

Fig. 5. Constraints for expressions and statements

and class via with clauses. Consider, for instance, the base program in Fig. 3. The method set (line 9) of class Lit has return type Exp. It updates the field val with the variable x of type Int, and returns this. Therefore *in class* Lit *the body of method* set *requires that field* val *must exist and be of type* Int, *and class* Lit *must implement (either directly or indirectly) interface* Exp. This requirement is encoded by the constraint:

$$\text{Lit with } \{\text{set with } \{\text{field}(\text{Lit}, \text{val}, \text{Int}), \text{subtype}(\text{Lit}, \text{Exp})\}\}$$

Program constraints can be straightforwardly checked against the *signature* of the corresponding program, which is a data structure containing the information provided by the program deprived of the bodies of its methods.

The constraints extracted from a delta, called *delta constraints*, contain delta operations on program constraints. Consider the deltas in Fig. 3. The delta Dadd in line 18 *adds the* Add *class*. This is encoded by the constraint:

$$\text{adds}(\text{Add with } \mathbf{C}) \tag{1}$$

where $\mathbf{C}$ are the constraints extracted from the body of the class Add. They also contain the following constraint:

$$\text{toString with } \{\text{meth}(\text{Exp}, \text{toString}, \emptyset \to \text{String})\} \tag{2}$$

stating that *body of method* toString *requires that method* toString *of type* $\emptyset \to$ String *must be defined in interface* Exp. The delta Dadd_NOprint in line 27 *removes the method* toString *from the class* Add, this is encoded by the constraint:

$$\text{modifies}(\text{Add with } \{\text{removes}(\text{toString})\}) \tag{3}$$

The *abstraction* of a program consists of its signature and constraints. The *delta abstraction table* (DAT) maps each delta name to a data structure that contains the signature and the constraints of the delta. For each product, the abstraction of the corresponding variant (recall that a variant is a FABS program) can be straightforwardly generated from the abstraction of the base program and the DAT: the signature of the variant is generated by applying the signatures of the activated deltas to the signature of the base program; and the constraints of the variant are generated by applying the constraints of the activated deltas to the constraints of the base program. Therefore, each variant can be type checked, without being generated, by generating and checking its abstraction (i.e., by checking its constraints against its signature). For instance, consider the product {Flit, Fadd} of the EPL (in Fig. 3): the deltas Dadd, Dlit_NOprint and Dadd_NOprint are activated and the constraints extracted from them are applied to the constraints extracted from the base program. Because, e.g., the constraint (3) is applied after the constraint (1), the constraint (2) is removed from the programs constraints generated for the variant. The resulting constraints are thus validated against the signature of that variant, in which neither Exp nor Lit have the method toString.

3.3   Type Checking Step (ii): Building the PFGT

Given a strongly unambiguous SPL (cf. Sect. 3.1), any total ordering of the deltas that is compatible with the canonical application ordering can be used to generate the variants. Each of these total orderings determines a set **S** that contains, for each product, the ordered sequence of the deltas activated by the product (note that different total orderings may generate the same set). The trie [15] for **S**, called the *product family generation trie* (PFGT), is a tree, where each edge is labeled by a delta, that represents all sequences in **S** by factoring out the common prefixes—the structure of the trie for a set of sequences **S** is uniquely determined by **S**. Moreover, each node of the PFGT that corresponds to a sequence in **S** is labeled by the associated product (by construction, these nodes include all the leaves).

The ABS toolchain generates the variants by applying the activated deltas according to a total ordering, that we call the *topological application ordering*, which is a topological sorting of the direct graph describing the canonical application ordering (this graph contains at least all the edges of the after graph, cf. Sect. 3.1). Our implementation of the SPL type checking mechanism (illustrated in Sect. 4) builds the PFGT for (the set **S** of sequences of deltas determined by) the topological application ordering.

3.4   Type Checking Step (iii): Checking All Variants

All the variant program abstractions can be efficiently generated and checked by traversing the PFGT in depth-first order and marking each node N with a program abstraction [12].

- The root node is marked with the abstraction of the base program.
- Each non-root node is marked with the program abstraction obtained by applying the abstraction of the delta that labels the edge between N and it parent to the program abstraction that marks N's parent.
- If N represents a product, the program abstraction generated for marking N is checked, thus establishing whether the associated variant is well-typed.
- If the generation of the program abstraction for N fails (i.e., the application of the delta abstraction that labels the edge entering N to the program abstraction marking N's parent fails), then the subtree with N as root is pruned, and an error message informs that the variants associated with the products in the subtree cannot be generated.

4   Integration into the ABS Toolchain

Until the release of version 1.4.2 in April 2017, the ABS toolchain was structured as a pipeline of three components:

1. The *Parser* component takes in input an ABS SPL (i.e., a set of files written in the different languages listed in Fig. 1) and produces the Extended Abstract Syntax Tree (E-AST) representing the artifact base—it also checks whether the `after` graph is acyclic and, if so, it computes the topological application ordering (cf. the explanation in last paragraph of Sect. 3.3).
2. The *Rewriter* component generates the variant corresponding to a given product: it applies the activated deltas to the base program to produce the Core AST (C-AST) of the variant.
3. The *Semantic Analysis and Backend* component supports analyzing the C-AST by using the different tools developed for the Core ABS language [6]. The first of the analysis to be performed is type checking.

In order to check that all variants can be generated and are well-typed Core ABS programs, the user had to generate all the variants and type check each of them in isolation using the Core ABS type checker. Moreover, there was no support for checking the unambiguity of the SPL.

Currently we have implemented part of the SPL checking mechanism illustrated in Sect. 3. Our implementation is available as a novel component in version 1.4.2 of the ABS toolchain. The novel component, called the *SPL Checking* component, is inserted into the pipeline between the Parser and the Rewriter components. We stress that, unlike in Sect. 3, the implementation is based not merely on FDABS, but on the complete ABS language.

4.1   An Overview of the Novel Component

The SPL Checking component performs the following steps:

1. A feature-based step that computes the signature of the base program and the DST (i.e., the signature of each delta)—cf. Sect. 3.2. Some errors in the artifact base can already be detected and reported during this step.
2. A step that, by using only the DST and the canonical partition, checks whether the SPL is strongly unambiguous—cf. Sect. 3.1.
3. A family-based step that (by using only configuration knowledge) builds the PFGT for the topological application ordering—cf. Sect. 3.3.
4. A product-based step that (by using only the signature of the base program, the DST and the PFGT) efficiently generates all the variant signatures (thus checking whether all the variants can be generated)—cf. Sect. 3.4.

It is worth observing that the signature of a variant contains enough information to check whether, e.g.: each interface occurring in some `implements` or `extends` clause, or in some method header or fields declaration is declared in the variant; the `extends` relation is acyclic; each interface has no (defined or inherited) incompatible method headers; each class implements the methods of the interfaces listed in its `implements` clause—we are currently working on extending step 4 above to perform these checks.

Moreover, we are also working on fully implementing the SPL type checking mechanism, i.e., on replacing steps 1 and 4 above by:

1′ A feature-based step that computes the abstraction of the base program and the DAT (i.e., the abstraction of each delta)—cf. Sect. 3.2. Some errors in the artifact base can already be detected and reported during this step.

4′ A product-based step that (by using only the abstraction of the base program, the DAT, and the PFGT) efficiently generates and checks all the variant abstractions (thus checking whether all the variants can be generated and are well-typed)—cf. Sect. 3.4.

4.2   On Building the PFGT

The PFGT, which caches and keeps track of common delta application sequences, is used to improve the efficiency of generating variant signatures (cf. Sect. 3.4). In order to build the PFGT we need to enumerate all the products of the SPL (cf. Sect. 3.3). μTVL supports feature attributes (Booleans and integers) as a way of permitting more fine-grained product specifications. An established approach [4] to determine all the products of a feature model with Boolean and integer attributes is to express it as a constraint satisfaction problem (CSP) over Boolean or integer variables. The solutions to the CSP are all the attributed products, i.e., all the attributed feature combinations allowed by the attributed feature model. The ABS toolchain[4] uses an off-the-shelf CSP library[5] for this task.

Even though ABS support feature attributes, we omit these when enumerating all solutions to the attributed feature model in order to build the PFGT, as they are irrelevant for type checking variants. This is due to the fact that, for each product with attributes, the set of the activated deltas is determined by the selected features alone, i.e., it is not possible to specify the activation of a delta based on the values of feature attributes. Feature attributes only influence the configuration to the extent of assigning concrete values to variables in the ABS source code—this is achieved by passing feature attributes as attributes to the activated deltas. The delta abstraction is built by abstracting away from these. The correct use of attributes can be checked separately, for each delta (together with its `after` clause and `when` clause) in isolation. A convenient side-effect of abstracting away attributes is that it may significantly reduce the number of products—consider, for example that the introduction of a single, unbound integer attribute multiplies the number of products by up to 2^{32}.

---

[4] ABS toolchain available at https://github.com/abstools/abstools.
[5] Choco Solver: http://www.choco-solver.org/.

5   Case Studies and Evaluation

We tested the SPL Checking component on two industrial SPLs implemented in ABS.

The first case study is provided by the Fredhopper Access Server (FAS), a distributed web-based software system for Internet search and merchandising, developed by Fredhopper B.V. (now ATTRAQT). In particular, we considered the Replication System, a subsystem for ensuring data consistency across the FAS deployment. This system has been described in more detail previously [26]. The version we tested includes a feature model with 8 features and 5 integer feature attributes. These are implemented with a core ABS program and 8 deltas, totaling about 2000 lines of ABS code. The feature model has 16 products when feature attributes are omitted. If feature attributes are considered, the number of products is 5500.

The second case study is provided by the FormbaR project [19], an ongoing effort to build a comprehensive model of railway operations for Deutsche Bahn AG. The current version of this ABS model includes a feature model with 5 features, a core program and 5 deltas, totaling about 3300 lines of code. The feature model is comparatively simple and only has 5 products; each product has one feature and the associated variant is generated by applying a single delta to the base program. The source code is available from the FormbaR project website.[6]

5.1   Error Reporting

If the ABS compiler (absc) detects a product line declaration in a given ABS source project, it automatically performs the SPL unambiguity checking and the SPL partial type checking. These checks capture two kinds of errors, respectively (cf. Sect. 4.1). First, in case SPL unambiguity cannot be ruled out, an error similar to the following is reported:

```
replication.abs:1419:0:The product line RS is potentially ambiguous:
    Deltas JCD and CD both target class RS.RSMain, method
    getSchedules, but their application order is undefined.
productline RS;
^
```

Second, in case the generation of the signature of a variant fails, an error message, such as the following, points to the problem.

```
replication.abs:1396:4:Field iterator could not be found. When
    applying delta JCD on top of CD >> JD >> RD >> core, while
    building product {RS,Client,JSched}.
    removes Int iterator;
---^
```

---

[6] FormbaR project: http://formbar.raillab.de/.

5.2   Performance

We measured the performance of the SPL unambiguity and partial type checking mechanism implementation and compared it against the performance of generating and fully type checking all variants of the respective SPL in sequence. The results of the experiments are summarized in Fig. 6—we used a 2013 laptop machine (Intel core i7 CPU at 2 GHz, 16 GB RAM). We found that SPL partial checking had little noticeable impact on the performance of the ABS compiler. For the FAS Replication System SPL it took just 0.643 s, of which 0.61 s were spent computing all solutions to the constraint satisfaction problem (i.e., to enumerate all the products), and 0.033 s were spent checking unambiguity and generating the signatures of all the 16 variants.

By comparison, generating a single variant of the FAS Replication System SPL took on average slightly over 5 s (we timed only the process of transforming the E-AST by applying deltas and subsequently type checking the C-AST). For all 16 different products obtainable by disregarding attributes, this process took 82 s. Before implementation of the SPL Checking component, no tool infrastructure existed to automatically type check the entire product line. Moreover no option to exclude feature attributes from variant generation was provided. It would have required the developer to manually build and subsequently check all 5500 products, which takes around 8 h.

	FAS Replication System	FormbaR
Solve CSP	0.610	0.540
Check unambiguity & build variant PSTs	0.033	0.026
SPL partial checking (total)	**0.643**	**0.566**
Build one variant (avg.)	5.130	0.020
Build variants	82.080	0.100
Solve CSP & build variants (total)	**82.690**	**0.640**

Fig. 6. Case studies: performance (numbers in seconds)

For the FormbaR SPL, currently a quite simple product line, where each product has a single feature and only one delta is applied to generate the associated variant, it took 0.1 s to generate all 5 variants. If we include the time to solve the CSP, then the whole process took 0.64 s. This is slightly less efficient than employing the SPL partial checking mechanism, which took 0.566 s (including the time to solve the CSP).

5.3   Discussion

According to the numbers above the SPL partial checking mechanism exhibits a significant performance advantage (with respect to generating all variants and fully type checking each of them in isolation) for all but very simple SPLs. Our evaluation also shows that the most performance-critical task of SPL partial checking is solving the CSP in order to enumerate all products. For a product line with hundreds or thousands of products, this task could potentially take too long to be practical. We plan to approach this problem from two angles. First, we see potential for optimization of the CSP, and will consider the alternative of SAT (which has shown promising performance according to related studies [14, 24]), as this has not been a focus of our attention so far. Second, we will explore solving simplified CSPs corresponding to partially configured feature modes in case of too large solution spaces.

6   Related Work

SPL implementation approaches can be classified into three main categories [22]: *annotative approaches* expressing negative variability; *compositional approaches* expressing positive variability; and *transformational approaches* expressing both positive and negative variability.

DOP is a transformational approach. Notably, it is an extension of *Feature-Oriented Programming* (FOP, see [2, Sect. 6.1] and [3]), a compositional approach, where deltas are associated one-to-one with features and have limited expressive power: they can add and modify program elements, however, they cannot remove them. In annotative approaches all variants are included within the same model (often called a 150% model). A prominent example of SPL annotative implementation mechanism is represented by C preprocessor directives (#define FEATURE and #ifdef FEATURE).

We refer to [25] for a survey on SPL analyses (cf. the brief discussion at the beginning of Sect. 3). Here we discuss a type checking mechanism for FOP SPLs that has been implemented for the AHEAD Tool Suite [24], and a type checking mechanism for delta-oriented SPLs that we have recently proposed [10].

The AHEAD Tool Suite [3] supports FOP SPLs of Java programs. Thaker et al. [24] illustrates the implementation of a family-based approach for type checking AHEAD SPLs. The approach comprises: (i) a family-feature-based step that computes for each class a stub (which contains a stub declaration for each field or method declaration that could appear in that class) and compiles each feature module in the context of all stubs; and (ii) a family-based step that infers a set of constraints that are combined with the feature model to generate a formula whose satisfiability implies that all variants can be successfully generated and compiled. The first step requires that all the field and method declarations that could appear in a class C in some variant must be "type compatible", e.g., for each field name f all declarations of field with name f that may appear in C in some variant must have the same type. The type checking approach presented in Sect. 3 do not suffer of this limitation. However, it involves an explicit iteration over the set of products, which becomes an issue when the number of products is huge (a product line with n features can have up to 2^n products). The approach by Thaker et al. [24] does not require an explicit iteration over the set of products, however it requires to check the validity of a propositional formula (which is a co-NP-complete problem). Thaker et al. [14, 24] report that the performance of using SAT solvers to verify the propositional formulas (a SAT solver can be used to check whether a propositional formula is valid by checking whether its negation is unsatisfiable) for four non-trivial product lines was encouraging and that, for the largest product line, applying the approach was even faster than generating and compiling a single product. The empirical evaluation (cf. Sect. 5) of our partial implementation for ABS (cf. Sect. 4) of the feature-product-family approach for delta-oriented SPLs originally formalized for IFΔJ [5, 12] (that is reformulated for FDABS in Sect. 3) exhibits a similar performance increase with respect to generating and checking each variant in isolation.

Delaware et al. [14] provide a formal foundation for the approach implemented by Thaker et al. [24]. They formalize a feature-family-based type checking approach for the LIGHTWEIGHT FEATURE JAVA (LFJ) calculus, which models FOP for the LIGHTWEIGHT JAVA (LJ) [23] calculus. The approach, which does not suffer of the "type compatible" limitation of the approach by Thaker et al. [24], comprises: (i) a feature-based step that uses a constraint-based type system for LFJ to analyze each feature module in isolation and infer a set of constraints for each feature module; and (ii) a family-based step where the feature model and the previously inferred constraints are used to generate a formula whose satisfiability implies that all variants are well-typed.

Recently, Damiani and Lienhardt [10] proposed a feature-family-based type checking approach that provides an extension to DOP of the two steps of the approach by Delaware et al. [14] together with a preliminary step, called partial typing, which provides early detection of some errors by analyzing each delta with respect to the class, field and method declarations occurring in the whole artifact base.[7] The approach has been designed to take advantage of automatically checkable DOP guidelines that make an SPL more comprehensible and type checking more efficient (see also [11]). Both the approach and the guidelines are formalized by means of IFΔJ.

7   Conclusion

We presented an extension of the ABS toolchain with an SPL unambiguity and type checking mechanism. Currently we have implemented only part of this mechanism (cf. Sect. 4.1). Our implementation is integrated in version 1.4.2 of the ABS toolchain, released in April 2017. We are currently working on fully implementing the SPL type checking mechanism and improving the efficiency of enumerating all the product of the SPL. Our evaluation, that used two industrial case studies, showed significant performance and usability advantages over an entirely product-based type checking approach that involves building all SPL

---

[7] Partial typing guarantees that variants that can be generated and have their inner dependencies satisfied are well-typed, thus providing early detection of some errors— however, because it does not use feature model and configuration knowledge, it cannot guarantee that each variant can be generated and do not contain references to classes, fields or methods that are not defined in the variant.

variants. We found that 95% of the performance cost of the implemented SPL checking comes from solving the CSP necessary to enumerate all products. The actual unambiguity and partial type checking implementation is very efficient and takes only few milliseconds. This result raises our confidence that an implementation of the full SPL checking mechanism will remain similarly performant. We also plan to extend the SPL Checking component of the ABS toolchain by implementing the feature-family type checking mechanism and the automatically checkable DOP guidelines that we have recently proposed [10,11] (see Sect. 6). Our goal is to tame complexity of SPL type checking by tool support for DOP guidelines enforcement and orchestration of different type checking approaches.

Acknowledgments. We thank Eduard Kamburjan for help with the FormbaR case study, and the anonymous reviewers for comments and suggestions.

References

1. Albert, E., de Boer, F.S., Hähnle, R., Johnsen, E.B., Schlatte, R., Tapia, S.L.T., Wong, P.Y.H.: Formal modeling and analysis of resource management for cloud architectures: an industrial case study using real-time ABS. SOCA **8**(4), 323–339 (2014)
2. Apel, S., Batory, D., Kästner, C., Saake, G.: Feature-Oriented Software Product Lines: Concepts and Implementation. Springer, Heidelberg (2013)
3. Batory, D., Sarvela, J.N., Rauschmayer, A.: Scaling step-wise refinement. IEEE Trans. Softw. Eng. **30**, 355–371 (2004)
4. Benavides, D., Trinidad, P., Ruiz-Cortés, A.: Automated reasoning on feature models. In: Pastor, O., Falcão e Cunha, J. (eds.) CAiSE 2005. LNCS, vol. 3520, pp. 491–503. Springer, Heidelberg (2005). doi:10.1007/11431855_34
5. Bettini, L., Damiani, F., Schaefer, I.: Compositional type checking of delta-oriented software product lines. Acta Informatica **50**(2), 77–122 (2013)
6. Bubel, R., Montoya, A.F., Hähnle, R.: Analysis of executable software models. In: Bernardo, M., Damiani, F., Hähnle, R., Johnsen, E.B., Schaefer, I. (eds.) SFM 2014. LNCS, vol. 8483, pp. 1–25. Springer, Cham (2014). doi:10.1007/978-3-319-07317-0_1
7. Clarke, D., Diakov, N., Hähnle, R., Johnsen, E.B., Schaefer, I., Schäfer, J., Schlatte, R., Wong, P.Y.H.: Modeling spatial and temporal variability with the HATS abstract behavioral modeling language. In: Bernardo, M., Issarny, V. (eds.) SFM 2011. LNCS, vol. 6659, pp. 417–457. Springer, Heidelberg (2011). doi:10.1007/978-3-642-21455-4_13
8. Clements, P., Northrop, L.: Software Product Lines: Practices and Patterns. Addison-Wesley Longman Publishing Co., Inc., Boston (2001)
9. Damiani, F., Hähnle, R., Kamburjan, E., Lienhardt, M.: A unified and formal programming model for deltas and traits. In: Huisman, M., Rubin, J. (eds.) FASE 2017. LNCS, vol. 10202, pp. 424–441. Springer, Heidelberg (2017). doi:10.1007/978-3-662-54494-5_25
10. Damiani, F., Lienhardt, M.: On type checking delta-oriented product lines. In: Ábrahám, E., Huisman, M. (eds.) IFM 2016. LNCS, vol. 9681, pp. 47–62. Springer, Cham (2016). doi:10.1007/978-3-319-33693-0_4

11. Damiani, F., Lienhardt, M.: Refactoring delta-oriented product lines to enforce guidelines for efficient type-checking. In: Margaria, T., Steffen, B. (eds.) ISoLA 2016. LNCS, vol. 9953, pp. 579–596. Springer, Cham (2016). doi:10.1007/978-3-319-47169-3_45

12. Damiani, F., Schaefer, I.: Family-based analysis of type safety for delta-oriented software product lines. In: Margaria, T., Steffen, B. (eds.) ISoLA 2012. LNCS, vol. 7609, pp. 193–207. Springer, Heidelberg (2012). doi:10.1007/978-3-642-34026-0_15

13. de Boer, F., Clarke, D., Helvensteijn, M., Muschevici, R., Proença, J., Schaefer, I.: Final Report on Feature Selection and Integration, March 2011. Deliverable 2.2b of project FP7-231620 (HATS). http://www.hats-project.eu

14. Delaware, B., Cook, W.R., Batory, D.: Fitting the pieces together: a machine-checked model of safe composition. In: Proceedings of ESEC/FSE 2009. ACM (2009). doi:10.1145/1595696.1595733

15. Fredkin, E.: Trie memory. Commun. ACM **3**(9), 490–499 (1960)

16. Hähnle, R.: The abstract behavioral specification language: a tutorial introduction. In: Giachino, E., Hähnle, R., Boer, F.S., Bonsangue, M.M. (eds.) FMCO 2012. LNCS, vol. 7866, pp. 1–37. Springer, Heidelberg (2013). doi:10.1007/978-3-642-40615-7_1

17. Helvensteijn, M., Muschevici, R., Wong, P.Y.H.: Delta modeling in practice: a Fredhopper case study. In: Proceedings of VAMOS 2012, pp. 139–148. ACM (2012). doi:10.1145/2110147.2110163

18. Igarashi, A., Pierce, B., Wadler, P.: Featherweight Java: a minimal core calculus for Java and GJ. ACM TOPLAS **23**(3), 396–450 (2001)

19. Kamburjan, E., Hähnle, R.: Uniform modeling of railway operations. In: Artho, C., Ölveczky, P.C. (eds.) FTSCS 2016. CCIS, vol. 694, pp. 55–71. Springer, Cham (2017). doi:10.1007/978-3-319-53946-1_4

20. Lopez-Herrejon, R.E., Batory, D., Cook, W.: Evaluating support for features in advanced modularization technologies. In: Black, A.P. (ed.) ECOOP 2005. LNCS, vol. 3586, pp. 169–194. Springer, Heidelberg (2005). doi:10.1007/11531142_8

21. Schaefer, I., Bettini, L., Bono, V., Damiani, F., Tanzarella, N.: Delta-oriented programming of software product lines. In: Bosch, J., Lee, J. (eds.) SPLC 2010. LNCS, vol. 6287, pp. 77–91. Springer, Heidelberg (2010). doi:10.1007/978-3-642-15579-6_6

22. Schaefer, I., Rabiser, R., Clarke, D., Bettini, L., Benavides, D., Botterweck, G., Pathak, A., Trujillo, S., Villela, K.: Software diversity: state of the art and perspectives. Int. J. Softw. Tools Technol. Transf. **14**(5), 477–495 (2012)

23. Strniša, R., Sewell, P., Parkinson, M.: The Java module system: core design and semantic definition. In: Proceedings of OOPSLA 2007, pp. 499–514. ACM (2007)

24. Thaker, S., Batory, D., Kitchin, D., Cook, W.: Safe composition of product lines. In: Proceedings of GPCE 2007, pp. 95–104. ACM (2007). doi:10.1145/1289971.1289989

25. Thüm, T., Apel, S., Kästner, C., Schaefer, I., Saake, G.: A classification and survey of analysis strategies for software product lines. ACM Comput. Surv. **47** (2014)

26. Wong, P.Y., Albert, E., Muschevici, R., Proença, J., Schäfer, J., Schlatte, R.: The ABS tool suite: modelling, executing and analysing distributed adaptable object-oriented systems. J. Softw. Tools Technol. Transf. **14**, 567–588 (2012)

Safety-Critical Systems

Generalised Test Tables: A Practical Specification Language for Reactive Systems

Bernhard Beckert[1], Suhyun Cha[2], Mattias Ulbrich[1], Birgit Vogel-Heuser[2], and Alexander Weigl[1(✉)]

[1] Karlsruhe Institute of Technology, Karlsruhe, Germany
{beckert,ulbrich,weigl}@kit.edu
[2] Technical University of Munich, Munich, Germany
suhyun.cha@tum.de, vogel-heuser@ais.mw.tum.de

Abstract. In industrial practice today, correctness of software is rarely verified using formal techniques. One reason is the lack of specification languages for this application area that are both comprehensible and sufficiently expressive. We present the concepts and logical foundations of generalised test tables – a specification language for reactive systems accessible for practitioners. Generalised test tables extend the concept of test tables, which are already frequently used in quality management of reactive systems. The main idea is to allow more general table entries, thus enabling a table to capture not just a single test case but a family of similar behavioural cases. The semantics of generalised test tables is based on a two-party game over infinite words.

We show how generalised test tables can be encoded into verification conditions for state-of-the-art model checkers. And we demonstrate the applicability of the language by an example in which a function block in a programmable logic controller as used in automation industry is specified and verified.

1 Introduction

Complex industrial control software often drives safety-critical systems, like automated production plants or control units embedded into devices in automotive systems. Such controllers have in common that they are *reactive systems*, i.e., that they periodically read sensor stimuli and cyclically execute the same piece of code to produce actuator signals.

Usually, in practice, the correctness of implementations of reactive systems *is not* verified using formal techniques. What *is* used instead in industrial practice today is testing, where individual test cases are used to check the reactive system under test [11]. Main reasons why formal methods are not popular are: (a) It is difficult to adequately formulate the desired temporal properties. (b) There is

Research supported by the DFG (German Research Foundation) in Priority Programme SPP1593: Design for Future – Managed Software Evolution (VO 937/28-2, BE 2334/7-2, and UL 433/1-2).

N. Polikarpova and S. Schneider (Eds.): IFM 2017, LNCS 10510, pp. 129–144, 2017.
DOI: 10.1007/978-3-319-66845-1_9

a lack in specification languages for reactive systems that are both sufficiently expressive and comprehensible for practitioners.

Test cases are commonly written in the form of *test tables*, in which each row contains the input stimuli for one cycle and the expected response of the reactive system. Thus, the whole table captures the intended behaviour of the system (the sequence of actuator signals) for one particular sequence of input signals.

In this paper, we present a novel specification language called *generalised test tables* (gtts) which lifts the principle of test tables to an expressive means for temporal specification of reactive systems. With a gtt one can describe an *entire family* of test cases with a single table.

The specification language comprised of gtts is designed to preserve the intuitiveness and comprehensibility of (non-generalised) concrete test tables – in particular for system design engineers who are experts in test case specification but are not familiar with formal temporal specification. To this avail, the generalisations are defined as conceptional extensions of notation already present in concrete test tables. The features that go beyond the concrete case are chosen such that essential characteristics of concrete test tables are preserved. Moreover, concrete test tables are a special case of gtts. We argue that, thus, gtts are still intuitive for an engineer. The characteristics of concrete test tables that we deem essential and that are preserved in gtts are:

1. Every signal/actuator cycle corresponds to one row in the test table.
2. Rows in the test table are traversed sequentially (no jumping around).
3. Every row formalises a local implication of the form: "If the signal values adhere to the input constraint, then the actuator signals adhere to the output constraint."

The main features of generalised test tables that go beyond concrete tables are (a) generalisations of notational elements known from concrete tables and (b) concepts adopted from other well-known table formalisms like spreadsheets.

The main contributions of this paper are: (1) the concept of gtts as a practical specification language for reactive systems (Sect. 3); (2) a formal semantics for gtts (Sect. 4), defined by means of a semi-deterministic input/output game; (3) a sound encoding for gtts into Büchi automata, together with optimisations (Sect. 5), which has been implemented (4) an extended example in which a realistic min/max function block, which is a typical example for the software driving automated production systems, is specified and verified using a gtt (Sect. 6).

2   The Basis: Concrete Test Tables

Concrete test tables – of which generalised test tables are an extension – describe a single test case for a reactive system. The rows of a concrete test table correspond to the successive steps performed by the system under test. The columns correspond to the system's variables. These are partitioned into *input* variables and *output* variables. In addition, there is a special column named DURATION.

The reactive systems we consider are executed cyclically, where each cycle is one step in the test. Cycles consume a fixed period of time, the *cycle time*. In each cycle, the concrete input values contained in the table row corresponding to that step are the stimuli for the system; and the system is expected to react with the output values contained in the same row. If the observed system response is different from the expectation for one or more of the rows in the test table, then the system violates the test case. The value of DURATION determines how long the system is to remain in the step, i.e., how often the row is to be repeated. DURATION is given as a number of cycles (it can also be given as a time constraint, which is transformed into cycles by division with the system's specific cycle time). A table row with a duration of n is equivalent to repeating that same row n times with a duration of 1.

	Inputs			Outputs			
#	A	B	C	X	Y	Z	DURATION
0	1	1	2	0	0	5	1
1	0	3	3	6	6	5	7
2	1	4	2	2	8	5	2

Fig. 1. Example for a concrete test table.

Example 1. Figure 1 shows an example for a simple concrete test table. The table has three input variables A, B, C and three output variables X, Y, Z, and describes a test case of 10 cycles (as the durations of the three rows add up to 10). In this example, all variables are of type integer; whereas in general, other types, such as Boolean variables, are also possible.

There is no restriction on the types of variables and their values that can be used in the tables. In the following, we use variables of type Boolean and integer; and the example in Sect. 6 uses bounded bit vector types.

3   The Concept of Generalised Test Tables

Generalising a test table and its specified test case is done by substituting concrete values in the table's cells by *constraint* expressions. Intuitively, a system satisfies a generalised test table if it responds to input values that adhere to the input constraints with output values that adhere to the output constraints. This generalises the meaning of concrete test cases were the constraints are unique values. Thus, a generalised test table specifies a – possibly infinite – set of concrete test tables. A detailed explanation of the semantics of generalised test table is given in Sect. 4.

In the following, we explain three generalisation concepts: (1) abstraction using constraint expressions (which is the basis of generalisation), (2) using references to other cells in constraint expressions, and (3) using generalisation in the duration columns of tables.

Abstraction using constraints. Instead of concrete values, we allow cells to contain constraints such as "$X > 0$", "$X + 1 = 4$", or "$X > 3 \land X < 10$." Besides the name of the variable that the cell corresponds to (e.g., X), the expressions can be built using all operators of the appropriate type ($+, *$ etc.), constant values $(0, 1, 2, \ldots)$, and predicates such as $=, >, \geq$ etc. In addition, logical operators $(\land, \lor$ etc.) can be used to combine several atomic constraints.

For convenience, we allow abbreviations (see Fig. 2): In the column for variable X, the constraint "$X < n$" can be written as "$<n$" and "$X = n$" simply as "n". We allow interval constraints $[n, m]$, which stand for "$X \geq n \wedge X \leq m$." And "–" is the constraint satisfied by all values ("don't care").

Abbrev.	Constraint
n	$X = n$
$< n$	$X < n$ (same for $>, \leq, \geq, \neq$)
$[m, n]$	$X \geq m \wedge X \leq n$
–	$X = X$ (don't care)

Fig. 2. Constraint abbreviations (X is the name of the variable that the cell corresponds to; n, m are arbitrary expressions of type integer).

References to other cells. A reactive system's behaviour depends both on the current and the previous input stimuli. Therefore, the expected values in the cells of a generalised test table are not independent of each other. We may want to specify that, e.g., for the value of input A being n, the value of output X is $n + 1$. For that purpose, we introduce two additional syntactical concepts to be used in constraints: global variables and references to other cells.

Global variables, denoted by lower-case letters, can be used in all constraints in any place where an expression of the corresponding type is expected. The value of a variable v is globally the same in all cells, in which v occurs. Thus, we can write p in a cell with input A (short for $A = p$) and $p + 1$ in a cell with output X (short for $X = p + 1$) to express that the value of output X is equal to $p + 1$ for the input A being of value p. Besides being the same in all cells, the value of a global variable is only restricted by the constraints, in which it occurs. Thus, for example, $X = p$ is equivalent to "don't care" if p does not occur in any other cell.

In addition to global variables, we allow references to other cells using the form "$X[-n]$", where X is a variable name and $n \geq 0$ is a concrete number. $X[-n]$ refers to the cell in the X-row n cycles before the current one. For references to other cells in the current cycle, we just write "X" as an abbreviation for "$X[-0]$", which refers the value of column X on the same row.

Thus, we can write "$A + 1$" in an X-cell to express that the output X is by one greater than the input A. To express that the value of Y increases by one in each cycle, we write $Y[-1] + 1$ in each Y-cell except for the first one.

References to other cycles are always relative to the current cycle – they are not given w.r.t. the start or end of the table. Absolute references to particular cells can be expressed using global variables. References to future cycles (both relative and absolute) could also be added – at least for static analysis – but are not covered in this paper.

Generalisation in the duration column. The DURATION variable defines the number of cycles for which a row is repeated. As a further generalisation concept, we allow the concrete values in the DURATION column to be replaced by constraints. However, in contrast to the columns for input and output variables, we only allow the DURATION column to contain constraints describing intervals; and they must not refer to other cells. Thus, constraints of the form "$[n, m]$" and "$\geq n$" are the only possibilities. We use "$*$" as a special "don't care" symbol for the duration column; it is equivalent to "≥ 0".

	Inputs			Outputs			
#	A	B	C	X	Y	Z	DURATION
0	1	1	2	0	0	–	1
1	–	p	p	$=2*p$	X	Z[−1]	≥ 6
2	–	p+1	–	[0,p]	>Y[−1]	2*Z>Y	*

Fig. 3. Example for a generalised test table with a global variable p.

Example 2. Figure 3 shows an example of a simple generalised test table, incorporating the generalisation concepts described above. Note that the concrete table depicted in Fig. 1 is one of the possible instances of the generalised test table given in Fig. 3, achieved by instantiating the global variable p with the value 3.

The first row expresses a cycle, which is executed once. It provides three concrete input values for the sensor inputs A, B, C, and expects the outputs X, Y to both be equal to 0, whereas the output value for Z can be of arbitrary value.

The input values for the second row are applied repeatedly for strictly more than five scan cycles (there is no upper bound). The input A is a "don't care" value, i.e., it can potentially be different for each cycle. The input values for B and C may also be arbitrary; however, they are bound to be equal to the global variable p. Hence, the values of B and C are the same in each of the cycles of the second table row. The output value of X is required to be identical to $2 * p$, i.e., twice the value of the input values for B, C. Moreover, Y is also required to be equal to $2 * p$, enforced by the reference to the X-cell. Finally, the value of output Z is equal to the one of the first row, as it is ensured by the back-reference $Z[-1]$, requiring the value in each cycle to be the same as that of the previous one.

For the third row – which does not correspond to the third cycle, but at least to the eighth cycle, as the second row is repeated at least six times – the inputs for A, C are arbitrary and B is equal to $p + 1$. The output value for X is an arbitrary one between 0 and p inclusively. The output Y contains a back reference to Y from the previous cycle. Thus, in the first cycle of the third row, Y is greater than $2 * p$ (as $Y = 2 * p$ from the second row's last cycle). The value of Y must then increase in each further cycle. The value of Z must be more than half the value for Y in order to satisfy the constraint $2 * Z > Y$. The third row may be repeated arbitrarily often, as indicated by the symbol $*$ in column DURATION. Note that no real system is able to fulfil the last row for an arbitrarily large number of steps, since the enforcement of strict monotonicity in Y must lead to an integer overflow at some point.

This paper introduces and describes the formal foundations of gtts and shows their principal suitability for formal specification and automatic verification. In a companion paper [12], the presentation focuses more on the adequacy and usability of the approach for engineers. A thorough empirical study which analyses the accessibility of the individual features by field engineers remains as future work.

4   Semantics of Generalised Test Tables

A gtt is a sequence of rows. Each row corresponds to three constraints: one for the input variables, one for the output variables, and one for duration of that row. Which part of a constraint is written in exactly which column is only relevant as long as abbreviations and syntactic sugar is used. For example, writing Y in the X-column of a table is expanded to $X = Y$, so the column is relevant. But it is irrelevant in which column we write a constraint like $X = Y$, that is not further expanded. This gives rise to the following definition, which basically just fixes notation:

Definition 1 (Generalized Test Table as Sequence of Constraints). *Let T be a generalised test table with m rows; let $InVar_T$ and $OutVar_T$ be the set of input variables resp. the set of output variables of T; and let $GVar_T$ be the set of global variables occurring in T. Then T is identified with the sequence*

$$(\phi_1, \psi_1, \tau_1) \cdots (\phi_m, \psi_m, \tau_m),$$

where ϕ_i is the conjunction of all constraints contained in cells in row i that correspond to input *variables, ψ_i is the conjunction of all constraints contained in cells in row i that correspond to* output *variables, and τ_i is the interval contained in the duration column at row i.*

The reactive systems whose behaviour is being specified by test tables can be formalised as functions from sequences of inputs to sequences of outputs. The possible inputs are elements of $I = I_1 \times \cdots \times I_k$ where the I_r are the value spaces of the input variables. And the possible outputs are elements of $O = O_1 \times \cdots \times O_l$ where the O_s are the value spaces of the output variables.

Definition 2 (Reactive system). *A reactive system is a history-deterministic function $p : I^\omega \to O^\omega$. That is, $i_1 \downarrow_n = i_2 \downarrow_n$ implies $p(i_1) \downarrow_n = p(i_2) \downarrow_n$ for all n, where $x \downarrow_n$ denotes the finite initial sub-sequence of x of length n.*

In the following, we often identify a reactive system p with the set of its possible traces, i.e., $p \subseteq (I \times O)^\omega$.

4.1   Unrolled Instances of Generalised Test Tables

The rows of gtts have a duration and may be repeated more than once. In a first step towards defining the semantics of gtts, we eliminate the indeterminism w.r.t. the repetition of rows and define the set of *unrolled instances* of a gtt by making the repetitions explicit. At the same time, we also instantiate the global variables contained in gtts with all their possible values.

Definition 3 (Unrolled Instances). *Let* $G = (\phi_1, \psi_1, \tau_1) \cdots (\phi_m, \psi_m, \tau_m)$ *be a gtt without global variables. The set* $D1(G)$ *of unrolled instances of* G *consists of all gtts*

$$(\phi_1, \psi_1, 1)^{T_1} \cdots (\phi_m, \psi_m, 1)^{T_m}$$

such that T_i *is in the interval* τ_i *(*$1 \leq i \leq m$*).*[1]

In the unrolled instances, the duration constraint is redundant (as it is always 1); in the following, we therefore write (ϕ_i, ψ_i) instead of $(\phi_i, \psi_i, 1)$.

Global variables are not considered in unrolled instances, as their semantics is defined via universal quantification: A system has to conform to the test table for all their instances (see Definition 5).

In general, the set of unrolled instances for a generalised test table is infinite. This does not pose a problem as the notion of unrolled instances is only used as a theoretical concept for defining the semantics of gtts.

4.2 Evaluation of Expressions

The evaluation of constraints that appear in unrolled instances of gtts is straight forward. Note that they do not contain global variables anymore as these have been instantiated during unrolling.

Definition 4. *Let* $v \in (I \times O)^*$ *be a partial trace of length* $n \geq 1$. *And let* $v{\downarrow}n = (i, o)$ *be the last element of the trace. Then, the valuation function* $[\![e]\!]_v$, *which assigns a value to every expression or formula* e, *is inductively defined by:*

$$[\![e \circ f]\!]_v = [\![e]\!]_v \circ [\![f]\!]_v \quad for \ \circ \in \{+, -, \leq, \wedge, \vee, \ldots\}$$
$$[\![X]\!]_v = i(X) \quad if \ X \in InVar$$
$$[\![X]\!]_v = o(X) \quad if \ X \in OutVar$$
$$[\![X[-k]]\!]_v = [\![X]\!]_{v{\downarrow}(n-k)} \quad if \ k < n$$
$$[\![X[-k]]\!]_v = [\![X]\!]_{v{\downarrow}1} \quad if \ k \geq n$$

4.3 Two-Party Game for Defining Test Conformance

The intuition behind the following definitions is the following: A reactive system p conforms to a gtt G if every trace $t \in p$ conforms to G, where a trace conforms to G if one of the following conditions holds: (a) the input/output pairs of t satisfy *all* rows of *at least one* unrolled instance of G, or (b) t fails to satisfy the input constraints of *all* unrolled instance of G. In the former case, the trace is covered by the specification described by G, in the latter case, the input sequence triggers an application scenario which is not covered by the specification.

Formally, we define the semantics of a gtt G by means of a game played between a challenger (that chooses the inputs) and the reactive system p under test (that chooses the outputs). The challenger can be identified with the environment of the system. The game is played operating on a set S of unrolled

---

[1] We use the notation $(\phi, \psi, \tau)^n$ do denote that the row (ϕ, ψ, τ) is repeated n times.

Input: A gtt T

$S \leftarrow D1(T)$

$v \leftarrow \epsilon$

$k \leftarrow 1$

5: **loop**

    Challenger chooses $i \in I$.

    System computes $o \in O$.

    $v \leftarrow v \cdot (i, o)$

10:    $S \leftarrow \{D \in S \mid v \models \phi_k$ for the k-th row $t_k = (\phi_k, \psi_k)$ in $D\}$

    if $S = \emptyset$ **then**

        terminate: *System wins*   ▷ Chosen input not covered by T

    end if

15:    $S \leftarrow \{D \in S \mid v \models \psi_k$ for the k-th row $t_k = (\phi_k, \psi_k)$ in $D\}$

    if $S = \emptyset$ **then**

        terminate: *Challenger wins*   ▷ Chosen output violates T

    end if

20:    **if** $\exists D \in S. \ |D| = k$ **then**

        terminate: *System wins*   ▷ Unrolled instance D has finished

    end if

    $k \leftarrow k + 1$

end loop

Fig. 4. Game between challenger and system w.r.t. a gtt T

instances of G from which in every round inconsistent and conflicting instances are removed.

The player removing the last consistent instance from S loses the game. In addition, the system can win by successfully reaching the end of one of the non-eliminated table instances.

Figure 4 shows the game's rules in algorithmic form. During the course of a game, S holds the set of unrolled instances of G which have not been eliminated, v holds the so far observed partial trace up to and including the current move, and k counts the iterations. Initially the set $S = D1(G)$ contains all unrolled instances of the gtt T (Line 2). In each round, the challenger chooses input values (Line 6), and the program under test computes its output from its internal state and the input values (Line 7). The functions which choose the input/output values depending on the observed partial trace are called *strategies*. Since reactive programs are deterministic, there is only one strategy for the program, which is encoded in its implementation. The challenger is not confined in its choices; there are many possible strategies for the challenger. Whenever S becomes empty, i.e., no unrolled instance of G satisfies the partial trace, the respective player loses the game: If this is caused by the input constraint ϕ_k being violated, the challenger loses and the system wins (Line 12). If S becomes empty because the output constraint ψ_k is violated, the system loses and the challenger wins (Line 17). If S contains a consistent unrolled instance which has been fully traversed (its length is the current iteration counter), then the partial trace v is a witness for the system conforming to the gtt. The system wins (Line 21).

A single game has three possible outcomes: Either (a) the challenger wins, or (b) the system wins, or (c) neither party wins (draw). In the case of a draw, the game is infinite, while a game where one player wins ends after a finite number of iterations.

A strategy for one party is called a winning strategy if it wins every possible game regardless of the other party's strategy. The definition of conformance to a gtt can now be defined based on who wins the games:

Definition 5 (Conformance). *The reactive system $P : I^\omega \to O^\omega$ strictly conforms to the gtt T iff its strategy is a winning strategy for the game shown in Fig. 4 for all instantiations of global variables, i.e., it is winning w.r.t. $\sigma(T)$ for all instantiations σ that replaces each global variable occurring in T by an element of its value space.[2] The reactive system P weakly conforms to T iff its strategy never loses.*

The difference between weak and strict conformance is that of whether the analysis of a system w.r.t. a test table successfully finishes after finitely many steps or whether the system is under consideration for infinitely many steps. For example, consider the very simple gtt shown in Fig. 5. Intuitively, it requires that – independently of the input – the output must eventually be 2 after an arbitrary number of cycles with output 1. The reactive system that always returns 1 (and never 2) does not have this property. Corre-

I	O	⊙
–	1	*
–	2	[1,1]

Fig. 5. Gtt illustrating the difference between strict and weak conformance

spondingly, it does not strictly conform to the table (it does not have a winning strategy). But it weakly conforms (it never loses either). This corresponds to the fact that by inspecting finite partial traces, one cannot decide whether or not this system violates the test table.

Any analysis that only considers partial traces (like run time monitoring or testing) can, in general, only test weak conformance. A static analysis, however, is able to analyse a reactive system w.r.t. strict conformance.

The definition of conformance (Definition 5) can be lifted to the case of non-deterministic reactive systems by requiring that *all* possible strategies of P must be winning strategies.

This semantics definition seems unnecessarily complicated, but an attempt to define it on the program traces is bound to fail as the implication of a violated constraint is different depending on whether it occurs on the input or on the output values: A gtt with constraint false on the input side is trivially satisfied, while false on the output side makes it unsatisfiable. Yet, both describe the same set of traces: the empty set.

---

[2] In fact, the global variables are replaced by constants representing values. We assume that every value can be represented by a constant.

5   Transforming Generalised Test Tables into Automata

In this section, we describe the construction of a Büchi automaton that logically encodes conformance to a gtt. In order to ease the presentation of this construction, we assume a normalised form of test tables which allow only a restricted form of duration constraints:

Definition 6 (Normalised gtt). *A gtt $G = (\phi_1, \psi_1, \tau_1) \cdots (\phi_m, \psi_m, \tau_m)$ is normalised if $\tau_i = [1,1]$, $\tau_i = [0,1]$, or $\tau_i = [0,\infty]$ $(1 \leq i \leq m)$.*

The syntactical restriction of normalised tables does not pose a limitation on the expressiveness of gtts due to the following observation:

Proposition 1. *For every gtt T there is a semantically equivalent normalised gtt T_0.*

The construction of such a normalised table T_0 for T is canonical: Every row with a finite duration interval $\tau = [a,b]$ is unrolled into b rows with the first a repetitions having duration $[1,1]$ and the remainder having duration $[0,1]$. If $\tau = [a,\infty]$, then the row is repeated a times with duration $[1,1]$ and once with duration $[0,\infty]$. Note that if T has m rows and the largest number in the duration constraints is n, then the normalised table has at most $m \cdot n$ rows.

Due to the intervals in the duration constraints, it is not automatically clear to which row a system cycle has to conform, and which the successor row of each row is (as intermediate rows may have zero duration). The set of possible successor rows $succ(k)$ for row k in a normalised gtt can be represented as

$$succ(k) = \{k+1\} \tag{1}$$
$$\cup \, (\text{if } k < m \wedge 0 \in \tau_{k+1} \text{ then } succ(k+1) \text{ else } \emptyset) \tag{2}$$
$$\cup \, (\text{if } \tau_k = [0,\infty] \text{ then } \{k\} \text{ else } \emptyset), \tag{3}$$
$$succ(0) = \{1\} \cup (\text{if } 0 \in \tau_1 \text{ then } succ(1) \text{ else } \emptyset).$$

In a normalised table, tha normalised gtt can be representede next row is always a possible successor row (1), but rows may be leapt over (2), or repeated (3). $succ(0)$ is the set of rows in which the table may begin. Figure 6 illustrates the row successor relation (right) for a normalised gtt (left).

Alphabet. The Büchi automata will accept ω-traces in $(I \times O)^\omega$ produced by a reactive system (Definition 2). The alphabet of the automata is defined over the

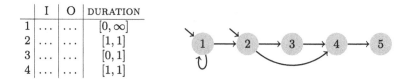

	I	O	DURATION
1	...	...	$[0,\infty]$
2	...	...	$[1,1]$
3	...	...	$[0,1]$
4	...	...	$[1,1]$

Fig. 6. A normalised table and the successor relation on its rows.

domains of input and output variables of the reactive system. In the following, we use Boolean formulas to describe subsets of the alphabet.

States. A gtt $G = (\phi_1, \psi_1, \tau_1) \cdots (\phi_m, \psi_m, \tau_m)$ with m rows results in an automaton with 2^{m+2} states. The states are characterised by vectors $(s_1, \ldots, s_{m+1}, fail)$ of Boolean variables, one for each row in G (s_1 to s_m), one indicating termination s_{m+1}, and one indicating failure ($fail$). Intuitively, s_k is true in a state iff the table is in a situation where the test table may have been executed by the trace up to the k-th row. The initial state $(s_1^0, \ldots, s_{m+1}^0, fail^0)$ is defined by

$$s_k^0 = \text{true iff } k \in succ(0) \text{ and } fail^0 = \text{false}. \tag{4}$$

State transition. Given a state $(s_1, \ldots, s_{m+1}, fail)$, its successor state $(s_1', \ldots, s_{m+1}', fail')$ is deterministically computed according to these equivalences:

$$\bigwedge_{k=1}^{m} \left(s_k' \leftrightarrow \bigvee_{i=1}^{m} (s_i \wedge k \in succ(i) \wedge \phi_i \wedge \psi_i) \right) \tag{5}$$

$$s_{m+1}' \leftrightarrow \left(s_{m+1} \vee \bigvee_{i=1}^{n} (s_i \wedge m+1 \in succ(i) \wedge \phi_i \wedge \psi_i) \right) \tag{6}$$

$$fail' \leftrightarrow \left(fail \vee \left(\bigvee_{i=1}^{m} (s_i \wedge \phi_i \wedge \neg\psi_i) \wedge \bigwedge_{i=1}^{m+1} \neg s_i' \right) \right) \tag{7}$$

The equivalences in (5) encode that the k-th row is active in the next step (variable s_k') if there is an active row i preceding k such that both its input constraint ϕ_i and output constraint ψ_i are satisfied. The same applies to the virtual row $m+1$ behind the table in (6). Here, additionally, once true, the variable s_{m+1} never falls back to false again. The *fail* flag indicating a specification violation is defined in (7). It is triggered whenever there is one active row i such that its input constraint ϕ_i is satisfied while the output constraint ψ_i is violated and there is no active row in the next step. Note that the equivalences above ensure the state transition system is always deterministic.

The acceptance condition remains to be described. By definition, a Büchi automaton accepts an infinite word if one state from the set of final states is traversed infinitely often. We construct two different such accepting sets of states: condition A_{WC} for weak conformance and A_C for strict conformance (the following formulas are identified with the set of states that satisfy them):

$$A_{WC} := \neg fail \qquad A_C := \left(\bigwedge_{i=1}^{m} \neg s_i \wedge \neg fail \right) \vee s_{m+1}$$

For weak conformance, the automaton accepts any trace that never have set the flag *fail* to true. For strict conformance, the automaton accepts a trace if it reaches a state in which s_{m+1} (the flag for finishing a table) is true or there is no active row anymore without failing (i.e., the challenger has lost).

The automata. Based on the above constructions, we can now define two Büchi automata. They share the state space, initial states (4), and transition function (5)–(7). The automaton $\mathcal{A}_{WC}$ for weak conformance uses A_{WC} as set of final states, the one for strict conformance uses A_C.

Proposition 2. *Let T be a normalised gtt (Definition 6).*
A reactive system P weakly conforms to T iff all traces of p are accepted by $\mathcal{A}_{WC}(T)$, i.e., $P \subseteq \mathcal{L}(\mathcal{A}_{WC}(T))$.
A reactive system P strictly conforms to T iff all traces of p are accepted by $\mathcal{A}_C(T)$, i.e., $P \subseteq \mathcal{L}(\mathcal{A}_C(T))$.

Extension for back references. The automata construction described above does not cover gtts with back-references of the form $v[-k]$.

To handle back reference, the state space needs to be enriched by additional variables. For any input or output variable v for which a back-reference $v[-k]$ occurs in a table, the state variables $v_1, \ldots, v_k$ are added. Moreover, the following equivalencies are added to the state transition:

$$v_1' = v \ \wedge \ \bigwedge_{i=2}^{k} v_i' = v_{i-1}$$

The expression $v[-c]$ then refers to the variable v_c for any constant $c \in \{1, ..., k\}$. The same construction is applied for each global variable (as global variables have the same value in all states).

Verifying system conformance. We provide two tools: the backend *geteta* for conformance verification of software for automated production systems, and *stvs* a graphical frontend for the creation of gtts and the inspection of counter examples. The implementation of *geteta* takes a gtt (encoded in XML), and a reactive system in Structured Text (ST), a textual programming language for automated production systems within the IEC standard 61131-3, and translate both to SMV file format. For the translation of ST source code, we use symbolic execution to compute the state relation of one system cycle into single static assignment form. For verification, we combine the model of the reactive system and the automaton representing the gtt into a product automaton, in which the inputs are chosen non-deterministically by the model checker. Links and further information are available on the companion website[3].

6   Experiment

We demonstrate the suitability of gtts for the specification and verification using a realistic example from the domain of automated production systems.

System under test. We consider an example system whose purpose is to watch over the input values and to raise a warning if they repeatedly exceed the previously learned range of allowed values. Such diagnosis functionality is common in

---

[3] Companion page: https://formal.iti.kit.edu/ifm17/.

#	Input			Output		⊙
	mode	learn	I	Q	W	
1	Active	–	–	0	true	–
2	Learn	true	q	0	false	1
3	Learn	true	p	0	false	1
4	Active	–	$[p,q]$	$[p,q]$	false	*
5	Active	–	$>q$	q	false	5
6	Active	–	$<p$	p	false	5

(a)

#	Input			Output		⊙
	mode	learn	I	Q	W	
1	Learn	true	q	0	true	1
2	Learn	true	p	0	true	1
3	Active	–	$>q$	q	false	10
4	Active	–	$>q$	q	true	≥ 1
5	Active	–	$[p,q]$	$[p,q]$	true	5
6	Active	–	$[p,q]$	$[p,q]$	false	≥ 1

(b)

Fig. 7. Two gtts for the specification of the `MinMaxWarning`'s behaviour

safety-critical applications. More precisely, the system under test is the function block `MinMaxWarning` written in ST. A function block declares its input, output and local variables. In the case of `MinMaxWarning`, the input variables `mode`, `learn`, `I` and the output variables `Q`, `W` are declared. `MinMaxWarning` learns the typical input values and warns the caller for subsequent outliers.

`MinMaxWarning` operates in two modes, `Active` and `Learn`, as selected by the caller via `mode`. During the learning phase, the function block learns the minimum and maximum values of the input values (`I`), if the `learn` flag is activated. When switched into the active phase, the function block checks that the input value (`I`) stays within the previously learned interval. The output value `Q` is equal to `I` if `I` is within the learned interval; otherwise, the nearest value from the interval is returned. If the input value keeps being out of range for a specified number of cycles, then the function block raises an alarm via the variable `W`. The alarm is reset after a certain cool down time if the input value falls back into the learned interval. An unlearned function block always signals a warning.

Test tables. The required functionality is partially described by the two gtts shown in Fig. 7. These tables have two global integer variables p, q. As p should represent the minimum input value, resp. q the maximum, we specify the constraint $p \leq q$ in the model checker. The waiting time before an alarm is raised is fixed to ten cycles, and the cool-down time to five cycles.

The first gtt (Fig. 7a) specifies a behaviour without warning. In the beginning, it is checked that the unlearned system returns the default constants ($Q = 0$ and $W = $ true; Row 1). This phase can be interrupted for switching into the learning mode (Rows 2 and 3). During learning, the system learns the minimum p and the maximum q input values. Subsequently, the system response is only allowed to be within this range. In Row 4, we test the non-warning case, in which only inputs between p and q are supplied. Rows 5 and 6 test for input values outside the range, and ensure that no warning is risen too early.

The second gtt (Fig. 7b) targets the case where warnings need to be given. We use the same initialisation, but require a warning due to a too high input (Rows 3 and 4). Rows 5 and 6 specify the cool-down within five cycles.

Verification. The verification system *geteta* that uses the construction from Sect. 5 and version 1.1.1 of the model-checker nuXmv [4], needs 0.53 CPU seconds for proving weak conformance of the first gtt and 0.63 CPU seconds for the second (median, $n = 6$). With the same setup, the verification of strict conformance takes 1.35 and 1.39 CPU seconds. Proving strict conformance requires an additional fairness condition to avoid infinite stuttering on the non-deterministic input variables. The experiments were run on a 3.20 GHz system with Intel Core i5-6500 and 16 GB RAM. The companion website provides the experiment files.

7   Related Work

A *Parnas table* is a tabular representation of a relation. Lorge et al. [10] use them in addition to first order logic for the specification of procedure contracts. In the *Software Cost Reduction* approach (SCR) [7], a collection of Parnas tables is used to specify a system's behaviour as a finite automaton. We follow a different approach with gtts: A system behaviour is specified as a sequence of admissible reactions to stimuli in the rows of a single table. Automata in SCR are deterministic while gtts are allowed to have non-deterministic transitions. Gtts allow the direct access to past values via back references or global variables; SCR requires an encoding of these values into the state. Both specification methods use tables as specification representation because of its accessibility for system engineers [7].

As an addition to the classical temporal specification languages CTL and LTL, Moszkowski [9], presents Interval Temporal Logic (ITL), which is ω-regular. ITL contains the chop-operator $(r_1; r_2)$ which – similar to our concept of rows – describes that there exists a point in time t s.t. until t the formula r_1 holds in all states and from t formula r_2 holds in all the following states. Obviously, we can encode a gtt T into an ITL by forming a disjunction of the generated normalised gtt of T (Definition 6). In general, the encoding results into an exponential blow-up. Armonie et al. [1] present *ForSpec Temporal Logic* (FTL) as an extension to LTL with logical and arithmetical operations and description of *regular events*. These regular events describes a finite regular language, similar to ITL and gtt. Additionally, FTL allows the composition with temporal connectives (a composition of gtts is possible on the automata level). Ljungkrantz et al. [8] propose ST-LTL, which enriches LTL with the arithmetical operators of Structured Text, syntactical abbreviations for specifying the rising or falling edges of variables, and access to previous variable value. To lower the obstacle for using formal specification in the development of critical software, like automated production systems, Dwyer et al. [6], Campos and Machado [3], and Bitsch [2] provide collections of specification patterns. The idea of specification patterns is that they cover the typical cases that arise from safety engineering. Additionally, their usage is simplified due to documentation and categorisations.

8   Conclusion

Gtts are a novel formal specification method for behavioural specifications of reactive systems. Their syntax is aligned with the concrete test tables and spreadsheet applications used in industry to ease the use of formal methods for software or mechanical engineers.

We have shown that it is possible to specify realistic software blocks from industry using gtts and verified them. Besides for verification at design time, gtts can also be used to generate checker code that monitors systems at runtime [5].

The concept of gtts is an important step towards the integration of formal methods into engineering automated production systems. Future work includes a user study on the accessibility of the features and an extension of the notation allowing the specification of software change during evolution.

References

1. Armoni, R., Fix, L., Flaisher, A., Gerth, R., Ginsburg, B., Kanza, T., Landver, A., Mador-Haim, S., Singerman, E., Tiemeyer, A., Vardi, M.Y., Zbar, Y.: The ForSpec temporal logic: a new temporal property-specification language. In: Katoen, J.-P., Stevens, P. (eds.) TACAS 2002. LNCS, vol. 2280, pp. 296–311. Springer, Heidelberg (2002). doi:10.1007/3-540-46002-0_21

2. Bitsch, F.: Safety patterns—the key to formal specification of safety requirements. In: Voges, U. (ed.) SAFECOMP 2001. LNCS, vol. 2187, pp. 176–189. Springer, Heidelberg (2001). doi:10.1007/3-540-45416-0_18

3. Campos, J.C., Machado, J.: Pattern-based analysis of automated production systems. IFAC Proc. Vol. **42**(4), 972–977 (2009)

4. Cavada, R., Cimatti, A., Dorigatti, M., Griggio, A., Mariotti, A., Micheli, A., Mover, S., Roveri, M., Tonetta, S.: The NUXMV symbolic model checker. In: Biere, A., Bloem, R. (eds.) CAV 2014. LNCS, vol. 8559, pp. 334–342. Springer, Cham (2014). doi:10.1007/978-3-319-08867-9_22

5. Cha, S., Ulewicz, S., Vogel-Heuser, B., Weigl, A., Ulbrich, M., Beckert, B.: Generation of monitoring functions in production automation using test specifications. In: 15th IEEE International Conference on Industrial Informatics, INDIN 2017, Emden, Germany. IEEE, 24–26 July 2017 (to appear)

6. Dwyer, M.B., Avrunin, G.S., Corbett, J.C.: Patterns in property specifications for finite-state verification. In: Proceedings of the 1999 International Conference on Software Engineering (IEEE Cat. No. 99CB37002), pp. 411–420, May 1999

7. Heitmeyer, C.L., Archer, M., Bharadwaj, R., Jeffords, R.: Tools for constructing requirements specifications: the SCR toolset at the age of ten. Int. J. Comput. Syst. Sci. Eng. **20**(1), 19–35 (2005)

8. Ljungkrantz, O., Åkesson, K., Fabian, M., Yuan, C.: A formal specification language for PLC-based control logic. In: 2010 8th IEEE International Conference on Industrial Informatics, pp. 1067–1072, July 2010

9. Moszkowski, B.: A temporal logic for multilevel reasoning about hardware. Computer **18**(2), 10–19 (1985)

10. Parnas, D.L., Madey, J., Iglewski, M.: Precise documentation of well-structured programs. IEEE Trans. Softw. Eng. **20**(12), 948–976 (1994)

11. Rösch, S.: Model-based testing of fault scenarios in production automation. Ph.D. thesis, Technische Universität München, München (2016)
12. Weigl, A., Wiebe, F., Ulbrich, M., Ulewicz, S., Cha, S., Kirsten, M., Beckert, B., Vogel-Heuser, B.: Generalized test tables: a powerful and intuitive specification language for reactive systems. In: 15th IEEE International Conference on Industrial Informatics, INDIN 2017, Emden, Germany. IEEE, 24–26 July 2017 (to appear)

Transient and Steady-State Statistical Analysis for Discrete Event Simulators

Stephen Gilmore[1], Daniël Reijsbergen[1], and Andrea Vandin[2(✉)]

[1] University of Edinburgh, Edinburgh, Scotland
[2] IMT School for Advanced Studies, Lucca, Italy
andrea.vandin@imtlucca.it

Abstract. We extend the model checking tool MultiVeStA with statistical model checking of steady-state properties. Since MultiVeStA acts as a front-end for simulation tools, it confers this ability onto any tool with which it is integrated. The underlying simulation models are treated as black-box systems. We will use an approach based on *batch means* using the ASAP3 algorithm. We motivate the work using two case studies: a biochemical model written in the Bio-PEPA language and an application from transport logistics.

Keywords: Statistical model checking · Steady-state · Batch means · MultiVeStA

1 Introduction

Statistical model-checking (SMC) [26,38] is a verification technique which is used for checking logical properties of formal models of large-scale systems. Based on analysis by simulation, statistical model-checking offers advantages over explicit-state model-checking because the absence of a formal representation of the reachable state-space of the system means that the approach scales better in supporting more detailed models of more complex systems, albeit at the cost of qualifying results with a statistical confidence. The SMC approach is well-suited to investigating transient (meaning, time-dependent) properties of systems.

Our focus is on *black-box systems*, which are those for which no knowledge of the internal state or transition structure is assumed. For these systems, conclusions about the satisfaction of formal system properties can only be based on observation traces, which in our case are obtained using system simulation. In this paper we extend an existing statistical model checker for black-box systems, MultiVeStA [31], by adding the ability to check steady-state (meaning, time-independent) properties of systems. The application of steady-state model checking to black-box systems is novel and is the main contribution of this paper.

Previous applications of SMC for black-box systems [11,32,37] have considered only transient properties. Conversely, existing SMC procedures for steady-state properties are only applicable to Markov chain models and the associated

© Springer International Publishing AG 2017
N. Polikarpova and S. Schneider (Eds.): IFM 2017, LNCS 10510, pp. 145–160, 2017.
DOI: 10.1007/978-3-319-66845-1_10

logics such as CSL [7] and UTSL [37], and are hence not sufficiently generic for black-box systems.

In particular, the current leading SMC model-checking techniques for steady-state analysis are the approach based on *regeneration cycles* which is implemented in the MRMC model-checker [23], and the approach based on *perfect simulation* which is found in [18].

These are not applicable in the context of black-box systems for the following reasons.

- The use of regeneration cycles requires that the state space has a pre-identified bottom strongly connected component (BSCC) structure – i.e., state space regions for which the probability of travelling from one region to another is 0 – and assumes that the system has a known regeneration state, which is not true for black-box systems, thereby making this approach inapplicable for our setting.
- The perfect simulation algorithm of [18] will exhibit either a time complexity which is linear in the state space size, or requires envelope computation which means that it is prohibitively expensive for use with black-box systems [12].

In this paper, we use the method of *batch means* [3,17]. Typical challenges facing the batch means method include the warm-up period, independence of the batches, and getting 'stuck' in a BSCC when more than one exists. To ameliorate these, we use an approach based on the ASAP3 [34] algorithm, which prescribes that we continue sampling until the batch means pass two statistical tests, one for normality and one for the absence of correlation between the means. To avoid the (rare) multiple-BSCC problem, one could further extend the algorithm with the method of independent replications [2].

The MultiVeStA tool which we extend here is a parametric simulation analyser which functions as a front-end for multiple discrete-event simulators by interactively asking them to produce observation traces which are then analysed. The logical query language underlying MultiVeStA, called MultiQuaTEx, allows the specification of expressions which map functions of state variables onto real numbers, thereby defining stochastic processes. In combination with a stopping criterion for individual runs, this defines a property specification language that generalises (the transient fragments of) other languages such as the logics PCTL [22] and CSL [6,7] for Markov chains, and UTSL [37] for general discrete-event systems (see discussion in [1]). However, MultiQuaTEx and UTSL currently both omit *steady-state* properties, which do not involve the value of a random variable at a (possibly random) stopping time, but rather its long-run average.

The parametric multi-simulator approach of MultiVeStA is validated using two case studies. The first is a model of local intracellular signalling reactions in the cAMP/PKA/MAPK pathway in neurons as studied in [15,27]. This model is introduced in Sect. 4.1 to facilitate explanation of the core concepts of MultiVeStA in the following sections. The second case study concerns a model for the performance analysis of a public transportation network in Edinburgh [29], parameterised using real-world GPS data. It is introduced in Sect. 5.

Information on how to replicate the experiments of this paper are available online at http://sysma.imtlucca.it/tools/multivesta/batchMeans.

2   Batch Means Method

The type of property that we are interested in is the steady-state value of a random variable F. To evaluate this property, we ask the simulator to generate a simulation run $(F(t))_{t \geq 0}$ such that $F(t)$ represents the value of F when the simulated time is t. Then we define the steady-state mean π_F as

$$\pi_F = \lim_{T \to \infty} \frac{1}{T} \int_0^T F(t)dt.$$

Using batch means, π_F is estimated for a large value of T rather than for the limit. Let B and b be positive integers (two parameters). A confidence interval for this value is then constructed by dividing the time interval $[0, T]$ into B batches of equal time length. We discard the first b batches to remove initialisation bias, and assume that the means of the remaining batches are normally distributed. The challenge is to find a T large enough (but minimal) for the assumptions of normality and lack of initialisation bias to be approximately valid.

We solve this using an approach based on the ASAP3 procedure [34]: we draw a moderately large number of events (4096 by default) and record the obtained simulated time T_1. We then draw B (default value: 256) batches of time length T_1 and discard the first b (default value: 4) batches. We then perform a test for normality on the remaining batches — we use the Anderson-Darling test, offered by the SSJ library [24,25]. If the test fails to reject the null hypothesis that the batch means are drawn from the normal distribution, we compute the correlation between subsequent batch means and determine whether this is smaller than a threshold value given in [34]. If so, we construct a confidence interval that corrects for this correlation. If not, we iteratively repeat the experiment for $T_i = 2T_{i-1}$ until both conditions are met. When both conditions are met, we continue sampling (increasing the time length of the batches) until the confidence interval width is smaller than δ, yielding a Chow-Robbins confidence interval that is asymptotically valid [21].

A pseudocode representation of such algorithm appears in Algorithm 1. In particular, Algorithm 2 details how the size of batches is initially computed, i.e., how the parameter T_1 mentioned above is calculated. Instead, Algorithm 3 details how the statistical quality of the batches is computed.

If the limit does not exist, then the confidence interval is expected to asymptotically widen, meaning that the procedure will not terminate. If the limit is not unique in the sense that different runs of the same procedure will yield different limits, owing to, for example, the existence of more than a single BSCC, then the method of *independent replications* [2] is to be preferred. We would like to stress again that the multiple-BSCC setting is rare in practice, and that the batch means is much faster than independent replications because the b warm-up batches only need to be drawn once rather than for every sample. In a general

---

Algorithm 1. Batch means algorithm

Require: B even (default: 256), variable of interest x
1: $T \leftarrow$ determineInitialBatchDuration()
2: $\mu \leftarrow (\mu_1, \ldots, \mu_B)$
3: **for** $i \in \{1, \ldots, B\}$ **do**
4:     $\mu_i \leftarrow$ drawBatch(x, T)
5: **end for**
6: $(a, \rho, d) \leftarrow$ performGoodnessOfFitTests(μ)
7: **while** $a > a^*$ **and** $\rho > \rho^*$ **and** $d > \delta$ **do**
8:     **for** $i \in \{1, \ldots, B/2\}$ **do**
9:         $\mu_i \leftarrow (\mu_{2i} + \mu_{2i+1})/2$
10:     **end for**
11:     $T \leftarrow 2T$
12:     **for** $i \in \{B/2 + 1, \ldots, B\}$ **do**
13:         $\mu_i \leftarrow$ drawBatch(x, T)
14:     **end for**
15:     $(a, \rho, d) \leftarrow$ performGoodnessOfFitTests(μ)
16: **end while**
17: **return** confidence interval based on μ, compensating for correlation

---

Algorithm 2. determineInitialBatchDuration()

Require: initial event number X (default: 4096)
1: $T \leftarrow 0$
2: $k \leftarrow X$
3: **while** $T = 0$ **do**
4:     **for** $i \in \{1, \ldots, k\}$ **do**
5:         simulator.takeStep()
6:     **end for**
7:     $T =$ simulator.getTime()
8:     $k \leftarrow 2k$
9: **end while**
10: **return** T

---

approach, the two methods can be integrated by starting with the method of independent replications, and switching to the method of batch means if the samples are judged to be sufficiently similar by a normality test.

Although our implementation allows experienced users to override the default parameters, it is not necessary for novice users to do so. There is typically no need to adjust the parameters B, b, and the initial number of events, because these only determine the number of initial runs; if this is chosen too low, the algorithm is designed to draw more samples. For the confidence level of the normality test, it is sufficient to choose a default value of 95% or 99%. (The confidence level for this test does not provide a strict bound anyway because it is conducted several times. In the early stages of the simulation, when the means are typically very unlike the normal distribution and strongly correlated, the test's p-value and therefore the probability of stopping prematurely tends

---

Algorithm 3. `performGoodnessOfFitTests()`

Require: batch means μ,
 1: $\mu' \leftarrow (\mu_{b+1}, \ldots, \mu_B)$
 2: $a \leftarrow$ `PerformNormalityTest`(μ')
 3: $\rho \leftarrow$ `PerformTestForAutocorrelation`(μ')
 4: $d \leftarrow$ `ComputeConfidenceIntervalWidth`(μ')
 5: **return** (a, ρ, d);

---

to be far below the threshold.) The only parameters that in all cases need to be set by the user are the confidence interval final width δ and confidence level α, which need to be set for most SMC procedures. Note that it is important to avoid choosing δ too low, because making it y times smaller will require roughly y^2 times as many samples.

3 MultiVeStA

This section introduces MultiVeStA [31], a Java framework for statistical model checking that can be easily integrated with existing discrete event simulators. MultiVeStA has been successfully applied to many scenarios, including: (by external users) contract-oriented middlewares [8], opportunistic network protocols [5], online planning [10], (by MultiVeStA's developers) software product lines [35,36], crowd-steering [28], public transportation systems [13,20], volunteer clouds [30], and swarm robotics [9].

MultiVeStA has a distributed architecture, making it possible for users to distribute simulations across a network of compute-servers. An in-depth discussion of MultiVeStA's architecture and of MultiQuaTEx is provided in [28,31].

The tool extends VeStA [1,33] and PVeStA [4], as discussed in [31]. More information on MultiVeStA and on the currently integrated simulators is available at http://sysma.imtlucca.it/tools/multivesta/.

3.1 Simulator Integration

MultiVeStA adopts a distinctive black-box approach: it does not require systems to be specified in a given system specification language, but rather it makes it possible to directly analyse models written for simulators which have been integrated with MultiVeStA. In particular, MultiVeStA interacts with underlying simulators by triggering basic actions such as:

- **reset**: reset the simulator to its "initial state", and update the seed used for pseudo-random sampling, necessary before performing a (new) simulation;
- **next**: perform one step of simulation; and
- **eval**: evaluate an observation in the current simulation state.

This is obtained by instantiating MultiVeStA's Java interface which contains three corresponding methods. As a consequence, MultiVeStA natively supports

```
1   public class SimulatorState extends NewState{
2
3       //Reference to the simulator
4       private Simulator simulator;
5
6       /* @param params Parameters provided to MultiVeStA */
7       public SimulatorState(ParametersForState params) {
8           super(params);
9           //Name of the (file with the) model to be analyzed
10          params.getModel();
11          //Optional string with simulator-specific parameters.
12          params.getOtherParameters();
13          //Optional evaluator of model-specific observations see [31]
14          params.getStateEvaluator();
15          //Read the model and initialize the simulator...
16      }
17
18      /* @param randomSeed The new seed for random generation */
19      public void setSimulatorForNewSimulation(int randomSeed) {
20          simulator.reset(randomSeed);
21      }
22
23      public void performOneStepOfSimulation() {
24          simulator.performOneStep();
25      }
26
27      /* @param obs a string representing the observation to be evaluated
28       * @return the value of the evaluated observation */
29      public double rval(String obs) {
30          simulator.eval(obs);
31      }
32  }
```

Listing 1. A skeleton of the adaptor between MultiVeStA and a simulator.

Java-based simulators. However, it has been also integrated with C-based simulators using the Java Native Interface (JNI) or Python-based simulators using the py4j libraries.

Similar in spirit to MultiVeStA is (the independently proposed) Plasmalab [11], a framework for SMC. The main difference lies in the property specification languages which are used (see [31]): temporal logics to estimate probabilities by Plasma-Lab, and MultiQuaTEx by MultiVeStA (Sect. 4.2). Plasma-lab offers further statistical analysis techniques including sequential hypothesis testing for transient properties, but crucially it does not support steady-state model checking, which is the main contribution of this paper.

After adding the MultiVeStA library to the classpath of the simulator, one has to extend the class NewState in order to provide the three functionalities above. Listing 1 provides a skeleton of such class. Essentially, this is an adaptor between MultiVeStA and the simulator, which just propagates the requests received from MultiVeStA to the simulator, and returns the obtained results. We note that the class stores a reference to the simulator (Line 4), in the form of an object of a class in the simulator's namespace.

The class constructor (Lines 7–16) should perform only actions that have to be done once (and not for individual simulation runs). For example, it might read the model from a file. The parameters provided by the user to MultiVeStA are collected in the object **params**, containing the name of the model to be analysed, simulator-specific parameters, and a model-specific state evaluator (see [31] for more details on the latter).

The method `setSimulatorForNewSimulation` (Lines 19–21) is invoked by MultiVeStA to reset the simulator for a new simulation, providing also the new random seed. During a simulation, the method `performOneStepOfSimulation` (Lines 23–25) is invoked by MultiVeStA to perform a simulation step.

The method `rval` (Lines 29–31) is invoked by MultiVeStA to evaluate observations of the current state of a simulation run. Typically, the method delegates the evaluation of the observations to the simulator, if possible, or deals only with observations common to all possible models that can be defined for the simulator (e.g., the current simulation time or the molecule count of a given chemical species in biological simulators), and invokes the state evaluator which is provided for any model-specific observations.

The state evaluator is not necessary if we know in advance all observations that can be computed for any model definable for the simulator, or if the evaluation of an observation can be delegated to the simulator. We have found in practice that the delegation of the evaluation to the simulator is often possible, and is the preferred option.

4   Analysis of a Biochemical Pathway Using MultiVeStA

In this section we show how transient and steady-state analysis of a well-known biological model from the literature can be performed using MultiVeStA.

4.1   Example 1: The cAMP/PKA/MAPK Biochemical Pathway

As our first example in this paper we consider a biochemical reaction pathway expressed in Bio-PEPA [16], a process-algebra-based framework for the modelling and the analysis (including stochastic simulation) of biochemical networks. The Bio-PEPA software [14] supports a range of both continuous and discrete simulators including accelerated stochastic simulation methods. MultiVeStA interoperates with the Direct Method implementation of the Gillespie stochastic simulation algorithm provided by the Bio-PEPA Eclipse Plugin as discussed in [20]. The particular Bio-PEPA model considered is the cAMP/PKA/MAPK pathway modelled as in [27], analysed with Bio-PEPA in [15]. A schematic presentation of the pathway is given in Fig. 1, taken from [15].

Three sub-networks can be identified in the pathway, highlighted in boxes with different colours. Each sub-network regards the activation of three molecules, namely *AC* (*adenylate cyclase*), *PKA* (*protein kinase A*) and *MAPK* (*mitogen-activated protein kinase*). We refer to [15] for a detailed presentation of the model. Here, we will show how MultiVeStA can be used to study the dynamics in terms of *activation* and *deactivation* of the enzyme *AC*, both as a function of time, and at steady state.

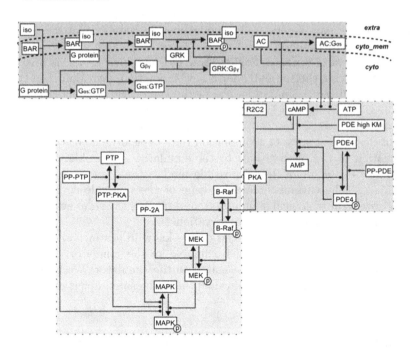

Fig. 1. Schematic representation of the cAMP/PKA/MAPK pathway (from [15]).

4.2 Transient Analysis with MultiVeStA

MultiVeStA offers a powerful and flexible property specification language, MultiQuaTEx [31], which allows the modeller to express transient properties to be verified. Intuitively, a MultiQuaTEx query specifies a random variable (representing, e.g., the number of active AC molecules at a certain point in time during a simulation).

The expected value of a MultiQuaTEx query is estimated as the mean $\overline{x}$ of n samples (taken from n simulations), with n large enough (but minimal) to guarantee that we can construct a $(1 - \alpha) \cdot 100\%$ confidence interval around $\overline{x}$ of width at most δ, for given α and δ. This means that, with a probability of at least $1 - \alpha$, the actual expected value belongs to the random interval $[\overline{x} - \frac{\delta}{2}, \overline{x} + \frac{\delta}{2}]$.

A MultiQuaTEx query might actually specify many random variables. An ensemble of simulation results computed by MultiVeStA can be reused multiple times to study each of the random variables in turn. Listing 2 depicts a MultiQuaTEx query for the cAMP/PKA/MAPK pathway.

We now overview MultiQuaTEx using the expression in Listing 2, defined for the above mentioned cAMP/PKA/MAPK pathway model. It studies the evolution over time of the fraction of active instances of adenylate cyclase (`AC_active`) over the total quantity of adenylate cyclase (`AC_active` + `AC_inactive`). A MultiQuaTEx query consists of a list of *MultiQuaTEx operators*, used in an `eval parametric` clause to specify the properties to be estimated.

```
1   fractionAtTime(t, act, inact) =
2       if{s.rval("time") >= t}
3           then s.rval(act) / (s.rval(act) + s.rval(inact))
4           else #fractionAtTime(t, act, inact)
5       fi;
6
7   eval parametric(E[fractionAtTime(t,"AC_active", "AC_inactive")],1.0,10.0,700.0);
```

Listing 2. A transient MultiQuaTEx query

Lines 1–5 define one MultiQuaTEx operator, `fractionAtTime`, with three parameters: `t`, `act` and `inact`. It is evaluated (in every simulation) as the fraction `act/(act + inact)` at time point `t`.

Line 7 instantiates `fractionAtTime`, specifying the properties to be evaluated: the (expected value of the) fraction of active AC from time point 1 to time point 700, with step 10. Many MultiQuaTEx operators can appear in an `eval parametric` clause, which is just syntactic sugar expanded into a list of `eval E[·]`. There will be 70 of these in the case of Listing 2, all evaluated using the same simulations.

A MultiQuaTEx operator consists of the following ingredients:

1. real-valued observations on the current simulation state (`s.rval`);
2. arithmetic expressions (Line 3);
3. conditional statements;
4. a one-step next operator which triggers the execution of a simulation step (the `#` symbol of Line 4);
5. recursion, used in Line 4 to evaluate the operator in the next simulation step.

This is general enough to express PCTL and CSL properties, as discussed in [1], however users must restrict themselves to queries that can be evaluated for each simulation in a finite number of simulation steps.

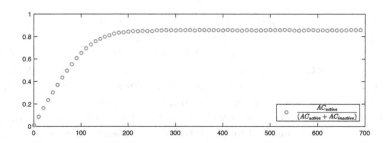

Fig. 2. Estimation of the transient MultiQuaTEx query from Listing 2.

Figure 2 depicts the estimation computed by MultiVeStA of the transient MultiQuaTEx query from Listing 2 for $\alpha = 0.05$ and $\delta = 0.01$ (meaning a 95% confidence interval of width at most 0.01). The analysis required 480 simulations, with a runtime of about 1000 s (without distributing the simulations) on a 2.6 GHz Intel Core i5 machine with 4 GB of RAM. A similar analysis has been performed in [15], studying how the fraction of active instances of AC (and of two additional molecules PKA and $MAPK$) changes over time. This has been done by running an arbitrary number of simulations with time horizon set to 700 s, and required a modification of the Bio-PEPA model to represent the fraction of active molecules directly within the model. Here, instead, we follow a separation-of-concerns approach, leaving the model unchanged and delegating to MultiQuaTEx the definition of the measures of interest. In addition, MultiVeStA gives a statistical assurance on the obtained measures.

4.3 Steady-State Analysis in MultiVeStA

The extension of MultiVeStA with steady-state capabilities required us to extend MultiQuaTEx correspondingly. Listing 3 provides a *steady-state* MultiQuaTEx query. It is similar to that in Listing 2, but it studies the fraction of active AC at steady state rather than at given time points.

```
1  fractionAtTime(act,inact) =
2      s.rval(act)/(s.rval(act)+s.rval(inact));
3
4  eval batchMeans(E[ fractionAtTime("AC_active","AC_inactive") ])  ;
```

Listing 3. A steady-state MultiQuaTEx query

The query is composed of two parts:

1. A list of MultiQuaTEx operators, where, differently from the transient case, the one-step next operator (#) is not allowed; and
2. the `eval batchMeans` clause, similar to the `eval parametric` one, which lists the properties to be estimated at steady state.

Intuitively, a steady-state MultiQuaTEx query defines a number of state observations. In order to estimate the value of each observation at steady state, we integrated within MultiVeStA the batch means methods described in Sect. 2. Intuitively, as depicted in Algorithm 1, we do not perform n independent simulations as in the transient case, but only a single long simulation, divided in n batches of equal time length, each of which gives a sample.

The time horizon is automatically chosen to be large enough (but minimal), to guarantee that we can construct an $(1-\alpha)\cdot 100\%$ confidence interval $[\bar{x}-\frac{\delta}{2}, \bar{x}+\frac{\delta}{2}]$ for the value at steady state of the property of interest, where $\bar{x}$ is the mean of the batch samples.

Figure 3 depicts the novel architecture of MultiVeStA. We see that MultiVeStA consists of two main macro-functionalities, transient analysis and steady-state one. Each functionality allows to parse and analyse the corresponding family of MultiQuaTEx queries. Both analysis interact with integrated simulators by using the adaptor interface discussed in Sect. 3.1. For easiness of presentation, the figure ignores the distributed architecture supporting the transient analysis.

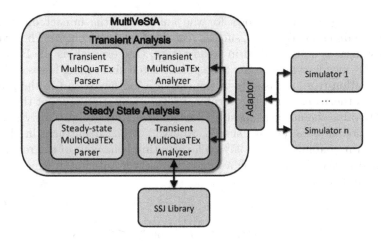

Fig. 3. The novel architecture of MultiVeStA

Figure 2 shows that the fraction of active adenylate cyclase (seems to) stabilize to about 0.855 after 300 s of simulated time. We can now confirm that this actually holds at steady state. Indeed, Listing 3 is estimated as 0.855 using the same confidence interval used for the transient case ($\alpha = 0.05$ and $\delta = 0.01$). This has been done by performing a simulation with time horizon of 14066 s. Notably, the steady-state analysis took only about 20 s, compared to the 1000 s required by the transient one. The transient analysis is slower even in the case where we attempt to reduce the computation time of the simulation by setting 300 as the simulation stop-time in Listing 2, obtaining a runtime analysis of about 486 s.

Finally, we remark that when using the Bio-PEPA tools alone it is not possible to perform any form of steady-state analysis, thus our integration of MultiVeStA with support for batch means provides analysis capabilities which are not provided by the Bio-PEPA Eclipse Plugin.

5   Example 2: Edinburgh Bus Simulator

Recently, many approaches have been provided to analyse models of public transportation systems parameterised using real-world GPS data (e.g., [19]). In this section we use MultiVeStA to study a model of a public city bus service in Edinburgh [29], obtained from GPS data. We consider the problem of guaranteeing a quality-of-service constraint required by the legislator. The recently submitted paper [29] presents a model of a bus service in Edinburgh, parameterised using real-world data. The model is used to evaluate the performance of bus networks. The software is particularly focussed on so-called *frequent* services, which means that more than six buses are scheduled to depart per hour. In this case, passengers are not expected to base their decision of when to arrive at a stop on an explicit timetable. Instead, performance is expressed in terms of the regularity of the *headways*, i.e., the inter-departure times at stops.

The parametric model allows for the analysis of the impact on headway regularity of different strategies, such as real-time headway control. The headway regularity measures are studied in steady state. One example is the Buses-Per-Hour (BPH) metric, which at any time point t is 0 if six or more buses arrived at a given location (e.g., a bus stop or the end of a journey stage) in the previous hour and 1 otherwise. Scottish government regulations stipulate that the steady-state BPH value should be at most 5%; meaning that a regulator arriving at the given location in steady state should observe six bus departures in the next hour with a probability of over 95%. The counting behaviour of the regulator is represented in the simulation by a forgetful observer automaton which behaves as described in Fig. 4.

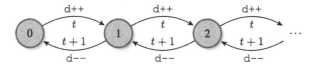

Fig. 4. Observers counting departures should note the times of departures and forget departures which are more than one hour old.

The BPH metric is expressed within MultiQuaTEx as displayed in Listing 4, where H_8 is a state observation evaluated within the bus simulator as the number of buses which arrived in the previous hour at the end of stage 8.

```
1   BPH8() = if {s.rval("H_8") < 6}
2            then 1
3            else 0
4         fi;
5
6   eval batchMeans(E[ BPH8() ]);
```

Listing 4. The MultiQuaTEx query for the BPH after stage/patch 8.

One question that is of interest to planners is how many buses need to be assigned to the route to meet the government regulations. An overview of the performance of a specific bus service in Edinburgh (namely the Airlink service) for different numbers of buses assigned to the route can be found in Table 1.

Each row of Table 1 contains estimates of the BPH metric at the end of a specific stage of the route roughly corresponding to the end of patch 8 in Fig. 5. This location is immediately after a busy junction in the city centre and the value of the BPH metric here is higher than at most other points along the route. The BPH metric expresses a penalty and so a higher value of the BPH metric signifies worse performance. The requirement for the frequent services such as the Airlink is that the width of the confidence interval around the satisfaction of the BPH requirement should be at most 0.05 — we see from the table that at least 9 buses are required to meet this criterion.

Table 1. Analysis of the performance of the Airlink service in Edinburgh for different numbers of buses assigned to the route.

#buses	C.I.	# iterations	runtime (s)
8	[0.5095, 0.5100]	4	306.2
9	[0.0110, 0.0119]	3	193.5

We display the BPH at the end of a specific stage — corresponding to a so-called *patch* — of the route. An example of a patch structure for the Airlink route is displayed in Fig. 5.

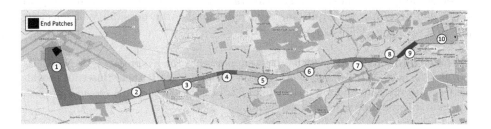

Fig. 5. One possible stage structure along the Airlink route in Edinburgh.

The default number of buses servicing the Airlink route is 11, and the value of the BPH metric is very low in this setting because, with so many buses serving the route, it is very unlikely that there will be fewer than six buses arriving in any given hour. From the table we see that government regulations would still be met if two buses were removed from the route: 11 buses are used, but 9 would be sufficient. Our analysis thus suggests that the bus company which operates this service could cut fuel costs and reduce atmospheric emissions of pollutants while continuing to satisfy the relevant performance requirements imposed in legislation.

6 Conclusions

In this paper we have extended a statistical model-checker with computational methods for the calculation of steady-state properties of dynamic systems viewed as black-box systems which offer no access to their internal structure or logic. The challenges of this setting are that we have only the perspective of an external observer, and can only express properties over the model outputs. The benefits of this approach are that the method is applicable to a wide range of simulators, across a wide range of modelling formalisms. In this paper we computed steady-state metrics of a model in a biochemical reaction simulator and a transportation system in a custom discrete-event simulator.

Working across formalisms in this way means that the MultiVeStA tool provides a transferrable statistical model-checking service which modellers can apply to their own preferred modelling formalism, allowing them to continue working with the modelling languages where they have accumulated experience, or which are best suited to the problem which is under study. In the future, we plan to further enrich the family of analysis techniques offered by MultiVeStA, and to apply the tool to further domains.

The provision of a query language such as MultiQuaTEx also supports the transferability of the MultiVeStA service to other formalisms in a way in which a specialised logic would not. Based on functions, conditional statements, and arithmetic expressions, MultiQuaTEx resembles a programming language more than a logic, making understanding and expressing properties easier for a practitioner because of the more accessible syntax which is used. In the future we plan to develop an editor for MultiQuaTEx, offering also the possibility of selecting among a set of predefined queries.

Acknowledgments. This work has been supported by the EU project QUANTICOL, 600708. The authors thank Bill Johnston and Philip Lock of Lothian Buses for providing access to the data and for their helpful feedback on parts of this research project, and Jane Hillston for her helpful comments.

References

1. Agha, G.A., Meseguer, J., Sen, K.: PMaude: rewrite-based specification language for probabilistic object systems. In: QAPL 2005. ENTCS, vol. 153(2), pp. 213–239. Elsevier (2006)
2. Alexopoulos, C., Goldsman, D.: To batch or not to batch? ACM Trans. Model. Comput. Simul. **14**(1), 76–114 (2004)
3. Alexopoulos, C., Seila, A.F.: Implementing the batch means method in simulation experiments. In: Proceedings of the 28th Conference on Winter Simulation, WSC 1996, pp. 214–221. IEEE Computer Society, Washington, DC (1996)
4. AlTurki, M., Meseguer, J.: PVeStA: a parallel statistical model checking and quantitative analysis tool. In: Corradini, A., Klin, B., Cîrstea, C. (eds.) CALCO 2011. LNCS, vol. 6859, pp. 386–392. Springer, Heidelberg (2011). doi:10.1007/978-3-642-22944-2_28
5. Arora, S., Rathor, A., Rao, M.V.P.: Statistical model checking of opportunistic network protocols. In: Proceedings of AINTEC 2015, pp. 62–68. ACM (2015)
6. Aziz, A., Sanwal, K., Singhal, V., Brayton, R.: Model-checking continuous-time Markov chains. ACM Trans. Comput. Logic (TOCL) **1**(1), 162–170 (2000)
7. Baier, C., Haverkort, B., Hermanns, H., Katoen, J.-P.: Model-checking algorithms for continuous-time Markov chains. IEEE TSE **29**(6), 524–541 (2003)
8. Bartoletti, M., Cimoli, T., Murgia, M., Podda, A.S., Pompianu, L.: A contract-oriented middleware. In: Braga, C., Ölveczky, P.C. (eds.) FACS 2015. LNCS, vol. 9539, pp. 86–104. Springer, Cham (2016). doi:10.1007/978-3-319-28934-2_5
9. Belzner, L., Nicola, R., Vandin, A., Wirsing, M.: Reasoning (on) service component ensembles in rewriting logic. In: Iida, S., Meseguer, J., Ogata, K. (eds.) Specification, Algebra, and Software. LNCS, vol. 8373, pp. 188–211. Springer, Heidelberg (2014). doi:10.1007/978-3-642-54624-2_10

10. Belzner, L., Hennicker, R., Wirsing, M.: OnPlan: a framework for simulation-based online planning. In: Braga, C., Ölveczky, P.C. (eds.) FACS 2015. LNCS, vol. 9539, pp. 1–30. Springer, Cham (2016). doi:10.1007/978-3-319-28934-2_1

11. Boyer, B., Corre, K., Legay, A., Sedwards, S.: PLASMA-lab: a flexible, distributable statistical model checking library. In: Joshi, K., Siegle, M., Stoelinga, M., D'Argenio, P.R. (eds.) QEST 2013. LNCS, vol. 8054, pp. 160–164. Springer, Heidelberg (2013). doi:10.1007/978-3-642-40196-1_12

12. Bušić, A., Gaujal, B., Vincent, J.-M.: Perfect simulation and non-monotone Markovian systems. In: Valuetools 2008. ICST (2008)

13. Ciancia, V., Latella, D., Massink, M., Paškauskas, R., Vandin, A.: A tool-chain for statistical spatio-temporal model checking of bike sharing systems. In: Margaria, T., Steffen, B. (eds.) ISoLA 2016. LNCS, vol. 9952, pp. 657–673. Springer, Cham (2016). doi:10.1007/978-3-319-47166-2_46

14. Ciocchetta, F., Duguid, A., Gilmore, S., Guerriero, M.L., Hillston, J.: The Bio-PEPA tool suite. In: QEST 2009, pp. 309–310 (2009)

15. Ciocchetta, F., Duguid, A., Guerriero, M.L.: A compartmental model of the cAMP/PKA/MAPK pathway in Bio-PEPA. In: Ciobanu, G. (ed.) MeCBIC 2009. EPTCS, vol. 11, pp. 71–90 (2009)

16. Ciocchetta, F., Hillston, J.: Bio-PEPA: a framework for the modelling and analysis of biological systems. TCS 410(33–34), 3065–3084 (2009)

17. Conway, R.W.: Some tactical problems in digital simulation. Manage. Sci. 10(1), 47–61 (1963)

18. Rabih, D., Pekergin, N.: Statistical model checking using perfect simulation. In: Liu, Z., Ravn, A.P. (eds.) ATVA 2009. LNCS, vol. 5799, pp. 120–134. Springer, Heidelberg (2009). doi:10.1007/978-3-642-04761-9_11

19. Gast, N., Massonnet, G., Reijsbergen, D., Tribastone, M.: Probabilistic forecasts of bike-sharing systems for journey planning. In: CIKM 2015, pp. 703–712 (2015)

20. Gilmore, S., Tribastone, M., Vandin, A.: An analysis pathway for the quantitative evaluation of public transport systems. In: Albert, E., Sekerinski, E. (eds.) IFM 2014. LNCS, vol. 8739, pp. 71–86. Springer, Cham (2014). doi:10.1007/978-3-319-10181-1_5

21. Glynn, P.W., Whitt, W.: The asymptotic validity of sequential stopping rules for stochastic simulations. Ann. Appl. Probab. 2, 180–198 (1992)

22. Hansson, H., Jonsson, B.: A logic for reasoning about time and reliability. Formal Aspects Comput. 6(5), 512–535 (1994)

23. Katoen, J.-P., Zapreev, I.S., Hahn, E.M., Hermanns, H., Jansen, D.N.: The ins and outs of the probabilistic model checker MRMC. Perform. Eval. 68(2), 90–104 (2011)

24. L'Ecuyer, P.: SSJ: Stochastic simulation in Java, software library (2016). http://simul.iro.umontreal.ca/ssj/

25. L'Ecuyer, P., Meliani, L., Vaucher, J.: SSJ: a framework for stochastic simulation in Java. In: Yücesan, E., Chen, C.-H., Snowdon, J.L., Charnes, J.M. (eds.) Proceedings of the 2002 Winter Simulation Conference, pp. 234–242. IEEE Press (2002)

26. Legay, A., Delahaye, B., Bensalem, S.: Statistical model checking: an overview. In: Barringer, H., et al. (eds.) RV 2010. LNCS, vol. 6418, pp. 122–135. Springer, Heidelberg (2010). doi:10.1007/978-3-642-16612-9_11

27. Neves, S.R., Tsokas, P., Sarkar, A., Grace, E.A., Rangamani, P., Taubenfeld, S.M., Alberini, C.M., Schaff, J.C., Blitzer, R.D., Moraru, I.I., Iyengar, R.: Cell shape and negative links in regulatory motifs together control spatial information flow in signaling networks. Cell 133(4), 666–680 (2008)

28. Pianini, D., Sebastio, S., Vandin, A.: Distributed statistical analysis of complex systems modeled through a chemical metaphor. In: HPCS 2014, pp. 416–423. IEEE (2014)
29. Reijsbergen, D., Gilmore, S.: An automated methodology for analysing urban transportation systems using model checking (2016). https://danielreijsbergen. files.wordpress.com/2016/10/bus_modelling1.pdf
30. Sebastio, S., Amoretti, M., Lluch Lafuente, A.: A computational field framework for collaborative task execution in volunteer clouds. In: SEAMS 2014, pp. 105–114. ACM (2014)
31. Sebastio, S., Vandin, A.: MultiVeStA: statistical model checking for discrete event simulators. In: Valuetools 2013, pp. 310–315. ACM (2013)
32. Sen, K., Viswanathan, M., Agha, G.: Statistical model checking of black-box probabilistic systems. In: Alur, R., Peled, D.A. (eds.) CAV 2004. LNCS, vol. 3114, pp. 202–215. Springer, Heidelberg (2004). doi:10.1007/978-3-540-27813-9_16
33. Sen, K., Viswanathan, M., Agha, G.A.: Vesta: a statistical model-checker and analyzer for probabilistic systems. In: QEST 2005, pp. 251–252 (2005)
34. Steiger, N.M., Lada, E.K., Wilson, J.R., Joines, J.A., Alexopoulos, C., Goldsman, D.: ASAP3: a batch means procedure for steady-state simulation analysis. ACM Trans. Model. Comput. Simul. 15(1), 39–73 (2005)
35. ter Beek, M.H., Legay, A., Lluch-Lafuente, A., Vandin, A.: Statistical analysis of probabilistic models of software product lines with quantitative constraints. In: SPLC 2015, pp. 11–15. ACM (2015)
36. ter Beek, M.H., Legay, A., Lluch Lafuente, A., Vandin, A.: Statistical model checking for product lines. In: Margaria, T., Steffen, B. (eds.) ISoLA 2016. LNCS, vol. 9952, pp. 114–133. Springer, Cham (2016). doi:10.1007/978-3-319-47166-2_8
37. Younes, H.L.S.: Probabilistic verification for "Black-Box" systems. In: Etessami, K., Rajamani, S.K. (eds.) CAV 2005. LNCS, vol. 3576, pp. 253–265. Springer, Heidelberg (2005). doi:10.1007/11513988_25
38. Younes, H.L.S., Simmons, R.G.: Probabilistic verification of discrete event systems using acceptance sampling. In: Brinksma, E., Larsen, K.G. (eds.) CAV 2002. LNCS, vol. 2404, pp. 223–235. Springer, Heidelberg (2002). doi:10.1007/3-540-45657-0_17

Algebraic Compilation of Safety-Critical Java Bytecode

James Baxter$^{(\boxtimes)}$ and Ana Cavalcanti

Department of Computer Science, University of York, York, UK
jeb531@york.ac.uk

Abstract. Safety-Critical Java (SCJ) is a version of Java that facilitates the development of certifiable programs, and requires a specialised virtual machine (SCJVM). In spite of the nature of the applications for which SCJ is designed, none of the SCJVMs are verified. In this paper, we contribute a formal specification of a bytecode interpreter for SCJ and an algebraic compilation strategy from Java bytecode to C. For the target C code, we adopt the compilation approach for icecap, the only SCJVM that is open source and up-to-date with the SCJ standard. Our work enables either prototyping of a verified compiler, or full verification of icecap or any other SCJVM.

1 Introduction

Java is widely used and there is interest in using it for programming safety-critical real-time systems. This has led to the creation of a variant of Java called Safety-Critical Java (SCJ) [16]. It is being developed by the Open Group under the Java Community Process as Java Specification Request 302. SCJ replaces Java's garbage collector with a system of scoped memory areas to allow determination of when objects are deallocated. It also introduces preemptive priority scheduling of event handlers to ensure predictable scheduling.

Due to these new mechanisms, SCJ requires a specialised virtual machine, although, since the syntax of Java is not modified, a standard Java compiler can be used to generate bytecode. There exist some SCJ virtual machines (SCJVMs) [1,22,27]; they all allow for code to be compiled ahead-of-time to a native language, usually C, since SCJ targets embedded systems with low resources. As far as we know, the icecap HVM [27] is the only publicly-available SCJVM that is up-to-date with the SCJ specification; it outputs production-quality code.

Neither icecap nor any of the other SCJVMs has been formally verified. In [3], we present a formal account of the services of an SCJVM. Here, we focus on the execution of Java bytecode and its compilation to native C code. We formalise the requirements for an SCJVM bytecode interpreter and a compilation strategy, using the algebraic approach [25] to verify compilation from bytecode to C, with icecap as a source of requirements for our specification. We use C as our target, following the scheme used by icecap that aims for portable native code that can

N. Polikarpova and S. Schneider (Eds.): IFM 2017, LNCS 10510, pp. 161–176, 2017.
DOI: 10.1007/978-3-319-66845-1_11

be easily integrated into existing systems. The decision to use bytecode rather than SCJ itself as our source ensures that we can rely on existing Java compilers and work ensuring their correctness. Our focus here is not the development of an SCJVM or compiler, but a technique that can be used to develop and verify an ahead-of-time compiling SCJVM implementation.

We use algebraic compilation, in which the semantics of the source and target languages are defined using the same specification language, and a compilation strategy is a procedure to apply compilation rules: refinement laws that address the program constructs independently. Implementing the rules using a rewrite engine can produce a prototype verified compiler. Algebraic compilation has been studied for imperative [25] and object-oriented languages [9], and for hardware compilation [21]. Here we use it, for the first time, to compile a low-level language, Java bytecode, to a high-level language, C. While Java bytecode has some high-level features, particularly its notion of objects, we view it as low-level since it is unstructured, with control flow managed using a program counter.

In summary, our main contributions here are

- a formal model of an SCJVM interpreter,
- a set of provably correct compilation rules for transforming this model, and
- a specification of a strategy for applying these rules to transform Java bytecode in the interpreter to a shallow embedding of C code.

All *Circus* models are mechanically checked by the CZT infrastructure, and some domain checks using Z/Eves are available. In doing this we also provide insights into the application of algebraic compilation to compile low-level source languages, and SCJ programs in particular, to high-level targets. While there is existing work on compiling Java to C [23,27,30], none of these works include verification of such a compilation.

In Sect. 2 we present SCJ and the *Circus* language that we use for refinement. Section 3 is an overview of our approach, whose main components are detailed in the subsequent sections: Section 4 describes our SCJVM model; Sect. 5 discusses the shallow embedding of C in *Circus*; and Sect. 6 describes our compilation strategy. Section 7 discusses some of our design decisions. We conclude in Sect. 8, where we discuss related and future work.

2   Preliminaries

We present SCJ in Sect. 2.1 and *Circus* in Sect. 2.2.

2.1   Safety-Critical Java

An SCJ program is structured as a sequence of missions. An instance of a class implementing an interface called `Safelet` defines the starting point of an SCJ program, via an initialisation method, and the definition of a mission sequencer that determines the sequence of missions of the program.

Each mission consists of a collection of schedulable objects, which include asynchronous event handlers that can be released aperiodically, in response to a release request, or periodically, at set intervals of time. Each of these schedulable objects is executed on a separate thread. These threads continue executing until the mission is signalled to terminate by one of its own schedulable objects.

Scheduling follows a preemptive priority policy. The threads eligible to run are placed into queues, with one queue for each priority. The thread at the front of the highest priority non-empty queue runs. A priority ceiling emulation system, whereby a thread's priority is raised when it takes a lock, avoids deadlock when it is interrupted by a thread of higher priority.

SCJ replaces the Java garbage collector with a system of memory areas. Different kinds of area are cleared at different times: the immortal memory is never cleared; the mission memory is cleared between missions; a per-release memory is local to an event handler and is cleared after each of its releases; and a private memory can be created and entered as needed.

SCJ uses an API that includes components that provide real-time clocks, support for raw memory accesses, and a lightweight input/output system. Some of the classes from the standard Java API are removed or restricted to ensure the classes required by SCJ are small enough for embedded systems.

2.2 *Circus*

We formalise the bytecode interpreter and our compilation strategy in *Circus* [20]. It is a refinement notation that combines the process-based style of CSP [24] with the data-based style of the Z notation [31]. It also includes programming constructs from Dijkstra's guarded command language [8]. *Circus* is appropriate for our work because it is a notation for refinement, which is a key part of the algebraic approach to verifying compilation, and it permits reasoning about parallelism. It also combines data and reactive behaviour, which enables us to pass from a bytecode program represented as data in an interpreter to a C program with the same control flow as the bytecode program.

Circus specifications define processes: basic or composed from other processes using CSP operators, such as parallel composition, sequence, and internal and external choice. Each process may have an internal state defined using Z and communicates with its environment via channels like a CSP process.

To illustrate the structure of a *Circus* model, we present in Fig. 1 a sketch of a simplified model for an SCJVM interpreter. Typically, a specification begins with type and channel declarations. The types are declared as in Z. Channels carry data of the type specified in their declaration. In our example, there are declarations for channels *getInstruction* and *getInstructionRet*, used to obtain the instruction for each address, provided externally in this simplified model.

The state of a process is defined by a Z schema; in the case of the *Interpreter* process, by the schema *InterpreterState*. The components of the state initially have arbitrary values; specific initial values can be defined through Z schemas, such as *InterpreterInit*, which specifies that the *frameStack* component is empty.

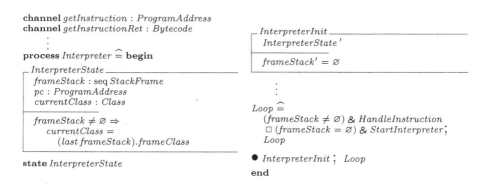

Fig. 1. A sketch of a simple interpreter process

The *Loop* action is defined using a CSP guarded choice that offers different actions depending on whether *frameStack* is empty. *Loop* then repeats via a sequential composition with a recursive call. The main action of a process specifies its behaviour at the end, after a spot. The main action of *Interpreter* initialises the state using *InterpreterInit* and then calls *Loop*.

For a full description of *Circus*, we refer to [20]. For a substantial example, we refer to [2], where we present our specification of the SCJVM services.

3   Our Approach to Algebraic Compilation

In the algebraic approach to compilation the source and target language semantics are embedded in the same specification language and compilation is proved correct by establishing a refinement. A series of compilation rules are applied according to a strategy to refine a source program into a representation of the target machine containing the instructions of the target code.

Here, we adapt the approach to deal with a low-level source language. Our approach can be viewed as the usual approach applied in reverse, starting with an interpreter containing the bytecode source program, and proving that it is refined by an embedding of the C code, as shown in Fig. 2. The core services of an SCJVM must be available for both the source and target codes.

For a low-level language, a deep embedding is the natural method for representing its semantics, since it is defined in terms of how it is processed by a (virtual) machine. For the C code we must choose whether to use a shallow embedding, representing C constructs by corresponding *Circus* constructs, or a deep embedding, creating a *Circus* model that interprets the C code.

We use a shallow embedding, since it allows existing algebraic laws for *Circus* to be used directly for manipulation of the C code and proof of the compilation rules. A deep embedding would require representing the syntax of C separately in *Circus* and rules for transforming the C code would have to be proved.

The shallow embedding approach is much easier to extend or adapt. If a larger subset of bytecodes needs to be considered or the target C code needs

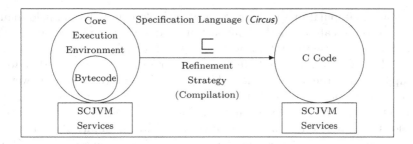

Fig. 2. Our algebraic approach

to be modified, in the worst case, we need more or different *Circus* compilation rules. There will be no need to extend the *Circus* model defining the C semantics.

In the next few sections, we describe Fig. 2 in more detail. A complete formal account of the components in Fig. 2 can be found in [2].

4   SCJVM and Interpreter Model

Our *Circus* model of the SCJVM has six components, each defined by a single *Circus* process. The first three components are the SCJVM services: the memory manager, the scheduler and the real-time clock. They support the execution of an SCJ program by the core execution environment and are unaffected by the compilation strategy, ensuring the memory management and scheduling models of SCJ are preserved by the compilation strategy.

The remaining components form the core execution environment (CEE), which manages the execution of an SCJ program. It is defined by a parallel composition of three *Circus* processes as shown below. Note that the parallelism here represents composition of requirements, not a requirement for a parallel implementation. In an implementation, such as icecap, these processes would be different parts of the program, which may be made up of C files or Java classes.

process $CEE(bc, cs, sid, initOrder) \; \widehat{=}$
   $ObjMan(cs) \parallel Interpreter(bc, cs) \parallel Launcher(sid, initOrder)$

CEE uses global constants that characterise a particular program: bc, recording the bytecode instructions, cs, recording information about the classes in the program, sid, recording the identifier of the **Safelet** class, and $initOrder$, a sequence of class identifiers indicating in which order the classes should be initialised. (For simplicity here, and in what follows, we write $\parallel$ to indicate a parallel composition, but omit the definition of the synchronisation sets.)

$ObjMan$ manages the cooperation between the SCJ program and the SCJVM memory manager, including the representation of objects. The SCJVM memory manager is agnostic as to the structure of objects.

$Interpreter$ and $Launcher$ define the control flow and semantics of the SCJ program. The interpreter is for a representative subset of Java bytecode that covers stack manipulation, arithmetic, local variable manipulation, field manipulation, object creation, method invocation and return, and branching. This covers the main concepts of Java bytecode. A full list of the instructions can be found in [2]. We do not include instructions for different types as that would add duplication to the model while yielding no additional verification power. We also do not include exception handling as SCJ programs can be statically verified to prove that exceptions are not thrown [11,17]. Furthermore, reliance on exceptions to handle errors has been discouraged by an empirical study due to the potential for errors in exception handling [26]. Errors caused in the SCJVM by an incorrect input program are represented by abortion.

The *Interpreter* interacts closely with the *Launcher*, which defines the flow of mission execution. The *Launcher* begins by creating an instance of the `Safelet` class and then executes programmer supplied methods using *Interpreter*.

We describe *Interpreter* in more detail, since it is a central target of the compilation. A simplified version of it is sketched in Sect. 2.2. In the full model the *Interpreter* is defined as the parallel composition of *Thr* processes.

process $Interpreter(bc, cs) \mathrel{\widehat{=}} \|\, t : TID \setminus \{idle\} \bullet Thr(bc, cs, t)$

There is one process $Thr(bc, cs, t)$ for each thread identifier t in the set TID, of thread identifiers, except the identifier of the *idle* thread. Each *Thr* process represents an interpreter for a separate thread, with thread switches coordinated by communication between threads. The state of each *Thr* process is defined by the *InterpreterState* schema in Fig. 1. The control flow of the main action of *Thr* is shown in Fig. 3. It consists of state initialisation as described by *InterpreterInit*, followed by a choice of two actions, *MainThread* and *NotStarted*, with *MainThread* representing the control flow for the main thread, and *NotStarted* for all other threads. The different behaviours are not described as separate processes because they are similar.

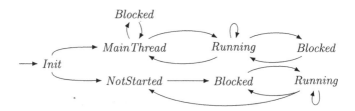

Fig. 3. The overall control flow of *Thr*

MainThread offers a choice of executing a method in response to a signal from the Launcher or switching to another thread. When it executes a method, *MainThread* creates a new Java stack frame (on *frameStack*) for the method and behaves as *Running*. It repeatedly handles bytecode instructions and polls the scheduler until *frameStack* is empty. Polling occurs inbetween bytecode instructions. (This assumption does not necessarily rule out compiler implementations that do not preserve atomicity, as discussed in Sect. 7.)

When a mission is initialised, the *Launcher* communicates with *ObjMan* to set up the memory areas for the mission's schedulable objects, and with the scheduler to start their associated threads. This causes the scheduler to signal that the threads are starting. With that, the instances of *Thr* associated with the started threads, which behave as the *NotStarted* action, create a new stack frame and behave as *Blocked*, each waiting for a request to switch to its thread.

After all the threads are started, the *Launcher* signals the scheduler to suspend the main thread, following which the scheduler signals the *Interpreter* to switch to a new thread. This causes the *Thr* process for the main thread to behave as *Blocked* and the *Thr* process for the new thread to behave as *Running*.

The compilation strategy refines the *CEE* process. Basically it transforms the *Thr* processes, with little change to the other processes. A complete model of the CEE, including the definition of *Thr*, can be found in [2].

5   Shallow Embedding of C in *Circus*

In our approach, compilation generates a C program represented by a *Circus* process. The particular definition of this process depends on the Java bytecode program, as defined by our constants bc and cs, that it implements. So, we refer to the *Circus* process as $CProg_{bc,cs}$, but note that it does not include any reference to these constants, since this is the process that represents the compiled program. For all values of bc and cs, $CProg_{bc,cs}$ has the structure defined below.

process $CProg_{bc,cs} \mathrel{\widehat{=}} \parallel t : TID \setminus \{idle\} \bullet CThr_{bc,cs}(t)$

The parallelism of C threads is represented by a *Circus* parallelism, like the parallelism of Java threads in the *Interpreter*. In $CProg_{bc,cs}$ there is a process $CThr_{bc,cs}$ for each identifier t in the set TID, except for the *idle* thread identifier.

The $CThr_{bc,cs}$ process has a similar structure to the *Thr* process presented in the previous section, except that the *Running* action is replaced with an *ExecuteMethod* action that executes the C function corresponding to a given method identifier. Within the body of $CThr_{bc,cs}$, each function of the generated C code is represented by a *Circus* action of the same name. The constructs within the C function are represented using *Circus* constructs.

The constructs we allow within a C function are conditionals, while loops, assignment statements, and function calls. These are comparable with those allowed in MISRA-C [18] and present in the code generated by icecap. These constructs can be represented by the corresponding constructs in *Circus*.

As each function in the C code is a *Circus* action, function calls are represented as references to those actions. Function arguments in C are passed by value, although those values may be pointers to other values. Accordingly, since our SCJVM model represents pointers explicitly, we represent function arguments using value parameters of the *Circus* action. Local variables of the function are represented using *Circus* variable blocks.

If a function has a return value, it is represented with a result parameter of the *Circus* action, with an assignment to that parameter at the end of the action representing return statements. It is not necessary to cater for return statements in the middle of a function as we have control over the structure of the functions. We follow guidelines for safety-critical uses of C variants, such as MISRA-C [18], and use a single return statement at the end of a function. A function with both a return value and arguments has its value parameters (representing the arguments) followed by the result parameter (representing the return value).

6   Compilation Strategy

Our compilation strategy refines the $CEE(bc, cs, sid)$ process defined in Sect. 4 to obtain a process that includes a representation of C code as described in Sect. 5. The overall theorem for the strategy is as follows.

Theorem 1 (Compilation Strategy). *Given bc, cs, sid and initOrder, there are processes $StructMan_{cs}$ and $CProg_{bc,cs}$ such that,*

$CEE(bc, cs, sid, initOrder)$
$\qquad \sqsubseteq StructMan_{cs} \parallel CProg_{bc,cs} \parallel Launcher(sid, initOrder).$

$StructMan_{cs}$ manages objects represented by C structs that incorporate the class information from cs, refining the process $ObjMan$, which handles abstract objects. $StructMan_{cs}$ has Z schemas representing struct types for objects of each class. These schemas contain the identifier *classid* of the object's class, so that polymorphic method calls can be made by choice over the object's class. There are also components for each of the fields of the object.

The schema types for each type of object are combined into a single free type $ObjStruct$. $StructMan_{cs}$ contains a map from memory addresses managed by the SCJVM to the $ObjStruct$ type, representing the C structs in memory, and provides access to the individual values in that map.

$CProg_{bc,cs}$ refines the *Interpreter*, with the *Thr* processes refined into the $CThr_{bc,cs}$ processes described in the previous section. This means that the threads from SCJ are mapped onto threads in C, since we do not dictate a particular thread switch mechanism in either the source or target models.

In order to apply the compilation strategy, the bc and cs inputs must conform to a few restrictions. The most important of these are the restrictions on the structure of control flow: each loop must have only a single exit and conditionals must have a single common end point for all branches. Recursion is also not allowed, directly or indirectly, since method calls cannot be handled unless control flow constructs and method calls in the called method have been introduced first. Finally, the program must be a valid program that could run in the interpreter described in Sect. 4.

The compilation strategy is split into three stages, each with a theorem describing it, for which the strategy acts as a proof. The proof of Theorem 1 is obtained by an application of the theorems for each stage. All the theorems and their proofs, with a full description of the stages, can be found in [2].

Each stage of the compilation strategy handles a different part of the state of the *Interpreter*: the *pc*, the *frameStack*, and objects. They operate over each of the *Thr* processes, managed by the SCJVM services.

The first stage introduces the control constructs of the C code. This removes the use of *pc* to determine the control flow of the program. The choice over *pc* values is replaced with a choice over method identifiers pointing to sequences of operations representing method bodies.

In the second stage, the information contained on the *frameStack*, which is the local variable array and operand stack for each method, is introduced in the C code. This is done by introducing variables and parameters to represent each method's local variables and operand stack slots. A data refinement is then used to transform each operation over the *frameStack* to operate on the new variables. The *frameStack* is then eliminated from the state.

In the final stage, the class information from *cs* is used to create a representation of C structs. This means that *ObjMan*, which has a very abstract representation of objects, is transformed into *StructMan*. The process for each thread is then made to access the structs for the objects in a more concrete way that represents the way struct fields are accessed in C code.

This yields final method actions of a form similar to that of the example shown below, which is taken from the **handleAsyncEvent()** method of a simple SCJ event handler class named **InputHandler**.

$$InputHandler\_HandleAsyncEvent \; \widehat{=}$$
$$\mathbf{val} \; var0 \bullet \mathbf{var} \; var1, stack0, stack1 : Word \bullet$$
$$stack0 := var0 \; ; \;\; Poll \; ; \;\; getObject!stack0 \longrightarrow getObjectRet?struct$$
$$\longrightarrow stack0 := (castInputHandler \; struct).input \; ; \; \ldots$$

The method is compiled to the action *InputHandler_HandleAsyncEvent*, with the implicit **this** parameter represented as a value parameter *var0*. The local variable (*var1*) and stack slots (*stack0* and *stack1*) are represented as *Circus* variables. The operations of the C code are composed in sequence, with an action named *Poll* that polls for thread switches between each operation. Stack operations are represented as assignments. For instance, $stack0 := var0$ arises from the compilation to load a local variable onto the stack. Access to objects is performed by communicating with $StructMan_{cs}$ to obtain the struct for the object, casting it to the correct type, and accessing the required value. Above, we obtain the value of the *input* field from an *InputHandler* object. The communication with $StructMan_{cs}$ is performed via the *getObject* channel and the function *castInputHandler* is used to map the *ObjectStruct* returned from the communication to a type representing an **InputHandler** object.

We illustrate our approach by giving further details about the first and most challenging stage of the strategy, elimination of program counter. The theorem

Algorithm 1. Elimination of Program Counter

1: EXPANDBYTECODE
2: INTRODUCESEQUENTIALCOMPOSITION
3: **while** ¬ ALLMETHODSSEPARATED **do**
4:     INTRODUCELOOPSANDCONDITIONALS
5:     SEPARATECOMPLETEMETHODS
6:     RESOLVEMETHODCALLS
7: **end while**
8: REFINEMAINACTIONS
9: REMOVEPCFROMSTATE

---

describing this stage is shown below, where $ThrCF$ is the result of transforming Thr to eliminate pc as indicated above and detailed in the sequel.

Theorem 2. $Thr(bc, cs, t) \sqsubseteq ThrCF_{bc,cs}(cs, t)$

The strategy for this stage is defined by Algorithm 1. Each of its steps is defined by its own algorithm, which details how the compilation rules are applied. The correctness of Algorithm 1 (and the other algorithms in the strategy) relies on the correctness proofs for the compilation rules, which are *Circus* laws. The algorithm forms the basis of a proof for Theorem 2 since it provides a strategy to apply the rules to refine $Thr(bc, cs, t)$ into $ThrCF_{bc,cs}(cs, t)$. All that then need be proved is that the algorithm does indeed yield *Circus* code of the correct form.

Algorithm 1 begins, on line 1, by expanding the semantics of each bytecode instruction (using a copy rule). Afterwards, sequential composition is introduced between bytecode instructions on line 2. Dependencies between methods must be considered in order to introduce the remaining control constructs, since method calls are handled by placing the method invocation bytecode in sequence with a call to a *Circus* action containing the body of the method being invoked. We say a method call for which this transformation has been done is *resolved*. Resolution is necessary to introduce a reference to the method action representing the C function for the method at the appropriate place in the control flow, after the value of pc has been set to the method's entry point by the invocation instruction.

The action containing the body of the method can only be created after loops and conditionals have been introduced and the method's body has been sequenced together into a single block of instructions. However, loops and conditionals can only be introduced when all the method calls in their bodies have been resolved (since method calls break up the body of a loop or conditional). For this reason, we perform loop and conditional introduction and method resolution iteratively, until all methods have had their control flow constructs introduced and their bodies copied into separate *Circus* actions. This occurs in the loop beginning at line 3 of Algorithm 1.

Within the loop (lines 4 to 6), loops and conditionals are first introduced to methods that have already had method calls resolved, on line 4. Methods that are in a form in which their control flow is described using C constructs are then copied into separate actions, on line 5. Calls to the separated methods are then resolved, introducing references to the newly created method actions, on line 6.

After all the methods have been copied into separate actions, the *MainThread* and *NotStarted* actions are refined to replace the choice over pc with a choice over method identifiers, on line 8. Finally, a data refinement is used to eliminate the pc from the state, on line 9.

In our example, the *InputHandler_HandleAsyncEvent* action is created in this stage as shown below. The control flow, mainly sequential composition, has been introduced, but the instructions are in the form of data operations over the *frameStack*. A call to the *InputStream_Read* method action can be seen here.

$$InputHandler\_HandleAsyncEvent \mathrel{\widehat{=}} HandleAloadEPC(0) \; ; \; Poll;$$
$$HandleGetfieldEPC(15) \; ; \; Poll \; ; \; HandleInvokevirtualEPC(33);$$
$$Poll \; ; \; InputStream\_Read \; ; \; Poll \; ; \; HandleAstoreEPC(1) \; ; \; \cdots$$

The algorithms for all stages of the strategy can be found in [2]. For illustration, we describe the INTRODUCESEQUENTIALCOMPOSITION procedure, referenced on line 2 of Algorithm 1. It begins with construction of a control flow graph for the program, which is then examined for nodes with a single outgoing edge leading to a node with a single incoming edge. Such nodes represent points at which simple sequential composition occurs, rather than more complex control flows such as loops and conditionals that are introduced later in the strategy. At these nodes, the compilation rule given by Rule 1 is applied.

Rule 1 (Sequence introduction). *If $i \neq j$ and*

$$\{frameStack \neq \varnothing\} \; ; \; A \quad = \quad \{frameStack \neq \varnothing\} \; ; \; A \; ; \; \{frameStack \neq \varnothing\}$$

then,

$$
\begin{array}{ll}
\mu X \bullet & \mu X \bullet \\
\quad \textbf{if } frameStack = \varnothing \longrightarrow \textbf{Skip} & \quad \textbf{if } frameStack = \varnothing \longrightarrow \textbf{Skip} \\
\quad [\!] \; frameStack \neq \varnothing \longrightarrow & \quad [\!] \; frameStack \neq \varnothing \longrightarrow \\
\qquad \textbf{if } \cdots & \qquad \textbf{if } \cdots \\
\qquad [\!] \; pc = i \longrightarrow & \qquad [\!] \; pc = i \longrightarrow \\
\qquad\qquad A \; ; \; pc := j \quad \sqsubseteq_A & \qquad\qquad A \; ; \; pc := j \; ; \; Poll \; ; \; B \\
\qquad [\!] \; pc = j \longrightarrow B & \qquad [\!] \; pc = j \longrightarrow B \\
\qquad \cdots & \qquad \cdots \\
\qquad \textbf{fi} \; ; \; Poll \; ; \; X & \qquad \textbf{fi} \; ; \; Poll \; ; \; X \\
\quad \textbf{fi} & \quad \textbf{fi}
\end{array}
$$

This rule, like many of the compilation rules, acts upon *Circus* actions of a generalised form. Where dots ($\cdots$) are shown on the left hand side the rule, it indicates that any syntactically valid *Circus* at that point may match the rule, but remains unaffected by the rule, as indicated by corresponding dots on the right hand side of the rule. The left hand side of this rule is in the form of the *Running* action, with a loop that continues until *frameStack* is empty and a choice over the value of pc to select the instruction to execute. The rule unrolls the loop, sequencing the instructions at $pc = i$ with the instructions executed after them at $pc = j$. An occurrence of *Poll* is placed inbetween to permit thread switches. The preconditions for the application of this rule are that i and j not be the same (since that would be a loop), and that the instructions at $pc = i$ preserve the nonemptiness of the *frameStack* (to fulfil the loop condition of *Running*).

We note that the pc assignment that causes the sequential composition remains in the code after the application of this rule. It is removed in the data refinement on line 9 of Algorithm 1, since removing it as part of the rule would complicate the preconditions.

The other compilation rules have a similar form to Rule 1 but introduce other constructs such as loops, conditionals, and method calls. An account of all the laws used in the strategy can be found in [2].

7   Discussion

Our work is the first on verified compilation from Java bytecode to C. Our results may be of value in the compilation of standard Java programs, but they are specific to SCJ. Although SCJ uses the same bytecode instructions as standard Java, SCJ does not have dynamic class loading, which substantially changes the semantics of the bytecode instructions. The class initialisers must also be executed at the start of the program and the program execution must be coordinated according to the SCJ mission paradigm, both performed by the *Launcher* in our model. Finally, the instructions must rely on the SCJVM services, so, for example, the **new** instruction must communicate with the SCJVM memory manager to ensure SCJ's memory model is followed.

We have also considered the introduction of control flow constructs to the compiled C code. This differs from previous work, which translates branch instructions in the bytecode using **goto** statements in the C code. Avoiding the use of **goto** statements permits more optimisation by the C compiler, makes the control flow of the code more readable, and brings the code in line with the restrictions of MISRA C. This has been one of the most challenging parts of our work, since we require a strategy for identifying the control flow constructs of the Java bytecode. In our strategy, we handle branches in the Java bytecode by analysing the structure of the control flow graph for each method. Unconditional jumps are handled in the same way as sequential composition, while conditional branches are handled by introducing C conditionals. Where the jump introduces a loop, we instead introduce looping constructs corresponding to C while loops.

We have also had to consider the difficulties raised by the features of Java when compiling bytecode. Chief among these is the issue of how inheritance and dynamic dispatch are handled. The class where a method is defined must be identified when it is invoked, since a method's bytecode instructions require constant pool information about the class in order to be executed correctly. Since SCJ requires that all classes be available before program execution, the possible classes for a particular method call can be determined statically. When there is a unique class (as will always be the case for `invokestatic` and `invokespecial` instructions), we can replace the method call with a reference to the correct method in the RESOLVEMETHODCALLS algorithm (line 6 of Algorithm 1). If there is no unique class then we must determine the set of all possible classes where it can be defined. In RESOLVEMETHODCALLS, we compute this set and replace the method call with a choice over the class identifier of the object, the branches of the choice corresponding to the possible methods.

In our strategy we do not handle recursion. This is not a strong restriction, since it is in line with the constraints imposed by MISRA C. Detecting recursion in object-oriented programs is complicated by dynamic dispatch, since mutual recursion may or may not arise depending on dynamic dispatch. However, the fact that SCJ does not allow dynamic class loading means that all the classes are available during compilation, which means dynamic dispatch is constrained by the classes available, making detection of potential recursion feasible.

SCJ also presents several issues of its own in terms of memory management and scheduling. These are handled by the SCJVM services part of our model However, there are many places where a program must interact directly with the SCJ infrastructure, such as entering memory areas or registering an event handler with its mission. To handle such interactions correctly we handle the calls to methods that cause these interactions in a special way, allowing them to interact with the *Launcher* and the SCJVM services.

In RESOLVEMETHODCALLS, we replace the calls to these special methods by communications with other components of the SCJVM. Since the *Launcher* and the SCJVM services remain unchanged throughout the strategy, these communications become calls to C functions in the SCJVM infrastructure. A similar system could be applied to handle native method calls, though we view that as future work since it is not a central part of the considerations for an SCJVM. Native methods would be represented via a shallow embedding in *Circus*, in the same way as the output of the compilation, but would be present before compilation with special handling given to calls to them in the interpreter.

The real-time requirements on SCJ scheduling also impose predictability, so that the bytecode instructions processed by the interpreter must appear to be atomic. This is specified in our model by only permitting thread switches inbetween bytecode instructions. This atomicity requirement is preserved throughout our strategy, and the behaviour of polling for thread switches remains inbetween the C code corresponding to each bytecode instruction.

However, an implementation is only required to have the same sequence of externally visible events as our C code model. This means that the thread switches will appear the same in a non-atomic implementation for most bytecode instructions. The bytecode instructions which have effects visible outside the *Interpreter*, which are the `new` instruction, the field access instructions, and instructions that invoke the special methods mentioned above, interact with shared memory and so do have an atomicity requirement. We can only verify an implementation that ensures such operations are not interrupted, usually by employing synchronisation. This is, of course, the case for icecap.

Our work can be used to verify an SCJVM that uses ahead-of-time compiling, or as a specification to create such an implementation. Since the compiled C code only uses core features of C and is compatible with MISRA C, it can be compiled by most C compilers. So, existing work on verification of C compilers, such as that of CompCert [13, 14], can be used to ensure correct execution of the SCJ program. Since SCJ does not modify the syntax of Java, existing Java compilers can be used to produce the bytecode handled by the strategy.

8   Conclusions

We have described our approach to algebraic compilation of SCJ bytecode. Compiler verification can be complex and, for some languages, compiler updates are common. So, it can be easier to verify properties of the compiler output. In the case of an SCJ compiler, however, SCJ is a controlled language and the core of Java bytecode it uses is fairly stable, as is the only fully compliant SCJVM. In addition, the algebraic approach allows for a modular compilation strategy composed of individual compilation rules. Thus, extending or handling any changes to SCJ would require only changing or adding some compilation rules. The parts of the strategy not directly involved with any changes may be left unchanged.

This compilation strategy is the final component needed to create SCJ programs with assurance of correct execution. Other work that contributes to this goal produces correct SCJ programs from *Circus* specifications [5,6], and verifies Java [9,12,15,28,29] and C [4,13,14] compilers. Together, these can ensure a complete chain of verification from SCJ programs to executable code.

The mapping from bytecode to C code used in icecap can be used as a basis for the construction of other compilers. A sound implementation can also be obtained by a mechanisation of the strategy via tactics of refinement in a rewriting engine such as Isabelle [19] or Maude [7].

The next stage of our work will be the formalisation and mechanisation of correctness proofs for our strategy. The strategy must also be evaluated by applying it to some examples of SCJ programs to ensure it can handle a wide range of SCJ programs. Further work in the future could include the extension of the strategy to cover more Java bytecode instructions or additional transformations such as code optimisations. Our work will eventually allow the formal verification of a complete SCJVM implementation, an effort that has started in [10].

Acknowledgements. The authors gratefully acknowledge useful feedback from Augusto Sampaio on the application of the algebraic approach. We also thank Andy Wellings for his advice on SCJ and Leo Freitas for his help with the use of Z/EVES and understanding of icecap. This work is supported by EPSRC studentship 1511661 and EPSRC grant EP/H017461/1.

References

1. Armbruster, A., Baker, J., Cunei, A., et al.: A real-time Java virtual machine with applications in avionics. ACM Trans. Embed. Comput. Syst. **7**(1), 5:1–5:49 (2007)
2. Baxter, J.: An Approach to verification of Safety-Critical Java Virtual Machines with Ahead-of-time compilation. Technical report, University of York (2017). www-users.cs.york.ac.uk/~jeb531/2017report.pdf
3. Baxter, J., Cavalcanti, A., Wellings, A., Freitas, L.: Safety-critical Java virtual machine services. In: JTRES 2015, pp. 7:1–7:10. ACM (2015)
4. Blazy, S., Dargaye, Z., Leroy, X.: Formal verification of a C compiler front-end. In: Misra, J., Nipkow, T., Sekerinski, E. (eds.) FM 2006. LNCS, vol. 4085, pp. 460–475. Springer, Heidelberg (2006). doi:10.1007/11813040_31
5. Cavalcanti, A., Wellings, A., Woodcock, J., Wei, K., Zeyda, F.: Safety-critical Java in circus. In: JTRES 2011, pp. 20–29. ACM (2011)
6. Cavalcanti, A., Zeyda, F., Wellings, A., Woodcock, J., Wei, K.: Safety-critical Java programs from Circus models. Real-Time Syst. **49**(5), 614–667 (2013)
7. Clavel, M., Durán, F., Eker, S., Lincoln, P., Martı-Oliet, N., Meseguer, J., Quesada, J.F.: Maude: specification and programming in rewriting logic. Theoret. Comput. Sci. **285**(2), 187–243 (2002)
8. Dijkstra, E.W.: Guarded commands, nondeterminacy and formal derivation of programs. Commun. ACM **18**(8), 453–457 (1975)
9. Duran, A.: An Algebraic Approach to the Design of Compilers for Object-Oriented Languages. Ph.D. thesis, Universidade Federal de Pernambuco (2005)
10. Freitas, L., Baxter, J., Cavalcanti, A., Wellings, A.: Modelling and verifying a priority scheduler for an SCJ runtime environment. In: Ábrahám, E., Huisman, M. (eds.) IFM 2016. LNCS, vol. 9681, pp. 63–78. Springer, Cham (2016). doi:10.1007/978-3-319-33693-0_5
11. Kalibera, T., Parizek, P., Malohlava, M., Schoeberl, M.: Exhaustive testing of safety critical java. In: JTRES 2010, pp. 164–174. ACM (2010)
12. Klein, G., Nipkow, T.: A machine-checked model for a Java-like language, virtual machine, and compiler. ACM Trans. Program. Lang. Syst. **28**(4), 619–695 (2006)
13. Leroy, X.: Formal verification of a realistic compiler. Commun. ACM **52**(7), 107–115 (2009)
14. Leroy, X.: A formally verified compiler back-end. J. Autom. Reason. **43**(4), 363–446 (2009)
15. Lochbihler, A.: Verifying a compiler for Java threads. In: Gordon, A.D. (ed.) ESOP 2010. LNCS, vol. 6012, pp. 427–447. Springer, Heidelberg (2010). doi:10.1007/978-3-642-11957-6_23
16. Locke, D., et al.: Safety-Critical Java Technology Specification. https://jcp.org/aboutJava/communityprocess/edr/jsr302/index2.html
17. Marriott, C.: Checking Memory Safety of Level 1 Safety-Critical Java Programs using Static-Analysis without Annotations. Ph.D. thesis, University of York (2014)
18. Motor Industry Software Reliability Association Guidelines: Guidelines for Use of the C Language in Critical Systems (2012)
19. Nipkow, T., Wenzel, M., Paulson, L.C. (eds.): Isabelle/HOL: A Proof Assistant for Higher-Order Logic. LNCS, vol. 2283. Springer, Heidelberg (2002)
20. Oliveira, M., Cavalcanti, A., Woodcock, J.: A UTP semantics for circus. Formal Aspects Comput. **21**(1–2), 3–32 (2009)
21. Perna, J.: A verified compiler for Handel-C. Ph.D. thesis, University of York (2010)

22. Pizlo, F., Ziarek, L., Vitek, J.: Real time Java on resource-constrained platforms with Fiji VM. In: JTRES 2009, pp. 110–119. ACM (2009)
23. Proebsting, T.A., Townsend, G., Bridges, P., et al.: Toba: Java for applications a way ahead of time (wat) compiler. In: Proceedings of the 3rd Conference on Object-Oriented Technologies and Systems (1997)
24. Roscoe, A.W.: Understanding Concurrent Systems. Texts in Computer Science. Springer, London (2011)
25. Sampaio, A.: An Algebraic Approach to Compiler Design. World Scientific, Singapore (1997)
26. Sawadpong, P., Allen, E.B., Williams, B.J.: Exception handling defects: an empirical study. In: HASE 2012, pp. 90–97. IEEE (2012)
27. Søndergaard, H., Korsholm, S.E., Ravn, A.P.: Safety-critical Java for low-end embedded platforms. In: JTRES 2012, pp. 44–53. ACM (2012)
28. Stärk, R., Schmid, J., Börger, E.: Java and the Java Virtual Machine. Springer, Berlin (2001)
29. Strecker, M.: Formal verification of a Java compiler in isabelle. In: Voronkov, A. (ed.) CADE 2002. LNCS (LNAI), vol. 2392, pp. 63–77. Springer, Heidelberg (2002). doi:10.1007/3-540-45620-1_5
30. Varma, A., Bhattacharyya, S.S.: Java-through-C compilation: an enabling technology for Java in embedded systems. In: Proceedings of the Conference on Design, Automation and Test in Europe, vol. 3, p. 30161. IEEE Computer Society (2004)
31. Woodcock, J., Davies, J.: Using Z: Specification, Refinement, and Proof. Prentice-Hall Inc., Upper Saddle River (1996)

Task-Node Mapping in an Arbitrary Computer Network Using SMT Solver

Andrii Kovalov[✉], Elisabeth Lobe, Andreas Gerndt, and Daniel Lüdtke

German Aerospace Center (DLR), Simulation and Software Technology,
Cologne, Germany
{andrii.kovalov,elisabeth.lobe,andreas.gerndt,daniel.luedtke}@dlr.de

Abstract. The problem of mapping (assigning) application tasks to processing nodes in a distributed computer system for spacecraft is investigated in this paper. The network architecture is developed in the project 'Scalable On-Board Computing for Space Avionics' (ScOSA) at the German Aerospace Center (DLR). In ScOSA system the processing nodes are connected to a network with an arbitrary topology. The applications are structured as directed graphs of periodic and aperiodic tasks that exchange messages. In this paper a formal definition of the mapping problem is given. We demonstrate several ways to formulate it as a satisfiability modulo theories (SMT) problem and then use Z3, a state-of-the-art SMT solver, to produce the mapping. The approach is evaluated on a mapping problem for an optical navigation application as well as on a set of randomly generated task graphs.

1 Introduction

In this paper we investigate the generation of optimal task-node mappings for a distributed system structured as a collection of communicating tasks which run on a computer network with an arbitrary topology. Our work is motivated by the existing project 'Scalable On-Board Computing for Space Avionics' (ScOSA) at the German Aerospace Center (DLR), however the proposed approach is not specific to this project and can be used for task-node mapping in various contexts.

1.1 ScOSA System Overview

The conventional way to design on-board computers for spacecraft is to have independent dedicated computers for various subsystems (payload, communication, attitude control, etc.) including the redundant counterparts for fault-tolerance. This conventional approach does not scale well under the increasing demands on the on-board data processing capabilities.

The project ScOSA at DLR aims at developing a scalable on-board computer system [15]. Most importantly, in a ScOSA system all computers are connected to a network that provides the computing power to all the on-board applications.

© Springer International Publishing AG 2017
N. Polikarpova and S. Schneider (Eds.): IFM 2017, LNCS 10510, pp. 177–191, 2017.
DOI: 10.1007/978-3-319-66845-1_12

Fig. 1. Example task graph (left) and network (right)

The applications for ScOSA are organized as directed graphs of tasks that send messages. An example of a task graph and a network structure is shown in Fig. 1.

In this example the first tasks (A and B) run periodically with certain periods. When they are finished, they send messages to the next tasks, which are triggered by these incoming messages, and so on. The tasks start either when they receive all messages that are not *optional*, or when they receive a *final* message, which triggers a task to start immediately. Every task is assigned to a particular processing node in the network. The messages can either be passed locally or sent over the network if the destination task is located on another node.

One of the important concepts in ScOSA is reconfiguration. There are special nodes ('Master' and 'Observers') that constantly monitor the state of the other nodes. If a failure is detected, a reconfiguration command is broadcast to the network, and the tasks are reassigned to the healthy nodes.

It was decided that ScOSA does not employ adaptive reconfiguration at runtime [15]. Instead, in order to achieve a higher degree of deterministic behavior, all possible configurations with their respective activation events have to be determined before launch of the spacecraft or during updates uploaded by ground control. In case of a failure, ground control needs to be able to understand and reproduce the behavior of the system, including the conducted reconfigurations, in order to resume normal operation of the spacecraft. As there could be many combinations of consecutive node failures, there is a need to automatically generate a large number of task-node mappings.

1.2   Mapping and Subsequent Model Checking

Our goal is to have a two-stage process shown in Fig. 2 where we first generate a mapping and then verify that this mapping cannot lead the system into an undesirable state. In this paper we only discuss the mapping problem; model checking will be the next step in our work.

Our approach is to formulate the mapping problem as a satisfiability modulo theories (SMT) problem, and then use a state-of-the-art optimizing SMT solver to solve it. We chose this approach instead of using heuristics (such as greedy algorithms) because of two reasons. First of all, it guarantees the optimal solution, and for our purposes we would prefer the best solution to a fast but suboptimal one. Secondly, we can later introduce some bounded model checking into the SMT-based mapping, for example to check that the first few runs of the task graph do not block the network. In the subsequent model checking step, we are planning to analyze more complex properties on a more detailed system model.

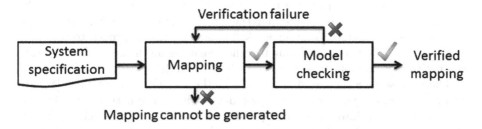

Fig. 2. Our proposed approach to generate and verify the mapping (in this paper only the mapping generation is discussed, model checking is future work).

The rest of the paper is structured as follows. Section 2 gives an overview of the existing work in task-node mapping, especially with the use of SMT solvers. In Sect. 3 we give a formal definition of our task-node mapping problem, which we then formulate as an SMT problem in Sect. 4. The approach is evaluated in Sects. 5 and 6 concludes the paper.

2   Related Work

The problem of mapping application tasks to hardware processing nodes is an important practical problem and has been studied for decades. Several formulations of it have been shown to be NP-complete [1,10], so it is usually solved by applying heuristics. A good overview of mapping algorithms is given in [9]. One of the widely used heuristics is a greedy heuristic. Lee and Aggarwal [11] show an approach where the initial mapping is produced with a greedy algorithm, and then improved with a series of pairwise exchanges. Other greedy algorithms are shown in [5,8]. The latter presents a hierarchical algorithm which treats the hardware as a tree and for each level of this tree divides the tasks into groups according to the communication patterns among them. Another algorithm [6] partitions the hardware graph based on the coordinates of the hardware nodes, which is practical for multiprocessor systems that have a grid or torus topology.

Genetic algorithms can also be used to search for an optimal mapping. In [12] a two-step genetic algorithm is shown that first maps the tasks to a set of node types using an average communication time, and then maps the tasks to the specific nodes considering the actual communication time between them. Another genetic algorithm [20] solves a slightly different problem, where not all the tasks are mapped to the nodes, but the ones that give the most value to the system.

The task-node mapping problem can also be addressed with the exhaustive search tools such as integer linear programming (ILP) or satisfiability modulo theories (SMT) solvers. In [1,17] an ILP-based approach is shown where the task-node mapping problem is first formulated as an integer linear program and then relaxed to a linear program (LP) which can be solved in polynomial time. The solution to the LP problem maps a subset of tasks to the nodes, and the exhaustive enumeration is used to map the remaining tasks (which is exponential in the number of nodes). Another work [21] uses an ILP approach to solve the problem of mapping and scheduling together, focusing on the network contention (competition of different messages for a physical link).

There are some SMT-based approaches to the task mapping problem [18,19]. In [19] the use of symmetries is explored to reduce search space. In [18] the problem is divided into the master problem of producing a mapping, and sub-problems for scheduling. In order to explore the whole search space and find the optimal solution, the previously found solutions are learned and excluded. An improvement of this approach in [13,14] integrates the analysis of the current partial mapping into the SAT solving process itself.

A somewhat similar approach is described in [2] where first, the mapping problem is solved with answer set programming, then the solution is refined for better schedulability (e.g. load balancing), and then the schedule is produced with an SMT solver.

A slightly different application model is taken in [4] where tasks are not strictly mapped to nodes, but can be executed on different nodes according to an SMT-generated schedule.

3   Formal Definition of the Problem

This section gives the formal definition of the task-node mapping problem.

3.1   Period Estimation for Event-Triggered Tasks

For our formal definition we treat all the tasks as periodic. However, a ScOSA application can consist of both periodic and aperiodic tasks, therefore we first need to estimate the periods of the event-triggered tasks. The periods of the time-triggered tasks are known. Then, if a task runs with period p, it sends an output message with period p. We assume the receiving task gets this message with period p and therefore runs with the same period.

If a task waits for multiple messages, it only can start when all the necessary messages have arrived. In this case its period is defined by the longest period of all the incoming messages. With this simple approach we can propagate the period information to all the tasks as illustrated in Fig. 3. This period propagation only works for task graphs that are either acyclic or all the backward messages are optional and do not affect the task periods. In real applications the task graphs can contain cycles, and the period estimation becomes more complex, especially with the use of *final* messages. Then, the task periods can be measured directly

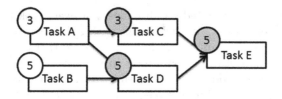

Fig. 3. Estimated periods of all the tasks in a task graph

on the actual running system or in a simulation, but this is out of scope of this paper.

3.2 Formulation of the Mapping Problem

Our formal definition of the problem is close to the one given in [10], but we also consider task utilization. The task graph is a directed graph (not necessarily connected) $TG = (T, E^T)$, where T is a set of tasks, and $E^T \subseteq T \times T$ is a set of edges representing message passing between the tasks.

Every task t has its worst case execution time $wcet_t$, its period p_t and the size of its output message m_t:

$$\forall t \in T : wcet_t > 0, p_t > 0, m_t \geq 0.$$

The utilization of the task t is then defined as $u(t) = wcet_t/p_t$. Utilization of the task is the fraction of its period when it is executing (the worst case time is chosen because we are targeting real-time systems).

Every task t that has outgoing edges in the task graph produces messages of size m_t greater than zero. We can say that all the other tasks (without outgoing edges) produce messages of zero size:

$$\forall t \in T : \begin{cases} m_t > 0, & \exists t' \in T : (t, t') \in E^T \\ m_t = 0, & \text{otherwise.} \end{cases}$$

The traffic tt between two tasks t and t' is then defined as

$$tt(t, t') = \begin{cases} 0, & (t, t') \notin E^T \\ m_t/p_t, & \text{otherwise} \end{cases}$$

and shows how much data task t is sending to task t' per time unit.

The communication network is represented as a graph $HN = (N, E)$ where N is a set of nodes and $E \subseteq \{\{n_1, n_2\} : n_1, n_2 \in N, n_1 \neq n_2\}$ is a set of network links. Every edge $e \in E$ has a bandwidth $b_e > 0$ which defines how much data this link can transfer in one time unit. In reality the actual bandwidth of a link depends on the number and size of the messages that are transferred via that link. For few large messages, a link usually shows higher bandwidth than for many small messages due to the overhead from packet headers.

Not all tasks can be executed on all nodes. For every task there is a subset of nodes that can execute it. We define this with a function of available nodes $an : T \to 2^N$. For a task t, $an(t) \subseteq N$ is a set of nodes that can execute t.

Next we consider routing. Every router in the network has a routing table that specifies the output ports for all possible destination nodes. For example, the network in Fig. 1 has no link between Node 2 and Node 3. One way to route messages from 2 to 3 would be via Node 4. In this case the routing table of the router in Node 2 would contain an entry saying that all messages for Node 3 should be sent to Node 4. We assume that the routing is consistent and is given as input. Formally, routing is defined as $R \in \{0,1\}^{(N \times N) \times E}$, with

$$R_{n,n',e} = \begin{cases} 1, & \text{if the data sent from node } n \text{ to node } n' \text{ passes edge } e \\ 0, & \text{otherwise.} \end{cases}$$

If a message is sent from node n to node n' that have a direct link between them, then $R_{n,n',e} = 1$ if and only if $e = \{n, n'\}$.

Our aim is to find a mapping function $m : T \to N$, where for a task t, $m(t) \in an(t)$ is a node on which the task is running.

We consider two additional constraints on this mapping function: on the network bandwidth and on the node load. Mappings should be avoided where the amount of traffic transferred on a link exceeds its bandwidth. Mappings where too many tasks are mapped to a single node should also be excluded.

For the bandwidth constraint we first define traffic between two nodes n and n' as

$$nn(n, n') = \sum_{\substack{t,t' \in T \\ m(t)=n \\ m(t')=n'}} tt(t, t').$$

The amount of traffic that passes through an edge e is

$$traffic(e) = \sum_{n,n' \in N} R_{n,n',e} \cdot nn(n, n').$$

The constraint on the edge bandwidth is then written as

$$\forall e \in E : traffic(e) \leq b_e.$$

The load on a node n is defined as

$$load(n) = \sum_{\substack{t \in T \\ m(t)=n}} u(t).$$

The constraint on the node load is then formulated as

$$\forall n \in N : load(n) \leq L$$

where L is the node load limit, which is some constant less than 1. This constant should allow for context switching and other overhead on the node that is not directly related to task execution. The constraint on node load might be more restrictive depending on the actual scheduling policy on the node (particularly, on preemption), but in our model we assume that if the mapping satisfies this constraint, the tasks are schedulable on the node.

In order to have a quality measure for a mapping, we use two objectives. The first objective is to minimize the total amount of traffic in the network *totalTraffic* with

$$totalTraffic = \sum_{e \in E} traffic(e).$$

The second objective is to minimize the maximal load among all the nodes *maxLoad* with

$$maxLoad = \max_{n \in N}(load(n)).$$

This objective aims to distribute the load evenly across all nodes.

There are of course other possible objectives for the mapping generation. For example, the fastest execution of the whole task graph. This would make the system respond to the external changes quicker. We could also have application-specific objectives, such as dedicate more resources for critical tasks.

4   SMT Formulation

To produce an optimal mapping with respect to the chosen objective, we use a state-of-the-art SMT solver Z3 [16], which has built-in optimization functionality [3]. This means the solver produces not just any satisfying assignment but an assignment that maximizes or minimizes a given objective function.

In this section we show how we formulated the problem of finding a task-node mapping as an SMT problem. In some cases we developed alternative ways of modeling particular aspects of the problem. We compare the performance of alternative approaches in Sect. 5.

4.1   Task-Node Mapping Variables

First of all, we need to create variables that define the mapping of tasks to nodes, which will be assigned as a solution to the mapping problem. We tried two alternative approaches - using boolean variables and integer variables.

Boolean Mapping Variables. With this approach we create $|T| \times |N|$ boolean variables TN_{tn}, where if this variable is *true* then task t is mapped to node n and *false* otherwise.

In order to make sure that a task is mapped to exactly one node, we include the following assertion for every $t \in T$:

$$\bigvee_{n \in N} \left(TN_{tn} \wedge \bigwedge_{n' \in N \setminus \{n\}} \neg TN_{tn'} \right).$$

Additionally, we need to constrain the available nodes for every task t with the following assertion:

$$\bigvee_{n \in an(t)} TN_{tn}.$$

Integer Mapping Variables. Another approach is to create one integer variable TN_t for every task t that is equal to index i of the mapped node $m(t)$. For every TN_t the constraints are defined with following assertions:

$$(TN_t \geq 1) \wedge (TN_t \leq |N|),$$

$$\bigvee_{n_i \in an(t)} (TN_t = i).$$

In the rest of the section, we will use boolean mapping variables. The corresponding expressions for integer mapping variables are easy to formulate.

4.2 Link Bandwidth Constraints

To formulate the link bandwidth constraints, we first convert the task-task traffic into node-node traffic. The amount of traffic between the tasks is known and given as input, but the actual traffic at the links depends on the mapping.

$|N| \times |N|$ variables $NNtraffic_{nn'}$ represent the amount of traffic from node n to node n':

$$NNtraffic_{nn'} = \begin{cases} 0, & n = n' \\ \sum_{t \in T} \sum_{t' \in T} \mathrm{ite}(TN_{tn} \wedge TN_{t'n'}, tt(t,t'), 0), & n \neq n', \end{cases}$$

where TN_{tn} is a boolean mapping variable, $tt(t, t')$ is the amount of traffic from task t to task t', and ite() is an 'if-then-else' function, which returns the second or the third argument depending on whether the first argument is true or false.

The link traffic for every link $e \in E$ is represented with variable $Ltraffic_e$, which is the sum of all node-node traffic amounts, where the route between the nodes passes e. This amount should not exceed the bandwidth of the link:

$$Ltraffic_e = \sum_{\substack{(n,n') \in N \times N \\ R_{n,n',e}=1}} NNtraffic_{nn'},$$

$$Ltraffic_e \leq b_e.$$

As mentioned, the real bandwidth decreases with the increase of the number of messages that are passed via the link. For applications with many small messages, this can be modeled by counting the number of messages contributing to the link traffic, and then decreasing the bound depending on this number.

4.3   Node Load Constraints

We represent the load on the nodes with $|N|$ variables $NodeLoad_n$ that are defined for every node n as follows:

$$NodeLoad_n = \sum_{t \in T} ite(TN_{tn}, u(t), 0),$$

$$NodeLoad_n \leq L,$$

where L is a constant defining the limit on the node load. It is also possible to assign individual load limits to different nodes to model nodes with different performance.

4.4   Objective Functions

The two objectives that we consider are the minimization of the total network traffic and the minimization of the highest node load (load balancing). The first objective function can be formulated as follows

$$\sum_{e \in E} Ltraffic_e.$$

For the second objective we need to minimize the highest node load among all the nodes. We first define the function $\max(x, y)$, and then use it to get the highest load among all nodes

$$\max(x, y) = ite(x > y, x, y)$$

The highest node load is defined as follows and can then be minimized

$$maxNodeLoad$$
$$= \max(NodeLoad_1, \max(NodeLoad_2, \ldots \max(NodeLoad_{m-1}, NodeLoad_m) \ldots))$$

4.5   Variable Types

Another practical question of SMT formulation is what type of variables to use for numerical values, as Z3 supports both real and integer variables. In our model we have numeric values for traffic amounts and task utilization values. Our first approach is to encode everything with real variables with their actual values.

Another approach would be to round all the values and encode them as integers. However, for the task utilization it is not practical because the values are between 0 and 1. Instead of just rounding, we multiply the real values by a factor such as 100 or 1000, and then round them. Depending on the factor, we might lose precision and, presumably, the performance might be different. We evaluate both approaches, and discuss the results in the following section.

5   Evaluation

In this section we compare the task-node mapping performance with different variations of the SMT formulation, show the application of our mapping approach to an existing optical navigation system, and estimate the scalability of the approach. All the described experiments were performed with an off-the-shelf laptop with 16 GB RAM and a quad-core 2.6 GHz processor using Z3 version 4.5.0 on generated SMT-LIB files (without explicitly specified logic).

5.1   Performance Comparison of Different SMT Formulations

In order to understand how the runtime of Z3 depends on the SMT formulation, we took several random task graphs and solved them with all the SMT formulations discussed in the previous section for both our objective functions using the four-node network from Fig. 1. We took three task graphs with 10 tasks and three task graphs with 15 tasks, all of which were satisfiable. In each of these two groups there was one instance with a low load on the network (total task utilization of around 25% of the maximum load; total traffic in the task graph around 25% of the total bandwidth summed over all links), one with medium load (task utilization and total traffic of around 50%), and one with high load (task utilization and total traffic of around 75%). The running times are shown in Table 1. The rows show different SMT formulations, and the columns show different mapping problem instances. The SMT formulations differ in the type of mapping variables (see Subsect. 4.1) and the type of numerical variables (see Sect. 4.5).

Table 1. Mapping time in seconds of different SMT encodings for instances with different numbers of tasks (10 tasks and 15 tasks) and different loads on the network (L - low load, M - medium load, H - high load, around 25, 50, 75 % of maximum load respectively). # - incorrect mapping, * - suboptimal mapping.

Mapping variables	Numeric variables	Traffic minimization						Node load minimization					
		10 tasks			15 tasks			10 tasks			15 tasks		
		L	M	H	L	M	H	L	M	H	L	M	H
Boolean	Int(*100)	0.1	2.6	0.7	(#)0.2	(#)0.5	0.9	(*) 6.8	2.8	2.9	2.9	10.2	(*) 17.1
	Int(*1000)	0.2	1.4	0.7	0.3	3.5	1.2	10.7	4.8	3.4	17.8	25.3	91.5
	Int(*10000)	0.2	0.3	1.0	0.5	23.6	1.4	10.9	4.5	4.4	38.8	67.9	109.9
	Real	1.0	0.3	1.6	0.5	29.6	1.9	12.8	7.3	5.3	39.5	92.0	200.5
Integer	Int(*100)	0.2	1.1	0.8	(#)1.2	(#)2.1	1.1	(*) 7.2	3.5	3.7	3.6	11.3	(*) 25.4
	Int(*1000)	0.9	1.4	1.0	1.9	11.2	1.6	12.4	5.2	4.6	21.6	35.7	(*)156.9
	Int(*10000)	1.1	0.3	1.3	2.4	10.2	2.0	15.7	5.1	5.4	50.1	110.4	224.5
	Real	0.2	0.3	1.8	2.6	21.1	2.4	18.8	8.8	7.0	58.7	116.8	367.7

We can draw several rather straightforward conclusions from the measurements in Table 1. First of all, it is better to use boolean variables rather than integer variables to represent the mapping itself. For almost all cases the mapping with boolean mapping variables ran faster than with integers.

Secondly, the mapping runs faster if the numerical values are modeled as integers rather than reals, and the runtime depends on the precision of the integer representation. For example, if real values are multiplied by 100 and rounded, the mapping runs quicker, however due to rounding errors the produced mapping might be incorrect (violating initial constraints) or not optimal. As shown in Table 1, this was observed in several cases for multiplication by 100 and once for multiplication by 1000.

Thirdly, the level of load on the network created by the task graph does not seem to be a critical factor influencing the mapping time. For the load balancing objective, among the instances with 15 tasks, the hardest one seems to be the instance with high load, whereas for instances of size 10, the low-load instance took the most time to solve. Moreover, for the traffic minimization objective, the mid-load instance appears to be the hardest among the instances of size 15.

The mapping for the traffic minimization objective is significantly faster than for the load balancing objective, on average about 30 times faster. This is probably caused by the way the load balancing objective was specified. The nested max() function results in many if-then-else statements, whereas the traffic objective is a simple sum.

5.2   Task-Node Mapping for the ATON Application

We evaluated our task-node mapping approach with the existing application 'Autonomous Terrain-based Optical Navigation' (ATON) [7], which is expected to run on the ScOSA platform in the future. ATON is a navigation system, currently developed at DLR. It is designed to provide a navigation solution for a precise landing on the Moon or other celestial bodies. It consists of the following sensors: an inertial measurement unit (IMU), two cameras, a laser altimeter and an (emulated) star tracker. The system was recently tested on an unmanned aerial vehicle (UAV) in a closed-loop scenario. The ATON software consists of several modules for absolute (crater navigation) and relative (feature tracking) navigation. The navigation filter combines the results of the sensors and software modules and provides a position, velocity and attitude estimation. The task graph for this application is shown in Fig. 4. We estimated the periods for non-sensor tasks using the approach described in Subsect. 3.1.

The majority of the data is sent from Camera tasks to Undistortion tasks (camera images with high frequency), and from Undistortion to Crater navigation (undistorted images with lower frequency). The Crater navigation tasks receive more inputs than they are able to process. In practice, this means that when a Crater navigation task finishes, it starts processing the latest received image immediately, thus creating a full load on a node. To model this, we trigger the Crater navigation tasks on every fourth incoming message because the execution time of Crater navigation is slightly less than the time of arrival of four incoming messages.

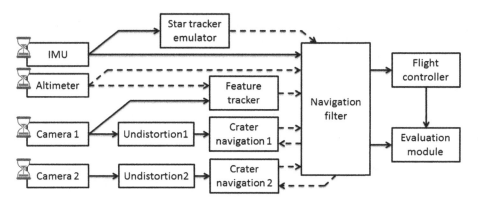

Fig. 4. Autonomous Terrain-based Optical Navigation (ATON) application task graph. Dashed lines show optional messages that are not required to start a task.

The mapping for the ATON task graph and our four-node example network from Fig. 1 is shown in Fig. 5. We calculated mappings for the two objectives discussed above: traffic minimization and load balancing. They took 0.4 and 1.8 s respectively. The load balancing is not an appropriate objective in this case because the Crater navigation tasks use all the capacity of their nodes, so the maximal node load, which is minimized, will always be the same. The traffic minimization, on the other hand, shows good results: the tasks with the most communication are colocated (Camera and Undistortion tasks).

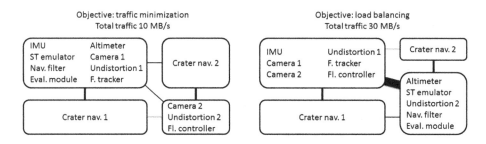

Fig. 5. ATON mapping to a four-node network with two different objectives. The width of lines between the nodes corresponds to the amount of exchanged data. The gray lines show that there is no data transfer between the nodes.

5.3   Remarks on Scalability

In order to evaluate the scalability of our approach, we generated a number of random task graphs of different sizes. We generated 10 task graphs for each problem size (5, 10, 15, 20 tasks) and took the average mapping time, excluding few instances that were unsatisfiable (in which case the solving ran under a second). The graph of average mapping times is shown in Fig. 6. There is a

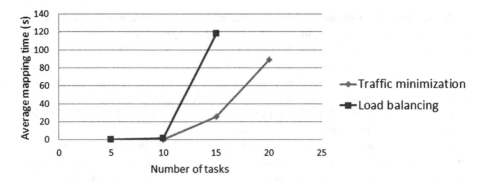

Fig. 6. Mapping time for different number of tasks with different objectives.

significant variation of solving time even for the same problem size. For example, the time for load balancing with 15 tasks ranges from 1.4 s to 8.7 min.

It is clear that the scalability of this approach is limited because the search space and the runtime grow exponentially with the number of tasks. For t tasks and n nodes there are n^t possible mappings, so even for rather simple cases with 4 nodes and 20 tasks we have to search within a large state space. Considering that some instances are mapped significantly faster than others, our best guess is that this approach can be practical for some instances of up to 30–50 tasks.

This is of course true for any exact optimization solution. When the problem instance is too large for an exact method, the only solution is to use approximate approaches such as search heuristics or genetic algorithms.

6   Conclusions and Future Work

We have demonstrated an application of SMT solving to produce a task-node mapping between tasks that run periodically in a distributed system, and the available processing nodes that are connected to a network with an arbitrary topology.

We formally defined the task-node mapping problem originating from our project ScOSA, showed how to translate this problem into an SMT problem, and solved it with the state-of-the-art SMT solver Z3.

In order to evaluate our approach, we used it to map the tasks of an existing application in a reasonable time. Additionally, we evaluated the scalability of the approach by running it on generated problem instances of different sizes.

As a result, the SMT-based approach proved to be suitable for the topology-aware mapping problem and practical for many problem sizes, which we suppose to have in ScOSA.

Our practical recommendations on SMT modeling to achieve some speedup are as follows. First, it appears to be better to use boolean encoding of an integer index variable rather than straightforward integer encoding. Second, it is advantageous to round numerical values to integers (however, with lower precision there is a risk of getting incorrect or suboptimal mapping).

A number of questions, however, remain for the future work. First of all, we need to compare our approach to the other approaches listed in Sect. 2. Secondly, we need to evaluate how accurately our model with periodic tasks reflects the actual system containing both time-triggered and event-triggered tasks. Additionally, it would be interesting to investigate if the solving time depends on the topology of the task and network graphs.

In the future, the task-node mapping will be extended with model checking to support the systems engineering for future ScOSA systems. For the mapping we consider a rather simple model of the system and the network. In the subsequent model checking, we are planning to analyze more complicated properties on a more precise system model such as message delivery times considering the routers' behavior and the routing protocol, time bounds on failure detection, absence of 'reconfiguration races' where different reconfigurations are triggered simultaneously, time bounds on the reconfigurations, application-specific properties.

Our long-term goal is to create a tool where the user inputs the network structure, the task graphs, requirements and constraints, and gets a collection of optimal mappings that satisfy the requirements, if such mappings exist.

References

1. Baruah, S.: Task partitioning upon heterogeneous multiprocessor platforms. In: Proceedings of the 10th IEEE Real-Time and Embedded Technology and Applications Symposium, RTAS 2004, pp. 536–543 (2004)
2. Biewer, A., Andres, B., Gladigau, J., Schaub, T., Haubelt, C.: A symbolic system synthesis approach for hard real-time systems based on coordinated SMT-solving. In: 2015 Design, Automation Test in Europe Conference Exhibition (DATE), pp. 357–362 (2015)
3. Bjørner, N., Phan, A.-D., Fleckenstein, L.: vZ - an optimizing SMT solver. In: Baier, C., Tinelli, C. (eds.) TACAS 2015. LNCS, vol. 9035, pp. 194–199. Springer, Heidelberg (2015). doi:10.1007/978-3-662-46681-0_14
4. Cheng, Z., Zhang, H., Tan, Y., Lim, Y.: SMT-based scheduling for multiprocessor real-time systems. In: 2016 IEEE/ACIS 15th International Conference on Computer and Information Science (ICIS), pp. 1–7 (2016)
5. Cruz, E.H.M., Diener, M., Pilla, L.L., Navaux, P.O.A.: An efficient algorithm for communication-based task mapping. In: 2015 23rd Euromicro International Conference on Parallel, Distributed, and Network-Based Processing, pp. 207–214 (2015)
6. Deveci, M., Rajamanickam, S., Leung, V.J., Pedretti, K., Olivier, S.L., Bunde, D.P., Çatalyürek, U.V., Devine, K.: Exploiting geometric partitioning in task mapping for parallel computers. In: 2014 IEEE 28th International Parallel and Distributed Processing Symposium, pp. 27–36 (2014)
7. Franz, T., Lüdtke, D., Maibaum, O., Gerndt, A.: Model-based software engineering for an optical navigation system for spacecraft. In: Deutscher Luft-und Raumfahrtkongress. Braunschweig, Germany, September 2016
8. Glantz, R., Meyerhenke, H., Noe, A.: Algorithms for mapping parallel processes onto grid and torus architectures. In: Proceedings of the 2015 23rd Euromicro International Conference on Parallel, Distributed, and Network-Based Processing, PDP 2015, pp. 236–243. IEEE Computer Society, Washington, DC (2015)

9. Hoefler, T., Jeannot, E., Mercier, G.: An overview of process mapping techniques and algorithms in high-performance computing. In: Jeannot, E., Zilinskas, J. (eds.) High Performance Computing on Complex Environments, pp. 75–94. Wiley (2014)

10. Hoefler, T., Snir, M.: Generic topology mapping strategies for large-scale parallel architectures. In: Proceedings of the International Conference on Supercomputing, ICS 2011, pp. 75–84. ACM, New York (2011)

11. Lee, S.Y., Aggarwal, J.K.: A mapping strategy for parallel processing. IEEE Trans. Comput. **C–36**(4), 433–442 (1987)

12. Lei, T., Kumar, S.: A two-step genetic algorithm for mapping task graphs to a network on chip architecture. In: Proceedings of the Euromicro Symposium on Digital System Design, pp. 180–187 (2003)

13. Liu, W., Gu, Z., Xu, J., Wu, X., Ye, Y.: Satisfiability modulo graph theory for task mapping and scheduling on multiprocessor systems. IEEE Trans. Parallel Distrib. Syst. **22**(8), 1382–1389 (2011)

14. Liu, W., Yuan, M., He, X., Gu, Z., Liu, X.: Efficient SAT-based mapping and scheduling of homogeneous synchronous dataflow graphs for throughput optimization. In: 2008 Real-Time Systems Symposium, pp. 492–504 (2008)

15. Lüdtke, D., Westerdorff, K., Stohlmann, K., Börner, A., Maibaum, O., Peng, T., Weps, B., Fey, G., Gerndt, A.: OBC-NG: towards a reconfigurable on-board computing architecture for spacecraft. In: 2014 IEEE Aerospace Conference, pp. 1–13 (2014)

16. de Moura, L., Bjørner, N.: Z3: an efficient SMT solver. In: Ramakrishnan, C.R., Rehof, J. (eds.) TACAS 2008. LNCS, vol. 4963, pp. 337–340. Springer, Heidelberg (2008). doi:10.1007/978-3-540-78800-3_24

17. Potts, C.: Analysis of a linear programming heuristic for scheduling unrelated parallel machines. Discrete Appl. Math. **10**(2), 155–164 (1985)

18. Satish, N., Ravindran, K., Keutzer, K.: A decomposition-based constraint optimization approach for statically scheduling task graphs with communication delays to multiprocessors. In: 2007 Design, Automation Test in Europe Conference Exhibition, pp. 1–6 (2007)

19. Tendulkar, P., Poplavko, P., Maler, O.: Symmetry breaking for multi-criteria mapping and scheduling on multicores. In: Braberman, V., Fribourg, L. (eds.) FORMATS 2013. LNCS, vol. 8053, pp. 228–242. Springer, Heidelberg (2013). doi:10.1007/978-3-642-40229-6_16

20. Wang, L., Li, Z., Song, M., Ren, S.: A genetic algorithm based approach to maximizing real-time system value under resource constraints. In: 2012 IEEE 31st International Performance Computing and Communications Conference (IPCCC), pp. 285–294 (2012)

21. Yang, L., Liu, W., Jiang, W., Li, M., Yi, J., Sha, E.H.M.: Application mapping and scheduling for network-on-chip-based multiprocessor system-on-chip with fine-grain communication optimization. IEEE Trans. Very Large Scale Integr. (VLSI) Syst. **24**(10), 3027–3040 (2016)

Concurrency and Distributed Systems

Analysis of Synchronisations in Stateful Active Objects

Ludovic Henrio[1], Cosimo Laneve[2,3], and Vincenzo Mastandrea[1,3(✉)]

[1] Université Côte d'Azur, CNRS, I3S, Sophia Antipolis, France
ludovic.henrio@cnrs.fr, mastandr@i3s.unice.fr
[2] University of Bologna, Bologna, Italy
cosimo.laneve@unibo.it
[3] INRIA-Focus, Sophia Antipolis, France

Abstract. This paper presents a static analysis technique based on effects and behavioural types for deriving synchronisation patterns of stateful active objects and verifying the absence of deadlocks in this context. This is challenging because active objects use futures to refer to results of pending asynchronous invocations and because these futures can be stored in object fields, passed as method parameters, or returned by invocations. Our effect system traces the access to object fields, thus allowing us to compute behavioural types that express synchronisation patterns in a precise way. The behavioural types are thereafter analysed by a solver that discovers potential deadlocks.

1 Introduction

Active objects are a programming model that unifies the models of actors and objects. In this model, method invocations are *asynchronous*: an object that invokes a method does not release the control and is free to continue processing – the invocation is "not blocking". The returned value of an invocation is bound to a pointer, called *future*, which is used by the caller to access the value. The access to a future triggers a synchronisation [4,12,16].

Active objects are gaining prominence because they provide a high-level multitasking paradigm easier to program than explicit threads. For this reason, they are a pervasive Symbian OS idiom [15] and have been adopted in several languages and libraries, such as Akka [18], an actor library for Java and Scala [10], or in ABS [12], and in ProActive [4]. In active object languages, futures are first class values; therefore they can be sent as arguments of method invocations, returned by methods, or stored in object fields. In this context, the analysis of synchronisation patterns is challenging because the context where synchronisation, i.e. future access, occurs can be different from the context where the future is created. For example, the synchronisation of a future stored in a field happens when the value stored in the field is necessary; at this point, the execution of the corresponding method must finish before the value of the future can be accessed.

This work was partially funded by the ANR project ANR-11-LABX-0031-01.

N. Polikarpova and S. Schneider (Eds.): IFM 2017, LNCS 10510, pp. 195–210, 2017.
DOI: 10.1007/978-3-319-66845-1_13

This paper presents a static analysis technique for finding synchronisation patterns and detecting deadlocks in stateful active objects. Our analysis is expressed on an active model called **gASP** that features implicit synchronisation on futures (called *wait-by-necessity*) and does not require any specific type for futures. With wait-by-necessity, the execution is only blocked when a value to be returned by a method is needed to evaluate a term. This programming abstraction allows the programmer not to worry about placing synchronisation points: the synchronisation will always occur as late as possible. The strengths of this analysis are: the precise management of object states and their update, the tracking of futures passed by method invocations or stored in fields, and the support for infinite states. This paper extends previous works [6,8] with the handling of stateful objects by tracing the effects of methods on fields, including the storage of futures inside object fields.

To illustrate synchronisation in active objects, consider the example below.

```
1   Int n                                8   //MAIN
2   addToStore(Int x){                   9   { Store = new Act(0);
3     count = n + 1;                      10      x = Store.addToStore(1);
4     n = this.store(x,count);            11      x = x + 1; // needed to
5     return count }                                      avoid conflicts
6   store(Int x, Int y){                  12      k = Store.addToStore(4) }
7     /* storing x */ return y }
```

This program creates an active object, calls the **addToStore** method asynchronously twice. To prevent non-deterministic results, and to ensure the order of execution of requests, we synchronise on the result of the first invocation (Line 11) before triggering the second one. Synchronisation is expressed by any operation accessing the method result, a specific synchronisation operation is not necessary in **gASP** even if it could be added. The **addToStore** method triggers an invocation to the **store** method and counts the number of stored elements. Our analysis is able to detect that a deadlock is possible if the second invocation to **addToStore** is executed before the method **store**. The analysis reveals by a circular dependency where the single thread of the active object is waiting for the value of **n** inside **addToStore**, the effect analysis reveals that **n** contains the result of the **store** method, and thus **store** must be executed to resolve the dependency. The analysis also discovers that if Line 11 is omitted then the two concurrent **addToStore** requests lead to a non-deterministic object state (one of the states being undesired).

The typing technique is based on an *effect system* that traces the accesses to fields (e.g. read and write access to **n** in the example), and a *behavioural system* that discovers the synchronisation patterns of active objects. The effect type records if a field is read or write, and which parameters are used by each method. It is used to identify conflicting field accesses, e.g. one invocation reading a field and a parallel one writing a new future in the same field. The effect type records the usage of parameters because they correspond to synchronisations that create a dependency between tasks. Also we mark an accessed future as "already synchronised" to avoid synchronising it multiple times. Because futures are implicit and pervasive we use a novel technique where "everything is a future", this enables precise tracking of futures and prevent multiple synchronisation of the same future hold by several variables. The analysis detects and excludes program with non-deterministic effects. It could be extended to non-deterministic programs by associating multiple values to each variable, merging the different environments when non-determinacy is detected. This is not studied here, it would make the analysis less precise and the formalisation more complex.

The behavioural types define the synchronisation patterns. They are expressed in a modelling language that is an extension of *lams* [7,13], which are conjunctions and disjunctions of object dependencies and method invocations. Like in [6], to deal with method returning futures, we use a place-holder that represents the object that will access a future . Actually, our types extend those of [6] with so-called *delegations* that represent side-effects of methods on argument fields. If a method stores a future f in the field of an argument, then the next access to the field should occur after the end of the method (to prevent read/write conflicts) and should be bound to the future. As the future f is generally not known when typing, we create a delegation which represents this future. We introduce the notation *method ⤳ object. field_name* for delegations.

The analysis of the behavioural type is performed by the solver defined in [6], which detects circularities in the graph of dependencies, highlighting potential *deadlocks* caused by erroneous synchronisation patterns. The behavioural type system specifies a set of pairwise dependencies between futures, some of them being delegations; the analysis unfolds this set of dependencies to find the potential circularities in the program execution. We prove that our analysis finds all the potential deadlocks of a program.

Section 2 presents gASP. Section 3 describes our type system and Sect. 4 presents our analysis technique. Section 5 provides related work and a conclusion. Due to space limitation, this paper only contains the crucial points of the formalisation; technical details and proofs can be found in [11].

2   The Active Object Model gASP

Syntax. The language gASP has types T that may be either Int or a class Act. Extending this work to several classes is not problematic. We use x, y, k, $\cdots$ to range over variable names. The notation $\overline{T\ x}$ denotes any finite sequence of *variable declarations* $T\ x$, separated by commas. A gASP program is a sequence of variable declarations $\overline{T\ x}$ (fields) and method definitions $T\ \mathtt{m}(\overline{T\ y})\ \{\ s\ \}$, plus a main body $\{\ s'\ \}$. The syntax of gASP body is defined by the following grammar:

$$
\begin{array}{llll}
s ::= & \mathtt{skip}\ \mid\ x = z\ \mid\ \mathtt{if}\ e\ \{\ s\ \}\ \mathtt{else}\ \{\ s\ \}\ \mid\ s\ ;\ s\ \mid\ \mathtt{return}\ v & & \text{statements} \\
z ::= & e\ \mid\ v.\mathtt{m}(\overline{v})\ \mid\ \mathtt{new}\ \mathtt{Act}(\overline{v}) & & \text{expressions with side effects} \\
e ::= & v\ \mid\ v \oplus v & & \text{expressions} \\
v ::= & x\ \mid\ \mathtt{null}\ \mid\ \textit{integer-values} & & \text{atoms}
\end{array}
$$

Expressions with side effects include asynchronous method calls $v.\mathtt{m}(\overline{v})$, where v is the invoked object and $\overline{v}$ are the arguments of the invocation. Operations taking place on different active objects occur in parallel, while operations in the same active object are sequential. Terms z also include $\textbf{new Act}(\overline{v})$ that creates a new active object whose fields contain the values $\overline{v}$. A (pure) expression e may be a simple term v or an arithmetic or relational expression; the symbol $\oplus$ range over standard arithmetic and relational operators. Without loss of generality, we assume that fields and local variables have distinct names.

Semantics. The semantics of $\textsf{gASP}$ uses two sets of names: *active object names*, ranged over by α, β, . . . , and *future names*, ranged over by f, g, ...
 The runtime syntax of $\textsf{gASP}$ is:

$$
\begin{array}{llll}
cn & ::= & f(w) \mid f(\bot) \mid \alpha(a,p,\overline{q}) \mid cn\ cn & \text{configurations} \\
w & ::= & \alpha \mid f \mid v & \text{values and names} \\
p,q & ::= & \{\ell \mid s\} & \text{processes} \\
a,\ell & ::= & \overline{x} \mapsto \overline{w} & \text{memories}
\end{array}
$$

Configurations, denoted cn, are non empty sets of active objects and futures. Active objects $\alpha(a,p,\overline{q})$ contain a name α, a memory a recording fields, a running process p, and the set of processes waiting to be scheduled $\overline{q}$. The element $f(\cdot)$ represents a *future* which may be an actual value (called *future value*) or $\bot$ if the future has not yet been computed. A name, either active object or future, is *fresh* in a configuration if it does not occur in the configuration. Memories a and ℓ (where ℓ stores local variables) map variables into values or names. The following auxiliary functions are used: $dom(\ell)$ returns the domain of ℓ; $fields(\texttt{Act})$ is the list of fields of $\texttt{Act}$; $\ell[x \mapsto v]$ is the standard map update; $a + \ell$ merges the mappings a and ℓ, it is undefined if $a(x) \neq \ell(x)$ for some x. We use the following notation: $(a + \ell)[x \mapsto w] = a' + \ell'$ implies $a' = a[x \mapsto w]$, if $x \in \mathrm{dom}(a)$, or $\ell' = \ell[x \mapsto w]$, otherwise. The evaluation of an expression, denoted $[\![e]\!]_{a+\ell}$, returns the value of e by computing the expression, retrieving the values stored in $a + \ell$; $[\![\overline{e}]\!]_{a+\ell}$ returns the tuple of values of $\overline{e}$. Finally, if $\texttt{m}$ is defined by $T\,\texttt{m}(\overline{T\ x})\ \{\,s\,\}$ then: $\mathrm{bind}(\alpha,\texttt{m},\overline{w},f) = p$ where p is a process in the following shape $\{\,[\,\texttt{destiny} \mapsto f,\ \texttt{this} \mapsto \alpha,\ \overline{x} \mapsto \overline{w}\,]\mid s\,\}$, where the special variable $\texttt{destiny}$ records the name of the future currently computed.

 The operational semantics of $\textsf{gASP}$ is defined by a transition relation between configurations. Figure 1 shows the essential rules of the semantics, all the rules can be found in [6,11]. Rule UPDATE replaces the future reference by its value, it can be triggered at any time when a future value is known. The new value may be also a future. Rule SERVE schedules a new process to be executed, which is taken from the set q of waiting processes. Rule ASSIGN stores a value or a name into a local variable or a field (*cf.* definition of $a + \ell$). The evaluation of $[\![e]\!]_{a+\ell}$ may require synchronisations: if e is an arithmetic expression, the operands must be evaluated to integers, and, if an operand is a future, the rule can only be applied *after this future has been evaluated and updated*. The $\texttt{if}$ statement is omitted here but the evaluation of the condition must result in a boolean which may trigger a synchronisation. Note that this semantics ensures the strong encapsulation of objects: an active object can only assign its

$$\frac{w \text{ is not a variable}}{[\![w]\!]_\ell = w} \qquad \frac{x \in dom(\ell)}{[\![x]\!]_\ell = \ell(x)} \qquad \frac{[\![v]\!]_\ell = k \quad [\![v']\!]_\ell = k'}{[\![v \oplus v']\!]_\ell = k''} \qquad \frac{\text{SERVE}}{\alpha(a, \varnothing, \overline{q} \cup \{p\}) \to \alpha(a, p, \overline{q})}$$

$$\frac{\text{UPDATE}}{\substack{(a+\ell)(x) = f \\ (a+\ell)[x \mapsto w] = a' + \ell' \\ \alpha(a, \{\ell \mid s\}, \overline{q}) \, f(w) \\ \to \alpha(a', \{\ell' \mid s\}, \overline{q}) \, f(w)}} \qquad \frac{\text{ASSIGN}}{\substack{[\![e]\!]_{a+\ell} = w \\ (a+\ell)[x \mapsto w] = a' + \ell' \\ \alpha(a, \{\ell \mid x = e \; ; \; s\}, \overline{q}) \\ \to \alpha(a', \{\ell' \mid s\}, \overline{q})}} \qquad \frac{\text{RETURN}}{\substack{[\![v]\!]_{a+\ell} = w \quad \ell(\text{destiny}) = f \\ \alpha(a, \{\ell \mid \text{return } v\}, \overline{q}) \, f(\bot) \\ \to \alpha(a, \varnothing, \overline{q}) \, f(w)}}$$

$$\frac{\text{NEW}}{\substack{[\![\overline{v}]\!]_{a+\ell} = \overline{w} \quad \beta \text{ fresh} \quad \overline{y} = fields \\ \alpha(a, \{\ell \mid x = \text{new } \text{Act}(\overline{v}) \; ; \; s\}, \overline{q}) \\ \to \alpha(a, \{\ell \mid x = \beta \; ; \; s\}, \overline{q}) \, \beta([\overline{y} \mapsto \overline{w}], \varnothing, \varnothing)}}$$

$$\frac{\text{INVK}}{\substack{[\![v]\!]_{a+\ell} = \beta \quad [\![\overline{v}]\!]_{a+\ell} = \overline{w} \quad \beta \neq \alpha \\ f \text{ fresh} \quad bind(\beta, \text{m}, \overline{w}, f) = p' \\ \alpha(a, \{\ell \mid x = v.\text{m}(\overline{v}) \; ; \; s\}, \overline{q}) \, \beta(a', p, \overline{q'}) \\ \to \alpha(a, \{\ell \mid x = f; s\}, \overline{q}) \, \beta(a', p, \overline{q'} \cup \{p'\}) \, f(\bot)}}$$

Fig. 1. Evaluation function and semantics of gASP (excerpt) - full version in [11].

own fields. The initial configuration of a gASP program with main body $\{s\}$ is: $main([\overline{x} \mapsto \overline{0}], \{[\text{destiny} \mapsto f_{main}, \text{this} \mapsto main] \mid s\}, \varnothing)$ where $main$ is a special active object, $\overline{x} = fields$, and f_{main} is a future name. As usual, $\to^*$ is the reflexive and transitive closure of $\to$.

Analysed Programs. In order to simplify the technical details, we will consider gASP programs that verify the following restrictions:

(i) object fields and method returned values are of type Int (at runtime they can be either futures or integer values);

(ii) the futures created in a method must be either returned or synchronised or stored in a field of a parameter (or *this*).

Constraint (i) can be checked by a standard type checker, and (ii) can be verified by a simple static analyser. In particular, (ii) prevents computations running in parallel without any means to synchronise on them. Technically, admitting futures that are never synchronised requires to collect the corresponding behaviours and add them to any possible continuation, like in [8].

Deadlocks. In gASP, when computing an expression, if one of the elements of the expression is a future then the current active object waits until the future has been updated. If the waiting relation is *circular* then no progress is possible. In this case all the active objects in the circular dependency are *deadlocked*. We formalise the notion of deadlock below. Let *contexts* $C[\,]$ be the following terms

$$C[\,] ::= \quad x = [\,] \oplus v \; ; \; s \quad \mid \quad x = v \oplus [\,] \; ; \; s \quad \mid \quad \text{if } [\,] \{s'\} \text{ else } \{s''\} \; ; \; s$$
$$\mid \quad \text{if } [\,] \oplus v \{s'\} \text{ else } \{s''\} \; ; \; s \quad \mid \quad \text{if } v \oplus [\,] \{s'\} \text{ else } \{s''\} \; ; \; s$$

As usual, $\mathcal{C}[e]$ is the context where the hole $[\,]$ of $\mathcal{C}[\,]$ is replaced by e.

Let $f \in destinies(\overline{q})$ if there is $\{\ell|s\} \in \overline{q}$ such that $\ell(\text{destiny}) = f$.

Definition 1 (Deadlocked configuration). *Let* cn *be a configuration containing* $\alpha_0(a_0, p_0, \overline{q_0}), \cdots, \alpha_{n-1}(a_{n-1}, p_{n-1}, \overline{q_{n-1}})$. *If, for every* $0 \leq i < n$,

1. $p_i = \{\ell_i \mid C[v]\}$ *where* $[\![v]\!]_{a_i + \ell_i} = f_i$ *and*
2. $f_i \in destinies(p_{i+1}, \overline{q_{i+1}})$, *where* $+$ *is computed modulo* n

then cn *is* deadlocked.

A program is deadlock-free *if all reachable configurations are deadlock free.*

Queue with Non Deterministic Effects. Since gASP is stateful, it is possible to store futures in object fields and to pass them around during invocations. Therefore, computing the value of a field is difficult and, sometimes, not possible because of the nondeterminism caused by the concurrent behaviours. To be precise enough, we restrict the analysis to programs where method invocations only create request *queues with deterministic effects*.

Definition 2. *An active object* $\alpha(a, p, \overline{q})$ *has a queue with deterministic effects if when a process in* $\overline{q}$ *write on a field all the other process in the queue do not perform neither read nor writes on the same field.*

A configuration cn *has deterministic effects if every active object of this configuration has a queue with deterministic effects. A* gASP *program has deterministic effects if any reachable configuration has deterministic effects.*

Example. The execution of the program shown in the introduction reaches the following configuration after the first execution of the **addToStore** method (future f), at the point where either the method **store** (future g) or **addToStore** (future h) can be served: $main(\,[n \mapsto 0], \varnothing, \varnothing\,)$ $f(1)$ $g(\bot)$ $h(\bot)$ $\alpha(\,[n \mapsto g\,], \varnothing, \{body\text{-}of\text{-}\mathsf{store}\}, \{body\text{-}of\text{-}\mathsf{addToStore}\}\,)$.

From this point, if α serves the invocation of **addToStore** we reach a deadlock because the execution of **addToStore** needs to know the value of the field **n** (to execute Line 4) but the method **store** can only be served after the termination of the current method. If **store** is served first, then when the execution of **addToStore** occurs, the future stored in the field **n** is already computed therefore the expression **n + 1** can be solved and the program terminates.

3   Behavioural Type System

In this section we define a type system that associates abstract descriptions, called *behavioural types* to gASPprograms. This association is done by recording several information: (1) *effects on object fields* to enforce consistency of read/write operations between methods invoked in parallel on the same active object; (2) *dependencies between active objects* and *between futures and active objects* to enforce consistency of synchronisation patterns. The analysis is performed following the program structure and verifying that the types of methods match previously declared types. From the explicit type system presented below, an inference system can be defined in a standard way. Note that it is not possible to infer at static time which variables contain a future. Consequently, we consider all stored values as futures and some of corresponding values will be already synchronised when created. It is therefore important to distinguish *future names* that are identifiers and *future types* that are values corresponding to futures; the environment will map future identifiers to future types.

Analysed Properties. The goal of the type system is to verify the deadlock freedom of gASP programs. Since gASP is stateful, deadlocks might be caused by accesses to futures stored in object fields. Therefore, the type system must also compute the *effects* of statements on active object fields (and expose them in types of methods so that the analysis is compositional). It is worth noticing that in gASP, because of concurrency, the computations are non-deterministic and the effects on fields may be indeterminate. Our type system also verifies whether the analysed program might exhibit such a non-deterministic behaviour.

Types. Types are either basic types, future types or behavioural types. They are defined as follows:

$$
\begin{array}{llll}
b & ::= \square \mid \alpha[\overline{x{:}f}] & & \text{basic type} \\
f & ::= b \mid \lambda X.\mathtt{m}(f, \overline{g}, X, \Gamma, E) \mid f \rightsquigarrow g.x & & \text{future type} \\
\kappa & ::= \star \mid \alpha \mid X & & \text{synchronisers} \\
L & ::= 0 \mid (\kappa, \alpha) \mid f_\kappa \mid L + L \mid L \,\&\, L & & \text{behavioural type}
\end{array}
$$

Basic types b are used for values or parameters; they may be either primitive type, i.e. integer, $\square$ or an object type $\alpha[\overline{a:f}]$. Future types f include basic types, invocation results, and delegations. The invocation result $\lambda X.\mathtt{m}(f, \overline{g}, X, \Gamma, E)$ represents the value computed by a method invocation, where $f, \overline{g}$ are the arguments of the invocation (f is the future of the called object), X, called *handle*, is a placeholder for the object that will synchronise with the invocation, the environment Γ and the effects E record the state changes performed by the method, they are discussed in the following. The delegation $f \rightsquigarrow g.x$ represents a method side effect, namely the value that is written by the method corresponding to f in the field x of the argument g. In the type system we also use "check-marked" future types, noted $f^{\checkmark}$, to represent a future value that has been already synchronised. We use $f^{[\checkmark]}$ to range over both future types and "check-marked" future types.

Behavioural types include 0, the empty dependency, and (κ, α) that means: if κ is instantiated by an object β, then β will need α to be available in order to proceed its execution. Behavioural types also include *synchronisation commitments* f_κ, whose meaning depends on the value of κ: $f_\star$ means that the invocation related to f is potentially running in parallel; f_α means that the active object α is waiting for the result of the invocation corresponding to f; f_X represents the return of a future f, where the handle X will be replaced with the name of the object that will synchronise on the result of f. The types $L \,\&\, L'$ is the behaviour of two statements of types L and L' running in parallel; $L + L'$ is the behaviour of two statements (of types L and L') running in sequence (regardless of the order).

We will shorten $L_1 \& \cdots \& L_n$ into $\&_{i \in \{1..n\}} L_i$ and $L_1 + \cdots + L_n$ into $\sum_{i \in \{1..n\}} L_i$. The operations "$\&$" and "$+$" on behavioural types are associative, commutative with 0 being the identity. The operator "$\&$" has precedence over "$+$".

Environments. Environments, noted Γ, Γ', $\cdots$, are maps from variables to future names $(x \mapsto f)$, from future names to future types, check-marked or not $(f \mapsto \mathtt{f}^{[\checkmark]})$, and from method names to their signatures.

The image of an environment Γ is noted $\mathrm{im}(\Gamma)$; the restriction of Γ to a set S of names is noted $\Gamma|_S$; the difference operation the difference operation $\Gamma \setminus x$ defined as $\Gamma|_{\mathrm{dom}(\Gamma) \setminus x}$. The following functions on Γ are also used:

- $names(\Gamma) = \mathrm{dom}(\Gamma) \cup \{\alpha \mid \alpha[\overline{x : f}]^{[\checkmark]} \in \mathrm{im}(\Gamma)\}$;
- $obj(\overline{f})$ (resp. $int(\overline{f'})$) is a subset of $\overline{f}$ such that for each $f' \in obj(\overline{f})$ (resp. $f' \in int(\overline{f})$) we have $\Gamma(f') = \alpha[\cdots]$ (resp. $\Gamma(f') \neq \alpha[\cdots]$) for some α;
- $Fut(\Gamma)$ is the set of future names in $\mathrm{dom}(\Gamma)$; $aFut(\Gamma)$ and $sFut(\Gamma)$ are the subset of $Fut(\Gamma)$ that contain future names f such that $\Gamma(f)$ is respectively not-check-marked or check-marked;
- $unsync(\Gamma) = \&_{f \in aFut(\Gamma)} f_\star$ is the parallel behaviour of the method invocations which are not-yet-synchronised;
- $\Gamma[f^\checkmark]$ returns the environment $\Gamma[f \mapsto \mathtt{f}^\checkmark]$ when $\Gamma(f)$ is either $\mathtt{f}$ or $\mathtt{f}^\checkmark$;
- $\Gamma(f.x) = \begin{cases} g & \text{if } \Gamma(f) = \alpha[\cdots, x{:}g, \cdots] \\ undefined & \text{otherwise} \end{cases}$
- $\Gamma[f.x \mapsto g]$ returns the environment such that $\Gamma(f.x) = g$, assuming that $f \in \mathrm{dom}(\Gamma)$ and $x \in fields(\mathtt{Act})$; $\Gamma[f.x \mapsto g]$ is defined like Γ elsewhere;
- $\Gamma_1 =_{\mathrm{unsync}} \Gamma_2$ whenever $\Gamma_1(f) = \Gamma_2(f)$ for every f in $aFut(\Gamma_1) \cup aFut(\Gamma_2)$.

Effects. Effects are functions, noted E, A, $\cdots$, that map future names to a set of field names labelled either with $\mathtt{r}$ (read) or with $\mathtt{w}$ (write). For example, consider $\mathtt{m}$ a method with effect E, and f one of its arguments, $E(f) = \{x^\mathtt{w}, y^\mathtt{r}\}$ means that $\mathtt{m}$ writes on the field x of the object that is the value of f and reads on the field y. Let $\mathtt{h}$ range over $\{\mathtt{r}, \mathtt{w}\}$; if $x^\mathtt{h} \in E(f)$, we use the notation $E(f.x) = \mathtt{h}$. With an abuse of notation, we also write $x \in E(f)$ if $E(f) = \{x_1^{\mathtt{h}_1}, \cdots, x_n^{\mathtt{h}_n}\}$ and $x \in \{x_1, \cdots, x_n\}$ (therefore $x \notin E(f)$ also when $E(f)$ is undefined). In the example in the introduction, the method $\mathtt{addToStore}$ has the effect $[g \mapsto [n^\mathtt{w}]$ where g represents the current object ($\mathtt{this}$). The set $\{\mathtt{r}, \mathtt{w}\}$ with the ordering $\mathtt{r} < \mathtt{w}$ is a lattice, therefore we use the operation $\sqcup$ for least-upper bound. We also use few auxiliary operations that are shown in Fig. 2: *update operation with upper bound*[1]; *effects of unsynchronised methods*[2]; *compatibility*[3]; effect instantiation taking into account effect compatibility[4]. We extend the definition of the operation $\sqcup$ and $\#$ from effects to sets of effects iterating them for all the element of the sets pairwise.

$$E[f.x \mapsto^{\sqcup} \mathtt{h}](f.x) = \begin{cases} \mathtt{h} \sqcup \mathtt{h}' & \text{if } E(f.x) = \mathtt{h}' \\ \mathtt{h} & \text{if } x \notin E(f) \text{ and } x \in \textit{fields}(\mathtt{Act}) \\ \textit{undefined} & \text{otherwise} \end{cases} \tag{1}$$

$$\textit{Effects}(\Gamma) = \bigsqcup \{E \mid \Gamma(f) = \lambda X.\mathtt{m}(\overline{g}, X, \Gamma_\mathtt{m}, E)\} \tag{2*}$$

$$x^\mathtt{h} \# y^{\mathtt{h}'} = \begin{cases} \textit{true} & \text{if } x \neq y \text{ or } (x = y \text{ and } \mathtt{h}' = \mathtt{r} = \mathtt{h}) \\ \textit{false} & \text{otherwise} \end{cases} \tag{3}$$

$$\textit{instanceof}(E, \sigma)(f) = \begin{cases} \bigsqcup_{g \in \sigma^{-1}(f)} E(g) & \text{if } \forall f_1, f_2 \in \sigma^{-1}(f).f_1 \neq f_2 \Rightarrow E(f_1) \# E(f_2) \\ \textit{undefined} & \text{otherwise} \end{cases} \tag{4**}$$

Fig. 2. Auxiliary functions for effects - full version in [11]. (*We notice that $\Gamma(f)$ is not check-marked, **The usage of *instanceof* is illustrated in the description of T-METHOD-SIGN).

Judgements. The judgements used in the type system are:

- $\vdash \mathtt{m} : (f, \overline{g}, \Gamma_\mathtt{m}, X) \rightarrow (E, A)$ instantiates the method signature of m, where $f, \overline{g}$, X are the *formal parameters*, $\Gamma_\mathtt{m}$ is the part of environment accessible from the method parameters which are objects: $\Gamma_\mathtt{m} = (\Gamma|_{f \cup obj(\overline{g})})$, where Γ is the environment at invocation point. E, A are the environments storing the effects of m: E stores the effects that happen before m is synchronised, A stores the effects of the methods invoked by m and not synchronised in its body;
- $\Gamma, E \vdash x : f \;\triangleright\; E'$ for typing values and variables with future names, where E' is the update of E
- $\Gamma \vdash f : \mathtt{f}$ for typing future names with future types;
- $\Gamma, E \;^\oplus\vdash_S e : \mathsf{L} \;\triangleright\; \Gamma', E'$ for typing synchronisations, where S is the set of arguments of the current method, L is the behavioural type, and Γ' and E' are the updates of Γ and E respectively;
- $\Gamma, E, A \vdash_S z : f, \mathsf{L} \;\triangleright\; \Gamma', E', A'$ for typing expressions with side effects z;
- $\Gamma, E, A \vdash_S s : \mathsf{L} \;\triangleright\; \Gamma', E', A'$ for typing statements s.

Type System. We assume that every environment Γ is such that $\Gamma(\square) = \square^\checkmark$ and $\Gamma(\textit{this}) = \alpha[\cdots]$, where α is the active object running the current method. The typing rules are shown in Fig. 3 and the most rellevant ones are discussed.

Rule (T-FIELD) models the reading of a field (of the *this* actor). The preconditions verify that the access is compatible with the effects of not yet synchronised invocations in Γ and those in A (that will not be synchronised). We notice that there is no compatibility check with effects in E and E is updated with the new access (performing the upper bound with the old value). Rule (T-METHOD-SIGN) instantiates a method signature according to the invocation parameters. In particular, the rule also covers the case when two parameters have the same value thanks to the *instanceof* function. In the signature, each parameter has a fresh name, but upon invocation, new conflicts might be created by the fact that two different parameters are actually the same object. In this case, we prevent the instantiation of the invocation if a conflict might occur. For example, if the signature of a method m is such that $\Gamma(\mathtt{m}) = (f, f', X, \Gamma') \rightarrow ([f \mapsto \{x^\mathtt{r}\}, f' \mapsto \{x^\mathtt{w}\}]$

fields and method names: $\Gamma \vdash x : \mathsf{b}$ and $\vdash \mathtt{m} : (\overline{f}, X, \Gamma') \to (E, A)$

(T-FIELD)
$$\frac{\Gamma(this.x) = f \qquad E' = E[this.x \mapsto^{\sqcup} r]}{\Gamma, E \vdash x : f \ \triangleright \ E'}$$

(T-METHOD-SIGN)
$$\frac{\Gamma(\mathtt{m}) = (\overline{f}, X, \Gamma') \to (E, A) \qquad \sigma \ renaming \qquad E' = instanceof(E, \sigma) \qquad A' = instanceof(A, \sigma)}{\vdash \mathtt{m} : (\sigma(\overline{f}), \sigma(X), \Gamma'') \to (E', A')}$$

synchronizations: $\Gamma, E \ ^{\oplus}\!\vdash_S \ x : \mathsf{L} \ \triangleright \ \Gamma', E'$

(T-SYNC-INVK)
$$\frac{\begin{array}{c} \Gamma \vdash this : \alpha[\cdots]^{\checkmark} \qquad \Gamma, E \vdash x : f \ \triangleright \ E' \\ \Gamma \vdash f : \lambda X.\mathtt{m}(\overline{f'}, X, \Gamma_{\mathtt{m}}, E_{\mathtt{m}}) \qquad \Gamma' = \Gamma[f^{\checkmark}][h^{\checkmark}]^{h \in dom(E_{\mathtt{m}})} \\ \Gamma'' = \Gamma'([g.y \mapsto g'][g' \mapsto f \rightsquigarrow g.y])^{y^{\mathtt{w}} \in E_{\mathtt{m}}(g), \ g' \ fresh} \end{array}}{\Gamma, E \ ^{\oplus}\!\vdash_S \ x : f_{\alpha} \ \& \ unsync(\Gamma'') \ \triangleright \ \Gamma'', E' \sqcup E_{\mathtt{m}}|_S}$$

(T-SYNC-FIELD)
$$\frac{\Gamma \vdash this : \alpha[\cdots]^{\checkmark} \qquad \Gamma, E \vdash x : f \ \triangleright \ E' \qquad \Gamma \vdash f : g \rightsquigarrow this.x \qquad \Gamma' = \Gamma[f^{\checkmark}]}{\Gamma, E \ ^{\oplus}\!\vdash_S \ x : f_{\alpha} \ \& \ unsync(\Gamma') \ \triangleright \ \Gamma', E'}$$

expressions with side effects: $\Gamma, E, A \vdash_S z : f, \mathsf{L} \ \triangleright \ \Gamma', E', A'$

(T-EXPRESSION)
$$\frac{\Gamma, E \ ^{\oplus}\!\vdash_S \ v : \mathsf{L} \ \triangleright \ \Gamma', E' \qquad \Gamma', E' \ ^{\oplus}\!\vdash_S \ v' : \mathsf{L}' \ \triangleright \ \Gamma'', E''}{\Gamma, E, A \vdash_S v \oplus v' : \Box, \mathsf{L} + \mathsf{L}' \ \triangleright \ \Gamma'', E'', A}$$

(T-INVK)
$$\frac{\begin{array}{c} \Gamma, E \vdash v : f \ \triangleright \ E \qquad \Gamma \vdash f : \beta[\cdots]^{\checkmark} \qquad \Gamma, E \vdash \overline{v} : \overline{f'} \ \triangleright \ E' \qquad \overline{h} = f \cup obj(\overline{f'}) \\ \vdash \mathtt{m} : (f, \overline{f'}, X, \Gamma|_{\overline{h}}) \to (E_{\mathtt{m}}, A_{\mathtt{m}}) \qquad g \ fresh \qquad \overline{g'} = \overline{f'}[^{\Box}/_{int(sFut(\Gamma))}] \qquad \Gamma_{\mathtt{m}} = (\Gamma|_{\overline{h}})[^{\Box}/_{int(sFut(\Gamma))}] \\ \Gamma' = \Gamma[g \mapsto \lambda X.\mathtt{m}(f, \overline{g'}, X, \Gamma_{\mathtt{m}}, E_{\mathtt{m}})] \qquad (Effects(\Gamma')(h') \ \# \ y^{(E_{\mathtt{m}} \sqcup A)(h' \cdot y)})^{h' \in dom(E_{\mathtt{m}} \uplus A) \ \wedge \ y \in fields(\mathtt{Act})} \end{array}}{\Gamma, E, A \vdash_S v.\mathtt{m}(\overline{v}) : g, g_* \ \& \ unsync(\Gamma) \ \triangleright \ \Gamma', E', A \sqcup A_{\mathtt{m}}}$$

statements $\Gamma, E, A \vdash_S s : \mathsf{L} \ \triangleright \ \Gamma', E', A$

(T-ASSIGN-FIELD-EXP)
$$\frac{\begin{array}{c} x \in fields(\mathtt{Act}) \qquad \Gamma, E, A \vdash_S z : f, \mathsf{L} \ \triangleright \ \Gamma', E', A' \\ Effects(\Gamma')(this) \ \# \ x^{\mathtt{w}} \qquad A'(this) \ \# \ x^{\mathtt{w}} \end{array}}{\Gamma, E, A \vdash_S x = z : \mathsf{L} \ \triangleright \ \Gamma'[this.x \mapsto f], E'[this.x \mapsto^{\sqcup} \mathtt{w}], A'}$$

(T-RETURN-FUT)
$$\frac{\Gamma, E \vdash v : f \ \triangleright \ E' \qquad \Gamma \vdash f : \mathsf{f} \qquad \Gamma(future) = X \qquad \mathsf{L} = unsync(\Gamma \setminus f)}{\Gamma, E, A \vdash_S return \ v : f_X \ \& \ \mathsf{L} \ \triangleright \ \Gamma, E', A}$$

methods: $\Gamma \vdash \mathtt{m} \ (\overline{T \ x})\{s\} : (\overline{x'}, X) \to (\nu \ \overline{\varkappa})(\Gamma' \cdot \Gamma'' \cdot \mathsf{L})$ and $\Gamma \vdash \overline{Int \ a}, \overline{M} \ \{s\} : (\mathcal{L}, \Gamma' \cdot \mathsf{L})$

(T-METHOD)
$$\frac{\begin{array}{c} \Gamma(\mathtt{m}) = (this, \overline{f}, X, \Gamma_{\mathtt{m}}) \to (E, A) \qquad \overline{g} = int(\overline{f} \cup names(\Gamma_{\mathtt{m}})) \\ \Gamma + \Gamma_{\mathtt{m}} + \overline{x} : \overline{f} + \overline{g} : \Box + future : X, [this \mapsto \varnothing], \varnothing \vdash_{dom(\Gamma_{\mathtt{m}})} s : \mathsf{L} \ \triangleright \ \Gamma', E, A' \qquad \overline{w} = flat(this, \overline{f}, \Gamma_{\mathtt{m}}) \\ \overline{\varkappa} = names(\Gamma') \setminus names(\Gamma_{\mathtt{m}}) \qquad A = A' \sqcup \bigsqcup_{h \in dom(\Gamma')} \left\{ \left(E_{\mathtt{m}'}|_{\{this, \overline{f}\}} \right) \mid \Gamma'(h) = \lambda Y.\mathtt{m}'(\overline{f}, Y, \Gamma_{\mathtt{m}'}, E_{\mathtt{m}'}) \right\} \end{array}}{\Gamma \vdash \mathtt{m} \ (\overline{T \ x})\{s\} : (\overline{w}, X) \to (\nu \ \overline{\varkappa})(\Gamma'|_{\overline{\varkappa}} \cdot \Gamma'|_{obj(\overline{f})} \cdot \mathsf{L} \& (X, \alpha))}$$

Fig. 3. Typing rules -full version in [11].

or $\Gamma(\mathtt{m}) = (f, f', X, \Gamma') \to ([f \mapsto \{x^{\mathtt{w}}\}, f' \mapsto \{x^{\mathtt{w}}\}]$, the type system is not able to instantiate the method invocation $\lambda X.\mathtt{m}(g, g, X, \Gamma'', E_{\mathtt{m}})$ because of potential conflicts: two operations of write on the same object appeared due to the aliasing created between parameters.

In gASP, synchronisations are due to the evaluation of expressions e that are not variables. We use the notation $^{\oplus}\!\vdash$ for these judgments. Overall, we parse the expression and the leaves have two cases: either the future is synchronised (check-marked) or not. In this last case, there are three sub-cases, according to the future corresponds to an invocation – rule (T-SYNC-INVK) –, or to a field –

rule (T-SYNC-FIELD) –, or to a method's argument – rule (T-SYNC-PARAM). We discuss (T-SYNC-INVK), the other ones are similar. In this case, the future f bound to x is synchronised – henceforth its result is check-marked in the environment. Correspondingly, the futures that are synchronised by f, namely those that are recorded in the effect E_m, are synchronised as well. Finally, the rule records in the environment the updates of arguments' fields. Technically this is done using the delegation future type. The behavioural type collects the futures of methods that are running in parallel and f, which is annotated with the synchronising actor name α. This type will allow us to compute the dependencies of the parallel methods during the analysis.

In the example of the introduction, Line 11 triggers a synchronisation with the first execution of addToStore. As a consequence of the application of the rules (T-EXPRESSION) and (T-SYNC-INVK), n now points to a not-yet-known future of the form $f \rightsquigarrow g.n$; this future will be mapped during analysis to the first invocation to store.

The rule (T-INVK) creates a new future g corresponding to the invocation and stores it in Γ, after having computed the instance of the method signature. The last premise verifies the compatibility between the effects of the invoked method and those of the other running methods (the current one and the not-yet synchronised ones). The behavioural type collects futures of methods that are running in parallel, including g, which is created by the rule. The future g is not annotated with any actor name because invocation does not introduce any dependency. The substitution on second line replaces synchronised futures by □ to prevent additional synchronisations on these futures.

The behavioural type of statements is a sum of types that are parallel composition of synchronisation dependencies and unsynchronised behaviours. The rules are almost standard. We discuss the rule for returning a future – rule (T-RETURN-FUT). In this case, the returned value is an unsynchronised future f, therefore the synchronisation of f is bound to the synchronisation of the method under analysis. For this reason, the behavioural type is f_X, where X is the placeholder for the active object synchronising the method currently analysed. The rest of the behavioural type collects the unsynchronised behaviour.

In (T-METHOD), the premises verify the consistency of the typing of m in the environment with the typing of its body. In particular, the asynchronous effects of m must be the sum of the asynchronous ones in its body, i.e. A', plus the effects of the invocations that have not been synchronised. We notice that the behavioural type of the method has arguments that are structureless: object are removed and replaced by their flattened version, where the fields are removed and the corresponding values are lifted as arguments, this operation is fulfilled by the function *flat*. We also notice that the behavioural type of the body s is extended with a dependency (X, α). This dependency will be instantiated by the synchronising object when it is known. The behavioural type of a method has the shape $(\Gamma \cdot \Gamma' \cdot \textsf{L})$. The environment Γ defines fresh names created in the body of the method, it maps future names to either future results $\lambda X.\text{m}(\overline{g}, X, \Gamma'', E)$ or delegations $f \rightsquigarrow g.x$ or object types $\alpha\overline{[a:f]}$. The environment Γ' records the updates to the arguments $\overline{f}$ performed by the method, and L is the behavioural type of the body of the method. To make the rule TR-METHOD easier to read we let Γ and Γ' contain more information than we require in the behavioural type analysis, this is the reason why will be used a simplified form of this environment. Instead of Γ will be used Θ which does not define a mapping between future names and object types and future results do not present information about effects $(\lambda X.\mathtt{m}(\overline{g}, X, \Gamma''))$, and Γ' will be renamed as Φ.

Finally, a *behavioural type program* is a pair $(\mathcal{L}, \Theta \cdot \mathsf{L})$, where $\mathcal{L}$ maps *method names* m to *method behaviours* $(\overline{w}, X) \to (\nu \overline{\varkappa})(\Theta' \cdot \Phi \cdot \mathsf{L}')$, $\overline{w}, X$ are the *formal parameters* of m, Θ', Φ and L are the same as above. The last two elements, namely Θ and L, are the *environment* and the *type* of the main body.

The fact that $\Gamma \vdash \{\overline{\mathtt{Int}\ x}, \overline{M}\}\{s\}$ implies that any configuration reached evaluating the program has deterministic effects.

Example. The behavioural type of the program of Sect. 1 is of the form: $(\mathcal{L}, \Theta \cdot f_\star + f_{main} + f'_\star)$ where:

$$\Theta = [\ f \mapsto \lambda X.\mathtt{addToStore}(g, \Box, X, [\ g \mapsto \alpha[n{:}\Box]^\checkmark\ ], [\ g \mapsto [n^\mathtt{w}]\ ]),\ g' \mapsto f \rightsquigarrow g.n,$$
$$f' \mapsto \lambda X.\mathtt{addToStore}(g, \Box, X, [\ g \mapsto \alpha[n{:}g']^\checkmark\ ], [\ g \mapsto [n^\mathtt{w}]\ ])\ ].$$

We observe that the behavioural type of the main function performs two invocations of $\mathtt{addToStore}$. The first invocation is performed on the object α where the field n stores a value $(g \mapsto \alpha[n{:}\Box]^\checkmark)$, indeed at that point $n = 0$. The second invocation is performed on the same object but n stores the value written by the first invocation: in Θ we have the delegation $g' \mapsto f \rightsquigarrow g.n$ and in the second method invocation the object field n maps to g'. We can also notice that the first invocation has been synchronized, indeed the presence of the delegation in the environment indicates that the rule (T-SYNCH-INVK) has been applied. Both invocations of the $\mathtt{addToStore}$ method write on the field n of the object g, and the effect of both invocations is $[g \mapsto [n^\mathtt{w}]]$.

As stated above, $\mathcal{L}$ stores the behavioural type for each method of the program, then we have an entry for $\mathtt{addToStore}$ and $\mathtt{store}$.
$\mathcal{L}(\mathtt{addToStore}) = (\beta, this, g, f, X) \to (\nu\ f')(\Theta_\mathrm{add} \cdot \Phi_\mathrm{add} \cdot \mathsf{L}_\mathrm{add})$ where
$\mathsf{L}_\mathrm{add} = (\ g_\alpha + f'_\star + f'_X\ )\&(X, \beta)\qquad \Phi_\mathrm{add} = [\ this \mapsto \beta[n{:}f']\ ]$
$\Theta_\mathrm{add} = [\ f' \mapsto \lambda X.\mathtt{store}(this, f, \Box, X, [\ this \mapsto \beta[n{:}g]^\checkmark\ ], \varnothing)\ ]$
The behavioural type shows that the method $\mathtt{addToStore}$ performs three main actions. The first action is the possible synchronization, expressed by g_α, where g is one of the parameters. The second action is the invocation of the method $\mathtt{store}$ corresponding to future f'. The third action returns the result of the invocation of $\mathtt{store}$; expressed by the term f'_X stating that the f' is returned.

Concerning $\mathtt{store}$ we have: $\mathcal{L}(\mathtt{store}) = (\gamma, this, f, g, X) \to (\varnothing \cdot \varnothing \cdot (X, \gamma))$.

4   Behavioural Type Soundness and Analysis

The type system defined in Sect. 3 can be extended to configurations, see [11]: the judgment we use is $\Gamma \vdash cn : \mathsf{K}$ where K is a parallel composition of $\Theta \cdot \mathsf{L}$, one for

BT-FUN
$$\Theta(f) = \lambda X.\mathbf{m}(\overline{f}, X, \Gamma)$$
$$\mathcal{L}(\mathbf{m}) = (\overline{w}, Y) \rightarrow (\nu \overline{\varkappa})(\Theta' \cdot \Phi \cdot \mathsf{L})$$
$$\kappa \text{ is either } \star \text{ or an object name}$$
$$\overline{\varkappa'} \text{ fresh } \quad \Theta'' = \Theta + \Theta'[\overline{\varkappa'}/\overline{\varkappa}][^{flat(\overline{f},\Gamma)}/\overline{w}]$$
$$\mathsf{L}' = \mathsf{L}[\overline{\varkappa'}/\overline{\varkappa}][^{\kappa}/Y][^{flat(\overline{f},\Gamma)}/\overline{w}]$$
$$\overline{\Theta \cdot C[f_\kappa] \rightarrow \Theta'' \cdot C[\mathsf{L}']}$$

BT-FIELD
$$\Theta(f) = f' \rightsquigarrow g.x \quad \Theta(f') = \lambda X.\mathbf{m}(\overline{f}, X, \Gamma)$$
$$\mathcal{L}(\mathbf{m}) = (\overline{w}, Y) \rightarrow (\nu \overline{\varkappa})(\Theta' \cdot \Phi \cdot \mathsf{L})$$
$$\Phi' = \Phi[\overline{\varkappa'}/\overline{\varkappa}][^{flat(\overline{f},\Gamma)}/\overline{w}] \quad \Phi'(g.x) = h$$
$$\overline{\Theta \cdot C[f_\kappa] \rightarrow \Theta \cdot C[h_\kappa]}$$

Fig. 4. Behavioural type reduction rules

each configuration element. The soundness of the type system is demonstrated by a subject reduction theorem expressing that if a runtime configuration cn is well typed and $cn \rightarrow cn'$ then cn' is well typed as well. While the theorem is almost standard, we cannot guarantee type-preservation, instead we exhibit a relation between the type of cn and the type of cn'. Informally, this relation connects (i) the presence of a deadlock in a configuration with the presence of circularity in a type and (ii) the presence of a circularity in the evaluation of K' with the circularities of the evaluation of K.

The evaluation of a behavioural types is defined by a transition relation between types $\Theta \cdot \mathsf{L}$ that follows the rules in Fig. 4 and includes a specific rule for delegation types. We use *type contexts*:

$$C[\,] ::= \quad [\,] \mid \mathsf{L} \,\&\, C[\,] \mid C[\,] \,\&\, \mathsf{L} \mid \mathsf{L} + C[\,] \mid C[\,] + \mathsf{L}$$

Overall, BT-FUN and BT-FIELD indicate that the behavioural type semantics is simply the unfolding of function invocations and the evaluation of delegations. More precisely, rule BT-FUN replaces a future with the the body of the corresponding invocation. The environment Θ is augmented with the names defined in this body. Note that Θ'' is well-defined because $\text{dom}(\Theta) \cap \text{dom}(\Theta'[\overline{\varkappa'}/\overline{\varkappa}][^{flat(\overline{f},\Gamma)}/\overline{w}]) = \varnothing$ and $(flat(\overline{f}, \Gamma) \cup \overline{w}) \cap \overline{\varkappa'} = \varnothing$. The behavioural type L' is defined by a classical substitution. The substitution $[^{flat(\overline{f},\Gamma)}/\overline{w}]$ replaces active object and future names in $\overline{w}$. This substitution can generate terms of the form $\square_\alpha$, those terms can safely be replaced by 0. Rule BT-FIELD computes futures f bound to delegations $f' \rightsquigarrow g.x$, i.e. when the invocation corresponding to f' has updated the field x of the argument g; it retrieves the instance of Φ in the method of f' and infers h, the future written in the accessed field.

Definition 3. *Let* $\mathsf{L} \equiv_d \mathsf{L}'$ *whenever* L *and* L' *are equal up-to commutativity and associativity of "*$\&$*" and "*$+$*", identity of* 0 *for* $\&$ *and* $+$, *and distributivity of* $\&$ *over* $+$, *namely* $\mathsf{L} \,\&\, (\mathsf{L}' + \mathsf{L}'') = \mathsf{L} \,\&\, \mathsf{L}' + \mathsf{L} \,\&\, \mathsf{L}''$.
The behavioural type L *has a circularity if there are* $\alpha_1, \cdots, \alpha_n$ *and* $C[\,]$ *such that* $\mathsf{L} \equiv_d C[(\alpha_1, \alpha_2) \,\&\, \cdots \,\&\, (\alpha_n, \alpha_1)]$.
A type $\Theta \cdot \mathsf{L}$ *has a circularity if* $\Theta \cdot \mathsf{L} \rightarrow^* \Theta' \cdot \mathsf{L}'$ *and* L' *has a circularity.*

Below we write $\Gamma \vdash cn : \Theta \cdot \mathsf{L}$ to say that the configuration cn has type $\Theta \cdot \mathsf{L}$ in the environment Γ. This judgment requires an extension of the type system in Fig. 3 to configurations (see [11]). The main properties of the type system and its extension to configurations are stated below.

Theorem 1. *Let P be a* gASP *program and suppose that $\Gamma \vdash P:(\mathcal{L},\Theta \cdot L)$, then:*

1. *$\Gamma \vdash cn : \Theta \cdot L$ where cn is the initial configuration;*
2. *if $cn \to^* cn'$ then there are Γ', Θ' and L' such that $\Gamma' \vdash cn' : \Theta' \cdot L'$ and if $\Theta' \cdot L'$ has a circularity then also $\Theta \cdot L$ has a circularity.*
3. *if $\Theta \cdot L$ has no circularity then P is deadlock-free.*

Our technique reduces the problem of detecting deadlocks in a gASP program to that of detecting circularities in a behavioural type. It is worth to notice that these types have models that are infinite states because of recursion and creation of new names. Notwithstanding this fact, the problem of absence of circularities in a behavioural type is decidable. The solver uses a fixpoint technique that is defined in [7,13], which has been adapted to the types of this paper in [6].

Example. We show how a circularity appears when we apply the reduction rule on the illustrative example. The behavioural type of the example was shown in Sect. 3, we start from the behavioral type of the main function and describe the main reduction steps.

We focus on the third term $(f'_\star)$ that refers to the second method invocation of addToStore. The rule BT-FUN replaces the behavioural type of method invocation $f'_\star$ with the body of addToStore properly instantiated. Here the method invocation related to f' is $\Theta(f') = \lambda X.\mathtt{addToStore}(\cdots)$, we take the behavioural type $\mathsf{L_{add}}$, build the substitution $[^h/_{f'}][^\star/_X][^{\alpha,g,g',\Box}/_{\beta,this,g,f}]$ that instantiates the parameters adequately, and obtain the behaviour: $(g'_\alpha + h_\star + h_X)\,\&(\star,\alpha)$, additionally $\Theta' = \Theta + \Theta'_{add}$ where Θ'_{add} is obtained from Θ_{add} applying the same substitution. Finally we can apply BT-FUN and obtain the reduction $\Theta \cdot (f_\star + f_{main} + f'_\star) \to \Theta' \cdot (f_\star + f_{main} + (g'_\alpha + h_\star + h_X)\,\&(\star,\alpha))$.

We then focus on the term g'_α that refers to the synchronization of the field n during the execution of the second invocation of addToStore. The type associated to g' ($\Theta'(g') = f \rightsquigarrow g.n$) denotes that, when typing, we don't know the method invocation related to the future stored in n, we only know that the method invocation related to f has stored a future inside n. To solve this delegation and then discover the name of the future stored in the that field we apply the rule BT-FIELD and obtain: $\Theta' \cdot (\cdots + (g'_\alpha + h_\star + h_X)\,\&(\star,\alpha)) \to \Theta' \cdot (\cdots + (h'_\alpha + h_\star + h_X)\,\&(\star,\alpha))$. This reduction only replaces g'_α with h'_α where $h' = \Phi'_{add}(g.n)$ and Φ'_{add} corresponds to the instantiation of Φ_{add} accordingly to the invocation related to f: $\Theta(f) = \lambda X.\mathtt{addToStore}(g,\Box,X,[g \mapsto \alpha[n:\Box]^{\checkmark}])$ with the substitution $[^h/_{f'}][^{\alpha,g,\Box,\Box}/_{\beta,this,g,f}]$.

Now we focus on the term h'_α and, as in the first step, we can apply the rule BT-FUN we replace h'_α with the behavioral type of store opportunely instantiated and obtain: $\Theta' \cdot (\cdots + (h'_\alpha + h_\star + h_X)\,\&(\star,\alpha)) \to \Theta' \cdot (\cdots + ((\alpha,\alpha) + h_\star + h_X)\,\&(\star,\alpha))$ as the behavioural type of store is reduced to a pair.

The circularity (α,α) highlights a potential deadlock in our program. Indeed the method store is called on α and then the result of this invocation is awaited in the method `addToStore` in α, as no further order is ensured on the execution of these requests, this circularity indeed reveals a potential deadlock.

5   Concluding Remarks

This article defines a technique for analysing deadlocks of stateful active objects that is based on behavioural type systems. The technique also takes into account stateful objects that store futures in their fields. This required us to analyse synchronisation patterns where the future synchronisation occurs in a different context from the asynchronous invocation that created the future. The behavioural types that are obtained by the type system are analysed by a solver that detects circularities and identifies potential deadlocks.

To deal with implicit futures, we use a novel paradigm in our analyses, that consider *"every element as a future"*. This also allows us to deal with aliasing and with the fact that the future updates are performed on place at any time.

Related Work. Up-to our knowledge, the first paper proposing effect systems for analysing data races of concurrent systems dates back to the late 80's [14]. In fact, our approach of annotating the types to express further intentional properties of the semantics of the program is very similar to that of Lucassen and Gifford. The first application of a type and effect system to deadlock analysis is [3]. In that case programmers must specify a partial order among the locks and the type checker verifies that threads acquire locks in the descending order. In our case, no order is predefined and the absence of circularities in the process synchronisations is obtained in a post-typing phase. In [5], the authors generate a finite graph of program points by integrating an effect and point-to analysis for computing aliases with an analysis returning (an over-approximation of) points that may run in parallel. In the model presented in [5], future are passed (by-value) between methods only as parameters or return values, the possibility of storing future in object field is treated as a possible extension and not formalized. Furthermore this aspect is not considered combined to the possibility of having infinite recursion. However, [5] analyses *finite* abstraction of the computational models of the language. In our case, the behavioural type model associated to the program handles unbounded states.

Model checking is often used to verify stateful distributed systems. In particular, [17] uses the characteristics of actor languages to limit, by partial order reduction, the model to check. [1] provides an parametrised model of an active object application that is abstracted into a finite model afterwards. Contrarily to us, these results are restricted to a finite abstraction of the state of the system. Two articles [2,9] translate active objects into Petri-nets and model-check the generated net; these approaches cannot verify infinite systems because they would lead to an infinite Petri-net or an infinite set of colours for the tokens.

We refer the interested reader to [8] (Sect. 8) for a further comparison of alternative analysis techniques.

References

1. Ameur-Boulifa, R., Henrio, L., Kulankhina, O., Madelaine, E., Savu, A.: Behavioural semantics for asynchronous components. J. Logical Algebr. Methods Program. **89**, 1–40 (2017)
2. Boer, F.S., Bravetti, M., Grabe, I., Lee, M., Steffen, M., Zavattaro, G.: A petri net based analysis of deadlocks for active objects and futures. In: Păsăreanu, C.S., Salaün, G. (eds.) FACS 2012. LNCS, vol. 7684, pp. 110–127. Springer, Heidelberg (2013). doi:10.1007/978-3-642-35861-6_7
3. Boyapati, C., Lee, R., Rinard, M.C.: Ownership types for safe programming: preventing data races and deadlocks. In: Proceedings of the OOPSLA 2002 (2002)
4. Caromel, D., Henrio, L., Serpette, B.P.: Asynchronous sequential processes. Inf. Comput. **207**(4), 459–495 (2009)
5. Flores-Montoya, A.E., Albert, E., Genaim, S.: May-happen-in-parallel based deadlock analysis for concurrent objects. In: Beyer, D., Boreale, M. (eds.) FMOODS/FORTE 2013. LNCS, vol. 7892, pp. 273–288. Springer, Heidelberg (2013). doi:10.1007/978-3-642-38592-6_19
6. Giachino, E., Henrio, L., Laneve, C., Mastandrea, V.: Actors may synchronize, safely! In: Proceedings of PPDP 2016. ACM (2016)
7. Giachino, E., Kobayashi, N., Laneve, C.: Deadlock analysis of unbounded process networks. In: Baldan, P., Gorla, D. (eds.) CONCUR 2014. LNCS, vol. 8704, pp. 63–77. Springer, Heidelberg (2014). doi:10.1007/978-3-662-44584-6_6
8. Giachino, E., Laneve, C., Lienhardt, M.: A framework for deadlock detection in core ABS. Softw. Syst. Model. **15**(4), 1013–1048 (2016)
9. Gkolfi, A., Din, C.C., Johnsen, E.B., Steffen, M., Yu, I.C.: Translating active objects into colored petri nets for communication analysis. In: Proceedings of the FSEN 2017. LNCS. Springer (2017)
10. Haller, P., Odersky, M.: Scala actors: unifying thread-based and event-based programming. Theoret. Comput. Sci. **410**(2–3), 202–220 (2009)
11. Henrio, L., Laneve, C., Mastandrea, V.: Analysis of synchronisation patterns in stateful active objects. Research report, I3S; Inria - Sophia antipolis (2017). https://hal.archives-ouvertes.fr/hal-01542595
12. Johnsen, E.B., Hähnle, R., Schäfer, J., Schlatte, R., Steffen, M.: ABS: a core language for abstract behavioral specification. In: Aichernig, B.K., Boer, F.S., Bonsangue, M.M. (eds.) FMCO 2010. LNCS, vol. 6957, pp. 142–164. Springer, Heidelberg (2011). doi:10.1007/978-3-642-25271-6_8
13. Kobayashi, N., Laneve, C.: Deadlock analysis of unbounded process networks. Inf. Comput. **252**, 48–70 (2017)
14. Lucassen, J.M., Gifford, D.K.: Polymorphic effect systems. In: Proceedings of POPL 1988, pp. 47–57. ACM Press (1988)
15. Morris, B.: The Symbian OS Architecture Sourcebook: Design and Evolution of a Mobile Phone OS. Wiley, Hoboken (2007)
16. Niehren, J., Schwinghammer, J., Smolka, G.: A concurrent lambda calculus with futures. Theoret. Comput. Sci. **364**(3), 338–356 (2006)
17. Sirjani, M.: Rebeca: theory, applications, and tools. In: Boer, F.S., Bonsangue, M.M., Graf, S., Roever, W.-P. (eds.) FMCO 2006. LNCS, vol. 4709, pp. 102–126. Springer, Heidelberg (2007). doi:10.1007/978-3-540-74792-5_5
18. Wyatt, D.: Akka Concurrency. Artima (2013)

BTS: A Tool for Formal Component-Based Development

Dalay Israel de Almeida Pereira[(✉)], Marcel Vinicius Medeiros Oliveira,
Madiel S. Conserva Filho, and Sarah Raquel Da Rocha Silva

Universidade Federal do Rio Grande do Norte, Natal, Brazil
{dalayalmeida,madiel}@ppgsc.ufrn.br, marcel@dimap.ufrn.br,
sarahraquelrs@gmail.com

Abstract. In previous work we have presented a CSP based approach for developing component-based asynchronous systems, $\mathcal{BRIC}$, which guarantees deadlock freedom by construction. It uses CSP to specify the constraints and interactions between the components to allow a formal verification of the composition's behaviour. Following this work, we also proposed an efficient approach for ensuring livelock analysis by construction. In this work we present a tool that automates the verification of component composition by automatically generating and checking the side conditions imposed by both approaches. The tool also includes a support to $\mathcal{BRICK}$, an optimisation of $\mathcal{BRIC}$, that enriches the components with metadata containing additional useful information, which considerably reduces the costs of the composition verifications.

Keywords: Component-based systems · CSP · Compositional analysis · Deadlock verification · Livelock verification

1 Introduction

The use of increasingly complex applications is demanding a greater investment of resources in software development processes. Component-based System Development (CBSD) [15] has emerged as a promising approach for mastering this complexity. In this paradigm, the system is divided into independent pieces of software (components) that can interact and communicate with each other, yielding a more complex system. A component is a composition unity with contractually specified interfaces and with explicit context dependencies.

Although CBSD has improved the final quality of systems and the organisation of the development process, it usually lacks formalisation. This is still a major source of problems specially for reliable systems. In order to improve reliability, formal methods arise as an interesting development approach for critical systems helping to solve some of the problems in the development cycle.

CSP [14] is a formal notation used to model concurrent and reactive applications where processes interact with each other exchanging messages. The use of CSP allows us to identify problems such as deadlock and livelock. CSP has a set of tools that facilitate its use like the refinement model-checker FDR4 [21].

© Springer International Publishing AG 2017
N. Polikarpova and S. Schneider (Eds.): IFM 2017, LNCS 10510, pp. 211–226, 2017.
DOI: 10.1007/978-3-319-66845-1_14

In [20], Ramos presented an approach, $\mathcal{BRIC}$, for the trustful and systematic development of component-based systems for CSP models, considering a grey-box style of composition [9]. In $\mathcal{BRIC}$, component compositions are achieved using four predefined rules that impose restrictions on the basic components. Once the restrictions are satisfied, deadlock freedom is ensured by construction. Ramos also provided an extension of $\mathcal{BRIC}$, $\mathcal{BRICK}$, that inserts metadata inside the components as a way to decrease the number and the complexity of the verifications when composing the components.

$\mathcal{BRICK}$ has proved to be efficient in the verification of deadlock freedom [17]. The absence of livelock, however, is trivially ensured, since the basic components are, by definition, livelock-free, and no operator that may introduce such a behaviour can be used. In [11], we considered black-box compositions in $\mathcal{BRICK}$, a component notion that seems to be better aligned to CBSD, where the internal services of components are hidden from its environment: we presented a technique for constructing livelock-free $\mathcal{BRICK}$ systems using local analysis.

The use of $\mathcal{BRICK}$ demands considerable effort for specifying components and their compositions to ensure the correctness of the whole specification. This can make its practical application too complex and cumbersome. This paper presents BTS ($\mathcal{BRICK}$ Tool Support), a tool that provides a simpler way to create and compose $\mathcal{BRICK}$ components. More importantly, it provides a complete and automated analysis of components and compositions, making the development process safer and much more efficient, reducing development costs.

In Sect. 2, we introduce CSP. $\mathcal{BRICK}$ is described in Sect. 3. Section 4 presents BTS. Its evaluation is described in Sect. 5. Finally, we draw our conclusions and discuss about related and future work in Sect. 6.

2   CSP

CSP [14] is one of the most well established formalisms for describing and analysing concurrent systems. It is used to model applications where independent components (processes) interact with each other and with the outer world exchanging messages (events).

In CSP, the basic processes are $STOP$ and $SKIP$. The former represents a deadlocked process, the latter simply terminates successfully. Given an event a in the interface of a process P, the prefixing $a \rightarrow P$ is initially able to perform a, after which it will behave like P. Strictly speaking, the semantics of CSP does not differentiate inputs from outputs. However, the prefixing operator can also be used to denote directional communication. The process $c!v \rightarrow P$ sends the value v via channel c and behaves as P afterwards. On the other hand, the process $c?x \rightarrow P$ receives a value on channel c and assigns it to the implicitly declared variable x, which can be used in the subsequent behaviour P.

CSP also provides notations to describe different paths of behaviour. The external choice $P \,\square\, Q$ initially offers the initial events of both processes, P and Q. The environment makes the choice of synchronisation. It can be thought as buttons being offered to a client (a user) that will decide which one to press.

$datatype\ EV = up\ |\ down$
$datatype\ LF = thinks\ |\ eats$
$channel\ fk1, fk2,$
$\qquad pfk1, pfk2 : EV$
$channel\ life : LF$

$Fork =$
$\quad (fk1.up \rightarrow fk1.down \rightarrow Fork)$
$\quad \Box\ (fk2.up \rightarrow fk2.down \rightarrow Fork)$
$Phil =$
$\quad life.thinks \rightarrow pfk1.up \rightarrow$
$\quad pfk2.up \rightarrow life.eats \rightarrow$
$\quad pfk1.down \rightarrow pfk2.down \rightarrow Phil$

Fig. 1. The CSP Specification of the Dining Philosophers

The internal choice $P \sqcap Q$ is completely out of the environment's control. This is a non-deterministic choice, since the system will internally decide its behaviour: it will be ready to perform the initial events from just one of the processes.

Two processes can be composed in Interleave. In $P \ ||| \ Q$, the processes P and Q execute concurrently, but they do not synchronise on any event. It is also possible to compose two processes in parallel synchronising in a specific set of event cs. In $P\ [|\ cs\ |]\ Q$, the processes P and Q are executed concurrently and synchronise on the events in cs; any other events are executed independently.

Throughout this paper, we use a classical concurrency example, the dining philosophers [22]. In this example, a group of philosophers is seated at a round table to eat. Each pair of philosophers has a fork between them. Each philosopher must pick up two forks before eating and puts them back down afterwards. The CSP specification of this example is presented in Fig. 1.

The process $Fork$ offers an external choice between the events $fk1.up$ and $fk2.up$, where $fk1$ and $fk2$ are channels of type EV. This process ensures that two philosophers cannot hold the same fork simultaneously. The process $Phil$ represents the life cycle of a philosopher: before eating, the philosopher thinks and then he picks up the forks. After eating he puts the forks back down.

The process $P \setminus cs$ behaves like the process P but hides the set of events cs from the environment. Finally, the renaming $P[[a \leftarrow b]]$ behaves like P, but the occurrences of the event a are replaced by occurrences of the event b.

There are many well-established semantic models of CSP, one of them is the traces model $(\mathcal{T})$. In this model, the set $traces(P)$ contains all possible sequences of events in which P can engage.

Using FDR4 [21], we may automatically verify interesting properties of the processes. For instance, the assertion $assert\ P : [deadlock\ free]$ can be used in FDR4 to verify if the process P is deadlock-free. Using other assertions, we may also check for livelock freedom, determinism and process refinement.

3 $\mathcal{BRIC}$

$\mathcal{BRIC}$ [20] is a method for trustful and systematic development of component based systems. It describes components as contracts and imposes restrictions to component compositions in order to guarantee the safety of the final results.

$\mathcal{BRIC}$ provides four composition rules (two binary rules and two unary rules), each one with specific well defined conditions for valid applications. In what follows, the definition of $\mathcal{BRIC}$ component contracts is presented in Sect. 3.1 and the instatiation of such contracts is presented in Sect. 3.2. The Sect. 3.3 presents the composition rules and, finally, we present an extension to $\mathcal{BRIC}$, called $\mathcal{BRICK}$, in Sect. 3.4.

3.1 Component Contract

A component contract in $\mathcal{BRIC}$ is defined by a behaviour $\mathcal{B}$ (described in CSP), a set of channels $\mathcal{C}$, a set of data types $\mathcal{I}$, and a total function $\mathcal{R} : \mathcal{C} \to \mathcal{I}$ from channels to their types. The behaviour of the contract must be an I/O process, a restricted form of CSP processes P, in which:

- whenever an event $c.x$ is in the alphabet of P (α_P), c is either an input or an output channel of P;
- P has infinite traces (but finite state space);
- P is divergence free;
- P is input deterministic, that is, after every trace of P, if a set of input events of P may be offered to the environment, they may not be refused by P after the same trace;
- P is strongly output decisive, that is, all choices (if any) among output events on a given channel in P are internal.

Due to space restrictions, we refrain from presenting all formal definitions and proofs, which can be found elsewhere [20].

In our example, we define two contracts to represent forks and philosophers:

$$Ctr_{Fork} = \langle Fork, \{fk1 \to EV, fk2 \to EV\}, \{EV\}, \{fk1, fk2\}\rangle$$
$$Ctr_{Phil} = \langle Phil, \{lf \to LF, pfk1 \to EV, pfk2 \to EV\}, \{LF, EV\}, \{lf, pfk1, pfk2\}\rangle$$

3.2 Component Instantiation

Usually, a component is defined once and reused multiple times, and in different contexts. In this work, we represent these contexts as sets of channels. Since channels represent interaction points of the component, and each channel is used to communicate with a single component in the environment, replacing these channels makes the contract interact with another environment.

For illustration purposes, we develop a dining table with 2 philosophers and 2 forks. The contracts of the philosophers Ctr_{Phil_1} and Ctr_{Phil_2} instantiate the channels $pfk1$, $pfk2$ and $life$ with communications on channels pfk and lf. Similarly, the contracts of the forks Ctr_{Fork_1} and Ctr_{Fork_2} instantiate the channels $fk1$ and $fk2$ with communications on channels fk. In order to distinguish actions from each philosopher on each fork, there are two integers on the type of channels fk and pfk standing for the fork and for the philosopher. The type of channel lf is the philosopher's identifier. For example, the contracts Ctr_{Fork_1} and Ctr_{Phil_1} are defined as follows:

$$Ctr_{Fork_1} = \left\langle \begin{array}{l} Fork[[fk1 \leftarrow fk.1.1, fk2 \leftarrow fk.1.2]], \\ \{fk.1.1 \rightarrow EV, fk.1.2 \rightarrow EV\}, \{EV\}, \{fk.1.1, fk.1.2\} \end{array} \right\rangle$$

$$Ctr_{Phil1} = \left\langle \begin{array}{l} Phil_1[[life \leftarrow lf.1, pfk1 \leftarrow pfk.1.1, pfk2 \leftarrow pfk.2.1]], \\ \{lf.1 \rightarrow LF, pfk.1.1 \rightarrow EV, pfk.2.1 \rightarrow EV\}, \{LF, EV\}, \\ \{lf.1, pfk.1.1, pfk.2.1\}) \end{array} \right\rangle$$

3.3 Composition Rules

The composition rules ensure, by construction, deadlock-free compositions in $\mathcal{BRIC}$ [20]: interleave, communication, feedback and reflexive.

The Interleave composition $Ctr_1 [|||] Ctr_2$ aggregates two independent components with disjoint alphabets. After composition, these components do not communicate with each other. In our example, philosophers and forks can be interleaved separately: $Forks = Ctr_{Fork_1} [|||] Ctr_{Fork_2}$ and $Phils = Ctr_{Phil_1} [|||] Ctr_{Phil_2}$. These compositions are valid because the contracts have disjoint alphabets.

The communication composition $Ctr_1[ic \leftrightarrow oc]Ctr_2$ is based on the traditional way to compose two components (Ctr_1 and Ctr_2), using two channels (ic and oc), one from each component. In order to attach the channels, their protocols must have been defined. A *protocol* is an I/O process that inputs on a single unique communication channel and outputs on another single unique communication channel. Using these protocols, we can verify the compatibility between two contracts, ensuring that the outputs of each process are always accepted by the other process: no information generated (an output) by a process is leaked, but accepted by its peer in the communication.

In our example, we are able to compose the contracts *Forks* and *Phils* using the communication composition: $PComm = Forks[fk.1.1 \leftrightarrow pfk.1.1]Phils$.

$\mathcal{BRIC}$ unary compositions enable the construction of systems with cyclic topologies, assembling two channels of the same component. As a result, due to the existence of possible cycles, new conditions are required to preserve deadlock freedom. The unary compositions rules are feedback and reflexive.

The feedback composition $Ctr[ic \hookrightarrow oc]$ is the simpler unary composition, in which two channels (ic and oc) of the same component are assembled, but do not introduce a new cycle [20]. However, in order to attach two channels of the same component using feedback, these channels must be independent. A channel ch_1 is independent (or decoupled) of a channel ch_2 in a process when any communication of ch_2 does not interfere with the order of events communicated by ch_1. It means that they are independently offered to the environment.

The contract *PComm* contains all forks and philosophers. The channels $fk.2.2$ and $pfk.1.2$, however, are independent in *PComm* because they occur in the interleaved sub-components *Forks* and *Phils*, respectively. We may, therefore,

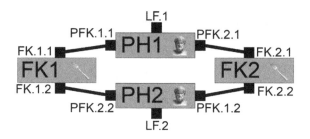

Fig. 2. Structure of the dining philosophers

connect these channels using Feedback: $PFeed_1 = PComm[pfk.1.2 \hookrightarrow fk.2.2]$. The channels $fk.2.1$ and $pfk.2.1$ are also independent in $PFeed_1$. Intuitively, their connection do not introduce a cycle; we may, therefore, connect these channels using the Feedback composition: $PFeed_2 = PFeed_1[pfk.2.1 \hookrightarrow fk.2.1]$.

The reflexive composition $Ctr[ic \hookrightarrow oc]$ deals with more complex systems that indeed present cycles of dependencies in the topology of the system structure. This rule connects dependent channels ic and oc, which may introduce undesirable cycles of dependencies among the communication of events in the system. In order to verify the compatibility between distinct channels of the same component, this rule does not compare the communication between two protocols but the communication between events of the same process (the behaviour of the component), which tends to be more costly when compared to the previous composition rules. So, although the feedback composition is more demanding, requiring the composing channels to be decoupled, its verification tends to be less costly than the reflexive composition, which makes a global verification.

We conclude our example using the reflexive composition to connect the channels $fk.1.2$ and $pfk.2.2$: $PSystem = PFeed_2[fk.1.2 \hookrightarrow pfk.2.2]$. This connection could not be achieved using feedback because the two channels are not independent in $PFeed_2$. Intuitively, their connection introduces a cycle that causes the dependence between these channels. A representation of the complete example is presented on Fig. 2.

3.4   Component Metadata

$\mathcal{BRICK}$ enriches components with metadata in a way to decrease the number of verifications made when composing them, since some properties of the new components can be predicted (using their parents) and maintained on the metadata. There are four types of metadata that can be inserted in a component contract: protocols, dual-protocols, context processes and decoupled channels. A dual-protocol DP, related to a channel ch, is a deadlock-free protocol such that, given a protocol P related to the same channel ch, $inputs(P) = outputs(DP)$, $outputs(P) = inputs(DP)$, $traces(DP) = traces(P)$. Context Processes are a metadata information that represents all the possible communications between a protocol P and another process compatible with it, which allows us to restrict proofs concerning communication via a specific protocol.

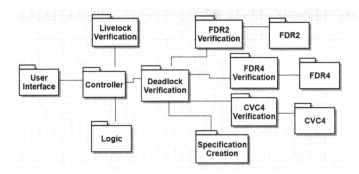

Fig. 3. The architecture of *BTS*

In a contract, one can define a protocol, a dual protocol and a context process for each channel. So, this information is stored as three different relations between channels and protocols, dual-protocols and context processes, respectively. The decoupled channels are stored by a symmetric binary relation on the set of channels of the contract. In this case, a relation between two channels means that these channels are decoupled inside the contract.

The metadata is recalculated in every composition from the composing components in a way the user will never have to describe them again. The use of metadata decreases the number and the complexity of verifications, since the user is giving more information about the components. Instead of checking compatibility among protocols in a process P, we check this on protocols within the metadata. Furthermore, instead of verifying the independence between channels in a process, we verify it directly on relations between channels within the metadata. In this way, we perform lightweight verifications as demonstrated in [17].

In [19], we presented a list of CSP assertions that mechanise the side conditions of the composition rules. Using these assertions, we can verify the correctness of the compositions. We also described which of these assertions may be verified using SMT solvers at a cost close to zero. Finally, we also described the assertions that can be discarded when using metadata. Based on these results, we developed a tool that assists development using the *BRICK* approach. The tool, which we describe in the following section, provides an interface for defining and composing component contracts, and more importantly, it automatically verifies the correctness of the components contracts and their compositions.

4   *BRICK* Tool Support

The practical use of *BRICK* tends to be exhaustive and too complex to be handled manually. In order to make it applicable, we developed *BTS*[1], a tool that assists the systematic and trustful *BRICK* development of component-based systems. The tool automatically generates most of the CSP specification

---

[1] Available at: https://goo.gl/yZEvHp.

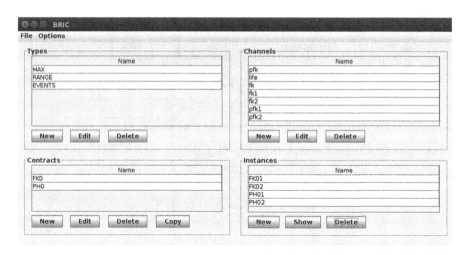

Fig. 4. The home screen of the BTS tool

and verifies the whole specification in order to guarantee deadlock and livelock freedom based on the $BRICK$ theory.

BTS achieves these automatic verifications by communicating with FDR (for refinement, deadlock-freedom and livelock-freedom assertions) and the SMT solver CVC4 [4] (for predicates on set theory). Regarding FDR, BTS is able to interact with FDR2 and FDR4 [21]. This is because, although FDR4 has come with some interesting improvements like concurrent verifications, in our experience, for small systems FDR2 tended to be faster than FDR4, as presented and explained in Sect. 5. Furthermore, by maintaining the possibility of using FDR2 we were able to compare their efficiency for our approach.

The SMT solvers VeriT [7] and Z3 [16] were also considered to achieve the verifications of the predicates on set theory. However, these verifications required the tool to support set theory. CVC4 accepts SMT-LIBv2 (satisfiability modulo theories Library version 2) [5] as input language, a standard already used in other tools (like CRefine [13] and Rodin [10], for instance). Although this standard has no native support to the set theory, CVC4 contains such an extension to this SMT language, making it possible to make the verifications we required.

Developed in Java, BTS runs on Windows and Linux and its architecture is composed by five main modules: a user interface (GUI); a controller that intermediates the interaction between the GUI and the other modules; a logic model that specifies and coordinates the basic structures; a livelock verification module; and a deadlock verification module. The latter is divided into a specification creation module and modules that communicate with the external tools (FDR2, FDR4, and CVC4). The architecture of BTS is presented in Fig. 3.

Using BTS, the user follows a sequence of steps to specify a system. The home screen (Fig. 4) shows four lists to which we may add elements. They contain types, channels, contracts and instances of the specification. The user must first define the types of information used in the system and then, he can define channels, which may contain one or more types. A component contract definition contains some of these channels and types previously defined. The contract instantiation requires a contract and a new set of channels.

In the home screen, a user can also choose how the tool handles verifications. In order to guarantee deadlock-freedom, *BTS* verifies automatically components and compositions using one of the following tools or combination of tools: FDR2 only, FDR4 only, FDR2 with CVC4, or FDR4 with CVC4. In order to make verifications in FDR, the tool generates the CSP script containing all the assertions (as presented in [19]), sends it to FDR, processes the results and presents them to the user in a simpler manner. Using CVC4, *BTS* generates SMT scripts for some of these verifications and sends them to this solver rather than using FDR. The benefits of using the SMT solver are presented in the Sect. 5.

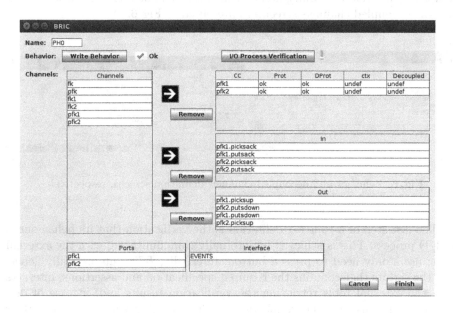

Fig. 5. Contract definition screen

In type creation, the user must specify its name and its definition. In *BTS*, only four types can be used: integer, boolean, interval of integers or datatype (a specific set of atomic constants like, for instance, *EV* and *LF* in our example). The channel definition requires a name and the types of the communication values. After defining types and channels, the user is ready to define contracts.

The contract definition first requires its name and its CSP behaviour. The contract channels can be chosen from the list of channels. It is also possible to define them as input or output and to define the communication channels (specifying events from the channels). The contract screen also allows the definition of metadata information (protocols, dual protocols, context processes and decoupled channels) by double-clicking on a cell of the table as presented in Fig. 5, which contains, in our example, the contract of one of the philosophers.

The specification of the contract's behaviour, protocols, dual protocols, and context processes are done using CSP processes. The decoupled channels are defined by just pairing the channels from the list of the existing channels. All metadata is verified immediately after their definition. All these verifications require internal interactions with the external tools.

Channels with undefined protocol or dual-protocol cannot be used in compositions. However, the absence of a context process and decoupled channels for a channel will not prevent compositions on this channel. In this case, verifications will simply be more costly because BTS will be using the $BRIC$ approach rather than the more efficient $BRICK$ approach. Nevertheless, this change is completely internal and transparent to the user. The behavior definition screen and the decoupled channels screen are presented in Fig. 6.

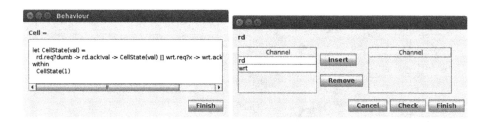

Fig. 6. Behavior and decoupled channels definition screens, respectively

The last step of a contract definition is the verification that its behaviour is an I/O process. This is achieved by internally communicating with the external tools; users only need to press a button. Internally, BTS automatically generates the scripts that contains the required specification and assertions, interacts with the external tools retrieving the verification results and, in case of definition errors, displays the verification results (possibly with errors and their details). Figure 7 presents the sequence diagram that describes the verification of a contract using FDR4 and CVC4 at the same time.

In our example, using BTS, we defined a contract that describes the behaviour of a philosopher and a contract that describes the behaviour of a fork. Each of these contracts were then instantiated twice (forks $FK01$ and $FK02$ and philosophers $PH01$ and $PH02$) as presented in Fig. 4. The contract instantiation screen allows us to rename every channel and to define the name of the new instance. BTS automatically verifies the validity of the new contracts.

Two instances can be composed using BTS. For that, users simply select the contracts to be composed, the channels on which they will communicate (except for Interleaving), the rule of composition and the type of verification (deadlock, livelock or both). Our tool automatically verifies the specification and displays the results to the end user. The result of a successful composition adds the newly created component to the list of components instances and removes the composing contracts from this list. Errors are detailed to the user.

In our example, we composed the two philosophers using the interleave composition. Similarly, we achieved the composition of the two forks. These compositions resulted in two different components, one for the forks and one for the philosophers. The composition of these components was achieved using the communication composition (composing the channels fk.1.1 from a fork and pfk.1.1 from a philosopher) resulting in a single component. For this reason, all remaining compositions were unary compositions. We used feedback compositions attaching channels pfk.1.2 with fk.2.2, and fk.2.1 with pfk.2.1. The last composition was a reflexive composition because the last two channels, fk.1.2 and pfk.2.2, were no longer independent as explained in the last section.

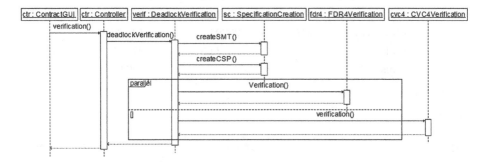

Fig. 7. Sequence diagram of a contract verification in *BTS*

The livelock analysis is not performed using FDR or CVC4. Instead, we have implemented an independent module in *BTS* that automates our livelock technique for *BRIC* as presented in [11], which proved to be more efficient than FDR4. The basic principle of this strategy is to use the minimum sequences that lead the behaviour of the contracts back to its initial state as a way to find the possibility of livelock performing a local analysis. Considering only these finite sequences that represent infinite behaviours, we are able to preserve the absence of livelock when *BRIC* components are being composed.

The use of metadata in *BTS* alleviates the verification of some of the side conditions during contract definition. Furthermore, some of these side conditions are verified during the contract definition and are not repeated. *BTS* also recalculates the new component metadata based on the metadata of the composing components. In our approach, composing components can only be instantiations of previously defined components contracts. The metadata of different contract instances do not need to be verified because, as discussed in [20], this verification needs only to be made once on the original component contract metadata.

5 Evaluation

The evaluation of *BTS* was based on a classical case study: the dining philosophers described in [20]. In this case study, the tool was capable of creating and verifying the CSP scripts correctly. Using *BTS*, the definition of types, channels, interfaces, contracts and instances were achieved using *BTS*'s user interface. We compared the verification time using the different tools and their combinations, using an AMD Phenom(tm) II X4 B97 Processor 3.20 GHz, with 16Gb RAM, running Ubuntu 14.10. All results are presented in Table 1 and Fig. 8.

Table 1. Time effort in the dining philosophers *BTS* (ms))

	FDR2	FDR4	FDR2 + CVC4	FDR4 + CVC4
2 Phils	1686.33	3297.33	850.00	1872.00
3 Phils	6423.66	7918.33	1361.33	3064.33
4 Phils	413792.33	215915.33	2629.00	5138.33
5 Phils	-	-	15883.66	14018.33
6 Phils	-	-	203064.33	115086.00

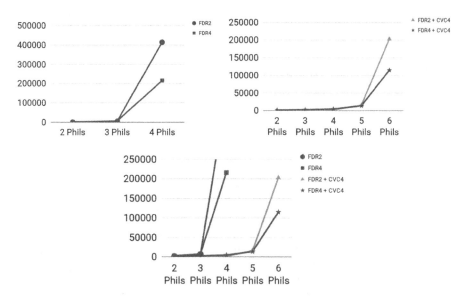

Fig. 8. Comparison between the different tools used in our case study

In examples with less philosophers, FDR2 performs better than FDR4, even when we use CVC4 together with these tools. The reason of this difference resides on the fact that FDR4 makes a type check of the entire CSP specification before any other verification, while FDR2 only checks the processes used inside the assertions. However, as we can see on the diagrams of the Fig. 8, as we add more philosophers to the case study, FDR4 tends to perform better, since the time spent on type checking is no more relevant. We can also observe that, using CVC4 together with FDR, we decrease even more the time spent in verifications.

As we can see in the diagrams, the verifications present an exponential growth, which indicates scalability issues. The work presented in [17], which also made a similar study and identified, as expected, the reflexive composition as the bottleneck, presents an approach that allows these verifications to be carried out in linear time. The adaptation of *BTS* in order to include the theories presented in [17] is in our near future research agenda.

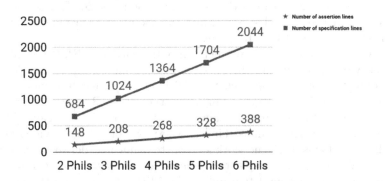

Fig. 9. Number of assertion and specification lines created by *BTS* in our case study

In our case study, the tool generated hundreds of CSP specification and assertion lines (see Fig. 9). For example, for six philosophers, the tool automatically created 388 assertion lines and more than 2044 specification lines, which contains both the specification the user inserted directly and the specification the tool automatically created. These numbers clearly demonstrate the amount of exhaustive work that *BTS* automatises, which would be made manually otherwise. In order to present the verification results to the user, *BTS* also analyses the FDR and CVC4 outputs and presents them, hiding specification details.

6   Conclusion

In this work we presented a tool that automates the systematic construction of trustworthy component-based systems, which makes use of CSP, SMT, FDR and CVC4 to generate the formal specifications of the system and verify them automatically. Using BTS, one can avoid specifying a system using the *BRICK* approach manually. Furthermore, the tool also verifies the system automatically in a transparent manner, which makes the development process more efficient.

The tool was evaluated by a classical case study, in which *BTS* successfully generated and verified all the specifications and assertions in a transparent manner to the user. Besides, we also verified the *BTS*'s scalability by adding more components to the system and comparing the time spent in verification.

BTS is the first tool that automates the $\mathcal{BRICK}$ approach. A few number of tools, however, have been created to automate formal approaches for specifying component based models. Some of the existing tools are [6,23,25], which use existing approaches ([1,8,12], respectively) for creating and verifying component based developments. The advantage of $\mathcal{BRICK}$'s is the use of CSP whose expressiveness allows us to describe a larger number of systems when compared to other approaches. The use of protocols in $\mathcal{BRICK}$ is another advantage since it alleviate the costs of verification. These protocols are not used in [1,8,12]. Furthermore, [1,12] are applied only to embedded and distributed systems and [8] does not present efforts to allow the reuse of components. $\mathcal{BRICK}$ is not limited to embedded or distributed systems, and the use of protocols and the reuse of components are some of its advantages.

The work presented in [17] presents an optimisation to $\mathcal{BRICK}$ that makes use of behavioral patterns to reduce even more the composition verification costs. The introduction of this approach to *BTS* is in our research agenda. We also intend to evaluate *BTS* with two more case studies: the Ring Buffer [18], which was used to evaluate the initial versions of the tool [24], and the leadership election protocol [2], an algorithm used in B&O networks of audio and video systems, in which products inside the network are able to define a leader (usually the most stable product) in order to assist the *dynamic global system configuration*.

Finally, we aim at completely hiding the CSP notation from the user. This will be achieved with the development of a new user interface for *BTS* using graphical notations like Reo [3] to define component behaviours and integration, which would be internally translated into CSP.

References

1. Åkerholm, M., Carlson, J., Fredriksson, J., Hansson, H., Håkansson, J., Möller, A., Pettersson, P., Tivoli, M.: The save approach to component-based development of vehicular systems. J. Syst. Softw. **80**(5), 655–667 (2007)
2. Antonino, P.R.G., Oliveira, M.M., Sampaio, A.C.A., Kristensen, K.E., Bryans, J.W.: Leadership election: an industrial sos application of compositional deadlock verification. In: Badger, J.M., Rozier, K.Y. (eds.) NFM 2014. LNCS, vol. 8430, pp. 31–45. Springer, Cham (2014). doi:10.1007/978-3-319-06200-6_3
3. Arbab, F.: Reo: a channel-based coordination model for component composition. Mathematical Struct. Comput. Sci. **14**(03), 329–366 (2004)
4. Barrett, C., Conway, C.L., Deters, M., Hadarean, L., Jovanović, D., King, T., Reynolds, A., Tinelli, C.: CVC4. In: Gopalakrishnan, G., Qadeer, S. (eds.) CAV 2011. LNCS, vol. 6806, pp. 171–177. Springer, Heidelberg (2011). doi:10.1007/978-3-642-22110-1_14
5. Barrett, C., Stump, A., Tinelli, C.: The smt-lib standard: Version 2.0 (2010). www.SMT-LIB.org

6. Beneš, N., Brim, L., Černá, I., Sochor, J., Vařeková, P., Zimmerová, B., et al.: The coin tool: modelling and verification of interactions in component-based systems. Electronic Notes in Theoretical Computer Science, pp. 221–225 (2008)

7. Bouton, T., Caminha B. de Oliveira, D., Déharbe, D., Fontaine, P.: veriT: an open, trustable and efficient SMT-solver. In: Schmidt, R.A. (ed.) CADE 2009. LNCS, vol. 5663, pp. 151–156. Springer, Heidelberg (2009). doi:10.1007/978-3-642-02959-2_12

8. Brim, L., Černá, I., Vařeková, P., Zimmerova, B.: Component-interaction automata as a verification-oriented component-based system specification. ACM SIGSOFT Softw. Eng. Not. **31**, 4 (2005)

9. Bruin, H.: A grey-box approach to component composition. In: Czarnecki, K., Eisenecker, U.W. (eds.) GCSE 1999. LNCS, vol. 1799, pp. 195–209. Springer, Heidelberg (2000). doi:10.1007/3-540-40048-6_15

10. Butler, M., Hallerstede, S.: The rodin formal modelling tool. In: BCS-FACS Christmas 2007 Meeting-Formal Methods In Industry, London (2007)

11. Filho, M.S.C., Oliveira, M.V.M., Sampaio, A., Cavalcanti, A.: Local livelock analysis of component-based models. In: Ogata, K., Lawford, M., Liu, S. (eds.) ICFEM 2016. LNCS, vol. 10009, pp. 279–295. Springer, Cham (2016). doi:10.1007/978-3-319-47846-3_18

12. Object Management Group. The Common Object Request Broker (CORBA): Architecture and Specification. Object Management Group (1995)

13. Gurgel, A.C., Castro, C.G., Oliveira, M.V.M.: Tool support for the circus refinement calculus. ABZ **8**, 349–349 (2008)

14. Hoare, C.A.R.: Communicating sequential processes. Commun. ACM **21**(8), 666–677 (1978)

15. McIlroy, M.D., Buxton, J.M., Naur, P., Randell, B.: Mass-produced software components. In: Proceedings of the 1st International Conference on Software Engineering, Garmisch Pattenkirchen, Germany. sn (1968)

16. Moura, L., Bjørner, N.: Z3: an efficient SMT solver. In: Ramakrishnan, C.R., Rehof, J. (eds.) TACAS 2008. LNCS, vol. 4963, pp. 337–340. Springer, Heidelberg (2008). doi:10.1007/978-3-540-78800-3_24

17. Oliveira, M.V.M., Antonino, P.R.G., Ramos, R.T., Sampaio, A.C.A., Mota, A.C., Roscoe, A.W.: Rigorous development of component-based systems using component metadata and patterns. Formal Aspects Comput., 1–68 (2016)

18. Oliveira, M.V.M., Sampaio, A.C.A., Antonino, P.R.G., Oliveira, J.D., Filho, M.C., Bryans, J.: Compositional analysis and design of CML models. Technical Report D24.4, COMPASS Deliverable (2014)

19. Oliveira, M.V.M., Sampaio, A.C.A., Antonino, P.R.G., Ramos, R.T., Cavancalti, A.L.C., Woodcock, J.C.P.: Compositional Analysis and Design of CML Models. Technical Report D24.1, COMPASS Deliverable (2013)

20. Ramos, R., Sampaio, A., Mota, A.: Systematic development of trustworthy component systems. In: Cavalcanti, A., Dams, D.R. (eds.) FM 2009. LNCS, vol. 5850, pp. 140–156. Springer, Heidelberg (2009). doi:10.1007/978-3-642-05089-3_10

21. Gibson-Robinson, T., Armstrong, P., Boulgakov, A., Roscoe, A.W.: FDR3 — a modern refinement checker for CSP. In: Ábrahám, E., Havelund, K. (eds.) TACAS 2014. LNCS, vol. 8413, pp. 187–201. Springer, Heidelberg (2014). doi:10.1007/978-3-642-54862-8_13

22. Roscoe, A.W., Hoare, C.A.R., Bird, R.: The Theory and Practice of Concurrency, vol. 1. Prentice Hall, Englewood Cliffs (1998)

23. Sentilles, S., Pettersson, A., Nystrom, D., Nolte, T., Pettersson, P., Crnkovic, I.: Save-ide-a tool for design, analysis and implementation of component-based embedded systems. In: Proceedings of the 31st International Conference on Software Engineering, pp. 607–610. IEEE Computer Society (2009)
24. Silva, S.R.R.: Bts: uma ferramenta de suporte ao desenvolvimento sistemático de sistemas confiáveis baseados em componentes. Master's thesis, Universidade Federal do Rio Grande do Norte (2013)
25. Sy, O., Bastide, R., Palanque, P., Le, D., Navarre, D.: Petshop: a case tool for the petri net based specification and prototyping of corba systems. In: Petri Nets 2000, p. 78 (2000)

Testing and Verifying Chain Repair Methods for Corfu Using Stateless Model Checking

Stavros Aronis[1]($^{\boxtimes}$), Scott Lystig Fritchie[2], and Konstantinos Sagonas[1]

[1] Department of Information Technology, Uppsala University, Uppsala, Sweden
{stavros.aronis,kostis}@it.uu.se
[2] VMware, Cambridge, MA, USA
sfritchie@vmware.com

Abstract. Corfu is a distributed shared log that is designed to be scalable and reliable in the presence of failures and asynchrony. Internally, Corfu is fully replicated for fault tolerance, without sharding data or sacrificing strong consistency. In this case study, we present the modeling approaches we followed to test and verify, using Concuerror, the correctness of repair methods for the Chain Replication protocol suitable for Corfu. In the first two methods we tried, Concuerror located bugs quite fast. In contrast, the tool did not manage to find bugs in the third method, but the time this took also motivated an improvement in the tool that reduces the number of traces explored. Besides more details about all the above, we present experiences and lessons learned from applying stateless model checking for verifying complex protocols suitable for distributed programming.

1 Introduction

This work began, as is often the case, around a whiteboard where a group of engineers were discussing distributed protocols used in cloud systems. Diagrams for two particular protocols were drawn, one for Chain Replication (Sect. 2.1) and one for Corfu (Sect. 2.3), a recently proposed variant of Chain Replication. Both protocols have been studied in research papers, but at the heart of the whiteboard discussion were protocol extensions to repair data after a replica crash; an area of less scientific scrutiny, but of obvious importance to implementors.

The discussion started with one particular replica repair method, known to work well when used in the original Chain Replication [16]. Corfu [13] is similar, but not identical to Chain Replication, therefore warranting an investigation about whether the differences are significant enough to cause that particular method to break in some cases. The verdict of the whiteboard discussion was that, indeed, there exists an execution scenario that violates safety in Corfu, and this same scenario could not manifest when repairing replicas in a system using the original Chain Replication algorithm. A different method was therefore proposed, which would not suffer from that particular weakness. Was this method correct however? No such verdict could be reached at the whiteboard discussion, as is again often the case.

© Springer International Publishing AG 2017
N. Polikarpova and S. Schneider (Eds.): IFM 2017, LNCS 10510, pp. 227–242, 2017.
DOI: 10.1007/978-3-319-66845-1_15

A stateless model checking tool like Concuerror (Sect. 3) should, at least in principle, also be able to find the bug that was discovered at the whiteboard discussion for the first method, and was therefore tried by one of the engineers. After creating executable models of CORFU and the replica repair extension (Sect. 4), the bug was indeed found by the tool. A model for the second repair method was therefore created and tested. After a few iterations, the tool managed to find a scenario that showed that this method was also erroneous. The engineer shared this (un)fortunate discovery on Twitter[1] catching the attention of Concuerror's developers, who were intrigued by the tweet and contacted him for more information about that particular use of their tool and for his experiences.

A fruitful collaboration began. At the engineer's end, several variations of repair techniques were devised and modeled, with new flaws in them found quickly by the tool. Eventually, a technique emerged that appeared to be safe. At the other end, the developers of Concuerror used this case study as inspiration to design and implement an improvement to the partial order reduction techniques that the tool employs (Sect. 5.1) and to also evaluate how effective a particular search space bounding technique was for finding bugs.

In this paper, we retell the story, starting with an overview of Chain Replication and CORFU (Sect. 2), including the ideas related to chain repair, followed by a brief overview of stateless model checking and Concuerror (Sect. 3). In the same section, we also briefly describe the main ideas behind the partial order reduction and bounding techniques that Concuerror uses to make testing and verification more effective. We then describe the initially used model, starting from the correctness properties that should hold and explaining in detail the various parts of the model that are related to them (Sect. 4). The chain repair methods are then described together with performance results that show the time and effort involved to find bugs in these methods or verify their correctness. The paper continues by describing and justifying refinements that were applied to the model, as well as an improvement that was implemented in Concuerror to increase its effectiveness (Sect. 5). All these enabled Concuerror to verify the correctness of the final repair method. The paper ends by reviewing related work (Sect. 6) and offering some final remarks (Sect. 7).

2   Chain Replication

Chain Replication [16] is a variation of leader/follower replication that supports linearizable single objects. In this section, we first describe the basic Chain Replication algorithm, including how repair of a failed server can be performed after the server restarts. Then, we describe a variation of the algorithm, which is used by the CORFU distributed log [13], and finally explain how porting the same repair technique to CORFU can lead to problems (e.g., linearizability violations).

---

[1] @slfritchie: "I was all ready to have a celebratory "New algorithm works!" tweet. Then the DPOR model execution w/Concuerror found an invalid case. Ouch." (https://twitter.com/slfritchie/status/745863131407220737).

2.1 Basic Algorithm

In Chain Replication's leader/follower protocol, all replica servers are arranged in an ordered list of *head*, *middle*, and *tail* servers. The head server is the leader; all other servers are followers. Clients send update operations to the head server.

If the head server rejects an update operation, it sends an error back to the client. If the operation is accepted, the head server does not reply, but sends state update requests down the chain. Each follower server (if any) records the update requests to their respective local data stores and then forwards the requests downstream, in the same order they were received. After an update has been stored by the last server in the chain, the tail server sends a successful acknowledgment (ack) to the client. Thus, for a single update to a chain of length three, four messages are required: client → head, head → middle, middle → tail, and tail → client.

Clients send read-only operations to the tail server, which is also the linearization point for all replicas. If the tail server stores a value, then all other servers upstream in the chain must already store that value or a newer one.

Note that a chain of length one is a single server that acts in both head and tail roles.

2.2 Chain Repair

The Chain Replication paper [16] is clear about what is required to shorten a chain when a server crashes or is otherwise stopped. It also discusses how to reintroduce a crashed server back into the chain, but omits details that an implementor must be aware of to maintain Chain Replication's linearizable consistency guarantee.

A naïve repair method might take the following steps:

1. stop all surviving servers in the chain, e.g., $[S_{head}^a, S_{tail}^b]$,
2. copy S_{tail}^b's update history to the server under repair S_{repair}^c, then
3. restart all servers with a chain configuration of $[S_{head}^a, S_{middle}^b, S_{tail}^c]$.

This offline repair method is easy, but sacrifices cluster availability. Online repair is desirable, but we also wish to preserve Chain Replication's property of linearizable reads by sending only one query to a chain member.

The Chain Replication repair technique used by HibariDB [7] starts a repair with a transition from chain $[S_{head}^a, S_{tail}^b] \Rightarrow [S_{head}^a, S_{tail}^b, S_{repair}^c]$, where S^c is the crashed server. Read queries ignore the server under repair; they are sent to the tail server as usual. Updates are sent to the head server and propagate down the entire chain; replies are sent by S_{repair}^c. While this intermediate chain configuration is in place, a separate process aynchronously copies missing data from S_{tail}^b to S_{repair}^c. When all missing history items have been copied to the server under repair, all servers in the chain enter read-only mode. A flush command is sent by the head to force all pending writes down the chain to the tail. When the corresponding ack from the tail is received by the head, then we know that all update log histories must be equal: $S_{head}^a = S_{tail}^b = S_{repair}^c$. Finally, the chain transitions to $[S_{head}^a, S_{middle}^b, S_{tail}^c]$, and then read-only mode is canceled.

2.3 Chain Replication in CORFU

The design of the CORFU system [13] uses Chain Replication with three changes, related to what we described so far. First, the responsibility for implementing replication is moved to the client. CORFU servers do not communicate with each other, so it is impossible for them to implement the original Chain Replication protocol. Instead, the replication logic is embedded in the client. Thus, for a single update to a CORFU chain of length three, six messages are involved, in three pairs between each of client ↔ head, client ↔ middle, and client ↔ tail.

The second change is that CORFU's servers implement write-once semantics. Clients may not replace or overwrite a previously written value.

Third, CORFU builds upon standard Chain Replication by identifying each chain configuration by an epoch number. All clients and servers are aware of the epoch number, and all client operations include the epoch number. If a client operation contains a different epoch number, the operation is rejected by the server. A server temporarily stops service if it receives a newer epoch number from a client. When any participant detects a change of epoch, it can retrieve the new configuration from a dedicated cluster layout configuration service.

2.4 Chain Repair Techniques for CORFU

Since CORFU's servers do not communicate directly with each other as HibariDB's servers do, the "read-only mode + sync flush down the chain" technique used by HibariDB cannot be directly applied to CORFU. Consider a scenario where a chain is undergoing repair during epoch #5 and there exist two clients, C_w and C_r. We are interested in the value of some piece of data, which starts with an *old* value (i.e., not_written, since each key can only be written once). Client C_w is writing a *new* value to the cluster. This scenario is illustrated in Fig. 1.

epoch #5	S^a_{head} value=*new*	S^b_{tail} value=*old* or value=*new*	S^c_{repair} value=*old*
epoch #6	S^a_{head} value=*new*	S^b_{middle} value=*new*	S^c_{tail} value=*old* or value=*new*

Fig. 1. An epoch & chain configuration change while a *new* value is written to the chain.

While epoch #5 is in effect, reads are sent to server S^b, which is in the tail role. All read operations during epoch #5 will return either the *old* or *new* value. If a client can read the *new* value, then all later reads will also read the *new* value. However, client C_w should also write to S^c, which is beyond the current tail. This operation can unfortunately be delayed by the network.

The repairer is not influenced by the new value, and can therefore change the cluster configuration to epoch #6. A race condition becomes possible. In epoch #6, S^c will receive read queries because it has the tail role. Now our writing and reading clients can race: if C_w is too slow to complete the write—disregarding even that it also has a wrong epoch number—then C_r can read the *old* value from the new tail cluster. Back during epoch #5, it was possible to read the *new* value. If we can now read the *old* value in epoch #6, then it looks like the value has gone "backwards in time". Such time travel violates the linearizability property. It is exactly this race condition that was discovered at the whiteboard discussion in the story of the introduction.

HibariDB's repair technique works because the head server knows about all pending writes: the head sends its flush message down the chain, and a final ack sent by the tail is eventually received by the head. HibariDB also stops new writes during the transition process. When the flush's ack is received by the head, all servers have the same update log history.

In contrast, CORFU has no central coordinator like HibariDB's head server. Can we use a variation of this HibariDB's repair technique without also introducing direct server $\leftrightarrow$ server communication? Does a variation exist that does not require tracking the state of all writing clients to orchestrate their behavior?

Let us briefly overview a particular testing and verification technique and tool that we can employ to answer these questions.

3 Stateless Model Checking, Erlang, Concuerror and Bounding

The problem of verification and testing of distributed systems and their algorithms is difficult, since one must consider all the different ways in which the involved entities can interact. *Model checking* techniques can explore the state space of a program that implements such an algorithm systematically, verifying that each reachable state satisfies some given properties. However, applying model checking to programs of realistic size is problematic, as it entails capturing, encoding and storing a large number of states.

Stateless model checking [10], also known as *systematic concurrency testing*, avoids this obstacle by exploring the state space of a program without explicitly storing intermediate global states. A special run-time scheduler drives program execution, recording operations that can be affected by the interaction between involved entities. State capturing is not needed, because if all such operations are executed in the same order from the initial state, then any previously encountered state can be reached again. Thus the effort of testing and verification can focus only on those operations. Stateless model checking has been successfully implemented in tools such as VeriSoft [11], CHESS [14] and Concuerror [12]. The last tool is specific to programs written in Erlang.

Erlang is an industrially relevant programming language based on the actor model of concurrency [2]. In Erlang, actors are realized by language-level processes implemented by the runtime system instead of being directly mapped to operating system threads. Each Erlang process has its own private memory area (stack, heap and mailbox) and communicates with other processes via asynchronous message passing with *copying semantics*. Processes then consume messages using *selective receive*, i.e., they can select which message to pick from their mailbox using pattern matching. The use of message passing for inter-process communication, rather than shared memory, makes distribution transparent. It also makes Erlang suitable for modeling distributed systems. Erlang has all the ingredients needed for concurrency via message passing and most of the ingredients (e.g., reads and writes to data stored in shared ETS tables, etc.) needed for concurrent programming using shared memory.

The tool we will employ, Concuerror [4], is a stateless model checking tool for finding errors in Erlang programs or verifying their absence[2]. Given a program and a test to run, Concuerror uses a dynamic exploration algorithm to systematically explore the execution of the test under conceptually all process interleaving. To achieve this, the tool performs a code rewrite that inserts instrumentation at code points where processes can yield control back to the scheduler during their execution. The instrumentation that Concuerror uses is selective (i.e., it takes place only at points that involve process actions that inspect or update some concurrency-related primitive that accesses VM-level data structures that are shared by processes) and allows Concuerror to control the scheduling when the program is run, without having to modify the Erlang VM in any way. Concuerror supports the complete Erlang language and can instrument and test programs of any size, automatically including any libraries they use.

Since the number of global states that can be reached due to different scheduling decisions in stateless model checking can be exponential in the number of execution steps, systematic concurrency testing algorithms use techniques such as *partial order reduction (POR)* and *bounding* to reduce the size of the search space.

Partial Order Reduction. POR techniques define equivalence classes among traces, based on the happens-before relation between the operations that occur in them [9]. POR algorithms aim to explore just one trace in each such equivalence class. Reversing the order of execution for a pair of racing operations that exists in an explored trace is a simple way to obtain a trace that belongs to a different equivalence class. Dynamic POR techniques start by executing an arbitrary scheduling and then explore additional traces, justified by the existence of races between actually executed operations. The exploration continues 'by need', trying to examine a minimal number of traces. Several DPOR algorithms have been proposed, including the *Optimal-DPOR* algorithm [1], a provably optimal DPOR algorithm that Concuerror is using.

Bounding. Even when using POR techniques, the exploration needs to examine a lot of complex interleaving of processes, as a direct result of reversing every possible pair of racing instructions. Bounding techniques try to limit the complexity of the explored traces in order to expose bugs that are "shallower". In order to do that, they impose constraints on how processes can be scheduled. Exploration begins with a budget which is expended whenever such a scheduling constraint is violated.

Preemption bounding [15] limits the number of times the scheduler can preempt (i.e., interrupt) a process in order to run other processes. The justification is that common patterns of concurrency bugs require few scheduling constraints and these in turn

---

[2] More information about Concuerror is at http://parapluu.github.io/Concuerror.

can be related to few preemptions [3, 18]. Delay bounding [6] is another bounding technique that forces the scheduler to always schedule the first non-blocked process out of a total order of all processes. The bound here is the number of times this order can be violated. Concuerror employs *exploration tree bounding*, a bounding technique that restricts the number of times a DPOR algorithm can consider schedulings different from the "first" one. In implementations of stateless model checking with DPOR, the first scheduling that is explored is usually the same as the one chosen under preemption bounding: a round-robin scheduling, in which processes execute without preemptions until they block. Exploration tree bounding limits the number of times exploration can 'diverge' from that first scheduling, and essentially combines the benefits of Optimal-DPOR (i.e., never even start to explore a trace if one that belongs to the same equivalence class has been already explored) with some of the benefits of delay bounding.

Having described our platform we now move on to the description of our models.

4   Modeling CORFU

In this section, we describe our modeling approach for verifying the correctness of methods for chain repair suitable for CORFU. We first list the correctness properties that we are interested in. We continue by describing how we model a number of servers and clients of CORFU using Erlang, followed by how we model each of the chain repair methods we want to test/verify. Finally, we give a short initial evaluation of the modeling. This section gives a faithful account of the engineer's initial effort, before the developers of Concuerror were involved.

4.1   Correctness Properties

We are interested to verify that CORFU servers and clients do not suffer from scenarios such as the one described earlier as "a value traveling backwards in time during a chain repair". More formally, we want the following correctness properties to hold.

Immutability: Once a value has been written in a key, no other value can be written to it.
Linearizability: If a read operation sees a written value for some particular key, subsequent read operations for that key must also see the same value.

4.2   Initial Model

A high-level view of the CORFU system that is modeled is the following: A number of stable servers (one or two suffice) will undergo a chain repair procedure to have a single additional server added to their chain. Concurrently, two other clients will try to write two different values to the same key, while a third client will try to read the key twice.

We make some assumptions about the state prior to running a repair simulation. At some earlier time, all servers were connected in the cluster's single chain. Then one server crashed, causing the chain to be shortened. The procedure to shorten the chain is well-understood and known to be safe, so it is excluded from the model. We also use only a single key/value pair in the store, corresponding to a single address in the CORFU log, as the aforementioned correctness properties impose constraints on just a single key (i.e., log address) in the CORFU system. We assume that none of the servers in the chain had a value for the key before the crash. After the crash, we assume that the crashed server restarts with an empty local data store. The repairing process, as well as writer and reader clients are all assumed to be concurrent and freely interleaved; strict ordering of operations exists only within a particular client, e.g., between the two read operations performed by the reader or between the steps of the repairing process.

This model, which in the rest of the paper we refer to as the *Initial Model*, is sufficient to reveal bugs in two of the chain repair methods we tested. Refinements of the initial model will be described later (Sect. 5.2), when we present the effort that went into the verification of the third repair method.

Servers and Clients in the Model. All servers and clients of the CORFU system are modeled as Erlang processes. These processes exchange messages corresponding to requests sent by clients to the servers and the respective server replies, as well as notifications to a central coordinator. All processes are running concurrently, allowing all possible interleaving between events to occur. As mentioned, Concuerror's scheduler can switch between processes at *every* point where instrumentation is added, and this ability can mimic the effect of network delays at any point in our model and the resulting message reordering. We are not interested in lost messages.

The types of processes used in the model are the following:

1. Central coordinator. This is the top process of the model and is responsible for spawning and setting up every other process (servers and clients), monitoring when all the clients are done and collecting their results, using assertions to check the correctness properties, and doing final cleanups (i.e., shutting down the servers). It is used as a modeling convenience; no such coordinator exists in a CORFU system.
2. CORFU log servers. These processes mimic the protocol and behavior specified by the servers in the CORFU system. There may be two or three of these processes: one for the server under repair, and the rest representing the healthy chain.
3. The layout server process. This process offers the cluster layout configuration service mentioned earlier. A "layout" data structure normally determines the chain order for each segment of the CORFU distributed log. In our model we assume that the layout contains only a single chain, and that reads and writes are to a single key; other aspects of the full CORFU system's layout structure are out of scope. Each layout change moves the system to a new epoch.
4. CORFU reading client. This is a process that attempts to read data twice. It must never experience "time travel" behavior by witnessing a written value followed by a not_written value (i.e., linearizability violation). Also, it should never witness two different written values (i.e., immutability violation).
5. CORFU writing clients. We have two writer client processes in the model, each attempting to write a value different from that of the other and report back to the coordinator. At most one such client is permitted to succeed.
6. The data repair process. This process executes all steps required for copying data to the server under repair and lengthening the chain afterwards. The steps required were described in general in Sect. 2.4, and are described in more detail below.

Coordinator's Details. The model includes an initialization and shutting down phase in which the coordinator sets up the servers and waits for all clients to complete their execution before shutting down the servers. Shutting down the servers is not strictly necessary, since Concuerror is always able to reset the state of the system before starting new schedulings, but we include it since a "cleanup phase" is common in testing.

When the clients are done, they send a message back to the coordinator, including information about the results of their operations. Specifically for the writers, the coordinator uses these results to determine whether more than one write was successful, violating the immutability property from the writers' point of view. The coordinator also inspects whether the log is left at a consistent state, with either no value written to the key, or a singular value being written consistently to a prefix of the chain.

CORFU *Log and Layout Servers' Details.* Servers never initiate any communication and only respond to requests by clients. As explained earlier, log servers know the current epoch and will notify clients that are trying to communicate using a wrong epoch number. Log servers support read and write operations for keys as well as epoch (and layout) update operations, while the layout server supports layout read and update operations.

CORFU *Clients' Details.* Clients communicate with log servers directly to read or write data. Write operations are sent to every server in the chain, while read requests are sent to the tail server only. We assume that clients begin with knowledge of the healthy chain of servers. If a client request is answered with the information that their epoch is wrong, they communicate with the layout server to get an update and use this information consistently to continue their operation.

Valid replies to a write request are ok, meaning that the write was successful, or written, which denotes that the key already had a value. Valid replies to a read request are not_written, which denotes that no value exists, or {ok, Val} where Val is the value read. A client request may also be left incomplete, signaled by a starved reply: too many concurrent layout changes have interrupted the request. In our model, the retry limit is higher than the number of layout changes performed by the repairing process.

Repair Process' Details. The data repair process executes the following steps: First, it changes the layout to include the crashed server in some place in the chain, depending on the repair method, without changing the head or tail servers. At that stage, read operations are still sent to the tail server, ignoring the server under repair, even in cases where it will eventually be in the tail position. On the other hand, write operations must succeed in all servers (including the server under repair) to be considered successful.

Second, the data repair process copies data from the tail server to the server under repair. In the model, the repair process needs to copy a single key's worth of data. We know the identity of server of the data source (tail), the destination (repair), and the one data key that we need to sync; all are hard-coded into the repair process. The outcome of any race between the repairer and the regular writer processes is checked for correctness at the end of model execution by the coordinator.

Third and last, after a successful second phase, the layout is once more changed to include the repaired server in its final place in the chain.

We will test three repair methods, differing in where the recovered server is placed in the chain: the head, the tail or an intermediate position. In the last case, we will test a configuration with two initially healthy servers, in which the position of the repaired server will be just between them, as well as a configuration with only one healthy server, which we will have to "logically split in two" to make space for the server under repair.

4.3 Method 1: Add Repaired Server at End of Chain

Repair using the "end of chain" method is starting from a $[S^a_{head}, S^b_{tail}]$ layout, transitioning to a $[S^a_{head}, S^b_{tail}, S^c_{repair}]$ layout, doing the value copying from S^b and then changing layout again to shift S^b to a middle role and S^c to the new tail: $[S^a_{head}, S^b_{middle}, S^c_{tail}]$.

This method is vulnerable to the race condition described in detail in Sect. 2.4. If we find the same bug in our model, we have some confidence that Concuerror is indeed a suitable tool to investigate correctness of methods for chain repair.

4.4 Method 2: Add Repaired Server at Start of Chain

This second repair technique is a variation of the first. Instead of putting the server under repair at the end of the chain, we put it at the beginning. The chain's configuration during the middle epoch looks like this: $[S^c_{repair}, S^a_{head}, S^b_{tail}]$. A write operation during repair in this chain configuration must be sent to S^c and then propagate down the chain to the other servers. Reads are always served by the tail S^b and the repair value is also copied from there. A writer trying to communicate with server S^a after repair has started will be notified that this is no longer the head and will have to ask for a layout update.

4.5 Method 3: Add Repaired Server in the Middle

In the final technique, the server under repair is placed in the middle of the chain. Our intuition suggests that this should be a safe thing to do. The original Chain Replication protocol has no direct contact between a client and a server in the middle of the chain. There should be no opportunity for a reader client to witness a consistency violation.

For CORFU's variant of Chain Replication, the client does interact with middle servers: the client cannot act upon the effect of a write unless the update is successful at all servers in the chain, applied serially in the chain's order.

This method uses three epochs of chain configuration: (i) epoch #1: $[S^a_{head}, S^b_{tail}]$, (ii) epoch #2: $[S^a_{head}, S^c_{repair}, S^b_{tail}]$, and (iii) epoch #3: $[S^a_{head}, S^c_{middle}, S^b_{tail}]$.

There is only one small problem with this method. What if the healthy chain is of length one? How can we insert the repaired server into the middle of a too-short chain? The proposed solution is to split the single server of the healthy chain into two logical servers: a logical head and a logical tail. The data stores of the two logical roles have different implementations.

For the logical tail role, the data store remains the same as CORFU's normal disk-based store. The differences are applicable only in the context of the head role's store.

Table 1. Runs of the methods using bounded and unbounded exploration.

Method	Bounded exploration			Unbounded exploration		
	Bug?	Traces	Time	Bug?	Traces	Time
1 (Tail)	Yes	638	57 s	Yes	3 542 431	144 h
2 (Head)	Yes	65	7 s	Yes	389	26 s
3 (Middle)	No	1257	68 s	No	>30 000 000	>750 h

The logical head role's store is split into a conceptual RAM-based and a disk-based store. If a key is unwritten, the value of an update operation is first written to the RAM-based half of the store. Later, if and when the update reaches the logical tail role, the value is written to the disk-based half of the store and the key is deleted from the RAM store. If the repair process is interrupted for any reason, the RAM store is discarded, and the next epoch change will fall back to a chain containing only the healthy server.

4.6 An Evaluation of the Repair Methods on the Initial Model

Let us see where we are so far. Table 1 shows the experimental results of running each of the three methods on the initial model using a standard desktop and the current version of Concuerror. We run Concuerror in two modes: (i) using exploration tree bounding (we used a bound of at most 4) in order to check for bugs, and (ii) without bounding the exploration, i.e., using the tool for verification. We explain our findings below.

Method 1: Add Repaired Server at End of Chain. When this model is executed, Concuerror finds the linearization violation described earlier. The reader process sees the value written by a writer in the tail of epoch #2, but after the repair process is completed, and moves the servers to epoch #3 (without copying that value) the reader's second read runs ahead of the writer and finds a non-written entry in the added server, since the writer has not yet also written there. The bug is found quite fast (in under a minute) when using bounded exploration. In contrast, without a bound, many more traces are explored before the bug is found and the hunt lasts for several days.

Method 2: Add Repaired Server at Start of Chain. Concuerror finds a case analogous to the problem of Method 1, where trouble happens immediately after an epoch change. Two different bugs are detected, depending on whether bounding is used or not.

In bounded exploration, the buggy trace, which is found very fast, involves a process scheduling that permits both writer processes to write different values to S^a and S^c: one during epoch #1 and the other immediately after the transition to epoch #2. Thus, Concuerror finds that the log history invariant outlined in Sect. 2.1 is violated. Recall that CORFU's server implements a write-once store. CORFU's write-once enforcement means that nobody can overwrite or replace the conflicting value that is now in the middle of the chain at S^a. Similarly, the bad value written at S^c cannot be altered.

In unbounded exploration the bug found is different. One of the writers starts a write, but is interrupted, so the write never reaches the tail server. Then the repair process starts, notifying the servers in the chain about the new head. The writer finds out about the new head and starts the write again from the top of the chain. The server under repair is not initialized and reports that the writer knows a newer layout, so it repeatedly denies its requests until the writer starves. The remaining clients finish with the new server unwritten at the head and a value committed at the second position (by the writer's first attempt). At this state, any subsequent writer can immediately move the system to a bad state (succeeding with a different value on the new head, and failing at the second server since a value is already there).

This scenario is arguably fixable if the layout server notifies the repaired server (that is to become the new head) before the other servers in the chain. However, this fix is still vulnerable to the repaired server accepting a value to its unwritten entry, which the repairer will not see at the tail, just as before.

Method 3: Add Repaired Server in the Middle. For the third method, we used the model of transition from 1-to-2 servers. Concuerror's bounded exploration did not find any trace that violates either Chain Replication's invariants or CORFU's invariants. This result is encouraging, but full verification was not achieved: unbounded exploration ran for many days without exhausting the search space.

Let us summarize the results of our evaluation so far: (1) Concuerror was able to detect problems in buggy methods fairly quickly. (2) In the first method, bounding was crucial for finding the bug in reasonable time. (3) The third method could not be verified.

5   Optimization and Refinements

Since full verification of the third method was not possible with the initial model, we describe the actions we took to increase the effectiveness of our approach: an optimization of the tool and two refinements of the model. Both were direct results of our investigation of the traces explored by Concuerror.

5.1   Optimization: Avoid Reordering the Delivery of Unrelated Messages

One of the design choices of Erlang's message passing mechanism, namely the fact that at the point when a process receives a message the contents of its mailbox are checked in the order of their arrival, can lead to a very simple race scenario: If multiple messages can match a `receive` statement, the message placed first in the mailbox will be the one selected. If the order of delivery is different, `receive` will pick a different message.

To be sound, Concuerror detects such races and explores all possible orders of delivery for such messages. However, Concuerror's original implementation had not been optimized to detect cases where a `receive` statement is written in a way such that only particular messages can be received, regardless of the delivery of other messages. Instead, the tool treated any two messages that were delivered to the same process as "possibly racing".

In our model, once a client process C has executed its code, it has to notify the coordinator process with a {done,C,...} message. Even though the coordinator is written in a way such that each such message can only be received by one particular `receive` statement (using a particular C value), Concuerror originally explored all possible orders of delivering such messages. This introduces a multiplicative factor in the number of traces that need to be explored, which is factorial in the number of clients.

To avoid this unnecessary exploration, we extended Concuerror with the ability to take into account the `receive` patterns used when a message is received when determining which other messages are racing with that message's delivery. As a trivial example of the usefulness of the extension, we note that the extended version of Concuerror will not try different delivery interleavings for messages that are never retrieved from a process' mailbox. The technical aspects of the implementation are beyond the scope of this paper, but its benefits will become evident in the final evaluation.

5.2 Two Refinements of the Model

Conditional Read. In the initial model, the reader issues two read requests, with the intent to detect values that change or disappear. Either bug observation is possible only if the first read operation sees a value written (from either writer). There exist, however, cases where the first read is either observing the location as not yet written, or is starved altogether. Issuing another read request in such cases cannot expose any bugs and only results in exploring unnecessary traces when interleaving this second read request.

In order to avoid such unnecessary exploration, we have refined the reader client so that it only attempts a second read operation if such an operation can actually reveal bugs: namely only if the first read operation sees some written value.

Convert Layout Server to an ETS Table. A second refinement of the model is to simplify the modeling of the communication with the layout server. The reader and writer clients communicate with the layout server just to read epoch and layout information, and in the initial model this communication is implemented with messages. Concuerror, even with the optimization described in Sect. 5.1, must explore both orderings in which requests from different clients arrive to the layout server; the server's `receive` patterns should be able to handle any client's request.

To avoid reorderings of requests that are layout read operations, and therefore *commutable*, we changed the modeling of the layout server to instead use a shared memory location in the Erlang Term Storage area for the layout information. Concuerror's knowledge of operations that conflict with each other is precise enough to not treat read operations to such a location as racing. Therefore it does not need to reverse them and explore "the other" trace. There will of course still be races involving the layout server: the repairing process has to write to the same shared memory location when changing epochs, introducing races with any read requests.

5.3 Evaluation of the Effect of the Optimization and Refinements

Recall that the only two cases where Concuerror did not complete in reasonable time was when bounding was not used. More specifically, Concuerror took a lot of time to find a bug in Method 1 and could not verify the correctness of Method 3.

For Method 3, applying the optimization and the two refinements above is sufficient. With these changes, Concuerror can verify that the new model has no bugs in 48 h, after exploring 3 931 413 traces. We did not evaluate the effect of each change on its own, since the required time is significantly larger (e.g., not using the optimization of Sect. 5.1 with four clients sending done messages back to the supervisor, conceptually leads to the exploration of 4! = 24 times as many traces).

Table 2. Evaluation of improvements applied on Method 1, without bounding.

Optimization (Sect. 5.1)	Refinements (Sect. 5.2)		Traces	Time
	Cond. read	ETS layout		
✗	✗	✗	3 542 431	144 h
✓	✗	✗	151 923	5 h 30 m
✗	✓	✗	3 787	6 m 20 s
✓	✓	✗	212	19 s
✗	✗	✓	1 059 043	29 h 40 m
✓	✗	✓	47 148	1 h 05 m
✗	✓	✓	5 239	5 m 20 s
✓	✓	✓	289	18 s

For Method 1, we show more detailed results in Table 2. The message delivery order optimization reduces the time to the first bug to 5 h 30 m (151 923 traces) and the reader refinement even more so: a bug is found in 6 m 20 s (3 787 traces). When used together, these improvements can find a bug in the method in just 19 s (only 212 traces are explored). The layout server refinement is not so effective on its own and its application slightly increases the number of traces when combined with the reader refinement. With all three changes, the traces are shorter (no back and forth communication with an extra server) and thus the bug is found slightly faster (in 18 instead of 19 s) even though slightly more traces (289) are explored.

6   Related Work

An approach similar to ours has been described in the presentation of the P# language [5], which is suitable for designing asynchronous systems modeled as state machines. This modeling is very appealing for systems such as CORFU and indeed the chain replication algorithm has been included in the evaluation of the language. However, the bug-finding capabilities of the P# runtime are based on either depth-first systematic testing (without POR or our improvements for message passing), or random testing (which cannot be used for verification). Moreover the focus of the evaluation of chain replication is not on chain repair methods.

A different approach, used in the verification of distributed databases (including ones based on chain replication), has been to write a rigorous formal specification of the system and then use techniques such as temporal logic [8] or proof assistants [17] to complete the verification, possibly extracting an executable implementation from the specification. In contrast, our technique is using a simple, directly executable simulation of the system and all safety properties are described as plain, non-sophisticated assertions.

7 Concluding Remarks

We have described our experiences from using stateless model checking to test the correctness of three repair methods for the Chain Replication algorithm used in CORFU. Using a fairly straightforward model written in Erlang, we were able to find bugs in the first two repair methods using Concuerror, some more quickly detectable after applying a simple bounding technique. In an attempt to verify the correctness of the third repair method, we also designed and implemented an optimization for Concuerror, based on a particular pattern found in Erlang programs, and two techniques for refining the model. These changes allowed us to verify the correctness of the third chain repair method in reasonable time.

Acknowledgments. This work was supported in part by the Swedish Research Council and carried out within the Linnaeus centre of excellence UPMARC, Uppsala Programming for Multicore Architectures Research Center.

References

1. Abdulla, P., Aronis, S., Jonsson, B., Sagonas, K.: Optimal dynamic partial order reduction. In: Proceedings of the 41st ACM SIGPLAN-SIGACT Symposium on Principles of Programming Languages, POPL 2014, pp. 373–384. ACM, New York (2014). doi:10.1145/2535838.2535845
2. Armstrong, J.: Erlang. Commun. ACM **53**(9), 68–75 (2010)
3. Burckhardt, S., Kothari, P., Musuvathi, M., Nagarakatte, S.: A randomized scheduler with probabilistic guarantees of finding bugs. In: Proceedings of ASPLOS, ASPLOS XV, pp. 167–178. ACM, New York (2010). doi:10.1145/1736020.1736040
4. Christakis, M., Gotovos, A., Sagonas, K.: Systematic testing for detecting concurrency errors in Erlang programs. In: Sixth IEEE International Conference on Software Testing, Verification and Validation (ICST 2013), pp. 154–163. IEEE Computer Society (2013)
5. Deligiannis, P., Donaldson, A.F., Ketema, J., Lal, A., Thomson, P.: Asynchronous programming, analysis and testing with state machines. In: Proceedings of the 36th PLDI, PLDI 2015, pp. 154–164 (2015). doi:10.1145/2737924.2737996
6. Emmi, M., Qadeer, S., Rakamarić, Z.: Delay-bounded scheduling. In: Proceedings of the 38th Annual ACM SIGPLAN-SIGACT Symposium on Principles of Programming Languages, POPL 2011, pp. 411–422. ACM, New York (2011)
7. Fritchie, S.L.: Chain replication in theory and in practice. In: Proceedings of the 9th ACM SIGPLAN Workshop on Erlang, Erlang 2010, pp. 33–44. ACM, New York (2010). doi:10.1145/1863509.1863515
8. Geambasu, R., Birrell, A., MacCormick, J.: Experiences with formal specification of fault-tolerant file systems. In: IEEE International Conference on Dependable Systems and Networks With FTCS and DCC, DSN 2008, pp. 96–101. IEEE (2008)
9. Godefroid, P.: Partial-Order Methods for the Verification of Concurrent Systems: An Approach to the State-Explosion Problem. Springer-Verlag New York Inc., Secaucus (1996)

10. Godefroid, P.: Model checking for programming languages using VeriSoft. In: Proceedings of the 24th ACM SIGPLAN-SIGACT Symposium on Principles of Programming Languages, POPL 1997, pp. 174–186. ACM, New York (1997). doi:10.1145/263699.263717
11. Godefroid, P.: Software model checking: the VeriSoft approach. Form. Methods Syst. Des. **26**(2), 77–101 (2005). doi:10.1007/s10703-005-1489-x
12. Gotovos, A., Christakis, M., Sagonas, K.: Test-driven development of concurrent programs using Concuerror. In: Proceedings of the 10th ACM SIGPLAN Workshop on Erlang, Erlang 2011, pp. 51–61. ACM, New York (2011). doi:10.1145/2034654.2034664
13. Malkhi, D., Balakrishnan, M., Davis, J.D., Prabhakaran, V., Wobber, T.: From Paxos to CORFU: a flash-speed shared log. SIGOPS Oper. Syst. Rev. **46**(1), 47–51 (2012). doi:10.1145/2146382.2146391
14. Musuvathi, M., Qadeer, S., Ball, T., Basler, G., Nainar, P.A., Neamtiu, I.: Finding and reproducing heisenbugs in concurrent programs. In: Proceedings of the 8th USENIX Conference on Operating Systems Design and Implementation, OSDI 2008, pp. 267–280. USENIX Association, Berkeley (2008)
15. Qadeer, S., Rehof, J.: Context-bounded model checking of concurrent software. In: Halbwachs, N., Zuck, L.D. (eds.) TACAS 2005. LNCS, vol. 3440, pp. 93–107. Springer, Heidelberg (2005). doi:10.1007/978-3-540-31980-1_7
16. van Renesse, R., Schneider, F.B.: Chain replication for supporting high throughput and availability. In: Proceedings of the 6th Conference on Symposium on Operating Systems Design & Implementation, OSDI 2004, pp. 91–104. USENIX, Berkeley (2004)
17. Schiper, N., Rahli, V., van Renesse, R., Bickford, M., Constable, R.L.: Developing correctly replicated databases using formal tools. In: 2014 44th Annual IEEE/IFIP International Conference on Dependable Systems and Networks (DSN), pp. 395–406. IEEE (2014)
18. Thomson, P., Donaldson, A.F., Betts, A.: Concurrency testing using controlled schedulers: an empirical study. ACM Trans. Parallel Comput. **2**(4), 23:1–23:37 (2016). doi:10.1145/2858651

Synthesizing Coalitions for Multi-agent Games

Wei Ji[1,2], Farn Wang[3], and Peng Wu[1,2(✉)]

[1] State Key Laboratory of Computer Science, Institute of Software,
Chinese Academy of Sciences, Beijing, China
{jiwei,wp}@ios.ac.cn
[2] University of Chinese Academy of Sciences, Beijing, China
[3] Deptartment of Electrical Engineering, National Taiwan University,
Taipei, Taiwan
farn@ntu.edu.tw

Abstract. We present *Temporal Cooperation Logic with Coalition Variables* (*TCLX*), for the synthesis of coalitions of unknown sizes to achieve temporal objectives in multi-agent games. TCLX extends *Temporal Cooperation Logic* (*TCL*) by allowing existentially quantified variables for agent sets and operators for set relations. Even though TCLX is shown more expressive than TCL and incomparable with AMC, GL, and ATL* in expressiveness, the verification complexities of TCLX are still maintained as those of TCL, i.e., EXPTIME-complete for model-checking and 2-EXPTIME-complete for satisfiability checking. We then extend the on-the-fly model-checking algorithm of TCL for implementing a TCLX model-checker. Our implementation is experimented with three benchmark models in the context of network security, software development, and marketing promotion. The experiment results show the broad applicability and promises of TCLX in synthesizing coalitions for multi-agent systems.

1 Introduction

Over the last decade, significant progress has been observed in game theory and temporal logics for modelling and verifying multi-agent systems. The model-checking technology can thus be employed to verify whether a multi-agent system model satisfies specification properties expressed in temporal logics, such as *alternating-time temporal logic* (*ATL*), *ATL**, *alternating μ-calculus* (*AMC*), *game logic* (*GL*) [1], *strategy logic* (*SL*) [4,14–16], *basic strategy interaction logic* (*BSIL*) [19], and *temporal cooperation logic* (*TCL*) [6]. These game temporal logics can express the cooperation of known agents in a coalition to achieve a goal. For example, an NBA coach can put down the TCL specification ⟨Bryant, Jeremy⟩((⟨+Durant⟩□¬*foul*) ∧ (⟨+Boozer⟩□◇*rebounds*)) for a game plan to win a game. This formula specifies that Kobe Bryant and Jeremy Lin

This work is partially supported by the National Key Basic Research Program of China under Grant No. 2014CB340701, and the National Key Research and Development Program of China under Grant No. 2017YFB0801900.

N. Polikarpova and S. Schneider (Eds.): IFM 2017, LNCS 10510, pp. 243–259, 2017.
DOI: 10.1007/978-3-319-66845-1_16

are both on the court with the following two options: (1) Kevin Durant is also on the court so that fouls will never be made; and (2) Carlos Boozer is also on the court so that many rebounds can be obtained.

However, the above temporal logics require the explicit specification of agents in a coalition and lack the flexibility for solving the new business challenges shown below.

- An NBA coach needs to assemble a team with diverse skills and good health conditions from a roster of players to maximize the opportunity of winning a game. But there are too many combinations that seem viable. The coach need efficient decision support.
- Facing an outbreak of Dengue fever, a disease-control agency need appropriate its limited budget to certain stations and villages so that the disease can be best contained. However the decision is not easy since many factors, including the distribution of the reported cases, the facilities in the stations, the traffics among the villages, and the profile of the populations, need be considered.

As can be seen from the above examples, in a more general setting, support is really needed in synthesizing an appropriate coalition, together with strategies for agents in the coalition, to achieve their goals. In this work, we propose *Temporal Cooperation Logic with Coalition Variables* (*TCLX*) to support such a need. TCLX is an extension of TCL, which is in turn an extension of ATL. For example, let X, Y, Z denote variables of agent sets. The TCLX formula $\langle X \rangle (\text{Bryant} \in X \wedge |X| \leq 2 \wedge \langle +Y \rangle (|Y| \leq 3 \wedge \Box \neg foul) \wedge \langle +Z \rangle (|Z| \leq 3 \wedge \Box \Diamond rebounds))$ specifies that the coach prefers two coalitions, $X \cup Y$ and $X \cup Z$, in a game with the following constraints: (1) both coalitions need Kobe Bryant and may share another player; (2) the coalition $X \cup Y$ always guarantees no foul; and (3) the coalition $X \cup Z$ always guarantees getting rebounds infinitely often. Given a game graph that models the playbooks of the coach and the opponent team, the skills and the health conditions of the players, a model-checker can thus support synthesizing the appropriate values of X, Y, and Z for the coach's goal.

The theoretical contributions of this work are as follows:

- TCLX is more expressive than TCL, and incomparable with AMC, GL, and ATL* in expressiveness.
- The satisfiability and model-checking problems of TCLX are 2-EXPTIME-complete and EXPTIME-complete, respectively, the same as those of TCL.

Thus, TCLX gains additional expressiveness over TCL without sacrificing the worst-case complexity of verification. We endeavoured to implement a TCLX model-checker and experiment with 15 TCLX properties against three game models. The model checking experiments show further promise of TCLX for real-world applications.

Related Work. Module checking has been proposed to verify whether an open system satisfies a specification property expressed in a temporal or strategic logic [7,8,11]. ATL, ATL*, AMC, and GL were presented with strategy quantifier $\langle\!\langle A \rangle\!\rangle$, where A is a finite set of agents [1]. A very expressive extension to ATL* was introduced with other players' strategies and memory constraints [2]. The model-checking problem of this extension has been shown to be decidable. Expressive constraints on strategies in concurrent games were proposed by extending μ-calculus with decision modalities [17]. The decidability of satisfiability problems in this direction was reported with new context constraints, e.g., bounding the number of moves by agents [12].

SL was introduced, allowing for the first-order quantification over strategies [4]. The decision procedure is however non-elementary. Fragments of SL were identified with 2-EXPTIME model-checking algorithms [14–16]. BSIL, a fragment of SL, was identified with only PSPACE model-checking complexity [19]. It can express certain useful properties that ATL*, AMC, and GL cannot. BSIL was also extended to TCL, which is strictly more expressive than BSIL [6]. The model-checking problem of TCL is however EXPTIME-complete. A coalition structure generation problem of a multi-agent system focuses on partitions of agents that can fulfill a combinatorial optimization objective [18], while the TCLX framework aims to synthesize dynamic coalitions fulfilling a temporal cooperation objective.

The rest of this paper is organized as follows. Section 2 presents the system model for TCLX, i.e., concurrent game graphs, while Sect. 3 defines the syntax and semantics of TCLX. Section 4 discusses the expressiveness of TCLX. Sections 5 and 6 respectively establish the complexity of the TCLX satisfiability and model-checking problem. Then, we present our implementation of the TCLX model-checker and report our experiments in Sect. 7. The paper is concluded in Sect. 8 with future work.

2   System Model

2.1   Motivating Example

Consider a vendor that intends to promote sales of her new product via a social network shown in Fig. 1a. A node represents a village. A single individual can be regarded as a village with only one inhabitant. Other than the vendor, there are three more individuals Ana, Bob, and Cindy, and five villages v1, ..., v5. Inside each node, we label the size of the population of the corresponding village below its name.

Suppose Ana, Bob, and Cindy are celebrities (or people with special power in spreading incoming messages). The neighboring villages of a celebrity can be regarded as the fan communities of the celebrity. The fans can easily follow their favorite celebrities' suggestions. The label on an arrow in Fig. 1a represents the action that the destination node receives a message from the corresponding source node. A celebrity can receive messages from the vendor or another celebrity, and can simultaneously send out messages to some of her/his fan communities. The vendor would need to decide which (and how many) celebrities she should hire so that the new product information can reach the maximum number of fans under budgetary and regulatory constraints, e.g., the maximum number

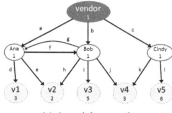

(a) A social network

villages	r			q_1			q_2			q_3			q_4			q_5			q_6			q_7		
vendor	0	1	0	0	0	1	0	0	1	0	0	1	0	0	1	0	0	1	0	0	1	0	0	1
Ana	1	0	0	0	1	0	1	0	0	0	1	0	0	1	0	1	0	0	0	1	0	0	1	0
Bob	1	0	0	1	0	0	0	1	0	0	1	0	1	0	0	0	1	0	0	1	0	0	1	0
Cindy	1	0	0	0	1	0	1	0	0	1	0	0	0	1	0	1	0	0	1	0	0	1	0	0
v_1	3	0	0	3	0	0	3	0	0	3	0	0	1	2	0	3	0	0	3	0	0	1	2	0
v_2	2	0	0	2	0	0	2	0	0	2	0	0	0	2	0	1	1	0	1	1	0	1	1	0
v_3	5	0	0	5	0	0	5	0	0	5	0	0	5	0	0	2	3	0	2	3	0	1	4	0
v_4	3	0	0	3	0	0	3	0	0	3	0	0	1	2	0	0	3	0	0	3	0	0	3	0
v_5	6	0	0	6	0	0	6	0	0	6	0	0	1	5	0	6	0	0	6	0	0	6	0	0

(b) States, each of which is a 9 × 3 matrix with the first, second, and third columns respectively for the numbers of inhabitants in modes S, I and R.

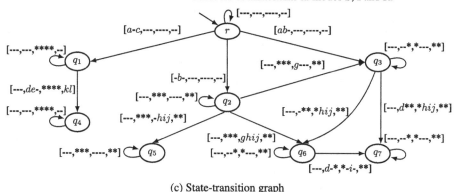

(c) State-transition graph

Fig. 1. A multi-agent game

of celebrities that she can hire. We aim to design a framework to technically support such a need in the general setting of social networks.

SIR model [10] is the most popular model in social network computing. Each individual can be in one of the three modes: S (susceptible), I (infected), or R (recovered). A village may own an internal mechanism so that its inhabitants may distribute over various modes at a moment. Thus, we can build a finite behavior model of the dynamics of marketing promotion upon a social network. Herein, we use counter-abstraction [5] to model the villages. For each village, we only record the respective number of inhabitants in mode S, I, and R, as shown in Fig. 1b.

Then, Fig. 1c shows such a finite behavior model, a concurrent game graph. It defines the behavioral structure among the states, represented by the ovals. The arrows in Fig. 1c represent state transitions labeled with move vectors modelling concurrent message spreading. We use a word like "xyz" to denote the simultaneous actions by an agent. Let '-' denote "*no move*" and '*' denote "*any move*". The move labels for communities v1,...,v5 are omitted in the move vectors because these communities always make no move. For example, on the arrow from state q_1 to q_4, the move vector [---, de-, ****, kl] indicates that in this transition, no action is made by the vendor (and the inhabitants in communities v1,...,v5), only actions d, e are by Ana respectively to v1 and v2, any action can be by Bob, and only actions k, l are by Cindy respectively to v4 and v5. It can be seen that such a game graph can flexibly and conveniently model various interaction scenarios in many application domains.

2.2 Concurrent Game Graphs

Let d denote a vector of dimension m and $d[a]$ denote its a-th element for $a \in [1, m]$. Let $\mathcal{AP}$ be a set of atomic propositions. A concurrent game graph of m agents (indexed $1, \ldots, m$, respectively) is defined as a tuple $\mathcal{G} = \langle \mathcal{Q}, r, \lambda, \Sigma, \delta \rangle$, where

- $\mathcal{Q}$ is the set of states, with $r \in \mathcal{Q}$ the *initial state* (or *root*) of $\mathcal{G}$;
- $\lambda : \mathcal{Q} \to 2^{\mathcal{AP}}$ is a proposition labeling function;
- $\Sigma = S_1 \times \ldots \times S_m$ is a set of move vectors, where S_a is a set of moves available to agent $a \in [1, m]$.
- $\delta : \mathcal{Q} \times \Sigma \to \mathcal{Q}$ is a transition function such that $\delta(q, d)$ is the successor state reached from state $q \in \mathcal{Q}$ on move vector $d \in \Sigma$.

For the convenience of presentation and proof, δ is assumed total, i.e., defined for all states and move vectors. In practice, when a move vector is not admitted, we may introduce an artificial failure state as the destination state or add a self-loop transition for the move vector. Let $E_\mathcal{G} = \{(q, \delta(q, d)) \mid q \in \mathcal{Q}, d \in \Sigma\}$ be the set of labeled transitions.

An infinite path $\rho = q_0 q_1 \cdots$ is a *play* in $\mathcal{G}$ if for every $k \in \mathbb{N}$, $(q_k, q_{k+1}) \in E_\mathcal{G}$. A *play prefix* is a play of finite length. The length of a play prefix $\pi = q_0 \cdots q_k$, denoted $|\pi|$, is defined as $k + 1$. A play can be viewed as an *infinite* play prefix with length ∞. Given a play or a play prefix $\rho = q_0 q_1 \cdots$ and $0 \leq j < |\pi|$, let $\rho(j) = q_j$. For a play prefix π, let $last(\pi)$ denote the last state in π, i.e., $\pi(|\pi| - 1)$. Given a play (prefix) ρ and $0 \leq h < k < |\pi|$, let $\rho[h, k]$ denote $\rho(h) \cdots \rho(k)$. If ρ is a play, then $\rho[h, \infty)$ denotes the infinite tail $\rho(h)\rho(h + 1) \cdots$.

A *strategy* for an agent a is a function from $\mathcal{Q}^*$ to S_a. A *coalition* α is a partial mapping from $[1, m]$ to strategies. Let $defined(\alpha) \stackrel{\text{def}}{=} \{a \mid 1 \leq a \leq m, \alpha(a) \text{ is defined}\}$. An agent a is *in a coalition* α if $a \in defined(\alpha)$. A play ρ is *compatible* with a coalition α if for every $k \in \mathbb{N}$, there exists a $d \in \Sigma$ such that $\delta(\rho(k), d) = \rho(k + 1)$ and for every $a \in defined(\alpha)$, $\alpha(a)(\rho[0, k]) = d[a]$.

3 TCLX

TCLX extends the *strategy interaction quantification* of TCL with coalition variables in the declaration of strategies.

Syntax. A TCLX formula ϕ is constructed with the following three syntax rules:

$$\phi ::= p \mid \neg\phi_1 \mid \phi_1 \vee \phi_2 \mid \langle X \rangle \psi$$
$$\psi ::= \eta \mid \psi_1 \vee \psi_2 \mid \psi_1 \wedge \psi_2 \mid \langle -X \rangle \psi_1 \mid \langle +X \rangle \psi_1 \mid \bigcirc \psi_1 \mid \eta U \psi_1 \mid \eta W \psi_1$$
$$\eta ::= \phi \mid c \in X_1 \mid |X_1| \sim c \mid |X_1| \sim |X_2| \mid X_1 \subseteq X_2$$
$$\mid \eta_1 \vee \eta_2 \mid \eta_1 \wedge \eta_2 \mid \langle -X \rangle \eta_1 \mid \bigcirc \eta_1 \mid \eta_1 U \eta_2 \mid \eta_1 W \eta_2$$

where X, X_1, and X_2 are coalition variables that range over sets of agent indices,

c is an integer constant, and $\sim$ is one of $\leq, <, =, \neq, >$, and $\geq$. Standard short-hands like Boolean conjunction, implication, and always modality ($\square$) can be adopted as follows.

$$true \equiv p \vee (\neg p) \qquad \Diamond \phi_1 \equiv true\,\mathrm{U}\phi_1 \qquad \phi_1 \wedge \phi_2 \equiv \neg((\neg\phi_1)\vee(\neg\phi_2))$$
$$false \equiv \neg true \qquad \square\phi_1 \equiv \phi_1\mathrm{W}false \qquad \phi_1 \Rightarrow \phi_2 \equiv (\neg\phi_1) \vee \phi_2$$
$$\langle A\rangle\psi \equiv \langle X\rangle(\psi \wedge |X| = |A| \wedge \textstyle\bigwedge_{a\in A} a \in X)$$
$$\langle +A\rangle\psi \equiv \langle +X\rangle(\psi \wedge |X| = |A| \wedge \textstyle\bigwedge_{a\in A} a \in X)$$
$$\langle -A\rangle\psi \equiv \langle -X\rangle(\psi \wedge |X| = |A| \wedge \textstyle\bigwedge_{a\in A} a \in X)$$

Formula ϕ, ψ, and η are respectively called *state* formulas, *tree* formulas, and *path* formulas. Given a formula like $\langle X\rangle\psi$ (respectively, $\langle +X\rangle\psi$ or $\langle -X\rangle\psi$), ψ is called the *scope* of X. Intuitively,

- $\langle X\rangle$ is a *coalition binder* (*CB*) that cancels bindings of strategies to all agents, finds a set A of agents for X, and declares a new set of strategies bound to the agents in A to enforce the scope of X.
- $\langle +X\rangle$ is a *coalition interacter* (*CI*) that finds a set A of agents for X, and declares a new set of strategies bound to the agents in A to enforce the scope of X. Any strategy binding inherited from the ancestor scopes that conflicts with the new strategy bindings are overridden.
- $\langle -X\rangle$ is a *coalition releaser* (*CR*) that finds a set A of agents for X and cancels their inherited strategy bindings from the ancestor scopes, if any.

If there are two declarations with the same variable names, the inner one overrides the outer one in the inner scope. For example, in the formula $\langle X\rangle \bigcirc (p \wedge \langle +X\rangle(|X| < 3 \wedge q\mathrm{U}w))$, the X in $|X| < 3$ refers to the one declared in CI $\langle +X\rangle$. In practice, we can use the positions of the coalition variables in a TCLX formula to tell one from another. For example, the formula $\langle X\rangle((\langle +Y\rangle\square p) \wedge \langle +Y\rangle(\Diamond q \wedge \langle X\rangle \bigcirc \neg p))$ can be equivalently rewritten as $\langle X_1\rangle((\langle +X_2\rangle\square p) \wedge \langle +X_3\rangle(\Diamond q \wedge \langle X_4\rangle \bigcirc \neg p))$ in TCLX. For the convenience of presentation, we assume that no two coalition variables are the same in a TCLX formula without loss of generality.

As in TCL [6], we do not allow universal CIs and CRs in the syntax of TCLX as the respective duals of existential CIs and CRs, because such duals result in a too succinct fragment of the strategy logic with non-elementary model-checking complexity. In general, the model-checking complexity is exponential to the number of alternations between existential and universal quantifications. As a consequence, negations in front of existential CIs and CRs are also not allowed since universal CIs and CRs can be encoded as the negations of existential CIs and CRs.

Semantics. Due to the design of TCLX, strategy bindings can only effectively happen when either a non-trivial CB or a non-trivial CI is interpreted. As the introduction of additional strategies through a non-trivial CI is governed by a *positive* Boolean combination, all strategy selections can be performed concurrently. This leads us to the concept of coalition schemes. Let $\mathrm{Var}(\phi)$ be the set of coalition variables in a TCLX formula ϕ. For a set of m agents, a *coalition scheme* σ of ϕ is a mapping from $\mathrm{Var}(\phi)$ to subsets of $[1, m]$. Let $\sigma(\phi)$ be the

TCL formula identical to ϕ except that every $X \in Var(\phi)$ is replaced by $\sigma(X)$. The existence of a coalition scheme refers to all the strategies introduced by the CBs or CIs in a TCLX formula, but only the strategies introduced by the respective CB and the CIs in its scope are relevant. Note that it suffices to introduce new strategies at the points where eventualities become true for the first time, because the validity of a TCLX state formula cannot depend on that of the left-hand side of an until (U) or a weak until (W) *after* the first time it has been satisfied. Therefore, the strategies do not really depend on the positions in a play in which they are invoked, and hence we can guess them up-front.

The semantics of TCLX also follows the assumption of ATL/ATL*, i.e., the number of agents (concurrency size) in a game graph must be fixed. Let $\alpha_1\alpha_2$ denote the update of partial function α_1 with partial function α_2, i.e., if agent a is defined in α_2, $\alpha_1\alpha_2(a) = \alpha_2(a)$; else if a is defined in α_1, $\alpha_1\alpha_2(a) = \alpha_1(a)$; otherwise, a is undefined in $\alpha_1\alpha_2$. Let $[X \mapsto A]$ denote a partial function that only maps X to A.

We say that a concurrent game graph $\mathcal{G} = \langle \mathcal{Q}, r, \lambda, \Sigma, \delta \rangle$ satisfies a TCLX formula ϕ at a state $q \in \mathcal{Q}$ with a coalition scheme σ and a coalition α, denoted $\mathcal{G}, q \models_\sigma^\alpha \phi$, where σ is used to evaluate the coalition variables, and α directs the moves of the present coalition. Formally, $\mathcal{G}, q \models_\sigma^\alpha \phi$ is true iff the following inductive constraints hold.

- $\mathcal{G}, q \models_\sigma^\alpha p$ iff $p \in \lambda(q)$.
- $\mathcal{G}, q \models_\sigma^\alpha \neg\phi_1$ iff $\mathcal{G}, q \models_\sigma^\alpha \phi_1$ is false.
- $\mathcal{G}, q \models_\sigma^\alpha \phi_1 \vee \phi_2$ iff $\mathcal{G}, q \models_\sigma^\alpha \phi_1$ or $\mathcal{G}, q \models_\sigma^\alpha \phi_2$.
- $\mathcal{G}, q \models_\sigma^\alpha \langle X \rangle \psi$ iff there exists a coalition β such that for all plays ρ from q compatible with β, ψ is satisfied by ρ with coalition scheme $[X \mapsto defined(\beta)]$, denoted $\rho \models_{[X \mapsto defined(\beta)]}^\beta \psi$.

Given a tree or path formula ψ, a play ρ, and a coalition scheme σ and a coalition α, $\rho \models_\sigma^\alpha \psi$ iff the following inductive constraints hold.

- $\rho \models_\sigma^\alpha \phi$ iff $\mathcal{G}, \rho(0) \models_\sigma^\alpha \phi$.
- $\rho \models_\sigma^\alpha \psi_1 \vee \psi_2$ iff $\rho \models_\sigma^\alpha \psi_1$ or $\rho \models_\sigma^\alpha \psi_2$.
- $\rho \models_\sigma^\alpha \psi_1 \wedge \psi_2$ iff $\rho \models_\sigma^\alpha \psi_1$ and $\rho \models_\sigma^\alpha \psi_2$.
- $\rho \models_\sigma^\alpha \bigcirc \psi_1$ iff $\rho[1, \infty) \models_\sigma^\alpha \psi_1$.
- $\rho \models_\sigma^\alpha \eta U \psi_1$ if there exists a $k \in \mathbb{N}$ such that $\rho[k, \infty) \models_\sigma^\alpha \psi_1$ and for all $j \in [0, k-1]$, $\rho[j, \infty) \models_\sigma^\alpha \eta$.
- $\rho \models_\sigma^\alpha \eta W \psi_1$ iff $\rho \models_\sigma^\alpha \eta U \psi_1$ or for all $k \in \mathbb{N}$, $\rho[k, \infty) \models_\sigma^\alpha \eta$.
- $\rho \models_\sigma^\alpha \langle -X \rangle \psi_1$ iff there exists a set $A \subseteq [1, m]$ and a coalition β identical to α except that for all $a \in A$, $\beta(a)$ is undefined, such that for all plays ρ' compatible with β starting at $\rho(0)$, $\rho' \models_{\sigma[X \mapsto A]}^\beta \psi_1$.
- $\rho \models_\sigma^\alpha \langle +X \rangle \psi_1$ iff there exists a coalition β such that for all plays ρ' compatible with $\alpha\beta$ starting at $\rho(0)$, $\rho' \models_{\sigma[X \mapsto defined(\beta)]}^{\alpha\beta} \psi_1$.
- $\rho \models_\sigma^\alpha c \in X_1$ iff $c \in \sigma(X_1)$.
- $\rho \models_\sigma^\alpha |X_1| \sim c$ iff $|\sigma(X_1)| \sim c$.
- $\rho \models_\sigma^\alpha |X_1| \sim |X_2|$ iff $|\sigma(X_1)| \sim |\sigma(X_2)|$.
- $\rho \models_\sigma^\alpha X_1 \subseteq X_2$ iff $\sigma(X_1) \subseteq \sigma(X_2)$.

Then, a concurrent game graph $\mathcal{G} = \langle \mathcal{Q}, r, \lambda, \Sigma, \delta \rangle$ satisfies a TCLX formula ϕ, denoted $\mathcal{G} \models \phi$, iff $\mathcal{G}, r \models_{[]}^{[]} \phi$, where $[]$ is the empty function undefined on everything.

4   Expressiveness of TCLX

Note that we follow the tradition of ATL [1] and use game graphs of fixed concurrency sizes to establish our expressiveness result. Formulas ϕ_1 and ϕ_2 respectively of two languages are *equivalent* if for every game graph $\mathcal{G}$ and every state q of $\mathcal{G}$, q satisfies ϕ_1 if and only if q satisfies ϕ_2. A formula ϕ is *not expressible in L* if there is no formula in L equivalent to ϕ. A language L_1 is *as expressive as* another language L_2 if for every formula $\phi_2 \in L_2$, there is a formula $\phi_1 \in L_1$ equivalent to ϕ_2. L_1 is *more expressive than* L_2 if L_1 is as expressive as L_2 while L_2 is not as expressive as L_1.

We show in this section that TCLX is more expressive than TCL, and incomparable with AMC, GL, and ATL*. Intuitively, a formula like $\langle X \rangle \psi$ (respectively, $\langle +X \rangle \psi$ or $\langle -X \rangle \psi$) is true if and only if there is a set A of agent indices such that $\langle A \rangle \psi$ (respectively $\langle +A \rangle \psi$ or $\langle -A \rangle \psi$) is true according to the TCL semantics. In fact, TCL can be viewed as a subclass of TCLX. For example, the TCL formula $\langle 1 \rangle \Diamond ((\langle +2 \rangle \bigcirc p) \wedge \langle 2, 3 \rangle \Box q)$ is equivalent to $\langle X \rangle (1 \in X \wedge |X| = 1 \wedge \Diamond ((\langle +Y \rangle (2 \in Y \wedge |Y| = 1 \wedge \bigcirc p)) \wedge \langle Z \rangle (2 \in Z \wedge 3 \in Z \wedge |Z| = 2 \wedge \Box q)))$. With such translation, it is clear that every TCL formula can be reduced in linear time to an equivalent TCLX formula, and Lemma 1 can be established.

Lemma 1. *TCLX is at least as expressive as TCL.*   □

Let $c_{\max}(\phi)$ be the greatest integer constant used in formula ϕ. Let $c_{\max}(\phi) = 0$ if no integer constant exists in ϕ. For example, $c_{\max}(\langle X \rangle (3 \in X \wedge \langle +Y \rangle (|Y| < 6 \wedge \Box p))) = 6$.

Lemma 2. *The TCLX formula $\xi : \langle X \rangle (|X| \leq 1 \wedge \bigcirc p)$ is not expressible in TCL.*

Proof. For every TCL formula ϕ, we build two game graphs G_1, G_2 in Fig. 2 that ϕ cannot distinguish, while ξ can. In this figure, an edge label $[*, \ldots, *, a, b]$ means all the move vectors, of which the last two elements are a and b in sequence, can trigger the labelled transition. Note that an agent index constant in a TCL formula can only occur in an agent index set A in a quantifier like $\langle A \rangle, \langle +A \rangle$ or $\langle -A \rangle$. The game graphs G_1, G_2 are both for $c_{\max}(\phi) + 1$ agents. It is apparent that G_1 does not satisfy ξ, while G_2 does.

Let K be the set of agent index constants used in ϕ. Note that $c_{\max}(\phi) + 1 \notin K$. According to the semantics of TCL, there must be a path subformula ψ of ϕ, a coalition scheme σ, and a subset $V \subseteq Var(\phi)$ with the following constraints.

- ψ is in the scope of the variables in V;
- Exactly one of $G_1, r, \sigma \models \psi$ and $G_2, r, \sigma \models \psi$ is true. (Note that in TCL, $G_1, r, \sigma \models \psi$ means ψ is true along every play compatible with σ from r in G_1.)

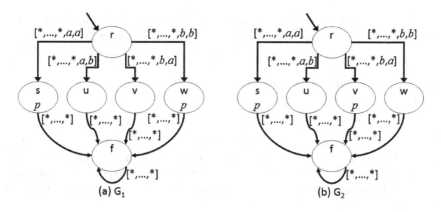

Fig. 2. Game graphs for the expressiveness of TCLX

However, $c_{\max}(\phi) + 1 \notin \bigcup_{X \in V} \sigma(X)$ and agent $c_{\max}(\phi) + 1$ is not involved in the strategies of agents in $\bigcup_{X \in V} \sigma(X)$ to enforce ψ. Without the cooperation by agent $c_{\max}(\phi) + 1$, ψ cannot distinguish G_1 and G_2 at r with σ since all the trace sets of agents $1, \ldots, c_{\max}(\phi)$ are the same $\{\{p\}\emptyset^*, \emptyset^*\}$. The lemma is thus proven. □

We close this section by remarking on the incomparability of TCLX with AMC, GL, and ATL* in expressiveness. The argument pretty much follows the related lemmas in [6,19] that show $\langle 1 \rangle ((\langle +2 \rangle \Diamond p) \wedge \langle +2 \rangle \Diamond q)$ is inexpressible in AMC, GL, and ATL* while some formulas respectively in AMC, GL, and ATL* are inexpressible in TCL.

5   Satisfiability of TCLX

The key observation is that if two agents in a game graph $\mathcal{G}$ always agree to, or not to, enforce path properties with respect to every coalition, we can reduce $\mathcal{G}$ to a $\mathcal{G}'$, in which the two agents behave as one agent and every other agent behaves the same as in $\mathcal{G}$. For example, if agents 2 and 3 are such coalition partners in $\mathcal{G}$, and are not constants used in a TCLX formula ϕ, we can construct a $\mathcal{G}'$ with agents 2 and 3 replaced with a new agent $(2, 3)$ such that for every pair of moves e and f issued by agents 2 and 3, respectively, in a transition in $\mathcal{G}$, agent $(2, 3)$ issues move (e, f) in the corresponding transition in $\mathcal{G}'$. Then we can show that $\mathcal{G}$ satisfies ϕ if and only if $\mathcal{G}'$ satisfies ϕ.

This observation sheds light on the finite structure of coalition schemes in satisfying a TCLX formula ϕ. The finite structure is indeed the intersection relation among all the values assigned to the coalition variables. Given a coalition scheme σ of ϕ, a group of agent indices greater than $c_{\max}(\phi)$ that agree in enforcing path obligations according to σ can be identified as a subset of $Var(\phi)$.

Example 1. For the TCLX formula $\phi = \langle X \rangle (1 \in X \wedge \Diamond ((\langle +Y \rangle \Box p) \wedge \langle +Z \rangle \Diamond q))$, suppose we have a game graph $\mathcal{G}$ of five agents and a coalition scheme σ such *that* $\sigma(X) = \{1, 2, 3, 4\}$, $\sigma(Y) = \{2, 3\}$, *and* $\sigma(Z) = \{2, 3\}$. *As can be seen, both* 1 *and* 4 *are in* $\sigma(X)$, *both* 2 *and* 3 *are in* $\sigma(X), \sigma(Y)$, *and* $\sigma(Z)$, *while* 5 *is in none of* $\sigma(X)$, $\sigma(Y)$, *and* $\sigma(Z)$. *Thus, agents* 1 *and* 4 *are identified with* $\{X\}$, *agents* 2 *and* 3 *are identified with* $\{X, Y, Z\}$, *while agent* 5 *is identified with the empty set. This matches our observation that agents* 1 *and* 4 *can be merged to one agent in* σ, *and so can agents* 2 *and* 3. □

The reduction by merging agents can be repeated until there are no more than $2^{|\operatorname{Var}(\phi)|}$ agents. However, we only merge those agents with indices greater than $c_{\max}(\phi)$. This is because if we also merge agents with indices no greater than $c_{\max}(\phi)$, we would have to reduce ϕ by lowering some agent index constants in ϕ. Such reduction can be messy and does not affect the complexity of the satisfiability problem.

Suppose $\mathcal{G}$ is a game graph of m agents and there are agent indices a, b such that $c_{\max}(\phi) < a < b \leq m$ and for every $X \in \operatorname{Var}(\phi)$, $a \in \sigma(X)$ if and only if $b \in \sigma(X)$. Let $\operatorname{merge}([e_1, \ldots, e_m], a, b) = [f_1, \ldots, f_{m-1}]$ with $f_a = (e_a, e_b)$ and the following restrictions.

- For every $i \in [1, a-1] \cup [a+1, b-1]$, $e_i = f_i$.
- For every $i \in [b+1, m]$, $e_i = f_{i-1}$.

Then, we define $\operatorname{merge}(\mathcal{G}, a, b) = \langle m - 1, \mathcal{Q}, r, \lambda, \Sigma', \delta' \rangle$ and coalition $\operatorname{merge}(\sigma, a, b)$ out of $\mathcal{G}$ and σ as follows.

- $\Sigma' = \{\operatorname{merge}([e_1, \ldots, e_m], a, b) \mid [e_1, \ldots, e_m] \in \Sigma\}$.
- $\delta(q, [e_1, \ldots, e_m]) = \delta'(q, \operatorname{merge}([e_1, \ldots, e_m], a, b))$ for any $q \in Q$ and $[e_1, \ldots, e_m] \in \Sigma$.
- $\operatorname{merge}(\sigma, a, b)(X) = (\sigma(X) \cap [1, b-1]) \cup \{c - 1 \mid c \in \sigma(X) \cap [b+1, m]\}$ for any $X \in \operatorname{Var}(\phi)$.

The following lemma shows the sufficiency and necessity for the satisfaction of ϕ by $\operatorname{merge}(\mathcal{G}, a, b)$.

Lemma 3. *Assume a TCLX formula* ϕ, *a game graph* $\mathcal{G}$, *agent indices* a, b, *and a coalition scheme* σ *such that* $c_{\max}(\phi) < a < b$ *and for every coalition variable* $X \in \operatorname{Var}(\phi)$, $a \in \sigma(X)$ *if and only if* $b \in \sigma(X)$. *Then,* $\mathcal{G} \models \sigma(\phi)$ *if and only if* $\operatorname{merge}(\mathcal{G}, a, b) \models \phi$.

Proof. In the "only if" direction, given a strategy-pruned tree T of $\mathcal{G}$ as an evidence for the satisfaction of $\sigma(\phi)$ in TCL, we can construct a strategy-pruned tree, isomorphic to T, of $\operatorname{merge}(\mathcal{G}, a, b)$ as an evidence for the satisfaction of $\operatorname{merge}(\sigma, a, b)(\phi)$ in TCL. The construction is obvious from the definitions of $\operatorname{merge}(\mathcal{G}, a, b)$ and $\operatorname{merge}(\sigma, a, b)$. The "if" direction can be proved in a similar way. □

Lemma 3 leads to the following lemma for the finite models of TCLX formulas.

Lemma 4. *Given a satisfiable TCLX formula* ϕ, *there is a game graph with no more than* $2^{|\operatorname{Var}(\phi)|} + c_{\max}(\phi)$ *agents satisfying* ϕ.

Proof. Suppose that we have a game graph $\mathcal{G}$ of $m > 2^{|\text{Var}(\phi)|} + c_{\max}(\phi)$ agents and a coalition scheme σ such that $\mathcal{G} \models \sigma(\phi)$. Then, there must be two agent indices $a, b > c_{\max}(\phi)$ such that for every coalition variable X of ϕ, $a \in \sigma(X)$ if and only if $b \in \sigma(X)$. According to Lemma 3, we can reduce $\mathcal{G}$ to a game graph of $m - 1$ agents that also satisfies ϕ. By repeating this reduction step, eventually we can obtain a game graph of no more than $2^{|\text{Var}(\phi)|} + c_{\max}(\phi)$ agents that satisfies ϕ. □

Then, we can establish the main theorem of this section in the following.

Theorem 1. *The satisfiability problem of TCLX is 2-EXPTIME-complete.*

Proof. This problem is 2-EXPTIME-hard since every TCL formula can be straightforwardly reduced to a TCLX formula in linear time and the TCL satisfiability problem is 2-EXPTIME-complete.

Given a satisfiable TCLX formula ϕ, Lemma 4 indicates that there is a game graph $\mathcal{G}$ of no more than $2^{|\text{Var}(\phi)|} + c_{\max}(\phi)$ agents satisfying ϕ. Then, there must be a satisfying coalition scheme σ of $\mathcal{G}$ for ϕ such that $\mathcal{G} \models \sigma(\phi)$ in the TCL semantics. This implies that we can enumerate all the values of coalition schemes to search for σ as an evidence for the satisfaction of ϕ by $\mathcal{G}$. The value of one coalition variable is a subset of at most $2^{|\text{Var}(\phi)|} + c_{\max}(\phi)$ agent indices. Thus, the total enumeration is of size $2^{|\text{Var}(\phi)|(2^{|\text{Var}(\phi)|} + c_{\max}(\phi))}$ and of doubly exponential complexity. This means that we can break the satisfiability problem of ϕ to doubly exponentially many instances of the TCL satisfiability problem. Since the TCL satisfiability problem is 2-EXPTIME-complete, the satisfiability problem of TCLX can also be answered in 2-EXPTIME. Thus, the TCLX satisfiability problem is 2-EXPTIME-complete. □

6 TCLX Model-Checking

TCLX model-checking problem is EXPTIME-hard since TCLX can be viewed as a super-class of TCL, of which the model-checking problem is EXPTIME-complete.

If a TCLX formula ϕ is satisfied by a game graph $\mathcal{G}$ of m agents, then there must be a coalition scheme σ such that $\mathcal{G} \models \sigma(\phi)$ in the TCL semantics. This implies that we can build an EXPTIME algorithm for model-checking ϕ by repetitively calling an EXPTIME TCL model-checking algorithm as a subroutine, as shown in Algorithm 1, for each value of σ. The correctness of the algorithm is straightforward according to the TCLX semantics. Thus we do not provide the proof in this paper.

Altogether the number of valuations of all the coalition variables at the for-loop in Algorithm 1 is $(2^m)^{|\text{Var}(\phi)|} = 2^{m|\text{Var}(\phi)|}$. Thus, model-checking a TCLX formula ϕ can be done in EXPTIME if we call an EXPTIME algorithm for the model-checking of the TCL formula $\sigma(\phi)$. This observation leads to the following theorem.

Theorem 2. *The model-checking problem of TCLX is EXPTIME-complete.* □

Algorithm 1. modelCheck($\mathcal{G}, \phi$)

---

for every subset $A_1, \ldots, A_n$ of $[1, m]$ for variable $X_1, \ldots, X_n$ in Var(ϕ) respectively **do**
  Construct σ such that for every $i \in [1, m]$, $\sigma(X_i) = A_i$.
  if $\mathcal{G} \models \sigma(\phi)$ /* by calling the TCL model-checking algorithm in [6] */ **then return** *true*
  end if
end for
return *false*

---

7   Implementation and Experiments

We implemented a TCLX model-checker by extending the on-the-fly model-checking algorithm in [6]. In evaluating a state formula $\langle X \rangle \psi$, a tree formula $\langle +X \rangle \psi$, or $\langle -X \rangle \psi$, we replace the evaluation procedure in the TCL model-checking algorithm by a loop that for every value A of X, uses this procedure to evaluate ψ. Three game models are built in our experiments: a network security system, a software development project, and the marketing promotion model described in Sect. 2.1. Each model is checked against five TCLX properties of various syntax structures by our TCLX model-checker.

Network Security. Figure 3 defines a typical network attack and defense game model with three attackers (agents 1, 2, 3) and one administrator (agent 4). This is inspired from the network security game presented in [13]. The administrator manages a Web server with an HTTP service and an FTP service to support Web pages and data access. On the contrary, agent 1 can perform an HTTP attack (h) to deface the website, or to launch other attacks through implanted viruses; agent 2 can perform an FTP attack (f) to steal the confidential data on the server through implanted sniffer programs; while agent 3 is the attacker that can plant viruses or sniffer programs (p) into the hacked server. Apparently, the attackers need to form a coalition to attack the server.

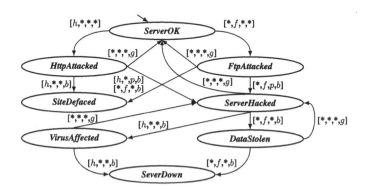

Fig. 3. Network security game graph

The administrator may perform well to repair the hacked server successfully, or fail to do so. These two kinds of responses to the attacks are abstracted as the moves g and b of the administrator, respectively. The self-loop transitions due to the unadmitted move vectors are omitted in Fig. 3, as well as in Fig. 4.

TCLX properties (1)–(5) in Table 1 are designed to verify the robustness of the Web server under the maintenance of the administrator. We reuse the name of a state as its atomic proposition label. Propositions *ServerOK*, *SiteDefaced*, *SeverDown*, *DataStolen*, and *VirusAffected* indicate that the server runs normally, the website is defaced, the server is broken down, the confidential data is stolen, and that a virus is implanted, respectively. The website is fine (*SiteOK*) unless it is defaced or the server is down.

Property (1) queries for exactly one agent that the administrator may fail to stop from defacing the website or breaking down the server. Agent 1 is a solution agent that can achieve this objective alone. Property (2) queries for at most two agents that the administrator may fail to stop from stealing the confidential data. Agents 2 and 3 can form a solution coalition to achieve this objective. Property (4) queries for exactly one agent that can steal the confidential data totally on its own, with keeping the server running normally, while property (5) queries for a coalition of agents that can steal the confidential data without agent 3. Both properties are false. This highlights the significance of a coalition with agent 3. Property (3) is designed for state *VirusAffected*, at which a virus is implanted. It means to check whether the administrator may recover the affected server back to normal. At state *VirusAffected*, the administrator can perform well on his responsibility.

Table 1. TCLX Properties used for the three game models

$\langle 4\rangle\langle +X\rangle(\|X\| == 1 \wedge \Diamond(SiteDefaced \vee SeverDown))$	(1)
$\langle 4\rangle\langle +X\rangle(\|X\| \leq 2 \wedge \Diamond DataStolen)$	(2)
$\langle\emptyset\rangle\Box(VirusAffected \rightarrow \langle 4\rangle\Diamond ServerOK)$	(3)
$\langle X\rangle(\|X\| == 1 \wedge (SiteOK \text{ U } (SiteOK \wedge DataStolen)))$	(4)
$\langle X\rangle(3 \notin X \wedge \Diamond DataStolen)$	(5)
$\langle 5\rangle \bigcirc (\langle X\rangle\Diamond Success) \vee \langle 5\rangle \bigcirc \Diamond Failure$	(6)
$\langle\emptyset\rangle\Box(Imp_{01} \rightarrow \langle X\rangle(X \subseteq \{1,2\} \wedge \langle +Y\rangle(Y \subseteq \{3,4\} \wedge \Diamond Success)))$	(7)
$\langle 3,4\rangle \bigcirc (\langle X\rangle\Diamond Success)$	(8)
$\langle\emptyset\rangle\Box\left(\begin{array}{l}(Testing_{11} \vee Testing_{01} \vee Testing_{10} \vee Testing_{00}) \rightarrow \\ \langle X\rangle(\|X\| == 1 \wedge (3 \in X \vee 4 \in X) \wedge \bigcirc(Success \vee Failure))\end{array}\right)$	(9)
$\langle X\rangle(\|X\| < 5 \wedge \Diamond Success)$	(10)
$\langle X\rangle(\|X\| < 4 \wedge \Diamond q_7)$	(11)
$\langle X\rangle(\|X\| < 3 \wedge \Diamond q_5 \wedge \langle -Y\rangle \bigcirc (\|Y\| == 1 \wedge q_2))$	(12)
$\langle X\rangle(\|X\| == 1 \wedge \langle +Y\rangle(\{2,3\} \subseteq Y \wedge \Diamond q_4))$	(13)
$\langle X\rangle(\|X\| == 1 \wedge \Diamond(\langle +Y\rangle \bigcirc (\|Y\| == 1 \wedge q_6)))$	(14)
$\langle X\rangle(\|X\| < 2 \wedge \bigcirc(\langle +Y\rangle \bigcirc (\|Y\| == 1 \wedge \langle +Z\rangle \bigcirc (\|Z\| == 1 \wedge q_6))))$	(15)

Software Development. Software development is teamwork. A software project team needs to cooperate closely to release a software product in time. In Fig. 4, we model as a concurrent game a typical software development process of a project team with 5 engineers. Agents 1 and 2 are responsible for software design and implementation; agents 3 and 4 are testing engineers; while agent 5 is the project manager in charge of requirement analysis and software design. We abuse the move g (respectively, d) to denote that an agent delivers an excellent (respectively, poor) performance of his duty.

The perfect work-flow in the game goes through states $Requirement$, $Design_1$, Imp_{11}, $Testing_{11}$, and $Success$ in sequence, when all the agents act responsibly. Otherwise, the project may fail to release ($ReleaseFailed$) due to a poor requirement analysis (via state $Design_0$), a poor design (via state Imp_{01} or Imp_{00}), a poor implementation (via state $Testing_{01}$, $Testing_{10}$, or $Testing_{00}$), or a poor test. The project fails ($Failure$) if it reaches $ReleaseFailed$ or is blocked before release. In these circumstances, the team may rely on the design, implementation, or testing engineers (whichever applicable) to save the project from failing. For example, at state $Testing_{01}$, a good test by agents 3 and 4 can help agents 1 and 2 to fix bugs in a poor implementation, and to deliver a nice implementation for testing at state $Testing_{11}$. However, a poor requirement analysis will lead the project towards failure inevitably via state $Design_0$.

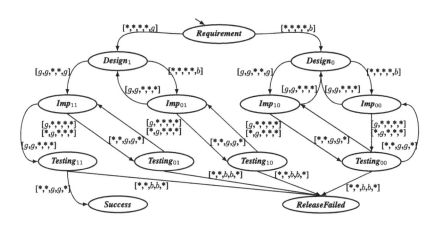

Fig. 4. Software development game graph

TCLX properties (6)–(10) in Table 1 are designed to verify the performance of the whole team. At state $Requirement$, property (6) means that the project manager (i.e., agent 5) can lead to a next state where a coalition of team members can enforce the success of the project, or to a next state where the project is destined to fail. The team itself is the maximum coalition for the success of the project. At state Imp_{01}, property (7) queries for a coalition with only design, implementation and testing engineers that can remedy a poor design and lead the project towards success. Agents 1, 2, 3, and 4 constitute the maximum coalition for this objective. Note that state Imp_{01} implies that the project manager has fully and precisely analyzed the requirements of the project. At state *Requirement*, property (8) means that the testing engineers can lead to a next state where a coalition of team members can enforce the success of the project, while property (10) queries for a coalition with some but not all engineers that can cooperate together to ensure the success of the project, irrespective of the performance of the rest engineers. At any of states $Testing_{11}$, $Testing_{01}$, $Testing_{10}$, or $Testing_{00}$, property (9) queries for a testing engineer who can solely determine the success or failure of the project. These three properties are false with respect to the corresponding states. This confirms the importance of teamwork for a software development project.

Marketing Promotion. We also verify the motivating example shown in Sect. 2.1 with TCLX properties (11)–(15) in Table 1. These properties relate the coverage of the vender's new product message with the celebrities that can help spread it. For instance, only Bob (i.e., agent 3) receives the message at state q_2, then forwards it to his fans at state q_5. At state q_4 (respectively, q_7), Ana (i.e., agent 2) and Cindy (respectively, Bob) receive the message, as well as their fans; while at state q_6, Ana, Bob, and Bob's fans receive the message, but not Ana's fans.

Property (11) queries for a coalition of at most three agents that can spread the message toward state q_7. Property (12) queries for a coalition of at most two agents that can spread the message toward state q_5, and can do so to a next state q_2 by removing exactly one agent from the coalition. Property (13) queries for a coalition with Ana and Bob that can spread the message toward state q_4. Property (14) queries for an agent that can eventually form a coalition with another agent to spread the message to a next state q_6; while Property (15) queries for an agent that can form a coalition incrementally in two steps to reach this state. The solution coalitions to these properties indicate the key celebrities and communities for marketing promotion, which is of great interest to the vender of the new product.

Table 2 presents the verification results for the 15 TCLX properties. All the experiments are conducted on a Ubuntu 11.04 machine with a Core i7 CPU and 8 GB memory. The top five, middle five, and bottom five rows of the table data are respectively for the network security system model, the software development project model, and the marketing promotion model. For each game model, column $|\mathcal{G}|$ shows, from top to bottom, the number of its agents, the number of its states, and the number of its transitions. For example, the first game model has 4 agents, 8 states, and 15 transitions. Column *space* shows the size of the solution space for each property. For a game model with m agents, the size of the solution space for a TCLX property with n coalition variables is 2^{mn}. Column *result* reports the model checking result of each property, while column *solution* presents the solution to each property (if applicable) yielded by our model-checker. Column *time* shows the average time usage in seconds for verifying each property. All the TCLX properties are verified 5 times for statistical accuracy.

Table 2. Experiment results (time in seconds)

property	$|\mathcal{G}|$	space	result	solution	time
(1)	4	16	true	$X = \{1\}$	0.76
(2)	8	16	true	$X = \{2,3\}$	0.31
(3)	15	1	true	no coalition variable	0.08
(4)		16	false	no solution	0.73
(5)		16	false		0.25
(6)	5	32	true	$X = \{1,2,3,4,5\}$	0.57
(7)	13	1024	true	$X = \{1,2\}, Y = \{3,4\}$	5.68
(8)	23	32	false	no solution	0.29
(9)		32	false		1.12
(10)		32	false		0.53
(11)	9	512	true	$X = \{1,2,3\}$	0.68
(12)	8	262144	true	$X = \{1,3\}, Y = \{3\}$	32.12
(13)	18	262144	true	$X = \{1\}, Y = \{2,3,4\}$	93.13
(14)		262144	true	$X = \{1\}, Y = \{3\}$	56.69
(15)		134217728	true	$X = \{1\}, Y = \{2\}, Z = \{3\}$	6772

The above model checking results and solutions match with the expectations. These experiment results demonstrate the diverse requirements on coalitions that can be expressed with TCLX on top of their temporal cooperation objectives. Coalitions can be static (one-shot) or dynamic in the sense that coalitions are formed along the behavioral evolution of agents. Both sorts of coalitions fit in the logic framework of TCLX, while the TCLX model checker can manage to synthesize satisfying coalition schemes (if any) in an on-the-fly manner. The exponential growth on the time usages in Table 2 is mainly caused by the increasing number of the coalition variables in the TCLX formulas, due to the enumeration nature of the implementation. Future effort will be devoted to improve the TCLX model checker by exploiting the high efficiency of symbolic verification techniques [3,9].

8   Conclusion

We have investigated the influences of using coalition variables in TCL for more expressiveness from the perspectives of both theory and implementation. Coalition variables are interpreted over the subsets of the agents in a concurrent game, and characterize the existence of agent coalitions for achieving the underlying TCL properties. Our experiments show a good potential of the approach in real-world applications. Integration of coalition and strategy representation, reasoning, and synthesis would be interesting for future work. It would be also interesting to see whether more expressiveness can be added without sacrificing verification efficiency.

References

1. Alur, R., Henzinger, T.A., Kupferman, O.: Alternating-time temporal logic. J. ACM **49**(5), 672–713 (2002)
2. Brihaye, T., Costa, A., Laroussinie, F., Markey, N.: ATL with strategy contexts and bounded memory. In: Artemov, S., Nerode, A. (eds.) LFCS 2009. LNCS, vol. 5407, pp. 92–106. Springer, Heidelberg (2009). doi:10.1007/978-3-540-92687-0_7
3. Bulling, N., Jamroga, W.: Alternating epistemic μ-calculus. In: IJCAI, pp. 109–114 (2011)
4. Chatterjee, K., Henzinger, T.A., Piterman, N.: Strategy logic. Inf. Comput. **208**, 677–693 (2010)
5. Emerson, E.A., Trefler, R.J.: From asymmetry to full symmetry: new techniques for symmetry reduction in model checking. In: Pierre, L., Kropf, T. (eds.) CHARME 1999. LNCS, vol. 1703, pp. 142–157. Springer, Heidelberg (1999). doi:10.1007/3-540-48153-2_12
6. Huang, C.-H., Schewe, S., Wang, F.: Model-checking iterated games. In: Piterman, N., Smolka, S.A. (eds.) TACAS 2013. LNCS, vol. 7795, pp. 154–168. Springer, Heidelberg (2013). doi:10.1007/978-3-642-36742-7_11
7. Jamroga, W., Murano, A.: On module checking and strategies. In: AAMAS, pp. 701–708 (2014)
8. Jamroga, W., Murano, A.: Module checking of strategic ability. In: AAMAS, pp. 227–235 (2015)
9. Jones, A.V., Knapik, M., Penczek, W., Lomuscio, A.: Group synthesis for parametric temporal-epistemic logic. In: AAMAS, pp. 1107–1114 (2012)
10. Kermack, W.O., McKendrick, A.G.: A contribution to the mathematical theory of epidemics. Proc. R. Soc. A Math. Phys. Eng. Sci. **115**(772), 700 (1927)
11. Kupferman, O., Vardi, M.Y., Wolper, P.: Module checking. Inf. Comput. **164**(2), 322–344 (2001)
12. Laroussinie, F., Markey, N.: Satisfiability of ATL with strategy contexts. In: GANDALF, EPTCS, vol. 119, pp. 208–223 (2013)
13. Lye, K.W., Wing, M.J.: Game strategies in network security. Int. J. Inf. Secur. **4**(1), 71–86 (2005)
14. Mogavero, F., Murano, A., Perelli, G., Vardi, M.Y.: What makes ATL* decidable? A decidable fragment of strategy logic. In: Koutny, M., Ulidowski, I. (eds.) CONCUR 2012. LNCS, vol. 7454, pp. 193–208. Springer, Heidelberg (2012). doi:10.1007/978-3-642-32940-1_15
15. Mogavero, F., Murano, A., Sauro, L.: On the boundary of behavioral strategies. In: LICS, pp. 263–272 (2013)
16. Mogavero, F., Murano, A., Vardi, M.Y.: Reasoning about strategies. In: FSTTCS, pp. 133–144 (2010)
17. Pinchinat, S.: A generic constructive solution for concurrent games with expressive constraints on strategies. In: Namjoshi, K.S., Yoneda, T., Higashino, T., Okamura, Y. (eds.) ATVA 2007. LNCS, vol. 4762, pp. 253–267. Springer, Heidelberg (2007). doi:10.1007/978-3-540-75596-8_19
18. Rahwan, T., Michalak, T.P., Wooldridge, M., Jennings, N.R.: Coalition structure generation: a survey. Artif. Intell. **229**, 139–174 (2015)
19. Wang, F., Schewe, S., Huang, C.H.: An extension of ATL with strategy interaction. ACM Trans. Program. Lang. Syst. (TOPLAS) **37**(3), 9 (2015)

Program Verification Techniques

Hoare-Style Reasoning from Multiple Contracts

Olaf Owe[✉], Toktam Ramezanifarkhani[✉], and Elahe Fazeldehkordi[✉]

Department of Informatics, University of Oslo, Oslo, Norway
{olaf,toktamr,elahefa}@ifi.uio.no

Abstract. Modern software is often developed with advanced mechanisms for code reuse. A software module may build on other software modules or libraries where the source code is not available. And even if the source code is known, the binding mechanism may be such that the binding of methods is not known at verification time, and thus the underlying reused code cannot be determined. For example, in delta- oriented programming the binding of methods depends on the ordering of deltas in each product, making modular reasoning non-trivial. Similar problems occur with traits and subclassing. Reasoning inside a module must then be based on partial knowledge of the methods, typically given by contracts in the form of pairs of pre- and post-conditions, and one may not derive new properties by re-verification of the (unavailable) source code.

In the setting of Hoare logic, this gives some challenges to general rules for adaptation that goes beyond traditional systems for Hoare logic. We develop a novel way of reasoning from multiple contracts, which makes the traditional adaptation rules superfluous. The problem we address does not depend on the choice of programming language. We therefore focus on general rules rather than statement-specific rules. We show soundness and completeness for the suggested rules.

Keywords: Hoare logic · Multiple contracts · Contract-based verification · Contract-based specification · Adaptation · Unavailable source code · Soundness · Completeness

1 Introduction

We consider an open world program development environment where a program may depend on program parts that are not yet known or available. For instance, in software product lines based on delta-oriented programming [25] the binding of methods depends on the ordering of deltas, which may differ from product to product. In a method definition in a delta, the special notation *original* binds to the previous version of the same method in the delta closest in the delta-ordering of the product. Thus for a given delta the binding of method calls is not known, and reasoning about the delta must be based on the contracts about methods

This work is supported by the Norwegian NRC projects *IoTSec: Security of IoT* and *DiversIoT*.

N. Polikarpova and S. Schneider (Eds.): IFM 2017, LNCS 10510, pp. 263–278, 2017.
DOI: 10.1007/978-3-319-66845-1_17

of underlying modules. Similar complications are caused by *traits* [12,27]. And for class-based programs with inheritance and late binding, the binding of calls (including self calls) may not be known at verification time. In these settings, it is important to be able to reason about the program in a modular fashion, based on contracts representing partial knowledge of methods for which the binding is not known.

Contract-based specification is well known from the work on design by contract by Meyer [18] and has been adopted in several languages and frameworks, including Eiffel [19] and SPEC# [3]. In this paper we will focus on contract-based verification, i.e., reasoning from contracts rather than reasoning about verifying contracts. We assume that a given program part (such as a method) is specified by a set of contracts, and consider a Hoare style reasoning framework. A contract may give partial knowledge of a program part, and we assume that a given program part may have *several contracts*, possibly accumulated over time as more knowledge becomes available.

A Hoare triple $\{P\}\, s\, \{Q\}$ characterizes the effect of a program (part) s by means of a precondition P and a postcondition Q, where both P and Q may refer to program variables as well as additional non-program variables, so-called *logical variables* [15]. The intuitive meaning of this triple is that if the program s is executed from a state ("the prestate") where P holds and the execution terminates, then Q will hold in the final state ("the poststate"). The pair (P, Q) is called a *contract* for s.

Example 1. For instance, the contract $(x < 0,\ x < 0)$ expresses that if the program variable x is negative in the prestate, it will also be negative in the poststate (if any), and the contract $(x > 0,\ x > 0)$ similarly restricts the final value of x when positive in the prestate. The contract $(x = 0,\ x = 0)$ characterizes the final value of x when its starting value is 0. All three contracts are examples of invariants. Using a logical variable y', the combination of the contracts $(x < 0 \wedge y = y',\ y = y')$ and $(x \geq 0 \wedge y = y',\ y = y' + x)$ gives full information about the final value of the program variable y.

The combination of all five example contracts above should imply the two following contracts (of which the latter is an invariant):

$$(y = y',\ x < 0 \wedge y = y' \vee x \geq 0 \wedge y = y' + x) \tag{1}$$

$$(x = 0 \wedge y = y',\ x = 0 \wedge y = y') \tag{2}$$

Traditionally, Hoare logics are used to deal with one contract per program. An occurrence of s may have a program environment which needs some adjustment or adaptation of the contract. The simplest way of adjustment is provided by the well-known Rule of Consequence:

$$(\text{CONSEQUENCE})$$

$$\frac{P' \Rightarrow P \qquad \{P\}\, s\, \{Q\} \qquad Q \Rightarrow Q'}{\{P'\}\, s\, \{Q'\}}$$

However, this rule is not suitable when s is used in a context where the assertions talk about more variables than the contract of s, nor when the precondition of the contract is not satisfied. For instance, from the contracts given above, we may not derive contract 1 nor 2 by the consequence rule alone. Moreover, if we use the conjunction rule on the contracts $(x > 0, x > 0)$, $(x < 0, x < 0)$, and $(x = 0, x = 0)$, we get false in the precondition. If we use the disjunction rule, we get true in the postcondition. Neither gives any information, so we need better ways to combine the information in several contracts.

Adaptation rules give more freedom in the reasoning, by allowing different preconditions and postconditions for different reuses (i.e., occurrences) of s. For instance, we may try to prove the example above, or we may try to find a precondition P such that $\{P\}\, s\, \{x = x' \wedge y = y' + x\}$ is satisfied for s as in the example. The original adaptation rule suggested by Hoare [16] can be formulated as

$$\text{(ADAPTATION)}$$
$$\frac{\{P\}\, s\, \{Q\}}{\{\exists \overline{z}.\, (P \wedge \forall \overline{w}.\, (Q \to R))\}\, s\, \{R\}}$$

where $\overline{w}$ is the list of program variables that may be changed by s and $\overline{z}$ is list of logical variables in (P, Q) but not in R. As shown in [20], this adaptation rule is sound and relatively complete, although the precondition is not the weakest possible formulation. As discussed in [1], the precondition may be weakened to $\forall \overline{w}'(\forall \overline{z}.\, P \Rightarrow Q_{\overline{w}'}^{\overline{w}}) \Rightarrow R_{\overline{w}'}^{\overline{w}})$, where $Q_{\overline{w}'}^{\overline{w}}$ denotes Q with all free occurrences of $\overline{w}$ replaced by $\overline{w}'$ (given that the lists $\overline{w}$ and $\overline{w}'$ have the same length). In this precondition, $\overline{z}$ are the logical variables in P and/or Q.

However, we are still not able to handle multiple contracts, and for the example above, we may still not derive contract 1 nor 2. Special adaptation rules considering the case of multiple contracts have been suggested, and will be discussed in the next section.

The contribution of this paper is to reconsider Hoare-style reasoning supporting reasoning from contracts when the program text is not available or known, allowing multiple contracts. Traditionally, completeness of Hoare logics assume that all parts of the program text are available, and thus may be used to re-verify different contracts when needed. We suggest a new approach for adaptation. We first introduce a rule called the *normalization rule*, which is simpler then the adaptation rule. We then introduce a generalized version of the rule, called the *generalized normalization rule*, for dealing with multiple contracts. The combination of the generalized normalization rule and the consequence rule forms a complete set of general reasoning rules. We prove soundness and completeness of these rules, and show that the (most expressive) adaptation rule and its generalization to multiple contracts, as well as other general rules, can be derived easily.

2   Reasoning About Multiple Contracts

In order to use a contract in program reasoning, one needs to know an overapproximation of the set of program variables that may be changed by the program, called the *var* set. This may be part of a contract. However, when considering delta-oriented programming, or object-oriented inheritance, a redefined method may involve variables that were not known when the original contract was formulated. This makes it impossible to restrict the *var* set for contracts that are intended to be reused/inherited. In this case an underestimation of the set of read-only variables can be valuable [8]. Instead of letting the contract specify the *var* set, one may overapproximate the set of program variables that may change for each call. As different choices of programming languages may require different kinds of specification of *var* sets, we will not impose a fixed way of specifying *var* sets, but assume that a *var* set $\overline{w}$ and a set of read-only variables $\overline{v}$ can be determined statically for each occurrence of a program/call specified by a contract.

Thus, for each occurrence of a program we let $\overline{w}$ denote the (finite) set of program variables that may be changed by a program s, and $\overline{v}$ denote the complementary set of program variables that may not be changed by s. In addition to the program variables, a contract may talk about logical variables, which are here denoted by the symbol z or by primed versions of the program variables.

Consider the case that several contracts may be assumed (or have been proved) for a given program, or method body, s. This can be expressed by a set of triples $\{P_i\} s \{Q_i\}$ for $1 \leq i \leq N$. How can we make use of this knowledge? The following adaptation rule expresses how to exploit the knowledge of several such triples. For any assertion R the rule allows us to derive a precondition of s with exactly R as the postcondition:

$$\text{(GENERALIZED ADAPTATION)}$$
$$\frac{\{P_i\} s \{Q_i\} \quad \text{for } 1 \leq i \leq N}{\{\forall \overline{w}' . (\bigwedge_i \forall \overline{z_i} . (P_i \Rightarrow Q_{i\overline{w}'}^{\overline{w}})) \Rightarrow R_{\overline{w}'}^{\overline{w}}\} s \{R\}}$$

where $\overline{w}'$ are fresh logical variables, $\overline{z_i}$ the logical variables in (p_i, q_i), and $\overline{w}$ variables that may be updated by the method. A similar rule for right-constructive reasoning was suggested in [29].

Example 2. Given the Hoare triples

$$\{x \geq 0\} s \{x \geq 0\} \quad \text{and} \quad \{x \leq 0\} s \{x \leq 0\}$$

How can we combine this knowledge in one Hoare triple? The generalized adaptation rule gives $\{\forall x' . (x \geq 0 \Rightarrow x' \geq 0) \land (x \leq 0 \Rightarrow x' \leq 0) \Rightarrow R_{x'}^x\} s \{R\}$. Taking R as $(x' \geq 0 \Rightarrow x \geq 0) \land (x' \leq 0 \Rightarrow x \leq 0)$, the precondition becomes

$$\forall x' . ((x \geq 0 \Rightarrow x' \geq 0) \land (x \leq 0 \Rightarrow x' \leq 0)) \Rightarrow ((x' \geq 0 \Rightarrow x' \geq 0) \land (x' \leq 0 \Rightarrow x' \leq 0))$$

which is implied by $x = x'$. By the consequence rule we may then derive

$$\{x = x'\} s \{(x' \geq 0 \Rightarrow x \geq 0) \land (x' \leq 0 \Rightarrow x \leq 0)\}$$

Thus, the generalized adaptation rule is able to handle this example, as well as contracts 1 and 2. However, it has some drawbacks. The rule is quite complicated. In particular, the precondition of the conclusion has non-trivial nesting of implications and quantifiers. The quantifier on each $\overline{z}_i$ is essentially an existential quantification (when lifted out of the implicant). In addition the rule is specialized to the setting of left-constructive reasoning (for a given postcondition R), and the usage of logical variables in R leads to rather complicated reasoning. A typical case appears when showing that the precondition of a given contract (for a given program) implies the precondition generated by left-constructive rules; in this situation the generalized adaptation rule leads to reasoning with existential quantifiers that can be non-trivial (for humans as well as automated tools).

2.1 Semantics

The validity of a Hoare triple $\{P\}\, s\, \{Q\}$ is denoted $\models\{P\}\, s\, \{Q\}$ and is defined as follows:

$$\models\{P\}\, s\, \{Q\} \equiv \forall \overline{z}, \overline{v}, \overline{w}', \overline{w}''.\ (\overline{v}, \overline{w}'[\![s]\!]\overline{w}'') \wedge P\frac{\overline{w}}{\overline{w}'} \Rightarrow Q\frac{\overline{w}}{\overline{w}''}$$

where $[\![s]\!]$ is the input/output relation defined by the program s, and where $\overline{z}$ is the list of logical variables occurring in P and/or Q, $\overline{v}$ is the list of program variables that may not change in s, $\overline{w}$ is the list of program variables that may change in s, and $\overline{w}'$ and $\overline{w}''$ are lists of logical variables distinct from $\overline{z}$ (of same length and types as $\overline{w}$).

The logical variables $\overline{w}'$ denote the prestate values of variables that may change in s and $\overline{w}''$ that of the poststate. The semantical meaning of a program s is here formalized as an input/output relation, which for a given state (i.e., values of $\overline{v}$ and $\overline{w}$) gives the possible output states, restricted to variables that may change ($\overline{w}$). Thus, $\overline{v}, \overline{w}'[\![s]\!]\overline{w}''$ expresses that if s starts in the prestate $\overline{v}, \overline{w}'$, then $\overline{v}, \overline{w}''$ is the poststate for some terminating execution of s. If no output states exists the program does not terminate normally. (Non-deterministic non-termination is then not captured, but since we deal with partial correctness, this can be ignored.) We assume a fixed interpretation of data types and related functions.

2.2 Normalization Rules

For $\overline{z}, \overline{v}, \overline{w}, \overline{w}', \overline{w}''$ as above, the definition of validity gives that $\models\{P\}\, s\, \{Q\}$ is the same as

$$\forall \overline{z}, \overline{v}, \overline{w}', \overline{w}''.\ (\overline{v}, \overline{w}'[\![s]\!]\overline{w}'') \wedge (\overline{w}=\overline{w}')\frac{\overline{w}}{\overline{w}'} \Rightarrow (P\frac{\overline{w}}{\overline{w}'} \Rightarrow Q)\frac{\overline{w}}{\overline{w}''}$$

since $P\frac{\overline{w}}{\overline{w}'}$ has no free w and since $(\overline{w} = \overline{w}')\frac{\overline{w}}{\overline{w}'}$ is equivalent to true. This can be reformulated as

$$(\overline{v}, \overline{w}'[\![s]\!]\overline{w}'') \wedge (\overline{u} = \overline{u}')\frac{\overline{w}}{\overline{w}'} \Rightarrow (\forall \overline{z}.\ P\frac{\overline{u}}{\overline{u}'} \Rightarrow Q)\frac{\overline{w}}{\overline{w}''} \tag{3}$$

for all $\overline{v}, \overline{w}', \overline{w}''$, where $\overline{u}$ is a sublist of $\overline{w}$ that includes all program variables occurring in P, and $\overline{u}'$ is the corresponding sublist of $\overline{w}'$. Then $P\frac{\overline{w}}{\overline{w}'}$ is the same as

$P^{\overline{u}}_{\overline{u}'}$. By the definition of validity, Eq. 3 is the same as $\models\{\overline{u} = \overline{u}'\}s\{\forall\overline{z}.\ P^{\overline{u}}_{\overline{u}'} \Rightarrow Q\}$. Thus we have proved

$$\models\{P\}\,s\,\{Q\} \Leftrightarrow \models\{\overline{u} = \overline{u}'\}\,s\,\{\forall\overline{z}.\ P^{\overline{u}}_{\overline{u}'} \Rightarrow Q\}$$

for $\overline{u}'$ not occurring in P nor Q. And thereby, we have proved the validity of the rule

(NORMALIZATION)
$$\frac{\{P\}\,s\,\{Q\}}{\{\overline{u} = \overline{u}'\}\,s\,\{\forall\overline{z}.\ P^{\overline{u}}_{\overline{u}'} \Rightarrow Q\}}$$

where $\overline{z}$ is the list of logical variables in (P,Q), $\overline{u}$ is a list of program variables including those in P, and $\overline{u}'$ is fresh (i.e., does not occur in P nor Q), and where the double line means that the rule can be used both ways, which is the case here since the validity of the premise is equivalent to that of the conclusion. We may choose $\overline{u}$ as exactly the program variables in P (in order to get simple preconditions), or as $\overline{w}$ (in order to easily compare different normalized triples). When no variable in $\overline{w}$ occur in P, the precondition $\overline{u} = \overline{u}'$ may be replaced by *true*, and $P^{\overline{u}}_{\overline{u}'}$ reduces to P.

This rule is useful since the precondition is incorporated in the postcondition, and thus *we can compare two Hoare triples by simply comparing their normalized postconditions* (choosing $\overline{u}$ as $\overline{w}$ so that the preconditions are the same). The rule basically expresses the strongest postcondition of a program s. Since the rule may be used backwards, we implicitly have the rule

(BACKWARD NORMALIZATION)
$$\frac{\{\overline{u} = \overline{u}'\}\,s\,\{\forall\overline{z}.\ P^{\overline{u}}_{\overline{u}'} \Rightarrow Q\}}{\{P\}\,s\,\{Q\}}$$

where $\overline{u}$ is a list of program variables including those in P, $\overline{u}'$ is fresh (i.e., not occurring in P or Q) and $\overline{z}$ is a list of logical variables. In this rule, there is no restriction on $\overline{z}$, apart from being a list of logical variables disjoint from $\overline{u}'$.

The Generalized Normalization Rule. When dealing with a number of contracts for the same program, we propose the following generalization of the normalization rule, which combines the information in a set of contracts for a given program s into one normalized triple:

(GENERALIZED NORMALIZATION)
$$\frac{\{P_i\}\,s\,\{Q_i\}\ \text{for each i} \in I}{\{\overline{u} = \overline{u}'\}\,s\,\{\bigwedge_{i\in I} \forall\overline{z_i}.\ P_{i\overline{u}'}^{\overline{u}} \Rightarrow Q_i\}}$$

where $\overline{u}$ includes the program variables in any P_i.

Since the rule is two-way, there is no information loss in applying the rule. When the rule is used forwards, knowledge from multiple contracts is combined, and when used backwards, the individual contracts can be recreated.

Proof of Soundness. By the same argumentation as above, the validity of each premise i can be expressed as

$$(\overline{v}, \overline{w}'[\![s]\!]\overline{w}')' \wedge (\overline{u} = \overline{u}')\frac{\overline{w}}{\overline{w}'} \Rightarrow (\forall \overline{z_i} . \; P_{i\overline{u}'}^{\overline{u}} \Rightarrow Q_i)\frac{\overline{w}}{\overline{w}''}$$

with $\overline{v}, \overline{w}', \overline{w}''$ universally quantified, and thus we have

$$(\overline{v}, \overline{w}'[\![s]\!]\overline{w}'') \wedge (\overline{u} = \overline{u}')\frac{\overline{w}}{\overline{w}'} \Rightarrow \bigwedge_{i \in I}(\forall \overline{z_i} . \; P_{i\overline{u}'}^{\overline{u}} \Rightarrow Q_i)\frac{\overline{w}}{\overline{w}''}$$

(for all $\overline{v}, \overline{w}', \overline{w}''$), which is equivalent to the validity of the conclusion. Thus the validity of the premises for all i is equivalent to the validity of the conclusion.□

Note that the rule may be used backwards, and thereby possibly obtaining triples that were not known before, for instance after reorganizing the postcondition (as illustrated below).

(BACKWARD GENERALIZED NORMALIZATION)

$$\frac{\{\overline{u} = \overline{u}'\} \, s \, \{\bigwedge_{i \in I} \forall \overline{z_i} . \; P_{i\overline{u}'}^{\overline{u}} \Rightarrow Q_i\}}{\{P_i\} \, s \, \{Q_i\} \text{ for each } i \in I}$$

Example 2 reconsidered. Reconsider the two triples

$$\{x \geq 0\} \, s \, \{x \geq 0\} \text{ and } \{x \leq 0\} \, s \, \{x \leq 0\}.$$

The generalized normalization rule gives the triple:

$$\{x = x'\} \, s \, \{(x' \geq 0 \Rightarrow x \geq 0) \wedge (x' \leq 0 \Rightarrow x \leq 0)\}$$

which is a more direct and explicit result than the one obtained above by the generalized adaptation rule. Furthermore, the postcondition can be reformulated as

$$(x' \geq 0 \Rightarrow x \geq 0) \wedge (x' \leq 0 \Rightarrow x \leq 0) \wedge (x' = 0 \Rightarrow x = 0)$$

Backward generalized normalization gives the new triple $\{x = 0\} \, s \, \{x = 0\}$. This derivation was clearly simpler than with generalized adaptation.

The Generalized Consequence Rule. By combining the generalized normalization rule with the consequence rule, we obtain a generalized consequence rule

(GENERALIZED CONSEQUENCE)

$$\frac{\{P_i\} \, s \, \{Q_i\} \text{ for each } i \in I \quad (\bigwedge_{i \in I} \forall \overline{z_i} . \; P_{i\overline{u}'}^{\overline{u}} \Rightarrow Q_i) \Rightarrow (\forall \overline{z} . \; P_{\overline{u}'}^{\overline{u}} \Rightarrow Q)}{\{P\} \, s \, \{Q\}}$$

(where the free variables in the second premise are implicitly universally quantified). This rule may be used for adaption of known contracts to a specific context. As opposed to all the adaptation rules mentioned above, this rule is agnostic to whether the verification strategy is left-constructive, right-constructive, or top-down (using the terminology of [7]). The generalized normalization rule can directly be used for bottom-up verification.

Example 1 reconsidered. We investigate if we can derive the proposed contracts 1 and 2 assuming x and y are the only program variables. The given contracts are

$$(x < 0,\ x < 0)$$
$$(x > 0,\ x > 0)$$
$$(x = 0,\ x = 0)$$
$$(x < 0 \wedge y = y',\ y = y')$$
$$(x \geq 0 \wedge y = y',\ y = y' + x)$$

According to the generalized consequence rule, we need to show that each of

$$x < 0 \wedge y = y' \vee x \geq 0 \wedge y = y' + x$$

(from contract 1) and

$$\forall z.\ x' = 0 \wedge y' = z \Rightarrow x = 0 \wedge y = z$$

(from contract 2) follows from the conjunction $(x' < 0 \Rightarrow x < 0) \wedge (x' > 0 \Rightarrow x > 0) \wedge (x' = 0 \Rightarrow x = 0) \wedge (\forall z.\ x' < 0 \wedge y' = z \Rightarrow y = z) \wedge (\forall z.\ x' \geq 0 \wedge y' = z \Rightarrow y = z + x)$ (reflecting the five given contracts). Note that the logical variable y' appearing in in the contracts becomes quantified according to the second premise of the generalized consequence rule. We rename this quantified variable to z, to adhere to the naming convention of the rule. For the case of contract 1, the implication follows by considering the cases $x' < 0$ and $x' \geq 0$. For the case of contract 2, the implication follows by lifting the quantifier on z in the implicand to the outermost level, and instantiating the last quantified z in the implicant (from the fifth contract) to that z.

3   Derivation of General Reasoning Rules

We now consider the reasoning system formed by the *generalized normalization rule* and the *consequence rule*. We illustrate that by these two rules we may quite easily derive common general reasoning rules. We derive below the common rules considered in the classical survey of Apt [1], namely the invariance axiom, substitution rules I and II, conjunction rule, invariance rule, and the elimination rule. According to [1] these rules ensure completeness. We also add some other relevant rules.

3.1   Derivation of Three Instantiation Rules

Assume the triple $\{P\}\ s\ \{Q\}$ is given. We may derive $\{\bar{u} = \bar{u}'\}\ s\ \{\forall \bar{z}.\ P^{\bar{u}}_{\bar{u}'} \Rightarrow Q\}$ by the normalization rule. By the consequence rule, we obtain $\{\bar{u} = \bar{u}'\}\ s\ \{(P^{\bar{u}}_{\bar{u}'})^{\bar{z}}_{\bar{e}} \Rightarrow Q^{\bar{z}}_{\bar{e}}\}$ where $\bar{e}$ is any expression list, possibly referring to program variables. The two substitutions may be merged since $\overline{u}$, $\overline{u}'$, and $\overline{z}$ are disjoint. In the case that Q does not refer to $\overline{z}$, we get $\{P_{\overline{e}}^{\overline{z}}\}$ s $\{Q\}$ by the normalization rule used backwards (which eliminates the substitution on $\overline{u}$). And in the case that the expression list $\overline{e}$ does not refer to program variables that may be changed by s (i.e., $\overline{w}$), the substitution on $\overline{z}$ commutes with the substitution on $\overline{u}$, and we get $\{\overline{u} = \overline{u}'\}$ s $\{(P_{\overline{e}}^{\overline{z}})_{\overline{u}'}^{\overline{u}} \Rightarrow Q_{\overline{e}}^{\overline{z}}\}$, which is equivalent to $\{P_{\overline{e}}^{\overline{z}}\}$ s $\{Q_{\overline{e}}^{\overline{z}}\}$ by the normalization rule used backwards.

Thus we have derived the three rules below (letting $\overline{z}$ denote the logical variables in (P, Q)):

For any expression list $\overline{e}$, including program variables and logical variables, we have

(NORMALIZED SUBSTITUTION)

$$\frac{\{P\} \, s \, \{Q\}}{\{\overline{u} = \overline{u}'\} \, s \, \{P_{\overline{u}',\overline{e}}^{\overline{u},\overline{z}} \Rightarrow Q_{\overline{e}}^{\overline{z}}\}}$$

where the substitutions on $\overline{u}$ and $\overline{z}$ are simultaneous.

For an expression list $\overline{t}$ without program variables, we have

(SUBSTITUTION I)

$$\frac{\{P\} \, s \, \{Q\}}{\{P_{\overline{t}}^{\overline{z}}\} \, s \, \{Q_{\overline{t}}^{\overline{z}}\}}$$

Note that program variables $\overline{v}$, not modified by s, may occur in $\overline{t}$.

For the case that $\overline{z}$ does not occur in Q, we have

(SUBSTITUTION II)

$$\frac{\{P\} \, s \, \{Q\}}{\{P_{\overline{e}}^{\overline{z}}\} \, s \, \{Q\}}$$

with $\overline{e}$ as above (no restrictions).

3.2   Deriving the Elimination Rule

The *Elimination Rule* states that logical variables in the precondition, not occurring in the postcondition, may be bound by an existential quantifier in the precondition:

(ELIMINATION)

$$\frac{\{P\} \, s \, \{Q\}}{\{\exists \overline{z} . \, P\} \, s \, \{Q\}}$$

where $\overline{z}$ are logical variables not occurring in the postcondition Q.

We derive this rule from the normalization rule. The premise is equivalent to $\{\overline{u} = \overline{u}'\}$ s $\{\forall \overline{z}, \overline{z}' . \, P_{\overline{u}'}^{\overline{u}} \Rightarrow Q\}$ where $\overline{z}'$ is the list of logical variables occurring in Q. We may simplify this normalized triple to $\{\overline{u} = \overline{u}'\}$ s $\{\forall \overline{z}' . \, (\exists \overline{z} . \, P_{\overline{u}'}^{\overline{u}}) \Rightarrow Q\}$, which again is the same as $\{\exists \overline{z} . \, P\}$ s $\{Q\}$, using the normalization rule backwards. Thus we have proved Rule of Elimination, using only the normalization rule.

3.3 Deriving the Invariance Axiom and Rule

The so-called *Invariance Rule* states that one may strengthen both a pre- and postcondition by a predicate R that does not refer to the program variables $\overline{w}$:

$$\text{(INVARIANCE)}$$
$$\frac{\{P\}\, s\, \{Q\}}{\{P \wedge R\}\, s\, \{Q \wedge R\}}$$

Let R be without occurrences of the program variables $\overline{w}$. We may prove the invariance rule by observing that the premise is (by the normalization rule) equivalent to $\{\overline{u} = \overline{u}'\}\, s\, \{\forall \overline{z}.\ P^{\overline{u}}_{\overline{u}'} \Rightarrow Q\}$ and that the conclusion is equivalent to $\{\overline{u} = \overline{u}'\}\, s\, \{\forall \overline{z}, \overline{z}'.\ P^{\overline{u}}_{\overline{u}'} \wedge R \Rightarrow Q \wedge R\}$ where $\overline{z}'$ are the additional logical variables of R. By Rule of Consequence, it suffices to prove that the former postcondition implies the latter, which is trivial.

Next, we derive the *Invariance Axiom*

$$\{P\}\, s\, \{P\}$$

for P without occurrences of $\overline{w}$. Normalization gives $\{\text{true}\}\, s\, \{P \Rightarrow P\}$ since $P^{\overline{u}}_{\overline{u}'}$ reduces to P because P is without occurrences of $\overline{w}$ and therefore also $\overline{u}$, and since in this case the precondition $\overline{u} = \overline{u}'$ may be replaced by *true*. The rest is trivial, assuming the axiom $\{\text{true}\}\, s\, \{\text{true}\}$.

Furthermore, we can derive the *Trivial Axiom*

$$\{\text{true}\}\, s\, \{\text{true}\}$$

from any contract (p, q). By consequence we derive $\{\textit{false}\}\, s\, \{\text{true}\}$ from $\{p\}\, s\, \{q\}$, and by normalization we obtain $\{\text{true}\}\, s\, \{\textit{false} \Rightarrow \text{true}\}$ since *false* does not refer to any program variables. Then $\{\text{true}\}\, s\, \{\text{true}\}$ follows by consequence.

3.4 Deriving the Improved Adaptation Rule

The improved adaptation rule is given by

$$\text{(IMPROVED ADAPTATION)}$$
$$\frac{\{P\}\, s\, \{Q\}}{\{\forall \overline{w}'.\ (\forall \overline{z}.\ P \Rightarrow Q^{\overline{w}}_{\overline{w}'}) \Rightarrow R^{\overline{w}}_{\overline{w}'}\}\, s\, \{R\}}$$

Derivation: The premise is equivalent to $\{\overline{w} = \overline{w}'\}\, s\, \{\forall \overline{z}.\ P^{\overline{w}}_{\overline{w}'} \Rightarrow Q\}$. The conclusion is equivalent to $\{\overline{w} = \overline{w}'\}\, s\, \{(\forall \overline{w}''.\ (\forall \overline{z}.\ P^{\overline{w}}_{\overline{w}'} \Rightarrow Q^{\overline{w}}_{\overline{w}''}) \Rightarrow R^{\overline{w}}_{\overline{w}''}) \Rightarrow R\}$. By first order logic, the latter postcondition can be reformulated as $\exists \overline{w}''.\ (\forall \overline{z}.\ P^{\overline{w}}_{\overline{w}'} \Rightarrow Q^{\overline{w}}_{\overline{w}''}) \Rightarrow R^{\overline{w}}_{\overline{w}''}) \Rightarrow R$, and it can then be derived from $((\forall \overline{z}.\ P^{\overline{w}}_{\overline{w}'} \Rightarrow Q) \Rightarrow R) \Rightarrow R$, since in general $(\exists w''.\ A)$ follows from A (where A here is $((\forall \overline{z}.\ P^{\overline{w}}_{\overline{w}'} \Rightarrow Q^{\overline{w}}_{\overline{w}''}) \Rightarrow R^{\overline{w}}_{\overline{w}''}) \Rightarrow R)$. By the consequence rule, this condition follows from $\forall \overline{z}.\ P^{\overline{w}}_{\overline{w}'} \Rightarrow Q$, which is the normalized postcondition established from the premise. Since the preconditions $(\overline{w} = \overline{w}')$ are the same, we have thus derived the conclusion of the adaptation rule from $\{P\}\, s\, \{Q\}$.

3.5 Deriving the Generalized Adaptation Rule

For the situation where a number of Hoare triples are known for a program s, we may derive the following adaptation rule, generalized to multiple specifications:

$$(\text{GENERALIZED ADAPTATION})$$

$$\frac{\{P_i\}\,s\,\{Q_i\} \quad \text{for all } i}{\{\forall \overline{w}'.\;(\bigwedge_i \forall \overline{z_i}.\; P_i \Rightarrow Q_{i\overline{w}'}^{\overline{w}}) \Rightarrow R_{\overline{w}'}^{\overline{w}}\}\,s\,\{R\}}$$

Given the premise $\{P_i\}\,s\,\{Q_i\}$ for all i, the generalized normalization rule gives $\{\overline{w} = \overline{w}'\}\,s\,\{\bigwedge_i \forall \overline{z_i}.\; P_{i\overline{w}'}^{\overline{w}} \Rightarrow Q_i\}$.

Using this result, the derived improved adaptation rule (of Sect. 3.4) gives $\{\forall w''.\;(\overline{w} = \overline{w}' \Rightarrow \bigwedge_i \forall \overline{z_i}.\;(P_{i\overline{w}'}^{\overline{w}} \Rightarrow Q_{i\overline{w}''}^{\overline{w}})) \Rightarrow R_{\overline{w}''}^{\overline{w}}\}\,s\,\{R\}$.

Using $\overline{w} = \overline{w}'$, we may replace $P_{i\overline{w}'}^{\overline{w}}$ by P_i and then eliminate $\overline{w} = \overline{w}'$ by Rule Substitution II (of Sect. 3.1), replacing $\overline{w}'$ by $\overline{w}$. The desired conclusion follows by renaming the quantified variable $\overline{w}''$ to $\overline{w}'$.

3.6 Deriving the Conjunction Rule

The *Conjunction Rule* is given by

$$(\text{CONJUNCTION})$$

$$\frac{\{P_i\}\,s\,\{Q_i\} \quad \text{for all } i}{\{\bigwedge_i P_i\}\,s\,\{\bigwedge_i Q_i\}}$$

As above, the premise gives (by generalized normalization):
$\{\overline{w} = \overline{w}'\}\,s\,\{\bigwedge_i \forall \overline{z_i}.\; P_{i\overline{w}'}^{\overline{w}} \Rightarrow Q_i\}$ which implies $\{\overline{w} = \overline{w}'\}\,s\,\{\forall \overline{z}.\;(\bigwedge_i P_{i\overline{w}'}^{\overline{w}}) \Rightarrow \bigwedge_i Q_i\}$ where $\overline{z}$ is the list of all logical variables, considering all premises. By backward normalization we obtain the desired conclusion.

4 Completeness

We show that the combination of the generalized normalization rule and rule of consequence is relatively complete. Since we only look at general rules, we do not define a specific programming language. Assume that a set of contracts (P_i, Q_i) is given for s. If the program text of s is not known, we may not re-verify s to obtain other contracts upon need. Therefore completeness needs to entail that if $\models\{P_i\}\,s\,\{Q_i\}$ (for all i) implies $\models\{P\}\,s\,\{Q\}$, we should be able to prove $\{P\}\,s\,\{Q\}$ from $\{P_i\}\,s\,\{Q_i\}$, using only generalized normalization and rule of consequence.

Theorem 1 (*Completeness*). *Consider a given non-empty set of contracts* (P_i, Q_i) *for a statement s. If validity of the contracts implies validity of* $\{P\}\,s\,\{Q\}$, *then* $\{P\}\,s\,\{Q\}$ *can be proved by generalized normalization and consequence, assuming* $\{P_i\}\,s\,\{Q_i\}$ *for each i.*

Proof. Since the generalized normalization rule can be used both ways, reasoning from several contracts can be reduced to reasoning from one contract. And similarly since the normalization rule can be used both ways, it suffices to consider normalized triples.

It therefore remains to show that if $\models\{\overline{w} = \overline{w}'\}$ s $\{R\}$ implies $\models\{\overline{w} = \overline{w}'\}$ s $\{R'\}$, then we may prove $\{\overline{w} = \overline{w}'\}$ s $\{R'\}$ given a proof of $\{\overline{w} = \overline{w}'\}$ s $\{R\}$, where R is $\bigwedge_i(\forall\overline{z}\,.\,P_i\frac{\overline{w}}{\overline{w}'} \Rightarrow Q_i)$ and R' is $\forall\overline{z}\,.\,P'\frac{\overline{w}}{\overline{w}'} \Rightarrow Q'$. It suffices to show $R \Rightarrow R'$ since then we can use the consequence rule to obtain the desired result. By the definition of validity given in Sect. 2.1, we have that $\forall\overline{v}, \overline{w}', \overline{w}''\,.\,(\overline{v}, \overline{w}'[\![s]\!]\overline{w}'') \Rightarrow R\frac{\overline{w}}{\overline{w}''}$ implies $\forall\overline{v}, \overline{w}', \overline{w}''\,.\,(\overline{v}, \overline{w}'[\![s]\!]\overline{w}'') \Rightarrow R'\frac{\overline{w}}{\overline{w}''}$. Consider $\overline{v}, \overline{w}', \overline{w}''$ such that $\overline{v}, \overline{w}'[\![s]\!]\overline{w}''$. We then have that $R\frac{\overline{w}}{\overline{w}''}$ implies $R'\frac{\overline{w}}{\overline{w}''}$, thus $\forall\overline{v}, \overline{w}', \overline{w}''\,.\,R\frac{\overline{w}}{\overline{w}''} \Rightarrow R'\frac{\overline{w}}{\overline{w}''}$. We may rename $\overline{w}''$ to $\overline{w}$. It follows that R implies R', and thus $\{\overline{w} = \overline{w}'\}$ s $\{R'\}$ follows by rule of consequence from $\{\overline{w} = \overline{w}'\}$ s $\{R\}$, which holds by assumption.   □

The theorem may be extended to empty contract sets when adding {true} s {true} as an axiom. Note that the completeness proof is not depending on a particular programming language, since we only talk about a given (unavailable) program s. We have assumed that the assertion language includes first order logic, but it may not contain the semantic (meta-)relation $[\![s]\!]$.

For a given programming language and reasoning system that is sound and relatively complete in the sense of Cook [6] when allowing re-verification of programs, we obtain a sound and relatively complete system for reasoning from sets of contracts without re-verification, when adding the generalized normalization rule (and rule of consequence if not already in the system).

5   Related Work

The use of multiple contracts has profound effect on the success of modern software engineering methods supporting various forms of code reuse. Contract-based verification is known though several reasoning frameworks, including proof replay [4], proof reuse [14,24], and proof transformations [26]. Our focus is on contract-based verification, without considering a specific programming language. We therefore focus on general reasoning rules for an arbitrary program. A number of works have considered the problem of adaptation in Hoare-style reasoning and the related soundness and completeness issues. The basic adaptation rules have been discussed in the introduction, and a number of general rules have been discussed in Sect. 3. We refer to Apt and Olderog [1,20] for further overview.

In [23] Pierik and deBoer consider the problem of adaptation for object-oriented programs, based on a closed world assumption. In contrast, the current work is based on an open word assumption, supporting modular reasoning. For object-oriented systems, a behavioral specification of the methods of an interface has the dual role of a contract, on one hand stating implementation requirements to any class implementing the interface, and on the other hand stating properties that classes using objects of the interface may rely on. A well-known problem here is that a behavioral specification of a method of an interface cannot be based on the fields of an implementation as they are not visible in the interface. A possible solution is to use an abstraction of the state, for instance expressed by means of the communication history as in [7], giving rise to completeness [9].

In [5] Bijlsma et al. consider contract-based verification of methods, and formulate a rule similar to the improved adaptation rule (Sect. 3.4). They show that the rule is maximally strong, assuming a single contract. They use the example contract $(z \leq x \leq z + 1, \ y = z \vee y = z + 1)$ to show difficulties with logical variables. Two instantiations of this contract are needed in order to derive the contract $(x = 0, \ y = 0)$. In our case this is possible due to the universal quantifier on $\overline{z}$ in the postcondition of the normalization rule.

A different form of adaptation, based on functional abstraction, is given in [21] and studied in [7]. Functional abstraction assumes that the underlying programming language is deterministic. A deterministic program s is equivalent to if t_s then $\overline{w} := f_s(\overline{v}, \overline{w})$ else abort fi for some termination condition t_s and some *effect function* f_s, i.e., a function from the input state to the output state (restricted to $\overline{w}$). Then adaptation reduces to $\{t_s \Rightarrow R^{\overline{w}}_{f_s(\overline{v},\overline{w})}\} \ s \ \{R\}$ where t_s and f_s are symbols, and where the precondition is the weakest possible. Given $\{P\} \ s \ \{Q\}$ we have $t_s \wedge P \Rightarrow Q^{\overline{w}}_{f_s(\overline{v},\overline{w})}$, which provides axiomatic knowledge of the symbols f_s and t_s. For instance, the contract above gives the axiom $t_s \wedge z \leq x \leq z + 1 \Rightarrow (f_s(x,y) = z \vee f_s(x,y) = z + 1)$. And functional adaptation with postcondition $y = 0$ gives $\{t_s \Rightarrow f_s(x,y) = 0\} \ s \ \{y = 0\}$, which may be reduced to $\{x = 0\} \ s \ \{y = 0\}$, using the axiom and the consequence rule. This approach trivially extends to the case of multiple contracts, letting each contract generate an axiom. However, the approach does not deal with non-deterministic programs.

Reasoning from multiple contracts has been discussed in the setting of modular and incremental reasoning about class inheritance, for the approach of lazy behavioral subtyping [10,11]. Here the set of contracts for a method will in general increase when moving down in the class hierarchy, which makes it necessary to deal with sets of contracts. A notion of *entailment* and an entailment relation $(\twoheadrightarrow)$ were introduced, letting $\{..., (p_i, q_i), ...\} \twoheadrightarrow (p, q)$ be defined as $(\bigwedge_i \forall \overline{z_i} . \ P_i{}^{\overline{w}}_{\overline{w}'} \Rightarrow Q_i) \Rightarrow (\forall \overline{z} . \ P^{\overline{w}}_{\overline{w}'} \Rightarrow Q)$ (using our notation). Thus entailment is conceptually similar to the generalized consequence rule. However, the work in [10,11] did not focus on Hoare logic rules, and completeness and soundness of entailment were not discussed.

Our normalization rule is basically expressing the strongest postcondition of a given program, a notion which is well-known in Hoare-style reasoning. Triples expressing the strongest postcondition for preconditions of the form $\overline{w} = \overline{w}'$, known as *most general formulas*, have been used in completeness proofs for specific programming languages [1]. A general rule similar to the normalization rule (called Hoare-SAT) is given by Zwiers et al. in [29]. In contrast to our rule, the conclusion is not expressed as a Hoare triple, but rather as a sat-specification relating programs and predicates in a complementary formalism. Furthermore, sat-specifications are able to deal with multiple specifications. Adaptation can then be made by switching from Hoare logic to sat-specifications and back. However, the given *Strong SP adaptation* rule is more complex than our generalized normalization rule since it deals with an arbitrary R, and is similar to the generalized adaptation rule (except from being right-constructive).

Apart from the rules in [10,11,29], there seems to be limited results on Hoare-style reasoning from multiple contracts about the same program (or method). And these rules have rather complex conditions i.e., the precondition is complicated in the rule for left-constructive verification strategy, and the postcondition is complicated in the rule for right-constructive verification. These rules are awkward to use with other strategies – in this case the sat-relations would be more flexible. However, the usage of sat-relations involves switching between several formal program reasoning systems (Hoare logic and the sat system). The generalized normalization rule suggested here is simpler then the ones mentioned and more universally applicable, and it allows adaptation without leaving the setting of Hoare logic.

The reasoning problem considered here is specific to contracts based on pre- and postconditions. As we have seen, there is some flexibility in formulating a pre- and postcondition pair without changing the semantics of the contract. However, the rule of consequence is not insensitive to this flexibility since this rule is based on separate comparison of preconditions and postconditions. Furthermore, the addition of several contracts is not straight forward. In the setting of relational calculus, a contract is basically expressed by a single input/output relation (apart from restrictions of variable sets), and thus the sensitivity to different formulations of pre/postcondition pairs is not an issue. Implication between input/output relations corresponds to semantical entailment. In fact the rule for reasoning about *entailment* of multiple contracts used in lazy behavioral subtyping [10], was derived from relational calculus. And also the sat system of [29] is similar to relational calculus. The general rules for relational calculus of programs is simpler than for Hoare logic. Framing of sets of program variables is possible [22]. On the other hand, the notions of pre- and postconditions are useful for specification, and the notions of data invariants, class invariants and loop invariants are expressed more naturally in Hoare logic, and Hoare logic is in general well understood.

The present approach is limited to partial correctness. The normailzation rule is problematic in a total correctness setting, unless a special symbol expressing termination is added (as in [21]). Calculi for contracts based on *refinements* [2,13,17,28], allow reasoning about contracts without mentioning a program, and allow combination of multiple contracts. Furthermore, this setting can deal with both total and partial correctness. Our work is however dedicated to the setting of Hoare-style logics.

6   Conclusions

The present study is triggered by recent work in software engineering methodology, such as software product lines, program evolution, as well as new modularity mechanisms and techniques for dealing with object-orientation and inheritance. The needs of these approaches motivate renewed focus on general reasoning rules, in particular with the added complexity of multiple contracts about the same program. We have not seen a discussion for Hoare Logic on completeness of contract-based verification for the case of multiple contracts. And in this case the importance of simplicity is a concern in itself, since the rules tend to become complex.

We consider partial correctness reasoning and suggest a novel set of general rules, based on generalized normalization (and rule of consequence), and prove soundness and completeness. Normalization is clearly simpler than traditional adaptation and other comparable rules. The generalized normalization rule has only one quantifier, which is a universal quantifier, and no nested implications. The methodology given by comparing normalized postconditions gives a simple and efficient approach to reasoning from sets of contracts, which is also suitable for automatic verification.

Acknowledgment. The authors are indebted to the reviewers for their valuable comments.

References

1. Apt, K.R.: Ten years of Hoare's logic: a survey - part I. ACM Trans. Program. Lang. Syst. **3**(4), 431–483 (1981)
2. Back, R.-J., Butler, M.: Exploring summation and product operators in the refinement calculus. In: Möller, B. (ed.) MPC 1995. LNCS, vol. 947, pp. 128–158. Springer, Heidelberg (1995). doi:10.1007/3-540-60117-1_8
3. Barnett, M., Leino, K.R.M., Schulte, W.: The Spec# programming system: an overview. In: Barthe, G., Burdy, L., Huisman, M., Lanet, J.-L., Muntean, T. (eds.) CASSIS 2004. LNCS, vol. 3362, pp. 49–69. Springer, Heidelberg (2005). doi:10.1007/978-3-540-30569-9_3
4. Beckert, B., Hähnle, R., Schmitt, P.H.: Verification of Object-oriented Software: The KeY Approach. Springer, Heidelberg (2007)
5. Bijlsma, A., Matthews, P.A., Wiltink, J.G.: A sharp proof rule for procedures in WP semantics. Acta Inform. **26**(5), 409–419 (1989)
6. Cook, S.A.: Soundness and completeness of an axiom system for program verification. SIAM J. Comput. **7**(1), 70–90 (1978)
7. Dahl, O.-J.: Verifiable Programming. International Series in Computer Science. Prentice Hall, Englewood Cliffs (1992)
8. Damiani, F., Dovland, J., Johnsen, E.B., Owe, O., Schaefer, I., Yu, I.C.: A transformational proof system for delta-oriented programming. In: Proceedings of the 16th International Software Product Line Conference, vol. 2 (SPLC 2012), pp. 53–60. ACM (2012)

9. Din, C.C., Owe, O.: A sound and complete reasoning system for asynchronous communication with shared futures. J. Log. Algebr. Methods Program. **83**(5–6), 360–383 (2014)
10. Dovland, J., Johnsen, E.B., Owe, O., Steffen, M.: Lazy behavioral subtyping. J. Log. Algebr. Program. **79**(7), 578–607 (2010)
11. Dovland, J., Johnsen, E.B., Owe, O., Steffen, M.: Incremental reasoning with lazy behavioral subtyping for multiple inheritance. Sci. Comput. Program. **76**(10), 915–941 (2011)
12. Ducasse, S., Nierstrasz, O., Schärli, N., Wuyts, R., Black, A.P.: Traits: a mechanism for fine-grained reuse. ACM Trans. Program. Lang. Syst. **28**(2), 331–388 (2006)
13. Groves, L.: Refinement and the Z schema calculus. Electron. Notes Theor. Comput. Sci. **70**(3), 70–93 (2002). REFINE 2002 (The BCS FACS Refinement Workshop)
14. Hähnle, R., Schaefer, I., Bubel, R.: Reuse in software verification by abstract method calls. In: Bonacina, M.P. (ed.) CADE 2013. LNCS, vol. 7898, pp. 300–314. Springer, Heidelberg (2013). doi:10.1007/978-3-642-38574-2_21
15. Hoare, C.A.R.: An axiomatic basis for computer programming. Commun. ACM **12**(10), 576–580 (1969)
16. Hoare, C.A.R.: Procedures and parameters: an axiomatic approach. In: Engeler, E. (ed.) Symposium on Semantics of Algorithmic Languages. LNM, vol. 188, pp. 102–116. Springer, Heidelberg (1971). doi:10.1007/BFb0059696
17. Mahony, B.P.: The least conjunctive refinement and promotion in the refinement calculus. Formal Aspects Comput. **11**(1), 75–105 (1999)
18. Meyer, B.: Applying "design by contract". IEEE Comput. **25**(10), 40–51 (1992)
19. Meyer, B.: Eiffel: The Language. Prentice Hall, Englewood Cliffs (1992)
20. Olderog, E.-R.: On the notion of expressiveness and the rule of adaptation. Theoret. Comput. Sci. **24**(3), 337–347 (1983)
21. Owe, O.: Notes on partial correctness. Research Report 26, Department of Informatics, University of Oslo (1977)
22. Owe, O.: On practical application of relational calculus. Research Report, Department of Informatics, University of Oslo (1992)
23. Pierik, C., de Boer, F.S.: Modularity and the rule of adaptation. In: Rattray, C., Maharaj, S., Shankland, C. (eds.) AMAST 2004. LNCS, vol. 3116, pp. 394–408. Springer, Heidelberg (2004). doi:10.1007/978-3-540-27815-3_31
24. Reif, W., Stenzel, K.: Reuse of proofs in software verification. Sadhana **21**(2), 229–244 (1996)
25. Schaefer, I., Bettini, L., Bono, V., Damiani, F., Tanzarella, N.: Delta-oriented programming of software product lines. In: Bosch, J., Lee, J. (eds.) SPLC 2010. LNCS, vol. 6287, pp. 77–91. Springer, Heidelberg (2010). doi:10.1007/978-3-642-15579-6_6
26. Schairer, A., Hutter, D.: Proof transformations for evolutionary formal software development. In: Kirchner, H., Ringeissen, C. (eds.) AMAST 2002. LNCS, vol. 2422, pp. 441–456. Springer, Heidelberg (2002). doi:10.1007/3-540-45719-4_30
27. Schärli, N., Ducasse, S., Nierstrasz, O., Black, A.P.: Traits: composable units of behaviour. In: Cardelli, L. (ed.) ECOOP 2003. LNCS, vol. 2743, pp. 248–274. Springer, Heidelberg (2003). doi:10.1007/978-3-540-45070-2_12
28. Ward, N.: Adding specification constructors to the refinement calculus. In: Woodcock, J.C.P., Larsen, P.G. (eds.) FME 1993. LNCS, vol. 670, pp. 652–670. Springer, Heidelberg (1993). doi:10.1007/BFb0024672
29. Zwiers, J., Hannemann, U., Lakhneche, Y., Stomp, F., de Roever, W.-P.: Modular completeness: integrating the reuse of specified software in top-down program development. In: Gaudel, M.-C., Woodcock, J. (eds.) FME 1996. LNCS, vol. 1051, pp. 595–608. Springer, Heidelberg (1996). doi:10.1007/3-540-60973-3_109

A New Invariant Rule for the Analysis of Loops with Non-standard Control Flows

Dominic Steinhöfel[(⊠)] and Nathan Wasser

Department of Computer Science, TU Darmstadt, Darmstadt, Germany
steinhoefel@cs.tu-darmstadt.de, nate@sharpmind.de

Abstract. Invariants are a standard concept for reasoning about unbounded loops since Floyd-Hoare logic in the late 1960s. For real-world languages like Java, loop invariant rules tend to become extremely complex. The main reason is non-standard control flow induced by return, throw, break, and continue statements, possibly combined and nested inside inner loops and try blocks. We propose the concept of a *loop scope* which gives rise to a new approach for the design of invariant rules. This permits "sandboxed" deduction-based symbolic execution of loop bodies which in turn allows a modular analysis even of complex loops. Based on the new concept we designed a loop invariant rule for Java that has full language coverage and implemented it in the program verification system KeY. Its main advantages are (1) much increased comprehensibility, which made it considerably easier to argue for its soundness, (2) simpler and easier to understand proof obligations, (3) a substantially decreased number of symbolic execution steps and sizes of resulting proofs in a representative set of experiments. We also show that the new rule, in combination with fully automatic symbolic state merging, realizes even greater proof size reduction and helps to address the state explosion problem of symbolic execution.

1 Introduction

In the past decades, *deductive software verification* [9] techniques evolved from theoretical approaches reasoning about simple while languages [13] to systems such as Spec# [2], Frama-C [7], OpenJML [6] and KeY [1] which are capable of proving complex properties about programs in industrial programming languages such as C, C# and Java [11,16]. Naturally, the complexity of the languages is reflected in the complexity of the verification, raising the question: How can we adequately handle language complexity, while restraining the negative impact of overly complex verification procedures on comprehensibility and performance?

Prominent deductive verification techniques comprise verification condition generation and Symbolic Execution (SE). The scope of this work is the latter. As opposed to concrete execution, SE [8] treats inputs to a program as abstract symbols as long as they are not assigned a concrete value; thus, programs can be analyzed for all possible input values. Whenever the execution depends on the concrete value of a symbolic variable, it makes a case distinction, following

© Springer International Publishing AG 2017
N. Polikarpova and S. Schneider (Eds.): IFM 2017, LNCS 10510, pp. 279–294, 2017.
DOI: 10.1007/978-3-319-66845-1_18

each possible branch independently. The outcome of SE is a Symbolic Execution Tree (SET). We distinguish two types of SE approaches: (1) *Lightweight* SE has its applications in bug finding or, for instance, concolic testing [14]. Programs are instrumented by replacing data types with symbolic representations or by the addition of function calls to the SE engine, which is in turn backed by an external SMT solver. Lightweight SE has been employed in the analysis of whole software libraries [4]. Example systems include KLEE [4] and Java PathFinder [17]. (2) *Heavyweight* SE can be used to prove complex functional properties about programs which are executed by a symbolic interpreter. A strong focus is put on *modularity*: e.g., single methods may be thoroughly analyzed independently from the concrete code of others. To achieve this, the analysis depends on specifications such as method contracts and loop invariants. Heavyweight SE systems can rely on an external solver, or be integrated with an internal theorem proving engine. Due to high computation time and the effort required for creating specifications, they do not scale to complete libraries, and are instead employed to assert strong guarantees about critical routines [11] or to build powerful tools like symbolic debuggers [12]. Example systems encompass KeY [1], VeriFast [21] and KIV [20]. In this paper, we consider heavyweight SE.

Heavyweight SE is strongly affected by both the performance and comprehensibility aspects phrased in the question at the beginning: The number of branches in an SET grows exponentially in the number of static branching points in the analyzed program, which is referred to as the *path explosion problem* in literature [5]. Additionally, proving the validity of complex properties may require interaction with the prover, for which it is essential that the proof is transparent and understandable to the user.

For reasoning about unbounded loops, invariants are standard since Hoare logic [13] and play a central role in heavyweight SE systems. This paper pushes forward a new kind of *loop invariant rule* tackling the aforementioned problems by integrating a novel program abstraction, which we refer to as *loop scopes*, and an automatic predicate abstraction-based state merging technique exploiting existing specification elements for infering predicates while maintaining precision.

Standard loop invariant rules require certain contorted maneuvers to deal with abnormal control flow induced, e.g., by breaks and exceptional behavior; these measures include non-trivial code transformation or a regime based on a multitude of artificial flags. Our approach avoids this by realizing a "sandboxing" technique: Loop bodies are encapsulated inside loop scopes, the semantics of which allow for a graceful and modular handling of nested loops and complex, irregular control flow. The loop bodies themselves do not have to be changed. Our implementation and evaluation for the heavyweight SE system KeY demonstrates that the loop scope invariant rule contributes to significantly shorter SETs that are moreover better understandable for a human observer. The integration of state merging helps to reduce proof sizes even further.

The idea of loop scopes appeared first in [22] and is not yet published. Our additional contributions are (1) a definition of the semantics of loop scopes and an outline of a soundness proof for the invariant rule (Sect. 3), (2) the implementation and experimental evaluation of the rule (Sect. 4), and (3) a predicate abstraction-based approach for merging SE states arising from the execution of loops with non-standard control flow (Sect. 5).

2   Program Logic for Symbolic Execution

One convenient approach to concisely describe heavyweight SE is the formalization of SE steps as rules in a formal calculus. For expressing our concepts, we chose Java Dynamic Logic (JavaDL) [1], a program logic for Java (the main concepts of which can be straightforwardly extended to other sequential languages like C#). JavaDL is an extension of first-order logic for formulating assertions about program behavior; programs and formulas are integrated within the same language. To this end, JavaDL contains *modalities* for expressing partial and total correctness, where the latter also includes proving that the program terminates. For simplicity, we restrict ourselves to the former in this paper: $[p]\varphi$ expresses that *if* the program p terminates, then the formula φ holds.

The JavaDL calculus is a *sequent calculus* in which, as usual, rules consist of one conclusion and at least one premise, and are applied bottom-up. The SE rules of the calculus operate on the first *active* statement *stmt* in a modality $[\pi \, stmt \, \omega]$. The nonactive prefix π consists of sequences of opening braces, beginnings "try {" of try-catch-finally blocks, or special constructs like the loop scopes introduced in this paper. The postfix ω denotes the "rest" of the program; in particular, it contains closing braces corresponding to the opening braces in π.

Example 1. Consider the following modality, where the active statement i = 0; is wrapped in a labeled try-finally block, and the nonactive prefix π and the "rest" ω are the indicated parts of the program:

$$\big[\underbrace{\texttt{l:\{try \{}}_{\pi} \; \underbrace{\texttt{i = 0;}}_{stmt} \; \texttt{j = 0;\}} \; \underbrace{\texttt{finally \{k = 0;\}\}}}_{\omega}\big]$$

The sequent i $< 0 \vdash [\pi$ i = 0; $\omega](i \doteq 0)$, embedding this modality, intuitively expresses "when started in a state where i is negative, 'π i = 0; ω' either does not terminate, or terminates in a state where i is zero (since Java is deterministic)". The SE rule applicable to the sequent, assignment, transforms the active statement into a state-changing *update*. Below, we show the definition of this rule on the right and its application on the sequent on the left (Γ and Δ are placeholders for sets of formulas):

$$\frac{\text{i} < 0 \vdash \{\text{i} := 0\}[\pi \, \omega](\text{i} \doteq 0)}{\text{i} < 0 \vdash [\pi \, \text{i = 0;} \, \omega](\text{i} \doteq 0)} \qquad \left[\begin{array}{c} \text{assignment} \\ \dfrac{\Gamma \vdash \{\text{x} := expr\}[\pi \, \omega]\varphi, \Delta}{\Gamma \vdash [\pi \, \text{x = } expr; \, \omega]\varphi, \Delta} \end{array}\right]$$

The above example employed another syntactical category of JavaDL called *updates*, which denote state changes. *Elementary* updates x := t syntactically represent the states where the program variable x attains the value of the term t.

Updates can be combined to *parallel* updates $x := t_1 \,\|\, y := t_2$, and can be *applied* to terms and formulas, where we write $\{\mathcal{U}\}\varphi$ for applying the update $\mathcal{U}$ to the formula φ. Semantically, φ is then evaluated in the state represented by $\mathcal{U}$. For a full account of JavaDL, we refer the reader to [1].

3   The Loop Invariant Rules

In the verification of sequential programs, and also in SE, the treatment of loops is one of the most crucial issues. Loops with a fixed upper bound on the number of iterations can be handled by *unwinding*. Whenever this bound is not known a priori, often *loop invariant rules* are employed. The "classic" loop invariant rule has the following shape [1,8], where *Inv* is a supplied loop invariant:

loopInvariant

$$
\frac{\begin{array}{ll}
\Gamma \vdash \{\mathcal{U}\}\, Inv, \Delta & \text{(initially valid)} \\
\Gamma \vdash \{\mathcal{U}\}\,\{\mathcal{U}_{havoc}\}((Inv \wedge se \doteq TRUE) \rightarrow [body]Inv), \Delta & \text{(preserved)} \\
\Gamma \vdash \{\mathcal{U}\}\,\{\mathcal{U}_{havoc}\}((Inv \wedge se \doteq FALSE) \rightarrow [\pi\,\omega]\varphi), \Delta & \text{(use case)}
\end{array}}{\Gamma \vdash \{\mathcal{U}\}\,[\pi\ \texttt{while}(\ se\ )\ body\ \omega]\varphi, \Delta}
$$

Loop invariant rules are based on an inductive argument: We have to prove that the invariant is *initially valid* and to show that it is *preserved* by an arbitrary iteration. Afterward, we may assume it for the execution of the remaining program $[\pi\,\omega]$ (*use case*). Since *preserved* and *use case* are to be proven in symbolic states where an arbitrary number of loop iterations has already been executed, potentially invalidating all information in the context, the context has to be *masked*. To this end, an "anonymizing" update $\mathcal{U}_{havoc}$ is added, which overwrites all variables/heap locations that are modified in the loop body with fresh symbols. In the context of simplistic programming languages, where only side-effect free expressions se are allowed for loop guards and there is no way of abruptly escaping the loop, this rule is already sufficient. For a language like Java, we need to take into account that loop guards might be complex expressions with side effects and exceptional behavior, and the execution might escape the loop in consequence of `returns`, `continues`, `breaks`, or thrown exceptions.

In the basic invariant rule loopInvariant, the loop body is executed outside its context $[\pi\,\omega]$. Consequently, information about how to handle `break`, `continue` and `return` statements is no longer present, and a direct extension of the rule that takes abrupt termination into account has to apply suitable program transformations to the loop body adding an encoding of this information. A fundamentally different approach based on four additional *labeled* modalities is discussed in detail in [22]; it requires five branches and is inherently incomplete. The approach implemented in the KeY system and described in [1] wraps the loop body in a labeled `try-catch` statement; `breaks`, `returns` and `continues` are transformed into labeled `breaks` before which corresponding flags are set that describe the respective nature of the loop termination. Thrown exceptions are caught in the catch block and assigned to a new variable which makes the exception available in the post condition of the *preserved* branch. An example for this transformation is given later in Example 3. The resulting invariant rule has the following form (the loop guard is executed twice in the preserved and use case branches since it may have side effects):

loopInvTransform

$$\frac{\begin{array}{ll} \Gamma \vdash \{\mathcal{U}\}\, Inv, \Delta & \text{(initially valid)} \\ \Gamma \vdash \{\mathcal{U}\}\, \{\mathcal{U}_{havoc}\}((Inv \wedge [\mathtt{b}=nse]\mathtt{b} \doteq TRUE) \;\rightarrow\; \overline{[\mathtt{b}=nse;\, body]}\widehat{Inv}), \Delta & \text{(preserved)} \\ \Gamma \vdash \{\mathcal{U}\}\, \{\mathcal{U}_{havoc}\}((Inv \wedge [\mathtt{b}=nse]\mathtt{b} \doteq FALSE) \;\rightarrow\; [\pi\; \mathtt{b}=nse;\; \omega]\varphi), \Delta & \text{(use case)} \end{array}}{\Gamma \vdash \{\mathcal{U}\}\, [\pi\; \mathbf{while}\,(\; nse\;)\; \{\; body\; \}\, \omega]\varphi, \Delta}$$

Here, $\overline{\mathtt{b}=nse;\, body}$ is the result of the mentioned program transformation, where Boolean flags brk and rtrn indicate that the loop has been left by a break or return statement, and the exception variable exc stores a thrown exception. The post condition $\widehat{Inv}$ of the *preserved* case has the following shape:

$$\begin{array}{ll} (\mathtt{exc} \neq null \;\rightarrow & [\pi\; \mathbf{throw}\; \mathtt{exc};\, \omega]\varphi) \\ \wedge\, (\mathtt{brk} \doteq TRUE \;\rightarrow & [\pi\; \omega]\varphi) \\ \wedge\, (\mathtt{rtrn} \doteq TRUE \;\rightarrow & [\pi\; \mathbf{return}\; \mathtt{result};\, \omega]\varphi) \\ \wedge\, (normal \;\rightarrow & Inv) \end{array}$$

where *normal* is equivalent to $\mathtt{brk} \doteq FALSE \wedge \mathtt{rtrn} \doteq FALSE \wedge \mathtt{exc} \doteq null$. The special variable result is assigned the returned values in the transformed loop body. This approach has several drawbacks:

Exceptions in guards. While loopInvTransform allows the loop guard *nse* to have side effects, it may not terminate abruptly. Relaxing this restriction introduces additional complexity.

Multiple reasons for loop termination. In practice, there might be multiple reasons for abrupt loop termination. For instance, while attempting to return an expression including a division by zero, an exception will be thrown which ultimately causes the loop termination. In Java, the "return attempt" as a reason for the loop termination will be completely forgotten; when using the above invariant rule, however, two of the conjuncts in $\widehat{Inv}$ apply.

Understandability. Due to the applied program transformation, the generated proof sequents are harder to understand for a human user, and also harder to describe in theory. Furthermore, the *preserved* case may also include the necessity to show the post condition φ. This may be considered as counter-intuitive since it is, theoretically, in the responsibility of the *use case*.

Repeated evaluation of loop guard. The loop guard has to be evaluated four times according to the rule. This may constitute a performance problem in the verification process, since the guard might be a complex expression including, for instance, method calls and array accesses.

Moreover, program transformation of Java code is generally an intricate and error-prone task. Subsequently, we introduce a new syntactical entity called *loop scope*. Loop scopes constitute a program abstraction which "sandboxes" loop bodies, thus facilitating a modular analysis of loops requiring very little program transformation. This new concept gives rise to a new kind of loop invariant rule.

Our proposed invariant rule is based on *(indexed) loop scopes* [22]. Definition 1 establishes *loop scope statements* as an extension to Java. We loosen the usual restriction that the label of a `continue` statement has to directly refer to a loop to allow for pushing leading loop labels inside loop scopes.

Definition 1 (Loop Scope Statements). *Let* x *be a program variable of type* `boolean`, *and* p *be a Java program. A* loop scope statement *is a Java statement of the form* $\circlearrowleft_x p \circ$. *We call* x *the* index *variable of the loop scope and* p *its body. Inside* p, *we allow labeled* `continue` *statements referring to arbitrary Java blocks.*

Definition 2 provides a scoping notion for `continue`s in loop scopes, which is needed for defining the semantics in Definition 3.

Definition 2 (Scope of Loop Scope Statements). *Let* p *be the body of a loop scope statement* lst. *A* `continue` *statement inside* p *is in the* scope *of* lst *iff it occurs on the top level, i.e., not nested inside a loop or loop scope in* p. *A labeled* `continue` *statement* `continue` l *is in the scope of* lst *iff the label* l *(1) is declared inside* p *and (2) refers to a top-level block in* p.

Definition 3 (Semantics of Loop Scope Statements). *Let* lst *be a loop scope statement with index* x *and body* p. lst *is* exited *by* `throw` *and (labeled)* `continue` *and* `break` *statements that are not caught by an inner* `catch` *or loop (scope) statement, or if there is no remaining statement to execute. Its semantics coincides with the semantics of* p, *except that upon exiting the loop scope,* x *is updated to (1)* `false` *if the exit point is a labeled or unlabeled* `continue` *statement in the scope of* lst, *and to (2)* `true` *for all other exit points. Furthermore, exiting the loop scope with* x `==` `false` *also leads to exiting the whole program.*

Example 2. Consider the program

```
try { ⟲x 1:{ y += 2; continue 1; f(); } ○ } finally {y = 0;}
```

Following Definition 3, it is semantically equivalent to "`y += 2; x = false;`", since `y += 2;` does not exit the loop scope and the `continue` statement is in its scope.

We use the semantics of loop scopes (i.e., x is `false`, or $FALSE$ in JavaDL, iff the loop continues with another iteration) to distinguish the *preserved* and the *use case* part in the second branch of our rule loopScopeInvariant (Fig. 1, next page), which subsumes the respective branches of loopInvTransform. The rule can be extended to a version for total correctness by reasoning about a well-founded relation [1]. Here, x is a fresh program variable, $\mathcal{U}_{havoc}$ an anonymizing update, and $n \geq 0$ is the number of labels in front of the loop. The program transformation performed by the rule is minimal. We merely (1) transform the `while` to an `if`, (2) push any labels inside, (3) add a trailing `continue` after the loop body, and (4) wrap the resulting `if` statement in a loop scope. Appending the `continue` statement ensures that the active statement of all final states arising loopScopeInvariant

$$\frac{\begin{array}{l} \Gamma \vdash \{\mathcal{U}\}Inv, \Delta \qquad\qquad\qquad\qquad\qquad \text{(initially valid)} \\[2pt] \Gamma, \{\mathcal{U}\}\{\mathcal{U}_{havoc}\}Inv \vdash \Delta, \{\mathcal{U}\}\{\mathcal{U}_{havoc}\}[\pi\ \circlearrowleft_{\mathbf{x}} \qquad \text{(preserved \& use case)} \\[2pt] \quad \texttt{if } (nse) \\ \quad l_1 : \ldots l_n : \ \{ \\ \qquad body \\ \qquad \texttt{continue}; \\ \quad \}\ \circlearrowleft\ \omega]((\mathbf{x} \doteq TRUE \to \varphi)\ \wedge\ (\mathbf{x} \doteq FALSE \to Inv)) \end{array}}{\Gamma \vdash \{\mathcal{U}\}[\pi\ l_1 : \ldots l_n : \ \texttt{while } (nse)\ \{\ body\ \}\ \omega]\varphi, \Delta}$$

Fig. 1. The loop scope invariant rule

after the execution of *body* is either a (labeled) break or continue, or a throw or return statement. The typical case where the loop scope has an empty body is the one that never entered the if statement, which corresponds to the case of regular loop termination due to an unsatisfied loop guard – the classic "use case" (the only other case is a labeled break referring to a label pointing to the loop). The following theorem states the validity of the rule loopScopeInvariant.

Theorem 1. *The rule* loopScopeInvariant *is* sound, *i.e., if the "initially valid" and "preserved & use case" premises are valid, then also the conclusion is valid.*

Proof Sketch. The proof follows the usual inductive argument: The invariant has to hold upon entering the loop (ensured by the validity of the "initially valid" case) and after an arbitrary loop iteration. The latter is asserted by the semantics of the loop scope along with the addition of the continue statement and the post condition conjunct $\mathbf{x} \doteq FALSE \to Inv$: Since the second premise of the rule is valid, we know that whenever the loop is resuming with another iteration (and $\mathbf{x} \doteq FALSE$), the invariant is preserved. Furthermore, for the cases that the loop is exited, it holds that $\mathbf{x} \doteq TRUE$ and thus that the conclusion φ of $\mathbf{x} \doteq TRUE \to \varphi$, the post condition of the method, is true. Therefore, we can conclude the validity of the rule's conclusion.

Example 3. Figure 2 depicts a synthetic example of a while loop with non-standard control flow taken from [1], as well as the "preserved" branch for the invariant rule loopInvTransform and the "preserved & used" branch for loopScopeInvariant, applied on the sequent $\Gamma \vdash \{\mathcal{U}\}$ [while (x>=0) {...}], Δ. Not only is the outcome for loopScopeInvariant already shorter and easier to read, but it also subsumes the "use case" branch of loopInvTransform which is not contained in Fig. 2. Also, the context $\pi\ \omega$ can constitute a Java program of arbitrary length. Since it occurs inside the additional modalities of the post condition in the "preserves" branch of loopInvTransform, this can significantly blow up the resulting sequent and therefore render the sequent even harder to understand. We additionally emphasize that loopScopeInvariant is easier to realize in systems like Hoare logic that do not allow more than one modality, which is required by loopInvTransform.

```
while (x >= 0) {
  if(x == 0) break;
  if(x == 1) return 42;
  if(x == 2) continue;
  if(x == 3) throw e;
  if(x == 4) x = -1;
}
```

(a) Loop with non-standard control flow.

$\Gamma, \{\mathcal{U}'\}Inv \vdash \{\mathcal{U}\} \{\mathcal{U}_{havoc}\}($
$\quad [\pi$ boolean ls; $\circlearrowleft_{ls}$
```
  if (x >= 0) {
    if(x == 0) {
      break;
    } if(x == 1) {
      return 42;
    } if(x == 2) {
      continue;
    } if(x == 3) {
      throw e;
    } if(x == 4) { x = -1; }
    continue;
  }
```
$\quad\} \circlearrowleft \omega] ((ls \doteq TRUE \rightarrow \varphi) \wedge$
$\qquad (ls \doteq FALSE \rightarrow Inv))), \Delta$

(b) "preserved & used" branch of an application of loopScopeInvariant.

$\Gamma \vdash \{\mathcal{U}\} \{\mathcal{U}_{havoc}\} (Inv \wedge [b=x>=0]b \doteq TRUE \rightarrow$
$\quad [b=x>=0;$
$\quad$ loopBody: {
```
    try {
      boolean brk=false, rtrn=false;
      Throwable exc=null;
      if(x == 0) {
        brk=true; break loopBody;
      } if(x == 1) {
        result=42; rtrn=true;
        break loopBody;
      } if(x == 2) {
        break loopBody;
      } if(x == 3) {
        throw e;
      } if(x == 4) { x = -1; }
    } catch(Throwable e) {
      exc = e;
    }
```
$\quad] (exc \neq null \rightarrow \quad [\pi$ throw exc; $\omega]\varphi)$
$\quad \wedge (brk \doteq TRUE \rightarrow \quad [\pi \omega]\varphi)$
$\quad \wedge (rtrn \doteq TRUE \rightarrow [\pi$ return result; $\omega]\varphi)$
$\quad \wedge (exc \doteq null \wedge brk \doteq FALSE \wedge$
$\qquad rtrn \doteq FALSE \rightarrow Inv)$
$\quad), \Delta$

(c) "preserved" branch of an application of loopInvTransform.

Fig. 2. While loop with non-standard control flow and resulting sequents after an application of loopInvTransform and loopScopeInvariant on it.

Of course, we need to treat loop scope statements in a sound manner according to their semantics (Definition 3). There are eight cases which we have to consider; those are distinguished by the currently active statement inside the loop scope, which can be: (1) empty, (2) an unlabeled continue, (3) a labeled continue, (4) an unlabeled break, (5) a labeled break, (6) a return for a void method, (7) a return for a non-void method, or (8) a throw statement. Figure 3 shows those new calculus rules. We discuss the most interesting cases; for a full account as well as for the additionally relevant, already existing rules, see [19].

The rules labeledBreakIndexedLoopScope and labeledContinueIndexedLoopScope address the cases where a labeled break or continue reaches the loop scope. This only ever happens if the label is not addressing the current loop (or, for that matter, any block or inner loop inside the current loop): Otherwise, the already existing calculus rules of KeY will eventually transform the labeled to an unlabeled statement. If one of the two rules is applicable, the loop is definitely exited (and thus, the loop scope removed and x set to true), and the labeled break or continue statement is left for further processing outside this loop scope.

throwIndexedLoopScope
$$\frac{\Gamma \vdash \{\mathcal{U}\}[\pi \; \mathtt{x = true; \; throw} \; se; \; \omega]\varphi, \Delta}{\Gamma \vdash \{\mathcal{U}\}[\pi \; \circlearrowleft_x \; \mathtt{throw} \; se; \; p \; \circlearrowright \; \omega]\varphi, \Delta}$$

emptyReturnIndexedLoopScope
$$\frac{\Gamma \vdash \{\mathcal{U}\}[\pi \; \mathtt{x = true; \; return}; \; \omega]\varphi, \Delta}{\Gamma \vdash \{\mathcal{U}\}[\pi \; \circlearrowleft_x \; \mathtt{return}; \; p \; \circlearrowright \; \omega]\varphi, \Delta}$$

returnIndexedLoopScope
$$\frac{\Gamma \vdash \{\mathcal{U}\}[\pi \; \mathtt{x = true; \; return} \; se; \; \omega]\varphi, \Delta}{\Gamma \vdash \{\mathcal{U}\}[\pi \; \circlearrowleft_x \; \mathtt{return} \; se; \; p \; \circlearrowright \; \omega]\varphi, \Delta}$$

labeledBreakIndexedLoopScope
$$\frac{\Gamma \vdash \{\mathcal{U}\}[\pi \; \mathtt{x = true; \; break} \; l_i; \; \omega]\varphi, \Delta}{\Gamma \vdash \{\mathcal{U}\}[\pi \; \circlearrowleft_x \; \mathtt{break} \; l_i; \; p \; \circlearrowright \; \omega]\varphi, \Delta}$$

labeledContinueIndexedLoopScope
$$\frac{\Gamma \vdash \{\mathcal{U}\}[\pi \; \mathtt{x = true; \; continue} \; l_i; \; \omega]\varphi, \Delta}{\Gamma \vdash \{\mathcal{U}\}[\pi \; \circlearrowleft_x \; \mathtt{continue} \; l_i; \; p \; \circlearrowright \; \omega]\varphi, \Delta}$$

emptyIndexedLoopScope
$$\frac{\Gamma \vdash \{\mathcal{U}\}[\pi \; \mathtt{x = true}; \; \omega]\varphi, \Delta}{\Gamma \vdash \{\mathcal{U}\}[\pi \; \circlearrowleft_x \; \circlearrowright \; \omega]\varphi, \Delta}$$

unlabeledBreakIndexedLoopScope
$$\frac{\Gamma \vdash \{\mathcal{U}\}[\pi \; \mathtt{x = true}; \; \omega]\varphi, \Delta}{\Gamma \vdash \{\mathcal{U}\}[\pi \; \circlearrowleft_x \; \mathtt{break}; \; p \; \circlearrowright \; \omega]\varphi, \Delta}$$

continueIndexedLoopScope
$$\frac{\Gamma \vdash \{\mathcal{U}\}[\mathtt{x = false};]\varphi, \Delta}{\Gamma \vdash \{\mathcal{U}\}[\pi \; \circlearrowleft_x \; \mathtt{continue}; \; p \; \circlearrowright \; \omega]\varphi, \Delta}$$

Fig. 3. Calculus rules for loop scope removal

Due to the loop scope semantics (Definition 3), an unlabeled active continue statement has to trigger a leaving of the loop scope (removing the execution context $\pi \; \omega$) and the setting of the index variable to false. This is realized by the rule continueIndexedLoopScope, which distinguishes it from all the others that keep the context and set the index to true. It is applied either when the additional continue statement added after the loop body is reached, i.e. in the case of normal control flow, or in the case of an (unlabeled, or labeled and referring to the current loop) continue statement within the loop body.

4 Evaluation

We implemented the loop scope invariant rule for KeY, a deductive program verification system for JavaDL based on heavyweight symbolic execution. Its calculus rules for the SE of Java programs cover most sequential Java features, such as inheritance, dynamic dispatch, reference types, recursive methods, exceptions, and strings (we refer the reader to [1] for a full account). Prior to that, the system was based on the loop invariant rule loopInvTransform (see Sect. 3). In the remainder of this section, we refer to the previous rule implemented in KeY as the "old" rule and to our implementation of the loop scope invariant rule as the "new" rule. Our experimental evaluation is based upon a sample of 54 Java programs (containing loops) of varying size which are shipped with KeY as examples. Each of these examples can be solved fully automatically by KeY. For the evaluation, we created two proof versions: One with the old, and one with the new rule. We then compared the numbers of proof nodes and SE steps for each example. Table 1 depicts the results for 44 of the examples. Negative numbers indicate a better performance of the new rule. We left out some small examples for space reasons; the complete table and the KeY proof files can be found on our web page key-project.org/papers/loopscopes.

Figure 4 contains box plots for the percentage difference of the numbers of proof nodes and SE steps between the old and the new rule. The bars in the

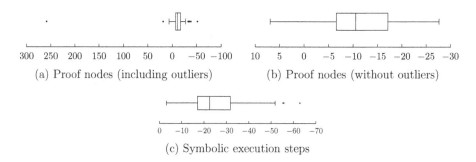

(a) Proof nodes (including outliers)   (b) Proof nodes (without outliers)

(c) Symbolic execution steps

Fig. 4. Box plots visualizing the percentage difference in the number of proof nodes/SE steps between the old and the new rule.

middle of the box represent the median, the box itself the midspread (the middle 50%), and the whiskers point to the last items that are still within 1.5 of the inter quartile range of the lower/upper quartile. The examples which are not covered by the whiskers, the outliers, are signified as points.

Overall, we saved between 3% and 63% of *SE steps*, the median is 27. Of all examples, 50% are in the range of 17% and 32% of saved steps. This is mostly due to the overhead of the fourfold evaluation of loop guards in the old rule. Considering the total number of saved *proof steps*, the situation is more complex. While for 50% of all examples, the number of proof steps can be reduced by 7% to 16% when using the new rule, we have seven outliers, and in total four examples where the number of nodes is higher in the proof with the new rule.

Of those, the "coincidence_count" example with an increase of 258.88% is most surprising. The reason is not the SE, since even in this example we saved 27.14% of SE steps. We discovered that the increased number of proof nodes is due to disadvantageous decisions of KeY's strategies: From situations in the compared proofs where the sequents were equal up to renaming of constants and ordering of formulas, the strategies made significantly worse decisions in the proof with the new rule. We made similar observations for the remaining three negative examples as well as for the positive outlier "jml-information-flow". Exemplarily for "coincidence_count" and "jml-information-flow", we were able to underpin the assumption that the extreme loss/gain in performance is due to (fixable) disadvantageous strategy decisions by pruning the longer proofs at the interesting positions, performing a few simple steps manually and starting the strategies again. The resulting proof size savings fit the expectations. We reported those examples to the KeY team as benchmarks for tuning the strategies.

Some of the positive outliers are more interesting: In the "lcp" example, the loop condition is extremely complex, which is why the new rule performs much better. The "ArrayList.remove.0" example contains two nested loops. The application of an invariant rule to the inner loop is superfluous, since the specific method contract constituting the proof goal already facilitates closing the proof without considering the inner loop. Still, the strategies choose to apply an

Table 1. 44 out of 54 experimental results (including all negative results), ordered by the percentage of proof nodes saved. The outliers are discussed in Sect. 4.

Problem	Proof Nodes Old Rule	New Rule	% Difference # Nodes	Symb.Ex.Steps Old Rule	New Rule	% Difference # Symb.Ex.Steps
coincidence_count	14.199	50.957	258.88%	210	153	-27.14%
ArrayList.remove.1	12.269	14.575	18.80%	258	191	-25.97%
saddleback_search	30.119	32.203	6.92%	235	181	-22.98%
list_recursiveSpec	5.243	5.557	5.99%	184	170	-7.61%
removeDups	19.891	19.736	-0.78%	373	308	-17.43%
ArrayList_add	6.451	6.380	-1.10%	458	444	-3.06%
polishFlagSort	4.299	4.242	-1.33%	93	83	-10.75%
ArrayList_concatenate	23.205	22.585	-2.67%	641	564	-12.01%
list_recursiveSpec	6.131	5.937	-3.16%	216	184	-14.81%
BinarySearch_search	4.462	4.269	-4.33%	182	149	-18.13%
MemoryAllocator_alloc	1.067	1.003	-6.00%	90	77	-14.44%
reverseArray	5.348	4.997	-6.56%	151	139	-7.95%
Node_search	7.768	7.256	-6.59%	97	57	-41.24%
gcdHelp-post	2.634	2.456	-6.76%	39	28	-28.21%
Queens_isConsistent	3.677	3.420	-6.99%	167	135	-19.16%
ArrayList.enlarge	3.051	2.824	-7.44%	106	79	-25.47%
ArrayList.contains	2.414	2.225	-7.83%	98	60	-38.78%
UpdateAbstraction_ex9_secure	1.457	1.319	-9.47%	183	162	-11.48%
MemoryAllocator_alloc_unsigned	1.362	1.232	-9.54%	91	78	-14.29%
ArrayList_enlarge	2.764	2.499	-9.59%	152	125	-17.76%
arrayMax	1.921	1.734	-9.73%	97	72	-25.77%
arrayFillNonAtomic	5.376	4.852	-9.75%	294	268	-8.84%
ArrayList_enlarge	3.195	2.871	-10.14%	157	130	-17.20%
SumAndMax_sumAndMax	4.101	3.676	-10.36%	140	114	-18.57%
ArrayList.add	2.302	2.060	-10.51%	144	131	-9.03%
LinkedList_get_normal	6.889	6.160	-10.58%	184	159	-13.59%
removeDups_arrayPart	1.735	1.533	-11.64%	102	89	-12.75%
reverseArray2	2.224	1.964	-11.69%	134	110	-17.91%
selection_sort	5.512	4.829	-12.39%	278	205	-26.26%
ArrayList.remFirst	2.485	2.175	-12.47%	168	133	-20.83%
loop2	1.032	892	-13.57%	83	57	-31.33%
AddAndMultiply_add	1.351	1.165	-13.77%	109	83	-23.85%
permissions_method3	1.656	1.401	-15.40%	91	57	-37.36%
contains	1.021	863	-15.48%	73	49	-32.88%
project	6.137	5.088	-17.09%	433	293	-32.33%
for_Array	827	684	-17.29%	95	68	-28.42%
ArrayList_get	1.830	1.496	-18.25%	157	121	-22.93%
sum1	939	753	-19.81%	85	58	-31.76%
sum3	820	646	-21.22%	100	58	-42.00%
ArrayList_contains_dep	6.069	4.393	-27.62%	396	213	-46.21%
ArrayList.remove.0	3.689	2.473	-32.96%	186	69	-62.90%
jml-information-flow	48.215	31.659	-34.34%	474	369	-22.15%
lcp	3.132	1.927	-38.47%	235	104	-55.74%
for_Iterable	622	300	-51.77%	130	58	-55.38%

invariant rule. While in the case of the new rule, this is not very costly and the proof can be closed without any further branching, the proof with the old rule spends a lot of proof steps for the use case of the inner loop.

5   Exploiting Invariants: Integration of State Merging

As mentioned in the introduction, one of the main bottlenecks of symbolic execution is the *path explosion problem* [5]. In [18], a general lattice-based framework for merging states in SE is proposed and implemented for KeY. SE states sharing the same program counter (the same remaining program to execute) can be merged together using one of the state merging techniques conforming with the framework. The most common techniques are *if-then-else merging*, where the precise values of differing program variables in the merged states are remembered and distinguished by the respective path conditions, and *predicate abstraction*.

```
/*@ public normal_behavior
  @ requires arr != null;
  @ ensures \result == -1 ||
  @     arr[\result] == elem;
  @*/
public int partiallyUnrolledFindBrk(
    int[] arr, int elem) {
  int i = -1, res = -1;
  /*@ loop_invariant
    @   (\forall int k; k <= i && k >= 0;
    @     arr[k] != elem) &&
    @   i >= -1 && i <= arr.length &&
    @   (res == -1 || arr[res] == elem);
    @ decreases arr.length - i + 1;
    @*/
  while (++i < arr.length) {
    if (i + 3 < arr.length) {
      if (arr[i] == elem) {
        res = i; break;
      } else if (arr[i + 1] == elem) {
        res = i + 1; break;
      } else if (arr[i + 2] == elem) {
        res = i + 2; break;
      } else if (arr[i + 3] == elem) {
        res = i + 3; break;
      } else {
        i += 3; continue;
      }
    }

    if (arr[i] == elem)
      res = i; break;
  }

  return res;
}
```

Listing 1. Find method using break statements to escape the loop

```
/*@ public normal_behavior
  @ requires arr != null;
  @ ensures \result == -1 ||
  @     arr[\result] == elem;
  @*/
public int partiallyUnrolledFindRtrn(
    int[] arr, int elem) {
  int i = -1;
  /*@ loop_invariant
    @   (\forall int k; k <= i && k >= 0;
    @     arr[k] != elem) &&
    @   i >= -1 && i <= arr.length;
    @
    @ decreases arr.length - i + 1;
    @*/
  while (++i < arr.length) {
    if (i + 3 < arr.length) {
      if (arr[i] == elem) {
        return i;
      } else if (arr[i + 1] == elem) {
        return i + 1;
      } else if (arr[i + 2] == elem) {
        return i + 2;
      } else if (arr[i + 3] == elem) {
        return i + 3;
      } else {
        i += 3; continue;
      }
    }

    if (arr[i] == elem)
      return i;
  }

  return -1;
}
```

Listing 2. Find method using return statements to directly return the result

The easiest (and automatic) state merging technique is the if-then-else method, which though only partially improves the situation, since at the end, if-then-else expressions will be split up again. Conversely, predicate abstraction is a strong technique, which though requires the user to supply abstraction predicates by JML annotations; the automatic generation of those predicates is, similar to loop invariant inference, a difficult task, and not yet implemented for KeY. However, when merging states resulting from the execution of loops with abrupt termination (and not arbitrary states, e.g., resulting from a split after an if statement), we can *automatically* exploit the loop invariant as well as the post condition for the method to generate suitable abstraction predicates that can be employed for predicate abstraction. Based on [18], we implemented this approach for KeY (available at key-project.org/papers/loopscopes). When applying our loop invariant rule, the appropriate merge points and inferred abstraction predicates are registered and taken into account by the automatic strategies. Once all execution paths until a merge point are explored, they are merged based on this information. We describe how to infer the predicates along an example.

Listings 1 and 2 contain similar, "partially unrolled" methods for finding an element in an integer array. The methods are fully specified in JML and can be proven by KeY. As long as possible, they search the next three array positions for the sought-after element. In Listing 1, the control flow breaks out of the loop once that the element is found; in Listing 2, the element is directly returned. SE produces proof goals for each `break`/`return` statement, which can be merged.

In Listing 1, the states after each break only differ in the value of the variable `res`, since `i` is not needed anymore after the loop and is removed. For each state, the part of the invariant talking about `res` has to hold: `res == -1 || arr[res] == elem`. From this formula, we create a unary abstraction predicate $P_{break}(v) \equiv v \doteq -1 \lor arr[v] \doteq elem$. KeY is able to show in a background proof that this predicate holds for `res` in each state and uses it to abstract away from the concrete values in the merged state. Thus, we save 194 proof nodes (6.3%) and 23 symbolic execution steps (11.6%). Compared to using the *old* invariant rule, we save 21.0%/45.8% of proof nodes/symbolic execution steps.

For Listing 2, we can do something similar based on the post condition of the method. The states after the return statements differ in the returned value. We generate an abstraction predicate from the post condition of the method by substituting the JML expression \result by the parameter of the predicate: $P_{return}(v) \equiv v \doteq -1 \lor arr[v] \doteq elem$. The obvious equivalence of P_{break} and P_{return} is due to fact that (almost) the method's whole behavior is realized in the loop. KeY proves this property true for each returned value in the return states and merges the states based on the abstraction predicate. We obtain a reduction of 164 proof nodes (6.2%) and 20 symbolic execution steps (10.0%); and 10.5%/31.7% compared to the old invariant rule.

6   Related Work

It is natural to compare our work with other heavyweight SE systems like Veri-Fast and KIV. For VeriFast, an SE system for C, we unfortunately could not find any work formally explaining the handling of irregular control flow in loops; the most formal paper we encountered [21] is based on a reduced language without throws, breaks and continues. KIV is a deductive verification system which has been extended by an SE calculus covering Java Card in a PhD thesis by Stenzel [20]. Their calculus is also a variant of Dynamic Logic. Its most significant difference to JavaDL is the *flattening* (sequential decomposition) of statements. This implies that the system cannot use inactive prefixes, but instead includes *mode information* in a store shared by multiple modalities, and multiple artificial statements dealing with method returns and abrupt termination. Interestingly, their loop invariant rule bears a strong resemblance to the one proposed by us. Where we decide whether to prove the invariant or the "use case" based on the loop scope index, they decide based on the evaluation of the loop guard and on the mode information. But there are some relevant aspects which distinguish this work from ours: (1) The rule in KIV requires substantially more program transformation due to the flattening. Moreover, we can directly treat continue statements, whereas they are transformed to labeled breaks in KIV. One of their arguments is that continues are problematic for loop unwinding; however, as discussed in [22], loop scopes can also be employed in that context, making the transformation superfluous. (2) In [20], the rule circumvents the need for anonymization by dropping the preconditions Γ, which makes it necessary to also encode information about the initial state in the invariant, thus bloating it more than necessary. (3) After an abrupt termination, KIV has to process all subsequent modalities until an appropriate "catcher" statement appears. Our approach simply exits the loop scope, which emphasizes the advantages of the "sandboxing" technique. (4) Our work is, to the best of our knowledge, the only one comparing the performance of a "classic" invariant rule to one of this style, and the only one integrating an invariant rule with symbolic state merging. Current versions of KIV can no longer parse Java programs, hence it was not possible to practically examine the implemented rule.

A lot of work on the verification of sequential programs is based on Verification Condition Generation (VCG). ESC/Java(2) [10] and its successor Open-JML [6] generate verification conditions for annotated Java programs. The Frama-C plugins Jessie and Krakatoa [15] translate annotated C and Java programs into the Why [3] language. Boogie [2] generates verification conditions for Spec#. In these approaches, the verification works via a translation to an intermediate language. The way loops are commonly translated ("loop framing", [2]) is structurally similar to our approach: The invariant is asserted initially, accessed locations are anonymized and the invariant is assumed for the anonymized state; finally, the invariant is asserted after executing the loop body. The handling of abnormal control flow depends on the translation into the intermediate language; usually, this remains rather underspecified in the literature. According to a personal communication with David R. Cok, exceptions in OpenJML result in gotos to basic blocks for catch statements or exceptional exit from the procedure; breaks and continues likewise branch to dedicated blocks. Generally, verification conditions consist of one huge implication per method, including one conjunct for each program block ending in a goto. While probably being beneficial for the performance of VCG approaches, this impedes the traceability of problems. Conversely, Symbolic Execution (SE) produces many small proof obligations. Our approach targets a middle course. It is based on SE, but reduces the number of proof goals through abstraction-based state merging, while increasing understandability by using a loop invariant rule with a simple semantics. Additionally, we require very little program transformation. The translation into an intermediate language may mitigate language complexity; however, it can require compromises concerning soundness [10] and, in any case, is a non-trivial and error-prone task [15] which is difficult to prove sound.

7   Future Work and Conclusion

We have introduced the concept of a *loop scope* for the deduction-based symbolic execution of loops in industrial sequential programming languages. Building on this, we have presented a loop invariant rule which we implemented for the program verification system KeY. Our rule is sound, efficient, and produces understandable proof obligations. We integrated the new rule with a novel, fully automatic abstraction-based state merging technique based on abstraction predicates inferred from existing loop invariants and method post conditions. The performance improvement is beneficial for automatic proof attempts, where thresholds on time or number of proof steps may otherwise lead to early termination.

The loop scope invariant rule is scheduled to replace the existing rule in KeY in the next public release. We are planning to also release our state merging approach to the public after having performed a more extensive case study.

References

1. Ahrendt, W., Beckert, B. (eds.): Deductive Software Verification - The KeY Book. LNCS, vol. 10001. Springer, Cham (2016). doi:10.1007/978-3-319-49812-6
2. Barnett, M., Chang, B.-Y.E., DeLine, R., Jacobs, B., Leino, K.R.M.: Boogie: a modular reusable verifier for object-oriented programs. In: Boer, F.S., Bonsangue, M.M., Graf, S., Roever, W.-P. (eds.) FMCO 2005. LNCS, vol. 4111, pp. 364–387. Springer, Heidelberg (2006). doi:10.1007/11804192_17
3. Bobot, F., Filliâtre, J.C., et al.: Why3: Shepherd your herd of provers. In: Boogie 2011: First International Workshop on IVL, pp. 53–64 (2011)
4. Cadar, C., Dunbar, D., et al.: KLEE: unassisted and automatic generation of high-coverage tests for complex systems programs. In: 8th USENIX Conference on OSDI, pp. 209–224. USENIX Association, Berkeley (2008)
5. Cadar, C., Sen, K.: Symbolic execution for software testing: three decades later. Commun. ACM **56**(2), 82–90 (2013)
6. Cok, D.R.: OpenJML: software verification for Java 7 using JML, OpenJDK, and Eclipse. In: Proceedings of the 1st Workshop on FIDE, pp. 79–92 (2014)
7. Cuoq, P., Kirchner, F., Kosmatov, N., Prevosto, V., Signoles, J., Yakobowski, B.: Frama-C. In: Eleftherakis, G., Hinchey, M., Holcombe, M. (eds.) SEFM 2012. LNCS, vol. 7504, pp. 233–247. Springer, Heidelberg (2012). doi:10.1007/978-3-642-33826-7_16

8. Dannenberg, R., Ernst, G.: Formal program verification using symbolic execution. IEEE Trans. Softw. Eng. **SE–8**(1), 43–52 (1982)

9. Filliâtre, J.C.: Deductive software verification. Int. J. Softw. Tools Technol. Transf. (STTT) **13**(5), 397–403 (2011)

10. Flanagan, C., Saxe, J.B.: Avoiding exponential explosion: generating compact verification conditions. SIGPLAN Not. **36**(3), 193–205 (2001)

11. Gouw, S., Rot, J., Boer, F.S., Bubel, R., Hähnle, R.: OpenJDK's Java.utils.Collection.sort() is broken: the good, the bad and the worst case. In: Kroening, D., Păsăreanu, C.S. (eds.) CAV 2015. LNCS, vol. 9206, pp. 273–289. Springer, Cham (2015). doi:10.1007/978-3-319-21690-4_16

12. Hentschel, M., Hähnle, R., Bubel, R.: Visualizing unbounded symbolic execution. In: Seidl, M., Tillmann, N. (eds.) TAP 2014. LNCS, vol. 8570, pp. 82–98. Springer, Cham (2014). doi:10.1007/978-3-319-09099-3_7

13. Hoare, C.A.R.: An axiomatic basis for computer programming. Commun. ACM **12**(10), 576–580 (1969)

14. Jaffar, J., Murali, V., et al.: Boosting concolic testing via interpolation. In: Proceedings of 9th Joint Meeting on FSE, pp. 48–58. USA. ACM, New York (2013)

15. Marché, C., Paulin-Mohring, C., et al.: The KRAKATOA tool for certification of JAVA/JAVACARD programs annotated in JML. J. Logic Algebr. Program. **58**(1–2), 89–106 (2004)

16. Pariente, D., Ledinot, E.: Formal verification of industrial C code using Frama-C: a case study. In: Proceedings of the 1st International Conference on FoVeOOS, p. 205 (2010)

17. Păsăreanu, C.S., Visser, W.: Verification of Java programs using symbolic execution and invariant generation. In: Graf, S., Mounier, L. (eds.) SPIN 2004. LNCS, vol. 2989, pp. 164–181. Springer, Heidelberg (2004). doi:10.1007/978-3-540-24732-6_13

18. Scheurer, D., Hähnle, R., Bubel, R.: A general lattice model for merging symbolic execution branches. In: Ogata, K., Lawford, M., Liu, S. (eds.) ICFEM 2016. LNCS, vol. 10009, pp. 57–73. Springer, Cham (2016). doi:10.1007/978-3-319-47846-3_5

19. Steinhöfel, D., Wasser, N.: A new invariant rule for the analysis of loops with non-standard control flows. Technical report, TU Darmstadt (2017). http://tinyurl.com/loop-scopes-tr

20. Stenzel, K.: Verification of Java card programs. Ph.D. thesis, University of Augsburg, Germany (2005)

21. Vogels, F., Jacobs, B., et al.: Featherweight VeriFast. LMCS **11**(3), 1–57 (2015)

22. Wasser, N.: Automatic generation of specifications using verification tools. Ph.D. thesis, Technische Universität Darmstadt, Darmstadt, January 2016

Triggerless Happy

Intermediate Verification with a First-Order Prover

YuTing Chen$^{(\boxtimes)}$ and Carlo A. Furia

Chalmers University of Technology, Gothenburg, Sweden
yutingc@chalmers.se
http://bugcounting.net

Abstract. SMT solvers have become *de rigueur* in deductive verification to automatically prove the validity of verification conditions. While these solvers provide an effective support for theories—such as arithmetic—that feature strongly in program verification, they tend to be more limited in dealing with first-order quantification, for which they have to rely on special annotations—known as *triggers*—to guide the instantiation of quantifiers. Writing effective triggers is necessary to achieve satisfactory performance with SMT solvers, but remains a tricky endeavor—beyond the purview of non-highly trained experts.

In this paper, we experiment with the idea of using *first-order provers* instead of SMT solvers to prove the validity of verification conditions. First-order provers offer a native support for unrestricted quantification, but have been traditionally limited in theory reasoning. By leveraging some recent extensions to narrow this gap in the Vampire first-order prover, we describe a first-order encoding of verification conditions of programs written in the Boogie intermediate verification language. Experiments with a prototype implementation on a variety of Boogie programs suggest that first-order provers can help achieve more flexible and robust performance in program verification, while avoiding the pitfalls of having to manually guide instantiations by means of triggers.

1 The Trouble with Triggers

Deductive verification reduces the problem of assessing the correctness of a program to checking the *validity* of logic formulas known as *verification conditions* (VCs). VCs normally include both first-order quantification and theory-specific fragments: quantifiers naturally express specification properties of the program under verification—such as its heap-based memory model, or an inductive definition of "sortedness"; logic theories, on the other hand, are needed to reason efficiently about basic data types—most notably, integers. Having both kinds of logic in the same formulas aggravates the already challenging problem of automated reasoning.

SMT solvers are the tools of choice to check the validity of VCs, and in this role they are part of nearly every verification toolchain. Such solvers expressly target combinations of decidable logic theories (the "T" in SMT is for "theory") on

© Springer International Publishing AG 2017
N. Polikarpova and S. Schneider (Eds.): IFM 2017, LNCS 10510, pp. 295–311, 2017.
DOI: 10.1007/978-3-319-66845-1_19

which they achieve a high degree of automation; in contrast, they tend to struggle with handling the complex usages of quantification that are often necessary for expressing VCs but render logic undecidable. The practical solution that has been adopted in most SMT solvers is to use *triggers* [7]—heuristics that guide the instantiation of quantifiers. Triggers are specific to the axioms that define the predicates used in a formal specification; as such, they are additional annotations that must be provided for verification. Writing triggers that achieve good, predictable performance remains a highly specialized skill—a bit of a black art that only few researchers are fluent in.[1]

In contrast to SMT solvers, first-order theorem provers support, as the name suggests, first-order quantification natively and without particular restrictions. First-order provers have not been often used in program verification for a number of reasons, including the more spectacular performance improvements of SAT/SMT solvers, and the lack of out-of-the-box support for theory-specific reasoning. More recently, however, these limitations have started to mollify, and the best first-order provers have become flexible tools with some effective support for arithmetic and other commonly used theories. Encouraged by these improvements, in this paper we probe the feasibility of *using first-order provers in lieu of SMT solvers* to check the validity of VCs *for the deductive verification* of programs.

To make our contributions applicable to the verification of a variety of programming languages, we target the popular *intermediate verification language Boogie*—which we outline in the motivating examples of Sect. 2. Boogie is both a language and a tool: Boogie the language combines an expressive typed logic and a simple imperative procedural programming language, and Boogie the tool generates VCs from Boogie programs in a form suitable for SMT solvers; the Boogie language also includes syntax for triggers, which are passed on to the back-end solver to help handle quantifications.

We developed a technique and a tool called BLT (Boogie less triggers), which inputs Boogie programs and generates VCs in a subset of the TPTP (Thousands of Problems for Theorem Provers) format [23] that is suitable for first-order provers. In Sect. 3 we describe the salient features of the first-order encoding, and the key challenges we addressed to produce VCs that are tractable. To this extent, we specifically took advantage of some recent features of TPTP supported by the Vampire prover [12,13] to encode imperative code effectively. Based on experiments involving 126 Boogie programs, in Sect. 4 we demonstrate how BLT can achieve better stability and flexibility in a variety of situations that depend on triggers when analyzed using the SMT solver Z3 (Boogie's default back-end solver).

The main advantage of using a first-order prover is that complex quantifications are handled by the prover without requiring trigger annotations—thus helping increase the degree of automation, and reduce the expertise required to use verification technology proficiently. In Sect. 6 we discuss some outstanding

---

[1] Section 5 outlines the relatively few works that deal with trigger selection explicitly.

challenges of improving the flexibility of deductive verification that we intend to address to extend the present paper's work in this direction.

In the paper, "Boogie" refers to the behavior of the Boogie tool with its standard back-end Z3, whereas "BLT" refers to the behavior of the BLT tool, which also inputs Boogie programs but feeds VCs to the Vampire first-order prover. To simplify the presentation, we often attribute to Boogie qualities that more properly belong to Boogie used in combination with Z3—namely, the effect of triggers.

Tool availability. The tool BLT and the examples used in the paper are available as open source at: https://emptylambda.github.io/BLT/.

2   Motivating Examples

This section discusses examples of programs where the outcome of verification using Boogie (with Z3 as back-end solver) crucially depends on triggers; BLT, which generates VCs for the Vampire first-order prover, is not affected by triggers, and thus behaves in a more predictable and robust way on such examples. Section 4 discusses a more extensive experimental evaluation.

Matching triggers. Boogie dispatches VCs to an SMT solver, which may need help to decide how to instantiate universally quantified variables while searching for a proof. A *trigger* (also called *matching pattern*) is a directive to the SMT solver on how to instantiate quantifiers to create new terms based on the terms that are already in the proof space. A trigger $\langle f(x) \rangle$, associated with a universally quantified variable x, instructs the SMT solver to instantiate x with the value E whenever the ground term $f(E)$ is in the proof state. Picking suitable triggers is not trivial, as it risks introducing problems in opposite directions: triggers that are too permissive generate otiose terms that may slow down a proof, or even set off an infinite loop of term generation; triggers that are too specific miss terms that are necessary for a proof, and thus ultimately reduce the level of proof automation. To make things even more complicated, SMT solvers introduce their own default triggers when no user-supplied triggers are available, which renders the whole business of understanding and selecting triggers a mighty tricky one.

Linked lists. In the example of Fig. 1a, inspired by one of Boogie's online examples[2], next is a map from nodes of type ref to their successors in a chain of linked nodes—a straightforward model of a heap-allocated linked list. Function dist defines that the distance between two nodes from and to is the number of hops following next from one node to the other. Procedure length computes such distance with a simple loop that starts from a given node head and follows next until it reaches a nil node—indicating the end of the list. If the list is *acyclic*—an assumption we encode with the invariant head≠cur (declared as free, and thus assumed without checking it)—length satisfies its specification that it returns

---

[2] http://www.rise4fun.com/Boogie/5I.

```
type ref;
const nil: ref;
const next: [ref] ref;

function dist(from, to: ref) returns (int);
axiom ( ∀ from, to: ref • ⟨dist(from, to)⟩
  (from = to ⟹ dist(from, to) = 0) ∧
  (from ≠ to ⟹ dist(from, next[to])
                 = dist(from, to) + 1) );

procedure length(head: ref) returns (len: int)
  ensures len = dist(head, nil); {
  var cur: ref;
  cur, len := head, 0;
  while (cur ≠ nil)
    free invariant head ≠ cur;
    invariant len = dist(head, cur);
    { cur, len := next[cur], len + 1; }
}
```

(a) Length of a linked list.

```
const a: [int] int;

axiom (∀ i: int •   // a is sorted
         0 ≤ i ⟹ a[i] < a[i+1]);

function hash(int) returns (int);
axiom (∀ x, y: int •
         x > y ⟹ hash(x) > y);

procedure ah(k: int) returns (h: int)
  requires k ≥ 0;
  ensures h > a[k];
{ h := hash(a[k+1]); }
```

(b) Reasoning about hash functions.

Fig. 1. (a): trigger ⟨dist(from, to)⟩ in the axiomatic definition of function dist is required to prove that the loop invariant in procedure length holds initially. (b): axiomatic definitions of sortedness and of hashing are ineffective in proofs even if they are semantically sufficient to verify procedure ah.

the value dist(head,nil). Still, without trigger ⟨dist(from, to)⟩, Boogie fails to verify the procedure; precisely, it cannot prove that the loop invariant holds *initially*—that is, that 0 = dist(head, head)—even if this is a mere application of the base case in dist's axiomatic definition.

For a successful correctness proof, Boogie requires either that the axiom defining dist be split into two axioms—one for the base case and one for the inductive case—or that the trigger ⟨dist(from, to)⟩ be added to dist's definition. Even this simple example indicates that predicting the behavior of quantifier instantiation, and the need for triggers, imposes an additional burden to users, and renders the verification process less robust. In contrast, BLT verifies the very same example without any user-provided suggestions about how to instantiate quantifiers, and without depending on the axioms being in a specific form.

Hash functions and sortedness. Using quantified formulas with SMT solvers often leads to *brittle* behavior: changes to a formula that do not affect its semantics may make it significantly less effective in proofs. Take the example of Fig. 1b, where map a models an unbounded integer array whose elements are *sorted* in strictly increasing order. Function hash has the property that the hash of an integer x is greater than any integer smaller than x. By combining these two properties, it should be possible to verify procedure ah, which inputs a nonnegative integer k and returns the hash of a[k + 1]—which has to be greater than a[k]. Boogie, however, fails verification of ah's postcondition.

In an attempt to help the SMT solver, we may try to add triggers to the axioms in the example. However, we cannot add triggers to the axiom about hash: in order to be sufficiently discriminating [2,7], a trigger must mention all quantified variables (x and y in this case), cannot use theory-specific interpreted symbols (such as $\langle x > y \rangle$), because matching does not know about function symbols interpreted by some theory, and cannot mention variables by themselves (such as $\langle x, y \rangle$), because a variable by itself would match any ground term. Since y only appears by itself or in arithmetic predicates, no valid user-provided trigger involving y can be written. What about adding triggers to the axiom that declares a sorted? Here the only sensible trigger is a[i], which however results in a *matching loop*: an infinite chain of instantiations that quickly saturate the proof space.

As observed elsewhere [17,18] and part of the folklore, an equivalent definition of sortedness that works much better with SMT solvers uses two quantified variables:

$$\forall \; i, j: \mathtt{int} \bullet 0 \leq i \land i < j \implies a[i] < a[j] \tag{1}$$

Boogie can verify ah if we use the definition of sortedness in (1) instead of the one in Fig. 1b. Somewhat surprisingly, Boogie can also verify ah if we use the same definition as in Fig. 1b but we add it as a *precondition* to ah rather than as an axiom. In contrast, BLT easily verifies any of these semantically equivalent variants: while first-order theorem provers are not immune from generating infinite fruitless instantiations, their behavior does not incur the brittleness that derives from depending on suitable triggers—that are neither too permissive nor too constraining.

3   Encoding Boogie in TPTP

In order to use first-order provers to verify Boogie programs, we define a semantic-preserving translation $\mathcal{T}$ of the Boogie language into TPTP—the standard input format of first-order theorem provers.

As a result of continuous evolution, TPTP has become a sizable language that aggregates several different logic fragments, going well beyond classic first-order predicate calculus. We loosely use the name TPTP to refer to the specific subset targeted by our translation, which mainly consists of a monomorphic many-sorted first-order logic, augmented with the so-called FOOL fragment: a first-class Boolean sort and polymorphic arrays. Our translation is informed by the recent support for FOOL [13] added to the Vampire automated theorem prover, so that we can use it in our experiments as an effective back-end to verify Boogie programs.

Boogie combines a typed logic and a simple imperative programming language; Sect. 3.1 discusses the translation of the former, and Sect. 3.2 the translation of the latter. We outline the essential features of Boogie and TPTP as we describe the translation $\mathcal{T}$.

3.1   Declarative Constructs

Types. Boogie's *primitive types* include int (mathematical integers) and bool (Booleans), which naturally translate to TPTP's integer type $int and Boolean type $o. Vampire reasons about terms of type $int using an incomplete first-order axiomatization of Presburger arithmetic, sufficient to handle common usages in program analysis.

A Boogie *user-defined type* declaration type t introduces an uninterpreted type t, expressed in TPTP by a type entity t of type $tType, which represents the type of all primitive uninterpreted types.

A Boogie *map type* $[t_1, \ldots, t_n]$ u corresponds to a mapping $t_1 \times \cdots \times t_n \to u$, which translates to a curried *array type* $\mathcal{T}(t_1) \to \cdots \to \mathcal{T}(t_n) \to \mathcal{T}(u)$ in TPTP:

$$\mathcal{T}\big([t_1, \ldots, t_n] \ u\big) = \begin{cases} \$array(\mathcal{T}(t_n), \mathcal{T}(u)) & n = 1 \\ \mathcal{T}\big([t_1]([t_2, \ldots, t_n]u)\big) & n > 1 \end{cases}$$

We currently do not support other Boogie types—notably, reals, bitvectors, and polymorphic types and type constructors.

Declarations. TPTP declarations are expressions of the form $\ell(I, K, D)$, where ℓ denotes a specific subset of TPTP, I is an identifier *of the declaration*, K is the kind of declaration (type, axiom, or conjecture), and D is the actual declaration. Here we simply write tptp for ℓ and omit the identifier I—which is not used anyway. Then, a *constant* declaration const c: t in Boogie translates to the TPTP declaration tptp(type, c:$\mathcal{T}$(t)). An *axiom* axiom ax in Boogie translates to a TPTP axiom tptp(axiom, $\mathcal{T}$(ax)). Section 3.2 describes other kinds of declarations, used to translate imperative constructs.

Functions. Mathematical functions are part of both Boogie and TPTP; thus the translation is straightforward: function declarations translate to function declarations

$$\mathcal{T}\big(\text{function } f(a_1: t_1, \ldots, a_n: t_n) \text{ returns } (u)\big)$$
$$= \text{tptp(type, } f:(\mathcal{T}(t_1) \circ \cdots \circ \mathcal{T}(t_n)) \mapsto \mathcal{T}(u)) \qquad (2)$$

and function definitions are axiomatized.

Expressions. *Boolean* connectives translate one-to-one from Boogie to TPTP. The *integer* operators $+$ and $-$ translate to built-in binary functions $sum and $difference; similarly, integer comparison uses built-in functions such as $less and $greatereq, with obvious meaning. The equality and non-equality symbols have the same meaning in Boogie and in TPTP: x = y iff x and y have the same type and the same value.

Boogie *map expressions* translate to nested applications of TPTP's $select and $store, which behave according to the axiomatization of FOOL [13]:

$$\mathcal{T}\big(m[e_1, \ldots, e_n]\big) = \begin{cases} \$select(\mathcal{T}(m), \mathcal{T}(e_n)) & n = 1 \\ \mathcal{T}\big((m[e_1])[e_2, \ldots, e_n]\big) & n > 1 \end{cases}$$

$$\mathcal{T}\big(m[e_1, \ldots, e_n := e]\big) = \begin{cases} \$store(\mathcal{T}(m), \mathcal{T}(e_n), \mathcal{T}(e)) & n = 1 \\ \mathcal{T}\big(m[e_1 := (m[e_1])[e_2, \ldots, e_n := e]]\big) & n > 1 \end{cases}$$

where m is an entity of type $[t_1, \ldots, t_n]$ u.

Quantifiers. *Quantified* logic variables must have identifiers starting with an uppercase letter in TPTP, and thus $\mathcal{T}$ may rename logic variables. As we repeatedly mentioned, triggers (associated with quantifiers) have no use in TPTP and thus the translation drops them.

3.2   Imperative Constructs

Variables. Program variables encode state, which is modified by computations. In the logic representation, a Boogie program variable `var v: t` translates to the TPTP declaration `tptp(type, v:`$\mathcal{T}$`(t))`, which corresponds to a free logic variable of given type. Indeed, constants and program variables have the same TPTP representation, with VCs encoding the effects of computations in a purely declarative way.

Procedures. Boogie's imperative constructs define procedures, each consisting of a signature, a specification, and an implementation, as shown in Fig. 2a. Each procedure determines a set of VCs that encode the correctness of the procedures's implementation against its specification.

Figure 2b shows the TPTP translation $\mathcal{T}(p)$ of p, which consists of three parts:

1. The input/output arguments of p, which are encoded as if they were global program variables; since each procedure is translated independent of the others, there is no risk of interference.
2. The precondition of p (`requires R`), which is encoded as an axiom.
3. The actual VCs of p, which are encoded as a TPTP conjecture expressing that the implementation B determines a sequence of states that end in a state satisfying p's postcondition (`ensures E`).
   In the rest of this section, we define the predicate transformer $\tau(S, Q)$, which behaves like a weakest precondition calculation [11] of predicate Q through Boogie statement S.

If a theorem prover can prove the conjecture from the given axioms, the implementation of p is (partially) correct against its specification.[3] Figure 3b shows the complete translation of the example in Fig. 1b, including functions, axioms, arrays, and assignments.

Sequential composition. The encoding of statements is naturally compositional:

$$\tau(S \; ; \; T, Q) = \tau(S, \tau(T, Q))$$

Assignments. The encoding of assignments uses the *let-in* construct:

$$\tau(v := e, Q) \quad = \quad \$\mathtt{let}(\mathcal{T}(v) \triangleq \mathcal{T}(e), Q)$$

---

[3] The typechecker establishes the correctness of a procedure's `modifies` clause, so that the prover can just rely on it. This is possible because Boogie's variables cannot be aliased.

```
// signature
procedure p(a₁: t₁,...,aₙ: tₙ)              % p's arguments as variables:
  returns (b: u)                            𝒯(var a₁: t₁, ..., aₙ: tₙ, b: u)
  // specification:                            % precondition (requires):
  requires R modifies M ensures E           tptp(axiom, 𝒯(R))
  // implementation:                           % verification conditions:
  { B }                                     tptp(conjecture, τ(B,𝒯(E)))
```

(a) Generic Boogie procedure p.   (b) Encoding of p's VCs in TPTP.

Fig. 2. General structure for the translation of a Boogie procedure.

which roughly corresponds to introducing a fresh variable v', defining its value according to $\mathcal{T}(e)$, and replacing every free occurrence of $\mathcal{T}(v)$ in Q by v'.

The encoding of nondeterministic assignments ("havoc") uses the derived scheme $\tau(\text{havoc } v, Q) = \tau(v := v', Q)$, where v' is a locally fresh variable—introduced by the translation—of the same type as v without other constraints on its value.

Passive statements. The encoding of assertions and assumptions follows the standard weakest precondition rules:

$$\tau\big(\text{assert } b, Q\big) \quad = \quad \mathcal{T}(b) \wedge Q$$
$$\tau\big(\text{assume } b, Q\big) \quad = \quad \mathcal{T}(b) \implies Q$$

Procedure calls. A *call* `call r := p(e₁,...,eₙ)` to procedure p in Fig. 2a desugars the call using standard *modular verification semantics*, where the callee's effects within the caller are limited to what the callee's specification declares:

$$\tau\big(\text{call } r := p(e_1, \ldots, e_n), Q\big)$$
$$= \tau\big(\text{assert } R(e_1, \ldots, e_n); \text{ havoc } r, M; \text{ assume } E(e_1, \ldots, e_n, r), Q\big)$$

Loops. Encoding a loop $\tau\big(\text{while } (b) \text{ invariant } J \{ L \}, Q\big)$ involves three logically conjoined conditions:

1. *Initiation* checks that the invariant holds upon entering the loop: $\mathcal{T}(J)$.
2. *Consecution* checks that the invariant is maintained by the loop:
   $\tau(\text{havoc } \theta(L); \text{ assume } b \wedge J; L, \mathcal{T}(J))$ where $\theta(L)$ are the *targets* of the loop body—variables that may be modified by L; these are just the variables that appear as targets of assignments, as arguments of havoc statements, or in the modifies clauses of procedures called in L.
3. *Closing* checks that the invariant establishes Q (the loop's postcondition):
   $\tau(\text{havoc } \theta(L); \text{ assume } \neg b \wedge J, Q)$.

The tool BLT generates a TPTP conjecture for each of these conditions, which are proved independently; thus, in case of failed verification, we know which VC

```
% fresh variables cur_ and len_
tptp(type, cur_: ref).
tptp(type, len_: $int).
% VC checking "closing" of the loop
tptp(conjecture, $let(
    % initial assignments
    cur ≜ head; len ≜ 0,
    % generic number of loop iterations
    $let([cur, len] ≜ [cur_, len_],
    % assume exit condition
    (~(cur ≠ nil) ∧
    % assume invariant
    (len = dist(head, cur)) ∧ (head ≠ cur)))
    % assert postcondition
    ⟹ (len = dist(head, nil))))).
```

(a) TPTP translation of one VC of Fig. 1a.

```
% array a
tptp(type, a: $array($int, $int)).
% a is sorted
tptp(axiom, ∀[I: $int]: ($lesseq(0, I) ⟹
    $less($select(a, I), $select(a, $sum(I, 1)))))).
% function hash
tptp(type, hash: $int ↦ $int).
% property of hash
tptp(axiom, ∀[X: $int, Y: $int]:
    ($greater(X, Y) ⟹ $greater(hash(X), Y))).
% input argument k, return argument h
tptp(type, k: $int). tptp(type, h: $int).
% precondition (requires)
tptp(axiom, $lesseq(0, k)).
% VC
tptp(conjecture, $let(
    h ≜ hash($select(a, $sum(k, 1))),
    $greater(h, $select(a, k))))).
```

(b) TPTP translation of Fig. 1b.

Fig. 3. Excerpts of BLT's TPTP encoding of the examples in Fig. 1.

failed verification. Figure 3a shows the VC corresponding to *closing* of procedure length's loop from Fig. 1a.

Abrupt termination. Statements such as goto and return make imperative code less structured, and complicate the encoding of VCs. We currently do not support goto and break, whereas we handle return statements: for every simple path π on the control-flow graph of the procedure p being translated that goes from p's entry to a return statement, we generate the additional VC $\tau(\widetilde{\pi}, \mathcal{T}(\mathsf{E}))$—where E is p's postcondition and $\widetilde{\pi}$ is the sequence of statements on π, suitably modified to account for conditional branches and loops. For brevity we omit the uninteresting details.

Conditionals. TPTP includes the conditional *expression* $ite(b, then, else)$—which evaluates to then if b evaluates to true, and to else otherwise. Using $ite and first-order Booleans, we could encode the VC for a Boogie conditional *statement* as:

$$\tau\big(\text{if (b) then } \{ \text{ Th } \} \text{ else } \{ \text{ El } \}, Q\big) = \$ite(\mathcal{T}(\mathsf{b}), \tau(\mathsf{Th}, Q), \tau(\mathsf{El}, Q)) \quad (3)$$

As noted elsewhere [16], (3) tends to be inefficient because it duplicates formula Q, so that the generated VC is worst-case exponential in the size of the input program.

Instead of following [9,16]'s approach, based on passivization, we leverage another feature of FOOL, namely *tuples*, to build a VC whose size does not blow up. A code block is *purely active* if every statement it contains is an assignment or a conditional whose branches are purely active. Given a purely active code block B, $lhs(\mathsf{B})$ denotes the variables assigned to anywhere in B. Given a purely active conditional statement, we encode it using TPTP tuples and conditional expressions as:

$$\tau\big(\text{if (b) then \{ Th \} else \{ El \}}, Q\big) =$$
$$\text{\$let}([lhs(\mathsf{Th})] \oplus [lhs(\mathsf{El})] \triangleq \text{\$ite}(\mathcal{T}(\mathsf{b}), \tau(\mathsf{Th}, [lhs(\mathsf{Th})]), \tau(\mathsf{El}, [lhs(\mathsf{El})])), Q) \quad (4)$$

Operator $\oplus$ denotes a kind of tuple concatenation where variables that appear in both tuples only appear once in the concatenation; for example $[\mathsf{x,y,z}] \oplus [\mathsf{x,w,z}] = [\mathsf{x,y,z,w}]$. In the right-hand side of (4), τ applies to the assignments in the *then* and *else* branches of the conditional and, recursively, to nested conditionals. Expressions of the form $\tau(\mathsf{B}, [lhs(\mathsf{B})])$ indicate the formal application of the predicate transformer τ on a *tuple* of variables instead of a proper predicate;[4] the semantics of *let-in* with tuples is such that every variable that is not explicitly assigned a value in the *let* part stays the same: $\text{\$let}([\mathsf{x}_1, \ldots, \mathsf{x}_n] \triangleq [\,], e)$ is equivalent to $\text{\$let}([\mathsf{x}_1, \ldots, \mathsf{x}_n] \triangleq [\mathsf{x}_1, \ldots, \mathsf{x}_n], e)$.

Finally, let us outline how to transform any conditional into purely active code. Since structured imperative Boogie code can be desugared into assignments (including the nondeterministic assignment havoc), passive statements, and conditionals, we only need to explain how to handle passive statements. The idea is to introduce a fresh Boolean variable α for every passive statement assume b: set α to true before the conditional; replace assume b by $\alpha := \mathsf{b}$; and add assume alpha after the conditional. Since α is fresh, it can be tested after the conditional in any order; since it is initialized to true it does not interfere with the other branch (where the assumption or assertion does not appear). The same approach works for assert passive statements. Overall, this encoding generates VCs of size *linear* in the size of the input program.

4   Implementation and Experiments

Implementation. We implemented the translation described in Sect. 3 as a command-line tool BLT. BLT is written in Haskell and reuses parts of Boogaloo's front-end [21] to parse and typecheck Boogie code. The translation is implemented as the composition of a collection of functions, each taking care of the encoding of one Boogie language features; this facilitates extensions and modifications in response to language and translation changes.

BLT inputs a Boogie file, generates its VCs in TPTP, feeds them to Vampire, and reports back the overall outcome. An option is available to choose between the *tuple-based* (4) and the *duplication-based* (3) encoding of conditionals; some experiments, which we describe later, compared the performance of these two encodings.

---

[4] Since τ is applied recursively as usual, consecutive assignments to the same variable translate to nested *let-ins* (see sequential composition and assignments rules).

4.1 Experimental Subjects

The experiments target Boogie programs in groups demonstrating different traits of the TPTP encoding of VCs and of BLT:

Group E consists of *examples* selected to demonstrate the impact of using triggers, and thus BLT's capability of handling quantifiers without triggers.

Group A is a selection of *algorithmic* problems (such as searching and sorting), which demonstrates to what extent BLT measures up to Boogie on problems in the latter's natural domain.

Group T is a selection of programs from Boogie's *test suite*,[5] which demonstrate BLT's applicability to a variety of features of the Boogie language.

Group S consists of few Boogie programs with a fixed structure and increasingly larger size, used to assess BLT's *scalability* and the efficiency of its generated VCs.

We wrote the programs in group E based on examples in the Boogie tutorial and in papers discussing trigger design [2,17,18,22]. We took the programs in group A from our previous work [10], with small changes to fit BLT's currently supported Boogie features. We retained in group T all test programs that only use language features currently fully supported by BLT, and do not target options or features of the Boogie tool—such as assertion inference or special type encoding—other than vanilla deductive modular verification. We constructed the programs in group S by repeating conditional assignments according to different, repetitive patterns (for example as a sequence of conditional increments to the same variable); the resulting programs allow us to empirically evaluate the size of the VCs generated by BLT, and to what extent Vampire can handle them efficiently. Table 1 shows some statistics about the size of the programs in each group, as well as that of the VCs generated by Boogie in SMT-LIB[6] and by BLT in TPTP. BLT's repository (https://emptylambda.github.io/BLT/) includes all Boogie programs used in the experiments.

4.2 Experimental Setup

All the experiments ran on a Ubuntu 14.04 LTS GNU/Linux box with Intel 8-core i7-4790 CPU at 3.6 GHz and 16 GB of RAM, with the following tools: Boogie 2.3.0.61016, Z3 4.3.2, and Vampire 4.0.

Each experiment targets one Boogie program and runs four verification attempts: (i) Boogie runs on b ($\checkmark_t$); (ii) Boogie runs on b with all *prover annotations (in particular, triggers) removed* ($\checkmark_0$); (iii) BLT runs[7] on b, encoding

---

[5] https://github.com/boogie-org/boogie/tree/master/Test.

[6] The size of the SMT-LIB encoding gives an idea of the *size* of the generated VCs, but in the experiments we used Boogie in its default mode where it feeds VCs directly through Z3's API.

[7] Remember that BLT always ignores triggers and other prover annotations in the Boogie input.

Table 1. Data for the Boogie programs used in the experiments and their translation to TPTP: for each GROUP, how many Boogie programs (#) the group includes, how many verification conditions (VCs) the programs determine in total (in BLT's encoding); the minimum m, mean μ, maximum M, and total Σ length of the programs in non-comment non-blank lines of code (BOOGIE (LOC)); the minimum m, mean μ, maximum M, and total Σ size in kbytes of the SMT-LIB encoding of the VCs built by Boogie (SMT-LIB), of the TPTP encoding of the VCs built by BLT using tuples (TPTP T.) and using duplication (TPTP D.).

			BOOGIE (LOC)				SMT-LIB (KBYTES)				TPTP T. (KBYTES)				TPTP D. (KBYTES)			
GROUP	#	VCs	m	μ	M	Σ	m	μ	M	Σ	m	μ	M	Σ	m	μ	M	Σ
E	9	19	13	20	49	181	2	3	7	26	1	2	8	15	1	2	8	16
A	10	42	17	44	152	439	3	14	80	144	2	17	102	166	2	17	104	172
T	56	279	6	29	137	1614	1	8	93	423	0	3	44	140	0	2	33	136
S	51	51	6	295	5122	15039	1	31	647	1574	0	68	1832	3493	0	$28{\cdot}10^3$	$7{\cdot}10^5$	$14{\cdot}10^5$

conditionals using tuples ($\checkmark$); (iv) BLT runs on b, encoding conditionals using duplication ($\checkmark_d$). We always used Boogie with the /noinfer option, which disables inference of loop invariants; since BLT does not have any inference capabilities, this ensures that we are only comparing their performance of VC generation and checking. We used different timeouts per verification condition in each group—E: 30 s; A: 180 s; T: 30 s; S: 300 s—while capping the memory to the available free RAM; BLT may use up to 30 s to generate VCs in each problem, although this time is measurable only in group S's scalability experiments.

Except to specify timeouts and the input format, we always ran Vampire with *default options*; in particular, we did not experiment with its numerous proof search strategies: while users familiar with Vampire's internals may be able to tweak them to get better performance in some examples, we want to focus on assessing the predictability of behavior when we use the first-order prover as a black box—in contrast to through lower-level annotations and directives.

4.3 Experimental Results

Table 2 shows the number of successful verification attempts in each case, as well as statistics on the wall-clock running time. The most direct comparison is between $\checkmark_0$ and $\checkmark$, which shows how BLT compares to Boogie without the help of triggers.

The experiments in **group E** highlight five cases where Boogie's effectiveness crucially depends on triggers; thus, BLT outperforms Boogie since it can prove all 19 VCs independent of triggers or other quirks of the encoding. The experiments in **group A** indicate that there remains a considerable effectiveness gap between Boogie and BLT when it comes to algorithmic reasoning, which is mainly due to first-order provers' still limited capabilities of reasoning about arithmetic and other theories that feature strongly in program correctness; the gap of performance (that is, running time) is instead mainly due to the fact that Vampire continues a proof attempt until reaching the given timeout, whereas

Table 2. A summary of the experimental comparison between Boogie and BLT: for each GROUP, how many verification conditions (VCs) are to be proved; the number of VCs verified by Boogie with user-defined triggers ($\checkmark_t$) and without triggers or other prover-specific annotations ($\checkmark_0$), and its the minimum m, mean μ, maximum M, and total Σ verification time (without triggers); the number of VCs verified by BLT, and the minimum m, mean μ, maximum M, and its total Σ verification time of the VCs with tuple-based encoding ($\checkmark$) and with duplication-based encoding ($\checkmark_d$).

GROUP	VCs	BOOGIE (WITH Z3)						BLT T. (WITH VAMPIRE)					BLT D. (WITH VAMPIRE)		
		$\checkmark_t$	$\checkmark_0$	m	μ	M	Σ	$\checkmark$	m	μ	M	Σ	$\checkmark_d$	μ	Σ
E	19	16	14	0.7	0.7	0.7	6.2	19	0.0	0.1	0.2	0.6	16	0.1	0.6
A	42	42	42	0.7	0.7	0.7	6.9	26	0.2	290.5	540.6	2904.7	24	258.1	2581.2
T	279	137	137	0.7	0.7	0.7	37.6	108	0.0	13.9	301.3	776.0	105	13.3	746.2
S	51	51	51	0.7	0.7	1.3	34.8	37	0.0	105.8	300.7	5393.8	48	20.7	1053.8

Z3 normally terminates quickly. The experiments in **group** T indicate that BLT provides a reasonably good coverage of the Boogie language, but is sometimes imperfect in reasoning about some features. Note that several of the programs in T are supposed to fail verification, and we observed that BLT's behavior is consistent on these—that is, it does not produce spurious proofs.[8]

Scalability. Let us look more closely into the experiments in **group** S, which assess the scalability of BLT, and compare its two encodings—tuple-based (4) and duplication-based (3)—of conditionals. Boogie scales effortlessly on these examples, so we focus on BLT's performance.

First, note that the two encodings yield similar performance in the program groups other than S, which do not include long sequences of conditional statements. More precisely, group S includes four families of programs; programs in each family have identical structure and different *size*, determined by a size parameter that grows linearly. Family S_v performs simple assignments on a growing number of *variables*; family S_a performs a growing number of *assignments* on a fixed number of variables; families S_i and S_n perform *conditional assignments* following different patterns—sequential and nested conditionals.

BLT scales as well as Boogie when we increase the number of variables or assignments (S_v and S_a): the verification time with both tools is essentially insensitive to input size and under one second per input program. In contrast, BLT's performance degrades significantly when we increase the number of conditionals, so that group S's numbers in Table 2 are dominated by the experiments in S_i and S_n. Figure 4 illustrates the different behavior of the two encodings in S_i (the results in S_n are qualitatively similar). As expected (Fig. 4, left), the tuple-based encoding scales with the input program size, whereas the

---

[8] While the total number of VCs verified by Boogie in group T (137) is the same with ($\checkmark_t$) and without ($\checkmark_0$) prover-specific annotations, the two sets are different: 13 VCs verify without annotations but do not verify with annotations because they correspond to tests that should fail with the annotations; another 13 VCs verify with annotations but not without them.

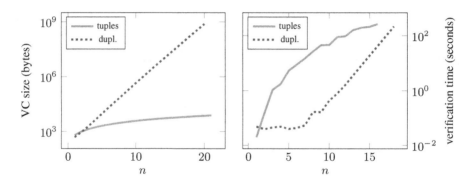

Fig. 4. Scalability of BLT on the programs of group S_i. Left: how the size of the VCs grows with the input size parameter n, in the tuple-based encoding (4) and in the duplication-based encoding (3). Right: how the verification time of the TPTP VCs grows with the input size parameter n, again in each encoding.

duplication-based encoding blows up exponentially—and in fact the largest example in this group can only be generated with the tuple-based encoding within 30 s. The verification time (Fig. 4, right) shows a somewhat more unexpected picture: Vampire can digest very large input files, and is generally faster on the wasteful duplication-based encoding; in contrast, reasoning about tuples requires much memory and is quite slow in these conditions. Extrapolating the trends in Fig. 4, it seems that the verification time of tuple-based VCs may eventually reach a plateau—even though is currently too large in absolute value to be practical.

We plan to experiment with different encodings of conditional statements to investigate ways of assuaging the current scalability limitations of BLT. It is however encouraging that BLT's performance on the smaller, yet more logically complex, examples in the other groups is often satisfactory.

5   Related Work

Triggers were first proposed by Greg Nelson in his influential PhD work [20]. Simplify [7] was the first SMT solver implementing those ideas; today, most widely used SMT solvers—including Z3 [6] and CVC4 [3]—support trigger annotations and include trigger-selection heuristics for when the input does not include such annotations.

As we repeatedly argued in this paper, triggers are indispensable as they increase the flexibility of SMT solvers—especially for program proving—but also introduce an additional annotation burden, and reduce the predictability and stability of provers. A key challenge in developing program provers based on SMT solvers is designing suitable triggers, but few publications deal explicitly with the problem of trigger selection—which thus remains a skill prohibitively difficult to master. Among these works, Spec# generates special triggers to support list comprehensions in specifications [17]; the Dafny verifier includes flexible strategies to generate triggers that avoid matching loops while also supporting calculations of ground facts from recursive definitions [2]; recently, Dafny has been extended with a mechanism that helps users design triggers in their verified programs [18]. The behavior of triggers has also been analyzed in the context of the VCC [5] and Why3 [8] verifiers.

First-order theorem provers approach the problem of checking validity using techniques, such as saturation, quite different from those of SMT solvers. As a result, they fully support complex usage of quantifiers, but they tend to struggle dealing with theories that are not practical to axiomatize—which has restricted their usage for program verification, where theory reasoning is indispensable for dealing with basic types. The results of the present paper rely on recent developments of the Vampire theorem prover [15], which have significantly extended the support for theory reasoning with a first-class Boolean sort and polymorphic arrays [13].

Others have used the Boogie *language* as input to tools other than the Boogie *verifier*, to extend the capabilities of verifiers using Boogie as intermediate representation. HOL-Boogie [4] uses a higher-order interactive prover to discharge Boogie's verification conditions; Boogaloo [21] and Symbooglix [19] support the symbolic execution of Boogie programs; Boogie2Why [1] translates Boogie into Why3, to take advantage of the latter's multi-prover support.

6   Discussion and Future Work

The experimental results detailed in Sect. 4 show the feasibility of using a first-order prover for program verification. The gap between BLT and Boogie is still conspicuous—both in applicability and in performance—but we must also bear in mind that most programs used in the experimental evaluation have been written expressly to demonstrate Boogie's capabilities, and thus it is unsurprising that Boogie works best on them. In Sect. 2, however, we have highlighted situations where Boogie's behavior becomes brittle and dependent on low-level annotations such as triggers; it is in these cases that a different approach, such as the one pursued by BLT, can have an edge—if not yet in overall performance at least in predictability and usability at a higher level.

BLT remains quite limited in scalability and theory reasoning compared to approaches using SMT solvers. Progress in both areas depends on improvements to the Boogie-to-TPTP encoding, as well as to the back-end prover Vampire. Only recently has Vampire been extended with support [13,14] for some of the TPTP features that the encoding described in Sect. 3 depends on; hence, BLT will immediately benefit from improvements in this area—in particular in the memory-efficiency of rules for tuple reasoning. As future work, we plan to fine-tune the TPTP encoding for performance; the experiments of Sect. 4 suggest focusing on finding a scalable encoding of conditionals. There is also room for improving the encoding based on static analysis of the source Boogie code—a technique that is used in different modules of the Boogie tool but not in any way by the current BLT prototype. Finally, we will extend the TPTP encoding to cover the features of the Boogie language currently unsupported—most notably, type polymorphism and gotos.

This paper's research fits into a broader effort of *integrating* different verification techniques and tools to complement each other's shortcoming. Our results suggest that it is feasible to rely on first-order provers to discharge verification conditions in cases where the more commonly used SMT solvers are limited by incompleteness and exhibit brittle behavior, so as to make verification ultimately more flexible and with a higher degree of automation.

Acknowledgments. We thank Evgenii Kotelnikov for helping us understand the latest features of Vampire's support for FOOL.

References

1. Ameri, M., Furia, C.A.: Why just Boogie? Translating between intermediate verification. In: Ábrahám, E., Huisman, M. (eds.) IFM 2016. LNCS, vol. 9681, pp. 79–95. Springer, Cham (2016). doi:10.1007/978-3-319-33693-0_6
2. Amin, N., Leino, K.R.M., Rompf, T.: Computing with an SMT solver. In: Seidl, M., Tillmann, N. (eds.) TAP 2014. LNCS, vol. 8570, pp. 20–35. Springer, Cham (2014). doi:10.1007/978-3-319-09099-3_2
3. Barrett, C., Conway, C.L., Deters, M., Hadarean, L., Jovanović, D., King, T., Reynolds, A., Tinelli, C.: CVC4. In: Gopalakrishnan, G., Qadeer, S. (eds.) CAV 2011. LNCS, vol. 6806, pp. 171–177. Springer, Heidelberg (2011). doi:10.1007/978-3-642-22110-1_14
4. Böhme, S., Leino, K.R.M., Wolff, B.: HOL-Boogie — an interactive prover for the boogie program-verifier. In: Mohamed, O.A., Muñoz, C., Tahar, S. (eds.) TPHOLs 2008. LNCS, vol. 5170, pp. 150–166. Springer, Heidelberg (2008). doi:10.1007/978-3-540-71067-7_15
5. Böhme, S., Moskal, M.: Heaps and data structures: a challenge for automated provers. In: Bjørner, N., Sofronie-Stokkermans, V. (eds.) CADE 2011. LNCS (LNAI), vol. 6803, pp. 177–191. Springer, Heidelberg (2011). doi:10.1007/978-3-642-22438-6_15
6. Moura, L., Bjørner, N.: Z3: an efficient SMT solver. In: Ramakrishnan, C.R., Rehof, J. (eds.) TACAS 2008. LNCS, vol. 4963, pp. 337–340. Springer, Heidelberg (2008). doi:10.1007/978-3-540-78800-3_24
7. Detlefs, D., Nelson, G., Saxe, J.B.: Simplify: a theorem prover for program checking. J. ACM **52**, 365–473 (2005)
8. Dross, C., Conchon, S., Kanig, J., Paskevich, A.: Reasoning with triggers. In: SMT. EPiC Series, pp. 22–31. EasyChair (2012)
9. Flanagan, C., Saxe, J.B.: Avoiding exponential explosion: generating compact verification conditions. In: POPL, pp. 193–205. ACM (2001)
10. Furia, C.A., Meyer, B., Velder, S.: Loop invariants: analysis, classification, and examples. ACM Comp. Sur. **46**(3) (2014)
11. Gries, D.: The Science of Programming. Springer, New York (1981)

12. Kaliszyk, C., Sutcliffe, G., Rabe, F.: TH1: the TPTP typed higher-order form with rank-1 polymorphism. In: PAAR at IJCAR. CEUR Workshop Proceedings, vol. 1635, pp. 41–55. CEUR-WS.org (2016)
13. Kotelnikov, E., Kovács, L., Reger, G., Voronkov, A.: The Vampire and the FOOL. In: SIGPLAN CPP, pp. 37–48. ACM (2016)
14. Kotelnikov, E., Kovács, L., Suda, M., Voronkov, A.: A clausal normal form translation for FOOL. In: GCAI. EPiC, vol. 41, pp. 53–71. EasyChair (2016)
15. Kovács, L., Voronkov, A.: First-order theorem proving and VAMPIRE. In: Sharygina, N., Veith, H. (eds.) CAV 2013. LNCS, vol. 8044, pp. 1–35. Springer, Heidelberg (2013). doi:10.1007/978-3-642-39799-8_1
16. Leino, K.R.M.: Efficient weakest preconditions. Inf. Process. Lett. **93**(6), 281–288 (2005)
17. Leino, K.R.M., Monahan, R.: Reasoning about comprehensions with first-order SMT solvers. In: SAC, pp. 615–622. ACM (2009)
18. Leino, K.R.M., Pit-Claudel, C.: Trigger selection strategies to stabilize program verifiers. In: Chaudhuri, S., Farzan, A. (eds.) CAV 2016. LNCS, vol. 9779, pp. 361–381. Springer, Cham (2016). doi:10.1007/978-3-319-41528-4_20
19. Liew, D., Cadar, C., Donaldson, A.F.: Symbooglix: a symbolic execution engine for Boogie programs. In: ICST, pp. 45–56. IEEE Computer Society (2016)
20. Nelson, C.G.: Techniques for program verification. Ph.D. thesis, Xerox PARC (1981). CSL-81-10
21. Polikarpova, N., Furia, C.A., West, S.: To run what no one has run before: executing an intermediate verification language. In: Legay, A., Bensalem, S. (eds.) RV 2013. LNCS, vol. 8174, pp. 251–268. Springer, Heidelberg (2013). doi:10.1007/978-3-642-40787-1_15
22. Rümmer, P.: E-matching with free variables. In: Bjørner, N., Voronkov, A. (eds.) LPAR 2012. LNCS, vol. 7180, pp. 359–374. Springer, Heidelberg (2012). doi:10.1007/978-3-642-28717-6_28
23. Sutcliffe, G.: The TPTP problem library and associated infrastructure. J. Autom. Reason. **43**(4), 337–362 (2009)

SemSlice: Exploiting Relational Verification for Automatic Program Slicing

Bernhard Beckert, Thorsten Bormer, Stephan Gocht, Mihai Herda[(⊠)],
Daniel Lentzsch, and Mattias Ulbrich

Karlsruhe Institute of Technology (KIT), Karlsruhe, Germany
{beckert,bormer,herda,ulbrich}@kit.edu, stephan.gocht@student.kit.edu,
d.lentzsch@web.de

Abstract. We present SemSlice, a tool which automatically produces
very precise slices for C routines. Slicing is the process of removing statements from a program such that defined aspects of its behavior are
retained. For producing precise slices, i.e., slices that are close to the
minimal number of statements, the program's semantics must be considered. SemSlice is based on automatic relational regression verification,
which SemSlice uses to select valid slices from a set of candidate slices.
We present several approaches for producing candidates for precise slices.
Evaluation shows that regression verification (based on coupling invariant inference) is a powerful tool for semantics-aware slicing: precise slices
for typical slicing challenges can be found automatically and fast.

1   Introduction

Program Slicing. Program slicing [18] removes statements from a program in
order to reduce its size and complexity while retaining some specified aspects of
its behavior. Slicing techniques (or similar data dependency analyses) are used
to optimize the result of compilers. Slicing is also a powerful tool for challenges
in software engineering such as code comprehension, debugging, and fault local-
ization, where the user is involved [3]. A recent study [6] shows that slicing can
improve programming skills in novice learners.

The Idea Behind SemSlice. Traditional slicing techniques use an over
approximation of dependencies in a program and thus produce imprecise, non-
minimal slices. SemSlice goes beyond purely syntactical dependency analysis
and takes the semantics of statements and expressions into account. It can thus
produce much more precise slices than related approaches. SemSlice is fully
automatic and does not require auxiliary annotations (like loop invariants etc.).
SemSlice finds slices by applying *regression verification* [7], an approach for
proving relational properties of programs, to check whether generated slice candidates are valid slices, i.e., are equivalent to the original program with respect
to the specified slicing criterion. Thus, the process has two steps: (1) The tool
generates a slice candidate, i.e., a sub-program of the original program that is not

© Springer International Publishing AG 2017
N. Polikarpova and S. Schneider (Eds.): IFM 2017, LNCS 10510, pp. 312–319, 2017.
DOI: 10.1007/978-3-319-66845-1_20

necessarily a valid slice for the given criterion. (2) The tool uses the existing but customized automatic relational verification engine to check whether the candidate is equivalent to the original program with respect to the criterion. This process is repeated and combined with syntactical slicing to iteratively refine obtained slices.

Handling Loops. Precise slices are particularly difficult to obtain for programs with loops. SemSlice provides a higher degree of automation compared to existing semantics-aware slicing frameworks [1, 11] which are based on inferred or user-provided *functional* loop invariants. In the context of slicing, functional loop invariants have disadvantages: In order to prove that at the location of the slicing criterion the relevant program variables have the same value, strong loop invariants are needed (they have to fix unique values for the variables). Moreover, a loop invariant for the original program needs not be a valid invariant for the sliced program; a different second invariant may be needed. SemSlice does not employ functional invariants but operates on *relational coupling loop invariants* which formalize the difference between two program variants and thus escape this dilemma.

Contribution. SemSlice demonstrates the feasibility of using relational verification to compute precise slices. The advantage of this approach is that the candidate generation engine does not need to care about the correctness of the candidates – that is handled by the relational verifier. In addition to the three heuristics for generating candidates described and evaluated in this paper, Sem-Slice can easily be extended with others. Thus, SemSlice provides a platform for relational verification based slicing for the software slicing community.

Structure of This Paper. The remainder of this paper is structured as follows. Section 2 introduces the concepts of program slicing and relational verification. The implementation of SemSlice is described in Sect. 3. The different approaches to generate slice candidates are introduced in Sect. 4. The paper is completed by a short evaluation in Sect. 5, a report on related tools in Sect. 6 and a conclusion in Sect. 7.

2   Background

2.1   Static Backward Slicing

SemSlice performs a variant of *static backward slicing* (as introduced by Weiser [18]), in which the *slicing criterion*—the specification of the behavioral aspects that must be retained—comprises a set of program variables and a location within the program. Statements which have no effect (a) on the value of the specified program variables at the specified point and (b) on how often the point is reached may be removed.

	(a)		(b)		(c)
1	`int f(int h, int N){`	1	`int f(int h, int N){`	1	`int f(int h, int N){`
2	`    int i = 0;`	2	`    int i = 0;`	2	`    int i = 0;`
3	`    int x = 0;`	3	`    int x = 0;`	3	`    int x = 0;`
4	`    while(i < N) {`	4	`    while(i < N) {`	4	`    while(i < N) {`
5	`        if(i < N - 1)`	5	`        if(i < N - 1)`	5	`        if(i < N - 1)`
6	`            x = h;`	6	`            skip;`	6	`            skip;`
7	`        else`	7	`        else`	7	`        else`
8	`            x = 42;`	8	`            x = 42;`	8	`            skip;`
9	`        i++;`	9	`        i++;`	9	`        i++;`
10	`    }`	10	`    }`	10	`    }`
11	`    return x;`	11	`    return x;`	11	`    return x;`
12	`}`	12	`}`	12	`}`

Fig. 1. (a) Original program, (b) Slice with respect to variable x at line 8, (c) Incorrect slice candidate

Formally, a *slice candidate* is a variant of the original program where zero or more statements have been replaced with the side-effect-free `skip` statement. A slice candidate is considered a *valid slice* if, given the same input to the slice candidate and original program, the following two conditions hold:

1. During execution of the slice candidate and the original program, respectively, the location specified in the slicing criterion is reached for the same number of times.
2. When the location is reached for the ith time in the original program and for the ith time in the slice ($i \geq 1$), each variable specified in the slicing criterion has the same value in the original program's state and in the slice's state.

Figure 1 shows an example of static backward slicing. The goal is to slice the C routine in Fig. 1a with respect to a slicing criterion, which requires the value of x at the **return** statement in line 11 to be preserved. A valid slice for this criterion is shown in Fig. 1b: The assignment in line 6 has been taken from the program. Instead of removing it, we have replaced it by a synthetic `skip` statement without effects to keep the program structure similar to the input program. This line has no effect on the value of x after the loop as x is always set to 42 in the last loop iteration. To show that this program is a slice of the original, an over approximating syntactical analysis (ignorant of the meaning of statements) is insufficient. A semantic analysis is required to determine that the last loop iteration always executes the else-branch. The slicing procedure needs to reason about loops and path conditions.

2.2 Relational Program Verification

Relational verification is an approach to prove specified relations between two given programs (or variants of the same program) to be valid. The tool that SEMSLICE relies on for relational verification is the automatic regression verification tool LLRÊVE [12], which takes two programs as input. If it terminates, the tool has either proved that the programs behave equivalently or it comes up with a counterexample input showing that the programs' semantics are different.

LLRÊVE operates on a generalized version of product programs [2] in which two programs are combined into one in order to be able to reason simultaneously about corresponding loops in the programs. Thus, the program behavior needs not be fully encoded into functional loop invariants, but only the relation between the two behaviors. Relying on relational coupling invariants allows the verification engine to automatically infer the needed abstractions (loop invariants and function summaries) in more cases than if functional abstractions are used. As an example, for proving that the candidate shown in Fig. 1b is a correct slice with respect to the given slicing criterion, our approach has inferred the following coupling invariant:

$$((N_1 - N_2 + i_2 - i_1 = 0) \wedge (N_1 - i_1 \geq 1))$$
$$\vee((N_1 - N_2 + i_2 - i_1 = 0) \wedge (x_1 = x_2))$$

Since our analysis considers two programs, the variable names occuring in the coupling invariant are annotated with 1 or 2 depending on which program they belong to. Note that the coupling invariant states that the value of x is the same in both programs (at the location specified by the slicing criterion).

3   Implementation

SEMSLICE[1] combines the slicing candidate generation with the existing tools clang, LLRÊVE, and ELDARICA. Its workflow is shown in Fig. 2. We implemented the candidate generation component and adapted LLRÊVE for checking slices candidates. The other components are used "of the shelf". A user-friendly web interface for SEMSLICE can be accessed at formal.iti.kit.edu/slicing.

Clang and LLVM. Clang[2] is a front end of the LLVM compiler infrastructure [14] and is used to compile C code into the LLVM intermediate representation (IR). The slicing process operates on the IR, and the resulting slice is also returned in IR. While a reverse transformation into C is possible in principle, it is currently not supported by the LLVM framework and adding this feature would require a significant effort. Building on top of LLVM reduces language complexity and allows us to use the API of LLVM which provides methods to modify the IR (e.g., to remove statements) and standard code analyses (like loop detection).

Candidate Generation. A duplicate of the original program is modified by removing statements to generate a slice candidate. The choice which statements are removed depends on the chosen candidate selection method (see Sect. 4). The process can be iterated; then the results of previously checked slice candidates are taken into consideration for generating new ones.

---

[1] The SEMSLICE source code is available at github.com/mattulbrich/llreve/tree/slicing.

[2] http://clang.llvm.org.

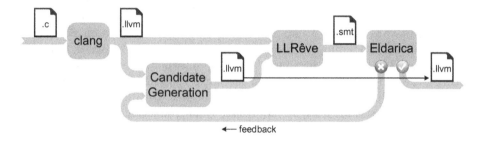

Fig. 2. SEMSLICE Architecture for finding a valid slice

LLRêve and Eldarica. SEMSLICE encodes the slicing criterion as a relational specification between the slice candidate and the original program in first order logic. From this input, LLRÊVE generates an SMT formula, more precisely a set of constrained horn clauses, in which the coupling invariants become uninterpreted predicate symbols to be inferred by the solver. ELDARICA [10], a state-of-the-art SMT solver, checks the formula for satisfiability, i.e., for existence of sufficiently strong relational invariants. If the formula is satisfiable, a valid slice has been found. It may be refined further or taken as the final result. Otherwise, ELDARICA may provide a counterexample, i.e., an input under which the criterion is evaluated differently in the slice candidate and the original program.

Implementation Aspects. LLRÊVE can only check relational specifications in the final states of the two programs. A slicing criterion, however, may refer to any point within the program. We have adapted the clause construction in LLRÊVE to allow for relational conditions to be checked within functions.

Since a valid slice requires by definition that the criterion's statement is reached equally often in program and slice, SEMSLICE enforces that all loops are iterated equally often by encoding this requirement into the proof obligation. This requirement is a little too strict: for a loop not containing the criterion, there might be a correct slice which iterates the loop less often, but cannot be validated with our technique. This requirement enforces the mutual termination property (i.e. the slice terminates iff the original program also terminates) of the original program and the slice candidate. If it were to be relaxed than our approach would be able to validate more candidates, however, the mutual termination property would have to be shown through other means.

4   Slice Candidate Generation

SEMSLICE provides three methods for candidate generation. They differ in time requirements, number of generated candidates, and precision.

The naive *brute forcing* (BF) approach generates all possible slice candidates. It is complete in the sense that it finds the smallest slice that can be validated with relational verification. Section 5 shows that it runs surprisingly fast on small programs, but due to the exponential number of slice candidates it does not scale.

Single statement elimination (SSE) successively removes statements from the program. If removing a statement yields an invalid slice, SSE reverts and tries removing another statement. This results in a quadratic number of LLRÊVE invocations. Thus, it scales better than brute forcing, but cannot remove groups of statements that cannot be removed individually like x:=x+50; x:=x-50.

Counterexample guided slicing (CGS) works in the opposite direction: It successively adds statements to a candidate until it can be proved valid. In case of an invalid slice candidate, CGS uses the counterexample provided by ELDARICA to choose which statements are to be added in the next iteration. In each iteration the slice candidates grow by at least one statement such that termination is guaranteed. On the considered examples, CGS terminates very fast after only a few iterations, but with potentially reduced precision compared to the other methods.

5   Evaluation

Table 1 shows an evaluation of SEMSLICE using a collection[3] of small but intricate examples (e.g., the example of Fig. 1 or a routine in which the same value is first added and then subtracted) that each focus on a particular challenge for semantics-aware slicing. Some are taken from slicing literature [1,4,8,11,17] while others were crafted by ourselves. The second column indicates the source of each example, the third the number of LLVM-IR statements in the program. For each candidate generation method from Sect. 2.1, the table lists the number of statements in the smallest slice found by SEMSLICE, the (wall) time needed by

Table 1. Evaluation

Original			BF			SSE			CGS		
Example	Source	#stmts	time(s)	#stmts	#calls	time(s)	#stmts	#calls	time(s)	#stmts	#calls
count_occurrence_error	self	50				13	42	11			
count_occurrence_result	self	50				16	44	13			
dead_code_after_ssa	[17]	4	<1	2	4	<1	2	4	<1	2	1
dead_code_unused_variable	self	3	<1	2	2	<1	2	3	<1	2	1
identity_not_modifying	[8]	8	<1	3	3	<1	7	5	<1	6	1
identity_plus_minus_50	[1]	5	<1	2	4	<1	5	4	<1	5	1
iflow_cyclic	[17]	18	62	14	2197	<1	16	6	<1	17	1
iflow_dynfamic_override	self	15	23	8	1298	<1	11	8	<1	12	1
iflow_endofloop (Fig. 1)	self	19	118	15	4065	<1	16	7	<1	18	2
intermediate	self	13	4	11	129	<1	12	5	<1	12	2
requires_path_sensitivity	[11]	20	647	16	26894	<1	17	10	<1	18	3
single_pass_removal	self	13	<1	3	7	<1	6	11	<1	8	1
unchanged_over_itteration	self	20	29	9	932	1	15	14	<1	20	2
unreachable_code_nested	self	10	<1	2	1	<1	9	1	<1	4	1
whole_loop_removable	self	20	15	8	469	<1	17	5	<1	17	2

[3] The benchmarks are available at github.com/ mattulbrich/llreve/tree/slicing/ slicing/testdata/benchmarks.

the tool, and the number of calls to the SMT solver. The experiments were conducted on a machine with an Intel Core I5-6600K CPU and 16GB RAM. The exponential brute forcing approach works satisfactorily fast on functions with up to 20 statements, and while it requires more time than the other approaches, it computes more precise slices.

Modern coding conventions [15, p. 34] suggest that functions should comprise at most some 20 lines of code, and our approach is capable to deal with challenges of that size. What hinders us slicing real-world programs is that SEMSLICE cannot yet deal with bit-operations, complicated heap structures, and deep calling hierarchies.

6   Related Work

Static slicing is an active research area, other semantic approaches have been published using abstract interpretation [9,16] or term rewriting [8,13]. In this section we focus on approaches with accessible tools.

GamaSlicer [5] features a graphical user interface and is designed for slicing Java programs annotated with JML. It provides multiple slicing algorithms, the most sophisticated one is *assertion based slicing* [1], which uses the specification as slicing criterion. A valid slice is obtained by removing statements from the original program such that the original specification still holds. Unlike SEMSLICE, this tool requires functional loop invariants from the user.

Tracer is a tool that runs in command line and computes slices for C programs based on *path sensitive backward slicing* [11]. It uses symbolic execution to find and remove unfeasible paths in a program and thereby increase precision compared to syntactic slicing. To cope with path explosion of the symbolic execution tree, parts of the tree are reused. This approach scales very well, but unfeasible data dependencies over multiple iterations of a loop like those in Fig. 1a cannot be detected.

7   Conclusion

We presented SEMSLICE, a fully automatic tool to compute slices using semantic information. The approach uses relational verification to show that a slice candidate is equivalent to the original program with respect to a slicing criterion. Three different approaches to compute slice candidates were introduced.

The presented approach works well on small, but intricate programs. To be able to treat larger programs with SEMSLICE, we will in future work combine the regression verification engine with other better scaling, but less precise regression verification tools.

As our approach builds on top of a relational verification engine that infers relational coupling invariants, functional loop invariants need not be specified. Our evaluation shows powerful and highly precise program slicing can be implemented by relying on relational verification. That indicates that relational verification is indeed a very useful basis for building formal program analysis tools.

References

1. Barros, J.B., Da Cruz, D., Henriques, P.R., Pinto, J.S.: Assertion-based slicing and slice graphs. Formal Aspects Comput. **24**(2), 217–248 (2012)
2. Barthe, G., Crespo, J.M., Kunz, C.: Relational verification using product programs. In: Butler, M., Schulte, W. (eds.) FM 2011. LNCS, vol. 6664, pp. 200–214. Springer, Heidelberg (2011). doi:10.1007/978-3-642-21437-0_17
3. Binkley, D., Harman, M.: A survey of empirical results on program slicing. Adv. Comput. **62**, 105–178 (2004)
4. Canfora, G., Cimitile, A., De Lucia, A.: Conditioned program slicing. Inf. Softw. Technol. **40**(11), 595–607 (1998)
5. da Cruz, D., Henriques, P.R., Pinto, J.S.: Gamaslicer: an online laboratory for program verification and analysis. In: Proceedings of the Tenth Workshop on Language Descriptions, Tools and Applications. p. 3. ACM (2010)
6. Eranki, K.L., Moudgalya, K.M.: Program slicing technique: a novel approach to improve programming skills in novice learners. In: Proceedings of the Conference on Information Technology Education. pp. 160–165. ACM (2016)
7. Felsing, D., Grebing, S., Klebanov, V., Rümmer, P., Ulbrich, M.: Automating regression verification. In: Proceedings of the International Conference on Automated Software Engineering, ASE 2014, pp. 349–360. ACM (2014)
8. Field, J., Ramalingam, G., Tip, F.: Parametric program slicing. In: Proceedings of the Symposium on Principles of Programming Languages, pp. 379–392. ACM (1995)
9. Halder, R., Cortesi, A.: Abstract program slicing on dependence condition graphs. Sci. Comput. Program. **78**(9), 1240–1263 (2013)
10. Hojjat, H., Konečný, F., Garnier, F., Iosif, R., Kuncak, V., Rümmer, P.: A verification toolkit for numerical transition systems. In: Giannakopoulou, D., Méry, D. (eds.) FM 2012. LNCS, vol. 7436, pp. 247–251. Springer, Heidelberg (2012). doi:10.1007/978-3-642-32759-9_21
11. Jaffar, J., Murali, V., Navas, J.A., Santosa, A.E.: Path-sensitive backward slicing. In: Miné, A., Schmidt, D. (eds.) SAS 2012. LNCS, vol. 7460, pp. 231–247. Springer, Heidelberg (2012). doi:10.1007/978-3-642-33125-1_17
12. Kiefer, M., Klebanov, V., Ulbrich, M.: Relational program reasoning using compiler IR. In: Blazy, S., Chechik, M. (eds.) VSTTE 2016. LNCS, vol. 9971, pp. 149–165. Springer, Cham (2016). doi:10.1007/978-3-319-48869-1_12
13. Komondoor, R.: Precise slicing in imperative programs via term-rewriting and abstract interpretation. In: Logozzo, F., Fähndrich, M. (eds.) SAS 2013. LNCS, vol. 7935, pp. 259–282. Springer, Heidelberg (2013). doi:10.1007/978-3-642-38856-9_15
14. Lattner, C., Adve, V.: Llvm: A compilation framework for lifelong program analysis and transformation. In: International Symposium on Code Generation and Optimization, CGO 2004, pp. 75–86. IEEE (2004)
15. Martin, R.C.: Clean Code: A Handbook of Agile Software Craftsmanship, 1st edn. Prentice Hall PTR, Upper Saddle River, NJ (2008)
16. Mastroeni, I., Nikolić, Đ.: Abstract program slicing: from theory towards an implementation. In: Dong, J.S., Zhu, H. (eds.) ICFEM 2010. LNCS, vol. 6447, pp. 452–467. Springer, Heidelberg (2010). doi:10.1007/978-3-642-16901-4_30
17. Ward, M.: Properties of slicing definitions. In: Ninth IEEE International Working Conference on Source Code Analysis and Manipulation, SCAM 2009, pp. 23–32. IEEE (2009)
18. Weiser, M.: Program slicing. In: Proceedings of the 5th International Conference on Software Engineering. pp. 439–449. IEEE Press (1981)

Formal Modeling

VBPMN: Automated Verification of BPMN Processes (Tool Paper)

Ajay Krishna[1], Pascal Poizat[2,3], and Gwen Salaün[1](✉)

[1] Univ. Grenoble Alpes, CNRS, Grenoble INP, Inria, LIG, 38000 Grenoble, France
Gwen.Salaun@inria.fr
[2] Université Paris Lumières, Univ Paris Nanterre, Nanterre, France
[3] Sorbonne Universités, UPMC Univ Paris 06, CNRS, LIP6 UMR7606, Paris, France

Abstract. Business process modeling is an important concern in enterprise. Formal analysis techniques are crucial to detect semantic issues in the corresponding models, or to help with their refactoring and evolution. However, business process development frameworks often fall short when it comes to go beyond simulation or syntactic checking of the models. In this paper, we present our VBPMN verification framework. It features several techniques for the automatic analysis of business processes modeled using BPMN, the *de facto* standard for business process modeling. As such, it supports a more robust development of business processes.

Keywords: Business processes · BPMN · Verification · Evolution · Tool · Process algebra · LNT · Labelled transition system · Model transformation

1 Introduction

Mastering business processes has become a central concern in companies and organizations. The modeling of these processes is the first step in order to refine, optimize, or make them evolve while reducing costs and increasing incomes. BPMN is a workflow-based notation that has been published as an ISO standard [9,11], and thus is used widely for business process modeling. Several frameworks have been developed in order to support the development of BPMN processes. They mostly provide modeling, simulation, or execution features. However, but for syntactic checking, these frameworks do not provide any advanced, *i.e.*, behavioral semantics-related, support for analyzing the process models.

In this paper, we present a verification framework, VBPMN, that is freely available for download [1]. It enables one to verify several properties of interest on BPMN processes. VBPMN relies on an intermediate process meta-model called PIF (Process Intermediate Format). This pivot meta-model, and its XML representation, open the way to the use of different process modeling notations as front-end. They also enable us to develop back-end connections to the input languages of several verification tools, and as a consequence to several kinds of

© Springer International Publishing AG 2017
N. Polikarpova and S. Schneider (Eds.): IFM 2017, LNCS 10510, pp. 323–331, 2017.
DOI: 10.1007/978-3-319-66845-1_21

verification. For now, we have focused on BPMN as a front-end, and on connection to the CADP verification toolbox [7] using one of the input languages it supports, LNT [3], and the SVL verification scripting language [6]. It is worth emphasizing that other modeling notations can be connected to PIF, *e.g.*, Event-driven Process Chains (EPC) or UML activity diagrams, since they share an important subset of concepts and associated semantics. Complementary back-ends are already under development, concretely, a transformation from PIF to the input language of an SMT solver to support data-flows and data constraints in processes, and a transformation from PIF to Maude to support the quantitative analysis of timed processes.

Figure 1 gives an overview of VBPMN. It comes with a Web application that takes as input BPMN-2.0-compliant business processes. The processes are first transformed into PIF. Then, from the PIF descriptions, models in LNT and model-specific verification scripts in SVL are generated. In the end, CADP is used to check either for functional properties of a given business process or for the correctness of the evolution of a business process into another one. This later kind of verification being supported by VBPMN is particularly helpful in order to improve a process *wrt.* certain optimization criterion.

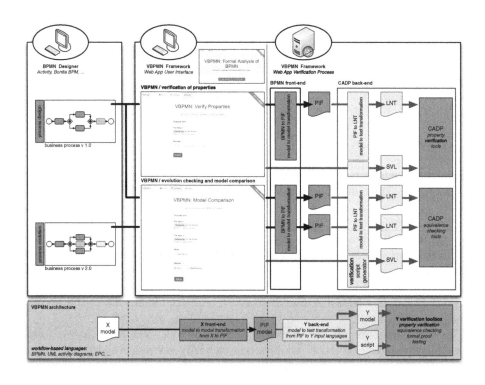

Fig. 1. Overview of VBPMN.

The rest of this paper is organized as follows. Section 2 introduces the models and languages supported by **VBPMN**. Section 3 gives an overview of the **VBPMN** Web application. In Sect. 4, we focus on the CADP back-end, on the properties it allows one to check, and we present experimental results. Section 5 concludes the presentation and sketches some perspectives for our work.

2   Models and Languages

VBPMN relies on an intermediate format, PIF. It allows one to support several modeling languages, *e.g.*, BPMN, and to target several verification tools, *e.g.*, the CADP toolbox using LNT and LTS formal descriptions. We present here the main models and languages currently supported in the framework.

BPMN. BPMN is an ISO/IEC standard since 2013 [9,11]. It is a workflow-based graphical notation (and an XML-based language) for modeling business processes whose development is supported by many designers and execution frameworks, *e.g.*, Activiti, Bonita BPM, or jBPM. In our work, we focus on the behavioral subset of BPMN which consists of start/end events, tasks, and gateways (exclusive, inclusive, and parallel). We support looping behaviors and unbalanced workflows, that is, gateways without an exact correspondence between split and merge gateways. We only require that BPMN processes are syntactically correct, which is enforced by the aforementioned BPMN designers.

PIF. PIF stands for Process Intermediate Format. We use it as a pivot meta-model and language in order to make our approach generic and extensible. PIF is based on the common constructs one finds in a workflow-based modeling language. The interest of such a pivot language is that several modeling languages can be used as input, *e.g.*, BPMN (that is supported by now), UML, or Event-driven Process Chains. Moreover, several verification techniques and tools can be connected to it as a back-end, *e.g.*, to deal with behavioral properties of models, or with extensions of such properties to time and data-related aspects.

LNT and LTS. We have focused so far on purely behavioral properties. Verification operates on Labelled Transition Systems (LTSs). This low-level model is especially convenient because there are many verification tools accepting this format as input, in particular in the model checking area. A translational semantics from PIF to LTSs was obtained indirectly using a model transformation from PIF to the LNT process algebra. LNT [3] is expressive enough to encode the expressiveness of the PIF constructs and LNT operational semantics maps to LTSs. Further, LNT is the input formalism of the CADP toolbox [7], which provides various kinds of analysis we reuse for formally analyzing the PIF descriptions resulting from our BPMN to PIF model transformation.

Transformations. VBPMN works thanks to several model transformations, as depicted in the generic architecture on the bottom of Fig. 1. We first use a model-to-model transformation in order to transform BPMN processes into PIF models. Then, we use a model-to-text transformation for generating from PIF models corresponding LNT specifications as well as CADP verification scripts in the SVL language [6]. These scripts automate the verification selected in the VBPMN Web interface (see Sect. 3 below for more details). Note that when one of the verification steps described in the SVL scripts fails, one gets a witness (*i.e.*, a counter-example) that is presented back in the Web interface so that the designer can use it to modify the erroneous process model.

3   Web Application

Business processes are usually designed by business analysts that may not be familiar with formal verification techniques and tools. Our goal is to enable one to take benefit from formal verification without having to deal with a steep learning curve. The VBPMN Web Application has been developed in this direction. It hides the underlying transformation and verification process, it provides the users with simple interaction mechanisms, and it generates analysis results that are easily relatable to the input process model(s). There are numerous tools supporting the modeling of business processes. Extending a specific one, *e.g.* the Eclipse BPMN designer, would limit the community that could use VBPMN. Therefore, we have decided to architecture it as a Web application.

Technology stack. The VBPMN Web application is hosted on a Tomcat application server. Its responsive UI invokes a RESTful API to trigger the transformation from BPMN to PIF and the verification of the process models. The use of such an API makes the platform more extensible – other people could build custom UIs using them. Internally, the API is built using the Jersey JAX-RS implementation. The model-to-model transformation from BPMN to PIF is realized at the XML level (both BPMN and PIF have XML representations) using a combination of JAXB and of the Woodstox Streaming XML API (StAX), which implements a pull parsing technique and offers better performance for large XML models. The model-to-text transformation from PIF to LNT and SVL is achieved using a Python script that can also be used independently from the Web application as a command-line interface tool.

User interface. One can choose either to verify some property or to check process evolution correctness. In the first case (Fig. 2, left), one has to upload the BPMN process model and specify the temporal logic formula for the property. In the later case (Fig. 2, right), one has to upload two BPMN processes, specify the evolution relation, and optionally give tasks to hide or to rename in the comparison (see [12] for the formal definition of the evolution relations). As a result one can visualize the LTS models that have been generated for the BPMN processes. Further, in case the verification fails, *i.e.*, either the property does not yield or the evolution is not correct, one gets a counter-example model.

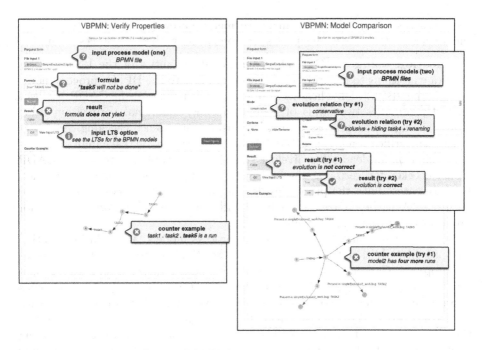

Fig. 2. VBPMN Web application in use.

4   CADP Back-End

The CADP back-end addresses business process verification using available model-checking and equivalence checking techniques in the CADP toolbox. This is achieved by transforming PIF models into LNT process algebraic descriptions, and by generating specific SVL verification scripts from UI inputs.

From PIF to LNT and SVL. The principle of the PIF to LNT transformation is to encode into LNT processes all the BPMN elements involved in a process model behavioral semantics, that is, all nodes (initial/end events, tasks, and gateways) and all sequences flows between nodes. This gives us a set of LNT processes that are then composed in parallel and synchronized accordingly to the BPMN execution semantics. For instance, after execution of a node, the corresponding LNT process synchronizes with the process encoding the outgoing sequence flow, which then synchronizes with the process encoding the node appearing at the end of this flow, and so on. More details on this encoding can be found in [12], which however applied only to balanced process workflows, *i.e.*, workflows where every split gateway of some kind (exclusive, parallel, inclusive) has a corresponding merge gateway of the same kind. This limitation is no longer present in VBPMN that now supports also unbalanced process workflows. This has been achieved by implementing in LNT a scheduler that runs in parallel with all other processes, keeps track of active flows, and interacts with some specific node processes, *e.g.*, those for inclusive merge gateways, in order to indicate them whether they have to expect synchronization with more processes or not.

Verification using CADP. The operational semantics of the LNT process algebra enables us to generate LTSs corresponding to the BPMN process model given in the VBPMN UI. These LTSs may then be analyzed using CADP. VBPMN currently provides two kinds of formal analysis: functional verification using model checking and process comparison using equivalence checking. As far as functional verification is concerned, one can for example use reachability analysis to search, *e.g.*, for deadlock or livelock states. Another option is to use the CADP model checker for verifying the satisfaction of safety and liveness properties. In these cases, since the properties depend on the input process, they have to be provided in the UI by the analyst, who can reuse well-known patterns for properties such as those presented in [4].

Process evolution takes as input two process models, an evolution relation and possibly additional parameters for the relation. Several evolution relations are proposed. Conservative evolution ensures that the observational behavior is strictly preserved. Inclusive evolution ensures that a subset of a process behavior is preserved in a new version of it. Selective evolution (that is compatible with both conservative and inclusive evolution) allows one to focus on a subset of the process tasks. It is also possible to have VBPMN work up-to a renaming relation over tasks. If the two input process models do not fullfil the constraints of the chosen evolution relation, a counter-example that indicates the source of the violation is returned by VBPMN in the UI. This helps the process analyst in understanding the impact of evolution and supports the refinement into a correct evolved version of a process model. All the evolution relations are checked using the CADP equivalence checker and SVL scripts for hiding and renaming.

Experiments. We used a Mac OS laptop running on a 2.3 GHz Intel Core i7 processor with 16 GB of memory. We carried out experiments on many examples taken from the literature or hand-crafted, and we present in Table 1 some of these results. For each process, the table gives the number of tasks (T), flows (F), gateways (exclusive, parallel, and inclusive, respectively), and two booleans indicating the presence of loops (L) and unbalanced workflow structure (U). The table finally presents the size of the generated LTS in terms of states and transitions (before and after minimization modulo branching equivalence [13]) as well as the computation time for obtaining the LTS model. We recall that one can use this LTS for analysis purposes using model checking available for instance in the CADP toolbox. All the examples presented in the table are compiled into LTS within a few seconds. The main factor of state space increase is the presence in the input process of parallel or inclusive gateways. Those gateways exhibit a high degree of parallelism and the enumeration of all possible executions result in larger LTSs. As far as the computation time is concerned, the number of parallel and inclusive gateways is again the main factor of explosion as shown in the last example of the table, which consists of several nested gateways. The presence of loops can also increase the size of the resulting LTS and of the computation time because this may induce additional executions to be explored.

Table 1. Experimental results.

Process description	Constructs							LTS (states/transitions)		Gen. time
	T	F	⊗	⊕	⊙	L	U	Raw	Min.	
Booking sys.	6	11	2	0	0	✓	×	29/29	8/9	6 s
Retry sys.	2	8	3	0	0	✓	✓	21/21	5/6	6 s
Leave man.	6	13	3	0	0	✓	✓	36/36	9/11	6 s
Acc. open. (1)	15	29	5	2	2	×	×	469/1,002	24/34	6 s
Acc. open. (2)	16	33	5	2	2	✓	×	479/1,013	26/37	7 s
Software dev.	6	19	7	0	0	✓	✓	40/42	12/16	6 s
Publishing sys.	12	31	7	2	2	✓	✓	3,038/9,785	32/63	7 s
Incident sys.	7	16	5	0	0	×	✓	39/41	11/13	6 s
Travel org.	6	14	0	0	4	×	✓	4,546/6,155	51/77	9 s
Lunch pay.	6	24	8	0	0	✓	✓	54/59	11/16	6 s
Hand-craft. (1)	20	38	0	8	0	×	×	577,756/3,388,390	334/1,174	26 s
Hand-craft. (2)	20	43	0	6	6	×	×	4,488,843/26,533,828	347/1,450	224 s

5 Concluding Remarks

In this paper, we have presented VBPMN, our tool for the analysis of business processes. VBPMN has a particular focus on BPMN since it is a standard, but it may indeed support as input any workflow-based language that can be transformed into the PIF meta-model and language. PIF is used as an intermediate between workflow notations and back-end formal frameworks, *i.e.*, formal models, equipped with associated verification techniques and tools. We have here focused on a transformation from PIF to LTS, which is, in practice, achieved via a transformation to the LNT process algebra and reusing the LTS semantics of LNT. These LTSs can then be analyzed using model and equivalence checking techniques thanks to the CADP toolbox. The overall analysis process provided by VBPMN is fully automated and freely available for download [1].

Related work. To the best of our knowledge, the existing industrial development frameworks for BPMN, such as Activiti or Bonita BPM, do not provide formal techniques for verifying business processes. If we broaden the scope, we can compare to LoLA, ProM, and VerChor.

LoLA can be used to check whether a Petri net satisfies some property, using reduction techniques and state space explicit exploration. It has been applied in various application domains and more specifically to the verification of the BPEL orchestration language, of Web service choreographies, and of business process models, see, *e.g.*, [5]. In comparison to LoLA-based works, VBPMN proposes specific analysis techniques for the verification of business process evolution.

ProM [2] is a platform for the development of state-of-the-art process mining techniques and tools. Process mining can be used to extract knowledge, *e.g.*, under the form of process models, from execution logs. It can also be used to monitor processes and detect deviations. VBPMN does not address mining from logs, and assumes models are given. The techniques we propose for evolution checking are somehow complementary to ProM where evolution can be tackled from a deviation point of view. BPMNDiffViz [10] combines process mining and the concept of edit distance for providing a similarity measure between two processes. On the contrary, VBPMN has a more qualitative vision of evolution using bi-simulations and pre-orders. The extension to quantitative evolution is definitely an interesting perspective for VBPMN.

The VerChor platform [8] aims at analyzing choreographies possibly described using BPMN choreography diagrams. An intermediate format and a transformation to LNT was used there too. However, the focus is complementary: process diagrams and the verification of properties and of evolution in VBPMN, versus choreography diagrams and the verification of choreography-specific properties (synchronizability and realizability) in VerChor. Further, VBPMN supports unbalanced workflows, while VerChor does not.

Future work. Our main perspective is to go beyond control-flow and behavioral analysis of BPMN, and to take into account data-flow and quantitative aspects. We are studying extensibility features for the PIF meta-model and language. Further, we are developing new back-ends from PIF to SMT solvers for data-flow aspects, and to statistical model-checkers for quantitative aspects.

References

1. VBPMN Framework. https://pascalpoizat.github.io/vbpmn/
2. Bose, R.P.J.C., Verbeek, E.H.M.W., Aalst, W.M.P.: Discovering hierarchical process models using ProM. In: Nurcan, S. (ed.) CAiSE Forum 2011. LNBIP, vol. 107, pp. 33–48. Springer, Heidelberg (2012). doi:10.1007/978-3-642-29749-6_3
3. Champelovier, D., Clerc, X., Garavel, H., Guerte, Y., Lang, F., McKinty, C., Powazny, V., Serwe, W., Smeding, G.: Reference Manual of the LNT to LOTOS Translator, Version 6.1. INRIA/VASY (2014)
4. Dwyer, M.B., Avrunin, G.S., Corbett, J.C.: Patterns in property specifications for finite-state verification. In: Proceedings of ICSE 1999, pp. 411–420. ACM (1999)
5. Fahland, D., Favre, C., Koehler, J., Lohmann, N., Völzer, H., Wolf, K.: Analysis on demand: instantaneous soundness checking of industrial business process models. Data Knowl. Eng. **70**(5), 448–466 (2011)
6. Garavel, H., Lang, F.: SVL: a scripting language for compositional verification. In: Kim, M., Chin, B., Kang, S., Lee, D. (eds.) FORTE 2001. IIFIP, vol. 69, pp. 377–392. Springer, Boston, MA (2002). doi:10.1007/0-306-47003-9_24
7. Garavel, H., Lang, F., Mateescu, R., Serwe, W.: CADP 2011: a toolbox for the construction and analysis of distributed processes. STTT **15**(2), 89–107 (2013)
8. Güdemann, M., Poizat, P., Salaün, G., Ye, L.: VerChor: a framework for the design and verification of choreographies. IEEE Trans. Serv. Compu. **9**(4), 647–660 (2016)
9. ISO/IEC: International Standard 19510, Information technology - Business Process Model and Notation (2013)
10. Ivanov, S., Kalenkova, A.A., van der Aalst, W.M.P: BPMNDiffViz: a tool for BPMN models comparison. In: Proceedings of BPMN 2015 Demo Session, CEUR Workshop Proceedings, BPMN 2015, vol. 1418, pp. 35–39 (2015). http://CEUR-WS.org

11. OMG: Business Process Model and Notation (BPMN) - Version 2.0, January 2011
12. Poizat, P., Salaün, G., Krishna, A.: Checking business process evolution. In: Kouchnarenko, O., Khosravi, R. (eds.) FACS 2016. LNCS, vol. 10231, pp. 36–53. Springer, Cham (2017). doi:10.1007/978-3-319-57666-4_4
13. van Glabbeek, R.J., Weijland, W.P.: Branching time and abstraction in bisimulation semantics. J. ACM **43**(3), 555–600 (1996)

How Well Can I Secure My System?

Barbara Kordy and Wojciech Widel[(✉)]

INSA Rennes, IRISA, Rennes, France
{barbara.kordy,wojciech.widel}@irisa.fr

Abstract. Securing a system, being it a computer network, a physical infrastructure or an organization, is a very challenging task. In practice, it is always constrained by available resources, e.g., budget, time, or man-power. An attack–defense tree is a security model allowing to reason about different strategies that an attacker may use to attack a system and potential countermeasures that a defender could apply to defend against such attacks. This work integrates the modeling power of attack–defense trees with the strengths of integer linear programming techniques. We develop a framework that, given the overall budget allocated for the system's protection, suggests which countermeasures should be implemented to secure the system in the best way possible. We lay down formal foundations for our framework and implement a proof of concept tool automating the solving of relevant optimization problems.

1 Introduction

The only system that is guaranteed to be fully secure is the empty system which does not provide any functionality. Any other system offering an actual service will always be vulnerable to attacks. These attacks may target the system's availability (e.g., denial of service attacks), its integrity (e.g., corruption of data leading to inaccurate or inconsistent results), or the confidentiality of the users' private information (e.g., stealing credentials necessary for authentication). To achieve their malicious goals, attackers, who might be external to the system or insiders, have a plethora of methods to choose from, including digital means, such as hacking, physical attacks, for instance, breaking in and stealing, as well as very powerful social engineering techniques relying on psychological manipulation. All these aspects must be taken into account while securing a system or a company. In addition, perfect security would require the system's owners to have unlimited resources, in terms of financial means and time, but in practice, this is never the case. This is where the risk analysis comes into play.

The crucial challenge in every risk assessment methodology is to exhaustively describe the attack scenarios corresponding to the most feared threats, in order to determine the most likely ones, and deploy relevant countermeasures, in such a way that the residual risks are acceptable. Attack–defense trees have been introduced in [6] as a formal solution to address this challenge and to support practical risk assessment methodologies.

An *attack–defense tree* (ADTree) is a graph-based model representing how an attacker may compromise a system and how a defender may protect it against

© Springer International Publishing AG 2017
N. Polikarpova and S. Schneider (Eds.): IFM 2017, LNCS 10510, pp. 332–347, 2017.
DOI: 10.1007/978-3-319-66845-1_22

potential attacks. ADTrees enhance the industrially recognized formalism of attack trees [8,10], by explicitly integrating the countermeasures and the counterattacks against these countermeasures to the model. Methods for quantitative analysis of ADTrees, e.g., [1,7], allow the modeler to analyze and quantify the effect of deploying a countermeasure, and to evaluate its consequences.

Several aspects can be taken into account while choosing the countermeasures to be implemented. One can be interested in minimizing the number of undefended attacks, minimizing the impact that the system would suffer from in a case of an attack, maximizing the minimal necessary investment of the attacker, etc. It turns out that all these problems might be modeled as integer linear programming problems [3].

The objective of this work is to develop a framework allowing a security expert to select the most pertinent set of countermeasures, in order to secure the analyzed system in the best way possible. This framework combines the modeling features of ADTrees with the potential of integer optimization techniques. Knowledge about possible attack strategies and the corresponding countermeasures is extracted from an attack–defense tree. This information is then used by integer optimization algorithms to select the most appropriate set of countermeasures. Our selection procedure is guided by practical constraints, such as the cost of individual actions of the attacker and the defender, the impact of an attack to the system, and the overall defense budget available.

Contribution. The main *scientific novelty* of this work is the development of the defense semantics for ADTrees, capturing possible strategies of a reasonable attacker and listing corresponding defender's strategies allowing to secure the analyzed system. The *practical contribution* is the formulation of security-relevant optimization problems in terms of integer programming and the implementation of a prototype tool to solve them. Our tool takes an ADTree as input and uses a free integer programming solver *lp_solve* [2] to output the optimal set of countermeasures to be implemented, according to a given optimization function.

Related work. The stimulus triggering the framework developed in this paper has been the work of Laura Albert McLay, an operations researcher working on cybersecurity problems. McLay investigates optimization techniques to distribute security budget amongst possible countermeasures and makes use of maximal coverage models to prioritize mitigations [12]. The major difference between our approach and the one of McLay is the way in which the link between potential attacks and the corresponding sets of countermeasures is tackled. In [12], this link is given as input to the problem. In our approach, this information is extracted from an ADTree in the form of its defense semantics. We propose an extraction algorithm which contributes to the development of formal foundations for ADTrees and, as such, is the main scientific contribution of this paper.

Optimization techniques have also been applied to attack–defense trees to address the problem of multi-objective evaluation of security using the concept of Pareto efficient solutions [1,11]. The goal of [11] is to identify optimal counter-measures that maximize the security performance, minimize the attack impact and minimize the defense cost. However, contrary to our approach, attack–defense trees used in [11] do not allow to model attacker's actions that would disable a countermeasure of the defender, which results in a less complex but also much less expressive model. The authors of [1] use Pareto frontier to devise a technique that optimizes several parameters, e.g., cost and probability, at once. ADTrees considered in [1] are similar to the ones used in our paper. However, this work does not consider coverage problems, as we do in the current work.

2   Security Modeling with Attack–defense Trees

We start by explaining the ADTree formalism and presenting the assumptions about the attacker and the defender considered in this work. Then, we introduce a formal semantics which allows us to take advantage of integer programming techniques to reason about attack–defense scenarios modeled with ADTrees.

2.1   Attack–defense Trees

Attack–defense trees (ADTrees) [6] are rooted trees with labeled nodes sup-porting representation and quantitative analysis of security scenarios involving two competing (sets of) actors – the attacker (denoted by A) and the defender (denoted by D). Labels of the nodes of an ADTree depict goals of the actors. One of the actors is trying to achieve a particular goal represented by the root node of the ADTree and the other actor is trying to hamper them from doing so.[1] The goal of a node in an ADTree can be refined into sub-goals, either in a *disjunctive* way (denoted by OR) or in a *conjunctive* way (denoted by AND). The meaning of an ADTree is based on the notion of *goal achievement*. A goal represented by a disjunctively refined node is achieved if at least one of the sub-goals rep-resented by its children is achieved. To achieve a goal of a conjunctively refined node, sub-goals of all of its children must be achieved. The goals represented by the labels of the non–refined nodes are called *basic actions*. They represent the actual actions that the attacker and the defender will perform to achieve their goals. In order to forbid an actor from achieving their goal, the other actor may apply a countermeasure (denoted by C). In the ADTree formalism, the nodes representing countermeasures can be disjunctively or conjunctively refined and they can again be countered. At most one countermeasure per node is allowed, thus different ways of countering the same goal are represented using a single countermeasure which is disjunctively refined. The goal of a countered node is achieved if the node's refinement (or the corresponding basic action in the case of a non-refined but countered node) is achieved *and* the goal of the countermeasure attached to the node is not achieved by the other actor.

---

[1] In [6], the root actor is called the *proponent* and the other actor is the *opponent*.

An illustrative toy ADTree is given in Fig. 1 and explained in Example 1. The following graphical conventions are used: nodes of the attacker are depicted using red circles and those of the defender using green rectangles; conjunctively refined nodes are marked by an arc connecting their children; nodes are connected to their countermeasures with the help of dotted edges.

Example 1. In the scenario represented with the ADTree from Fig. 1, Eve (the attacker) wants to get the password for Bob's Windows account. Eve can either perform a hacking-based attack or try to guess

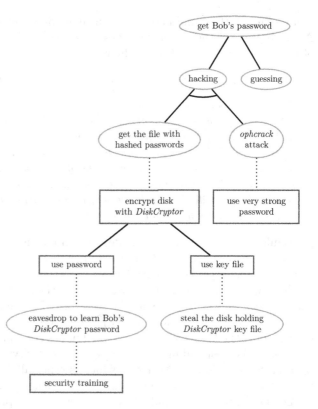

Fig. 1. ADTree for getting a password (Color figure online)

the password, perhaps by executing a brute-force search. To successfully perform the hacking attack, Eve needs to get the file with the hashed passwords stored in the memory of Bob's computer and then retrieve Bob's password from this file with the help of *ophcrack* [9] – a Windows password cracker for inversing hashes using rainbow tables. To prevent the theft of the password file, Bob (the defender) can encrypt the disk of his laptop using encryption software *DiskCryptor* [4]. *DiskCryptor* can be set up to work with a password or with a key file. In the first case, Bob needs to enter his *DiskCryptor* password before being redirected to the Windows login page. In the second case, Bob needs to boot from an external disk (e.g., CD or DVD) holding the correct key file. To overcome the disk encryption, Eve could eavesdrop on Bob entering his *DiskCryptor* password or steal the disk with the key file, respectively. Bob could follow a security training where he would learn that one should never enter his passwords while observed. Finally, to make the *ophcrack* attack impossible, Bob should use a very strong password which does not fall into the specification of available *ophcrack* tables.

Formally, an ADTree is defined using rooted, finite, labeled trees. We recall that a *tree* is an acyclic, connected graph having neither loops, i.e., edges starting and ending at the same node, nor multiple edges between two different nodes. A tree is finite if the set of its nodes is finite, and it is said to be rooted if one of its nodes is designated to be the root.

Definition 1. *An* ADTree *T is a tuple $T = (V, E, L, \lambda, \text{type}, \text{ref})$, where*

- *(V, E) is a rooted, finite tree,*
- *L is a set of labels representing the attacker's and the defender's goals,*
- *$\lambda: V \to L$ is a function that assigns labels to the nodes,*
- *type: $V \to \{A, D\}$ is a function assigning actors to the nodes, in such a way that every node has at most one child of the other type,*
- *ref: $V \to \{\text{OR}, \text{AND}, N\}$ describes a refinement of the node: we use OR for disjunctively and AND for conjunctively refined nodes, and N for the non-refined nodes, i.e., nodes holding basic actions.*

While labels of the refined nodes are important when creating an ADTree, they are not necessary for its analysis. For instance, if we assume that none of Bob's countermeasures was implemented in the scenario from Example 1, Eve would achieve her main goal by either getting the file with hashed passwords and running *ophcrack* or by guessing the password. This situation can be represented as $\text{OR}^A(\text{AND}^A(\text{hash}, \text{ophcrack}), \text{guess})$[2]. The actors' strategies can thus be fully expressed by the labels of the non-refined nodes combined using refinement operators of the corresponding refined nodes. This observation leads us to propose a term-based notation for ADTrees, which is especially useful in the case of large trees, where the graphical representation is neither convenient nor effective.

Let us denote by $\mathbb{B}^A$ and $\mathbb{B}^D$ the sets of labels representing basic actions of the attacker and the defender, respectively. We assume that $\mathbb{B}^A \cap \mathbb{B}^D = \emptyset$, and we set $\mathbb{B} = \mathbb{B}^A \cup \mathbb{B}^D$. Let $b^S \in \mathbb{B}^S$, for $S \in \{A, D\}$. ADTrees can be seen as terms generated by the following grammar.

$$T: : T^A \mid T^D$$
$$T^A: : b^A \mid \text{OR}^A(T^A, \ldots, T^A) \mid \text{AND}^A(T^A, \ldots, T^A) \mid C^A(T^A, T^D)$$
$$T^D: : b^D \mid \text{OR}^D(T^D, \ldots, T^D) \mid \text{AND}^D(T^D, \ldots, T^D) \mid C^D(T^D, T^A)$$

If the root of an ADTree has type A, then the tree is said to be of the *attacker's type*. Otherwise it is said to be of the *defender's type*. Terms of the form T^A (resp. T^D) represent trees of the attacker's (resp. defender's) type. The tree in Fig. 1 is of the attacker's type and it is represented with term (1).

$$T = \text{OR}^A\Big(\text{AND}^A\big(C^A(\text{hash}, T'), C^A(\text{ophcrack}, \text{strong})\big), \text{guess}\Big), \tag{1}$$

where T' is the following term representing the tree of the defender's type rooted in the 'encrypt disk with *DiskCryptor*' node

$$T' = \text{OR}^D\Big(C^D\big(\text{password}, C^A(\text{eavesdrop}, \text{sec-train})\big), C^D(\text{key-file}, \text{steal-kf})\Big).$$

---

[2] Here, as well as in the rest of the paper, we shorten the labels for better readability.

For the rest of this paper, we do a couple of assumptions. We identify ADTrees with the corresponding terms. To ease the presentation, we assume that the root actor (i.e., the proponent) is the attacker. Furthermore, we consider only ADTrees where all basic actions are independent. This implies that there are no multiple occurrences of the same label in a tree. Finally, it is assumed that both actors always succeed when executing their basic actions.

2.2   Formal Semantics

In order to formulate optimization problems related to attack–defense scenarios represented with ADTrees, we first need to extract potential attack and defense strategies from the ADTree, i.e., define the semantics of ADTrees. These strategies describe sets of actions allowing the attacker to achieve the root goal and the defender to make such an attack impossible or inefficient.

Let T be an ADTree. A *homogenous subtree* of T is a maximal subtree of T, such that all of its nodes are of the same type (A or D). Node designated to be the root of a homogenous subtree H of T is the one whose distance from the root of T is minimal among all nodes of H. Obviously, every ADTree can be partitioned in a unique way into homogenous subtrees: it suffices to remove all dotted edges connecting the nodes of the attacker with those of the defender. Since all of the nodes of a homogenous subtree are of the same type, homogenous subtrees do not use any C operators. We thus talk about homogenous subtrees of the attacker or of the defender.

Definition 2. *Let H be a homogenous subtree of the attacker (resp. defender). A minimal, wrt the inclusion, set of basic actions of the attacker (resp. defender) achieving the root goal of H is called an* attack *vector (resp.* defense *vector) in H.*

Example 2. The homogenous subtrees in our running example are

$$H_0 = \mathrm{OR}^{\mathrm{A}}(\mathrm{AND}^{\mathrm{A}}(\mathrm{hash}, \mathrm{ophcrack}), \mathrm{guess}) \qquad H_1 = \mathrm{strong}$$

$$H_3 = \mathrm{eavesdrop} \qquad\qquad\qquad H_2 = \mathrm{OR}^{\mathrm{D}}(\mathrm{password}, \mathrm{key\text{-}file})$$

$$H_4 = \mathrm{steal\text{-}kf} \qquad\qquad\qquad H_5 = \mathrm{sec\text{-}train}.$$

The left column gathers homogenous subtrees of the attacker and the right one of the defender. The attack vectors in the subtree H_0 are {hash, ophcrack} and {guess}. The defense vectors in H_2 are {password} and {key-file}.

Definition 3. *Let T be an ADTree.*

- *A set $D \subseteq \mathbb{B}^{\mathrm{D}}$ is called a* defense strategy *in T, if $D = \emptyset$ or if it is a union of defense vectors from some of the homogenous subtrees of T.*
- *A set $A \subseteq \mathbb{B}^{\mathrm{A}}$ is called an* attack strategy *in T, if there exists a defense strategy D in T, such that, with all of the countermeasures from D being employed, A is a minimal set of actions achieving the root goal of T. Such D is called a* witness *for attack strategy A.[3]*

---

[3] To avoid confusion, attack/defense strategies in an ADTree are denoted using capital letters and attack/defense vectors in its homogenous subtrees using lower case letters.

Example 3. The attack strategies in the tree T from Fig. 1 are

$$\{\texttt{guess}\}, \{\texttt{hash}, \texttt{ophcrack}\}, \{\texttt{hash}, \texttt{ophcrack}, \texttt{eavesdrop}\},$$
$$\{\texttt{hash}, \texttt{ophcrack}, \texttt{steal-kf}\}, \{\texttt{hash}, \texttt{ophcrack}, \texttt{eavesdrop}, \texttt{steal-kf}\}.$$

For instance, $\{\texttt{hash}, \texttt{ophcrack}, \texttt{eavesdrop}\}$ is an attack strategy because it represents a valid attack when the witness defense strategy $\{\texttt{password}\}$ is implemented. Likewise, $\{\texttt{hash}, \texttt{ophcrack}, \texttt{eavesdrop}, \texttt{steal-kf}\}$ is an attack strategy because the execution of all of these actions is a valid attack in the presence of the witness defense strategy $\{\texttt{password}, \texttt{key-file}\}$.

In contrast, the set $X = \{\texttt{hash}, \texttt{ophcrack}, \texttt{guess}\}$ is not an attack strategy in T, because it is not minimal. Indeed, for any defense strategy possible (including the empty strategy), $\texttt{hash}$ and $\texttt{ophcrack}$ can be removed from X and the root goal is still achieved with $\texttt{guess}$.

The reasoning in Example 3 shows that the attack strategies model a reasonable behavior of the attacker who, to achieve their goal, will not execute more actions than strictly necessary. In other words, every attack strategy in an ADTree T contains at most one attack vector from every homogenous subtree of T.

The set of all attack strategies in an ADTree T, that we denote by $\mathrm{AS}(T)$, can be obtained in a bottom–up manner using the rules given in Fig. 2, where $\bigotimes_{i=1}^{n} X_i = \{\bigcup_{i=1}^{n} x_i \mid x_i \in X_i\}$. It is important to notice that, in the case of the nodes of the form $\mathtt{OR}^{\mathtt{D}}(T_1^{\mathtt{D}}, \ldots, T_k^{\mathtt{D}})$, the union is taken over all subsets $I \subseteq \{1, \ldots, k\}$, including $I = \emptyset$.

$$\mathrm{AS}(\mathsf{b}^{\mathsf{A}}) = \{\{\mathsf{b}^{\mathsf{A}}\}\}, \qquad\qquad \mathrm{AS}(\mathsf{b}^{\mathsf{D}}) = \{\emptyset\},$$

$$\mathrm{AS}(\mathtt{OR}^{\mathtt{A}}(T_1^{\mathtt{A}}, \ldots, T_k^{\mathtt{A}})) = \bigcup_{i=1}^{k} \mathrm{AS}(T_i^{\mathtt{A}}), \qquad \mathrm{AS}(\mathtt{OR}^{\mathtt{D}}(T_1^{\mathtt{D}}, \ldots, T_k^{\mathtt{D}})) = \bigcup_{I \subseteq \{1, \ldots, k\}} \bigotimes_{i \in I} \mathrm{AS}(T_i^{\mathtt{D}}),$$

$$\mathrm{AS}(\mathtt{AND}^{\mathtt{A}}(T_1^{\mathtt{A}}, \ldots, T_k^{\mathtt{A}})) = \bigotimes_{i=1}^{k} \mathrm{AS}(T_i^{\mathtt{A}}), \qquad \mathrm{AS}(\mathtt{AND}^{\mathtt{D}}(T^1, \ldots, T^k)) = \bigcup_{i=1}^{k} \mathrm{AS}(T_i^{\mathtt{D}}),$$

$$\mathrm{AS}(\mathsf{c}^{\mathtt{A}}(T_1, T_2)) = \mathrm{AS}(T_1) \otimes \mathrm{AS}(T_2), \qquad \mathrm{AS}(\mathsf{c}^{\mathtt{D}}(T_1, T_2)) = \mathrm{AS}(T_1) \cup \mathrm{AS}(T_2).$$

Fig. 2. Rules for creation of attack strategies in an ADTree

Lemma 1. *Let T be an ADTree and A be an attack strategy in T. In addition, let H be a homogenous subtree of the attacker in T, with $\mathbb{B}_H$ being the set of all basic actions in H. Then the set $A \cap \mathbb{B}_H$ is either empty, or else it is exactly one attack vector in H.*

Proof. Let D_A be a witness for A, cf. Definition 3, and assume that the set $A \cap \mathbb{B}_H$ is not empty. Since A is a minimal strategy wrt D_A, the basic actions from $A \cap \mathbb{B}_H$ achieve the root of H, with the root of H being either the root of T, or else a countermeasure attached to one of the nodes achieved by D_A in T. From the minimality of A it also follows that if an action was removed from $A \cap \mathbb{B}_H$, then the root of H would no longer be achieved. Thus, $A \cap \mathbb{B}_H$ is an attack vector in H. □

The goal of the framework developed in this paper is to suggest to the defender an optimal way of securing a system. To do so, we need to link possible attack strategies describing how to attack the system with the corresponding defense strategies allowing to protect it. Unfortunately, previously proposed semantics for ADTrees do not achieve this, because they take the view of one actor only into account, as illustrated in Example 4.

Example 4. Consider the tree $T = \mathsf{C}^{\mathtt{A}}(\mathsf{b}, \mathsf{AND}^{\mathtt{D}}(\mathsf{b}_1, \mathsf{b}_2))$. There exist two (minimal) ways for the attacker to ensure that they achieve their goal: they need to execute action b and at the same time prevent the defender from executing either b_1 or b_2. Using the multiset semantics [6], this is modeled by the pairs $(\{\mathsf{b}\}, \{\mathsf{b}_1\})$ and $(\{\mathsf{b}\}, \{\mathsf{b}_2\})$. However, this interpretation does not give a recipe for a reasonable defender to counter the attack, which is executing both b_1 and b_2.

To make use of integer programming, we thus need to develop a new semantics for ADTrees, called *defense semantics for ADTrees*, expressing how the defender may prohibit a reasonable attacker from achieving their goal.

Definition 4. *The* defense semantics *of an ADTree T, denoted by $[\![T]\!]_{\mathcal{D}}$, is the set of all pairs (A, D), where A is an attack strategy in T and D is a minimal (with respect to inclusion) defense strategy in T, such that executing all actions from D makes it impossible for the attacker to achieve the goal represented by the root of T while realizing only the actions from A.*

In order to develop an algorithm constructing the defense semantics of an ADTree T, we first define the notion of countering attack and defense vectors.

Definition 5. *Let T be an ADTree, and $H^{\mathtt{A}}$ (resp. $H^{\mathtt{D}}$) be a homogenous subtree of T of the attacker's (resp. of the defender's) type. In addition, let a be an attack vector in $H^{\mathtt{A}}$ (resp. d be a defense vector in $H^{\mathtt{D}}$).*

We say that a set $S \subseteq \mathbb{B}^{\mathtt{D}}$ (resp. $S \subseteq \mathbb{B}^{\mathtt{A}}$) counters the attack vector a (resp. the defense vector d), if executing all actions from S makes it impossible for the attacker (resp. for the defender) to achieve the goal represented by the root of $H^{\mathtt{A}}$ (resp. $H^{\mathtt{D}}$) while executing only the actions from a (resp. from d).

In other words, S counters an attack vector a if, in the presence of the countermeasures from S, it is not sufficient to execute only the actions from a to achieve the root goal of the corresponding homogenous subtree. For instance, the attack strategy $\{\mathtt{hash}, \mathtt{ophcrack}, \mathtt{steal\text{-}kf}\}$ in the tree T from Fig. 1 counters the defense vector $\{\mathtt{key\text{-}file}\}$. Likewise, the defense vector $\{\mathtt{password}\}$ counters the attack vector $\{\mathtt{hash}, \mathtt{ophcrack}\}$.

Algorithm 1, where H_0 denotes the homogenous subtree of the attacker containing the root of an ADTree T, gives an algorithmic way of creating the defense semantics of T. In the corresponding lines, we indicate the steps the complexity of which is exponential wrt the number of nodes. Note however, that, for a given tree, these worst case scenario estimations will never hold for all of the lines at the same time, cf. Table 1 depicting a couple of empirical results.

Theorem 1. *Given AD Tree T, Algorithm 1 generates the semantics $[\![T]\!]_{\mathcal{D}}$.*

To prove Theorem 1, we need the following lemma which shows the uniqueness of the attack vector a' in line 14 of Algorithm 1.

Lemma 2. *Let T be an AD Tree and $(A, D) \in [\![T]\!]_{\mathcal{D}}$. For every defense vector $d \subseteq D$, there exists at most one attack vector $a \subseteq A$ countering d.*

Proof. Let $(A, D) \in [\![T]\!]_{\mathcal{D}}$ and let $d \subseteq D$ be a defense vector. By contraposition, suppose that there exist two distinct attack vectors a_1 and a_2 in A that counter d. Denote by N_d the set of nodes achieved by d, and by H_d the homogenous subtree containing N_d. By Lemma 1, a_1 and a_2 are attack vectors from distinct homogenous subtrees of T, say, H_1 and H_2, respectively. For $i \in \{1, 2\}$, denote by n_i the node of N_d, to which the root of H_i is attached. Let $n \in N_d$ be the lowest common ancestor of n_1 and n_2, i.e., the node that lies on the paths connecting n_1 and n_2 with the root of H_d, the distance of which from the root of H_d is maximal.

Let D_A be a witness for A. By definition of witness, neither $A \setminus a_1$ nor $A \setminus a_2$ achieves the root goal of T in the presence of the actions from D_A. Minimality of A wrt D_A implies that each of the nodes n_1, n_2, and n is achieved by D_A and that n is neither n_1 nor n_2. Furthermore it follows that n is an OR node. However, this means that achieving both n_1 and n_2 is not necessary for achieving n, which contradicts d being a defense vector in H_d. □

Proof of Theorem 1. Let $\text{Alg}(T)$ be the set constructed by Algorithm 1. We prove that $\text{Alg}(T) = [\![T]\!]_{\mathcal{D}}$.

First, let $(A, D) \in [\![T]\!]_{\mathcal{D}}$. By Definition 4 and Lemmas 1 and 2, the sets A and D can be represented as

$$A = a_0 \cup a_1 \cup \ldots \cup a_m \cup A', \quad D = d_0 \cup d_1 \cup \ldots \cup d_m, \qquad (2)$$

where a_0 is an attack vector in H_0, and for all $i \in \{0, \ldots, m-1\}$, d_i is a defense vector that counters a_i, and a_{i+1} is the unique attack vector in A countering d_i. Furthermore, defense vector d_m counters a_m and executing any of the attack vectors from A' has no impact on the defense vectors from D, and vice versa.

Let $i \in \{1, \ldots, m\}$. By lines 8–15, during the i-th execution of the **while** loop, the pair $(a_i, d_0 \cup \ldots \cup d_{i-1})$ is added to the NewCandidates set, with the latter becoming the Candidates set in line 19. When the algorithm enters the **while** loop for the $(m+1)$-th time and the aforementioned pair is considered in line 8, the defense vector d_m is identified in line 9 and the set D is added to the set MinDef. Then, the pair (A, D) is added to $\text{Alg}(T)$ in line 21.

Now, let $(A, D) \in \text{Alg}(T)$. Let $a_0 \subseteq A$ be the attack vector from line 5. Observe that the set D was built upon the pair $(a_0, \emptyset)$ by repeatedly identifying

---

Algorithm 1. Defense semantics for ADTrees

Input: ADTree T

Output: defense semantics $[\![T]\!]_{\mathcal{D}}$

1: Construct the set $AS(T)$ using the rules from Fig. 2 $\mathcal{O}(2^n)$
2: $[\![T]\!]_{\mathcal{D}} \leftarrow \emptyset$
3: **for** $A \in AS(T)$ **do** $\mathcal{O}(2^n)$
4:      MinDef $\leftarrow \emptyset$
5:      Candidates $\leftarrow \{(a_0, \emptyset) \mid a_0 \subseteq A$ is an attack vector in $H_0\}$
6:      **while** Candidates $\neq \emptyset$ **do**
7:          NewCandidates $\leftarrow \emptyset$
8:          **for** $(a, D) \in$ Candidates **do**
9:             Counter $\leftarrow \{d \mid d$ counters $a\}$ $\mathcal{O}(2^n)$
10:             **for** defense vector $d \in$ Counter **do** $\mathcal{O}(2^n)$
11:                 **if** d is not countered by A **then**
12:                     MinDef $\leftarrow$ MinDef $\cup \{D \cup d\}$
13:                 **else**
14:                     let a' be the unique attack vector in A that counters d
15:                     NewCandidates $\leftarrow$ NewCandidates $\cup \{(a', D \cup d)\}$
16:                 **end if**
17:             **end for**
18:          **end for**
19:          Candidates $\leftarrow$ NewCandidates
20:      **end while**
21:      $[\![T]\!]_{\mathcal{D}} \leftarrow [\![T]\!]_{\mathcal{D}} \cup \{(A, D) \mid D \in$ MinDef $\}$
22: **end for**
23: **return** $[\![T]\!]_{\mathcal{D}}$

---

a defense vector d_i countering the first element of the pair and an attack vector $a_{i+1} \subseteq A$ (if any) countering d_i, and then replacing the previous pair in the set of candidates as described in line 19. Hence, the sets A and D can be partitioned as in decomposition (2), and so $(A, D) \in [\![T]\!]_{\mathcal{D}}$.   □

Example 5. The defense semantics of our running tree T from Fig. 1 is

$$[\![T]\!]_{\mathcal{D}} = \{(\{\mathtt{hash}, \mathtt{ophcrack}\}, \{\mathtt{strong}\}),$$
$$(\{\mathtt{hash}, \mathtt{ophcrack}\}, \{\mathtt{password}\}),$$
$$(\{\mathtt{hash}, \mathtt{ophcrack}\}, \{\mathtt{key\text{-}file}\}),$$
$$(\{\mathtt{hash}, \mathtt{ophcrack}, \mathtt{eavesdrop}\}, \{\mathtt{strong}\}),$$
$$(\{\mathtt{hash}, \mathtt{ophcrack}, \mathtt{eavesdrop}\}, \{\mathtt{key\text{-}file}\}),$$
$$(\{\mathtt{hash}, \mathtt{ophcrack}, \mathtt{eavesdrop}\}, \{\mathtt{password}, \mathtt{sec\text{-}train}\}),$$
$$(\{\mathtt{hash}, \mathtt{ophcrack}, \mathtt{steal\text{-}kf}\}, \{\mathtt{strong}\}),$$
$$(\{\mathtt{hash}, \mathtt{ophcrack}, \mathtt{steal\text{-}kf}\}, \{\mathtt{password}\}),$$
$$(\{\mathtt{hash}, \mathtt{ophcrack}, \mathtt{steal\text{-}kf}, \mathtt{eavesdrop}\}, \{\mathtt{strong}\}),$$
$$(\{\mathtt{hash}, \mathtt{ophcrack}, \mathtt{steal\text{-}kf}, \mathtt{eavesdrop}\}, \{\mathtt{password}, \mathtt{sec\text{-}train}\})\}.$$

3   Security-Oriented Optimization Problems

We integrate the information captured by the defense semantics defined in the previous section with the integer linear programming. Linear programming is a standard approach to compute the best outcome, by optimizing a linear objective function subject to linear equality and linear inequality constraints. In our framework, the inequalities model the dependencies between attack strategies and defense strategies expressed by the defense semantics, the constraints related to the available budget, as well as cost and impact of individual actions of the attacker and the defender. Provided that the defender's budget is limited, they might not be able to implement all countermeasures at will. Our framework supports them in tackling the following types of the optimization problems

- *maximal coverage* – minimize the number of attack strategies that remain uncountered;
- *minimal impact* – minimize the impact of uncountered attack strategies;
- *maximal investment* – maximize the necessary investment of the attacker.

3.1   Mathematical Modeling

We start by fixing the notation that we employ in this section to model the optimization problems. Given an ADTree T, and its defense semantics $[\![T]\!]_{\mathcal{D}}$, let

- $\mathbb{B}^{\mathsf{D}} = \{\mathsf{b}_1^{\mathsf{D}}, \ldots, \mathsf{b}_p^{\mathsf{D}}\}$ be the set of basic actions of the defender present in T,
- $A_1, \ldots, A_n$ be the distinct attack strategies that appear in $[\![T]\!]_{\mathcal{D}}$,
- $D_1, \ldots, D_m$ be the distinct defense strategies that appear in $[\![T]\!]_{\mathcal{D}}$.

Furthermore, for $i \in \{1, \ldots, n\}$, $j \in \{1, \ldots, m\}$, and $k \in \{1, \ldots, p\}$, we set

$$P_{ij} = \begin{cases} 1, & \text{if } (A_i, D_j) \in [\![T]\!]_{\mathcal{D}} \\ 0, & \text{otherwise} \end{cases} \qquad y_{kj} = \begin{cases} 1, & \text{if } \mathsf{b}_k^{\mathsf{D}} \in D_j \\ 0, & \text{otherwise.} \end{cases}$$

For a basic action b^{S} of any of the actors $\mathsf{S} \in \{\mathsf{A}, \mathsf{D}\}$, we assume the cost of executing the action to be a non-negative real number $\mathrm{cost}(\mathsf{b}^{\mathsf{S}})$. Finally, the overall budget available to the defender is denoted by $\mathcal{B}$.

To model the different scenarios that may happen depending on which actions are and which are not executed, the following Boolean variables are defined

- $x_k = 1$, for $k = 1, \ldots, p$, if and only if the defender executes the action $\mathsf{b}_k^{\mathsf{D}}$,
- $f_j = 1$, for $j = 1, \ldots, m$, if and only if the defender does not execute at least one of the basic actions from the defense strategy D_j,
- $z_i = 1$, for $i = 1, \ldots, n$, if and only if the attack strategy A_i achieves the root node of T, in the presence of currently deployed countermeasures.

Optimization goal: minimize $\displaystyle\sum_{i=1}^{n} z_i$ $\hspace{3cm}$ (3)

Subject to: $\displaystyle\sum_{k=1}^{p} \text{cost}(\mathsf{b}_k^{\mathsf{D}}) x_k \leq \mathcal{B}$ $\hspace{3cm}$ (4)

$$f_j \geq \frac{\sum_{k=1}^{p} y_{kj}(1 - x_k)}{p}, \ 1 \leq j \leq m \qquad (5)$$

$$f_j \leq \sum_{k=1}^{p} y_{kj}(1 - x_k), \ 1 \leq j \leq m \qquad (6)$$

$$z_i \geq 1 + \sum_{j=1}^{m} P_{ij}(f_j - 1), \ 1 \leq i \leq n \qquad (7)$$

$$z_i \leq \frac{\sum_{j=1}^{m} P_{ij} f_j}{\sum_{j=1}^{m} P_{ij}}, \ 1 \leq i \leq n \qquad (8)$$

$x_k \in \{0,1\}, \ 1 \leq k \leq p, \qquad f_j \in \{0,1\}, \ 1 \leq j \leq m, \qquad z_i \in \{0,1\}, \ 1 \leq i \leq n.$

Fig. 3. Coverage problem modeled in terms of integer programming.

Coverage problem. We first focus on the problem of covering as many attack strategies as possible, provided the value of the defense budget $\mathcal{B}$.

Figure 3 gives the specification of the corresponding integer linear programming problem.

Inequality (4) ensures that the defender's investment cannot exceed their budget. The next two lines model the meaning of the variable f_j: inequalities (5) ensure that if the defender does not execute some of the actions from D_j, then $f_j = 1$; inequality (6) ensures that if $f_j = 1$, then the defender does not execute some action from D_j. Next, we model the meaning of z_i: inequalities (7) ensure that if the defender does not execute some action in any of the sets countering A_i (i.e., $f_j = 1$ for every j, such that $P_{ij} = 1$), then $z_i = 1$; and inequalities (8) ensure that if the defender executes all the actions from at least one of the sets D_j countering the attack strategy A_i (i.e., there exists j, such that $P_{ij} = 1$ and $f_j = 0$), then $z_i = 0$.

Remark 1. We notice that the number of elements in the set D_j can be expressed as $|D_j| = \sum_{k=1}^{p} y_{kj}$. Thus, the defender executes all of the actions from D_j, iff

$$\sum_{k=1}^{p} y_{kj} = \sum_{k=1}^{p} x_k y_{kj} \quad \text{which means} \quad \sum_{k=1}^{p} (1 - x_k) y_{kj} = 0. \qquad (9)$$

In consequence, if there exists j for which equality (9) holds and $P_{ij} = 1$, then the attacker cannot succeed by the attack strategy A_i. Conversely, if for all j with $P_{ij} = 1$, equality (9) does not hold, then the attacker can succeed with A_i. This explains the form of inequalities (5) and (6).

Observe that when the inequalities from Fig. 3 are expressed in a matrix form, say $M\hat{\mathbf{x}} \leq \hat{\mathbf{c}}$, where $\hat{\mathbf{x}} = (x_1, \ldots, x_p, f_1, \ldots, f_m, z_1 \ldots, z_n)$ and $\hat{\mathbf{c}}$ is a vector of

Table 1. Running time of the tool on randomly generated trees.

Size				Time in sec			
T	$AS(T)$	$[\![T]\!]_{\mathcal{D}}$	M	$AS(T)$	$[\![T]\!]_{\mathcal{D}}$	from $[\![T]\!]_{\mathcal{D}}$ to M	Solving
28	8191	53248	16409×8217	129.36	3.67	8.8	1152.22
80	3955	57508	7951×3997	0.02	4.1	4.5	0.58
80	3	99	81×76	>10800	0.01	<0.01	0.01
100	25	32	67×107	<0.01	0.06	<0.01	>3600
500	23	71	65×166	0.01	0.26	<0.01	0.01

constants, then the size of M is $(2m + 2n + 1) \times (p + m + n)$. For the completeness of presentation of results, sizes of corresponding matrices are included in Table 1.

Below, we investigate other optimization problems that fall into our setting.

Impact problem. Here it is assumed that every attack strategy A has assigned a value $\mathrm{Imp}(A)$ of it's impact when executed. The value of $\mathrm{Imp}(A)$ could be estimated by the security experts or expressed as the sum of impacts of basic actions composing the attack strategy A. The goal is to select the countermeasures to be implemented in such a way that the impact of uncountered attack strategies is minimal. The optimization goal from line (3) in Fig. 3 is replaced with

Optimization goal: minimize I

and the list of inequalities from Fig. 3 is extended with additional constraints

$$I \geq z_i \, \mathrm{Imp}(A_i), \ 1 \leq i \leq n, \tag{10}$$

ensuring that I is the maximum of the impacts of uncountered attack strategies.

Attacker's investment problem. We may use a similar technique to maximize the minimal necessary investment of the attacker in achieving their goal. In this case the optimization goal is replaced with

Optimization goal: maximize C

with respect to the same conditions as previously, extended with

$$C \leq z_i \, \mathrm{Cost}(A_i), \ 1 \leq i \leq n, \tag{11}$$

where $\mathrm{Cost}(A_i)$ is equal to the investment of the attacker they need to make in order to perform all basic actions from A_i, i.e. $\mathrm{Cost}(A_i) = \sum_{\mathsf{b}^{\mathsf{A}} \in A_i} \mathrm{cost}(\mathsf{b}^{\mathsf{A}})$.

Remark 2. The mathematical framework described in this section is generic and, as such, can be used to address not only problems relating to budget, impact, and monetary cost, but also to any other optimization problem expressed with the help of a linear function over the Boolean variables that we have defined in Sect. 3.1, subject to linear constraints. This is illustrated in Sect. 3.3, where we look for the optimal usage of available time.

3.2   Implementation

To validate the framework developed in this paper, we have implemented a proof of concept tool. It is programmed in Python and uses a free integer linear programming solver *lp_solve* [2]. Given an ADTree T, specified as in Definition 1, and the input values for the defense budget and cost, our prototype follows Algorithm 1 to construct the defense semantics $[\![T]\!]_\mathcal{D}$, and extracts the specification of the optimization problem of interest, as described in Sect. 3.1. The optimization problem is then solved using *lp_solve* and the optimal solution, i.e., the optimal value of the objective function together with the corresponding set of the defender's actions that need to be performed, is given as output.

We have tested the prototype on a computer running Intel Core i7–5600U CPU at 2.60 GHz dual core with 16 GB of RAM. ADTrees for the tests have been generated randomly to cover various possible cases.

The budget $\mathcal{B}$ has been set to be half of the sum of the costs of all basic actions of the defender.

Table 1 presents a sample of the obtained results. It compares the time spend on generation of the set $AS(T)$, generation of $[\![T]\!]_\mathcal{D}$, translation of the defense semantics into an integer programming problem specified by a matrix M, and solving the problem. In general, the most time-consuming of these steps are generation of $AS(T)$ and solving of the obtained optimization problem, since in the worst case they are both exponential in the number of nodes of T. In particular, the time necessary to generate $AS(T)$ depends exponentially on the maximum number of children of the OR^D nodes in T, cf. Fig. 2.

3.3   Countermeasure Optimization on the Running Example

We now illustrate the optimal countermeasure selection on our running scenario from Example 1. Here, the budget $\mathcal{B}$ represents the available time resources.

We suppose that the goal of Bob (the defender) is to *learn* how to secure his computer against the attacks depicted in the tree from Fig. 1. Bob is a busy person, so he can devote 50 min only to his learning process. He wants to know how he should spend this time in the most efficient way, i.e., so that he is able to minimize the number of unprevented attacks. To set up a password which is resistant to the *ophcrack* attack, Bob needs to understand how the rainbow table analysis works – this would take him 60 min. To be able to use *DiskCryptor*, 20 min are necessary to learn how to use it with a password and 30 min to master how to handle a key file. Finally, Bob can also follow the security training offered by his company, which lasts 25 min.

We have input these data to our tool and obtained a matrix of size 17×12. The tool solves the problem instantaneously and suggests that Bob should follow the security training and learn how to use *DiskCryptor* with a password, i.e., the optimal set of countermeasures is {password, sec-train} and it prevents all four attack strategies listed in Example 5. However, if the duration of the security training was 45 min, then the optimal set of countermeasures would be {password, key-file} which prevents three out of four attack strategies, namely {hash, ophcrack}, {hash, ophcrack, eavesdrop}, and {hash, ophcrack, steal-kf}.

4   Conclusion

The goal of the work presented in this paper has been to provide a framework to assist industry practitioners using ADTrees in performing their risk assessment evaluations. To achieve this, the security model of ADTrees is fused with optimization techniques. We rely on the expressive power of ADTrees to link potential attack and defense strategies and profit from the strengths of integer programming to select the most optimal sets of countermeasures. From a formal perspective, we introduce a novel defense semantics for ADTrees and thus contribute to the developments of mathematical foundations for this security model. To validate the usefulness of the proposed approach, we have implemented a proof of concept tool automating the computation of the defense semantics and the selection of the most appropriate set of countermeasures to be deployed.

As a next step, we will extend our framework to the probabilistic case, taking the probability with which actions are executed into account. We would also like to improve the worst case running time of our tool, by exploiting the possibility of using approximation algorithms. Finally, we plan to integrate this framework to ADTool, free software assisting creation and quantitative analysis of ADTrees [5].

References

1. Aslanyan, Z., Nielson, F.: Pareto efficient solutions of attack-defence trees. In: Focardi, R., Myers, A. (eds.) POST 2015. LNCS, vol. 9036, pp. 95–114. Springer, Heidelberg (2015). doi:10.1007/978-3-662-46666-7_6
2. Berkelaar, M., Eikland, K., Notebaert, P.: lp_solve: Open source (Mixed-Integer) Linear Programming system (2005). http://lpsolve.sourceforge.net/5.5/ version 5.5.2.5, Accessed Sep 2016
3. Chvátal, V.: Linear Programming. W.H Freeman, San Francisco (1983)
4. DiskCryptor: (2014). https://diskcryptor.net/ Accessed 17 March 2017
5. Gadyatskaya, O., Jhawar, R., Kordy, P., Lounis, K., Mauw, S., Trujillo-Rasua, R.: Attack trees for practical security assessment: ranking of attack scenarios with ADTool 2.0. In: Agha, G., Houdt, B. (eds.) QEST 2016. LNCS, vol. 9826, pp. 159–162. Springer, Cham (2016). doi:10.1007/978-3-319-43425-4_10
6. Kordy, B., Mauw, S., Radomirovic, S., Schweitzer, P.: Attack-defense trees. J. Log. Comput. 24(1), 55–87 (2014). doi:10.1093/logcom/exs029
7. Kordy, B., Pouly, M., Schweitzer, P.: Probabilistic reasoning with graphical security models. Inf. Sci. 342, 111–131 (2016). doi:10.1016/j.ins.2016.01.010
8. Mauw, S., Oostdijk, M.: Foundations of attack trees. In: Won, D.H., Kim, S. (eds.) ICISC 2005. LNCS, vol. 3935, pp. 186–198. Springer, Heidelberg (2006). doi:10.1007/11734727_17
9. Ophcrack: (2016). http://ophcrack.sourceforge.net/ Accessed 17 March 2017

10. Schneier, B.: Attack trees: modeling security threats. Dr. Dobb's J. Softw. Tools **24**(12), 21–29 (1999)
11. Shameli-Sendi, A., Louafi, H., He, W., Cheriet, M.: Dynamic optimal countermeasure selection for intrusion response system. IEEE J. TDSC **99**, 10–14 (2016). doi:10.1109/TDSC.2016.2615622
12. Zheng, K., McLay, L.A., Luedtke, J.R.: A budgeted maximum multiple coverage model for cybersecurity planning and management (2017, under submission)

MaxUSE: A Tool for Finding Achievable Constraints and Conflicts for Inconsistent UML Class Diagrams

Hao Wu[✉]

Department of Computer Science, National University of Ireland, Maynooth,
Maynooth, Republic of Ireland
haowu@cs.nuim.ie

Abstract. In the context of Model Driven Engineering (MDE), the structure of a system is typically described by using a UML class diagram annotated with a set of Object Constraint Language (OCL) constraints. These constraints specify rules that are not expressible by using structural features. These constraints can be conflicting, resulting in inconsistencies. When this happens, the existing tools terminate and provide no information about which constraints are achievable and which ones cause conflicts. In this paper, we present MaxUSE, a tool for finding achievable OCL constraints and conflicts for inconsistent UML class diagrams. MaxUSE integrates the USE modeling tool with a satisfiability modulo theories (SMT) solver. It finds a set of achievable constraints based on their rankings by casting to a weighted MaxSMT problem and at the same time locates constraint conflicts. We use an example to demonstrate MaxUSE's usage scenarios and discuss its usefulness to the community.

1 Introduction

Model-Driven Engineering (MDE) plays a significant role in modern software development by exploiting different abstract models. Among them, Unified Modeling Language (UML) is a common modeling language for modeling a system at an abstract level. It uses structure and behaviour diagrams to depict static and dynamic aspects of a system. For example, using class diagrams to model relationships between different entities and state machines to capture possible transitions from one state to another. On other hand, Object Constraint Language (OCL), a declarative language, is used to describe necessary rules that can not be expressed by UML diagrams. These rules impose additional constraints over different structural features to eliminate undesirable scenarios. Verifying consistency of a UML model therefore becomes a task of finding an *instance* that conforms to not only structural constraints but also OCL constraints.

Recently, a number of tools and approaches have been proposed to verify the consistency of a UML class diagram by employing formal verification techniques [1–4]. However, when a UML class diagram is inconsistent these tools typically have no knowledge about the constraints that cause conflicts. Knowing information about which constraints cause conflicts is very helpful for users

© Springer International Publishing AG 2017
N. Polikarpova and S. Schneider (Eds.): IFM 2017, LNCS 10510, pp. 348–356, 2017.
DOI: 10.1007/978-3-319-66845-1_23

to understand and fix their class diagrams. In practice, users may also wish to know how many constraints can be achieved in the current diagram, and use this information for further refining their class diagrams. For example, a user may be interested in fixing the minimum number of constraints that cause conflicts. In other scenarios, users may treat individual constraints differently based on their own domain-specific knowledge and look for an instance that satisfies the most important OCL constraints.

In this paper, we present MaxUSE, an automated tool for finding the set of achievable constraints based on user's rankings and constraint conflicts for inconsistent UML class diagrams. MaxUSE extends USE, an existing modeling tool, by integrating an SMT solver as its back-end reasoning engine. It finds the maximum total rank by solving a weighted MaxSMT problem and identify constraint conflicts by solving the set cover problem. Detailed theories and algorithms have been addressed in [5]. Here, we describe the integration of a modeling tool with an SMT solver (Sect. 2) and demonstrate MaxUSE's usage scenarios (Sect. 3) by illustrating it with an example.

2   Overall Architecture

MaxUSE is built on top of the USE modeling tool. It exploits USE's front-end to read in a UML class diagram annotated OCL constraints and generates SMT assertions that can be solved by an SMT solver. The overall architecture of MaxUSE, as shown in Fig. 1, consists of three layers: USE, Uran and Solver.

USE. USE is an open-source modeling tool that allows users to construct UML class diagrams in its own specification [6]. It also supports constraints written in OCL. USE provides a set of commands that enable users to construct object diagrams (instances) and check whether an object diagram (instance) conforms to its class diagram's structural and OCL constraints. To support ranked constraints, we change USE's front-end by modifying its grammars, UML and OCL metamodels (abstract syntax trees). We then implement two visitors that traverse and store each model feature, such as an association and a class invariant, into a temporal memory location that can be used by Uran.

Uran. Uran is an open-source project that aims to provide users with an engine for constructing and evaluating SMT2 assertions through well-defined APIs[1]. The purpose of Uran is to decouple assertion generation functionalities from modules that are designed for other purposes. This design allows users to freely modify and upgrade assertion generation to accommodate specific purposes without affecting other modules. Further, Uran directly interacts with an SMT solver via different APIs. Currently, Uran is able to communicate with the Z3 SMT solver. MaxUSE uses Uran API's to translate model features extracted from a USE specification to a set of predicates, functions and objects. It then outputs a set of well-formed SMT2 assertions associated with corresponding ranks.

---

[1] Available at: https://github.com/classicwuhao/uran.

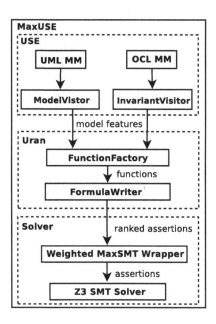

Fig. 1. The architecture of MaxUSE integrates with three layers: USE, Uran and Solver.

In other words, it formalises a UML class diagram with ranked OCL constraints into a weighted MaxSMT problem.

Solver. In order to solve this weighted MaxSMT problem, we implement a wrapper that iteratively calls the Z3 SMT solver until we find the optimal value. To reduce the number of calls to the solver, this wrapper uses a binary-search based algorithm to find the optimal value. Once an optimal values is found, we enumerate all possible ways of achieving this value by blocking all previous successful assignments until no more assignments can be found. Each assignment found by the solver is a weighted MaxSMT solution. Finally, we map each solution back to a corresponding model feature and generate a report. To find all constraint conflicts, we formalise the set of weighted MaxSMT solutions into the set cover problem and solve it using the algorithm described in [5]. Therefore, MaxUSE uses an SMT solver for computing both sets of achievable constraints and conflicts for inconsistent UML class diagrams.

3   Usage Scenarios

In this section, we illustrate three usage scenarios of using MaxUSE. The three scenarios discussed in this Section are based on the example shown in Fig. 2. This example uses a UML class diagram to represent a real world example of students in a university choosing multiple modules to study. This class diagram is enriched with 8 OCL constraints specified as class invariants ($inv1$ to $inv8$) under three classes. For example, each student must have a unique id number (*inv4*) and can only choose modules that are in their year (*inv5*). In this example, we use numbers 1 to 6 to distinguish a student's year, and students that are in year 6 are considered as research students. Thus, a university has some non-research and research students (*inv6*). All invariants except for *inv8* are ranked by using an integer value.

In this example, 7 (*inv1–inv7*) out of 8 class invariants are ranked. We consider a ranked class invariant as a *soft constraint*. This means that it might be switched off during the search for the maximum total rank. For example, *inv4* is a soft constraint and is ranked as 5. On the other hand, if an invariant is *not* ranked, then it is a *hard constraint* that must not be ignored during the search. For example, *inv8* in Fig. 2 must hold, no matter what. Therefore, this allows users to rank OCL constraints in a UML class diagram in 3 different ways: (1) not ranked at all (hard constraints only) (2) totally ranked (soft constraints only) (3) partially ranked (a mixture of soft and hard constraints).

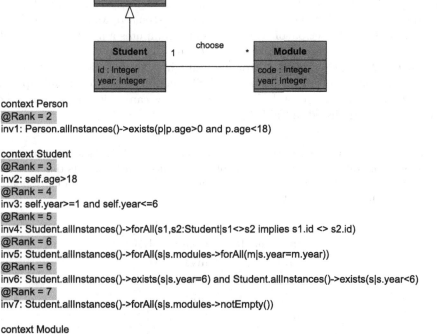

```
context Person
@Rank = 2
inv1: Person.allInstances()->exists(p|p.age>0 and p.age<18)

context Student
@Rank = 3
inv2: self.age>18
@Rank = 4
inv3: self.year>=1 and self.year<=6
@Rank = 5
inv4: Student.allInstances()->forAll(s1,s2:Student|s1<>s2 implies s1.id <> s2.id)
@Rank = 6
inv5: Student.allInstances()->forAll(s|s.modules->forAll(m|s.year=m.year))
@Rank = 6
inv6: Student.allInstances()->exists(s|s.year=6) and Student.allInstances()->exists(s|s.year<6)
@Rank = 7
inv7: Student.allInstances()->forAll(s|s.modules->notEmpty())

context Module
inv8: self.year>=1 and self.year<=5
```

Fig. 2. A UML class diagram annotated with ranked OCL constraints. The ranks are highlighted in the shaded area.

3.1 Verifying Consistency

If the set of OCL constraints is not ranked at all, then this means that every single constraint must hold. In this scenario, MaxUSE translates a UML class diagram with its OCL constraints to a set of SMT assertions. A UML class diagram is consistent iff generated SMT assertions are satisfiable. MaxUSE uses the Z3 SMT solver to determine the satisfiability of these assertions. In our example, MaxUSE is unable to find an instance that satisfy all 8 OCL constraints in Fig. 2, assuming that all constraints are hard constraints. This is due to 2 conflicts (sets): $(inv1, inv2)$ and $(inv5, inv6, inv7, inv8)$. In other words, removal of any elements in a conflict (set) makes the remaining elements achievable. For example, $inv5$, $inv7$ and $inv8$ are achievable if $inv6$ is removed from the class diagram.

3.2 Finding Achievable Constraints

In many practical situations, users may treat individual constraints differently. For example, a university may consider a registration procedure where students choosing some modules ($inv7$) is more important than choosing modules in their corresponding year ($inv5$). We thus allow users to freely rank individual constraints to distinguish their importance. In this scenario, MaxUSE calculates a total rank from the set of soft constraints and computes a maximum achievable rank by solving a weighted MaxSMT problem.

In Fig. 2, 7 ranked class invariants result in a total rank of 33. Since this UML class diagram is inconsistent, MaxUSE maximises this total rank up to 25. In fact, MaxUSE finds a total of two solutions that can achieve this value. These two solutions are listed in Table 1.

Table 1. Two solutions that can achieve a maximum rank of 25. Each solution contains a set of 5 achievable invariants out of 7 soft constraints. The invariants that cannot be met are marked with 0 in the "Rank" column. "NA" indicates that a corresponding class invariant is a hard constraint.

Solution 1		Solution 2	
Invariant	Rank	Invariant	Rank
inv1	**0**	**inv1**	**0**
$inv2$	3	$inv2$	3
$inv3$	4	$inv3$	4
$inv4$	5	$inv4$	5
$inv5$	6	**inv5**	**0**
inv6	**0**	$inv6$	6
$inv7$	7	$inv7$	7
$inv8$	NA	$inv8$	NA

MaxUSE finds a maximum of 5 achievable invariants out of 7 soft constraints in Fig. 2. Note that MaxUSE always first verifies the consistency of a UML class diagram. If the UML class diagram is consistent, then MaxUSE terminates since every constraint is achievable. In other words, MaxUSE finds the set of achievable (ranked) constraints only when a UML class diagram is *not* consistent.

3.3 Finding Constraint Conflicts

To find *all* conflicts among OCL constraints, MaxUSE first treats each constraint equally, then casts it to a MaxSMT problem[2] and solves it by using the Z3 SMT solver. Here, the returned solutions to MaxSMT is a set, namely they are MaxSMT solutions. Each MaxSMT solution in this set represents a way of achieving a maximum *number* of constraints. MaxUSE formalises this set of solutions into the set cover problem and solves it by using the algorithm in [5]. This algorithm is inspired by the work on using the set cover problem to model conflicts among SAT formulas [7]. Finally, MaxUSE interprets each solution to the set cover problem as a conflict.

For the class invariants in Fig. 2, MaxUSE finds a total of 8 possible ways of achieving a maximum number of 6 class invariants (shown in Table 2) and 2 conflicts: $(inv1, inv2)$ and $(inv5, inv6, inv7, inv8)$.

Table 2. A total of 8 MaxSMT solutions. Each one of them represents a way of achieving a maximum 6 number of class invariants shown in Fig. 2. We use a ✓ to indicate an invariant is achievable and a ✗ to denote an invariant that cannot be met.

	Inv1	Inv2	Inv3	Inv4	Inv5	Inv6	Inv7	Inv8
(1)	✓	✗	✓	✓	✗	✓	✓	✓
(2)	✓	✗	✓	✓	✓	✗	✓	✓
(3)	✓	✗	✓	✓	✓	✓	✗	✓
(4)	✓	✗	✓	✓	✓	✓	✓	✗
(5)	✗	✓	✓	✓	✗	✓	✓	✓
(6)	✗	✓	✓	✓	✓	✗	✓	✓
(7)	✗	✓	✓	✓	✓	✓	✗	✓
(8)	✗	✓	✓	✓	✓	✓	✓	✗

The first conflict is quite obvious and it is caused by the invariants $inv1$ and $inv2$ defined for the *age* attribute. However, the second conflict is not easy to identify. This conflict is caused by the invariants that there must exist some research and non-research students ($inv6$) choosing some modules ($inv7$) in their corresponding year ($inv5$). However, there are modules that are only available for non-research students ($inv8$: between year 1 and 5).

---

[2] Note that since the rank for each constraint is equal, this means that a weighted MaxSMT can be treated as a MaxSMT problem.

4   Usefulness

By integrating an SMT solver into a modeling environment, users are now able to use MaxUSE to tackle ranked OCL constraints in a UML class diagram. More importantly, when a UML class diagram is not consistent users no longer need to spend time on working out which constraints are achievable and which ones cause the conflicts. They can easily use MaxUSE to find out this information. In practice, this is a very effective and efficient way for further refining class diagrams. Further, our evaluation results in [5] suggest that MaxUSE scales reasonably well and the quality of computed constraint conflicts is high. Therefore, we believe that users from the software verification and Model Driven Engineering community can benefit from its capabilities.

5   Availability

MaxUSE is a free and open-source project hosted on GitHub under the GNU public license:

$$https://github.com/classicwuhao/maxuse$$

The repository is accompanied with detailed instructions and examples that show how to build and use MaxUSE. The implementation of MaxUSE consists of approximately Java 7000 lines of code. Currently, MaxUSE is command based and easy to install using the provided build script. In addition, the benchmark that we used for evaluating MaxUSE is also available in the repository.

6   Related Work

Even though a number of tools or approaches leverage the power of constraint solvers and theorem provers for verifying/reasoning UML models, they do not support ranked constrains and conflict finding [1–4,8–16]. To the best of our knowledge, MaxUSE is the first automated tool that supports finding achievable constraints (based on rankings) and conflicts for UML class diagrams.

The USE modeling tool takes a similar apporach to UML2Alloy. It integates with a relational model finder for verifying UML class diagrams [1,17]. However, the encodings used in the model finder are limited to boolean formulas, and thus they are not suitable for tackling numeric constraints. In particular, numeric ranks are defined for each OCL constraint. UML to CSP verifies EMF models by casting it to a Constraint Satisfaction Problem (CSP) [15,18–20]. However, they only allow users to check weak and strong satisfiability by generating a different number of instances for every class. The HOL-OCL tool encodes OCL into the Higher-order Logic (HOL) and uses Isabelle to reason about UML class diagrams [13]. Since Isabelle is an interactive theorem prover, the level of automation is quite limited and the feedback can be difficult to interpret by software engineers.

7   Conclusion

In this paper, we demonstrate how MaxUSE integrates an SMT solver into a modeling environment. This integration allows users to leverage efficient SMT solving to reason over ranked constraints defined in a UML class diagram. In addition, MaxUSE can significantly reduce the amount of effort in investigating inconsistencies in UML class diagrams by automatically finding the set of achievable OCL constraints and conflicts. In the future, we plan to build a plug-in for MaxUSE to allow us to exploit multiple SMT solvers for reasoning over a considerably large number of OCL constraints.

References

1. Kuhlmann, M., Hamann, L., Gogolla, M.: Extensive validation of OCL models by integrating SAT solving into USE. In: Bishop, J., Vallecillo, A. (eds.) TOOLS 2011. LNCS, vol. 6705, pp. 290–306. Springer, Heidelberg (2011). doi:10.1007/978-3-642-21952-8_21
2. Wille, R., Soeken, M., Drechsler, R.: Debugging of inconsistent UML/OCL models. In: 2012 DATE, pp. 1078–1083 (2012)
3. Wu, H., Monahan, R., Power, J.F.: Exploiting attributed type graphs to generate metamodel instances using an SMT solver. In: 7th TASE. Birmingham, UK (2013)
4. Dania, C., Clavel, M.: Ocl2msfol: A mapping to many-sorted first-order logic for efficiently checking the satisfiability of OCL constraints. In: 19th MoDELS, pp. 65–75. ACM (2016)
5. Wu, H.: Finding achievable features and contraint conflicts for inconsistent meta-models. In: 13th ECMFA (2017, to appear)
6. Gogolla, M., Büttner, F., Richters, M.: USE: A UML-based specification environment for validating UML and OCL. Sci. Comput. Program. **69**(1–3), 27–34 (2007)
7. Liffiton, M.H., Sakallah, K.A.: Algorithms for computing minimal unsatisfiable subsets of constraints. J. Autom. Reason. **40**(1), 1–33 (2008)
8. Beckert, B., Keller, U., Schmitt, P.H.: Translating the object constraint language into first-order predicate logic. In: FLoC @ 3rd Federated Logic Conferences, Denmark (2002)
9. Maraee, A., Balaban, M.: Efficient reasoning about finite satisfiability of UML class diagrams with constrained generalization sets. In: Akehurst, D.H., Vogel, R., Paige, R.F. (eds.) ECMDA-FA 2007. LNCS, vol. 4530, pp. 17–31. Springer, Heidelberg (2007). doi:10.1007/978-3-540-72901-3_2
10. Soeken, M., Wille, R., Drechsler, R.: Encoding OCL data types for SAT-based verification of UML/OCL models. In: Gogolla, M., Wolff, B. (eds.) TAP 2011. LNCS, vol. 6706, pp. 152–170. Springer, Heidelberg (2011). doi:10.1007/978-3-642-21768-5_12
11. Büttner, F., Egea, M., Cabot, J.: On verifying ATL transformations using 'off-the-shelf' SMT solvers. In: 15th MoDELS, pp. 432–448 (2012)
12. Clavel, M., Egea, M., de Dios, M.A.G.: Checking unsatisfiability for OCL constraints. ECEASST **24**, 13 (2009)
13. Brucker, A.D., Wolff, B.: HOL-OCL: A formal proof environment for UML/OCL. In: Fiadeiro, J.L., Inverardi, P. (eds.) FASE 2008. LNCS, vol. 4961, pp. 97–100. Springer, Heidelberg (2008). doi:10.1007/978-3-540-78743-3_8

14. Anastasakis, K., Bordbar, B., Georg, G., Ray, I.: UML2Alloy: A challenging model transformation. In: Engels, G., Opdyke, B., Schmidt, D.C., Weil, F. (eds.) MODELS 2007. LNCS, vol. 4735, pp. 436–450. Springer, Heidelberg (2007). doi:10.1007/978-3-540-75209-7_30

15. Beckert, B., Hähnle, R., Schmitt, P.H.: Verification of Object-Oriented Software: The KeY Approach. Springer, Berlin, Heidelberg (2007)

16. Wu, H.: Generating metamodel instances satisfying coverage criteria via SMT solving. In: The 4th MODELSWARD, pp. 40–51 (2016)

17. Torlak, E., Jackson, D.: Kodkod: A relational model finder. In: Grumberg, O., Huth, M. (eds.) TACAS 2007. LNCS, vol. 4424, pp. 632–647. Springer, Heidelberg (2007). doi:10.1007/978-3-540-71209-1_49

18. González Pérez, C.A., Buettner, F., Clarisó, R., Cabot, J.: EMFtoCSP: A tool for the lightweight verification of EMF models. In: SEMF: Rigorous and Agile Approaches, Zurich, Suisse (2012)

19. Cabot, J., Clarisó, R., Riera, D.: Verification of UML/OCL class diagrams using constraint programming. In: IEEE STV&V Workshop, pp. 73–80. IEEE Computer Society, Berlin, Germany (2008)

20. Cabot, J., Clarisó, R., Riera, D.: On the verification of UML/OCL class diagrams using constraint programming. J. Syst. Softw. **93**, 1–23 (2014)

Formal Verification of CNL Health Recommendations

Fahrurrozi Rahman and Juliana Küster Filipe Bowles[(✉)]

School of Computer Science, North Haugh, St Andrews KY16 9SX, UK
{fr27,jkfb}@st-andrews.ac.uk

Abstract. Clinical texts, such as therapy algorithms, are often described in natural language and may include hidden inconsistencies, gaps and potential deadlocks. In this paper, we propose an approach to identify such problems with formal verification. From each sentence in the therapy algorithm we automatically generate a parse tree and derive case frames. From the case frames we construct a state-based representation (in our case a timed automaton) and use a model checker (here UPPAAL) to verify the model. Throughout the paper we use an example of the algorithm for blood glucose lowering therapy in adults with type 2 diabetes to illustrate our approach.

Keywords: Formal verification · Controlled natural language · Timed automata · Health recommendations

1 Introduction

Understanding system requirements in software development is important because requirements constitute the foundation for the next phases. There are many ways to specify system requirements, but the most common way is to express them in natural language (NL). Undoubtedly, NL is the easiest way for stakeholders to communicate and understand the requirements of a system. However, the possible ambiguity of NL may lead to various interpretations of requirements, making it also difficult to find (among others) requirement inconsistencies, incompleteness or underspecification. Research on how to find defects in requirements captured in NL is needed as early as possible in the development process. The ability to eliminate defects early can reduce the cost of a later correction or rework, and reduce time spent in implementation and testing phases. Furthermore, our increasing reliance on software systems across a wide range of application domains including critical systems puts further pressure on the development of high quality and dependable software systems. The use of formal verification techniques to automatically identify inconsistencies or incomplete requirements is thus natural but not common at the level of NL requirements.

This research is partially supported by EPSRC grant EP/M014290/1.

N. Polikarpova and S. Schneider (Eds.): IFM 2017, LNCS 10510, pp. 357–371, 2017.
DOI: 10.1007/978-3-319-66845-1_24

Recent work by Carvalho [1] shows the use of natural language processing (NLP) and formal methods to automatically generate test cases from written software requirements. By contrast, our present focus is on the use of NLP in a different setting, namely for capturing healthcare recommendations. Clinical texts share the difficulties encountered in software requirements, since these are often ungrammatical, use telegraphic phrases with limited context and often lack complete sentence structure [2]. In addition, the common use of acronyms and abbreviations in clinical texts introduces further ambiguity.

In this paper, we explore the use of formal methods for the validation and verification of clinical texts when used to describe therapy algorithms. Inspired by the approach done by Carvalho et al. [1] for software requirements, we explore more complex cases of controlled natural language (CNL) as used in therapy algorithms. From each sentence in the therapy algorithm we automatically generate a parse tree and derive case frames. From the case frames we automatically construct a state-based representation, in our case a timed automaton [3], and use the model checker UPPAAL [4] to verify the model. We write queries in UPPAAL's logic, a subset of TCTL, on the one side to evaluate the approach, and on the other side to check properties of clinical interest. The choice of timed automata and UPPAAL is motivated by the fact that clinical texts sometimes make reference to timed and periodic events, and we want the added flexibility of probabilistic extensions available in the wide range of tools that are available in the UPPAAL family.

Our approach makes it possible to detect gaps and case omissions, helps to further clarify treatment steps, and in the long term could be useful for patients that want to understand the therapy underlying their disease and the options they may have. Similarly for clinicians and health care providers. Throughout the paper, we use the algorithm for blood glucose lowering therapy in adults with type 2 diabetes from the National Institute for Health and Care Excellence (NICE) to illustrate our approach. NICE[1] provides guidance and advice in the UK to improve health and social care, and publishes clinical pathways for the treatment of chronic conditions including diabetes, hypertension, cancer, and so on. This work is part of a more general aim to integrate formal techniques, such as model checkers and constraint solvers, to detect and resolve inconsistencies in health recommendations and clinical guidelines. This paper adds a NLP dimension to our previous work on detecting inconsistencies in treatments for patients with multimorbidities [5], and the use of theorem provers and constraint solvers to detecting inconsistencies in requirements and scenarios of execution [6,7].

This paper is structured as follows: we describe existing related work in Sect. 2, and the problem we are addressing with our proposed framework in Sect. 3. Section 4 presents the controlled natural language used to capture the sentences in a therapy algorithm, and Sect. 5 describes how case frames are generated. From the generated case frames we can further construct a timed automaton and use UPPAAL to verify it as described in Sect. 6. We conclude the paper with some discussion on future work in Sect. 7.

---

[1] More details on NICE available at www.nice.org.uk.

2   Background and Related Work

When describing related work, we focus on work closer to our own and hence current uses of NLP in healthcare on the one hand, and links between NLP and formal verification on the other hand.

Advances in natural language processing (NLP) have been sought with applications in many fields, and in particular have also found increased interest in healthcare applications in recent years. Within healthcare there are two broad areas where the use of NLP has been explored, namely in processing free text occurrences in electronic health records (EHRs) and pathology reports. For instance, it is the free text in EHRs for mental health patients that contains key information on the evolution of the patient's symptoms and medications, and pathology reports are still to date essentially text-based. The general benefits of NLP in healthcare are clear. Demner-Fushman [8] reports the adaptation of principal NLP strategies to develop clinical decision support (CDS) systems that may help in decision making—e.g. monitoring of clinical events, processing radiology/pathology text-based reports, or processing a mixture of clinical notes — for health care providers as well as the public. Through the use of CDS systems, clinicians can enter patient data to get advice concerning recommendations or assessments from the knowledge base. Incorporating accessible electronic health records (EHRs) in the system makes it possible to automatically generate reminders or alerts when some conditions are met. However, EHRs are often recorded as free narrative text created by clinicians and care providers which adds considerable challenges to introducing automated tools and techniques for creating usable and useful CDS systems.

The information contained in textual form in EHRs and examination reports can in some cases enable new research and links between diseases to be detected. For example, a study by Shah et al. [9] showed how applying text mining to 16 million EHRs led to the understanding that the use of Proton Pump Inhibitors (PPI) may increase the risk of Myocardial Infarction (MI). Although their finding still needs additional investigations, it has demonstrated how data mining can be used to identify drug safety signals by learning on multiple clinical data sources.

The mining system in [9] was built based on previous work [10] which had shown that relationships between adverse drug reactions and (as a consequence of) drug-drug interactions were detectable with high accuracy using a large corpus. Usually patients with multiple long term conditions are subject to multiple treatments and there is a risk of undetected adverse reactions to combinations of prescribed medications for different conditions. As an example, in Scotland, over half of all people with chronic conditions have comorbidities, and a recent survey indicated that medicines are implicated in 5–17% of hospital admissions, of which half are considered preventable [11].

Imler et al. [12] conducted a study to improve the (cost) effectiveness of colorectal cancer (CRC) screening and surveillance. Their aim was to create and test a system at various institutions and identify the necessary components for producing high quality guideline surveillance recommendations through the use of NLP. From 42,569 documents, 750 documents were randomly selected and split into training and test sets with ratio 1:2. From the 750 documents, five annotators would select 300 random documents each and then each document was annotated by two annotators. The annotating process would identify 19 features consisting of the category of colonoscopy (e.g. adenocarcinoma, advanced adenoma (AA), etc.), the location, and the counts of adenomas. From this more detailed analysis of the individual pathological findings and a variety of textual input, the accuracy of detecting CRC was 99.6%, of AA was 95%, of conventional adenoma was 94.6%, of advanced sessile serrated polyp (SSP) was 99.8% and of nonadvanced SSP was 99.2%.

In software engineering, Carvalho [1] has shown how to combine NLP and formal methods to automatically generate test cases from the written software requirements. The work proposes a framework to process and transform the requirement texts into a formalism called *data flow reactive system* (DFRS), which then is used to generate the test cases. In the DFRS the inputs and outputs of the system are modelled as signals, e.g. input signals from the sensors and output signals from the actuators. The system can also have timers to model time-based behaviour. As the input for the framework, the requirements are given in a controlled natural language (CNL) called SysReq-CNL, a subset of natural language tailored for generating unambiguous requirements. Every sentence is then parsed and structures called *case frames* are constructed from its parse tree following the case grammar theory [13]. In the case grammar theory, every sentence is analysed in terms of the thematic roles by each word or group of words, e.g. agent, patient, instrument, etc. For example, the thematic roles for "**the cat drinks milk**" are {**the cat/Agent**}, {**drinks/Action**}, and {**milk/Patient**}. Inside a case frame, the verb acts as the head of the frame and have several other thematic roles filled by the rest of the sentence elements. In Carvalho's approach, these case frames are transformed into the DFRS formalism and then translated into different target formal methods for verification to generate candidates for test cases. For example, the process algebra CSP [14] was used as the basis for generating test cases in [1]. Once the CSP specifications have been generated, the model checker FDR [15] can check the traces from the refinement property which then serve as test scenarios. In earlier work, DFRS had been transformed into other formalisms such as software cost reduction (SCR) [16], internal model representation (IMR) [17], and coloured Petri nets [18]. Independently of the formal approach used, the intention was always to generate test cases automatically.

Motivated to detect problems at an early stage of software development, Diamantopoulos [19] created a mechanism to automatically map requirements to formal representation through the use of ontologies and semantic role labelling. Comparatively to [1], their approach does not restrict the requirements to be written in a controlled language. From requirement sentences, several ontology concepts are inferred (i.e. project, requirement, actor, action, object, and property) using a model that has been trained from annotated software requirements. These ontology concepts can be used to trace the connection and relationship between them, and guide the translation of specifications to source code.

3   The Problem Domain and Framework

In this paper, we propose a framework to automatically generate logic-based statements from clinical texts—in this case a therapy algorithm— written in a controlled natural language, and enable formal verification of the algorithm. As an example of a therapy algorithm, we take a sample from the algorithm for blood glucose lowering therapy in adults with type 2 diabetes from NICE[2]. Figure 1 shows a portion of the discussed algorithm. We note that HbA1c refers to *glycated haemoglobin* which can be used to determine the average blood sugar levels of a person over a period of weeks/months, and is a common measure for diabetes. A normal value is below 42 mmol/mol.

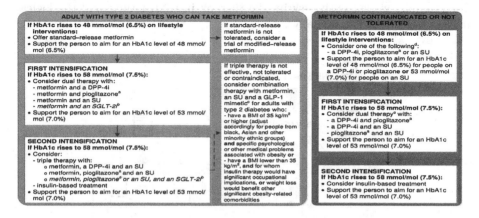

Fig. 1. A snippet of the blood glucose lowering therapy algorithm from NICE

To motivate our work, we want to check whether the therapy algorithm has inconsistencies (for example in the advised medications) and whether some cases (patient allergies or further long term conditions) are not considered and may leave a patient with no treatment options at all (or an option that may cause adverse drug reactions). In the future, we may also want to see if one therapy algorithm has conflicts with another algorithm for treating a different disease. Multimorbidity is increasing in the world, and hence a real concern in healthcare.

Our research is different from what we have discussed before because we do not deal with numerous patient records and clinical texts. Instead we currently only process a specific text related to handling a particular disease. Our approach also differs from [1] because we do not generate output in terms of steps for testing. We identify and verify discrepancies that may inherently be hidden inside therapy algorithms, and identify treatment options for patients with different circumstances.

To process the sentences in the therapy algorithm, we create a controlled natural language to standardise the structure of the sentences. Comparatively

---

[2] Full details are available at https://goo.gl/YDDtQY.

to [1], the sentence structure in a therapy algorithm is more complex because the value change is not always clearly visible (for instance *consider dual therapy with metformin and pioglitazone*) or the value changes in percentage (for instance, *aim for an HbA1c level of 53 mmol/mol (7.0%)*). Another difference is that the *agent* and the *patient* of the action are not explicitly stated. Here, we always assume that the agent is a doctor, or more generally a healthcare provider, and the patient is the patient under treatment. Furthermore, the conditions that need to be considered before giving a treatment may be nested and described in narrative form. The rules that we created are discussed in Sect. 4.

Our proposed framework is shown as a pipeline in Fig. 2 where the area inside the dashed border box indicates the system we have built. In our framework, light arrows show the automated steps whereas dark arrows imply manual processes. For example, we currently rewrite the therapy in CNL format and the logical queries for the model manually.

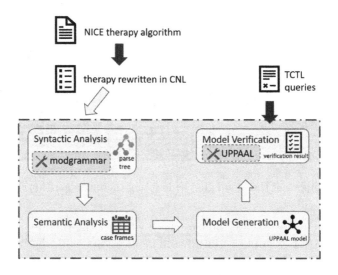

Fig. 2. The framework pipeline.

Before the therapy algorithm is processed, it is rewritten in CNL to conform with the grammar explained in the next section. Once all sentences are in agreement with the grammar, the Syntactic Analysis module will generate the parse trees with the help of an external library (indicated by the toolbox icon). The Semantic Analysis module will then construct the case frames by traversing the parse trees following some pre-defined rules explained in Sect. 5. The last two modules in the system deal with the UPPAAL model (a timed automaton). From the case frames, the Model Generation module generates the UPPAAL model as an XML file as discussed further in Sect. 6.1. Finally, the UPPAAL model is verified against queries specified in the temporal logic TCTL using the UPPAAL model checker (cf. Sect. 6.2).

4   Controlled Natural Language for Therapy Algorithms

In a therapy algorithm, we consider that every sentence has the following form:

number if conditions, the doctor shall: actions

The number in the beginning of every sentence is needed so we know its order when we generate the model automatically, as steps within a therapy algorithm follow a particular order. For example in Fig. 1, a first intensification can only happen after the patient has received a first treatment. Some considerations that we take when we transform all sentences into the standardised form are as follows: for every sentence, we add **the doctor** as the agent of the actions. In addition to explicitly showing who is responsible for a therapy, it is also needed to reduce the ambiguity from the missing information of who is responsible versus who receives the therapy.

Furthermore, if there is a list of choices (conditions or possible therapies), we transform it into

$$\{\text{choice}_1, \text{choice}_2, \cdots \text{choice}_n\}.$$

For example, the conditions in *"if triple therapy is not effective, not tolerated, or contraindicated"* and the advice *"consider therapy with a DPP-4i, pioglitazone, or an SU"* will be written as *"if triple therapy is {not effective, not tolerated, contraindicated}"* and *"consider therapy with {a DPP-4i, pioglitazone, an SU}"* respectively. This normalisation will ease us when we build the case frame from the parse tree.

Since our grammar is controlled and the lexicons are domain dependent (it is a medical therapy), we have specified in advance the vocabularies and their part-of-speech (POS) tags. Most of our lexical categories follow those by Carvalho [1] with some additional categories to simplify the parsing of the sentences and the case frame generation, such as **LBrace, RBrace, LPar, RPar,** and **Percent**. In addition to the lexical rules, we also follow Carvalho's [1] context free grammar (CFG) rules for our grammar with some modifications.

The start symbol of our grammar is **Advice** which is rewritten as

Number ConditionalClause Comma ActionClause

This means that the advice is in the form of actions guarded by conditions. Since we introduced a new rule to deal with a list of choices, we do not have the conjunctions of disjunctions anymore in our **ConditionalClause** as is visible by the absence of **Or** in our lexical rules. Our final grammar rules can be seen inside the *Grammar rule* box below.

After defining the lexical and grammar rules, the original sentences taken from the therapy algorithm are rewritten manually so they conform to the rules (as indicated by the black arrow in Fig. 2). For example, the original sentence after the first intensification for people who can take metformin in Fig. 1 is written as *"2 if HbA1c level rises to 58 mmol/mol (7.5%), the doctor shall: consider dual therapy with {metformin and a DPP-4i, metformin and pioglitazone, metformin and an SU, metformin and an SGLT-2i}, support to aim for an HbA1c level of 53 mmol/mol (7.0%)"*.

To parse the sentences, we use an external library in Python called modgrammar³ for building parsers using CFG definitions. In modgrammar, the rules are defined as Python classes making it possible to process the parse tree in terms of the underlying tree data structures. As the lexical rule is already predefined, we do not need to build a separate POS tagger to classify the tag for every word in the sentences because we can define the lexical rule in a similar manner as we defined the grammar rules.

Grammar rule

- **Advice** → Number? ConditionalClause Comma ActionClause
- **ConditionalClause** → Conj Condition
- **Condition** → NounPhrase VerbPhraseCondition
- **ActionClause** → NounPhrase VerbPhraseAction
- **VerbPhraseAction** → Shall Colon [VerbAction ToInfClause | VerbComplement | ChoiceAction ConditionalClause? sep=Comma]+
- **ChoiceAction** → LBrace PrepComplement [Comma VerbComplement]+ RBrace
- **VerbPhraseCondition** → VerbCondition Not? VerbComplement
- **ToInfClause** → To VBase VerbComplement
- **VerbComplement** → VariableState | ChoiceComplement | PrepComplement
- **PrepComplement** → [VariableState? Prep] VariableState | ChoiceComplement
- **ChoiceComplement** → LBrace VariableState [Comma VariableState]+ RBrace
- **PrepositionalPhrase** → Prep NounPhrase
- **VariableState** → AdjPhrase | NounPhrase
- **NounPhrase** → [Det? Adj* Noun PrepositionalPhrase*]+ [And NounPhrase+]*
- **VerbAction** → VBase
- **AdjPhrase** → [Adv?] Adj | VPart
- **VerbCondition** → VPre3 | VToBePre3
- **Noun** → Number | NSing | NPlur | Nmass

---

5   Case Frame Generation

After generating the parse tree, we construct automatically the case frames by traversing the parse tree. We follow eight thematic roles defined by Carvalho [1] with two additional roles: one for handling the nested condition in our sentences (CACT) and another one to mark the sequence of the sentence (NUM). The NUM role is useful in our case because the therapies are given in a sequence and we need to keep track of the order of their occurrence. For example, a value of 1 for NUM means the case frame is from the first sentence of the therapy, meanwhile 1.1 means the first alternative treatment for that first therapy. Apart from the NUM role, the thematic roles can be grouped into *action statements* and *conditional clause*. Here is a brief summary of each thematic role.

---

³ https://bitbucket.org/modgrammar/modgrammar.

- Action statement thematic roles
  1. *Action* (ACT): the action to be performed if the conditions are met. It is taken from the **VBase** or the **ToInfClause** inside **VerbPhraseAction**. Here, we only allow *consider, review, offer, support*, and *aim* for this category.
  2. *Agent* (AGT): the actor of the action. It is taken from the **NounPhrase** node found inside **ActionClause**. There is only one agent, i.e. the doctor.
  3. *Patient* (PAT): the entity affected by the action. It is taken from the **VariableState** node found inside **VerbComplement**.
  4. *To Value* (TOV): the value given to the patient. It is taken from the **VariableState** inside **PrepositionalComplement** or **ChoiceComplement**.
  5. *Nested Condition Action* (CACT): the additional condition for the action. For every ACT found, a list of CACT is created whose value could be empty, i.e. an empty list. It is taken from the **ConditionalClause** found inside **VerbPhraseAction**.
- Conditional clause thematic roles
  1. *Condition Action* (CAC): the action for the condition. The values are taken from all **VerbCondition** inside **ConditionalClause**.
  2. *Condition Patient* (CPT): the entity related to the condition. Because in the therapy algorithm there is only one entity related to the condition(s), its value is taken from the **NounPhrase** found in **ConditionalClause**.
  3. *Condition To Value* (CTV): the new value of the condition patient. It is taken from the **VariableState** in **VerbComplement** or **ChoiceComplement**, or from the **Noun** in **PrepComplement**.
  4. *Condition Modifier* (CMD): the modifier for the condition. The value is taken from the first **Noun** in **PrepComplement** if there are more than one.

Figure 3 shows an example of a case frame for the case when taking the first treatment in Fig. 1. The sentence is rewritten as *"1 if HbA1c level rises to 48 mmol/mol (6.5%) on lifestyle interventions, the doctor shall: offer standard-release metformin, support to aim for an HbA1c level of 48 mmol/mol (6.5%)."*

NUM:	1		
CONDITION #1 - Main Verb (CAC):	rises		
CPT:	HbA1c level	CTV:	48 mmol/mol (6.5%)
CMD:	on lifestyle interventions		
ACTION - Main Verb (ACT):	offer		
AGT:	the doctor	TOV:	-
PAT:	standard-release metformin	CACT:	-
ACTION - Main Verb (ACT):	aim		
AGT:	the doctor	TOV:	48 mmol/mol (6.5%)
PAT:	HbA1c level		

Fig. 3. Example of a case frame

6   Model Generation and Verification

In this paper, we generate state-based models automatically from an original description given in CNL, and verify the models with the model checker UPPAAL [4]. We first describe how models are generated.

6.1   Model Generation

UPPAAL is an integrated tool environment for modelling, validation and verification of real-time systems modelled as networks of timed automata. Timed automata (TA) [3] add the notion of time to standard automata (based on a finite set of states and labelled transitions between them) through a set of variables called *clocks*. Clocks are special variables which can be inspected or reset but not assigned a value. A time unit represents a second, minute or month, depending on what is a sensible unit for the model (note that there is no time in our therapy algorithm snippet). A constraint can be placed on *locations* (the term used for states in a TA) to denote a *location invariant* (to indicate for instance how long the automaton can remain in the location) and on transitions where it acts as a guard.

In UPPAAL we can create several instances of processes with the same behaviour. The behaviour is captured in a so-called template (a TA), and one or more instances of that template can be declared for runtime verification. In our example of a therapy algorithm for diabetes we need a template for the behaviour captured in the algorithm for treating diabetes, and an additional template to simulate a random change of the value of HbA1c in the blood.

The process of generating the diabetes automaton is done automatically by traversing the case frames for each sentence following the sequence number in the NUM role. This is shown as the Model Generation module in Fig. 2. We identified all variables from CPT and PAT roles and their values from the CTV and TOV respectively. If the value contains a number, the type of the variable is **int**, otherwise it is **bool**. For example, finding HbA1c can have value of 48, 53, and 58 made it an **int** variable. To model how HbA1c can change its value, we created a simple template that always increments the value of HbA1c. We assume $40 \leq HbA1c \leq 60$.

The locations are built sequentially from the first sentence to the last. Whenever the verb **rises** is found in CAC role, its CTV value is used as the upper limit for the current location's invariant and as the lower limit for the transition's guard to the next location. Updates in transitions are done by setting the boolean variable from PAT to **true**.

Figure 4 shows the model generated automatically. In this model, we only show the therapy path where standard-release metformin is tolerated, the first intensification and the second intensification. The locations have a location invariant on the value of HbA1c to indicate that if HbA1c rises above a certain value (for instance above 48 in the location Normal) then the location must be left and a treatment given. The different transitions between intensifications show the different options available and are dependant on the first treatment

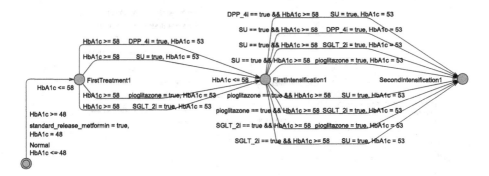

Fig. 4. Generated model for adults with type 2 diabetes that tolerate metformin

received (the taken medications are captured by a boolean variable with the same name and value true). The first alternative path where modified-release metformin is used will create a mirror of locations and transitions which only differs on the guard for the first transition. The full model is omitted here.

When investigating the generated model, we noticed that there is no transition that takes the system (in this case a potential patient) back to the initial state Normal. As it may be more realistic to assume that other factors (such as changing life style habits and diet) can have an effect and recovery is possible, we want to refine the model to take this into account. This means that the model should cover a situation where the patient's condition turns back to normal after a time under treatment. On the other side, this may not be a very frequent outcome and ideally we would like to quantify the likelihood of such a recovery to happen as opposed to a deterioration of the condition as given in the model of Fig. 4. This can be done with Probabilistic Timed Automata [20] which extend TA with probabilistic transitions. How to quantify such transitions is outside the scope of the present paper but should be informed by analysis of large datasets of records for patients with diabetes.

We modified the model generation process to create some branch points after a treatment is taken. A branch is created whenever we find the verb **aim** denoting the situation when the doctor tries to stabilise the HbA1c level after giving a treatment. At present, we give a value of 20 and 80 as the weight to go back to a normal state and to the next (deteriorated) state respectively. Figure 5 shows the graphical model with branch points. To keep the model more readable, we currently only show going back to a normal state, but further possible transition branches include returning to any other previous treatment state with different weights.

We note that the actual model generation is done by generating an xml file which can then be visualised in the tool as in Fig. 5 (after minor adjustments to take into account visual placement of the elements). The xml file contains all the information of locations, location invariants, transitions and variables, but can also given directly on the command line to the model checker for verification.

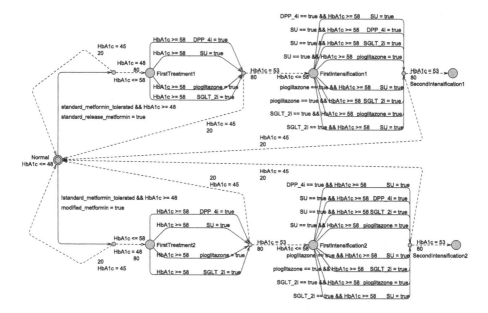

Fig. 5. Model with Branch Points

6.2   Model Verification

We have verified our model against some properties as shown in Table 1. The properties selected are used primarily to evaluate the approach. UPPAAL takes properties written in a restricted form of the temporal logic TCTL. The properties were verified against the model in Fig. 5 after an initial analysis of the original model and its refinement to include recovery. The property

```
A[] !diab.SecondIntensification1 && !diab.SecondIntensification2
```

illustrates the situation where a second intensification of the therapy has been reached (the property itself only holds iff second intensification is never reached, and the fact that it is not satisfied will result in a trace that shows a second intensification of the therapy being reached). Another similar property, A[] !deadlock, is not satisfied because the model at present and as generated from the therapy algorithm contains no further steps after second intensification and hence deadlocks at that point. This suggests that further discussions with clinicians are required to understand available options from that point and what is realistic.

From the model in Fig. 5, we can also see that there is a possibility of never reaching a first intensification shown by verifying the formulae:

```
E<> !diab.FirstIntensification1 && !diab.FirstIntensification2
```

The same is also true for second intensification. Again, these situations became possible because we added a scenario where the patient's condition improves after

Table 1. Verification result

UPPAAL queries	Verification result	Remark
`A[] !deadlock`	Not satisfied	There is a path that leads to a deadlock
`E<> !diab.FirstIntensification1 && !diab.FirstIntensification2`	Satisfied	There exists a path where first intensification is never reached
`E<> !diab.SecondIntensification1 && !diab.SecondIntensification2`	Satisfied	There exists a path where second intensification is never reached
`A[] !diab.SecondIntensification1 && !diab.SecondIntensification2`	Not satisfied	There is a path that reaches a second intensification
`diab.FirstIntensification2 --> diab.SecondIntensification2`	Not satisfied	There is a path in which a second intensification will never be reached from a first intensification

getting some treatment. The last property (which uses temporal implication)

```
diab.FirstIntensification2 --> diab.SecondIntensification2
```

also shows the possibility of never evolving to a second intensification after reaching the first intensification.

7   Conclusion

We have presented an approach to analyse therapy algorithms published by NICE automatically. Therapy algorithms contain instructions which we treat as CNL statements and from which we ultimately build a state-based representation, in our case a timed automaton, that can be analysed by a model checker such as UPPAAL. A particular problem that we wanted to investigate was how to detect inconsistencies and gaps in the treatment options. In particular, it was noted that the algorithm did not consider a possible recovery in the different treatment stages that a patient with type 2 diabetes may go through nor what happens after a second intensification (which creates a deadlock eventually).

In future work, and in collaboration with a general practitioner (GP), we will analyse EHRs for patients with diabetes in Scotland, in order to detect cases or treatments that are not currently captured in the guidelines, and extend the algorithm accordingly. More broadly, we also want to see if one algorithm may have conflicts with another from a different disease (cf. [5]).

Our long term goal is to build a framework of therapy models which can: (1) be used as a reference to give advice to clinicians and patients based on their current situation and future treatment options, and (2) compare the therapy algorithm with actual practice. For the latter, note that adding real data from EHRs will enable us to obtain models for current practice and allow us to contrast these with NICE guidelines and recommendations. In particular, the choice of timed automata and UPPAAL allows us to add further therapy algorithms as different templates which can then be composed together and verified directly. In addition, our models can be easily extended to incorporate probabilities on branched transitions to reflect real data from EHRs. Another possible direction to guarantee the scalability of our approach, consists of exploring links to constraint solvers such as Z3 (for cases of bounded model checking). We have used constraint solvers considerably in our work, including our recent work in [5, 7].

References

1. Carvalho, G.H.P.D.: NAT2TEST: Generating Test Cases from Natural Language Requirements based on CSP. Ph.D. thesis (2016)
2. Townsend, H.: Natural language processing and clinical outcomes: the promise and progress of NLP for improved care. J. AHIMA **84**(2), 44–45 (2013)
3. Alur, R., Dill, D.L.: A theory of timed automata. Theor. Comput. Sci. **126**, 183–235 (1994)
4. Behrmann, G., David, A., Larsen, K.G.: A tutorial on UPPAAL. In: Bernardo, M., Corradini, F. (eds.) SFM-RT 2004. LNCS, vol. 3185, pp. 200–236. Springer, Heidelberg (2004). doi:10.1007/978-3-540-30080-9_7
5. Kovalov, A., Bowles, J.K.F.: Avoiding medication conflicts for patients with multimorbidities. In: Ábrahám, E., Huisman, M. (eds.) IFM 2016. LNCS, vol. 9681, pp. 376–390. Springer, Cham (2016). doi:10.1007/978-3-319-33693-0_24
6. Bowles, J., Bordbar, B., Alwanain, M.: Weaving true-concurrent aspects using constraint solvers. In: Application of Concurrency to System Design (ACSD 2016). IEEE Computer Society Press, June 2016
7. Bowles, J.K.F., Caminati, M.B.: Mind the gap: addressing behavioural inconsistencies with formal methods. In: 23rd Asia-Pacific Software Engineering Conference (APSEC). IEEE Computer Society (2016)
8. Demner-Fushman, D., Chapman, W.W., McDonald, C.J.: What can natural language processing do for clinical decision support? J. Biomed. Inform. **42**(5), 760–772 (2009)
9. Shah, N.H., LePendu, P., Bauer-Mehren, A., Ghebremariam, Y.T., Iyer, S.V., Marcus, J., Nead, K.T., Cooke, J.P., Leeper, N.J.: Proton pump inhibitor usage and the risk of myocardial infarction in the general population. PLoSONE **10**(6), e0124653 (2015). 10.1371/journal.pone.0124653
10. LePendu, P., Iyer, S.V., Bauer-Mehren, A., Harpaz, R., Mortensen, J., Podchiyska, T., Ferris, T.A., Shah, N.H.: Pharmacovigilance using clinical notes. Clin. Pharmacol. Ther. **93**, 547–555 (2013). 10.1038/clpt.2013.47
11. Polypharmacy Guidance (2nd Edition). Scottish Government Model of Care Polypharmacy Working Group (2015)
12. Imler, T.D., Morea, J., Kahi, C., Cardwell, J., Johnson, C.S., Xu, H., Imperiale, T.F.: Multi-center colonoscopy quality measurement utilizing natural language processing. Am. J. Gastroenterol. **110**(4), 543–552 (2015). 10.1038/ajg.2015.51

13. Fillmore, C.J.: The case for case. In: Bach, E., Harms, R.T. (eds.) Universals in Linguistic Theory. Holt, Rinehart and Winston, London (1968)
14. Hoare, C.A.R.: Communicating Sequential Processes. Commun. ACM **21**(8), 666–677 (1978). doi:10.1145/359576.359585
15. Gibson-Robinson, T., Armstrong, P., Boulgakov, A., Roscoe, A.W.: FDR3 — a modern refinement checker for CSP. In: Ábrahám, E., Havelund, K. (eds.) TACAS 2014. LNCS, vol. 8413, pp. 187–201. Springer, Heidelberg (2014). doi:10.1007/978-3-642-54862-8_13
16. Carvalho, G., Falcão, D., Barros, F., Sampaio, A., Mota, A., Motta, L., Blackburn, M.: NAT2TEST$_{SCR}$: test case generation from natural language requirements based on SCR specifications. Sci. Comput. Program. **95**(Part3), 275–297 (2014). https://doi.org/10.1016/j.scico.2014.06.007
17. Carvalho, G., Barros, F., Lapschies, F., Schulze, U., Peleska, J.: Model-based testing from controlled natural language requirements. In: Artho, C., Öveczky, P. (eds.) Formal Techniques for Safety-Critical Systems. CCIS, vol. 419, pp. 19–35. Springer, Cham (2013). doi:10.1007/978-3-319-05416-2_3
18. Silva, B.C.F., Carvalho, G., Sampaio, A.: Test case generation from natural language requirements using CPN simulation. In: Cornélio, M., Roscoe, B. (eds.) SBMF 2015. LNCS, vol. 9526, pp. 178–193. Springer, Cham (2016). doi:10.1007/978-3-319-29473-5_11
19. Diamantopoulos, T., Roth, M., Symeonidis, A., Klein, E.: Software requirements as an application domain for natural language processing. Lang. Resour. Eval. **51**(2), 495–524 (2017)
20. Norman, G., Parker, D., Sproston, J.: Model checking for probabilistic timed automata. Formal Methods Syst. Des. **43**(2), 164–190 (2013)

Verified Software

Modular Verification of Order-Preserving Write-Back Caches

Jörg Pfähler$^{(\boxtimes)}$, Gidon Ernst, Stefan Bodenmüller, Gerhard Schellhorn,
and Wolfgang Reif

Institute for Software and Systems Engineering,
University of Augsburg, Augsburg, Germany
{pfaehler,ernst,bodenmueller,schellhorn,reif}@isse.de

Abstract. File systems not only have to be functionally correct, they
also have to be crash-safe: a power cut while an operation is running must
be guaranteed to lead to a consistent state after restart that loses as little information as possible. Specification and verification of crash-safety
is particularly difficult for non-redundant write-back caches. This paper
defines a novel crash-safety criterion that facilitates specification and
verification of order-preserving caches. A power cut is basically observa-
tionally equivalent to a retraction of a few of the last executed operations. The approach is modular: It gives simple proof obligations for each
individual component and for each refinement in the development. The
theory is supported by our interactive theorem prover KIV and proof
obligations for crash-safety have been verified for the Flashix flash file
system.

Keywords: Write-back caching · Crash-safe refinement · Flash file systems

1 Introduction

To be reliable, file systems have to be both functionally correct and crash-safe.
Functional correctness is typically expressed in terms of a high-level specification
of its operations, as given for example by the established POSIX standard [1].
Crash-safety is harder to prove, since it not only has to consider the states before
and after operations. Instead, a power cut that interrupts an operation in any
intermediate state must lead to a consistent state after reboot, where as little
information as possible has been lost.

We develop Flashix [18], a file system for flash memory that is verified with
the interactive theorem prover KIV [8] to be both functionally correct with
respect to POSIX and crash-safe. Flashix is strongly modular: it is hierarchically
composed of encapsulated components, which are formalized as data types [7,12]
extended by a specification of the effect of a power cut and subsequent recovery.

Supported by the Deutsche Forschungsgemeinschaft (DFG), "Verifikation von Flash-
Dateisystemen" (grants RE828/13-1 and RE828/13-2).

© Springer International Publishing AG 2017
N. Polikarpova and S. Schneider (Eds.): IFM 2017, LNCS 10510, pp. 375–390, 2017.
DOI: 10.1007/978-3-319-66845-1_25

Verifying crash-safety is critically affected by *caching* mechanisms employed by the implementation, as data structures in main memory are lost upon a power cut. Caches can be classified into *write-through* and *write-back* caches. The former can be reconstructed from persistent memory and are therefore fully redundant. Crash-safety is expressible by stating that the recovery operation restores the state from before the power cut. Losing a write-through cache due to a power cut is invisible to its clients (components that use the cache).

Write-back caches, on the other hand, lead to actual loss of data in the event of a power cut. The crash-safety of their clients then depends heavily on the exact nature of the data lost. Therefore the specification of the crash-safety of the cache needs to be propagated upwards through the component hierarchy.

Flashix is a log-structured file system. The log component appends log entries by using a write-back cache. It defers writes until the size of a page or sector is reached. This cache is *order-preserving*, i.e. the write operations to the storage device are in the same order as the writes to the cache. In our experience (Sect. 2 and [9]) if crash-safety is expressed as a *state-based* property, i.e. as a relation between the state before and after the power cut, it needs to be expressed on every level of abstraction, which complicates verification significantly.

The contribution of this paper is threefold. We propose a new correctness criterion for order-preserving caches called *quasi sequentially crash consistent*[1]. A storage system satisfies this criterion if a power cut takes the system's state backwards in time by retracting several system operations in order and by re-executing the earliest retracted operation. Secondly, we embed this *operations-based* property into the semantics of components (Sect. 3). This allows us to propagate it over component hierarchies implicitly via refinement (Sect. 4). The notion of refinement defined allows for substitution (Sect. 5). Section 6 shows that in practice considering the initial and final state of an operation's execution is sufficient for the verification of crash-safety. Finally, we implemented support for the proof obligations of the theory in our interactive theorem prover KIV [8] and applied it to the Flashix file system. All models, proofs and the executable code are available online.[2]

2   Motivation

The formal development of a software system usually starts with a specification of its desired behavior and properties, e.g. POSIX in the case of a file system. The implementation then comprises a hierarchy of components, stacked as indicated by Fig. 1, i.e., each implementation refines (dotted lines) a specification $Spec_i$. It is a client of ($-\otimes-$) an abstraction of one or more subcomponents

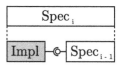

Fig. 1. Refinement

$Spec_{i-1}$. Either $Spec_{i-1}$ is refined further or serves as a specification for external components, e.g. the interface to flash hardware in the context of Flashix.

---

[1] The classification of Bornholt et al. [3] defines *sequential crash consistency*.

[2] http://www.isse.de/flashix.

state $block$: Array⟨Byte⟩

append(in buf: Array⟨Byte⟩, out err: Error)
  precondition
    $\# block + \# buf \leq$ BLOCK_SIZE
  atomic
    choose n: ℕ **with** $n \leq \# buf$ **in**
      $block := block \text{ ++ } buf[0\dots n]$
      $err := (n = \# buf) ?$ ESUCCESS : EIO

crash
  $block' = block\!\downarrow\!$PAGE_SIZE
  with domain $true$
synchronized
  $true$

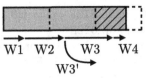

W1 W2 ⟍ W3 W4
W3'

Fig. 4. Alternative Re-Execution

// **same state & operations**

crash
  $block' = block$
  with domain $page\text{-}aligned(block)$
synchronized
  $page\text{-}aligned(block)$

Fig. 3. Explicit Specification   **Fig. 5.** Implicit Specification

Refinement guarantees that the final implementation has the properties of the top-level specification.

In [10] we have integrated the verification of crash-safety into this scheme: In addition to regular operations, each model is equipped with a specification of *resets*, which consist of the effect of crashes and their subsequent recovery, specified as a predicate over two states. We first illustrate this type of state-based specification with the Flashix write buffer [9] and then highlight a crucial problem with this approach and propose a different, operations-based specification.

The write buffer is visualized in Fig. 2. It alleviates the limitation that flash blocks can only be written sequentially and in page-sized chunks. The component keeps a page-sized buffer in RAM and writes it to flash as soon as the page-size is reached. A transactional log or journal uses the write buffer to record file system changes.

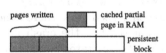

Fig. 2. Write buffer [9]

Explicit Reset Specification. Figure 3 depicts a first, natural abstraction of the write buffer that merges the cache and the contents of the flash block into one dynamically-sized array of bytes $block$. The **append** operation extends the contents of the abstract block by new data stored in buf. Since flash memory is inherently unreliable [20], the specification accounts for short writes that fail to persist the whole buf up to its size $\# buf$ and write just the subrange from 0 to n (n excluded) instead.[3] The specification is a program that cannot be interrupted by a power cut in an intermediate state, signified by the keyword **atomic**.

The effect of losing the cache is captured by the **crash** predicate. It restricts a transition from state s to s' of the system. In the case of the write buffer a prefix $block'$ of $block$ rounded down to the previous page boundary is taken,

---

[3] Note that the POSIX specification [1] explicitly permits such short writes to surface at the system interface.

where $block \downarrow \texttt{PAGE\_SIZE} = block[0...(\# block) \downarrow \texttt{PAGE\_SIZE}]$ for $n \downarrow \texttt{PAGE\_SIZE} = n - (n \bmod \texttt{PAGE\_SIZE})$.

The problem with the approach is that the data lost by the reset of the cache component $Spec_{i-1}$ (in Fig. 1) must be propagated explicitly to the levels of abstraction given by its direct client $Spec_i$, and then to its client's client, until the top-level specification. This is particularly problematic if the hierarchy is deep or, as is the case in Flashix, higher levels of abstraction can not naturally express the property. Therefore, we split the specification of a reset into 1. a retraction transition followed by a re-execution transition and 2. a crash transition.

Implicit Reset Specifications. Figure 4 shows an example with write operations W1 to W4. The operations and how far they filled the block is denoted by the start/end position of the arrows. Page boundaries are depicted as dotted lines. A power failure in the explicit approach (i.e., what effectively happens) removes the hatched part at the end of the block up to the last dotted line.

The effect can be explained *alternatively* by first reversing the effect of the last two operations W3 and W4 and subsequently re-executing the W3 operation (denoted by W3') on the same inputs, choosing the error path that writes only $n = (\# buf) \downarrow \texttt{PAGE\_SIZE}$ bytes. This alternative specification requires to define *synchronized* states that are resilient against crashes, i.e., a retraction is not allowed in such a state: Fig. 5 shows how these can be captured in the write buffer by a `synchronized` predicate over the state, where *page-aligned*(*block*) holds iff $\# block \bmod \texttt{PAGE\_SIZE} = 0$. Clearly, the alternative trace that executes W1, W2 and W3' is possible by the specification of the `append` operation. In a synchronized state there is no additional effect of a crash that must be modeled explicitly, i.e., the crash predicate of the implicit specification of Fig. 5 is just identity. In states outside of the domain of the crash predicate a crash can not occur.

By making the crash predicate partial, we mark the states of interest in which we *want* to consider crash transitions. Here, we use just the synchronized states, while in the general theory it is also possible to use a superset. We have to ensure that retracting operations and re-executing one operation actually targets a state in the domain of the (now partial) crash predicate. Informally, this is guaranteed when it can be proved that operations fall into two classes: *retractable* operations like W4, where a crash has the same effect before and after the operation, and *completable* operations like W3, which have an execution that leads to a state in the domain of the crash predicate.

We use both the implicit as well as the explicit specification as shown by Fig. 6. First, we abstract the write buffer implementation to the explicit specification with a normal refinement step (Theorem 1, Sect. 4). Then we introduce the implicit specification in a separate refinement step (Theorem 2, Sect. 4). In the semantics we define next, the retraction transition is then implicitly propagated upwards through the remaining

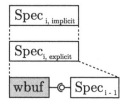

Fig. 6. Introducing Implicit Specifications

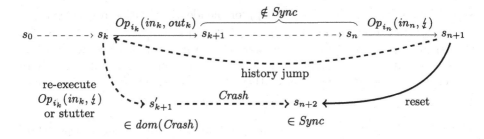

Fig. 7. Constructing a reset transition $s_{n+1} \longrightarrow s_{n+2}$.

refinement hierarchy automatically (Theorem 3, Sect. 5). Therefore only the (now trivial) crash predicate needs to be expressed on each layer of abstraction.

3   Components with Power Cuts

Systems considered in this work are hierarchically composed of encapsulated components, which are formally presented in terms of data types [7,12] extended by a specification of the effect of a power cut and subsequent recovery.

Definition 1 (Component). *A component $C = (S, In, Out, Init, Sync, Crash, (Op_i)_{i \in I})$ consists of a set of states S, inputs In and outputs Out, initial states Init, synchronized states Sync with $Init \subseteq Sync \subseteq S$, a relation $Crash \subseteq S \times Sync$ with $Sync \subseteq dom(Crash)$ describing the effect of a crash including its subsequent recovery,[4] and regular operations $Op_i \subseteq In \times S \times S \times (Out \uplus \{ \frac{1}{2} \})$. The value $\frac{1}{2}$ signifies that the operation was interrupted by a power cut.*

Operations are defined by programs that modify the state and compute an output from an input. Implementation programs may call operations of another (sub-)component as detailed in Sect. 5. A small-step semantics of the programs is given in [10]. Here, we abstract program runs to a relation Op_i between initial and final states. The crash and synchronized relation are given syntactically by the **crash** and **synchronized** predicate in Figs. 3 and 5.

A complete program run starting in state s with input in, finishing in state s' with output out is written $s \xrightarrow{Op_i(in, out)} s'$, which is equivalent to $(in, s, s', out) \in Op_i$, using the induced relation $Op_i(in, out) \subseteq S \times S$ as a label. Abbreviation $(s, s') \in Op_i(in)$ holds if there is any $out \neq \frac{1}{2}$ such that $(s, s') \in Op_i(in, out)$.

An incomplete run where the computation is interrupted by a power cut in an intermediate state s' (and the operation does not return a result) results in tuple $(in, s, s', \frac{1}{2}) \in Op_i$, written as $s \xrightarrow{Op_i(in, \frac{1}{2})} s'$, again using $Op_i(in, \frac{1}{2}) \subseteq S \times S$ as a label. It is reasonable to assume that a crash can happen in initial as well as final

---

[4] In the actual models recovery is a separate *operation* that runs directly after a crash and tries to restore the state. To keep the presentation brief, we combine the crash and recovery into one transition here.

states, i.e., we assume $Id_S \subseteq Op_i(in, \xi)$ for the identity relation resp. $Op_i(in) \subseteq Op_i(in, \xi)$. Interrupted steps in a run are followed by steps $s' \xrightarrow{\text{reset}} s''$ (detailed below), that model the *effect* of a power cut and its subsequent recovery.

The semantics of components is a set of runs, which are finite or infinite sequences of labeled transitions of these three kinds, which generalizes data types as used in Z [22] that have regular transitions $s \xrightarrow{Op_i(in,out)} s'$ only.

Definition 2 (Runs). *A run of the component C is given by a sequence of labeled state transitions $s_0 \xrightarrow{l_0} s_1 \xrightarrow{l_1} \cdots$ that starts in an initial state with $s_0 \in Init$ and consist of fragments for each (non-interrupted) state s_n:*

$$s_n \xrightarrow{Op_{i_n}(in_n,out_n)} s_{n+1} \quad \text{or} \quad s_n \xrightarrow{Op_{i_n}(in_n,\xi)} s_{n+1} \xrightarrow{\text{reset}} s_{n+2},$$

where $s_{n+1} \xrightarrow{\text{reset}} s_{n+2}$ picks an earlier state s_k from this run, optionally re-executes the corresponding k-th operation partially (ξ output), and applies the residual effect of crash & recovery, i.e., there is k with $k \leq n+1$ and s'_{k+1} s.t.:

- $s_{k'} \notin Sync$ for all k' with $k < k' \leq n+1$,
- $s_k \xrightarrow{Op_{i_k}(in,\xi)} s'_{k+1}$ and $k < n+1$ or $s_k = s'_{k+1}$,
- $(s'_{k+1}, s_{n+2}) \in Crash$

Figure 7 depicts how a transition $s_{n+1} \xrightarrow{\text{reset}} s_{n+2}$ (arrow →) is constructed by these three constituents (arrows ⇢).

We point out some aspects of Definition 2: Re-execution is optional and only permitted when at least one operation had been retracted by the jump ($k \neq n+1$). The state s_{n+2} will be synchronized as $Crash \subseteq S \times Sync$, implying that another crash does not go back further in the history. State s'_{k+1} must fall into the domain of $Crash$. This corresponds to the intuition that a power cut can be *observed in* or needs to be *considered in* states in $dom(Crash)$. Expressing the $Crash$-predicate on a selected subset of states is easier for the given component and its clients as we have motivated with Fig. 5. Retracting operations implies the existence of a different run without a jump that ends in the same state s_{n+2}:

$$s_0 \rightarrow \cdots \rightarrow s_k \xrightarrow{Op_{i_k}(in_k,\xi)} s_{k'+1} \xrightarrow{Crash} s_{n+2}. \tag{1}$$

A component where all states are synchronized ($Sync = S$) neither retracts nor re-executes operations. This view is used for the lowest level of specification, where the distinction between volatile and persistent memory is explicit, and the effect of a power cut is expressed as just forgetting data in volatile memory.

4   Crash-Safe Refinement

The observable behavior of a run is the sequence of its labels. Refinement is defined based on preserving observable behavior:

Definition 3 (Refinement). *A component C refines a component A, written $A \sqsubseteq C$, iff they have the same input and output set and the same index set of operations and for each run $cs_0 \xrightarrow{l_0} cs_1 \xrightarrow{l_1} \cdots$ of C there is a matching run $as_0 \xrightarrow{l_0} as_1 \xrightarrow{l_1} \cdots$ of A with the same labels.*

With these definitions it is now possible to express the correctness and crash-safety criterion we propose for file systems.

Definition 4 (Quasi Sequential Crash Consistency). *A file system is quasi sequentially crash consistent, iff it refines the POSIX component given in [11] augmented with synchronized states reached by successful calls to fsync or sync. The crash predicate discards open file handles and deletes orphaned files [10].*

Since our POSIX specification is a component as by Definition 1 its reset is allowed to retract operations, however, never across a successful call to fsync or sync. "Quasi" signifies that one re-execution is allowed, which is not allowed in Bornholt's definition of sequential crash consistency [3]. The Flashix file system is developed via incremental refinement of the POSIX component.

In general, a refinement step can change data representation as well as change the view of a crash, since only the observable behavior must be preserved. The generality of having both changes in abstraction is only needed for a uniform definition of refinement. In practice, refinements either change data representation, or the specification of a crash individually—several refinement steps can be combined transitively if needed. The following two subsections therefore consider the two types of refinement separately. Like in data refinement, refinement is typically proved using forward simulations. New proof obligations result from steps $s_n \xrightarrow{Op_j(in,\mathbf{t})} s_{n+1} \xrightarrow{\text{reset}} s_{n+2}$, therefore the proofs focus on these transitions.

4.1   Data Refinement and Propagation of Jumps

The proof obligations for changing data representation are just slightly more complex than data refinement. We denote with $R_1 \,\mathring{,}\, R_2$ the composition of two relations R_1 and R_2 and with $D \triangleleft R$ and $R \triangleright D$ the domain resp. range restriction of the binary relation R to the set D.

Theorem 1 (Data Refinement by Forward Simulation). *A refinement $A \sqsubseteq C$ is implied by a forward simulation $R \subseteq AS \times CS$ satisfying (for all $i \in I, in \in In, out \in Out$)*

1. $CInit \subseteq AInit \,\mathring{,}\, R$ (initialization)
2. $R \,\mathring{,}\, COp_i(in, out) \subseteq AOp_i(in, out) \,\mathring{,}\, R$ (correctness)
3. $ASync \,\mathring{,}\, R \subseteq CSync$ (synchronization)
4. $R \,\mathring{,}\, COp_i(in, \mathbf{t}) \,\mathring{,}\, CCrash \subseteq AOp_i(in, \mathbf{t}) \,\mathring{,}\, ACrash \,\mathring{,}\, R$ (crash)

The synchronization condition states that fewer states of component A are synchronized and the crash condition abstracts the remaining effect of a power cut.

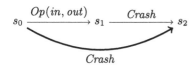

Fig. 8. Retractable before *Crash*

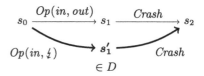

Fig. 9. *D*-Completable before *Crash*

Proof (of Theorem 1). The proof composes commuting diagrams as usual, starting with two related initial states given by 1. For regular transitions, proof obligation 2. gives the relevant commuting diagram. A history jump of component C is mapped to a history jump over the same number of operations in A. Condition 3. ensures that each unsynchronized state retracted by C can be retracted by A as well. Condition 4. commutes either the interrupted operation (when the jump is empty) or the re-execution jointly with the subsequent crash and recovery. □

4.2   Crash Refinement and Introduction of Jumps

Incrementally introducing history jumps is the second kind of refinement. It assumes that the data structures and operations are the same on both levels. The basic idea is to move parts of a power cut from a *Crash* transition to the jump transition by looking at the history fragment $s_n \xrightarrow{Op_i(in,out)} s_{n+1} \xrightarrow{Crash} s_{n+2}$ of the component before a crash transition and construct a different explanation of how the component ended up in s_{n+2}. This construction yields an alternative intermediate state s'_{n+1} from a set $D \subseteq dom(Crash)$, allowing us to simplify the crash transition to the relation $D \triangleleft Crash$ as in Fig. 5 for $D = page\text{-}aligned$.

Definition 5 (Retractable before *Crash*). *A transition* $s_0 \rightarrow s_1$ *is retractable before Crash, iff every state* s_2 *with* $(s_1, s_2) \in Crash$, *also satisfies* $(s_0, s_2) \in Crash$.

If an execution step is retractable before *Crash*, it did not have any immediate permanent effect and we can ignore that it ever took place directly before a crash happened. Figure 8 depicts this alternative execution in bold. This does not mean that the execution will never have a permanent effect. Any of the subsequent operations may very well persist the data of previous operations. In the example, the transition W4 in Fig. 4 is retractable before the crash of Fig. 3 that sets the state to *block* ↓ PAGE_SIZE.

Definition 6 (*D*-Completable before *Crash*). *A transition* $s_0 \xrightarrow{Op(in,out)} s_1$ *with out* $\in Out \uplus \{\frac{1}{2}\}$ *of an operation Op is called D-completable before Crash for some set* $D \subseteq dom(Crash)$, *iff for every state* s_2 *with* $(s_1, s_2) \in Crash$ *there is an execution* $s_0 \xrightarrow{Op(in,\frac{1}{2})} s'_1$ *with* $s'_1 \in D$ *and* $(s'_1, s_2) \in Crash$.

If a transition is D-completable before *Crash* it is possible to construct an alternative partial execution that ended in a D-state without any difference after a crash. Figure 9 also depicts this alternative execution in bold. Transition W3 in Fig. 4 for example is *page-aligned*-completable before the crash of Fig. 3 to *block* ↓ PAGE_SIZE and the depicted re-execution W3' is the alternative.

Definition 7 (D-Retractable before *Crash*). *An operation Op is D-retractable before Crash for some set $D \subseteq dom(Crash)$, iff every transition of Op is either retractable or D-completable before Crash, or equivalently:*

$$Op(in) \, {}^\circ_9 \, Crash \subseteq (Id_S \cup (Op(in, \notin) \rhd D)) \, {}^\circ_9 \, Crash \qquad \text{for all } in \in In$$

This lifts Definitions 5 and 6 to the level of one operation. For example, **append** of the write buffer is *page-aligned*-retractable before *block* ↓ PAGE_SIZE, since one can either retract the operation if it did not cross a page boundary or execute it in such a way that it writes up to the last page boundary.

The following theorem can be used to abstract an explicit crash specification as part of C to an implicit crash specification by A.

Theorem 2 (Implicit to Explicit Refinement). *The refinement $A \sqsubseteq C$ for*

$$C = (S, Init, In, Out, CSync, CCrash, (Op_i)_{i \in I}) \qquad \text{and}$$
$$A = (S, Init, In, Out, ASync, ACrash, (Op_i)_{i \in I})$$

with atomic operations Op_i for all $i \in I$ follows from

1. $dom(ACrash) \lhd CCrash \subseteq ACrash$
2. $ASync \subseteq CSync$
3. Op_i is $dom(ACrash)$-retractable before $CCrash$ for all $i \in I$

We usually apply Theorem 2 with crash predicates that satisfy the (stronger) condition $dom(ACrash) \subset dom(CCrash)$ to strengthen the crash transition, i.e., a crash can happen in fewer states of component A than of component C and is therefore simpler to express. This is compensated by farther jumps on the history of A in comparison to those of C as by 2. A has less synchronized states. These jumps are then easily propagated upwards over abstractions with Theorem 1.

Proof (of Theorem 2). We choose the run of C as the run of A and focus on the transitions of a power cut. Figure 10 depicts the situation before the power cut (omitting input and output labels), starting in a state s_0 where both C and A are synchronized. Such a state exists because at least in the initial state and after every power cut *both* components are synchronized. The three parts of the power cut transition of C are depicted in the figure starting in state s_n and ending in s_{n+1}. We construct a matching transition of A, depicted by arrows - ➔ in the figure. All operations that C retracts are also retracted by A (*history jump* from s_n to s_k). However, the history jump transition might be farther still (*history jump* from s_k to s_l). The idea is to determine a state

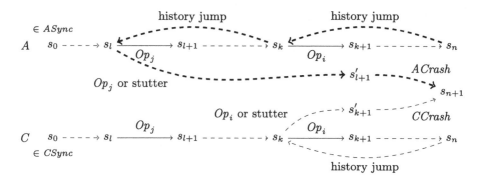

Fig. 10. From implicit to the explicit reset specification

$s'_{l+1} \in dom(ACrash)$ of component A with the properties shown in the figure: there is an additional second jump backwards to s_l and a re-execution that yields s'_{l+1}. The construction considers the $run \; s_0 \dashrightarrow s_k \xrightarrow{Op_i \; or \; stutter} s'_{k+1} \xrightarrow{CCrash} s_{n+1}$ of C implied by (1) of Sect. 3 that yields s'_{k+1}.

The existence of A's history jump and re-execution is proven by induction over k. If the sequence is empty ($k = 0$ and the transition stutters), then there is only a transition $s_0 \xrightarrow{CCrash} s_{n+1}$ starting from state s_0 with $s_0 \in ASync$. By proof obligation 1., $s_0 \xrightarrow{ACrash} s_{n+1}$ is the matching run of A: the additional history jump and re-execution transitions stutter. Otherwise, Op_i is $dom(ACrash)$-retractable before $CCrash$ and therefore the transition $s_k \xrightarrow{Op_i} s'_{k+1}$ is either:

- Retractable before $CCrash$ and therefore $s_0 \dashrightarrow s_k \xrightarrow{CCrash} s_{n+1}$ is also a valid run. The induction hypothesis gives a matching run of A and a history jump over m operations for this sequence. The history jump for the original sequence then is over $m + 1$ operations and we take the re-execution from the induction hypothesis which ends in the state s_{n+1}.
- $dom(ACrash)$-completable before $CCrash$ and $s_k \xrightarrow{Op_i} s''_{k+1} \xrightarrow{CCrash} s_{n+1}$ holds for some state $s''_{k+1} \in dom(ACrash)$. We choose $s'_{l+1} = s''_{k+1}$ and by proof obligation 1., $s_0 \dashrightarrow s_k \xrightarrow{Op_i} s'_{l+1} \xrightarrow{ACrash} s_{n+1}$ is a re-execution of A with $s'_{l+1} \in dom(ACrash)$ and the history jump stutters. $\qquad\square$

5   Component Hierarchies and Substitution

This section defines components $M(A)$ that use a subcomponent A (see Fig. 1), underlying several limitations to confine communication between M and A to the interface. Hierarchies allow us to split off a part M of the entire implementation and verify it based on a (possibly very abstract) component A. A can then be refined separately, without jeopardizing the correctness and crash-safety of M. This facilitates modular and incremental development of a large system.

Intuitively, M has volatile state only and the entire persisted state resides in its subcomponent A. Combined states of $M(A)$ are written $ms \oplus as$.

Definition 8 (Hierarchies). *The component $M(A) = (MS \times AS, In, Out, MInit \times AInit, MS \times ASync, MCrash \times ACrash, (MOp_i)_{i \in I})$ combines the state space of M and of its subcomponent A. The state of A is hidden from M (information hiding) and the interaction with A is accomplished via synchronous calls to A's operations in the programs MOp_i of M and observation of their inputs and outputs. The crash on the M part of the state must be arbitrary, i.e., $MCrash = MS \times MS$, and $M(A)$ is synchronized if and only if A is.*

Refinement is compatible with hierarchical composition, i.e., correctness and crash-safety of a component is preserved by substitution of its subcomponents.

Theorem 3 (Substitution). *If $CSync = CS$ and $A \sqsubseteq C$, then $M(A) \sqsubseteq M(C)$.*

The condition $CSync = CS$ states that every C state is synchronized, i.e., there are no backward jumps and no re-execution in C and likewise in the combined $M(C)$. The Theorem is applicable in practice, because we can substitute implementation machines, which are always synchronized, bottom-up.

Proof (of Theorem 3). Given a fixed, arbitrary run of $M(C)$ we derive a matching run of $M(A)$ with the same labels to satisfy Definition 3 in several steps: From each $M(C)$-transition, we extract the fine-grained steps of C corresponding to the calls of its operations. Concatenating these gives a run of C, which can be mapped to one of A *as a whole* by the assumption $A \sqsubseteq C$. Finally, the A run can be integrated back with M. The reset transitions reduces to two helper lemmas. Specifically, if C is an implementation component, then Lemma 1 maps the $M(C)$ crash to the C one.

Lemma 1. *If $ms \oplus cs \xrightarrow{\text{reset}} ms' \oplus cs'$, then $cs \xrightarrow{\text{reset}} cs'$ holds for all ms, ms'*

The converse (Lemma 2) lifts the matching A reset from as to as' back into the context.

Lemma 2. *If $as \xrightarrow{\text{reset}} as'$, then $ms \oplus as \xrightarrow{\text{reset}} ms' \oplus as'$ holds for all ms, ms'.*

Lemma 1 is trivial: the $M(C)$ reset transition has no back-jumps and is thus equivalent to $(cs, cs') \in CCrash$ by the restrictions of component composition of Definition 8. Note that in general, compositions $M(C)$ retract operations at a coarser granularity than C can do on its own, i.e., a reset of $M(C)$ cannot be explained with the help of a C-reset in the presence of back-jumps.

Lemma 2 guarantees that the back-jump induced by the reset transition of the abstract A is permitted by the semantics of $M(A)$. The proof can be followed alongside Fig. 11 to establish arrows $\longrightarrow$ from the given arrows $\dashrightarrow$. The first line shows the big-step semantics of $M(A)$ and the second line extracts the small-step semantics of the one operation MOp_i ($ms_0 \oplus as_0 = ms^k \oplus as^k$ and $ms_m \oplus as_m = ms^{k+1} \oplus as^{k+1}$). The history jump of A targets a state as_l in the

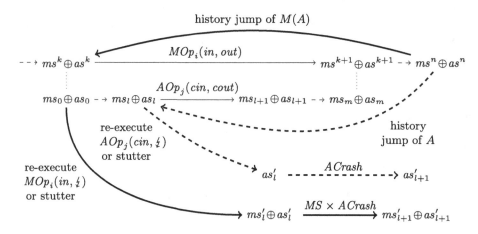

Fig. 11. Mapping a reset transition of a subcomponent A to one of $M(A)$.

middle of a previously execution operation MOp_i. The reset of $M(A)$ retracts to the state $ms^k \oplus as^k$ right before this call and then reaches the combined intermediate state $ms_l \oplus as_l$ by partial re-execution of the MOp_i potentially including a partial AOp_j from the A reset. In the resulting state $ms'_l \oplus as'_l$, the A crash is known and the M crash admits any desired successor anyway. □

6   *Crash*-neutrality

The proof obligations 4 of Theorem 1 consider intermediate states. In this section we adapt the criterion of *Crash*-neutrality from our previous work [10], allowing us to consider initial and final states of operations only. This reduces the difficulty and size of proofs by enabling standard techniques from sequential verification.

Informally, *Crash*-neutrality asserts that for any intermediate state a completion exists that does not modify the persistent memory any further. A component is *Crash*-neutral if all its operations are.

Definition 9 (*Crash*-Neutrality). *An operation Op is Crash-neutral if every partial execution $s \xrightarrow{Op(in,\fourteen)} s'$ with $s' \in dom(Crash)$, has a completion that terminates in a state s'' with the following property: for every state s_0 with $(s', s_0) \in Crash$ then $(s'', s_0) \in Crash$ holds, too.*

A useful shorthand to proving *Crash*-neutrality of $M(C)$ is given by the following lemmata. Its basic insight is that an operation is *Crash*-neutral if every small step of its program is *Crash*-neutral. Since all steps of M are either calls to C or just in-memory, it remains to ensure that C is *Crash*-neutral:

Lemma 3 (*Crash*-Neutrality of $M(C)$). *If C is Crash-neutral and all operation of M terminate, then $M(C)$ is Crash-neutral.* □

Lemma 4 (*Crash*-Neutrality of atomic *C*). *If every operation of *C* is atomic, then Crash-neutrality of *C* can be characterized by*

$$Crash \subseteq COp_i(in) \mathbin{;} Crash \qquad for \ all \ i \in I \ and \ in \in In \qquad \qquad \square$$

The append operation of the write buffer (see Fig. 3) is *Crash*-neutral, we simply choose $n = 0$ as the number of bytes written. With *Crash*-neutrality Theorem 1 can be reformulated such that only reasoning about initial and final states is necessary.

Theorem 4 (*Crash*-Neutral Data Refinement by Forward Simulation). *A refinement $A \sqsubseteq C$ for a CCrash-neutral component *C* is implied by a forward simulation $R \subseteq AS \times CS$ satisfying 1.–3. of Theorem 1 and*

$$4'. \ R \mathbin{;} CCrash \subseteq ACrash \mathbin{;} R \qquad \qquad (crash)$$

Proof. We consider the transition sequence $cs \xrightarrow{Op_i(in, \natural)} cs' \xrightarrow{reset} cs''$. If the history jump transition (and therefore the re-execute) stutter, we complete the operation $Op_i(in, \natural)$ by *CCrash*-neutrality and are still able to crash to cs'' afterwards. If we have a history jump, we complete the re-execution transition by *CCrash*-neutrality and are able to crash to cs'' afterwards. All relevant transitions for a forward simulation are explained by complete executions and we can use proof obligation 2 of Theorem 1 to find the matching abstract transition. $\square$

7 Related Work

We focus on techniques for the verification of crash behavior, comparison of Flashix to related efforts can be found in [9,11,18] and Lali's summary [14].

Bornholt et al. [3] define crash consistency models for file systems, based on operations that produce (potentially many) update events. A crash is then expressed by taking a prefix of the update events. The difference between their definition of sequential crash consistency [3, Definition 5] and quasi sequential crash consistency (Definition 4) is that we allow a re-execution that might produce different events and not just (a reordering of) a prefix, and we allow an additional effect of the crash afterwards. Update events have the same drawback as the explicit specification provided in Sect. 2. Their notion of crash consistency also omits orphaned files. Follow-up work [19] integrates crash-safety with simulation conditions similar to the ones we have given previously in [10]. This paper clarifies the adequacy of the simulation conditions wrt. a component semantics, which is not discussed in [19]. In particular, hierarchical composition of components has subtle effects of how exactly a crash and recovery must be organized that substitution is possible (Theorem 3).

Write-back caches where a crash affects multiple operations is discussed in [2,5,19], too. The abstract model of [2] keeps an explicit history back to the most recent flush as a list of higher-order state transformers. It is proved that the implementation of sync correlates to reducing the history to produce a current state. Chen's thesis [5] discusses a specification methodology of write-back caches that are not order-preserving. It is based on explicitly rewriting histories, although he lacks modular conditions as in Theorem 2.

In this paper as well as in [19] the intermediate steps of operations are summarized at the semantic level (as $Op(in, \natural)$ resp. $f(s, x, sync = false)$). Ntzik et al. [16] as well as Chen et al. [4,6] have developed Hoare-style proof rules that establish a user-provided invariant called "crash condition" over the intermediate states of a program that serves as the precondition of recovery. The latter work has produced the FSCQ file system that is verified with Coq. Maric and Sprenger [15] model crashes by exceptions that are triggered nondeterministically in the write operations of the hardware model to verify a redundant storage system. We have addressed this issue by a fine-grained semantics of programs in [10] which computes the crash condition symbolically.

Re-execution of operations underlies the "recoverability" criterion of Koskinen and Yang [13] at the level of entire programs. Their approach can be recast in our notation such that $Op(in, \natural) \, \S \, Crash$ establishes the precondition of the program, which can then be re-run to recover the intermediate state without runtime errors. Here, the purpose of re-execution is different: We use it as a specification mechanism to reach certain intermediate states.

8   Conclusion

In this paper we have defined an approach that facilitates the integration of order-preserving write-back caches into the hierarchical development of file systems. It is possible to verify functional correctness and quasi sequential crash consistency modularity. This enables modular, large-scale verification, which would otherwise be unrealistic to perform and hard to maintain.

We have reinterpreted the behavior of a crash in terms of the system's operations, so that at each level of abstraction a backward jump (induced by a crash) does not need to be expressed as part of the state. This allowed us to propagate the reset specification implicitly upwards through a refinement hierarchy. Obviously, it is necessary to capture the effect semantically to do this.

We implemented support for component specifications of Definition 1 and generate the proof obligations in our interactive theorem prover KIV [8]. We mechanized the verification of the Flashix file system, which provides quasi sequential crash consistency. Previously, we performed a verification of write-back caching for the two components above the write buffer, where the sequence of operations is mostly part of the state. The second component then flushed the write-back cache at the end of its operations, which we can avoid now. With the theory of this paper, the verification of the write buffer itself requires just little extra effort, due to the switch from the implicit to the explicit reset specification. However, the *specifications* (not the implementations) of all components above the write buffer greatly benefited in terms of verification effort. For the two abstractions directly above the write buffer we report a decrease of 40% resp. 17% of user interactions in the proofs (from 500 to 300 and from 1270 to

1050). Flashix is now significantly faster and more space efficient, due to fewer flushes.

The theory in this paper should be applicable to other file systems and achieve similar results, since all journaling and log-structured file systems [17,21] feature comparable write-back caches.

In future work, we plan to extend the theory to non-order-preserving caches by allowing commutations of operations.

References

1. The Open Group Base Specifications Issue 7, IEEE Std 1003.1, 2013 edn. The IEEE and The Open Group (2013)
2. Amani, S., Murray, T.: Specifying a realistic file system. In: Proceedings of Workshop on Models for Formal Analysis of Real Systems. Electronic Proceedings in Theoretical Computer Science, vol. 196, pp. 1–9. Open Publishing Association (2015)
3. Bornholt, J., Kaufmann, A., Li, J., Krishnamurthy, A., Torlak, E., Wang, X.: Specifying and checking file system crash-consistency models. In: Proceedings of ASPLOS, pp. 83–98. ACM (2016)
4. Chajed, T., Chen, H., Chlipala, A., Kaashoek, M.F., Zeldovich, N., Ziegler, D.: Certifying a file system using crash hoare logic: correctness in the presence of crashes. Commun. ACM **60**(4), 75–84 (2017)
5. Chen, H.: Certifying a crash-safe file system. Ph.D. thesis, Massachusetts Institute of Technology, Cambridge, MA, United States (2016)
6. Chen, H., Ziegler, D., Chlipala, A., Zeldovich, N., Kaashoek, M.F.: Using crash hoare logic for certifying the FSCQ file system. In: Proceedings of the Symposium on Operating Systems Principles (SOSP). ACM (2015)
7. de Roever, W.-P., Engelhardt, K.: Data Refinement: Model-Oriented Proof Methods and their Comparison. Cambridge University Press, Cambridge (1998)
8. Ernst, G., Pfähler, J., Schellhorn, G., Haneberg, D., Reif, W.: KIV-overview and verifythis competition. Softw. Tools Technol. Transf. (STTT) **17**(6), 677–694 (2015)
9. Ernst, G., Pfähler, J., Schellhorn, G., Reif, W.: Inside a verified flash file system: transactions and garbage collection. In: Gurfinkel, A., Seshia, S.A. (eds.) VSTTE 2015. LNCS, vol. 9593, pp. 73–93. Springer, Cham (2016). doi:10.1007/978-3-319-29613-5_5
10. Ernst, G., Pfähler, J., Schellhorn, G., Reif, W.: Modular, crash-safe refinement for ASMs with submachines. Sci. Comput. Program. (SCP) **131**, 3–21 (2016)
11. Ernst, G., Schellhorn, G., Haneberg, D., Pfähler, J., Reif, W.: Verification of a virtual filesystem switch. In: Cohen, E., Rybalchenko, A. (eds.) VSTTE 2013. LNCS, vol. 8164, pp. 242–261. Springer, Heidelberg (2014). doi:10.1007/978-3-642-54108-7_13
12. He, J., Hoare, C.A.R., Sanders, J.W.: Data refinement refined resume. In: Robinet, B., Wilhelm, R. (eds.) ESOP 1986. LNCS, vol. 213, pp. 187–196. Springer, Heidelberg (1986). doi:10.1007/3-540-16442-1_14
13. Koskinen, E., Yang, J.: Reducing crash recoverability to reachability. In: Proceedings of Principles of Programming Languages (POPL), pp. 97–108. ACM (2016)
14. Lali, M.I.: File system formalization: revisited. Int. J. Adv. Comput. Sci. **3**(12), 602–606 (2013)

15. Marić, O., Sprenger, C.: Verification of a transactional memory manager under hardware failures and restarts. In: Jones, C., Pihlajasaari, P., Sun, J. (eds.) FM 2014. LNCS, vol. 8442, pp. 449–464. Springer, Cham (2014). doi:10.1007/978-3-319-06410-9_31

16. Ntzik, G., da Rocha Pinto, P., Gardner, P.: Fault-tolerant resource reasoning. In: Feng, X., Park, S. (eds.) APLAS 2015. LNCS, vol. 9458, pp. 169–188. Springer, Cham (2015). doi:10.1007/978-3-319-26529-2_10

17. Rosenblum, M., Ousterhout, J.K.: The design and implementation of a log-structured file system. ACM Trans. Comput. Syst. (TOCS) **10**(1), 26–52 (1992)

18. Schellhorn, G., Ernst, G., Pfähler, J., Haneberg, D., Reif, W.: Development of a verified flash file system. ABZ 2014. LNCS, vol. 8477, pp. 9–24. Springer, Heidelberg (2014). doi:10.1007/978-3-662-43652-3_2

19. Sigurbjarnarson, H., Bornholt, J., Torlak, E., Wang, X.: Push-button verification of file systems via crash refinement. In: Symposium on Operating Systems Design and Implementation (OSDI). USENIX Association (2016)

20. Tseng, H-W., Grupp, L., Swanson, S.: Understanding the impact of power loss on flash memory. In: Proceedings of the Design Automation Conference (DAC), pp. 35–40. ACM (2011)

21. Tweedie, S.C.: Journaling the Linux ext2fs filesystem. In: The Fourth Annual Linux Expo (1998)

22. Woodcock, J., Davies, J.: Using Z: Specification, Proof and Refinement. Prentice Hall, Upper Saddle River (1996)

Formal Verification of ARP (Address Resolution Protocol) Through SMT-Based Model Checking - A Case Study -

Danilo Bruschi[1], Andrea Di Pasquale[1], Silvio Ghilardi[2], Andrea Lanzi[1],
and Elena Pagani[1(✉)]

[1] Università degli Studi di Milano, via Comelico 39, 20135 Milano, Italy
{danilo.bruschi,andrea.lanzi,elena.pagani}@unimi.it, spikey.it@gmail.com
[2] Università degli Studi di Milano, via Saldini 50, 20133 Milano, Italy
silvio.ghilardi@unimi.it

Abstract. Internet protocols are intrinsically complex to understand and validate, due both to the potentially unbounded number of entities involved, and to the complexity of interactions amongst them. Yet, their safety is indispensable to guarantee the proper behavior of a number of critical applications.

In this work, we apply formal methods to verify the safety of the Address Resolution Protocol (ARP), a standard protocol of the TCP/IP stack i.e. the communication protocols used by any Internet Host, and we are able to formally prove that the ARP protocol, as defined by the standard Request for Comments, exhibits various vulnerabilities which have been exploited since many years and still are the main ingredient of many attack vectors. As a complementary result we also show the feasibility of formal verification methods when applied to real network protocols.

Keywords: ARP · Man-in-the-Middle attack · Denial-of-Service attack · Formal verification · Model evaluation · Satisfiability Modulo Theories

1 Introduction

Core of this work is the Address Resolution Protocol (ARP), a standard protocol of the TCP/IP stack i.e. the set of communication protocols used by any Internet Host. More precisely, we apply a formal method to verify the safety property of ARP, where by safety we mean that no "bad things" happen during any protocol execution [18]. As far as we know, this is the first time that a formal method is successfully applied to the analysis of ARP. The work has been conducted by using the Model Checker Modulo Theories (MCMT) tool [15], which is a fully declarative and deductive symbolic model checker for safety properties of infinite state systems.

The ARP protocol plays a very critical role in the transmission phase of Internet messages as it converts the network (IP) address of a host into its

© Springer International Publishing AG 2017
N. Polikarpova and S. Schneider (Eds.): IFM 2017, LNCS 10510, pp. 391–406, 2017.
DOI: 10.1007/978-3-319-66845-1_26

corresponding hardware (MAC or Ethernet) address, which is the address we need to specify for communicating directly with a host. We briefly recall that IP addresses identify hosts in Internet and they are used "only" to route messages across the Internet. By contrast, MAC addresses identify hosts inside a Local Area Network (LAN) where they are physically connected. When a message has to be delivered to a host h, both its network and hardware addresses have to be known. Contrarily to network addresses which are usually publicly available (in particular in their symbolic form www.yyy.zzz), hardware addresses are not. Thus, ARP has been introduced for translating network addresses into hardware addresses. The protocol has been initially defined by Request for Comment (RFC) 826 [19], and subsequently redefined by RFC 3927 [11] and RFC 5227 [10], which have tried to settle some problems arising in the original formulation.

As many protocols of the TCP/IP stack, during the last twenty years ARP has been subverted in order to perform various forms of computer attacks [4,6,20]. The most prominent attack performed via ARP is the *Man-in-the-Middle* attack (MitM), in which an attacker can impersonate a victim's host and intercept/modify all the traffic directed to the victim's host. ARP hosts can also be victim of a *Denial-of-Service* attack (DoS). In this case, a malicious host m can continuously induce a victim host v to dismiss its current network address and to select a new one. While v does not own a stable address, it is not able to communicate.

In this paper, by using Satisfiability Modulo Theories (SMT), we will formally prove that the ARP protocol – as specified by the RFC documents – lacks safety properties, more precisely there exist protocol executions in which a MitM attack can be successfully perpetrated against some host. The same turns out to be true for a DoS attack.

2   Preliminaries on Formal Verification

The considered family of protocols belongs to the *infinite-state reactive parameterized systems*: although the behavior of a single host can be described by a finite state automaton, the number of components which constitute a system (i.e. a LAN), and whose behavior is determined by messages received by other system's components, is potentially infinite.

Various techniques have been introduced in the literature to handle safety verification for such parameterized systems (see [1–3,5,8,9], to name but a few entries). We chose the declarative approach of the *array-based systems* [12,14,16], because it offers a great flexibility and relies (at deductive engine level) on the mature technology offered by state-of-the-art SMT-solvers, which is gaining relevance. In array-based systems (see [13,15] for tool implementations), the state is represented by both global variables, and by array variables such that each array corresponds to a component of the state of the hosts, and the k-th element of an array a contains the value of component a for the host k. This representation is very natural, and eases the modeling process. A system is specified via a pair of formulæ $\iota(\underline{p})$ and $\tau(\underline{p}, \underline{p}')$, and a safety problem via a further formula $\upsilon(\underline{p})$, where

$\underline{p}$ is the set of parameters and array-ids, $\iota(\underline{p})$ is the state of possible initial states of the system, $\tau(\underline{p}, \underline{p}') := \bigvee_{i=1}^{n} \tau_i(\underline{p}, \underline{p}')$ symbolizes the possible state transitions of the system – according to the considered algorithm – modifying $\underline{p}$ into $\underline{p}'$, and $\upsilon(\underline{p})$ is the set *Bad* of states verifying the unsafe condition. Each transition $\tau_i \in \tau$ is composed by a *guard* and a set of updates: if the current values of parameters and arrays satisfy the guard, then the transition may fire and the updates are applied. More guards may be verified at the same instant; in this case, one of the corresponding transitions fires nondeterministically. A *safety model checking problem* is the problem of checking whether the formula

$$(\star)_n \qquad \iota(\underline{p}_0) \wedge \tau(\underline{p}_0, \underline{p}_1) \wedge \cdots \wedge \tau(\underline{p}_n, \underline{p}_{n+1}) \wedge \upsilon(\underline{p}_{n+1})$$

is satisfiable for some n, that is, whether a state in *Bad* can be reached from an initial state by applying the possible transitions. In order to verify whether a protocol is safe with respect to *Bad*, the tool we use in this work adopts a *backward reachability* policy. The search starts from *Bad* and, using the state transitions, for any element of *Bad* computes the pre-image, i.e. the set of states which can lead to *Bad*. For any set of obtained pre-images the same procedure is repeatedly applied, until one of the following two events occurs: either (i) a fixed point is reached (not intersecting initial states), meaning that the pre-image computation cannot reach other states different from the current ones, or (ii) an initial state is reached. In the former case, no formulæ of type $(\star)_n$ describing the reachability of *Bad* can be satisfied and the system is safe with respect to the property described by *Bad*. In the latter case, some formula of type $(\star)_n$ is satisfiable and the system is unsafe.

We used the Model Checker Modulo Theories (MCMT) tool [15]. MCMT is a fully declarative and deductive symbolic model checker for safety properties of infinite state systems whose state variables include arrays. Sets of states and transitions of a system are described by quantified first-order formulae *of special kinds*. The tool exploits decision procedures (as implemented in state of the art SMT solvers) to cope with satisfiability problems involving various datatypes like arrays, integers, Booleans, etc. Checks for safety and fix-points are performed by solving SMT problems (due to the special shape of the formulæ used to describe sets of states and transitions, such checks can be effectively discharged). Besides standard SMT techniques, efficient heuristics for quantifier instantiation, specifically tailored to model checking, are the heart of the system. Termination of the backward search is guaranteed only under specific assumptions, but it commonly arises in practice (for a full account of the underlying theoretical framework, the reader is referred to [16]). MCMT guarantees the safety of a protocol for any number N of system components.

The process of converting an algorithm into a MCMT model is performed manually: it requires deep comprehension of the algorithm, which must be broken down into its fundamental mechanisms and all possible cases, that are then translated into model transitions.

3   Address Resolution Protocol (ARP)

The main task of ARP is to enable a host h of a local network to discover, given the (32-bits) IP address of a host k (usually a well known data), the corresponding (48-bits) MAC address associated to k.[1] For efficiency reasons any host h maintains in a private data structure, known as ARP cache, all mappings $\langle$MAC, IP$\rangle$ it has so far discovered. Whenever h has to get in touch with host k, it will first look for k's MAC address in its own ARP cache. In case of failure it will initiate the ARP protocol, and it will proceed in the following way: h sends to all hosts in the LAN an *ARP request message*, asking for the MAC address of the owner of the address IP_k. Once k receives such a message it sends an *ARP reply* message, unicast to h, providing its own MAC address MAC_k. Once h receives the ARP reply it updates its own cache with the entry $\langle MAC_k, IP_k \rangle$. Similarly, k updates its own cache with the mapping $\langle MAC_h, IP_h \rangle$ provided by the ARP request from h. The same action is performed by other hosts already knowing h, so as to maintain their information updated. These operations are more precisely described in the following Algorithm 1. RFC 826 requires that ARP messages have a predefined format. The Ethernet header includes, among others, both the source and destination MAC address, eth_src and eth_dest respectively. The ARP message payload includes among others: the opcode identifying whether the message is a Request or a Reply, the source hardware (sha) and network (spa) addresses, and the target hardware (tha) and network (tpa) addresses, where *target* is the host destination of the ARP message.

3.1   ARP Formal Verification

In our verification, we assume that either (i) all hosts are honest, or (ii) one malicious host p_m exists, trying to perform a MitM attack against a victim p_v. Case (ii) is able to capture all the behaviors possible in real LANs. Indeed, real attackers focus on a specific victim, usually chosen after a preliminary analysis of the target LAN aiming at individuating the most vulnerable device in it. On the other hand, in case safety against MitM should be proved, any number of both attackers and victims should be checked. By contrast, we want to verify unsafety; hence, finding counterexamples with just one attacker is sufficient.

Honest hosts send Requests when they need to know the identity of a message destination; they manage ARP messages according to Algorithm 1. p_m may send either Requests or Replies at any time, containing fake information; it may also send unicast Requests to a specific host, not processed by other hosts. According to RFC 826 [19], we do not model cache entry expiration: at any time a host may generate a request even if the target information is already in its cache, as if its cache has expired in the past. We model the processing of one ARP message at a time. We take both the MAC address and the IP address of a host p_x to be

---

[1] We briefly recall that the MAC address of any device is hardwired into the device by its manufacturer, and is not publicly available.

Algorithm 1. Classical ARP (RFC 826 [19])

```
1: RequestGeneration()
2: when MAC address for some target IP needed do
3:     new ARP_pkt: ARP_pkt.opcode ← Request; ARP_pkt.spa ← myIP;
4:     ARP_pkt.sha ← myMAC; ARP_pkt.tpa ← targetIP; ARP_pkt.tha ← ⊥;
5:     broadcast ARP_pkt;
6: end do
7:
8: PacketReception()
9: when ARP_pkt received do
10:    Merge_flag ← false;
11:    if ARP_pkt.spa ≠ 0.0.0.0 ∧ ARP_pkt.spa ε ARP_cache then
12:        corresponding ARP_cache.sha ← ARP_pkt.sha;
13:        Merge_flag ← true;
14:    end if
15:    if ARP_pkt.tpa = myIP then
16:        if ARP_pkt.spa ≠ 0.0.0.0 ∧ not Merge_flag then
17:            ARP_cache ← ARP_cache ∪ ⟨ ARP_pkt.spa, ARP_pkt.sha ⟩;
18:        end if
19:        if ARP_pkt.opcode = Request then
20:            new ARP_pkt': ARP_pkt'.opcode ← Reply; ARP_pkt'.spa ← myIP; ARP_pkt'.sha ←
               myMAC;
21:            ARP_pkt'.tpa ← ARP_pkt.spa; ARP_pkt'.tha ← ARP_pkt.sha;
22:            send ARP_pkt to ARP_pkt.tha;
23:        end if
24:    end if
25: end do
```

equal to x. For the sake of space, in this section we just discuss the modeling of the unsafe case; the safe model is equal to the unsafe one without the transitions describing the p_m's behavior.[2] In the following, let N be the number of hosts.

In our models, the following global variables are used: φ indicates the current step of the computation, I counts the number of processes having processed the message in the current step; sh, sp and tp correspond to the sha, spa and tpa message fields respectively. The state of each process p_x is represented by the following array variables: $sm[x]$ indicates whether p_x must send a message; $cu[x]$ indicates whether p_x has processed the received message and possibly has updated its own cache. Both $sm[x]$ and $cu[x]$ are boolean variables. A MitM attack succeeds when in the ARP cache of some host $h \neq p_v$ the entry corresponding to p_v does not contain p_v's MAC address; such a situation is modeled by introducing the variables $CM[x]$ and $CP[x]$ which contain respectively the MAC address and IP address of p_v as contained in p_x ARP cache. For the sake of conciseness, in the transitions below we do not display the variables whose value stays unchanged.

The initial state satisfies:

$$\iota_1 := \varphi = 0 \wedge I = 0 \wedge sh = 0 \wedge sp = 0 \wedge tp = 0 \wedge$$
$$(\forall x.\ sm[x] = 0 \wedge cu[x] = 0 \wedge CM[x] = 0 \wedge CP[x] = 0) \tag{1}$$

that is, no message is around, no process has executed the current step, all caches do not contain any information about p_v, and no process has a message to send.

---

[2] Both source codes and results of all the models described in this work are available at http://homes.di.unimi.it/~pagae/ARPmodel/index.html.

The unsafe state capturing MitM attacks is described by the following formula:

$$v_M := \exists z.\ CM[z] = m \wedge CP[z] = v \tag{2}$$

that is, a process z exists whose cache entry for p_v was poisoned with the value of p_m.

The first three transitions model the `RequestGeneration()` procedure in Algorithm 1: we non-deterministically choose both the sender and the target of the new message. This is written as:

$$\tau_1 := \varphi = 0 \wedge \exists x, y.\ x \neq y \wedge \varphi' = 1 \wedge I' = 1 \wedge sm'[x] = 1 \wedge cu'[x] = 1 \wedge tp' = y$$

The sender parameters in the message are set in the next two transitions; in the former the host behaves honestly, in the latter the sender is p_m and generates a poisoned Request:

$$\tau_2 := \varphi = 1 \wedge \exists x.\ sm[x] = 1 \wedge \varphi' = 2 \wedge sp' = x \wedge sh' = x$$
$$\tau_3 := \varphi = 1 \wedge \exists x.\ sm[x] = 1 \wedge x = m \wedge \varphi' = 2 \wedge sp' = v \wedge sh' = m$$

If the source IP is different from that of p_v, a transition allows all processes to fire – one at a time – without changes to the cache entry concerning the victim:

$$\tau_4 := \varphi = 2 \wedge sp \neq v \wedge I < N \wedge \exists x.\ cu[x] = 0 \wedge \varphi' = 2 \wedge I' = I + 1 \wedge cu'[x] = 1$$

The same actions are performed (τ_6) when $sp = v$ but the host is not the target ($x \neq tp$) and it has nothing in its cache about p_v ($CP[x] = 0$). Otherwise, two cases must be considered. First, the receiving process is not the target but it has information about p_v in its cache, so it updates the cache entry:

$$\tau_5 := \varphi = 2 \wedge sp = v \wedge I < N \wedge \exists x.\ cu[x] = 0 \wedge CP[x] > 0 \wedge x \neq tp \wedge$$
$$\varphi' = 2 \wedge I' = I + 1 \wedge cu'[x] = 1 \wedge CP'[x] = sp \wedge CM'[x] = sh$$

Transitions τ_4-τ_6 model lines 10–14 of Algorithm 1. By contrast, if the host is the target (lines 15–18 of Algorithm 1), it must also generate a Reply, which is recorded by appropriately setting its $sm[x]$:

$$\tau_7 := \varphi = 2 \wedge sp = v \wedge I < N \wedge \exists x.\ cu[x] = 0 \wedge x = tp \wedge \varphi' = 2 \wedge$$
$$I' = I + 1 \wedge sm'[x] = 1 \wedge cu'[x] = 1 \wedge CP'[x] = sp \wedge CM'[x] = sh$$

When all hosts processed the Request, the Reply is sent (lines 19–23 of Algorithm 1). Two transitions describe this event: either the target generates a honest Reply (τ_8) or, if the target is p_m, it may generate a poisoned Reply. We report here just the latter; the former can be easily derived:

$$\tau_9 := \varphi = 2 \wedge I \geq N \wedge \exists x.\ cu[x] = 1 \wedge sm[x] = 1 \wedge x = m \wedge$$
$$\varphi' = 3 \wedge I' = 0 \wedge tp' = sp \wedge sp' = v \wedge sh' = m$$

Table 1. Results for the formal verification of ARP (RFC 826)

	MitM					
	Outcome	Time (s)	Max. depth	# nodes	SMT calls	# literals
No malicious	Safe	0.222	2	3	249	7
Broadcast p_m	Unsafe	0.211	5	12	395	10
Unicast p_m	Unsafe	0.150	5	12	457	10

According to [19], Replies are sent unicast (line 22 of Algorithm 1); hence, the message is processed just by the target (lines 15–18 of Algorithm 1), and afterwards a re-initialization – leaving caches unchanged – is performed before repeating all over again:

$$\tau_{10} := \varphi = 3 \wedge \exists x. \; x = tp \wedge \varphi' = 4 \wedge CP'[x] = sp \wedge CM'[x] = sh$$
$$\tau_{11} := \varphi = 4 \wedge \varphi' = 0 \wedge I' = 0 \wedge tp' = 0 \wedge sp' = 0 \wedge sh' = 0 \wedge$$
$$(\forall x. \; sm'[x] = 0 \wedge cu'[x] = 0)$$

Verification results. Table 1 shows the results obtained by running the described models on an Intel Core i7 running Linux Ubuntu 14.04 64 bits. We report the running time, the depth of the status tree, the number of tree nodes explored, the number of calls to the SMT solver, and the maximum number of literals in the constraint describing a node.

4 Link-Local Addresses

RFC 3927 [11] adds new functionalities to ARP for enabling the protocol to work in local networks where hosts may automatically configure their own network address interface, without human intervention. Address configuration is performed by randomly choosing an IP address in the range 169.254.1.0–169.254.254.255 and then verifying that the chosen address is not already in use by some other host.

Algorithm 2 describes RFC 3927. *All messages* – both Requests *and* Replies – *are broadcast.* A host h wishing to adopt a certain IP address ip probes it by broadcasting a Request with spa = 0.0.0.0 – which is an invalid address so as to avoid polluting caches if ip is already in use by another host – and tpa = ip. If h receives an ARP message with either spa = ip, or null spa and tpa = ip, it deduces that another host is using or probing ip and selects a different address. Otherwise, h *announces* that it will use ip by broadcasting a Request with both spa and tpa equal to ip, so as to overwrite previous ARP cache entries related to ip. From now on, for any received packet, h compares ip against the spa contained in the packet; if the two are equals, the address conflict detection (ACD) procedure is executed.[3] According to ACD, a host may try to defend its

---

[3] It is worth to notice that the lack of this check allowed the MitM attack in RFC 826 against the victim itself.

Algorithm 2. Dynamic configuration of Link-Local addresses (RFC 3927 [11])

```
 1: Select()
 2: when network interface becomes active do
 3:     myIP ← rand(seed(MAC, previous IP), 169.254.1.0, 169.254.254.255); Probing();
 4: end do
 5:
 6: Probing()
 7: new ARP_pkt: ARP_pkt.opcode ← Request; ARP_pkt.spa ← 0.0.0.0;
 8: ARP_pkt.sha ← myMAC; ARP_pkt.tpa ← myIP; ARP_pkt.tha ← 0;
 9: timer ← rand(0, PROBE_WAIT); count ← 0;
10: repeat
11:     when timeout do
12:         broadcast ARP_pkt; count++;
13:         if count < PROBE_NUM then
14:             timer ← rand(PROBE_MIN, PROBE_MAX);
15:         end if
16:     end do
17: until count < PROBE_NUM;
18: timer ← ANNOUNCE_WAIT;
19: when (ARP_pkt received s.t. (ARP_pkt.spa = myIP) ∨ (ARP_pkt.opcode = Request ∧
    ARP_pkt.spa = 0.0.0.0 ∧ ARP_pkt.tpa = myIP ∧ ARP_pkt.sha ≠ myMAC) do
20:     give myIP up; LimitConflicts(); //FAILURE!
21: end do
22: when timeout do
23:     conflict_num ← 0; Announce(ANNOUNCE_NUM); //SUCCESS!
24: end do
25:
26: Announce(limit)
27: count ← 0;
28: new ARP_pkt: ARP_pkt.opcode ← Request; ARP_pkt.spa ← myIP;
29: ARP_pkt.sha ← myMAC; ARP_pkt.tpa ← myIP; ARP_pkt.tha ← 0;
30: repeat
31:     broadcast ARP_pkt; count++; wait(ANNOUNCE_INTERVAL);
32: until count < limit;
33: ConflictDetection();
34:
35: ConflictDetection()
36: while true do
37:     when ARP_pkt received do
38:         if ARP_pkt.spa = myIP ∧ ARP_pkt.sha ≠ myMAC then
39:             ACD(); //CONFLICT!
40:         else
41:             ARP.PacketReception(ARP_pkt); //processing according to RFC 826
42:         end if
43:     end do
44: end while
45:
46: LimitConflicts()
47: conflict_num ++;
48: if conflict_num ≥ MAX_CONFLICTS then
49:     timer ← RATE_LIMIT_INTERVAL;
50: else
51:     timer ← 0;
52: end if
53: when timeout do
54:     Select();
55: end do
56:
57: ACD()
58: if want to defend ∧ current_time - start_defend > DEFEND_INTERVAL then
59:     start_defend ← current_time; Announce(1);
60: else
61:     give myIP up; start_defend ← 0; LimitConflicts();
62: end if
```

address at most once by sending a new Announce. If another conflict is detected, the host dismisses its own network address and selects a new one. In case of no conflict, the original ARP (Algorithm 1) is executed.

4.1 Verification of ARP as in RFC 3927

In order to analyze this protocol, three models have been developed:

M1: Probe and Announcement messages have been added to the ARP model, but *not* the address conflict detection mechanism

M2: the ACD mechanism has been modeled, with address give up in case of a detected conflict

M3: the ACD mechanism has been modeled, by introducing the defense procedure above mentioned in case a conflict is detected. When a second conflict is detected, the host – who already defended – dismisses the used address.

For all the three models the safety with respect to MitM attacks has been analyzed; for M2 and M3 we also investigated the safety property with respect to DoS attacks. No cache expiration is considered.

For the sake of space, we describe here just the more complex model, i.e. M3, and we focus on the new features introduced with respect to the ARP model as described in Sect. 3.1. This new model includes an additional global variable GA whose value indicates the type of message considered: Probe (1), Announce (2), Request (3), or unsolicited Reply (4) – not corresponding to any Request – from p_m. Additional local variables are: $st[x]$ which indicates the state of a host, that is, if it has to send the Probe (0), or the Announce (1), or its IP address is configured and it may send Requests (2). p_m may send any message independently of its own state. The variable $cd[x]$ indicates whether this is the first time that the host has detected a conflict and must thus defend. The variable $gu[x]$ indicates how many times a host gives up its current address. The new initial state is defined as:

$$\iota_2 := \iota_1 \wedge GA = 0 \wedge (\forall x. \; gu[x] = 0 \wedge cd[x] = 0 \wedge st[x] \geq 0 \wedge st[x] \leq 2)$$

where ι_1 is defined in Eq. (1). This formula provides the maximum generality as it does not force any initial state to the network hosts. The unsafe state for MitM, υ_M, is defined as in Eq. (2).

DoS attacks can be modeled by an host that dismisses its address an indefinite number of times. Yet, this is actually a *liveness* property that cannot be verified with the adopted technique. Hence, we shall re-write it as a weaker *safety* property, whose negation is:

$$\upsilon_D := \exists z. \; gu[z] \geq threshold \tag{3}$$

for some finite value of *threshold*. This is weaker than a DoS attack, as it says that a host dismisses its address a finite number of times. We discuss this aspect in more detail at the end of this section, when analyzing the verification results.

A description of the model now follows. In the first six transitions, we describe the event to be reproduced, amongst either generation of Probe, Announce or Request issued by a host,[4] or generation of an Announce, Request or unsolicited Reply from p_m. For the sake of space, we report here just the more complex case, that is, the generation of a Request:

$$\tau_3 := \varphi = 0 \wedge \exists x.\ st[x] = 2 \wedge \varphi' = 1 \wedge I' = 1 \wedge GA' = 3 \wedge sm'[x] = 1 \wedge$$
$$cu'[x] = 1 \wedge sh' = x \wedge sp' = x$$
$$\tau_7 := \varphi = 1 \wedge \exists x, y.\ x \neq y \wedge sm[x] = 1 \wedge \varphi' = 2 \wedge I' = 1 \wedge sm'[x] = 0 \wedge$$
$$cu'[x] = 1 \wedge tp' = y \wedge sp' = x \wedge sh' = x$$

The former transition selects the source while the latter selects the target. All other cases are modeled in one step, as just the source identifier must be indicated in the message, and lead to transitions guarded by $\varphi = 2$. Similarly for p_m's messages, where always $sp' = v \wedge sh' = m$.

Subsequently, there are eight transitions modeling the processing of the message generated by one of the first six transitions. The following cases are modeled as in the case of ARP (Sect. 3.1): (τ_8) Request processing when $sp \neq v$; (τ_9) $sp = v$ and the host is not the target but can update the cache; (τ_{10}) $sp = v$ and the host is not the target and cannot update the cache; (τ_{11}) $sp = v$ and the host is the target (but not the victim) that generates a Reply. Other four cases involve the victim in case the message is poisoned: p_v is the target of the message and detects the conflict; if this is the first conflict then it defends its address (τ_{13}), otherwise it discards the address (τ_{12}). Or, p_v detects the conflict but it is not the target. We analyze in more detail these latter cases, as they are more complex since two messages have to be modeled: both the target Reply and the victim defense.

The two messages cause different cache updates: if the target is different from p_v, its reply does not change the cache entries concerning the victim. Hence, they can be processed in whatever order, and we decided to model the processing of the Reply first. In case p_v renounces, the following transition applies:

$$\tau_{15} := \varphi = 2 \wedge I < N \wedge sp = v \wedge \exists x.\ cu[x] = 0 \wedge x \neq tp \wedge x = v \wedge cd[x] > 0$$
$$\wedge I' = I + 1 \wedge sm'[x] = 3 \wedge cu'[x] = 1 \wedge gu'[x] = gu[x] + 1 \wedge cd'[x] = 0$$

The value of $sm[x]$ is not changed afterwards and allows to remember – once all hosts have processed the Reply – that the victim has changed its address; $cd'[x]$ is reset because the victim is dismissing its current address, and it has not observed any conflict on the new address it is going to adopt. By contrast, in case p_v defends ($cd[x] = 0$), the transition τ_{14} is applied; such a transition is conceptually equal to τ_{15} apart for the assignments $sm'[x] = 5$ and $cd'[x] = 1$.

As for ARP, once all hosts processed the Request, the Reply is sent in broadcast, and consequently processed by all hosts. Four transitions (τ_{23}-τ_{26}) replicate for the Reply the same cases as for the Request modeled by transitions τ_8-τ_{11}

---

[4] Also p_m, who may nondeterministically behave honestly.

above described. Transitions τ_{27}-τ_{28} describe the cases in which p_v observes a poisoned Reply – generated by the malicious – and it either renounces or defends.

In the case p_v is the target of the Request and defends, no Reply is generated and the system goes to the defense modeling (fired by $sm'[x] = 4$). The defense is modeled by the following transitions:

$$\tau_{18} := \varphi = 2 \wedge I \geq N \wedge \exists x.\ cu[x] = 1 \wedge sm[x] = 4 \wedge \varphi' = 4 \wedge I' = 1 \wedge sm'[x] = 0$$
$$\wedge cu'[x] = 1 \wedge tp' = v \wedge sp' = v \wedge sh' = v \wedge (\forall y. y \neq x \wedge cu'[y] = 0)$$
$$\tau_{19} := \varphi = 4 \wedge I < N \wedge \exists x.\ cu[x] = 0 \wedge CP[x] > 0 \wedge I' = I + 1 \wedge$$
$$cu'[x] = 1 \wedge CM'[x] = sh \wedge CP'[x] = sp$$

The former describes the generation of the Announce after all hosts processed the Request. The latter describes the processing of the Announce on behalf of the receiving hosts having information for p_v. A transition τ_{20} describes the case of a host receiving an Announce but not having a cache entry for p_v, and thus skipping any processing. When all hosts processed the Announce, the system can restart:

$$\tau_{31} := \varphi = 4 \wedge I \geq N \wedge \exists x.\ cu[x] = 1 \wedge (\forall y. sm[y] = 0) \wedge \varphi' = 0 \wedge I' = 0 \wedge$$
$$GA' = 0 \wedge sm'[x] = 0 \wedge cu'[x] = 0 \wedge tp' = 0 \wedge sp' = 0 \wedge sh' = 0$$

The untouched variables are the cache, the state, the record of giveups and defenses occurred so far. A similar re-initialization is performed every time nothing harmful occurred. Transitions similar to τ_{18}-τ_{20} above apply when the target is different from p_v and all hosts already processed the Reply, and are fired by guards containing $sm[x] = 5$.

By contrast, if p_v renounces, this is modeled by a transition like this (triggered after all hosts processed a possible Reply):

$$\tau_{29} := \varphi = 3 \wedge I \geq N \wedge \exists x.\ cu[x] = 1 \wedge sm[x] = 3 \wedge \varphi' = 0 \wedge I' = 0 \wedge$$
$$GA' = 0 \wedge sm'[x] = 0 \wedge cu'[x] = 0 \wedge sp' = 0 \wedge sh' = 0 \wedge tp' = 0 \wedge$$
$$(\forall y.\ CM'[y] = 0 \wedge CP'[y] = 0)$$

which records that no host has information concerning the new address p_v is going to adopt.

Verification results. The first three lines in Table 2 show the outcome (Safe or Unsafe) obtained by running the described models for RFC 3927, and the running time; for DoS attack, a *threshold* = 5 was used. If no malicious host exists, the protocol is safe with respect to the MitM attack. By contrast, one malicious host sending either broadcast or unicast messages is able to pollute other processes caches. The three models reveal the impact of the different mechanisms adopted for ACD.

In M1, no ACD mechanism is implemented, that is, hosts do not check the spa field in incoming ARP messages. Hosts never dismiss their address and the

Table 2. Results of the verification of RFC 3927 (M1, M2, M3) and RFC 5227 (M4)

	MitM			DoS		
	no p_m	bcast p_m	ucast p_m	no p_m	bcast p_m	ucast p_m
M1	[S] 0.392 s	[U] 0.260 s	[U] 0.379 s	–	–	–
M2	[S] 0.268 s	[U] 0.439 s	[U] 0.311 s	[S] 0.330 s	[U] 44.85 s	[U] 104.93 s
M3	[S] 0.380 s	[U] 0.417 s	[U] 0.409 s	[S] 0.419 s	[U] 843.2 s	[U] 1716.8 s
M4	[S] 0.306 s	[U] 0.401 s	[U] 0.415 s	–	–	–

DoS attack cannot occur. By contrast, MitM may happen, and a counterexample provided by the prover – with p_m sending broadcast messages – consists in the following sequence of events: p_m generates an Announce with $sp = v$, $sh = m$ and $tp = v$. Any host h receiving it (*the victim included*) updates its cache with $CM[h] \leftarrow m$ and $CP[h] \leftarrow v$. When p_m sends unicast messages, the MitM attack is achieved with p_m sending a poisoned Request to a target that records the fake information in its own cache.

In M2, the protocol is proved unsafe with respect to MitM, and the following counterexample is supplied by the prover for p_m sending broadcast messages: p_m generates a poisoned Request to a random target $h \neq p_v$, containing $sp = v$ and $sh = m$; the target records in its cache $CM[h] \leftarrow m$ and $CP[h] \leftarrow v$. It is worth notice that the models do *not* capture the temporal duration of the attack, that is, the unsafe outcome of the model for MitM in M2 lasts for the time needed by p_v to configure a new IP address. Afterwards, entries still existing in some caches and coupling the MAC of p_m with the dismissed IP of p_v are refreshed as soon as p_v sends its own first Announce with its new address, and starts using it. By contrast, with ARP [19] the attack may last indefinitely. Similarly, if p_m sends unicast messages, the unsafe sequence of events is the same as for M1 above, the victim is unaware of the problem and never raises a conflict detection event.

In M2, the verification of the possibility of a DoS attack has been conducted with different values of *threshold* (see Eq. (3)). With threshold 20 and no constraints on the number of hosts, a sequence of 78 events is produced as counterexample, which clearly shows loops (Fig. 1): p_m sends an unsolicited (broadcast) poisoned Reply to a random target; p_v receives it and gives up. Afterwards, p_v takes another address but p_m sends a poisoned Announce with $tp = v$, $sp = v$, $sh = m$; p_v (which owns the target IP address) detects the conflicts and gives up again. The existence of loops shows that a sequence of events exists such that the host may indefinitely dismiss its address, thus implying that the DoS attack holds. With *threshold* = 20, running times were of 434.9 s. and 1171.6 s. for the broadcast and unicast case respectively.

In M3, MitM may arise and the counterexample supplied by the prover, when p_m generates broadcast messages, is the following: p_m generates a poisoned base Request to a random target h, with $sh = m$ and $sp = v$; the target receives such a Request and sets in its cache $CM[h] \leftarrow m$ and $CP[h] \leftarrow v$. The cache poisoning lasts until the victim defends by announcing its new IP address.

Fig. 1. M2 - Event loop in the verification of DoS attack for RFC 3927.

The unsafe sequence of events for p_m sending unicast messages is the same as for M1 and M2 above, and the same considerations apply. The verification of the DoS possibility is harder than before, due to the fact that a renounce may occur just *after* a previous conflict detection which the host coped with by defending. Hence, the sequences of events are longer and the prover has to explore a larger tree of possible sequences of events with more nodes of higher depth. Yet, with no constraints on the number of processes, we were able to achieve an unsafe outcome for v_D with *threshold* = 5; the prover supplied a sequence of events of length 49 involving a loop (Fig. 2). As for M2, the loop implicitly shows that the DoS attack may verify.

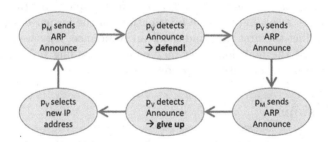

Fig. 2. M3 - Event loop in the verification of DoS attack for RFC 3927.

The highest computation complexity is reached by the M3 model verifying DoS, with p_m generating unicast messages: the maximum depth of the status tree is 49, the number of explored tree nodes is 8180, and 1355491 calls to the SMT solver are performed; the longest formula involves 26 literals. For the sake of space, all the results are reported in our website for interested readers.

5   Extended ARP: Address Conflict Detection

In order to deal with misconfigurations, RFC 826 [19] was further updated by RFC 5227 [10] which, with respect to RFC 3927, introduced a more aggressive Address Conflict Detection (ACD) mechanism. For the sake of brevity, in this section we just describe the differences with the latter, taking as reference Algorithm 2. According to RFC 5227, in the Select() procedure an address is assigned to a host in one out of three ways, namely: a static address is configured by a network administrator, or a dynamic address is supplied by either a

DHCP server or the Link-Local mechanism. Then, the `Probing()` procedure is run every time an interface is configured or booted. In RFC 5227, in case of conflict detection a host may (*i*) cease to use its IP address, or (*ii*) defend its address *once*, or (*iii*) defend its address *indefinitely*. In cases (i)-(ii), the behavior is exactly as in RFC 3927. Case (iii) is adopted e.g. when the host is a server needing to maintain its well-known stable address, and is not included in RFC 3927. In this case, the `Announce` procedure is called with *limit* = 1, and then the host continues using its IP address ignoring further conflicts. The `ACD()` procedure is modified accordingly, while the other procedures are equal in the two standards.

As a consequence of the above, cases (i)−(ii) are modeled by the M2 and M3 described in Sect. 4.1, while case (iii) is modeled by an additional model **M4** obtained from M3 by modifying the transitions where the victim dismisses its IP address so that the victim just fires without performing further actions.

Verification results. The last line of Table 2 reports the results obtained by running M4. The DoS attack cannot occur as hosts never dismiss their IP addresses. The sequence of events describing a MitM attack is the same whether p_m sends broadcast or unicast messages: p_m sends a poisoned Request to a target that pollutes its cache by recording the fake information. In the former case, the victim detects the conflict the first time and sends an Announce. Afterwards, it ignores the conflicts, and the malicious host may continue sending poisoned messages while the victim does not take any action.

6   Conclusions

In this paper, the modeling and formal verification of the three standard protocols for address resolution in Internet is described. The relevance of our work lies in two main achievements: first, under a practical point of view, our experiments formally show the weaknesses of currently adopted technologies with respect to security aspects, thus providing formal foundation to well known phenomena discovered and exploited by the underground community since many years. Second, the work highlights the maturity of existing formal approaches and tools in verifying the safety and correctness of real distributed systems. These approaches have been so far validated with several problems, included other network protocols (e.g. [7,17]). Yet, to the best of our knowledge, this is the first time that these techniques are applied to the analysis of ARP, with excellent results: the verification was possible for all deployed models, for any number N of system components, and within acceptable computation time.

In the future, we plan to apply these techniques to the verification of algorithms proposed in the literature but not yet standardized aiming at securing ARP – thus contributing to the development of safer networks – as well as possibly to other Internet protocols.

References

1. Abdulla, P.A., Delzanno, G., Henda, N.B., Rezine, A.: Regular model checking without transducers (on efficient verification of parameterized systems). In: Grumberg, O., Huth, M. (eds.) TACAS 2007. LNCS, vol. 4424, pp. 721–736. Springer, Heidelberg (2007). doi:10.1007/978-3-540-71209-1_56
2. Abdulla, P.A., Haziza, F., Holík, L.: All for the price of few. In: Giacobazzi, R., Berdine, J., Mastroeni, I. (eds.) VMCAI 2013. LNCS, vol. 7737, pp. 476–495. Springer, Heidelberg (2013). doi:10.1007/978-3-642-35873-9_28
3. Abdulla, P.A., Jonsson, B., Nilsson, M., Saksena, M.: A survey of regular model checking. In: Gardner, P., Yoshida, N. (eds.) CONCUR 2004. LNCS, vol. 3170, pp. 35–48. Springer, Heidelberg (2004). doi:10.1007/978-3-540-28644-8_3
4. Alqahtani, A.H., Iftikhar, M.: TCP/IP attacks, defenses and security tools. Int. J. Sci. Mod. Eng. (IJISME) 1(10) (2013)
5. Bardin, S., Finkel, A., Leroux, J., Schnoebelen, P.: Flat acceleration in symbolic model checking. In: Peled, D.A., Tsay, Y.-K. (eds.) ATVA 2005. LNCS, vol. 3707, pp. 474–488. Springer, Heidelberg (2005). doi:10.1007/11562948_35
6. Bellovin, S.M.: Security problems in the TCP/IP protocol suite. ACM SIGCOMM Comput. Commun. Rev. 19(2), 32–48 (1989)
7. Bhargavan, K., Obradovic, D., Gunter, C.A.: Formal verification of standards for distance vector routing protocols. J. ACM 49(4), 538–576 (2002)
8. Bloem, R., Jacobs, S., Khalimov, A., Konnov, I., Rubin, S., Veith, H., Widder, J.: Decidability of Parameterized Verification. Synthesis Lectures on Distributed Computing Theory. Morgan & Claypool Publishers, San Rafael (2015)
9. Bouajjani, A., Habermehl, P., Vojnar, T.: Abstract regular model checking. In: Alur, R., Peled, D.A. (eds.) CAV 2004. LNCS, vol. 3114, pp. 372–386. Springer, Heidelberg (2004). doi:10.1007/978-3-540-27813-9_29
10. Cheshire, S.: IPv4 Address Conflict Detection. RFC 5227, July 2008
11. Cheshire, S., Aboba, B., Guttman, E.: Dynamic Configuration of IPv4 Link-Local Addresses. RFC 3927, May 2005
12. Conchon, S., Goel, A., Krstic, S., Mebsout, A., Zaïdi, F.: Invariants for finite instances and beyond. In: Proceedings of FMCAD (2013)
13. Conchon, S., Goel, A., Krstić, S., Mebsout, A., Zaïdi, F.: Cubicle: a parallel SMT-based model checker for parameterized systems. In: Madhusudan, P., Seshia, S.A. (eds.) CAV 2012. LNCS, vol. 7358, pp. 718–724. Springer, Heidelberg (2012). doi:10.1007/978-3-642-31424-7_55
14. Ghilardi, S., Nicolini, E., Ranise, S., Zucchelli, D.: Towards SMT model checking of array-based systems. In: Armando, A., Baumgartner, P., Dowek, G. (eds.) IJCAR 2008. LNCS (LNAI), vol. 5195, pp. 67–82. Springer, Heidelberg (2008). doi:10.1007/978-3-540-71070-7_6
15. Ghilardi, S., Ranise, S.: MCMT: a model checker modulo theories. In: Giesl, J., Hähnle, R. (eds.) IJCAR 2010. LNCS (LNAI), vol. 6173, pp. 22–29. Springer, Heidelberg (2010). doi:10.1007/978-3-642-14203-1_3
16. Ghilardi, S., Ranise, S.: Backward reachability of array-based systems by SMT solving: termination and invariant synthesis. J. Log. Methods Comput. Sci. 6(4) (2010)
17. Islam, S.M.S., Sqalli, M.S., Khan, S.: Modeling and formal verification of DHCP using SPIN. Int. J. Comput. Sci. Appl. 3(6), 145–159 (2006)

18. Alford, M.W., Ansart, J.P., Hommel, G., Lamport, L., Liskov, B., Mullery, G.P., Schneider, F.B.: Formal foundation for specification and verification. In: Paul, M., et al. (eds.) Distributed Systems. LNCS, vol. 190, pp. 203–285. Springer, Heidelberg (1985). doi:10.1007/3-540-15216-4_15

19. Plummer, D.C.: An Ethernet Address Resolution Protocol - or - Converting Network Protocol Addresses to 48.bit Ethernet Address for Transmission on Ethernet Hardware. RFC 826, November 1982

20. Wagner, R.: Address Resolution Protocol Spoofing and Man-in-the-Middle Attacks. The SANS Institute, Reston (2001)

Certified Password Quality

A Case Study Using Coq and Linux Pluggable Authentication Modules

João F. Ferreira[1,2]([⊠]), Saul A. Johnson[1], Alexandra Mendes[1],
and Phillip J. Brooke[1]

[1] School of Computing, Teesside University, Middlesbrough TS1 3BX, UK
joao@joaoff.com, {Saul.Johnson,A.Mendes}@tees.ac.uk, pjb@scm.tees.ac.uk
[2] HASLab/INESC TEC, Universidade do Minho, 4704-553 Braga, Portugal

Abstract. We propose the use of modern proof assistants to specify, implement, and verify password quality checkers. We use the proof assistant Coq, focusing on Linux PAM, a widely-used implementation of pluggable authentication modules for Linux. We show how password quality policies can be expressed in Coq and how to use Coq's code extraction features to automatically encode these policies as PAM modules that can readily be used by any Linux system.

We implemented the default password quality policy shared by two widely-used PAM modules: *pam_cracklib* and *pam_pwquality*. We then compared our implementation with the original modules by running them against a random sample of 100,000 leaked passwords obtained from a publicly available database. In doing this, we demonstrated a potentially serious bug in the original modules. The bug was reported to the maintainers of Linux PAM and is now fixed.

Keywords: Password quality · Password policy · Verification · Security · Authentication · Coq · Proof assistant · Theorem prover · Linux · PAM

1 Introduction

Password quality is essential to keeping any password-protected system secure. If a password is easy to guess and an attacker gains authenticated access as a result, any security measures deployed to restrict access by unauthenticated users become irrelevant. From the perspective of the system, the attacker is indistinguishable from the legitimate user.

Without an enforced password quality policy, passwords created by users tend to be weak [11]. A password quality policy may mandate, for example, that all user passwords contain a mixture of upper case, lower case, and numeric characters in order to maximise the search space that a brute-force algorithm would need to examine in order to correctly guess a user's password. It is critical that the software that enforces these policies (the *password quality checker*) is

© Springer International Publishing AG 2017
N. Polikarpova and S. Schneider (Eds.): IFM 2017, LNCS 10510, pp. 407–421, 2017.
DOI: 10.1007/978-3-319-66845-1_27

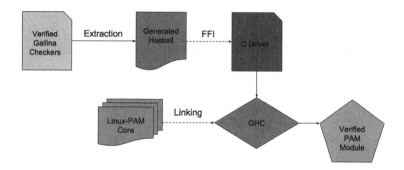

Fig. 1. An overview of the process of creating a verified PAM module.

both correct and configurable to keep up with the large body of ongoing research into password policy best-practises [7,28,32].

The importance of password quality checkers makes them an ideal candidate for formal verification. Using recent advances in code generation from theorem provers, it is now possible to transform high-level verified functional implementations into certified code that can be used in place of unverified procedural code to perform password quality checking. We therefore propose the use of modern proof assistants to formally verify password quality checkers. To demonstrate this, we use the Coq proof assistant [3] to specify, implement, and verify password quality checkers. We focus on Linux PAM [25,26], a widely-used implementation of pluggable authentication modules (PAM) for Linux. We show how we can define password quality policies in Coq and automatically encode them as Linux PAM modules that can readily be used. We document the process of extracting verified password quality assessment functions from a verified Gallina code base (Coq's specification language) into Haskell [19] and calling them via the Haskell foreign function interface (FFI) [13] from a driver written in C. Figure 1 provides an overview of this process. We implemented several PAM modules that perform password quality checking using verified code. In particular, we implemented a module identical to the default behaviour shared by two widely-used PAM modules designed to act as password quality checkers on Linux systems: *pam_cracklib* and *pam_pwquality*. In doing this, we demonstrated a potentially serious bug in the original PAM modules. The bug was reported to Linux PAM's maintainers and is now fixed.

In Sect. 2, we discuss password quality checking software, focusing on Linux PAM. Section 3 is about the use of Coq to specify, implement, and verify password quality checkers. We evaluate our work in Sect. 4 by comparing our implementation with *pam_cracklib* and *pam_pwquality*. We also demonstrate that the flexibility of our approach allows users to create verified password policies quickly and easily. After presenting related work in Sect. 5, we conclude the paper in Sect. 6.

2   Password Quality Checking Software

Password quality checking refers to techniques used to ensure that users do not create passwords that are vulnerable to brute-force attacks or guessing by a party with access to basic information about the user. For example, a user may be unable to create a password that is identical to their user name or email address, or that is too short. A range of other issues relate to passwords such as memorability, storage of passwords on systems, and other means to obtain passwords (such as snooping). We do not address these further in this work.

Password quality checking software often requires that an administrator provide a *password quality policy* which specifies the minimum characteristics of an acceptable password. A significant body of research is emerging that challenges conventional wisdom about what constitutes a secure password [28,32].

Linux PAM. We focus on Linux PAM [25,26], a widely-deployed open-source application that pulls together multiple authentication-related modules into one high-level API, allowing application developers to create programs that rely on various authentication services independently of the underlying implementations. Two well-known PAM modules that are used to indicate password quality are *pam_cracklib* and *pam_pwquality*. Both modules are written in C, use the same backend, and define the same default password quality policy (see Fig. 2). Figure 3 shows the type of code used in these modules to check whether a password is palindromic. Figure 3a shows a pure function named `palindrome` that returns 1 if the password given is a palindrome and 0 otherwise; Fig. 3b shows how the top-level function `password_check` uses `palindrome` to check if the *new password* is a palindrome (`msg` and _ are used for error control and internationalisation purposes respectively).

Since these modules are enabled by default in many popular Linux distributions, they are widely deployed. For example, in Red Hat Enterprise Linux 7 and in CentOS 7, the *pam_pwquality* PAM module replaced *pam_cracklib*, which was used up to version 6 as a default module for password quality checking [17]. It is estimated that CentOS is

---

Passwords must:
- − Not be identical to the previous password, if any.
- − Not be palindromic.
- − Not be a rotated version of the old password, if any.
- − Not contain case changes only in relation to the previous password, if any.
- − Have a Levenshtein distance of 5 or greater from the previous password, if any (*difok=5*).
- − Be at least 9 characters long (*minlen=9*), however:
- • Passwords may be 1 character shorter if they contain at least 1 lower case letter (*lcredit=1*).
- • Passwords may be 1 character shorter if they contain at least 1 upper case letter (*ucredit=1*).
- • Passwords may be 1 character shorter if they contain at least 1 digit character (*dcredit=1*).
- • Passwords may be 1 character shorter if they contain at least 1 other character (*ocredit=1*).
- • This shortening of minimum length will stack, making for a minimum length of 9 - 4 = 5 for passwords containing all 4 classes.
- • Effective minimum length is, then $M = m - c$ where M is the effective minimum length, m is the configured minimum length and c is the number of character classes present in the string.

Fig. 2. Default policy implemented by *pam_cracklib* and *pam_pwquality*.

```
static int palindrome(const char *new)
{
  int i, j;
  i = strlen(new);

  for (j = 0;j < i;j++)
    if (new[i - j - 1] != new[j])
      return 0;

  return 1;
}
```

(a) The **palindrome** function checks whether the argument string is palindromic.

```
static const char *password_check(
  pam_handle_t *pamh,
  struct cracklib_options *opt,
  const char *old, const char *new,
  const char *user)
{
  [...]
  newmono = str_lower(strdup(new));
  [...]

  if (!msg && palindrome(newmono))
    msg = _("is a palindrome");
  [...]
}
```

(b) The **password_check** function calls the function **palindrome** to check whether the proposed new password is palindromic.

Fig. 3. Two functions from *pam_cracklib.c*, one pure with only the new password accepted as a parameter, and one which drives the password checking process.

one of the most popular Linux distributions for web servers and is installed on millions of these worldwide[1].

3   Verified Password Quality in Coq

We now describe how we use Coq to specify, implement, and verify password checkers. We implement checkers as pure functional programs and demonstrate Coq's flexibility by showing different ways to specify them: often, we consider the functional programs to be *functional (executable) specifications*, but we can also specify checkers *by theorem* or *by property* (i.e. axiomatically). We conclude this section by describing how verified functional implementations can be extracted as Haskell code and linked with PAM modules that can be readily used.

3.1   Types and Password Checkers

In our model, we consider passwords to be Coq strings:

Definition Password := string.

Password checkers can be seen as functions from strings to booleans (e.g. the function **palindrome** in Fig. 3a is such a function). However, we want password checkers to take into consideration more elements, such as the previous password or the user's name (see the signature of **password_check** in Fig. 3b).

In our model, we consider the user's previous password and we encode this information in the type **PasswordTransition**:

```
Inductive PasswordTransition : Set :=
    PwdTransition : (option Password) -> Password -> PasswordTransition.
```

---

[1] See, for example, https://w3techs.com/technologies/details/os-linux/all/all, and http://www.computerworld.com/article/2468596/network-software/the-most-popular-linux-for-web-servers-is----.html.

An element of the type `PasswordTransition` represents an *old* password being changed into a *new* password. The old password is optional: if a user changes their password, the previous password is available as it must be entered to proceed; if an administrator changes the password of a user, that information is unlikely to be available. With these types defined, a password checker can be described as a function that takes a `PasswordTransition` and either succeeds or returns some error message. We define the type of a password checker as:

```
Definition CheckerResult := option ErrorMsg.
```

For example, a password checker that prevents passwords from being palindromes can be defined as:

```
Definition not_palindrome (pt : PasswordTransition) : CheckerResult :=
  if palindrome (new_pwd pt) then
    BADPWD: "The new password is a palindrome."
  else
    GOODPWD.
```

This defines a new password checker named `not_palindrome` whose behaviour is quite simple: if the new password (`new_pwd pt`) is a palindrome, then it should be rejected (with a specific error message). This checker depends on the function `palindrome`, which is discussed in the next subsection.

The reserved keywords `BADPWD` and `GOODPWD` are defined as symbolic abbreviations denoting the appropriate elements of type `CheckerResult`:

```
Notation GOODPWD := None.
Notation "BADPWD: msg" := (Some msg).
```

The palindrome checker uses only the new password and not the old password. This is not the general case: e.g., the old password is required when we do not want the new password to be a prefix of the old password (or vice-versa):

```
Definition prefix_old_pwd (pt : PasswordTransition) : CheckerResult :=
  NEEDS old_pwd FROM pt
    if (prefix (old_pwd pt) (new_pwd pt)) ||
       (prefix (new_pwd pt) (old_pwd pt))
    then
      BADPWD: "The new password is a prefix of the
               old password (or vice-versa)"
    else
      GOODPWD.
```

This password checker returns an error if the old password (`old_pwd pt`) is a prefix of the new password (`new_pwd pt`) or vice-versa. The checker depends on the function `prefix`, which is discussed in the next subsection. The body of this checker is prefixed by a new construct expressing that the old password is required to define the checker: `NEEDS old_pwd FROM pt`. The definition of `NEEDS` means that if the old password is undefined (e.g. if the administrator is changing the password of a normal user), then the check is disabled. Further, the function `old_pwd` is being exposed to the checker as a *local function*. This provides a safer way to access the old password, because using `old_pwd pt` without prefixing it with the `NEEDS` construct will result in a type error (caught at compilation time). In other words, the function `old_pwd` is only available in

contexts where the old password is defined, thus avoiding conditional boilerplate code
that checks whether the old password is defined.

3.2   Specification, Implementation, and Proofs

An advantage of defining password checkers in a proof engineering environment such
as Coq is that we can prove properties about implementations. For example, if we want
to prove that prefix_old_pwd is skipped when the old password is undefined, we can
state and prove a lemma as follows:

```
Lemma prefix_old_pwd_undefined: forall (pt: PasswordTransition),
    old_pwd_is_undefined(pt) = true  ->  prefix_old_pwd(pt) = GOODPWD.
Proof.
  intros. unfold old_pwd_is_undefined in H.
  (* Case analysis *)
  destruct pt. destruct o.
  (* Case 1 (trivial): old password is defined *)
  - congruence.
  (* Case 2: old password is undefined *)
  - unfold prefix_old_pwd. simpl. auto.
Qed.
```

The lemma simply states that if the old password is undefined[2], then the checker
prefix_old_pwd is disabled (i.e. it accepts all passwords). The proof is by case analysis
and is made simple by using tactics such as congruence, simpl, and auto.

In the context of our work, the most important aspect to verify is functional correctness. We have seen above that password checkers are functions from
PasswordTransition to CheckerResult that normally depend on inner pure functions.
For example, the checker not_palindrome depends on palindrome and prefix_old_pwd
depends on prefix. In general, when defining password checkers, we are interested in
proving that the inner pure functions are correct. In the remainder of this section,
we discuss different approaches to specify password checkers. The point of showing
different specification approaches is to demonstrate that writers of verified password
checkers can use their preferred style of specification (e.g. functional programmers will
probably prefer to write functional executable specifications).

Functional (executable) Specifications. As we are using a high-level functional
programming language to encode password checkers, we can give direct implementations of constructive or executable specifications [30,31]. E.g., the following definition
of palindrome acts both as specification and implementation:

```
Definition palindrome (s : string) : bool :=
    s ==_s (string_reverse s).
```

This definition is an implementation (i.e. it can be executed), but it also describes
the notion of palindrome: an arbitrary string s is a palindrome if and only if s is the
same as its reverse. Most programmers would be satisfied with this specification, but
because we are in a proof engineering environment, we can prove further properties;

---

[2] old_pwd_is_undefined(pt) is defined to return true when the old password is undefined and false otherwise.

an example is the following lemma stating that the function that reverses a string is involutive.

```
Lemma string_reverse_involutive : forall (s : string),
  string_reverse (string_reverse s) = s.
Proof.
  induction s as [| c s'].
  (* Base case *)
  - simpl. reflexivity.
  (* Inductive step *)
  - simpl. rewrite (string_reverse_unit (string_reverse s') c).
    rewrite IHs'. auto.
Qed.
```

The proof is by induction and uses the lemma **string_reverse_unit**, which states that for all strings s and characters c, we have:

$$string\_reverse(string\_append(s, c)) = string\_append(c, string\_reverse(s))$$

Specification by Theorem. A proof assistant like Coq also allows us to specify functions by capturing their specifications as theorems. E.g., the function **prefix**, used in the password checker **prefix_old_pwd**, can be specified as:

```
Theorem prefix_correct : forall s1 s2 : string,
  prefix s1 s2 = true  <->  substring 0 (length s1) s2 = s1.
```

This theorem states that a string **s1** is a prefix of a string **s2** if and only if **s1** is the substring of length **length s1** starting at position 0 of **s2** (i.e., for $k =$ **length s1**, the string composed by the k leftmost characters of **s2** is **s1**). This is proved in Coq's standard library.

Specification by Property. Strong specifications usually demand a greater proving effort: proofs are normally more complex and it is often the case that deeper knowledge of the proof assistant is required.

In some cases, it may be easier or desirable to prove properties that do not fully specify the implementation, but nevertheless increase our confidence in its correctness. For example, suppose that we define the Hamming distance [14,15] between two strings of equal length as follows:

```
Fixpoint hamming_distance (a b : string) : option nat :=
  match a, b with
    | EmptyString, EmptyString => Some 0
    | String ca a', String cb b' =>
      match hamming_distance a' b' with
        | None => None
        | Some n => Some ((nat_of_bool (negb (ca ==_a cb))) + n)
      end
    | _, _ => None
  end.
```

Instead of fully specifying this function, we increase our confidence in this implementation by proving properties the Hamming distance satisfies. For example:

```
Lemma hamming_distance_undefined_for_different_lengths : forall (a b : string),
  length a <> length b  <-> hamming_distance a b = None.

Lemma hamming_distance_defined_for_same_length : forall (a b : string),
  length a = length b  -> hamming_distance a b <> None.

Lemma hamming_distance_zero_for_identical : forall (s: string),
  hamming_distance s s = Some 0.
```

3.3 Password Policies and Code Extraction

Our framework mimics the behaviour of the PAM modules *pam_cracklib* and *pam_pwquality* in that password quality policies are lists of password checkers executed successively. E.g., the policy shown in Fig. 2 is defined as follows:

```
Definition pwd_quality_policy :=
  [ diff_from_old_pwd ; not_palindrome ; not_rotated ;
    not_case_changes_only ; levenshtein_distance_gt 5 ;
    credits_length_check 8 ].
```

This list, together with all its contents, is extracted into Haskell code by using Coq's code extraction mechanism [24]. Finally, the extracted Haskell code is linked with a C driver to create a PAM module that calls the Haskell code via Haskell's foreign function interface (FFI) [13]. In short, the C code calls each password checker with a password transition and reports the result to the user.

4   Evaluation

In this section, we evaluate our work by comparing the newly implemented verified PAM module to the original in terms of behaviour, performance, and compiled executable size. We describe the bug discovered in the original module, and demonstrate that the flexibility of our approach allows users to create verified password policies quickly and easily.

4.1 Experimental Setup

Using Vagrant, a virtual machine running Ubuntu 16.04 "Xenial" 64-bit with Coq v8.6 and the Glasgow Haskell Compiler v7.10.3 installed was created to provide a consistent testing environment [23]. An unmodified instance of this machine was used for every test run.

A random sample of 100,000 passwords was obtained from a publicly available database of ten million leaked passwords [5] using a Python script. An instance of the test machine was then configured to use each module in turn as the password quality checker for its native *passwd* executable, which handles user password changes. A set of shell scripts was created to run each password through this executable one at a time and record the results, which consist of feedback from the active PAM module about the strength of the submitted password. As the script terminates *passwd* after the first password entry, no actual password change was performed as the password must be entered twice (for confirmation) in order to effect one. Importantly, the passwords were checked on their own merit and not in the context of a password change; that is, the old password in use before the attempted password change was not taken into account during password quality checking. As a result of this, any password quality checks that compare the new password to the old password in any way were not in effect. This raw data was passed through a Python script which consolidated it into a CSV file ready for further analysis using spreadsheet software.

The behaviour of the verified module was then compared to the original module. All dictionary checks were disabled in the original module (and omitted from the verified module) prior to testing. All source code was maintained under source control on GitHub [22].

4.2   Experiment 1: Comparison with PAM Modules *pam_cracklib* and *pam_pwdquality*

The verified PAM module was first configured and built to implement the default policy shared by both *pam_cracklib* and its successor *pam_pwquality* (shown in Fig. 2 and encoded as shown in Sect. 3.3).

As expected, the verified module behaved identically to the original, accepting 56574 of the passwords in the database (that is, deeming them secure enough) with absolute consistency between them (i.e. the same passwords were accepted or rejected).

Aside from the behaviour of the module itself and whether or not it is written using verified code, there are other factors that may be considered when deciding on the most suitable module to use on any one system. For example, performance and executable size. In order to compare the performance of the verified module to the original module, each run of *passwd* during the experiment was timed and averaged to calculate an average checking time per password (Table 1).

Table 1. Average execution time for each test run.

Module	Description	Avg. time
pam_cracklib_nodict	Original C implementation of pam_cracklib with dictionary check disabled	0.00926278 s
pam_basic_pwd_policy	Verified module built with the default pam_cracklib default policy enabled (without dictionary check)	0.011845369 s

The average checking time for the verified module is around 1.28 times that of the unverified C module in all cases, but this difference is not as drastic as had been anticipated, considering that many algorithms in use within the verified module are not nearly as efficient as those in the original (compare the inefficient — yet easier to reason about — definition of palindrome shown in Sect. 3.2 to the implementation shown in Fig. 3a).

With regard to executable size, it is unsurprising that the compiled verified module is significantly larger than the original module (Table 2). The verified module is linked against several dependencies from both the Haskell and C standard libraries. The authors recognise, however, that on non-critical storage-constrained systems, it may be inconvenient to use an executable around 9 times the size of its unverified counterpart when its behaviour is expected to be identical.

Table 2. File size comparison between the original and verified modules.

File name	Description	File size
pam_cracklib_nodict.so	Original C implementation of pam_cracklib with dictionary check disabled	22384 bytes
pam_basic_pwd_policy.so	Verified module built with the default pam_cracklib default policy enabled (without dictionary check)	189688 bytes

4.3   Experiment 2: Increasing Password Entropy

Research into password complexity [16] has shown that it may become almost ubiquitously mandatory for users to create longer passwords that contain a good mixture of uppercase and lowercase letters, numbers, and symbols. It would not be unreasonable, then, for a system administrator to enforce a policy mandating that no passwords have more than two characters of the same class (i.e. type) in a row in an effort to boost entropy (see Table 3 for examples).

Table 3. Example of the status of different hypothetical passwords under the proposed policy.

Password	Accepted	Reason
1234Password	No	More than one number in a row, more than one lowercase letter in a row
1Ll4m4!Gg	Yes	No more than one number, uppercase letter, lowercase letter or symbol in a row
correcthorsebatterystaple	No	More than one lowercase letter in a row
Ab4kUs#!	No	More than one symbol in a row

In order to accomplish this using *pam_cracklib*, the *maxclassrepeat* option must be set to 1. After configuring the original *pam_cracklib* and the verified module in this way (using the policy from Fig. 2 with the additional constraint that no two consecutive characters may be of the same class), the test was run again over the same password database. In this case, the modules did not perform identically.

While the verified module predictably accepted only a tiny minority (371) of passwords, the original module exhibited exactly the same behaviour as before and accepted

56574 passwords. This result demonstrated the effects of a bug in *pam_cracklib*, specifically a check done inside *pam_cracklib.c* on line 411:

```
if ( opt->max_class_repeat > 1 && sameclass > opt->max_class_repeat) {
   return 1;
}
```

Rather than checking if the option max_class_repeat is set to a number greater than zero, the check is done against 1 instead (see highlighted code). This has the consequence of disabling the check entirely, which contradicts the documentation for the option and any intuition on the part of the system administrator.

This issue was raised on the Linux PAM GitHub repository [18], along with a pull request containing the fix. A project maintainer reviewed it to their satisfaction and merged the fix into the official repository, to be distributed in future releases. After the fix had been applied, the *pam_cracklib* module was compiled and tested again against the password database, this time functioning consistently with the verified module.

4.4   Experiment 3: A Simple Policy

To demonstrate the flexibility of our approach, we show that it is possible to quickly and easily compile a password quality checker PAM module drawing on specific research findings. Kelly et al. [21] suggest that the use of the *basic16* password policy (16 alphabetic characters) creates passwords that are more resilient against brute-force attacks than policies such as *comprehensive8* which allows for shorter (length 8), but more complex passwords containing a mixture of cases, numbers, and symbols.

The verified module was quickly reconfigured, rebuilt, and reinstalled with this new, very simple policy in place. In code, we simply alter the list of password quality checkers to apply only a length check and nothing more, before extracting the Coq code to Haskell and rebuilding the C driver:

```
Definition pwd_quality_policy := [
   plain_length_check 16
].
```

The policy makes use of the plain_length_check function that evaluates a password on length alone:

```
Definition plain_length_check (len : nat) (pt : PasswordTransition)
   : CheckerResult := if length (new_pwd pt) >=? len then GOODPWD
                      else BADPWD: "The new password is too short.".
```

The accompanying plc_correct lemma and proof certify that this function behaves correctly:

```
Lemma plc_correct: forall (len : nat) (pt : PasswordTransition),
      plain_length_check len pt = GOODPWD
<-> is_true (length (new_pwd pt) >=? len).
Proof. repeat (split; unfold plain_length_check;
               destruct (length (new_pwd pt) >=? len); crush). Qed.
```

In this case, because the function is very simple, the implementation is as complex as its specification. However, in general, this is not the case (see, for instance, the examples in Sect. 3). The proof is based on the definition of the function and a case analysis on the length of the new password. It also depends on the **crush** tactic from [10]. On running this newly-configured checker over the password database, 970 passwords were accepted while the rest were shorter than 16 characters in length and therefore rejected. Interestingly, the original *pam_cracklib* and *pam_pwquality* libraries can not be configured in this way without making changes at the source code level and recompiling, as various checks (**palindrome** being one example) cannot be disabled through configuration alone. While our approach also requires recompilation of the verified module, the scope of the required source code changes (modification of one list) is so small that it arguably amounts to little more than a configuration change. In this way, our approach is demonstrably more flexible than that taken by the original modules.

5   Related Work

To the best of our knowledge, this is the first effort in creating verified password quality checkers. The closest related work on provably improving the reliability of authentication systems is the body of work on verification of authentication protocols. For example, the work presented in [12,27] uses CSP and PVS to analyse and verify authentication properties. A very popular automatic cryptographic protocol verifier is ProVerif [4]. Uses of ProVerif include the verification of a user authentication protocol named oPass [29] and security properties of mutual-authentication and key-exchange protocols [6].

The work presented in this paper has been motivated by recent advances that make practical the verification of system security components [1]. In particular, we were inspired by approaches that are based on extracting (or generating) code directly from proof assistants. An example is FSCQ [8,9], the first file system with a machine-checkable proof (using Coq). Similarly to what we do, a Haskell implementation is extracted using Coq's extraction feature. Two additional examples are the implementation of a conference management system [20] and of a distributed social media platform [2], where code generation was also used to extract correct Scala implementations from Isabelle specifications.

6   Conclusion

Through this work, we have used the proof assistant Coq to create verified password quality checkers in the form of PAM modules with at least as much functionality (aside from dictionary checks) as *pam_cracklib* and *pam_pwquality* which are already widely deployed. We identified a potentially serious bug and we demonstrated that our framework can be used to easily create new certified password quality policies.

Despite the successes, limitations remain. While we use a code extraction approach that substantially reduces the size of the unverified code base, it does not eliminate it entirely. Some low-level unverified C code must still be written in order to call the extracted code in a useful context. Importantly, while the Gallina code is verified, the authors are not aware of any correctness proof of Coq's code extraction mechanism. Executable size is also greatly increased in the verified modules by almost an order of magnitude, which may place serious limitations on its use by storage-constrained systems.

The collection of proofs for the verified checkers is being constantly improved as part of an ongoing verification effort as we investigate potential future work in this area (see [22]). In particular, we aim at making most proofs as simple and automatic as possible. Nevertheless, as we demonstrated, the framework allows the creation of new policies that are completely verified. This work focuses on the specific and important area of verified password checking and we believe that it lays a foundation for further research in this area.

Future Work. A domain-specific language (DSL) is in development as a direct successor to this research which will allow Linux system administrators to quickly and easily express their ideal password quality policy and produce a verified password quality checker PAM module in one compilation step. We anticipate that this will offer a great deal of flexibility beyond the simple configuration options offered by existing password quality checking PAM modules.

In continuing this work, we hope to substantially reduce the size of the unverified C driver by stripping out functionality that is not absolutely necessary or that has been made redundant by our verification efforts. We also plan to verify other aspects of the PAM modules such as configuration option parsing as well as extend the functionality of the verified password quality checking code to include dictionary checks. An examination of the feasibility of adding Unicode support is also planned.

References

1. Appel, A.W.: Modular verification for computer security. In: IEEE 29th Computer Security Foundations Symposium (CSF), pp. 1–8 (2016)
2. Bauereiß, T., Gritti, A.P., Popescu, A., Raimondi, F.: CoSMeDis: a distributed social media platform with formally verified confidentiality guarantees. In: Security and Privacy (SP) (2017)
3. Bertot, Y., Castéran, P.: Interactive theorem proving and program development - Coq'Art: the calculus of inductive constructions. Springer Science & Business Media, Heidelberg (2013)
4. Blanchet, B., et al.: An efficient cryptographic protocol verifier based on prolog rules. In: CSFW, vol. 1, pp. 82–96 (2001)
5. Burnett, M.: Today i am releasing ten million passwords (2015). https://xato.net/today-i-am-releasing-ten-million-passwords-b6278bbe7495. Accessed 26 Apr 2017
6. Canetti, R., Herzog, J.: Universally composable symbolic analysis of mutual authentication and key-exchange protocols. In: Halevi, S., Rabin, T. (eds.) TCC 2006. LNCS, vol. 3876, pp. 380–403. Springer, Heidelberg (2006). doi:10.1007/11681878_20
7. National Cyber Security Centre: Password Guidance: Simplifying Your Approach (2016). https://www.ncsc.gov.uk/guidance/password-guidance-simplifying-your-approach. Accessed 26 Apr 2017
8. Chajed, T., Chen, H., Chlipala, A., Kaashoek, M.F., Zeldovich, N., Ziegler, D.: Certifying a file system using crash Hoare logic: correctness in the presence of crashes. Commun. ACM **60**(4), 75–84 (2017)
9. Chen, H., Ziegler, D., Chajed, T., Chlipala, A., Kaashoek, M.F., Zeldovich, N.: Using crash Hoare logic for certifying the FSCQ file system. In: Proceedings of the 25th Symposium on Operating Systems Principles, pp. 18–37. ACM (2015)
10. Chlipala, A.: Certified Programming with Dependent Types: A Pragmatic Introduction to the Coq Proof Assistant. MIT Press, Cambridge (2013)
11. Dell'Amico, M., Michiardi, P., Roudier, Y.: Password strength: an empirical analysis. In: INFOCOM, pp. 1–9, IEEE (2010)

12. Dutertre, B., Schneider, S.: Using a PVS embedding of CSP to verify authentication protocols. In: Gunter, E.L., Felty, A. (eds.) TPHOLs 1997. LNCS, vol. 1275, pp. 121–136. Springer, Heidelberg (1997). doi:10.1007/BFb0028390

13. Finne, S., Henderson, I.F., Kowalczyk, M., Leijen, D., Marlow, S., Meijer, E., Jones, S.P., Wallace, M.: The Haskell 98 Foreign Function Interface 1.0 An Addendum to the Haskell 98 Report (2002)

14. Hamming, R.W.: Coding and Theory. Prentice-Hall, Englewood Cliffs (1980)

15. Hamming, R.W.: Error detecting and error correcting codes. Bell Labs Tech. J. **29**(2), 147–160 (1950)

16. Inglesant, P.G., Sasse, M.A.: The true cost of unusable password policies: password use in the wild. In: Proceedings of the SIGCHI Conference on Human Factors in Computing Systems. ACM (2010)

17. Jahoda, M., Krátký, R., Prpič, M., Čapek, T., Wadeley, S., Ruseva, Y., Svoboda, M.: Red Hat Enterprise Linux 7 Security Guide (2017). https://access.redhat.com/documentation/en-US/Red_Hat_Enterprise_Linux/7/html/Security_Guide/index.html. Accessed 24 Apr 2017

18. Johnson, S.: Behavior of maxclassrepeat=1 inconsistent with docs (2017). https://github.com/linux-pam/linux-pam/issues/16. Accessed 31 Mar 2017

19. Jones, S.P.: Haskell 98 Language and Libraries: The Revised Report. Cambridge University Press, Cambridge (2003)

20. Kanav, S., Lammich, P., Popescu, A.: A conference management system with verified document confidentiality. In: Biere, A., Bloem, R. (eds.) CAV 2014. LNCS, vol. 8559, pp. 167–183. Springer, Cham (2014). doi:10.1007/978-3-319-08867-9_11

21. Kelley, P.G., Komanduri, S., Mazurek, M.L., Shay, R., Vidas, T., Bauer, L., Christin, N., Cranor, L.F., Lopez, J.: Guess again (and again and again): measuring password strength by simulating password-cracking algorithms. In: Security and Privacy (SP), pp. 523–537. IEEE (2012)

22. Software Reliability Lab. Verified PAM Cracklib (2017). https://github.com/sr-lab/verified-pam-cracklib. Accessed 05 Apr 2017

23. Software Reliability Lab. Verified PAM Environment (2017). https://github.com/sr-lab/verified-pam-environment. Accessed 30 Mar 2017

24. Letouzey, P.: Extraction in Coq: an overview. In: Beckmann, A., Dimitracopoulos, C., Löwe, B. (eds.) CiE 2008. LNCS, vol. 5028, pp. 359–369. Springer, Heidelberg (2008). doi:10.1007/978-3-540-69407-6_39

25. Morgan, A.G., Kukuk, T.: The Linux-PAM Module Writers' Guide (2010)

26. Samar, V.: Unified login with pluggable authentication modules (PAM). In: Proceedings of the 3rd ACM Conference on Computer and Communications Security, pp. 1–10 (1996)

27. Schneider, S.: Verifying authentication protocols in CSP. IEEE Trans. Softw. Eng. **24**(9), 741–758 (1998)

28. Shay, R., Komanduri, S., Durity, A.L., Huh, P.S., Mazurek, M.L., Segreti, S.M., Ur, B., Bauer, L., Christin, N., Cranor, L.F.: Designing password policies for strength and usability. ACM Trans. Inf. Syst. Secur. (TIS-SEC) **18**(4) (2016). Article no. 13

29. Sun, H.-M., Chen, Y.-H., Lin, Y.-H.: oPass: a user authentication protocol resistant to password stealing and password reuse attacks. IEEE Trans. Inf. Forensics Secur. **7**(2), 651–663 (2012)

30. Thompson, S.: Functional programming: executable specifications and program transformations. ACM SIGSOFT Softw. Eng. Notes **14**(3), 287–290 (1989)

31. Visser, J., Oliveira, J.N.F., Barbosa, L.S., Ferreira, J.F., Mendes, A.: CAMILA revival: VDM meets Haskell. In: 1st Overture Workshop. University of Newcastle TR Series (2005)
32. Zhang-Kennedy, L., Chiasson, S., van Oorschot, P.: Revisiting password rules: facilitating human management of passwords. In: APWG Symposium on Electronic Crime Research (eCrime), pp. 1–10. IEEE (2016)

Verification of STAR-Vote and Evaluation of FDR and ProVerif

Murat Moran[(⊠)] and Dan S. Wallach

Computer Science Department, William Marsh Rice University,
6100 Main St., Houston, TX 77005, USA
muratmoran@gmail.com, dwallach@gmail.com
https://www.cs.rice.edu

Abstract. We present the first automated privacy analysis of STAR-Vote, a real world voting system design with sophisticated "end-to-end" cryptography, using FDR and ProVerif. We also evaluate the effectiveness of these tools. Despite the complexity of the voting system, we were able to verify that our abstracted formal model of STAR-Vote provides ballot-secrecy using both formal approaches. Notably, ProVerif is radically faster than FDR, making it more suitable for rapid iteration and refinement of the formal model.

Keywords: Security protocols · Formal methods · Privacy · E-voting · STAR-Vote · FDR · ProVerif

1 Introduction

Security systems employ protocols to ensure their desired goals over a hostile network such as that the communication between agents is authenticated and/or the information that needs to be confidential is indeed confidential. They also aim to provide integrity, key distribution, non-repudiation, and other such properties. However, they are always a target for some malicious activity. Moreover, as the complexity of security-critical systems has grown, rigorous verification and secure implementation gains importance. In our case, cryptographic voting systems have multiple actors exchanging messages, to achieve a variety of important goals, requiring a careful system analysis to ensure there isn't a subtle problem. Formal methods has been shown to be a well suited methodology for analysis of cryptographic protocols, including famous results such as Lowe's attack [19] on the Needham-Schroeder public-key protocol (NSPK) [23]. Since then, formal methodologies have been applied in the analysis of a variety of cryptographic protocols, and also for electronic voting systems, using automated tools including FDR [21,22], ProVerif [2,13,24], Active Knowledge in Security Protocols (AKISS) [7], AVISPA [1], TA4SL [6] and Scyther [10].

Formal methods and their tools differ in their approaches to reasoning (e.g., BAN logic, theorem proving, or attack construction). However, all require the user to hold a deep understanding of how these tools work in order to reason

© Springer International Publishing AG 2017
N. Polikarpova and S. Schneider (Eds.): IFM 2017, LNCS 10510, pp. 422–436, 2017.
DOI: 10.1007/978-3-319-66845-1_28

about a system and its specification. Even to an experienced user, these tools raise a variety of challenges. Every tool differs in its expressiveness: the capability of a formal language while modeling protocols to capture their specifications. For example, some tools may not support automation of complex cryptographic primitives such as homomorphic encryption, as used by many voting schemes. Secondly, all model checking tools suffer from the general problem of state space explosion. Unlike toy security protocols, with only a few messages exchanged, analyzing complex security protocols can require computation exponential in the size of the protocol, exhausting finite computational resources, much less the patience of the user. Furthermore, some verifiers will cap the number of simultaneous adversaries or concurrent runs of the protocol, reducing the computational complexity but also possibly missing real-world vulnerabilities. Lastly, usability of the tools is very crucial. Some tools might merely say that a protocol is "correct" without offering a proof. Others might offer a counter-example to demonstrate a vulnerability, but that counter-example might require significant human effort to consider whether it applies or not to the "real" protocol.

In this article, we investigate the challenges in engineering automated analysis of complex security protocols, and evaluate FDR and ProVerif protocol verifiers through modeling and analysis of the STAR-Vote [4] voting system with respect to ballot-secrecy requirement. We have chosen these two verifiers as these tools are mature, widely accepted, and have been previously used for analysis of comparable systems.

STAR-Vote Overview. STAR-Vote [4] is a DRE-style electronic voting system, using human-readable paper and encrypted electronic records. STAR-Vote supports homomorphic tallying of votes and non-interactive zero knowledge (NIZK) proofs that ballots are well-formed. Voters have a receipt to verify their votes are counted-as-cast by visiting a block-chain "public bulletin board" structure. Similarly, voters can challenge machines to prove that any given encrypted vote is an accurate record of their intent [3], but challenged votes are not counted in the tally. STAR-Vote was designed around the requirements of Travis County (Austin), Texas by a collaboration between academics and the county elections staff. A variety of different cryptographic primitives are specified, including homomorphic encryption, NIZK proofs, and hash chains. STAR-Vote includes a controller operated by poll workers, multiple voting terminals operated by voters, and a ballot box which queries these machines before it will accept any given printed ballot. STAR-Vote is a perfect example of a complex security protocol, and it's valuable to apply formal modeling tools to understand its correctness.

From the voter's perspective, all of this complexity is hidden. Figure 1 shows a schematic diagram of the STAR-Vote system. An eligible voter goes to a polling station, authenticates to the election official and gets a 1D barcode encoding the voter's precinct and ballot style. This might involve an online database in cases where voters can go to multiple voting centers. STAR-Vote maintains an airgap between the voter registration database and the voting system, with the only data that crosses the boundary being the short barcode. The voter then presents the barcode to a poll worker at the controller machine, who scans it to learn the

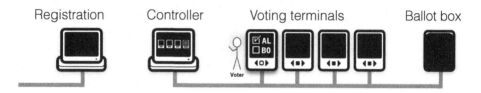

Fig. 1. A schematic diagram of STAR-Vote

voter's correct precinct and ballot style, and then prints a 5-digit unique code (also called a pin or token). The voter then carries this code to any open voting terminal and is presented with their proper ballot. When complete, the terminal prints a human-readable summary of the voter's choices, which the voter is to deposit in a ballot box, along with a receipt, which the voter can take home. This receipt corresponds to a hash of the ciphertext of the voter's selections which should also later appear on the web bulletin board (hereafter, "wbb"). The ballot box will refuse to accept anything other than a valid ballot, based on random ballot IDs printed on the ballot and verified with the networked voting machines, thus preventing some ballot stuffing attacks. A voter who recognizes a mistake on the printed ballot can also choose to "spoil" that ballot by taking it to the controller rather than depositing it. Needless to say, modeling the paper and electronic flow of messages in STAR-Vote is a complex task. Figure 2 illustrates a simplified STAR-Vote voting procedure capturing cryptographic message flow on the network. We will discuss the meanings of the relevant messages in the protocol as they arise in our analysis, but even to a quick glance, STAR-Vote is sufficiently complicated that we would expect to find challenges in its verification.

General Modeling Assumptions. In symbolic model checking, it is assumed that cryptographic primitives work perfectly. Hence, the system attacks that may be caused by cryptographic algorithms are not covered in our modeling. We treat cryptographic primitives as symbolic operations with the appropriate algebraic properties, such as; public key encryption: $E_{pk}(m)$ and digital signatures: $S_{sk}(m)$. Hence, an asymmetrically encrypted message can only be retrieved with the corresponding secret key. We abstract away some of the properties or components of the voting system that are analyzed due to either state explosion constraints or other limitations of our model checking tools. Our models consist of a limited number of agents. We could modify the model with an increased number of voters, candidates, voting terminals and precincts, but each would require a lot more space in the state base. Specifically for our STAR-Vote models in this paper; the homomorphic tallying of encrypted votes is abstracted away, which ensures that no single vote is decrypted, thus preserving privacy. ProVerif and FDR are both incapable of verifying homomorphic encryption. Hence, we consider an election scheme where all encrypted votes are published on the bulletin board after the election closed, decrypted individually and counted publicly in order to preserve anonymity of encrypted votes. Additionally, the voter verification and election integrity parts of the system are omitted as we focus solely on voter

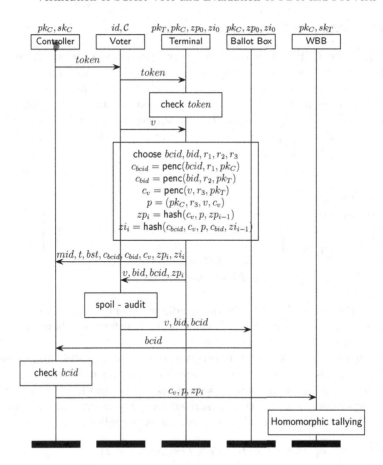

Fig. 2. A Simplified STAR-Vote voting procedure, where pk_C is controller's and pk_T is trustee's public key, bid and $bcid$ are the ballot and ballot cast identifiers respectively, r, zp_0, and zi_0 are random seeds, mid is voting terminal id. Additionally, penc models an encryption function and hash models a hashing function.

privacy, for instance; spoil-audit and hash-chain mechanisms, which do not leak privacy sensitive information.

2 STAR-Vote in Communicating Sequential Processes and FDR

The STAR-Vote Communicating Sequential Processes (CSP) model is explained in the followings[1].

---

[1] The complete machine readable CSP model is provided at https://muratmoran.com/publications/.

2.1   STAR-Vote CSP Model

Our STAR-Vote CSP model consists of five processes running in parallel: a controller process that controls the internal network, a voter process, a ballot marking device (voting terminal) process, an electronic ballot box process that can scan barcodes and sends scanned ballot cast ids to the controller, and a wbb process. Each CSP process has been modeled in a way that they all behave honestly and follow the process flow. As an example, the honest voter process behavior is modeled as the following:

$$
Voter(id) \mathrel{\widehat{=}}
$$

$$
\bigcap_{c \in \mathcal{C}}
\left(
\begin{array}{l}
choose.id.c \rightarrow \\
scomm.id.Term.c \rightarrow \\
\quad \underset{\substack{bid := Bids \\ bcid := Bcids \\ h := Hashchains}}{\square}
\left(
\begin{array}{l}
scomm.Term.id?(c, bid, bcid) \rightarrow \\
comm.Term.id?h \rightarrow \\
scomm.id.Box.Term.(c, bid, bcid) \rightarrow \\
closeElection \rightarrow STOP
\end{array}
\right)
\end{array}
\right)
$$

where id is the voter identity; c is the candidate; $Term$ is the voting terminal; Box is the ballot box process; bid is the ballot identifier; $bcid$ is the ballot cast identifier, and h is a hash chain of encrypted votes.

When defining processes and messages as in the voter process above, we need two different kinds of channel types; secret $scomm$ and public $comm$ channels in order to maintain the secrecy of security-sensitive information. The STAR-Vote voting system model is then described by the parallel composition of the processes that synchronize on common events as the following:

$$
System \mathrel{\widehat{=}} Voters \parallel Box \parallel Controller \parallel Terminal \parallel Wbb
$$

While modeling STAR-Vote, we encountered several difficulties due to the nature of FDR. Although, the aim here is to obtain a model that reflects real system behavior, we have to make a few simplifications to make the automated analysis possible with FDR model checker. In the voter process, for instance, we assume that the voter chooses the candidate that she would like to vote for before the election begins as FDR does not support revocation. This allows us to eliminate false positive attacks. In terms of randomness in choosing nonce-like terms, such as ballot ids and ballot cast ids, randomness is modeled as the non-deterministic choice of terms over a pre-determined set of terms. Lastly, in the original system, encrypted votes are submitted and publicized on the wbb along with non-interactive zero-knowledge proofs, which ensures that ballots are well-formed. However, in our model all ciphertexts and ballot forms are assumed to be well-formed as FDR does not support zero-knowledge proofs.

Intruder Model. In our analysis, we employed an active Dolev-Yao intruder [14] model in CSP, as adapted to voting systems in Moran and Heather [21]. The intruder model supports active intruder behavior: interacting with the protocol participants, overhearing communication channels, intercepting and spoofing any messages that the intruder has learned or generated from its prior knowledge. In this model, intruder processes have a set of deductions rules in order to compose and decompose messages, and a set *Ucomms*, as below, defining the unreliable channels on which the intruder can act. For instance, the following rules enable intruders to have access to any channels from and to the voter v_1, where the set *comms* is the union of all communication channels.

$$Ucomms = \bigcup(\{q.q'.f \mid q.q'.f \leftarrow comms, q \leftarrow \{v_1\}, q' \leftarrow agents\},$$
$$\{q.q'.f \mid q.q'.f \leftarrow comms, q \leftarrow agents, q' \leftarrow \{v_1\}\})$$

The system that will be analyzed is the parallel composition of the renamed voting system model *System*, which enables the messages flowing on unreliable channel to be taken or eavesdropped, and the intruder model *Intruder*. The resulting composition *System* $\parallel$ *Intruder* synchronizes on their common events. In the following section, we will define several sets like *Ucomms* for different intruder capabilities.

2.2   Analysis with FDR

In this section, we present the first automated analysis of STAR-Vote under an active Dolev-Yao intruder model and the anonymity specification given in [22]. Accordingly, the following trace equivalence should hold in order to verify that the voting system model *System* provides voter anonymity.

$$System_1 \setminus \{\mid scomm \mid\} \equiv_T System_2 \setminus \{\mid scomm \mid\},$$

where the processes $System_1$ and $System_2$ model two different system behavior: in the first v_1 votes for c_1 and v_2 for c_2, and in the second the voters vote other way around. Hence, the intruder with the available public information along with its prior knowledge cannot distinguish these two cases, then we say that the voting system does not leak any information that may link a voter to her cast vote. Here, what information is available to the intruder is defined by a set *Ucomms*, and also by masking or hiding the information that the intruder is not supposed to access.

There are numerous kinds of threat scenarios that we can model in this CSP framework by modifying *Ucomms*. Here, we present three of those cases, denoted as DY1, DY2 and DY3.

DY1: the intruder can observe only the public channels (*comm*), and not the channels that should be kept confidential, such as; the channels on which crucial ballot information and voters' choice of candidate are transmitted. Hence, we exclude such information from *Ucomms* set.

$$Ucomms = comms \setminus (comBallots \cup commCandidates)$$

DY2 (only 1 honest voter): the intruder can act as the Dolev-Yao intruder on all the channels except the voter v_1's communication channels—there exists only one honest voter and the rest is dishonest.

$$Ucomms = comms \setminus \bigcup(\{q.q'.f \mid q.q'.f \leftarrow comms, q \leftarrow \{v_1\}, q' \leftarrow \mathcal{A}\},$$
$$\{q.q'.f \mid q.q'.f \leftarrow comms, q \leftarrow \mathcal{A}, q' \leftarrow \{v_1\}\})$$

DY3 (only 1 dishonest voter): the intruder can act maliciously only on the channels of the voter v_3, who is collaborating with the intruder, and observe other public channels—there exist only 1 dishonest and at least 2 honest voters.

$$Ucomms = \bigcup(\{q.q'.f \mid q.q'.f \leftarrow comms, q \leftarrow \{v_3\}, q' \leftarrow \mathcal{A}\},$$
$$\{q.q'.f \mid q.q'.f \leftarrow comms, q \leftarrow \mathcal{A}, q' \leftarrow \{v_3\}\})$$

Our analysis found that STAR-Vote provides anonymity under active intruder models: DY1 and DY3, and produced privacy attacks against the system under DY2, all of which were as expected. (Why? Because when there's only one honest voter, the other voters can collude to know the subtotals of their own votes, and then infer the votes of the remaining honest voter.) To give an idea about overall verification times for FDR, Table 1 illustrates the verification times of the automated analysis of STAR-Vote under different intruder capabilities using an average laptop with Intel® Core™ i5 CPU 2.40 GHz, and 8 GB RAM. The longest run took just under three minutes. This is tolerable, but is far from ideal in terms of the engineering cycle time of evolving the model.

Table 1. The FDR verification times for STAR-Vote model under different Dolev-Yao capabilities

DY1			DY2			DY3		
Refine	States	Time	Refine	States	Time	Refine	States	Time
✓	128, 101	21 s	X	26	2 min 50 s	✓	95, 917	1 min 39 s

We also extended the model with ballot counting mechanism in the wbb process and measured FDR verification times using the same settings as before. As illustrated in Table 2, FDR verifies the model for DY1 and DY3 cases, but not DY2 as FDR crashes once 8 GB allocated memory runs out in 45 min. However, we were able to verify the extended model using a better server with 128 GB RAM in 2 h. Furthermore, when extending STAR-Vote CSP model by including a hash-chain mechanism, which is used in the original system for integrity purposes, even the server with 128 GB crashes before producing a result. Hence, automated verification of the STAR-Vote CSP model extended with more components (e.g., pins, hash-chain, and thresholded mechanisms) seems unrealistic.

Table 2. The FDR verification times for extended STAR-Vote model with *counting* mechanism under different Dolev-Yao capabilities. "'−'" means that FDR crashes before producing a result.

DY1			DY2			DY3		
Refine	States	Time	Refine	States	Time	Refine	States	Time
✓	$1,201,525$	23 min 1 s	−	−	−	✓	$95,917$	1 min 51 s

3 STAR-Vote in the Applied Pi Calculus and ProVerif

We briefly explain our STAR-Vote applied pi model in the followings[2].

3.1 STAR-Vote Model in Applied Pi

Similar to the CSP approach, we modeled the STAR-Vote voting system in the applied pi calculus by means of processes that intercommunicate, allowing verification by ProVerif. As with FDR, this process necessarily involves abstracting away some of the details. Initially, we modeled a set of cryptographic primitives Σ that are used in STAR-Vote, and it can be defined as the following;

$$\Sigma = \{\mathsf{ok}, \mathsf{pk}, \mathsf{hash}, \mathsf{sign}, \mathsf{dec}, \mathsf{penc}, \mathsf{zkp}, \mathsf{checksign}, \mathsf{checkzkp}\}$$

Function ok is a constant; pk, hash and checkzkp are unary functions; sign and dec are binary functions; penc, zkp and checksign are ternary. Accordingly, we have the following equations:

$$\mathsf{dec}(\mathsf{penc}(m, r, \mathsf{pk}(sk)), sk) = m \qquad (\text{E1})$$
$$\mathsf{checksign}(\mathsf{sign}(sk, m), m, \mathsf{pk}(sk)) = \mathsf{ok} \qquad (\text{E2})$$
$$\mathsf{checkzkp}(\mathsf{zkp}(\mathsf{pk}(sk), r, m, \mathsf{penc}(m, r, \mathsf{pk}(sk)))) = \mathsf{ok} \quad (\text{E3})$$

Equation E1 enables plaintext m to be extracted using the corresponding secret key sk, where r is a random seed. E2 allows digital signatures to be verified with an appropriate public key pk(sk). E3 allows non-interactive zero knowledge proof p to be verified.

For the model, we employ two channel types: public and private. The following process $V(c, b, v)$ models a simplified voter process behavior of STAR-Vote in the applied pi calculus, where v is the candidate of choice, c is a private channel between the voter and voting terminal, and b is a private channel between the voter and the ballot box:

$$
\begin{aligned}
V(c, b, v) ::= {}& \bar{c}\langle v \rangle. && \textit{voter enters her vote} \\
& c(v', bid, bcid, zp_i). && \textit{receives ballot summary and receipt } (zp_i) \\
& \text{if } v = v' && \textit{checks if her chosen candidate is on the ballot} \\
& \text{then } \bar{b}\langle (v, bid, bcid) \rangle. && \textit{and casts her ballot}
\end{aligned}
$$

---

[2] The actual applied pi model is provided at https://muratmoran.com/publications/ for brevity.

Likewise, the rest of the processes that comprise the STAR-Vote model (i.e., voting terminal (T), ballot box (B), controller (C) and web bulletin board (W) processes) are defined in terms of the grammar and equational theory above. The STAR-Vote pi calculus model $Star(sk_a, sk_c, v)$ is then described as the composition of these processes, and initialized with public-private key pairs (pk_a, sk_a) and (pk_c, sk_c) for election authority and controller respectively. The system then generates fresh seeds zp_0 and zi_0, and establishes private channels between trusted participants before the election as the following.

$$
\begin{aligned}
Star(sk_a, sk_c, v) ::= \ &\text{let } pk_a = pk(sk_a) \text{ in let } pk_c = pk(sk_c) \text{ in} \\
&\nu\, zp_0.\nu\, zi_0. \\
&\nu\, ch_{VT}.\nu\, ch_{VB}.\nu\, ch_{BC}. \\
&\nu\, ch_T C.\nu\, ch_{TW}.\nu\, ch_{CW}. \\
&(\\
&V(ch_{VT}, ch_{VB}, v)| \\
&T(ch_{VT}, ch_{TC}, ch_{TW}, pk_a, pk_c, sk_c, zp_0, zi_0)| \\
&B(ch_{VB}, ch_{BC}, pk_c, zi_0)| \\
&C(ch_{BC}, ch_{TC}, ch_{CW}, pk_c, sk_c)| \\
&W(ch_{CW}, ch_{TW}, sk_a, pk_c) \\
&)
\end{aligned}
$$

where ν is the name restriction (i.e., it creates new names).

Due to the limitations in ProVerif, we abstract away homomorphic encryption mechanism in STAR-Vote model. Using synchronization points in the model ensures that the intruder does not gain any information that can link encrypted votes with the plaintext equivalence. That is, the wbb waits until all the votes are decrypted, and then publishes all the plaintext votes. Is this simplification reasonable? Certainly they leave out security-critical aspects of the STAR-Vote design like the homomorphic tallying. If an actual election were conducted this way, a voter could use their receipt to prove to a third-party how they voted, and thus enable bribery or coercion of their vote. Nonetheless, the use of synchronization points presents a reasonable simulation of the constraints that an adversary might face with regard to attacking voter privacy, at least under the assumption that voters choose not to share their receipts. In a real election, a voter must be unable to compromise their privacy, *even if they want to*.

Intruder Model. Unlike the CSP approach, ProVerif does not need a separate implementation of an intruder model. ProVerif instead provides a standard Dolev-Yao intruder model, having access to all the public channels, and special functions to perform a number of malicious actions in order to violate voter privacy. That is, he can use anything available in the context. By specifying a private channel as public we can increase intruder's capabilities. Similarly, corrupt system participants such as voters and voting terminals can be modeled easily by either giving away their cryptographic keys or by publishing their private communication channels to the intruder.

3.2   Analysis with ProVerif

Vote-privacy (ballot-secrecy) is defined informally as "no party receives information which would allow them to distinguish one situation from another one in which two voters swap their votes"[13]. Formally, it is defined as:

Definition 1. *A voting protocol respects vote-privacy if*

$$S[V_A\{a/v\}|V_B\{b/v\}] \approx_l S[V_A\{b/v\}|V_B\{a/v\}]$$

for all possible votes a and b.

Recently, Blanchet and Smyth [5] have proposed an approach, based on barrier synchronization, to fully automate verification of this definition. It is implemented in the latest version of ProVerif, and supports automated verification of observational equivalence. Barrier synchronization ensures that ballot-secrecy holds by swapping outputs of both sides of the observational equivalence. In order to do that, a compiler first annotates barriers with data to be swapped and channels for sending and receiving data; the compiler then translates the biprocesses with annotated barriers into biprocesses without barriers.

We have used these barriers in our model for instance when describing the wbb process, which receives an individual encrypted vote and decrypts it. Hence, a synchronization point in between these two events is needed so that the order of the communication does not leak any information related to that particular vote. Definition 1 is reflected to ProVerif using a choice operator as:

$$Star(sk_a, sk_c, \mathsf{choice}[a, b]) \mid Star(sk_a, sk_c, \mathsf{choice}[b, a])$$

where ska and skc are authority's and controller's secret credentials, respectively, which are fed into the system, and a and b are candidate names.

Having described an abstract model of STAR-Vote, we were able to verify that our model satisfies the ballot-secrecy property using the ProVerif protocol verifier. With the same setting as in the CSP approach (the same laptop with 8 GB RAM), ProVerif takes around 1.45 s in total to verify our pi calculus model of this complex voting system protocol. ProVerif is also able to find possible attacks when, for instance, there exists a corrupt voting terminal and a ballot box by using the compromised information from these entities either by revealing corresponding secret keys or by making private channels public.

Extending the model in ProVerif is straightforward. We have also managed to verify two extended versions of this model: first one is extended with pins or tokens, which are given to voters by the controller for authorization purposes and then scanned to a voting terminal, and this version is verified in 9.8 s; the second one is extended with hash-chain mechanism, which requires two honest voter processes and other system participants processes extended for two voters. ProVerif verifies this extended model in 2.10 min using the same laptop.

4   Evaluation of the Tools: FDR and ProVerif

In this paper, having analyzed STAR-Vote voting system mechanically with FDR and ProVerif, we now share our experience with these two tools in this section with respect to expressiveness, usability and efficiency. The tools provide different approaches to protocol verification and make verification of complex security protocols easier than hand-proofs, but they may also suffer from the similar problems such as state explosion. We discuss some of the issues we encountered during our analysis in the following categories.

4.1   Expressiveness

We came across several inadequacy of the tools in expressing some of the system components, which needed to be abstracted away. For example, neither FDR nor ProVerif can verify homomorphic tallying. FDR furthermore cannot verify non-interactive zero knowledge proofs unlike ProVerif. Similarly, a typical voting system requirement, coercion-resistance, can be defined in CSP [15], but FDR does not support its mechanical verification. ProVerif can verify this property but we did not make it a focus of our verification efforts.

FDR is very expressive in its support for many different kinds of channels: public or private, blocked or spoofed, all of which can be defined in terms of functions and sets. ProVerif only supports public and private channels. In practice, this expressivity is necessary in FDR, which does not provide an adversary model, while ProVerif provides a Dolev-Yao adversary that does everything we need.

4.2   Usability

We found modeling and expressing protocol participants more straightforward with ProVerif than FDR. FDR frequently complains when the network of protocols is too complex to bring together. However they both guide the user well in finding bugs in the specification. FDR offers a sophisticated user interface, the ProBE CSP animator, which enables checking if processes behave as intended.

In terms of producing and interpreting counter-examples during the analysis, ProVerif *sometimes* produces a trace that leads to the attack when the verification does not hold; other times, ProVerif only says that a query does not hold, and terminates. Moreover, when ProVerif *does* return a counter-example trace, the task for the user to interpret the trace and locate why the attack occurs is often very difficult; we saw some traces that were 3–4 pages long. This also makes it difficult for a ProVerif user to distinguish whether a trace corresponds to a legitimate attack, since ProVerif can sometimes return false-positives; this might seem terrible, but it's essential to how ProVerif gains its runtime performance. On the other hand, FDR always produces a counter-example when there should be one, and tracing back the attack is smooth and straightforward.

In some cases ProVerif verified our model when it should not have, due to some minor, unrecognized bugs in our model, for instance; a type mismatching of functions or creating new names earlier in the model. Hence, it was not simple to find such bugs during modeling and verification, which may deceive an inexperienced user into analyzing incorrect model.

Lastly, consider the case of modeling a new voting system, starting from our existing STAR-Vote models in both FDR and ProVerif. How hard might it be to derive a new voting system model from our existing one? Code reuse would certainly be a valuable feature. We note that the ProVerif pi calculus model for STAR-Vote is around 100 lines of code while the CSP model is around 500 lines of code. This additional complexity in CSP comes largely from having to specify sets that are used to describe system participants and the intruder's behavior. ProVerif wins for having a generic intruder that we don't need to specify.

4.3   Efficiency

Verification times vary in FDR depending on the number of participants and whether the verification holds—results generated by FDR is not generic, and dependent of the number of concurrent participants in the protocols unlike ProVerif. We saw runtimes as fast 21 s, and we saw crashes which occurred after 17 h, and to even run that long we had to move to a much larger computer with 128 GB RAM. Needless to say, this can make for a frustrating user experience.

Table 1 displays verification times for FDR for scenarios with 2 or 3 voters, and Table 2 illustrates verification times for a model extended with pins. When we add an extra tallying mechanism in the model, the DY1 case increases from 21 s to 23 min with 10 times more states than before, and in the case of DY2 with tallying, FDR crashes after 45 min, on a laptop with 8 GB RAM, due to lack of memory. We verified this extended version with a bigger server with 128 GB. Additionally, when we extended the model further with hash chain mechanism FDR crashes even with the larger server after 17 h. Generally, the more ability given to intruder, the longer FDR takes to verify. We note that, to make verification more efficient, FDR3 and FDR4 offer multi-core parallelism features. Unfortunately, they don't support testing observational equivalence of complex models where the left hand side of the equivalence requires more than 10 million states.

We found that ProVerif operates very quickly with models of similar complexity to those we used in FDR. Verification took generally less than two seconds to complete, allowing us to rapidly iterate on our models. We verified two extended versions of the model with pins and hash-chain mechanism in 9.8 s and 2.10 min respectively.

In terms of man-hours, ProVerif can produce false-positive attacks due to its over-approximation [8]. Hence, dealing with such false positives takes enormous amount of man-hours and effort. However, FDR does not produce such false positives unless an intruder's power is adjusted improperly, but the user-defined intruder model requires careful attention, which is error-prone and takes a lot of time to integrate.

5   Related Work

To date, there have been a few attempts to compare automated security protocol verifiers in the literature. C. Meadows [20] compares the approaches followed in the tools NRL and FDR with the analysis of NSPK, and concludes that two tools are complementary. Hussain and Seret [16] presents a qualitative comparison between AVISPA and Hermes in terms of their complexity, ease to use and the conceptional differences between approaches (the comparison is not based on experiments). It is stated that Hermes is more suited for simple protocols, on the other hand, AVISPA is better for complex protocols where you would need scalability, flexibility, and precision. Cas J.F. Cremers *et al.* [11] first discuss the types of behavior restriction of the models used by the tools; Casper/FDR, ProVerif, Scyther and AVISPA back-end tools. Then, a performance comparison is made considering an analysis of secrecy and authentication properties. This is the only work that compares our chosen tools ProVerif and Casper/FDR[3]. However, the properties that we are dealing with in this paper is not considered since ProVerif was not able to check observational equivalence properties then. Dalal *et al.* [12] compare ProVerif and Scyther tools considering six different security protocols. The definitions of the models presented in the paper are not language specific, but pseudocode. Lafourcade *et al.* [18] analyze a number of protocols dealing with algebraic properties like Exclusive-Or and Diffie-Hellman and compare the results from different tools: OFMC, CL-Atse and XOR-ProVerif or DH-ProVerif in terms of efficiency. The properties that were checked are secrecy, authentication and also non-repudiation for one e-auction protocol. Cortier *et al.* [9] proposed a semi-automatic proof of vote privacy using type-based verification and the tool rF*, in which security properties and cryptographic functions are modeled in terms of refinement types. More recently, Lafourcade and Puys [17] focus on performance analysis of a number of tools including a ProVerif extension and analysis of 21 cryptographic protocols dealing with Exclusive-Or (xor) and exponentiation properties like Diffie-Hellman (DH). In the analysis, secrecy and authentication properties are considered. The tools have been evaluated in terms of execution time and memory consumption. It is stated that there is not a clear winner, but more recent tools tend to perform better.

6   Conclusion

In this paper, we have presented the first automated privacy verification of the STAR-Vote voting system along with an evaluation of two protocol verifiers: FDR and ProVerif. We verified that our STAR-Vote CSP and pi calculus models provide ballot-privacy, validating our previously informal design and providing further trustworthiness.

Throughout our analysis we had a chance to evaluate these two security protocol verifiers with respect to their expressiveness, usability, and efficiency. In

---

[3] Casper is a compiler that translates protocol description into the CSP language, which is then used by FDR.

terms of expressiveness, both tools need further research to pursue in automation of cryptographic primitives. Regarding usability, FDR offers more with its inbuilt tools to make sure the model behaves as expected, user interface and counterexamples, which are easy to interpret and trace back to what causes the failure. On the other hand, modeling with ProVerif is more straightforward and requires quite less effort than FDR does. About efficiency, ProVerif is very efficient and quite flexible in modeling and analyzing such complex systems despite the false-positives, which require a special attention. FDR with lazy spy intruder model is neither efficient nor scalable when analyzing such complex systems.

Overall, formal verification helps us understand how complex security protocols work and facilitate their analysis. However, it is still expensive in the sense that it requires a deep understanding of verification tools, experience and a huge amount of human effort.

Our future work will concentrate on improving the protocol verifiers ProVerif and FDR by finding techniques that allow us to automatically reason about other desired properties of e-voting systems such as election verifiability. Moreover, correctness of the intruder models of these two tools will be considered as a further research question. Lastly, a formal specification of system mechanisms that were abstracted away in this paper such as spoil-audit and risk-limiting audit for verifiability purposes can be pursued as future work.

Acknowledgments. This work was carried out under the NSF-funded Voting Systems Architectures for Security and Usability project. The principal author is also partly funded by TUBITAK. We would like to thank Ben Smyth, Olivier Pereira, and Thomas Gibson-Robinson for their helpful technical discussions.

References

1. Armando, A., et al.: The AVISPA tool for the automated validation of internet security protocols and applications. In: Etessami, K., Rajamani, S.K. (eds.) CAV 2005. LNCS, vol. 3576, pp. 281–285. Springer, Heidelberg (2005). doi:10.1007/11513988_27
2. Backes, M., Hritcu, C., Maffei, M.: Automated verification of remote electronic voting protocols in the applied pi-calculus. In: CSF (2008)
3. Benaloh, J.: Simple verifiable elections. In: Proceedings of the USENIX/ACCURATE Electronic Voting Technology Workshop (EVT 2006), Vancouver, B.C., Canada, June 2006
4. Benaloh, J., Byrne, M., Kortum, P.T., McBurnett, N., Pereira, O., Stark, P.B., Wallach, D.S.: STAR-Vote: a secure, transparent, auditable, and reliable voting system. CoRR, abs/1211.1904 (2012)
5. Blanchet, B., Smyth, B.: Automated reasoning for equivalences in the applied pi calculus with barriers. In: CSF (2016)
6. Boichut, Y., Heam, P.C., Kouchnarenko, O., Oehl, F.: Improvements on the Genet and Klay technique to automatically verify security protocols. In: Workshop on Automated Verification of Infinite States Systems (2004)
7. Chadha, R., Ciobâcă, Ş., Kremer, S.: Automated verification of equivalence properties of cryptographic protocols. In: Seidl, H. (ed.) ESOP 2012. LNCS, vol. 7211, pp. 108–127. Springer, Heidelberg (2012). doi:10.1007/978-3-642-28869-2_6

8. Chothia, T., Smyth, B., Staite, C.: Automatically checking commitment protocols in ProVerif without false attacks. In: Focardi, R., Myers, A. (eds.) POST 2015. LNCS, vol. 9036, pp. 137–155. Springer, Heidelberg (2015). doi:10.1007/978-3-662-46666-7_8

9. Cortier, V., Eigner, F., Kremer, S., Maffei, M., Wiedling, C.: Type-based verification of electronic voting protocols. In: Focardi, R., Myers, A. (eds.) POST 2015. LNCS, vol. 9036, pp. 303–323. Springer, Heidelberg (2015). doi:10.1007/978-3-662-46666-7_16

10. Cremers, C.J.F.: The scyther tool: verification, falsification, and analysis of security protocols. In: Gupta, A., Malik, S. (eds.) CAV 2008. LNCS, vol. 5123, pp. 414–418. Springer, Heidelberg (2008). doi:10.1007/978-3-540-70545-1_38

11. Cremers, C.J.F., Lafourcade, P., Nadeau, P.: Comparing state spaces in automatic security protocol analysis. In: Formal to Practical Security - Papers Issued from the 2005–2008 French-Japanese Collaboration (2009)

12. Dalal, N., Shah, J., Hisaria, K., Jinwala, D.: A comparative analysis of tools for verification of security protocols. IJCNS **3**(10), 779–787 (2010)

13. Delaune, S., Kremer, S., Ryan, M.: Verifying privacy-type properties of electronic voting protocols. J. Comput. Secur. **17**(4), 435–487 (2009)

14. Dolev, D., Yao, A.C.-C.: On the security of public key protocols. IEEE Trans. Inf. Theory **29**(2), 198–207 (1983)

15. Heather, J., Schneider, S.: A formal framework for modelling coercion resistance and receipt freeness. In: Giannakopoulou, D., Méry, D. (eds.) FM 2012. LNCS, vol. 7436, pp. 217–231. Springer, Heidelberg (2012). doi:10.1007/978-3-642-32759-9_19

16. Hussain, M., Seret, D.: A comparative study of security protocols validation tools: hermes vs. avispa. In: 2006 8th International Conference Advanced Communication Technology, vol. 1, pp. 303–308, 6 pages, February 2006

17. Lafourcade, P., Puys, M.: Performance evaluations of cryptographic protocols verification tools dealing with algebraic properties. In: Foundations and Practice of Security (FPS 2015), Clermont-Ferrand, France, October 2015

18. Lafourcade, P., Terrade, V., Vigier, S.: Comparison of cryptographic verification tools dealing with algebraic properties. In: Degano, P., Guttman, J.D. (eds.) FAST 2009. LNCS, vol. 5983, pp. 173–185. Springer, Heidelberg (2010). doi:10.1007/978-3-642-12459-4_13

19. Lowe, G.: An attack on the Needham-Schroeder public-key authentication protocol. Inf. Process. Lett. **56**(3), 131–133 (1995)

20. Meadows, C.A.: Analyzing the needham-schroeder public key protocol: a comparison of two approaches. In: Bertino, E., Kurth, H., Martella, G., Montolivo, E. (eds.) ESORICS 1996. LNCS, vol. 1146, pp. 351–364. Springer, Heidelberg (1996). doi:10.1007/3-540-61770-1_46

21. Moran, M., Heather, J.: Automated analysis of voting systems with dolev-yao intruder model. In: AVOCS 2013, September 2013

22. Moran, M., Heather, J., Schneider, S.: Verifying anonymity in voting systems using CSP. Formal Aspects Comput., 1–36 (2012)

23. Needham, R.M., Schroeder, M.D.: Using encryption for authentication in large networks of computers. Commun. ACM **21**(12), December 1978

24. Smyth, B.: Formal verification of cryptographic protocols with automated reasoning. Ph.D. thesis, School of Computer Science, University of Birmingham (2011)

Author Index

Althoff, Matthias 50
Aronis, Stavros 227

Baxter, James 161
Beckert, Bernhard 129, 312
Blom, Stefan 102
Bodenmüller, Stefan 375
Bormer, Thorsten 312
Bortolussi, Luca 3
Bowles, Juliana Küster Filipe 357
Brooke, Phillip J. 407
Bruschi, Danilo 391

Cavalcanti, Ana 18, 161
Cha, Suhyun 129
Chen, YuTing 295
Conserva Filho, Madiel S. 211

Da Rocha Silva, Sarah Raquel 211
Damiani, Ferruccio 111
Darabi, Saeed 102
de Almeida Pereira, Dalay Israel 211
Di Pasquale, Andrea 391

Ernst, Gidon 375

Fazeldehkordi, Elahe 263
Feldle, Jochen 50
Ferreira, João F. 407
Fritchie, Scott Lystig 227
Frohn, Florian 85
Furia, Carlo A. 295

Gerndt, Andreas 177
Ghilardi, Silvio 391
Giesl, Jürgen 85
Gilmore, Stephen 145
Gocht, Stephan 312
Groves, Lindsay 69

Henrio, Ludovic 195
Herda, Mihai 312
Hilgendorf, Eric 50

Huber, Monika 50
Huisman, Marieke 102

Immler, Fabian 50

Ji, Wei 243
Johnson, Saul A. 407

Keinholz, Jonas 50
Kordy, Barbara 332
Kovalov, Andrii 177
Krishna, Ajay 323

Laneve, Cosimo 195
Lanzi, Andrea 391
Lentzsch, Daniel 312
Li, Wei 18
Lienhardt, Michael 111
Linker, Sven 34
Lobe, Elisabeth 177
Lüdtke, Daniel 177

Mastandrea, Vincenzo 195
Mendes, Alexandra 407
Miyazawa, Alvaro 18
Moran, Murat 422
Muschevici, Radu 111

Nipkow, Tobias 50

Oliveira, Marcel Vinicius Medeiros 211
Oortwijn, Wytse 102
Owe, Olaf 263

Pagani, Elena 391
Pearce, David J. 69
Pfähler, Jörg 375
Poizat, Pascal 323
Policriti, Alberto 3

Rahman, Fahrurrozi 357
Ramezanifarkhani, Toktam 263
Reif, Wolfgang 375

Reijsbergen, Daniël   145
Ribeiro, Pedro   18
Rizaldi, Albert   50

Sagonas, Konstantinos   227
Salaün, Gwen   323
Schaefer, Ina   111
Schellhorn, Gerhard   375
Silvetti, Simone   3
Steinhöfel, Dominic   279

Timmis, Jon   18

Ulbrich, Mattias   129, 312
Utting, Mark   69

Vandin, Andrea   145
Vogel-Heuser, Birgit   129

Wallach, Dan S.   422
Wang, Farn   243
Wasser, Nathan   279
Weigl, Alexander   129
Wideł, Wojciech   332
Wu, Hao   348
Wu, Peng   243

Printed in the United States
By Bookmasters